Birgit Hellwig

A Grammar of Qaqet

D1674383

Mouton Grammar Library

Edited by
Georg Bossong
Bernard Comrie
Patience L. Epps
Irina Nikolaeva

Volume 79

Birgit Hellwig

A Grammar of Qaqet

DE GRUYTER
MOUTON

ISBN 978-3-11-073531-4
ISSN 0933-7636

Library of Congress Control Number: 2019933574

Bibliographic information published by the Deutsche Nationalbibliothek
The Deutsche Nationalbibliothek lists this publication in the Deutsche Nationalbibliografie; detailed bibliographic data are available on the Internet at http://dnb.dnb.de.

© 2020 Walter de Gruyter GmbH, Berlin/Boston
This volume is text- and page-identical with the hardback published in 2019.
Printing and binding: CPI books GmbH, Leck

www.degruyter.com

Acknowledgements

This grammar started out as a very rough sketch in 2011. Since then, it has matured considerably – thanks to many people who generously contributed to its making. I hope that I was able to do justice to all their thoughtful explanations, comments and advice, and that they feel their input is adequately reflected in the current version.

First and foremost, my thanks go to the Qaqet communities of Raunsepna, Lamarain and Kamanakam who have hosted and supported our research for many years now. Most of the research for this grammar was carried out in Raunsepna, and I want to especially acknowledge John Landi and Dorothy Naremetki, Bruno Lalem and Anna Nguinganan, Tony Alin, and Clara Langmetki: these six elders were the first to work with me in 2011, and they have stayed with the project ever since, extending their help to the other members of my team. Despite their busy schedules and community commitments, they would always make time for us, and their deep knowledge of their language and culture proved an invaluable source of inspiration. Over time, they encouraged more and more Qaqet to work with us – such that there are now over 200 Qaqet involved in the various projects: participating in audio and video recordings, transcribing and translating recordings, answering our questions and asking questions of their own, guiding the research into new directions, and contributing to this grammar. Many have become colleagues and friends in the process: I feel very fortunate and privileged that they have accepted us as guests among them, and decided to share aspects of their life with us.

In particular, two Raunsepna families have assumed central roles during our research: Paul Alin, Lucy Nguingi and their children; and Henry Lingisaqa, Marcella Tangil and their children. Their insights shape our project design and methodology, they make it possible to construct a longitudinal corpus of child language, they arrange our research schedule in the field and organize the many Qaqet research associates, and they continue such activities in our absence. I cannot thank them enough for their commitment and dedication, and it is fair to say that we would never have achieved our current state of knowledge without their help.

Many thanks are also due to the numerous people who regularly offer their time, expertise and company, patiently teaching us about their language and culture or simply stopping by for a chat: Francis Arum and his family; Utilia Avitki and Francis Kalang; Alois Balar and his family; Rose Boni, Damien Kereku and their family; Betty Dangas, Chris Philemon and their family; Andrew Durlaik; Stephen Ganinga; Andrew Guvangit; Martha Iaken and Caspar Mestaqaet; Anna Iarilmi, Clement Muaqanem and their family; Monica Ilas (from Lasrlem); Monica Ilas (from Lualait), Michael Wasupka and their family; Anna Kaqetki; Maria Karakmet; Bernard Karem; Jacob Kelile; Clara Kimas; Gloria Kuanas; Afra Kularek and Bonifaz Issa; Terry Kurukpet, Patrick Lemingel and their family; Angelika Kurlik and Ben Karliun; Cecilia Laniat; Roselyn Langmetki; Elizabeth Lara; Theckla Lasek; Paul Liosi; Balthasar Lua and his family; Alfons Malau; Bibiana Mali; Rose Mingas; Margaret Mitil, Vincent Depguasdarik and their family; Chris Mitparlingi, Martina Lurlki and their family; Erica Murumgi, Chris Srleqi and their family; Roberta Nakai, Caspar Panavu and their family; Angela Ngenaqa; Francisca Ngenara and Peter Saminga; Raphael Ngunaqa; Joseph Ngurengmes; Paula Nuvaqat and Alois Kemsarlem; Judith Rluses; Lucy Rluses and her family; Sara Puatbum; Selina Qiuaik, Chris Kereku and their family; Monica Sadi; Susan Sakalkal; Maria Salap and Raphael Nuavet; Rita Salap; Joana Samisim and her family; Joanita Sangunan and Felix Danly; Anna Savadi, Mathias Batnaqa and their family; Maria Savarin; Rebecca Savirian and her family; Lona Sinirang and Batlius Kabainga; Martin Srleqi and his family; Joana Stadi and Blasius Benga; Monica Sunun, Raphael Luangi and their family; Lucy Sutit and Frances Ngeligi; Rose Tamian; Terry Tamian and her family; Lucy Tena; Gertrud Trana; Ben Unduka; Caroline Unsim; Michael Vaka; and Francis Yalaqi.

My thanks also go to all the teachers at Raunsepna Elementary School and at Raunsepna Primary School for supporting our research, to Catherine Kusaiki and George Revesit Jr for supervising and training our many student helpers, and to all the students who contributed to our research, especially to Josephine Ani, Clementia Guailas, Samuel Hetla, Andrew Kaltumen, Ignasius Kasingimet, Bernard Kulap, Boniface Lan, Doreen Napait, Francisca Ngusurlki, Josephine Rami, Philipp Ramit, Jordan Revesit, Beno Sangarl, Job Saqaivuk, Conrad Solmet, Felix Takun and Steven Tiqa.

I am very grateful to the FMI (Filia Maria Immaculata) Sisters for their generous hospitality, and I thank Sr. Fidelis Rikie and Sr. Wilhelmina Sundu in Vunapope for making this possible, and Sr. Roselyne Tarur and Sr. Goretty Kuikui in Raunsepna for providing a welcoming and kind home to us. My thanks also go to the inhabitants of Raunsepna station for extending their friendship to us: the resident priest, the teachers, and the nurses and their families, including especially Sheila and Jefferson Marampau, Dorothy and Patrick Alvin, and Emma and Thomas. And many thanks to James and Ludwina Tapele and their family for always welcoming us en route to and from Raunsepna, providing a welcome and much-needed place of rest.

My research initially started out as a solitary endeavor, but the project gradually grew to include a team of researchers – each taking responsibility for different aspects of the overall research, contributing their own interests and expertise, and making the project their own. I want to thank them all for accompanying me and bearing with me for so long: Henrike Frye, who is researching child-directed speech in Raunsepna and Lamarain; Carmen Dawuda and Steffen Reetz, who are focusing on multilingualism in Kamanakam; Sonja Eisenbeiß and Evan Kidd, who are contributing their psycholinguistic expertise; and Alex Marley, who conducted a sociolinguistic survey of Raunsepna and Lamarain. Furthermore, a large number of student assistants and interns were, and still are, engaged in processing ca. 400 hours of natural and staged data: segmenting speech; computerizing and editing transcripts and translations;

glossing and annotating texts; converting, synchronizing and enhancing the technical quality of recordings; archiving and entering metadata. Many thanks to Janet Bachmann, Marijke Bosmans, Christoph Bracks, Pascal Coenen, Marc Heinrich, Miyuki Henning, Bettina Hipke, Patrick Jahn, Jan Junglas, Lukas Laureck, Manuel Lipstein, Medea Menzel, Katrin Obersteiner, Lena Pointner, Melanie Schippling, Jana Schmelzer, Gianna Urbanczik, Nataliya Veit, Katherine Walker, Lara Wenz, Anne Wiesner and Maria Zielenbach.

I am very grateful to a number of funding bodies for making our research possible. Our current project (*Language documentation and psycholinguistics: Documenting child language among the Qaqet of Papua New Guinea*) started in 2014 with generous funding from the Volkswagen Foundation's Lichtenberg program. It builds on a pilot project from 2013 (*Language socialisation and the transmission of Qaqet Baining (Papua New Guinea): Towards a documentation project*, funded by the Endangered Languages Documentation Programme) and on earlier research from 2011 to 2014 on the adult language (*Semantic categories: Exploring the history of the Baining languages of Island Melanesia*, funded by the Australian Research Council). I am also very grateful to the National Research Institute of Papua New Guinea, to the Office of the Provincial Administrator and to the Planning Office of East New Britain Province for endorsing and facilitating our research.

Having researched African languages for most of my academic life, it was not a matter of course that I should turn to a Papuan language in Papua New Guinea. The idea first emerged and took shape during the many interactions with colleagues and friends at the Centre for Research on Language Diversity at La Trobe University. I want to especially thank Tonya Stebbins for her enthusiastic descriptions of her own research among the related Mali Baining – without her, I would probably not have made the move to Papua New Guinea, and would never have met the Qaqet. And I want to thank Roger Wales for his power of persuasion and constant encouragement to integrate a child language perspective into my documentary and descriptive research. Even though this grammar is a grammar of the adult language, it has benefited from this new perspective – being able to draw on a large corpus of natural data, and gaining surprising insights on the adult grammar from child speech and child-directed speech.

Most of the grammar writing took place at the Department of Linguistics at the University of Cologne, and I could not have wished for a better place to do so. The university has a very active community of linguists, both at the department and across the faculty as a whole, with sometimes very different backgrounds and experiences – making our interactions stimulating and challenging at the same time, exposing us to new ways of thinking, encouraging us to think our ideas through, and broadening our overall perspectives. And all that in a very collegial atmosphere. Many thanks to the entire Cologne linguist community, and especially to Sonja Riesberg, Volker Unterladstetter and Claudia Wegener for their Papuan perspectives, to Trudel Schneider-Blum for reminding me of my Africanist background, to Gabriele

Schwiertz for her feedback on prosody and phonetics, to Dagmar Jung for the discussions on child language documentation, to Inge Molitor and Lena Wolberg for their unwavering and competent support, and to Nikolaus Himmelmann for being one of the driving forces behind this community and giving me the chance to participate in it.

Last but not least, many thanks to Bernard Comrie for reading the grammar cover to cover, and improving it with his helpful suggestions.

Amatlungena.

Contents

List of tables, figures and maps

Tables

Figures

Maps

Abbreviations and conventions

The interlinearization of examples follows the Leipzig Glossing Rules. The following abbreviations are used:

ART	article
ART.ID	article (inherently identifiable referents)
ASSOC	associative
AWAY	away from deictic center (directional)
BACK	back to deictic center (directional)
BEN	benefactive
COLL	collective
CONJ	conjunction
CONT	continuous (aspect)
DEM	demonstrative
DEONT	deontic
DIM	diminutive
DIR	directional
DIST	distal
DU	dual
EMPH	emphatic
EXC	excised (noun class)
EXT	extended (noun class)
F	feminine
FLAT	flat (noun class)
FUT	future
H	human
HERE	proximal (directional)
IDEOPH	ideophone
INTJ	interjection
INTRG	interrogative
IPFV	imperfective
LOC.PART	locative (location at part of a whole)
LONG	long (noun class)
M	masculine
N	neuter
NC	noun class
NCONT	non-continuous (aspect)
NEG	negation
NM	noun marker
NMLZ	nominalizer
NPST	non-past
NSPEC	non-specific
NUM	numeral
pfx	prefix
PL	plural
PLACE	locative (location at a place)
POSS	possessive

PROX	proximal
PST	past
PURP	purposive
RCD	reduced (noun class)
RECP	reciprocal
SBJ	subject (tr/intr)
sfx	suffix
SG	singular
SIM	simultaneous conjunction
THERE	distal (directional)
:AT	complex verb containing preposition 'at'
:IN	complex verb containing preposition 'in'
:LOC.PART	complex verb containing preposition ' LOC.PART'
:ON/UNDER	complex verb containing preposition 'on/under'
:PLACE	complex verb containing preposition 'PLACE'
:PURP	complex verb containing preposition or conjunction 'PURP'
:RECP	complex verb containing reciprocal
:SELF	complex verb containing reflexive
:SIDE	complex verb containing relational noun 'side'
:TO/WITH	complex verb containing preposition 'to/with'
:UP	complex verb containing directional 'up'
:??	complex verb containing an unknown element

Occasionally, constituents are overtly marked by means of square brackets. In such cases, the following abbreviations are used:

[...]ADJ	adjective
[...]ADV	adverb
[...]CONJ	conjunction
[...]DIR	directional
[...]INTRG	interrogative
[...]N	noun
[...]NP	noun phrase
[...]N.PROP	proper noun
[...]N.RELATOR	relational noun
[...]NUM	numeral
[...]OBJ	object
[...]PRED	predicate
[...]PTCL	particle
[...]PRO	pronoun
[...]QUANT	quantifier
[...]SBJ	subject
[...]V	verb

The following notation and transcription conventions are used when representing example sentences:

,	boundary of an intonation unit (as defined in chapter 2.3)
..	hesitation pause
(...)	omission of material

In all cases, the example source is added in brackets after the free translation. For the conventions, see chapter 1.2.

1 Introduction

This chapter gives an introduction to the Qaqet language and its speakers (section 1.1) and the fieldwork setting and data types (section 1.2). It also includes a brief typological profile situating Qaqet among the East Papuan languages and its Oceanic neighbors (section 1.3), and it presents the structure of the grammar (section 1.4).

1.1 The Qaqet language and its speakers

Qaqet is a non-Austronesian Baining language that is spoken by an estimated 15,000 people in the Gazelle Peninsula of Papua New Guinea's East New Britain Province. This section discusses the linguistic classification of Qaqet (section 1.1.1), summarizes previous research (section 1.1.2) and outlines aspects of the sociolinguistic landscape, situating the field sites within this larger setting (section 1.1.3).

1.1.1 Linguistic classification

Qaqet belongs to the Baining language family, which consists of six distinct languages: Qaqet [ISO 639-3: byx], Mali [gcc], Qairaq [ckr], Simbali [smg], Ura [uro] and possibly Makolkol [zmh]. There is not enough information available to determine Makolkol's genetic relationships with any certainty. All languages are minority languages spoken by small numbers of speakers, and Makolkol is probably extinct.

The Qaqet were the first Baining group to come into contact with the early explorers, missionaries and administrators, and the term 'Baining' was originally used in reference to them. To the extent that the other Baining groups became known to the colonial world, they were first thought to speak dialects of a single 'Baining' language. Today, as more linguistic information has become available, it is clear that they speak distinct, mutually not intelligible, languages.

The wider genetic affiliation of the Baining group remains unclear. They are negatively classified as non-Austronesian or non-Oceanic (or Papuan) and they are included within the geographically defined group of East Papuan languages. These are the approximately 25 non-Austronesian languages spoken in Island Melanesia, i.e., in the island region of Papua New Guinea (including New Britain, New Ireland, Milne Bay and Bougainville) and the Solomon Islands. Speakers of present-day East Papuan languages are the descendants of the first inhabitants of that region, with archaeological records dating back 30 to 35,000 years (Dunn, Reesink, and Terrill 2002; Spriggs 1997).

There have been attempts at establishing East Papuan as a genetic unit (Wurm 1982: 231–244), but the enormous time depth has left us very few potentially cognate items. Most authors therefore only posit smaller genetic groupings, arguing that the genetic unity of East Papuan as a whole cannot be proven by means of the comparative method (Foley 1986; Ross 2001, 2005). More recently, attention has shifted towards structural features, employing statistical models that have proved successful in the biological sciences. On this basis, Dunn et al. (2005, 2007, 2008) argue that the present-day distribution of such features constitutes evidence for either a genetic relationship or an early contact between speakers of East Papuan languages (i.e., a contact that considerably predates the much later contact to speakers of Oceanic languages) (but see Donohue and Musgrave 2007 for a critical review of this method).

The Baining languages are often grouped together with their immediate neighbors Taulil [tuh] and Butam [-] (probably extinct since the 1930s) (Foley 1986; Ross 2001: 309, 2005; Wurm 1982: 235–236), but the evidence from the comparative method is not strong (see especially Stebbins 2009a for an appraisal of the existing evidence). Taulil and Butam were not included in the study by Dunn et al. (2008) due to lack of data. The other East Papuan languages in the neighborhood, Kol [kol] and Sulka [sua] (spoken in East New Britain) and Kuot [kto] (spoken in New Ireland), are usually not grouped with the Baining languages, and are sometimes considered isolates. Structurally, there is evidence for grouping all the above languages, together with Anêm [anz] and Ata [ata] (spoken in West New Britain), into a single group encompassing all non-Austronesian languages of the Bismarck Archipelago (Dunn et al. 2008).

The vast majority of the Island Melanesia population today are speakers of Oceanic languages who started settling there around 3,200 years ago. This also includes the immediate neighbors of the Qaqet, the Tolai, who speak the Oceanic language Kuanua. Different from the genetic relationships among East Papuan languages, the relationships among the Oceanic languages are well understood (Lynch, Ross, and Crowley 2002). There has been a long history of contact, and there is considerable evidence for Oceanic borrowings into the lexicon and grammar of all Baining languages, and – to a lesser degree – evidence for borrowings from East Papuan (including Baining) into Oceanic (see section 1.3).

Qaqet is spoken over a large geographic area, and speakers consider there to be two major dialects: a northern dialect around the villages of Puktas and Lan (including coastal villages such as Kamanakam, and spreading inland towards Komgi), and a southern dialect around Raunsepna and Lamarain. Speakers comment especially on a salient phonological difference: the absence of /s/ in the northern dialect. In native Qaqet words, southern dialect /s/ corresponds to northern dialect /h/, e.g., /sləŋ/ ~ /hləŋ/ 'garden'. In integrated Tok Pisin loanwords, /s/ tends to correspond to /t/ (possibly because they were borrowed into the northern dialect via Kuanua, which also lacks /s/), e.g., /sup/ ~ /tup/ 'soap'. Otherwise speakers point to a large number of lexical differences, e.g., /ɣuldit/ (southern dialect) ~ /ɣalmin/ (northern dialect) 'frog'. However, the dialectal division is far from clear. The corpus for this grammar contains many instances of southern dialect speakers (born and raised in Raunsepna and Lamarain) who regularly use the northern phoneme /h/ or northern lexical items.

It seems likely that dialectal convergence has taken place, presumably because of the high mobility of Qaqet speakers (see section 1.1.3). The linguistic result is an exceptionally high level of variation: an apparently free alternation between /s/ and /h/, a large number of apparently synonymous lexical items, and also considerable variation in the realization of vowel phonemes and vowel sequences. It is possible that an in-depth dialectal or sociolinguistic study will be able to account for the attested distribution, but for the moment there does not seem to be any straightforward correlation with outside factors.

1.1.2 Previous research

The first anthropological notes on Qaqet Baining date back to the late 19th and early 20th century. They include reports from the *Hamburger Südsee Expedition* 1908–1910 (see Leipold 2008 for a description and contextualization of this expedition; pp. 170–176 on Baining), Parkinson's (1907) famous account of his long-term studies in that region (pp. 91–99 on Baining), and Burger's (1913) ethnographic descriptions of Baining and Taulil. Early notes on the Baining language are found in Parkinson (1907: 332–334) and Schmidt (1905). But the most important early records come from the Missionaries of the Sacred Heart (M.S.C.) priest Father Matthäus Rascher who lived among the northern Qaqet between 1896 and 1904. He wrote a first grammar of Qaqet: a handwritten manuscript (Rascher 1900), which was later edited and published (Rascher 1904); and he left us with numerous ethnographic notes and impressions of his life and missionary activities among the Qaqet (Rascher 1909). There also exist two early word lists (Stehlin 1905/1906; Volmer 1926), and a grammar sketch (Volmer 1928). And there is an early collection of traditional narratives, including both a Qaqet transcript and a German free translation (plus German word-by-word translations for some of the narratives) (Bley 1914).

Following up on these early linguistic contributions, Jim and Diana Parker from the Summer Institute of Linguistics (SIL) commenced their long-term work with the Qaqet in the 1970s. They have written a phonological sketch (Parker and Parker 1974) and a grammatical sketch (Parker and Parker 1977), and they have encouraged and contributed to a large number of Qaqet language publications. I have had access to a number of primers (Misaqi 1990; Parker, Simpson, and Cobb 1992; Tiqa, Kaltaumen, and Parker 1996), story and information booklets (Qaqet Literacy Project 2004a, 2004b, 2012, n.d.) and bible translations (PNG Bible Translation Association 1996, 2004a, 2004b, 2004c, 2005, 2006). There reportedly exist further primers, booklets and translations (Anon. 1984, 2006; Landi and Arigini 1983a, 1983b, 1983c, 1987a, 1987b, 1987c; Misaqi 1987; PNG Bible Translation Association 1976, 1978; Tiqa, Kaltaumen, and Parker 1983), but I have not been able to access them.

In addition to linguistic research, there has been considerable anthropological interest in the Baining. Following up on the early accounts, later missionaries have further contributed to our anthropological knowledge of different Baining groups, including the Qaqet Baining (e.g., Laufer 1946/1949, 1959a; Hesse and Aerts 1996; Hesse 2007). An excellent historical overview of missionary activities among the Qaqet is given in Hiery (2007). And a number of anthropologists have more recently published on the Qaqet, including Michael Dickhardt (2008, 2009, 2012), Jane Fajans (1983, 1985, 1993, 1997, 1998), Gail Pool (2015) and her husband Jeremy Pool (1984), and Marta Rohatynskyj (2000, 2001).

My own research with the Qaqet commenced in 2011, and subsequently included a team of researchers (see section 1.2). It resulted in transcribed and annotated corpora of natural speech, including both adult and child language. The corpora are archived with the Endangered Languages Archive (Hellwig 2012–2013) and with the Language Archive Cologne (Hellwig et al. 2014–2019). There also exist a sociolinguistic survey (Marley 2013) and a discussion of methodological aspects of our research (Hellwig, to appear).

Our modern linguistic knowledge of Baining languages is largely due to the work by Tonya Stebbins, who has extensively published on Mali Baining (Stebbins 2004, 2005, 2009a, 2009b, 2011; Stebbins and Planigale 2010; Stebbins and Tayul 2009, 2012). In addition, there exist publications on issues of language planning among the Qairaq (Schneider 2011, 2015) and on the morphophonology of Ura (Stanton 2007). To my knowledge, there are no linguistic resources available for either Simbali or Makolkol.

Turning to the other East Papuan languages of the region, a small number of linguistic analyses can be found. The early missionary Paul Futscher has done work on both Taulil and Butam, but unfortunately his work on Butam only survives in a later overview by Carl Laufer (Futscher 1959; Laufer 1950, 1959b, 1959c); there exists also a recent grammar of Taulil (Meng 2018). Our earliest knowledge on Sulka dates back to Müller (1915/16) and Schmidt (1904), followed by Schneider (1962), Tharp (1996) and finally Reesink (2005). Reesink (2005) also includes information on Kol. Finally, Kuot is known through the work of Chung and Chung (1996) and Lindström (2002; Lindström and Remijsen 2005).

Throughout the grammar, I draw on the above references to point out similarities and differences to Qaqet.

1.1.3 Sociolinguistic setting

The Baining are very likely the original inhabitants of the Gazelle peninsula of East New Britain Province, while other groups migrated there more recently (Stebbins 2009a). The dominant immigrant group, the Tolai, established a hierarchical relationship with the Baining. Adjacent communities were subjugated, had to pay tribute and take part in raids, while remote communities were the targets of such raids. During the colonial period, the Baining suffered epidemics and further stress through forced acculturation. The consequences were so dramatic that the missionaries of the mid-20th century spoke of the Baining as "a dying people" (Hiery 2007). Fortunately, their dire predictions did not come true. The various Baining groups, including the Qaqet, have recovered and today live a fairly autonomous life as highly mobile gardeners in the remote mountainous interior of the peninsula.

Today, there are only few outsiders in the remote Qaqet-speaking areas (Marley 2013): most marriages are intra-ethnic, and most outsiders live there only temporarily in an official capacity (as primary school teachers, nurses or church staff). As a result, Qaqet is still spoken regularly, and children still acquire it as their first languages. Outside of these remote settings, however, the Qaqet were, and still are, marginalized, and their society, culture and language are barely visible to the outside world. In the more accessible villages, they live permanently together with speakers of other languages, and their language is rapidly disappearing. Most adult Qaqet are multilingual and speak neighboring language(s), Kuanua, and the national lingua franca Tok Pisin (an English- and Kuanua-based creole). It is especially Tok Pisin that is increasingly endangering Qaqet and becoming the language of communication in all inter-ethnic contexts.

My and my team's research took place in both kinds of sociolinguistic landscapes: in the remote villages of Raunsepna and Lamarain and in the accessible village of Kamanakam.

Raunsepna is located in the mountainous interior of the Gazelle peninsula (with the geographical coordinates of -4,455352, 151,783302), and it borders the village of Lamarain (with the geographical coordinates of -4,471122, 151,791748). Its location is fairly remote and it can currently only be reached on foot (between 9 and 14 kilometers hike through rugged mountain territory, depending on the route taken). For a brief period (1980s until ca. 2005), four-wheel drive cars were able to reach the village on a rough road. Raunsepna is a major village in this part of the mountains. It is spread over a large area, encompassing several smaller autonomous communities (Merlalingi, Lasrlem, Kedel, Lualait, Lualait-Ranganan, Lualait-Anesmetki). In 2010, Dickhardt (2009: 137) counted 1,326 inhabitants, distributed over 238 households. At the center of Raunsepna is the so-called Station, which offers a number of central services that attract Qaqet from across the region: a primary school, a health post and a Catholic mission. Most non-Qaqet outsiders live at the Station: teachers, nurses, nuns and sometimes a priest, who are all temporarily stationed there and who are usually accompanied by a small number of family members. Outside of the Station, the population is almost exclusively Qaqet, with very few non-Qaqet spouses who have married into the community. It is not surprising that, in this kind of setting, the Qaqet language and culture have remained strong. Qaqet continues to be the dominant language spoken in all contexts that do not include outsiders, and children acquire Qaqet as their first language. All adults are bilingual in the lingua franca Tok Pisin, which they speak with non-Qaqet interlocutors. Children come into contact with Tok Pisin to varying degrees: through friends from the Station and from inter-ethnic marriages, and later through the elementary school (from around 6 to 7 years of age). But if they remain in the region, their dominant language continues to be Qaqet.

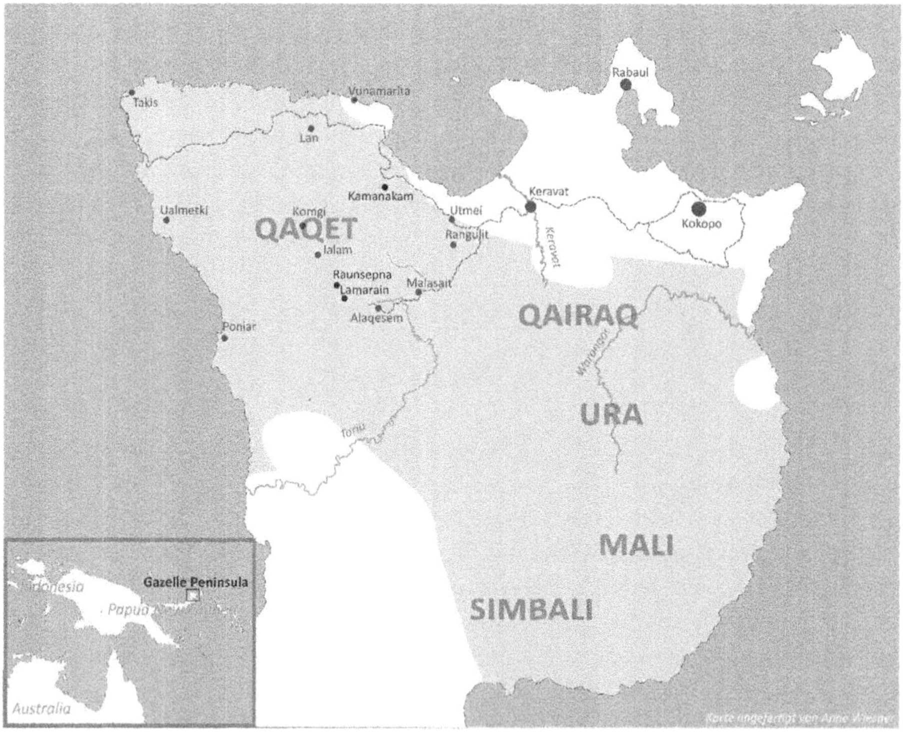

Map 1: The Qaqet area (Papua New Guinea, East New Britain, Gazelle Peninsula)

Villages such as Raunsepna and Lamarain are a new phenomenon and were established during the life-time of the oldest generation. The colonial administration created village structures and enforced settlement in them. Before, people lived highly mobile lives in small hamlets, pursuing slash-and-burn agriculture and hunting, and moving on as they created new gardens in the rain forest. People today still retain parts of this mobile life-style. Although they now own permanent homes in one of the new villages, they also maintain temporary homes in their various gardens in the mountains and on their plots along the coast. Different members of a family continue to move between these homes, settling for longer or shorter periods at any one of them. Most Qaqet continue to live as gardeners, supplemented with some hunting (of especially wild pigs, bandicoots, wallabies and cassowaries). They are famous in the entire region for growing taro and singapore (a type of taro) as well as peanuts (as a major cash crop). Their staple food also includes sweet potatoes, cassava, wild sugarcane (known in Tok Pisin as *pitpit*) and various kinds of leafy greens. Most have plots of land, known as *blocks*, at the more accessible coast where they plant cocoa and coconuts, which constitute their main source of cash income. These blocks are in the vicinity of villages like Kamanakam, allowing people to visit and interact with friends and relatives along the coast. But unlike the people of, e.g., Kamanakam, they do not consider the coast their home and they regularly spend time in Raunsepna-Lamarain.

While Qaqet remains strong in Raunsepna and Lamarain, its status in Kamanakam is much less stable. Kamanakam is located at the coast (at the geographical coordinates of -4,336388, 151,890085). The village is connected by road to the main towns of East New Britain – and although the road is in need of maintenance and, especially, bridgework, private cars and public transport regularly run on it. Kamanakam has a sizable Qaqet population that lives in close proximity to many non-Qaqet, including especially speakers of the Oceanic language Kuanua, but also large numbers from the Sepik and the Highlands areas of mainland Papua New Guinea. The non-Qaqet population initially came to work on the nearby plantations and to cultivate their own plots of land. By now, many of them have permanently settled and they have formed marriage and other interpersonal ties with the Qaqet community. As a result, Tok Pisin has become the dominant language of Kamanakam. Adult Qaqet still speak Qaqet in intra-ethnic settings – but such occasions are much fewer than in Raunsepna-Lamarain. And children grow up with both languages: they have various degrees of command of Qaqet, while their main language is Tok Pisin.

1.2 Fieldwork and data

The data for this grammar was collected during several research projects: a project on the adult language (2011–2014; funded by the Australian Research Council, FT0991412), a pilot project on child language (2012–2013; funded by the Endangered Languages Documentation Programme, SG0110), and a comprehensive project on language acquisition and socialization (2014–2019; funded by the Volkswagen Foundation's Lichtenberg Program, Az87100). At various points during the different projects, the research team also included the following researchers: Carmen Dawuda (constructing the child corpus in Kamanakam), Sonja Eisenbeiß and Evan Kidd (contributing psycholinguistic perspectives), PhD students Henrike Frye and Steffen Reetz, and MA student Alexandra Marley.

As introduced in section 1.1.3, research took place in two locations (Raunsepna-Lamarain and Kamanakam), but this grammar is largely based on the variety spoken in Raunsepna-Lamarain (unless stated otherwise). The reason is that the focus of our research in Kamanakam is on child language, i.e., most of the adult data, and especially all grammatical elicitation, comes from Raunsepna-Lamarain. There are some dialectal differences (see section 1.1.1) and the variety spoken in Kamanakam is heavily influenced by Tok Pisin. The relationship between Qaqet and Tok Pisin in Kamanakam is the topic of a separate PhD thesis within our project (Reetz, in prep.). This grammar is largely based on adult-to-adult interactions, although it occasionally draws on features attested in child language and in child-directed speech. An in-depth analysis of child-directed speech in Raunsepna-Lamarain is the topic of a separate PhD thesis (Frye, in prep.).

This grammar is based on elicited, staged and natural data, and the source of each example is stated following its free translation. In the case of elicitation, the source is specified as Speaker ID (see Tables 2 and 3 for information on the participants) plus date (e.g., AJL-15/06/2011 means that the data was elicited from AJL on 15 Jun 2011). This includes both written field notes and audio-recorded elicited words, paradigms, phrases and sentences. In the case of staged and natural data, the source is specified as text name plus segment reference (e.g., N11AAGBROTHERS-0039 refers to the 39th segment of the text labeled N11AAGBROTHERS). Segmentation is done on the basis of intonation units. The text name contains basic information on the text type, recording date and speaker. In most cases, it is made up of one letter for the text type (see Table 1 for the conventions), followed by two digits for the recording year, three letters for the ID of the speaker (if there is more than one speaker, the IDs of up to three speakers are added; if there are more than three speakers, the ID is noted as VAR 'various speakers'), and a short title. For example, N11AAGBROTHERS is a narrative about 'brothers', recorded in 2011 from the speaker AAG. Alternatively, natural examples are taken from the longitudinal child corpus, which also contains numerous adult-to-adult interactions. In this case, the text name starts with LONG (for longitudinal) and is followed by the ID of the focal child, the recording date in the format YYYYMMDD and a running number (e.g., LONGYJL20140903_1 refers to the longitudinal corpus of child YJL, recorded on 3rd of September 2014, part 1). Table 1 summarizes the types and amounts of textual data. Note that the longitudinal data is not yet transcribed in its entirety, and only a subset of about 60 hours was available to this grammar.

Texts collected until 2013 are archived with the Endangered Languages Archive (Hellwig 2012–2013), and texts collected from 2014 onwards are archived with the Language Archive Cologne (Hellwig et al. 2014–2019). Due to the sensitive nature of child data, only the adult texts are publically accessible.

A very large number of Qaqet contributed information and data to the different projects and thus ultimately to this grammar. Tables 2 and 3 list all adult and child participants, giving the following information: the participant's three-letter ID, their sex, their (approximate) date of birth, and their community of birth. Most of the participants were born in one of the smaller communities that together make up the village of Raunsepna (Merlalingi, Lasrlem, Kedel, Lualait and Lualait-Anesmetki) or in nearby Lamarain, and they continue to live in this area. If their exact community of birth is unknown, it was noted as Raunsepna. A few were born in other Qaqet villages (in Komgi and Malasait), but have now settled in Raunsepna. Throughout this grammar, as well as in the archived corpora, data is related back to the contributors by means of their three-letter ID.

Tab. 1: Overview of text types

Text type	Abbreviation (in text name)	Amount of data
Written texts & Translations	B ~ L	7 texts
Conversations	C	01:24:10 hours
Descriptions	D	00:10:47 hours
Interviews	I	02:12:14 hours
Narratives	N	00:58:48 hours
Procedural texts	P	01:00:51 hours
Story retellings	R	02:21:50 hours
Longitudinal data	Long	192:16:31 hours

Tab. 2: Participants (adults)

ID	Sex	(Approx.) date of birth	Community of birth
AAD	m	ca. 1980	Merlalingi
AAG	m	ca. 1982	Lasrlem
AAI	f	27 Aug 1979	Lualait
AAK	f	ca. 1960	Komgi
AAN	f	ca. 1943	Lualait
AAS	f	29 Jun 1980	Komgi
AAX	f	ca. 1950	Merlalingi
ABB	m	ca. 1977	Kedel
ABD	f	02 Jan 1980	Merlalingi
ABI	m	10 May 1985	Lasrlem
ABK	m	ca. 1982	Lamarain
ABL	m	1943	Lualait
ABS	m	1988	Komgi
ABU	m	ca. 1991	Raunsepna
AAD	m	ca. 1980	Merlalingi
ACB	m	1968	Merlalingi
ACG	f	2000	Lualait
ACL	f	ca. 1955	Merlalingi

ID	Sex	(Approx.) date of birth	Community of birth
ACM	m	21 Nov 1975	Lasrlem
ACP	m	11 Feb 1978	Merlalingi
ACS	m	ca. 1982	Merlalingi
ACT	m	ca. 1994	Raunsepna
ACU	f	ca. 1972	Merlalingi
ADK	m	09 Jan 1963	Merlalingi
ADN	f	ca. 1952	Komgi
AEL	f	1991	Lasrlem
AEM	f	01 Jan 1980	Merlalingi
AFD	m	1984	Lamarain
AFK	m	06 Jun 1980	Lasrlem
AFL	m	ca. 1980	Raunsepna
AFN	f	2000	Anesmetki
AFT	m	ca. 1998	Lualait
AFY	m	ca. 1982	Lualait
AGK	f	03 Dec 1984	Lualait
AGR	m	07 Jul 1993	Merlalingi
AGS	f	ca. 1995	Merlalingi
AGT	f	1993	Anesmetki
AHL	m	02 Apr 1986	Merlalingi
AHX	m	ca. 2000	Raunsepna
AIK	m	1997	Komgi
AJA	f	1994	Anesmetki
AJL	m	12 Mar 1952	Komgi
AJN	m	ca. 1982	Kedel
AJR	m	ca. 1996	Merlalingi
AJS	f	1979	Kedel
ALM	m	ca. 1980	Merlalingi
ALN	f	ca. 1994	Anesmetki
ALR	f	15 Apr 1976	Merlalingi
ALS	f	ca. 1989	Merlalingi
ALT	f	10 Jan 1985	Kedel
AMB	m	1970	Lasrlem
AME	f	ca. 1980	Lualait
AMI	f	06 Oct 1962	Lualait
AMK	f	ca. 1960	Lualait
AML	f	1991	Kedel
AMM	f	04 Sep 1991	Lualait

ID	Sex	(Approx.) date of birth	Community of birth
AMS	f	09 Sep 1980	Merlalingi
AMT	f	09 Feb 1990	Merlalingi
AMV	m	ca. 1982	Lamarain
AMW	m	08 Oct 1974	Merlalingi
APA	m	1982	Merlalingi
APL	m	23 Sep 1977	Merlalingi
APN	f	16 Feb 1985	Lasrlem
APP	m	ca. 1980	Raunsepna
APR	m	ca. 1998	Lasrlem
ARB	f	12 Sep 1977	Merlalingi
ARL	m	06 Sep 1979	Merlalingi
ARM	f	ca. 1990	Merlalingi
ARN	f	1982	Kedel
ARS	f	09 Dec 1983	Kedel
ART	f	30 Mar 1994	Kedel
ARV	m	ca. 1984	Merlalingi
ASB	f	ca. 1997	Merlalingi
ASG	m	ca. 1952	Kedel
ASH	m	16 Nov 1996	Kedel
ASQ	f	23 Jan 1981	Lualait
ASS	f	14 Jun 1990	Lasrlem
AST	m	1997	Merlalingi
ATA	m	ca. 1952	Merlalingi
ATK	f	27 Nov 1983	Merlalingi
ATT	f	1974	Kedel
AUA	f	1991	Lasrlem
AVD	m	07 Feb 1983	Lualait
AXA	m	ca. 2000	Raunsepna
AXG	f	ca. 1990	Raunsepna
AXK	m	ca. 2000	Raunsepna
AXP	f	ca. 1990	Raunsepna
AXT	m	ca. 1985	Raunsepna
BAK	f	20 Apr 1988	Lasrlem
BAM	m	ca. 1988	Lasrlem
BBK	m	1997	Merlalingi
BBL	m	ca. 1989	Merlalingi
BCK	f	ca. 1995	Merlalingi
BCL	f	1996	Anesmetki

ID	Sex	(Approx.) date of birth	Community of birth
BCM	m	ca. 1993	Komgi
BCP	m	20 Jun 1976	Kedel
BCS	m	ca. 1994	Raunsepna
BDN	f	ca. 1990	Raunsepna
BFN	m	23 Apr 1977	Lasrlem
BGR	m	ca. 1960	Merlalingi
BGS	m	ca. 1980	Merlalingi
BJA	f	1998	Anesmetki
BJR	f	Jun 1986	Merlalingi
BJS	f	1986	Kedel
BLN	f	May 1985	Merlalingi
BLT	f	22 Mar 1977	Kedel
BME	f	1986	Lasrlem
BMS	f	ca. 1964	Komgi
BPL	m	ca. 1982	Lualait
BRN	f	ca. 1998	Kedel
BRS	f	ca. 1968	Merlalingi
BRT	m	ca. 1998	Raunsepna
BXK	m	ca. 1985	Raunsepna
BXP	m	ca. 1985	Raunsepna
CAK	m	ca. 1998	Merlalingi
CBK	m	25 Jul 1993	Merlalingi
CBL	m	ca. 1997	Komgi
CCK	f	20 Feb 1988	Lamarain
CCL	m	ca. 1982	Merlalingi
CCM	m	1975	Lualait
CDN	f	ca. 1996	Lualait
CGS	f	02 Jun 1994	Merlalingi
CJR	f	ca. 2000	Kedel
CJS	m	1998	Malasait
CLS	f	07 Nov 1981	Lasrlem
CMS	f	1979	Komgi
CXK	m	ca. 1985	Raunsepna
DAK	m	1982	Lasrlem
DCK	m	17 Feb 1977	Lualait
DCM	m	02 Feb 1957	Lasrlem

Tab. 3: Participants (children)

ID	Sex	(Approx.) Date of Birth	Community
WCS	m	19 Jan 2010	Merlalingi
WMM	f	08 Jan 2012	Lualait
WMS	f	ca. 2008	Merlalingi
XAN	f	12 Apr 2011	Kedel
XAT	m	16 Jun 2013	Merlalingi
XBM	m	May 2016	Kedel
XCA	m	ca. 2000	Merlalingi
XCD	m	11 Feb 2004	Kedel
XCL	m	18 Jun 2013	Merlalingi
XCM	f	14 Nov 2003	Lualait
XCS	f	07 Jan 2004	Merlalingi
XEB	f	27 Nov 2010	Lasrlem
XEN	m	11 Jun 2016	Merlalingi
XFK	f	Mar 2009	Lualait
XMD	f	02 Mar 2015	Lasrlem
XMK	f	19 Apr 2009	Kedel
XMM	f	14 Apr 2008	Lualait
XMS	f	May 2014	Merlalingi
XMU	f	25 Jun 2011	Merlalingi
XPS	f	03 Sep 2015	Lasrlem
XRN	f	24 Apr 2014	Kedel
XSD	f	16 Feb 2006	Lualait
XVL	f	20 Jan 2016	Kedel
XXK	m	ca. 2014	Merlalingi
YAK	m	26 Feb 2008	Merlalingi
YAT	m	15 Oct 1998	Raunsepna
YBD	f	13 May 2010	Lualait
YBM	m	12 Nov 1999	Merlalingi
YBS	m	ca. 2014	Merlalingi
YCA	f	01 Jan 2000	Merlalingi
YCL	m	09 Jun 2001	Raunsepna
YCS	m	ca. 2002	Merlalingi
YDK	m	ca. 2008	Merlalingi
YDS	f	13 May 2013	Merlalingi
YGK	m	21 Sep 2007	Merlalingi
YGL	f	05 Jun 2006	Merlalingi

ID	Sex	(Approx.) Date of Birth	Community
YHK	f	24 May 2016	Lualait
YJL	f	20 Dec 2011	Merlalingi
YJS	f	ca. 2013	Merlalingi
YLP	m	17 Sep 2009	Merlalingi
YMM	f	26 Feb 2010	Merlalingi
YMN	f	26 Feb 2013	Lualait
YMS	f	27 Jan 2012	Merlalingi
YRA	m	27 Feb 2012	Merlalingi
YST	m	22 Oct 2010	Kedel
YXA	m	ca. 2014	Merlalingi
YXK	m	ca. 2006	Merlalingi
ZAE	m	21 Nov 2005	Lualait
ZAK	m	12 Jul 2001	Merlalingi
ZAL	m	ca. 2002	Lasrlem
ZAM	f	06 Feb 2000	Raunsepna
ZAP	m	Dec 2009	Lualait
ZAR	f	01 Feb 2008	Lasrlem
ZAT	m	ca. 2000	Raunsepna
ZBG	m	22 Jan 2016	Merlalingi
ZBK	f	12 Oct 2012	Merlalingi
ZBL	m	23 Oct 1998	Lasrlem
ZBM	m	27 Aug 1998	Lasrlem
ZBS	m	ca. 2000	Raunsepna
ZCA	m	05 May 1999	Merlalingi
ZCD	m	Jul 2000	Merlalingi
ZCK	f	20 May 2013	Lualait
ZCL	f	29 Jun 2001	Merlalingi
ZCN	m	Jul 2001	Anesmetki
ZCR	f	02 Feb 2011	Merlalingi
ZCS	f	ca. 2002	Merlalingi
ZDK	m	14 Dec 1999	Merlalingi
ZDL	m	08 Jan 2014	Merlalingi
ZDS	m	ca. 2005	Lualait
ZEA	f	08 Sep 2013	Lualait
ZEP	m	08 Nov 2015	Merlalingi
ZFI	f	ca. 2004	Merlalingi
ZFL	f	22 Oct 1998	Raunsepna
ZFM	m	06 Jun 2009	Merlalingi

ID	Sex	(Approx.) Date of Birth	Community
ZGD	f	ca. 2003	Raunsepna
ZGI	m	20 Feb 2013	Merlalingi
ZGK	f	Oct 2002	Anesmetki
ZGL	m	ca. 2000	Raunsepna
ZGM	m	ca. 2003	Raunsepna
ZGT	m	17 Sep 2009	Merlalingi
ZHK	f	ca. 2006	Merlalingi
ZIG	m	07 Oct 2015	Merlalingi
ZJD	m	ca. 2002	Lasrlem
ZJI	f	20 Feb 2006	Merlalingi
ZJK	f	16 Sep 2012	Lualait
ZJL	m	ca. 2006	Merlalingi
ZJN	f	19 Jun 1999	Raunsepna
ZJR	m	ca. 2004	Raunsepna
ZJS	m	10 May 2010	Merlalingi
ZJU	m	26 Sep 2000	Raunsepna
ZKL	m	2000	Kedel
ZKM	f	21 Sep 2007	Merlalingi
ZLB	m	Feb 2003	Merlalingi
ZLK	m	29 Mar 2016	Lualait
ZLP	f	ca. 2002	Raunsepna
ZMA	f	05 May 1998	Raunsepna
ZMB	m	ca. 2008	Merlalingi
ZMK	f	16 May 2001	Lasrlem
ZMM	m	17 Feb 2001	Lasrlem
ZMS	f	ca. 2006	Merlalingi
ZNK	m	2008	Kedel
ZNN	f	20 Sep 2013	Merlalingi
ZPI	f	ca. 2006	Merlalingi
ZPK	f	ca. 2006	Merlalingi
ZRA	f	ca. 2002	Raunsepna
ZRG	f	31 Dec 1998	Kedel
ZRK	f	14 Oct 2000	Raunsepna
ZRS	m	09 Apr 2000	Raunsepna
ZSD	f	ca. 2004	Raunsepna
ZSX	m	ca. 2006	Raunsepna
ZTT	f	15 Jun 2005	Merlalingi
ZTX	m	ca. 2007	Merlalingi

ID	Sex	(Approx.) Date of Birth	Community
ZVI	f	ca. 1998	Merlalingi
ZVK	f	Dec 2010	Kedel
ZXA	m	ca. 2011	Merlalingi
ZXK	m	ca. 2000	Raunsepna
ZXN	m	ca. 2004	Raunsepna
ZXP	f	ca. 1998	Raunsepna
ZXU	f	ca. 2011	Raunsepna

1.3 Typological profile

As outlined in section 1.1.1, it is not easy to establish genetic links between the East Papuan languages. There are, however, a number of typological features that are widespread amongst them and that are not widely shared with neighboring Oceanic languages. As Lindström et al. (2007: 128) note, "[t]he puzzle presented by these languages is their recurrent structural similarities together with the absence of formal correspondences (...)." This section summarizes the salient typological features of Qaqet, and places them in an East Papuan and areal perspective. For detailed accounts of their distribution in East Papuan and neighboring Oceanic, see Donohue and Musgrave (2007), Dunn, Reesink, and Terrill (2002), Dunn et al. (2008), Lindström et al. (2007), Reesink (2005), Ross (1996), Stebbins (2009a) and Terrill (2002).

Qaqet has a smallish phoneme inventory (16 consonant and 4 vowel phonemes) that includes a phonemic contrast between voiceless and voiced plosives, a phonemic contrast between /r/ and /l/, intervocalic lenition of voiceless plosives and the recent development of fricative phonemes from this process of lenition. The first two features are considered characteristic features of Oceanic, not of East Papuan (Dunn et al. 2008: 743). All four features are shared by the Baining languages and Kuot, but apparently not by the other East Papuan languages of the Bismarck Archipelago (Stebbins 2009a). Like many East Papuan languages (Lindström et al. 2007: 126), Qaqet has complex syllable structures, allowing for consonant clusters and word-final consonants. The prosodic structures of East Papuan languages are not well-understood, but there exists an excellent description of Kuot prosody (Lindström and Remijsen 2005). Qaqet differs from Kuot in that it does not have lexical stress, but it is otherwise remarkably similar to Kuot in its inventory of pitch movements that mark (mostly) the right edge of intonation units.

Overall, there is good evidence for the existence of different word classes (including the open classes of nouns, adjectives, verbs and adverbs). And although adjectives share morphosyntactic similarities with nouns, there are formal differences that justify setting up a distinct adjective class. The word classes are distinguished on the basis of their morphosyntactic properties, but there is one qualification to be added: many roots can occur underived in different word classes. This phenomenon is also attested in Mali Baining, and like Stebbins (2011: 58–59, 95–97), I consider it a case of conversion (not of acategoriality). Furthermore, there is also good evidence for the existence of phrases (with fixed and contiguous structures), including noun phrases. Nevertheless, there exists a small number of examples that deviate from the typical noun phrase structure, and some examples even show discontinuous structures. It is very likely that information structural constraints account for this variation, but the number of attested examples is too small to attempt larger generalizations.

In the nominal domain, Qaqet exhibits a number of characteristic East Papuan features (Dunn, Reesink, and Terrill 2002: 33–36; Dunn et al. 2008: 743; Stebbins 2009a; Terrill 2002). Most notably, nouns are marked for noun class (distinguishing two sex-based and six shape-based classes) and number (distinguishing singular, dual and plural), and the classes overtly appear in a large number of grammatical environments: as free pronouns and as arguments that developed from the free pronouns (object suffixes on verbs and prepositions); and on noun phrase elements agreeing with the noun (adjectives, the numerals 'one' and 'two', demonstratives, some indefinite pronouns, and the interrogative pronouns 'which' and 'who'). Furthermore, the noun classes are mapped onto a smaller system (labeled 'gender' throughout this grammar), which surfaces in the form of possessor indexes on possessed nouns, of subject indexes on verbs, and as associative pronouns. Both nominal classification and the dual/plural distinction are widespread among the East Papuan languages, and are largely absent from Oceanic. But although East Papuan languages tend to have some form of nominal classification, the formal and semantic properties of these systems are very different. The Qaqet system shares similarities with those of other Baining languages, but it remains to be seen whether similarities are also found with the other East Papuan languages of the Bismarcks.

In terms of noun phrase structure, Qaqet has pre-head determiners (demonstratives, indefinites and articles) and post-head adjectival and nominal (including numeral) modifiers. Post-head adjectives and numerals are shared by many East Papuan languages, while pre-head demonstratives are less common (albeit attested, too). The main evidence for Oceanic influence in this domain is the existence of definite and indefinite articles preceding the noun: articles are generally considered an Oceanic borrowing, which are now found in most East Papuan languages of New Britain.

In possessive noun phrases, Qaqet displays the typical Papuan order of the possessor preceding the possessed – despite not (or no longer) having the concomitant Papuan verb-final constituent order. Qaqet also does not have any possessive classifiers, which are typical of Oceanic languages (although they are largely absent in neighboring Oceanic languages, too). There is evidence for Qaqet having the category of inalienable possession (which is typical of Oceanic languages), but it only concerns a handful of items (a few kinship nouns, relational nouns and irregular proforms).

The category surfaces in the form of prefixes (and not suffixes, as would be typical for Oceanic).

Similarly, the pronominal categories are characteristic of East Papuan (Dunn, Reesink, and Terrill 2002: 40–41, 45–48; Stebbins 2009a): Qaqet has dedicated dual pronouns, and it shows no evidence for a distinction between inclusive and exclusive first person. Like in many other East Papuan languages, participants are indexed on the verb, but they are indexed by means of subject proclitics and object suffixes (and not by means of subject suffixes, as is otherwise the preference in East Papuan) (Dunn, Reesink, and Terrill 2002: 52–57; Dunn et al. 2008: 743).

In the verbal domain, Qaqet exhibits the typical lexicalization patterns reported for many Papuan languages (see, e.g., Foley 1986: 111–166). As such, verbs are highly compositional, consisting of simple verbs with general meanings that combine with other elements (usually prepositions, in the case of Qaqet) to form complex verbs with idiomatic, non-compositional, meanings. Similarly, Qaqet pays attention to many of the categories reported for other Papuan languages: it distinguishes continuous and non-continuous aspect (through distinct aspectual verb stems), and controlled and non-controlled events (through argument structure alternations). The only conspicuous absence is stem alternations that depend on the person and number of arguments – a pattern that is found in many East Papuan languages (Dunn, Reesink, and Terrill 2002: 38–57). While the semantic patterns seem to be of Papuan origin, their formal means of expression differ. In particular, verb serialization is not attested synchronically, and it cannot be identified as a source of lexicalization in the verb lexicon either. There is some evidence, though, that at least some particles and modifiers to the predicate originated in multi-verb constructions (possibly in serial verb constructions). Instead, Qaqet makes pervasive use of prepositions. It is possible to trace a diachronic development from prepositional phrases functioning as adjuncts via prepositions introducing arguments entailed by the verb semantics to particles and suffixes that have become lexicalized as parts of complex verbs.

More generally, prepositions are an areal pattern of the Bismarck Archipelago: they are not typical of (East) Papuan languages (which tend to have postpositions), and they are thus sometimes attributed to contact with Oceanic (Dunn, Reesink, and Terrill 2002: 33; Dunn et al. 2008: 743). Qaqet does not have any inherited postpositions, but there is a recent development from possessed nouns to relational nouns, which can arguably be analyzed as developing into postpositions.

Prepositions, relational nouns and adverbs predominantly convey spatial meanings. In addition, Qaqet has a complex and prevalent directional system that is based on the mountainous landscape, distinguishing 'down', 'up' and 'across'. This system is shared by the other Baining languages (Stebbins 2011: 192–206). Furthermore, Qaqet has a syntactically-defined word class of particles that expresses information on modality, time, aspect, discourse structure and speech act, and that plays an important role in structuring discourse. Again, Qaqet shares this word class with other Baining languages (Stebbins 2011: 93–94, 218–229).

Another shared areal pattern is clausal constituent order (Dunn, Reesink, and Terrill 2002: 32–33, 36–37; Dunn et al. 2008: 743): Qaqet has AVO ~ SV constituent order, i.e., it differs from the verb-final order otherwise widespread in (East) Papuan languages. This order is found in all clause types (affirmative and negative statements, questions and commands), and it is also found in one non-verbal construction (the locative construction). In addition, there are two non-verbal constructions (the equative and attributive constructions) that exhibit the reversed order of the predicate being followed by the subject.

As a consequence of its predominant verb-medial order, Qaqet does not have any clause chaining and/or switch reference, which is common in verb-final Papuan languages. Qaqet also does not employ multi-verb constructions synchronically, and, interestingly, there is also no clear evidence for subordination. Qaqet essentially combines main clauses with each other, indicating the different semantic relationships through a large number of conjunctions and particles.

1.4 Structure of the grammar

Following this introduction, Chapter 2 focuses on the phonology, presenting information on segmental phonology, syllable structure and prosody. Chapter 3 is organized around the noun phrase: it starts with a general discussion of word classes and phrase structure in Qaqet, and then discusses the possible heads of noun phrases (i.e., nouns, numerals and quantifiers, and pronouns), their determination (by means of demonstratives and articles) and their modification (by means of adjectives, nominal modifiers and adverbials), and finally describes possessive noun phrases and conjoined noun phrases. Chapter 4 continues the discussion of the nominal domain, focusing on the morphology and semantics of the noun class and gender systems. Chapter 5 is organized around the structure of the predicate. It outlines the predominant lexicalization patterns in the verbal lexicon, and then focuses on syntactic transitivity and semantic valency, discussing especially the role of prepositions in this domain. This chapter also introduces those tense/aspect and modifier categories that are marked within the predicate. Chapter 6 is a description of adverbials, covering relational nouns, adverbs and directionals. Note that prepositions and prepositional phrases are discussed in Chapter 5, and not taken up again in Chapter 6. Chapter 7 introduces the word class of particles, which plays an important role in structuring discourse. And chapter 8 focuses on clause structure, describing verbal and non-verbal clauses, clause linking as well as the structures of negative statements, questions and commands.

2 Phonology

This chapter discusses Qaqet phonology: the consonant and vowel phonemes (section 2.1), the syllable structures (section 2.2), and prosodic phenomena (section 2.3); section 2.4 summarizes the main phonological characteristics.

2.1 Phonemes, allophones and the orthography

This section describes the Qaqet phoneme inventory: it introduces the phonemes, presents evidence for their phonemic status and discusses their phonetic realizations and allophones. Section 2.1.1 introduces the consonants, and section 2.1.2, the vowels and diphthongs.

2.1.1 Consonants

Table 4 summarizes the consonant phonemes, including both their representation in the IPA and in the practical orthography (added in brackets if different from the IPA). This chapter uses IPA notation throughout, while the remainder of this grammar uses the orthography. With a few exceptions (as noted later in this chapter), the grammar follows the orthography developed by Parker and Parker (1974), which is used in the Qaqet translation of the New Testament (PNG Bible Translation Association 1996).

Tab. 4: Consonants and their orthographic representation

	labial	alveolar	retroflex	palatal	velar
plosive (voiceless)	p	t			k
plosive (voiced)[1]	^{n}b <b>	^{n}d <d>			^{n}g <g>
fricative	β <v>	s		[ʝ][3] <q>	ɣ <q>
nasal	m	n <n, nn>[2]		ɲ <ny>	ŋ <ng>
trill/flap		r	ɽ <rl>		
lateral		l			

[1]Prenasalization is represented throughout as /^{n}/, not reflecting the place of articulation (i.e., the notations /^{m}b/ and /^{ŋ}g/ are not used)
[2]/n/ is orthographically written <nn> before <g>, and <n> elsewhere.
[3][ʝ] is not a phoneme; it is included in this table because of its unexpected orthography.

Consonants can be realized with the secondary features of prenasalization, palatalization or labialization. However, this secondary articulation is not considered phonemic. All voiced plosives are realized prenasalized (see (iii) below), and prenasalization is not attested elsewhere. The phoneme /k/ (and its allophone [g]) are almost always realized palatalized in the environment of /i/ (see (i) below). And palatalization or labialization may occur as a variant realization of vowel sequences containing /i/ or /u/ respectively (see section 2.1.2).

This section presents the consonant phonemes in the following order: (i) voiceless plosives, (ii) fricatives, (iii) voiced plosives, (iv) nasals, and (v) liquids.

(i) Voiceless plosives: /p/, /t/, /k/

Qaqet has three voiceless plosives that contrast with each other in all environments. Table 5 gives (near-) minimal pairs for voiceless onsets and codas in the environment of different vowels.

Tab. 5: (Near) minimal pairs: Voiceless plosives

Onset consonant:						
	p__		t__		k__	
i	*pit*	up	*tit*	go.CONT	*ki*	3SG.F
u	*pusup*	up.above	*tu*	put.CONT	*kuɽi*	leave
ə	*pə*	PLACE	*tə*	PURP	*kəɽat*	bamboo
a	*panu*	up	*ta*	3PL.H	*ka*	3SG.M
Coda consonant:						
	__p		__t		__k	
i	*ⁿdip*	FUT	*ⁿdit*	stick/fill	*ⁿdik*	cut
u	*ⁿgurup*	rat	*rut*	belly	*karuk*	chicken
ə	*ɣəsəp*	heavy	*βəɽsət*	finish.NCONT	*səsək*	light
a	*ɣanap*	necks	*nat*	taros	*nak*	cry.NCONT

Phonetically, the voiceless plosives can be realized in different ways: released or unreleased, and aspirated or non-aspirated. Figure 1 exemplifies the most common realizations by means of the following example:

(1) *kʰəpɲip̚*
kə=pɲip
3SG.M.SBJ.NPST=die.CONT
'he is dying' (AJL-15/06/2011)

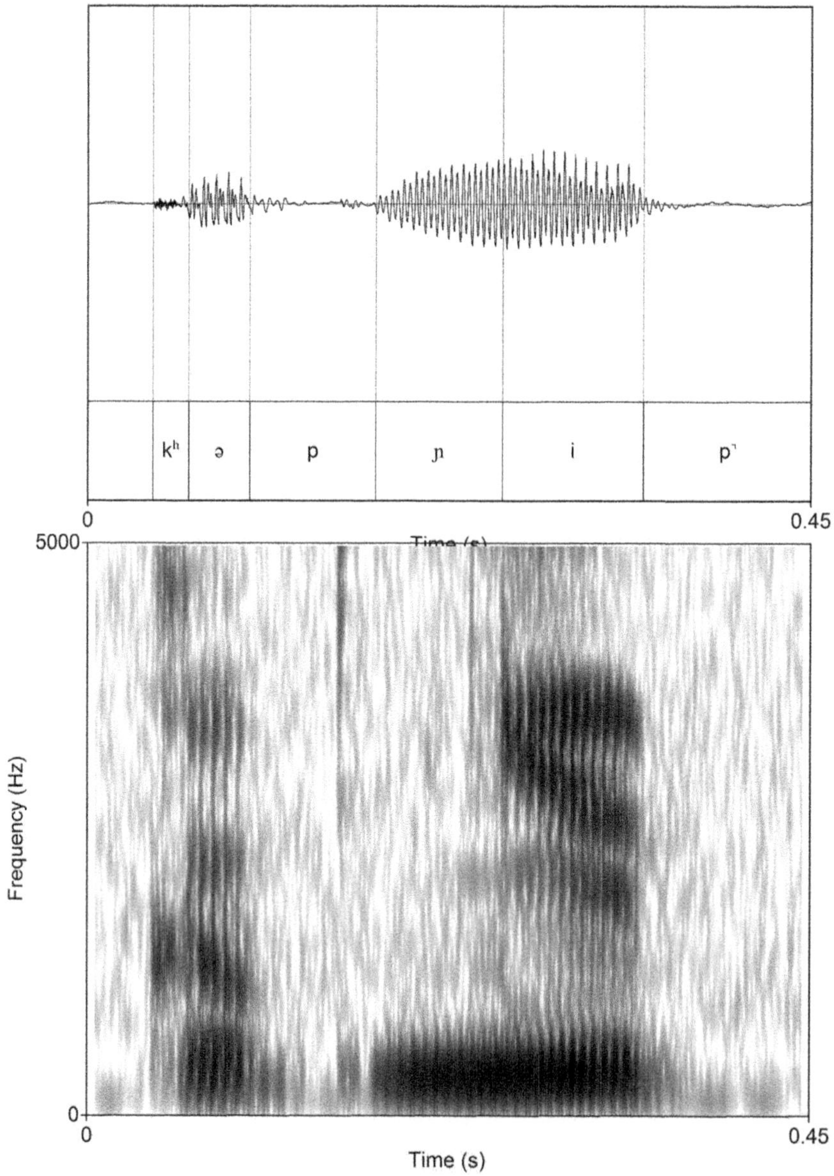

Fig. 1: Typical realization of voiceless plosives (male speaker: AJL)

In syllable onset position (as exemplified with word-initial /k/ [kʰ] in Figure 1), voiceless plosives are usually uttered released and aspirated – with a weak release burst and a short period of aspiration. In word-internal coda position (as exemplified with word-medial /p/ [p]), we still perceive a weak release burst, but usually no aspiration. And in word-final coda position (as exemplified with word-final /p/ [p̚]), the plosives often remain unreleased, and the place of articulation only leaves its traces in the formants of the preceding vowels. For example, we observe a lowering of formants 1, 2 and 3 in Figure 1, which is taken to be indicative of vowels preceding a labial plosive (following Ladefoged 2001: 48–52).

The realization of voiceless plosives thus depends largely on their position within the word: released and aspirated (word-initial and word-medial syllable onsets), released and non-aspirated (word-medial coda), and non-released (word-final coda). This distribution constitutes the default pattern, but variant realizations are attested. Such variation seems to be triggered by intonational phenomena occurring in particular at the right edge of intonation units (see section 2.3.1).

In addition, the plosive /k/ is almost always realized palatalized in the environment of the vowel /i/: as [k^j] preceding /i/ (e.g., in the pronoun /ki/ [k^{j}i] '3SG.F' or the noun class suffix /-ki/ [-k^{j}i] 'SG.F') and as [^{j}k] following /i/ (e.g., /laŋik/ [laŋi^{j}k] 'rope/vine' or /^{n}dik/ [^{n}di^{j}k] 'cut'). Palatalization usually takes the form of secondary articulation, but there are occasional realizations of /k/ (and its allophone [g]) as [c] (~ [ɟ]) (as in 2). Note that palatalization is not attested with any other plosive.

(2) *aβa ^{n}dəmɟi*
a=βa ^{n}dəm-ki
NM=trap-SG.F
'trap' (ATA-09/06/2011)

This type of palatalization is only attested in native Qaqet words and does not occur in Tok Pisin loanwords, thereby resulting in at least one minimal pair: Qaqet /liklik/ [li^{j}kli^{j}k] 'split/hit:REDUP' vs. Tok Pisin /liklik/ [liklik] 'little'. Furthermore, palatalization seems to be triggered by underlying vowels only, not by surface realizations. For example, it is observed to occur in (3a) (following the underlying morpheme /kia/ '3SG.F.SBJ'), but not in (3b) (following the underlying morpheme /ka/ '3SG.M.SBJ') – even though both are realized as [ki] in the context illustrated.

(3) a. *k^{j}iit*
kia=it
3SG.F.SBJ=chew.NCONT
'she chewed it' (AJL-02/06/2015)

b. *kiit*
ka=it
3SG.M.SBJ=chew.NCONT
'he chewed it' (AJL-02/06/2015)

Palatalization is widespread, but there are a few counter-examples, including at least one minimal pair: [si^{j}k] 'cut' vs. [sik] 'climb.NCONT'. The palatalization in the first word is expected, but its absence in the second word is not.

The phonetic realizations discussed so far (release, aspiration and palatalization) are largely predictable and thus not reflected in the practical orthography. The only problematic case here is palatalization and its (unexplained) absence in some cases, thus resulting in minimal pairs. Given the small number of cases involved, and especially given that they seem to be mainly restricted to loanwords, I tentatively do not analyze this contrast as a phonemic contrast.[1]

The voiceless plosives have two further predictable allophones, which are reflected in the orthography: a voiced allophone and a lenited allophone. All possibilities are summarized in Table 6. The allophone is noted in square brackets and its orthographic representation in angled brackets.

Tab. 6: Voiceless plosives, their allophones and their orthographic representation

	Following a nasal	Intervocalic	Elsewhere
/p/	[b] <b>	[β] <v>	[p] ~ [p̚] ~ [pʰ] <p>
/t/	[d] <d>	[r] ~ [ɾ] <r>	[t] ~ [t̚] ~ [tʰ] <t>
/k/	[g] <g>	[j̞] ~ [ɣ] <q>	[k] ~ [k̚] ~ [kʰ] ~ [kʲ] ~ [ʲk] <k>

The voiced and lenited allophones of /k/ are exemplified in Table 7 with the help of the noun class suffixes /-ka/ 'SG.M' and /-ki/ 'SG.F'. The phoneme /k/ is invariably realized as voiced [g] following a nasal, and as [k] following any other consonant. Intervocalically, it is almost always realized as [j̞] preceding /i/, and as [ɣ] preceding any other vowel. The complementary distribution of [j̞] and [ɣ] holds for the vast majority of cases, but there are some counter-examples. Most concern the sequence /uki/, which is realized [uj̞i] in some words (as in [ɣaruj̞i] 'scraper') and [uɣi] in others (as in [βuɣit] 'bamboo section'). For each word, only one of the two possible realizations is attested, i.e., the two realizations do not seem to be in free variation. It is likely that the unexpected velar realization [ɣ] is triggered by the preceding back vowel /u/. In addition, there are two further counter-examples: [aɣiapki] 'chicken' and [aɣipka] 'spear'. It is possible that synchronic /i/ in these words goes back to a vowel sequence */ai/ (see section 2.1.2 for the realization of vowel sequences). This analysis is supported by an attested alternative realization of one of the words, 'chicken', as [aɣaiapki].

1 It is possible that diachronic and comparative investigations will be able to explain cases without palatalization as, e.g., containing reflexes of a vowel other than */i/. But in the absence of such evidence, I prefer to treat such cases as unexplained counter-examples.

Tab. 7: Voiceless plosive /k/ and its allophones: An illustration

Following a nasal:						
m	*rim-ka*	[rimga]	taro	*am-ki*	[amgi]	mouth
n	*ɽan-ka*	[ɽanga]	pandanus	*nan-ki*	[nangi]	woman
ɲ	*ilaɲ-ka*	[ilaɲga]	toe	*ilaɲ-ki*	[ilaɲgi]	step/ladder
ŋ	^{n}*daŋ-ka*	[^{n}daŋga]	dog	^{n}*daŋ-ki*	[^{n}daŋgi]	bitch
Following any other consonant:						
plosive	*ilat-ka*	[ilatka]	sling	*aβət-ki*	[aβətki]	house
fricative	*is-ka*	[iska]	path	*aβis-ki*	[aβiski]	knife
liquid	^{n}*dul-ka*	[^{n}dulka]	stone	*laal-ki*	[laalki]	log
Intervocalic, following any of the vowels:						
i	*βɽi-ka*	[βɽiɣa]	cousin	*βɽi-ki*	[βɽiʝi]	cousin
u	*ɽu-ka*	[ɽuɣa]	flame	*ɣaru-ki*	[ɣaruʝi]	scraper
ə	*ɣulə-ka*	[ɣuləɣa]	clay	*ɣalə-ki*	[ɣaləʝi]	midriff
a	^{n}*baata-ka*	[^{n}baataɣa]	avocado	^{n}*gata-ki*	[^{n}gataʝi]	basket

Comparable voicing and lenition processes are attested for the other voiceless plosives, too. For example, the verb /tit/ 'go.CONT' is realized as [dir] ~ [diɽ] in example (4): the initial /t/ is voiced (following a nasal), and the final /t/ is lenited (in intervocalic position) (see also below for details on the realization possibilities).

(4) ^{n}*daβiandira*
^{n}*dap=ian=tit=a*
but=3DU.SBJ=go.CONT=DIST
'they go now' (N12BAMCAT-151)

Or the initial /p/ of the preposition /pət/ 'on/under' is realized as [b] following a nasal (as in [snanbət], from /snan-pət/ 'ask-on/under'), and as [β] in intervocalic position (as in [naβət], from /nə-pət/ 'from-on/under').

The voiced allophones originate through assimilation to the preceding voiced nasal, and the lenited allophones originate intervocalically through a process of voicing and lenition (from voiceless plosives to voiced fricatives and taps). A comparable allophony is attested for all Baining languages (Stanton 2007: 22–32; Stebbins 2009a:

226–227, 2011: 19–20, 22–23).[2] The realization of the lenited allophones varies between continuant (as [β], [r] ~ [ɾ], [ʝ] ~ [ɣ]) and approximant (as [ʋ], [ɹ], [j] ~ [ɰ]) in all languages, including Qaqet. In Qaqet, some friction is usually audible (albeit often weak), and I thus represent them as continuants throughout.

The above allophonic patterns are attested for all speakers and all speech styles (including both fast and slow speech, and both within and across word boundaries). They are not restricted to productive morphological processes either, but are found within monomorphemic words, too, e.g., we do not find sequences of nasals plus voiceless plosives. There are, however, a good number of voiceless plosives in intervocalic position that do not lenite. It is very likely that most of them originated from consonant clusters. Synchronically, such clusters arise transparently at the boundary of two morphemes. Example (5) illustrates the suffixation of /-ka/ 'SG.M' and /-ki/ 'SG.F' to roots ending in a plosive. In (5a), the root ends in /t/ and both plosives of the resulting cluster /tk/ are pronounced. In (5b), the root ends in /k/ and the resulting cluster of identical plosives /kk/ is not lenited (even though it now occurs in intervocalic position). Such clusters tend to be fairly long, as illustrated in Figures 2 and 3.

(5) a. *akəɽatka*
a=kəɽat-ka
NM=bamboo-SG.M
'bamboo' (AEM-07/06/2011)

b. *a ⁿduɽaikki*
a= ⁿduɽaik-ki
NM=chicken-SG.F
'chicken' (AEM-02/06/2011)

Figures 2 and 3 give the waveforms for examples (5a) and (5b). The two plosives of the /tk/ cluster (in Figure 2) are uttered individually (showing two release bursts) and have a combined length of 360ms. The /kk/ cluster (in Figure 3) shows only one release burst, and has an overall length of 200ms (with a long closure period plus aspiration following the release). As such, it is shorter than the consonant cluster /tk/, but longer than a simple plosive in other environments (e.g., the three plosives in Figure 1 above are all shorter than 100ms in duration). For the moment, such observations have to remain impressionistic, pending a systematic investigation into consonant length.

2 This allophony is not attested in Sulka, Taulil and Butam, the other East Papuan languages of East New Britain, but it is found in Kuot, the only East Papuan language on New Ireland (Lindström 2002: 88–91), from where it is said to have spread into neighboring Oceanic languages (Ross 1994: 566).

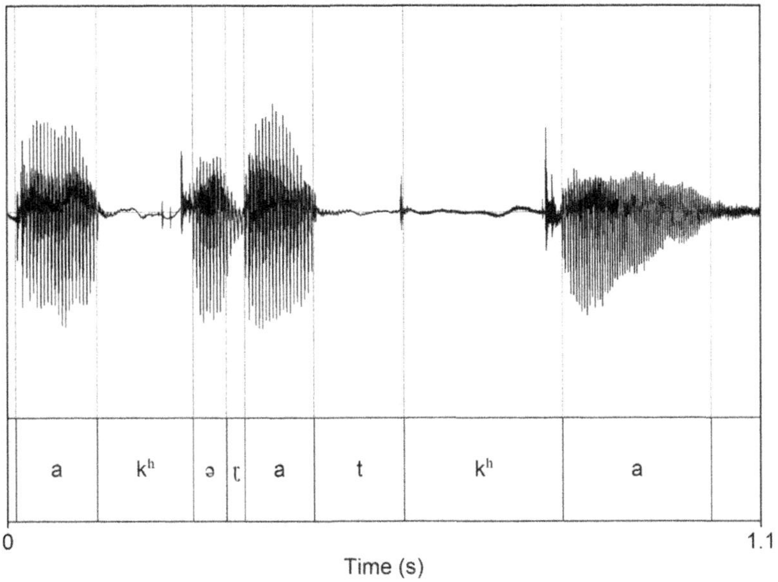

Fig. 2: Realization of adjacent non-identical plosives: /tk/ (female speaker: AEM)

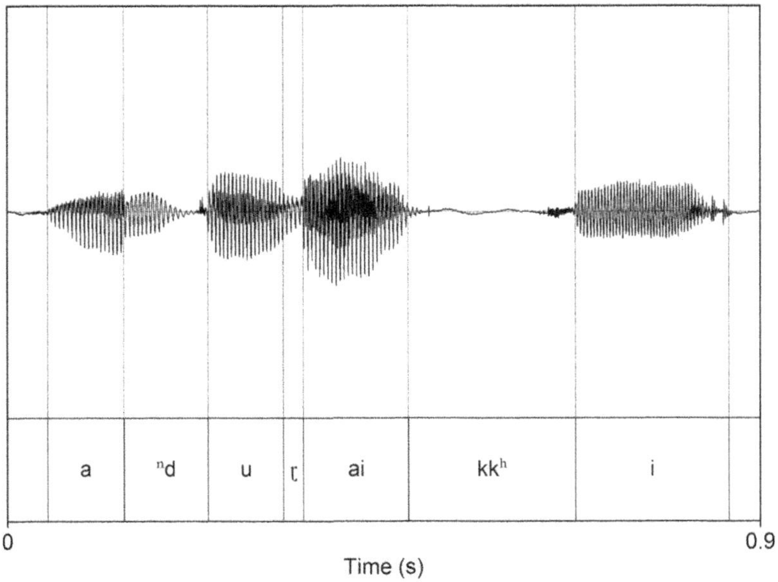

Fig. 3: Realization of adjacent identical plosives: /kk/ (female speaker: AEM)

There are a handful of examples where we would expect an intervocalic plosive to occur (because a root with a final plosive is followed by a suffix with an initial plosive), but which receive a lenited realization instead (as illustrated in 6a). Such cases could suggest that intervocalic plosives are instable. However, such unexpected lenition is only attested in very few lexemes, and it may be the result of a different diachronic development altogether: the widespread loss of a final vowel /a/ from roots (see chapter 4.1.1 for details and examples). This is shown in (6b), which illustrates a variant realization of the word in (6a). Here, the realization is indicative of a diachronic root */ɣuɽiɣa/ (retaining its final vowel). It is thus possible that the realization [aɣuɽiɣa] (in 6a) is a contracted version of [aɣuɽiɣaɣa] (in 6b).

(6) a. *aɣuɽiɣa (*aɣuɽikka)*
a=ɣuɽik-ka
NM=caterpillar-SG.M
'caterpillar' (ATA-09/06/2011)
b. *aɣuɽiɣaɣa*
*a=*ɣuɽiɣa-ka*
NM=caterpillar-SG.M
'caterpillar' (BCK-08/05/2015)

In fast speech, it is not uncommon for intervocalic consonant clusters to be simplified, losing their initial consonant. Such processes are attested regularly in synchronic clitic combinations. For example, the plosive /k/ in the pronoun /ka/ '3SG.M' lenites as expected when the pronoun follows a vowel-final conjunction (such as /^{n}də/ in 7a, resulting in [^{n}daɣa]). But when it follows a consonant-final conjunction (such as /^{n}dap/ in 7b), the final plosive of this conjunction frequently disappears, but the pronoun still retains its plosive consonant (resulting in [^{n}daka]). In such cases, the intervocalic plosive is not realized markedly longer.

(7) a. *^{n}dep ma ^{n}gət ^{n}daɣa..*
^{n}də=ip ma ^{n}gət ^{n}də=ka..
CONJ=PURP then CONJ=3SG.M.SBJ
'and then he..' (N12BAMCAT-200)
b. *^{n}dakakias*
^{n}dap=ka=kias
but=3SG.M.SBJ=actually
'but actually' (N12BAMCAT-164)

A comparable simplification of consonant clusters has probably taken place in the formation of aspectual verb stems. Present-day Qaqet marks aspectual distinctions primarily through a mutation of the initial consonant. In many cases, the first consonants of verbs alternate between simple lenited consonants (non-continuous stems) and simple plosive consonants (continuous stems) (see chapter 5.4.2). This distinction is meaningful and is retained in intervocalic environments (see also the discussion under (ii) below), as illustrated with the help of the frame /ka=VERB/

'3SG.M.SBJ=VERB' in Table 8. There is evidence that the continuous stem was originally formed by means of a prefix consonant. A handful of synchronic forms (e.g., the last three examples of Table 8) have preserved such an initial consonant cluster – usually as a free variant of a simple plosive. Most verbs, however, have lost the initial prefix consonant, but retained the plosive realization.

Tab. 8: Intervocalic voiceless plosives: Aspectual verb stems

Lenited (non-continuous stem) vs. plosive (continuous stem):		
ka=βəɽsət	*ka=pəɽsət*	finish
ka=ral	*ka=tal*	carry
ka=ɣuap	*ka=kuap*	tie
Lenited (non-continuous stem) vs. consonant cluster ~ plosive (continuous stem):		
ka=βəs	*ka=spəs* ~ *ka=pəs*	burn, close/thatch
ka=ran	*ka=tdan*	go inside
ka=ɣuip	*ka=pkuip* ~ *ka=kuip*	shake

Finally, voiceless plosives in loanwords never lenite, e.g., [apusi] 'cats' (from Tok Pisin /pusi/), [atrausel] 'tortoises' (from Tok Pisin /trausel/) or [akar] 'cars' (from Tok Pisin /kar/).

Given the above evidence, I assume that all present-day intervocalic voiceless plosives either originated in consonant clusters or else entered the language through loanwords. As is the case with all diachronic developments, some cases are no longer transparent, e.g., the intervocalic plosives in [akəɽat] 'bamboos' or [aɣuukuk] 'sweet potatoes' cannot be explained on the basis of our current knowledge. With the exception of intervocalic plosives at synchronic morpheme boundaries (as illustrated in Figure 3 above), none of these intervocalic plosives is realized markedly longer: this includes the simplified consonant clusters (example 7b), the plosives in continuous verb stems (Table 8), the plosives in loanwords, and the remaining unexplained plosives. Synchronically, there are thus many instances of non-geminated voiceless plosives in intervocalic position.[3]

3 The practical orthography does not distinguish between geminated and non-geminated plosives, and represents both as simple plosives (*p*, *t*, *k*). This is justified, as geminated and simple plosives do not contrast.

(ii) Fricatives: /β/, /s/, /ɣ/

The developments outlined under (i) have not only given rise to intervocalic plosives, but also to the phonemicization of lenited allophones in onset position (resulting in the fricative phonemes /β/ and /ɣ/, and in the trill phoneme /r/). The clearest evidence for this development comes from verbs. As illustrated in Table 8 above, initial plosives contrast with initial continuants to convey a synchronic aspectual distinction between continuous and non-continuous meanings. Diachronically, it is likely that both aspectual verb stems contained a plosive consonant. Since verbs are almost always preceded by a vowel-final subject index, these plosives would have usually occurred in intervocalic position. In the case of the non-continuous stems, the plosives would therefore have occurred lenited. But in the case of the continuous stems, the presence of consonantal prefixes would have prevented any lenition. As discussed above, most present-day continuous stems have now lost these consonantal prefixes, but they have retained the plosive realization of their initial consonants. That is, the aspectual distinction is maintained through contrasting an initial plosive (i.e., the former consonant cluster) with an initial continuant (i.e., the former lenited allophone). Synchronically, this contrast exists irrespective of the phonological environment: there are no contexts where the verb-initial continuants would receive a plosive realization, and the verb-initial plosives never lenite in intervocalic environments.

The evidence for a comparable phonemicization process in nouns is less conclusive. In terms of frequency, an exceptionally large number of noun roots seemingly begin with one of the lenited consonants.[4] It is likely that these consonants diachronically represent voiceless plosives, but it is unclear whether they should synchronically still be analyzed as voiceless plosives. The reason is that nouns are almost always preceded by a vowel-final article (including in their citation form), i.e., there are almost no contexts where an underlying voiceless plosive would be able to surface. The main exception here is the vocative context. For example, the citation form [aɣul^{n}dit] 'frogs' (from /a=kul^{n}dit/ 'NM=frog') contains an underlying root-initial plosive /k/, which only surfaces in the vocative (as in 8).

(8) *kul^{n}dit, ŋuluɲi ɣua?*
kul^{n}dit *ŋu=lu-ɲi* *kua?*
frog 1SG.SBJ.NPST=see.NCONT-2SG where
'frog, where are you (lit. I see you where)?' (AJL-28/05/2012)

Additional evidence comes from names, which usually consist of meaningful words (see chapter 3.2.1). For example, [aβilaŋəm] 'short tail' (from /a=pilaŋ-əm/ 'NM=tail-

4 Conversely, there are hardly any nouns that begin with a voiceless plosive – most attested examples are known loanwords, plus a few as yet unexplained forms.

SG.RCD') corresponds to the male name *Pilaŋəm* (retaining the initial /p/). Similarly, evidence comes from child-directed speech, where children's interlocutors sometimes omit the article and pronounce the underlying plosive, e.g., saying [kuukuk] instead of [aɣuukuk] 'sweet potatoes' (from /a=kuukuk/ 'NM=sweet.potato'). And finally, evidence comes from a handful of reduplicated roots, e.g., [aɣuilkuil] 'type of tree' is likely to be /a=kuil-kuil/ underlyingly: the first plosive /k/ is lenited as expected, but the reduplicated plosive /k/ is retained because it does not occur intervocalically.

Given the above evidence, it is tempting to speculate that all root-initial continuants in nouns are underlyingly voiceless plosives. Unfortunately, the majority of nouns are not attested in any of the contexts where an underlying plosive can surface, and it is therefore not clear if speakers analyze their initial continuants as lenited plosives. Given that the plosives never surface, it is equally possible that speakers analyze the continuants as the underlying phonemes. In the absence of psycholinguistic evidence, this issue cannot be resolved. The practical orthography adopts the policy of writing the continuant realization, but remains agnostic as to its phonemic status. This practice also includes all continuants that occur within morphemes, e.g., it is impossible to ascertain whether [β] in [aɣaβeet] 'forked sticks' (from /a=ɣaβiit/ 'NM=forked.stick') represents a phoneme /β/ or a phoneme /p/.

While the evidence from nouns thus remains inconclusive, the evidence from verbs is clear: synchronically, a phoneme /r/ (see (v) below for a discussion of liquids) and two fricative phonemes /β/ and /ɣ/ (with an allophone [j̥] preceding /i/) have to be posited, because they contrast with voiceless plosives in the same environment. Their occurrence is restricted to syllable onsets. This restriction is to be expected, given that they developed from plosives in intervocalic environments, i.e., from plosives in syllable onsets. As for their phonetic realizations, recall that they are realized with weak friction only (see the discussion under (i) above).

In addition, there exists a third fricative phoneme, /s/. Different from the other two fricatives, it is voiceless. Furthermore, it did not originate in lenited plosives, and thus does not show the same positional restrictions: it is attested in both onset and coda positions. It has a free variant [h] in all positions, e.g., [siɽək] ~ [hiɽək] 'throw, drop', [sləp] ~ [hləp] 'intensely', [asiɽik] ~ [ahiɽik] 'meat', [asləŋ] ~ [ahləŋ] 'garden', [nas] ~ [nah] 'self'. Speakers consider the realization [s] to be the southern Qaqet form, and [h] the northern Qaqet form (see chapter 1.1.1). However, there is considerable speaker variation, and the corpus contains many instances where southern dialect speakers pronounce [h], and northern speakers pronounce [s].

Table 9 gives some near-minimal pairs for fricatives in onset position, preceding different vowels.

Tab. 9: (Near) minimal pairs: Fricatives (onset)

	β_		s_		ɣ_ ~ ʝ_	
i	*siβit*	be.angry	*sisit*	ridge	*ŋariʝit*	five
u	*iβun*	rope.type	*suŋ*	quiet	*iaɣun*	moon
ə	*βəs*	burn.NCONT	*βəɽsəs*	loosen.NCONT	*laɣəs*	cucumber
a	*βalu*	slow.NCONT	*sa*	already	*ɣalun*	singapore

(iii) Voiced plosives: /^{n}b/, /^{n}d/, /^{n}g/

In addition to the above phonemes, Qaqet also has voiced plosives. In some cases, they are allophones of voiceless plosives following a nasal (see Table 6 above). But in other cases, they have to be considered phonemes. Table 10 gives (near) minimal pairs for different places of articulation: it contrasts voiceless plosives with voiced plosives and nasals in syllable onset position, and preceding different vowels. Table 11 then gives (near) minimal pairs for the voiced plosives contrasting with each other in syllable onset position.

Different from both voiceless plosives and nasals, they cannot occur in coda position.

Phonetically, voiced plosives are almost always realized prenasalized, and counter-examples are very rare. In intervocalic position, there are almost no counter-examples and a non-prenasalized realization only occurs occasionally as a free variant, e.g., [a^{n}baata] ~ [abaata] 'avocados'. If the plosive is preceded by another consonant, non-prenasalized variants tend to be more frequent. In the case of a preceding fricative /s/ or a preceding liquid /l/ or /ɽ/ (recall that the other fricatives and /r/ can only occur in syllable onsets), both realizations are attested in reasonable numbers, e.g., [as^{n}dəm] ~ [asdəm] 'ears'. In the case of a preceding nasal, it is impossible to determine (and probably irrelevant) whether prenasalization is present or absent. And in the case of a preceding voiceless plosive, prenasalization never occurs. For example, /ka=tdən/ '3SG.M.SBJ=come.CONT' is realized as [katdən] (never as *[kat^{n}dən]). This non-prenasalized realization is retained even if the preceding voiceless plosive is omitted: [kadən] (not *[ka^{n}dən]). This phenomenon is especially found in the case of continuous verb stems, such as /tdən/ 'come.CONT', which have lost – or are in the process of losing – their initial consonants (see the discussion of Table 8 above).

Tab. 10: (Near) minimal pairs: Voiceless plosives, voiced plosives, nasals (onset)

Labials:						
	p__		**^{n}b__**		**m__**	
i	*pit*	up	^{n}*bit*	bed	*mit*	across
u	*pusup*	up.above	^{n}*buɽəm*	many	*mu*	put.NCONT.PST
ə	*paɽsət*	finish.CONT	^{n}*bəɽtik*	loosen	*məɽ*	shit
a	*panu*	up	^{n}*bari*	bee	*mali*	search
Alveolars:						
	t__		**^{n}d__**		**n__**	
i	*tika*	EMPH	*pa*^{n}*di*	hopefully.PST	*ani*	maybe
u	*tu*	put.CONT	^{n}*duɽaik*	chicken	*nu*^{n}*gul*	boundary
ə	*tək*	put.CONT	^{n}*dəpguas*	three	*manəp*	down
a	*taɽik*	cross.CONT	^{n}*daɽik*	outside	*naɽip*	like
Velars:						
	k__		**^{n}g__**		**ŋ__**	
i	*ɽkiŋ*	tooth	*pa*^{n}*gin*	pumpkin	*ŋiŋ*	circle.CONT
u	*kua*	where	^{n}*gua*	1SG.POSS	*ŋua*	1SG
ə	*kəsna*	how.much	*a*^{n}*gəs*	year	*ŋət*	3N
a	*ka*	3SG.M	^{n}*galəp*	handle/club	*ŋarik*	arm/hand

Tab. 11: (Near) minimal pairs: Voiced plosives (onset)

	^{n}b__		**^{n}d__**		**^{n}g__**	
i	^{n}*bin*	step.CONT	^{n}*diŋ*	weave.CONT	^{n}*gil*	small
u	^{n}*buŋ*	break	*βu*^{n}*duŋ*	mosquito	*mu*^{n}*gun*	sit
ə	^{n}*bəɽtik*	loosen	^{n}*dəl*	knock	^{n}*gəl*	near
a	^{n}*bari*	bee	^{n}*daɣa*	taro	^{n}*galəp*	handle/club

Phonologically, prenasalized voiced plosives contrast with sequences of segmental nasals plus voiced plosives. Phonetically, the two cases tend to differ in duration (in that the du ration of prenasalization is shorter than that of segmental nasals), but this contrast is not always clear-cut and there are cases of potential ambiguity, i.e., where a sequence could be analyzed as either -VCV- (i.e., as -VC[^{n}b,^{n}d,^{n}g]V-) or as -VCCV- (i.e., -VC[nasal]C[b,d,g]V-). This overlap is illustrated in Table 12 with the help of a transparent morphological process: the suffixation of /-ki/ 'SG.F' to nouns whose base form is known to end in a nasal. Usually, this nasal is retained in the suffixed form, but there are occasional examples in the corpus, where a speaker utters a prenasalized plosive. Phonologically, this segmental nasal is present (as it causes the suffix /-ki/ to be realized as [-gi]), but phonetically it is not always realized as a segmental nasal. A similar variation is attested with loanwords, e.g., the Tok Pisin loan /pamken/ 'pumpkin' is realized in Qaqet by different speakers as [pamgin] ~ [pa^{n}gin].

Tab. 12: Realization of sequences of nasal plus plosive

Root	Root-SG.F	Realization	Gloss
^{n}gam	*^{n}gam-ki*	*^{n}gamgi* ~ *^{n}ga^{n}gi*	fruit
ulan	*ulan-ki*	*ulangi* ~ *ula^{n}gi*	eel
ilaɲ	*ilaɲ-ki*	*ilaɲgi* ~ *ila^{n}gi*	step/ladder
^{n}daŋ	*^{n}daŋ-ki*	*^{n}daŋgi* ~ *^{n}da^{n}gi*	bitch, female dog

(iv) Nasals: /m/, /n/, /ɲ/, /ŋ/

In addition to prenasalized plosives, Qaqet has four segmental nasals. Table 10 above has shown labial, alveolar and velar nasals contrasting with voiceless and voiced plosives; and Table 13 below illustrates contrasts among the four nasals, both in onset and coda positions.[5] The distribution of the palatal nasal /ɲ/ seems to be restricted: it contrasts with the other nasals in most environments, but not in the environment of /ə/. It is not clear whether it cannot occur in this environment, or whether its absence is a gap in the data set. The realization of /ə/ is exceptionally sensitive to its environment (see section 2.1.2), and it is possible that the presence of a palatal nasal triggers its realization as [i]. But there is currently no independent evidence for analyzing (some of) the /ɲi/ ~ /iɲ/ sequences as underlying */ɲə/ ~ */əɲ/ sequences.

5 The orthographic representation of nasals adopted in this grammar differs slightly from that proposed in Parker and Parker (1974). I write /ɲ/ as <ny> (not as <ng>), as I consider it to be contrastive to /ŋ/ <ng>, including in the environment of /i/. And I write /n/ as <nn> before <g> (to be able to distinguish the non-homorganic consonant sequence /ng/ <nng> from the simple phoneme /ŋ/ <ng>).

Tab. 13: (Near) minimal pairs: Nasals

Onset:				
	m__	n__	ɲ__	ŋ__
i	*miŋ*	*niŋ*	*ɲim*	*ŋiŋ*
	weave.NCONT.PST	fear.NCONT	look.NCONT	circle.CONT
u	*mu*	*nuⁿgul*	*ɲuuk*	*ŋu*
	put.NCONT.PST	boundary	2SG.SBJ.NPST: fetch.NCONT	1SG.SBJ.NPST
ə	*ləməŋ*	*ranəŋ*	*??*	*ŋən*
	chest	hold.NCONT		2PL
a	*ama*	*na*	*ɲa*	*ŋarik*
	ART	RECP	2SG.SBJ	arm/hand
Coda:				
	__m	__n	__ɲ	__ŋ
i	*ambim*	*ⁿbin*	*ⁿbiɲ*	*ⁿdiŋ*
	two.mouths	step.CONT	break	weave.CONT
u	*lum*	*ɣalun*	*ruɲga*	*luŋ*
	bamboo.section	singapore	knife	garden
ə	*aɽəmbəm*	*uɽən*	*??*	*ɽəŋ*
	thigh	prawn		back
a	*lamsaɣa*	*ulan*	*ilaɲ*	*laŋ*
	coconut	eel	leg/foot	shoulder

(v) Liquids: /r/, /ɽ/, /l/

Finally, Qaqet has three liquid phonemes: /r/, /ɽ/ and /l/. They all contrast in onset position, and the latter two also in coda position (as illustrated with near-minimal pairs in Table 14). Recall that /r/ originated as an allophone of /t/ in intervocalic environments. Synchronically, it has to be posited as a phoneme (like the fricatives /β/ and /ɣ/ ~ [j̰]) because it contrasts with plosives in the onset of verbs, and possibly also of nouns (see the discussion of Table 8 above). Its diachronic origin in an intervocalic environment is still reflected in the fact that it cannot occur in coda position.

Tab. 14: (Near) minimal pairs: Liquids

Onset:						
	r_		ɽ_		l_	
i	*ŋarik*	arm/hand	*taɽik*	cross.CONT	*lik*	split/hit
u	*rut*	belly	*ɽut*	steam	*ɣalut*	lizard
ə	*rən*	name	*ɽəŋ*	back	*aləŋ*	weakness
a	*ran*	go.inside. NCONT.FUT	*ɽan*	pandanus	*ulan*	eel
Coda:						
	_r		_ɽ		_l	
i	–		*miɽ*	market	*samil*	grasshopper
u	–		*ⁿduɽ*	tear	*ⁿdul*	stone
ə	–		*ɣaβəɽ*	hurry.NCONT	*ɣaβəl*	bush
a	–		*saŋaɽ*	catch.fish	*nal*	scraper

The phoneme /r/ is variably pronounced as either a trill [r] or a tap [ɾ]. Given its diachronic origin as a lenited sound, it is likely that it was originally realized as a tap. In present-day Qaqet, however, both realizations are attested in free variation, and this holds true for both the phoneme /r/ and the lenited allophone [r] of the phoneme /t/. There is considerable variation both across speakers (i.e., some are more likely to utter [r], and others, to utter [ɾ]) and within individual speakers. Qaqet trills are rarely produced with more than three periods of vibration, and taps seem to be always a possible alternative. Ladefoged and Maddieson (1996: 217) say that "[t]he aperture size and airflow must fall within critical limits for trilling to occur, and quite small deviations mean that it will fail. As a result, trills tend to vary with non-trilled pronunciations." Given this universal tendency, I analyze the phoneme /r/ (synchronically) as a trill. As for the realization of /ɽ/, is not entirely clear if it should be analyzed as a retroflex or postalveolar flap [ɽ] or as a lateral flap [ɺ]. This issue needs further investigation.

Different from the other liquids (and from all other consonants, but similar to the vowels), /ɽ/ can trigger lenition in a following voiceless plosive. Both within and across word boundaries, a following /p/ is always lenited to [β], e.g., /ⁿbaɽ-pik/ 'big-COLL.H' is invariably realized [ⁿbaɽβik]. A following /t/ or /k/, by contrast, is never lenited within a phonological word, e.g., /ⁿbaɽ-ta/ 'big-PL.H', /ⁿbaɽ-ka/ 'big-SG.M' and /ⁿbaɽ-ki/ 'big-SG.F' are realized as [ⁿbaɽta], [ⁿbaɽka] and [ⁿbaɽki] respectively. Across word boundaries, however, lenition is possible: although /t/ and /k/ are usually not lenited in this environment either, there do exist lenited examples. For example, /kəɽ tətuɣun/ 'they shall say' is sometimes realized as [kəɽ rətuɣun], and /kəɽ katit/ 'he shall go', as [kəɽ ɣatit]. It was not possible to determine any conditioning factors. There are indications, however, that /ɽ/ originated (at least in some cases) in /ra/ ~ /rə/ sequences (see chapter 3.5.1). Such an origin would explain the lenition of the following plosives. In subsequent developments, the phonemicization process would then have caused /ɽ/ to distribute like other consonants. But this process is presumably on-going: it first affected a following /t/ and /k/ (which only rarely lenite), but has not yet spread to /p/ (which always lenites).

2.1.2 Vowels

Qaqet has four short vowel phonemes, as summarized in Table 15 (with the orthographic representation added in brackets if different from the IPA). The vowels /i/, /u/ and /a/ can be realized long, and the vowels can combine to form diphthongs. Note that Qaqet does not have any short vowel phonemes /e/ and /o/. The latter is only attested in recent loanwords (e.g., /^{n}botol/ 'bottle', from Tok Pisin /botol/) and in non-native pronunciations of Qaqet names containing the phoneme /u/ (e.g., the Qaqet village of /kumgi/ [kʊmgi] is rendered /komgi/ in Tok Pisin). Phonetically, however, there are long vowels [ee] and [oo] that go back to /ii/, /ai/ and /au/.

This section discusses the attested vowels and vowel combinations in more detail, covering (i) short vowels, (ii) long vowels and (iii) diphthongs.

Tab. 15: Vowels and their orthographic representation

	Front	**Central**	**Back**
Close	i		u
Mid		ə <e>	
Open		a	

(i) Short vowels

Table 16 demonstrates the phonemic status of the short vowels with the help of (near) minimal pairs in different environments.

The two close vowels /i/ and /u/ are commonly realized as [ɪ] and [ʊ] in all contexts. The vowel /a/, by contrast, is realized over a fairly large vowel space. On the one hand, there is variation across speakers, covering both [a] and [ɐ] realizations. On the other hand, there are two environments that trigger regressive assimilation for all speakers. First, /a/ is invariably realized further back (as [ɑ]) before [ɣ], e.g. [ɑɣʊnaska] 'one' (from /a=ɣunas-ka/ 'NM=one-SG.M'). And second, it is realized further front (as [æ]) before a front vowel in the next syllable or before a palatal consonant. It is not entirely clear how far this assimilation spreads. It always affects the immediately preceding /a/, as in [aɲærikka] 'finger' (from /a=ɲarik-ka/ 'NM=hand-SG.M'). But there are also attested cases where it affects all preceding /a/ within a word, as in [ænængi] 'girl, woman' (from /a=nan-ki/ 'NM=woman-SG.F').

Tab. 16: (Near) minimal pairs: Vowels

i	ə	u	a
ki	*kə*	*kuɽi*	*ka*
3SG.F	3SG.M.SBJ.NPST	leave	3SG.M
ⁿdip	*ⁿdəpguas*	*andup*	*ⁿdap*
FUT	three	throw.NCONT	but
aβis	*βəs*	*βuska*	*βas*
knife	burn.NCONT	tastelessness	breadfruit
siŋ	*səŋ*	*suŋ*	*ɣuɽisaɲ*
chew.betelnut.NCONT	separate.NCONT	quiet	mud
arik	*arəpki*	*ⁿgurup*	*arapki*
supposing	axe	rat	boil
lim	*ɣaləm*	*lum*	*lamsaɣa*
young	piece.of.wood	bamboo.section	coconut
mit	*mət*	*ut*	*mat*
across	in	1PL	take.NCONT.PST

The vowel phoneme /ə/ is realized as the central vowel [ə] (but see below). It differs from the other vowels in that it is realized extremely short in the environment of a preceding and/or following sonorant. This even includes cases where /ə/ occurs at the right edge of an intonation unit: in this environment, all other vowels are predictably lengthened (see section 2.3.1). Despite the short duration of /ə/ in such environments, the syllable itself is not realized any shorter, as there is compensatory lengthening of the surrounding sonorants. The example below gives a minimal pair featuring a contrast between /ə/ (9a) and /a/ (9b). Figure 4 illustrates the short duration of /ə/ and the compensatory lengthening of the sonorants: *məs* has an overall duration of 340ms (with /ə/ being only 30ms long), while *mas* has an overall duration of 390ms (with /a/ being 120ms long).

(9) a. *kamᵊs*
ka=məs
3SG.M.SBJ=eat.NCONT.PST
'he ate' (AEM-02/06/2011)

b. *kamas*
ka=mas
3SG.M.SBJ=lie.NCONT.PST
'he lay down' (AEM-02/06/2011)

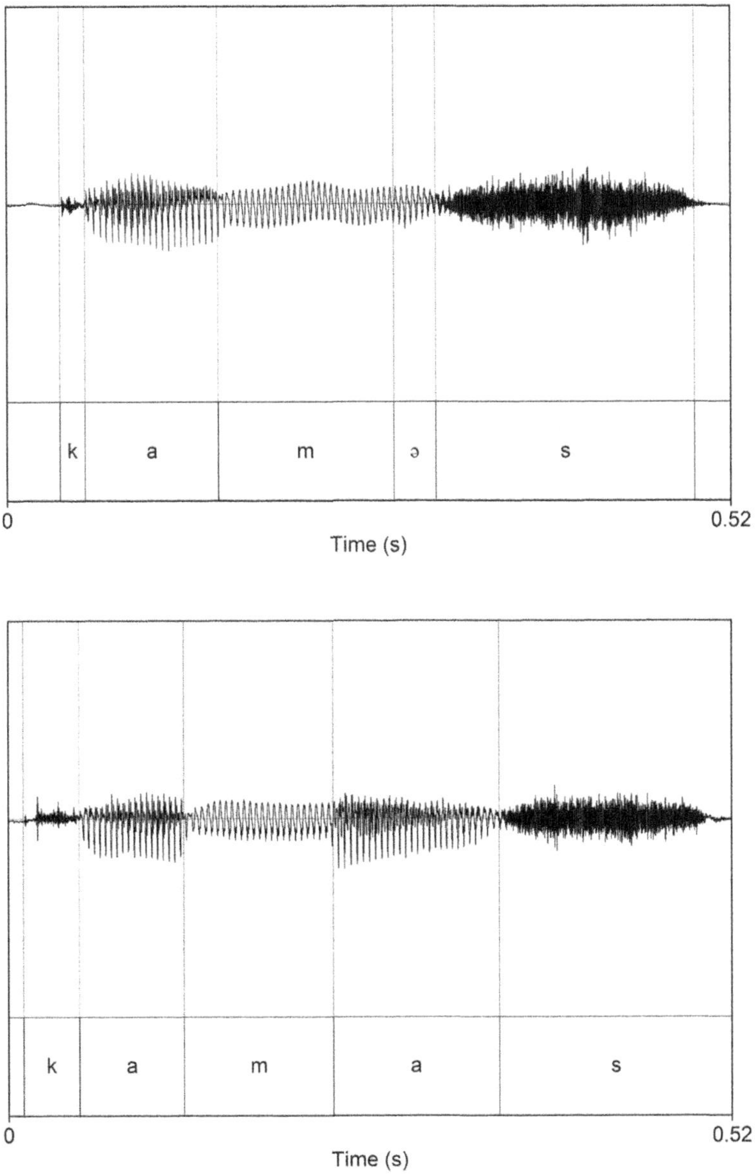

Fig. 4: Comparing the duration of /ə/ and /a/ (female speaker: AEM)

The phoneme /ə/ is exceptionally short in the environment of sonorants. This includes especially liquids, both preceding (Table 17a) and following liquids (Table 17b). But there are also many examples with nasals (Table 17c), and even with fricatives (Table 17d). In fast speech, /ə/ is frequently lost altogether. It is only between two plosives that the duration of /ə/ is longer and more comparable to that of other short vowels.

Tab. 17: Realization of /ə/ in the environment of sonorants and fricatives

	Realization		**Underlying form**	
17a	*amal^{ə}pka*	ten	*a=maləp-ka*	NM=ten-SG.M
17b	*ak^{ə}ɽat*	bamboo	*a=kəɽat*	NM=bamboo
17c	*aɣan^{ə}m*	neck	*a=ɣanəm*	NM=neck
17d	*aalaɣ^{ə}s*	cucumber	*a=alaɣəs*	NM=cucumber

Despite its short duration or even loss, /ə/ still triggers the lenition of an underlying intervocalic plosive, i.e., /ə/ behaves phonologically like the other three vowels and thus has to be analyzed as a phoneme (and not as an epenthetic vowel). For example, /p/ and /t/ in the clitic combination /sə=pət=a=NOUN/ 'to/with=on/under=NM=NOUN' would predictably first lenite (to [saβəra=NOUN]). Following that, /ə/ would either be realized exceptionally short or would be lost altogether, resulting in [saβ^{ə}ra=NOUN] ~ [saβra=NOUN].

In many cases, it is possible to posit an underlying vowel /ə/, since it surfaces in at least some contexts. For example, there are environments where /pət/ 'on/under' is overtly realized as [pət]. However, there are also words where the existence of /ə/ is doubtful, e.g., [sləŋ] ~ [s^{ə}ləŋ] 'garden', [mrənas] ~ [m^{ə}rənas] 'jump', or [βləŋ] ~ [β^{ə}ləŋ] 'kill'. Diachronically, these words probably contained a phonemic vowel /ə/, which was realized first as short [^{ə}] and later as zero. But synchronically, speakers almost always utter these words with an initial consonant cluster, and literate speakers do not write <e> /ə/ in such words. Given that there is no conclusive evidence, I tentatively analyze such cases as containing an initial consonant cluster.

The phoneme /ə/ has an allophone [ʊ], which is attested in the environment of the velar consonants /ɣ/ and /ŋ/ (either preceding or following), presumably assimilating in quality to the velars. For example, [amʊŋʊm] 'short tree' (from /a=məŋ-əm/ 'NM=wood-SG.RCD'). There are also a few cases where /ə/ assimilates to /u/ in the preceding or following syllable, e.g., [^{n}bʊɽʊm] /^{n}buɽəm/ 'many'. Like /ə/, it is realized extremely short. Given its short duration, I analyze such cases as allophones of /ə/ (rather than as instances of the phoneme /u/).

Conversely, there are indications that some instances of synchronic /ə/ developed from other vowel phonemes. The evidence here comes from vowel alternations in different forms of the word. Compare, e.g., /arəpki/ [arᵊpki] 'axe (SG)' with /arap/ [arap] 'axes (PL)'.

(ii) Long vowels

Vowel length is generally not distinctive in Qaqet. There are nevertheless some instances of contrasting long and short vowels – almost always at morpheme boundaries. When the vowels of two morphemes occur adjacently, they either form a diphthong (see (iii) below) or a long vowel. In such an environment, long vowels can then contrast with short vowels. For example, long vowels result when the article /a/ 'NM' cliticizes to a vowel-initial root (as illustrated in Table 18): [ee] (if the root starts in /i/), [oo] (if the root starts in /u/), and [aa] (if the root starts in /a/). In the last case, a long [aa] can contrast with a short [a] (where this article cliticizes to a consonant-initial root).

Tab. 18: Long vowels at morpheme boundaries: /a/ 'NM'

Vowel-initial roots			Consonant-initial roots		
[eelaɲ]	/a=ilaɲ/	leg/foot	–		
[oolan]	/a=ulan/	eel	–		
[aalingi]	/a=alin-ki/	sugarcane:SG.F	[alimgi]	/a=lim-ki/	young:SG.F

Similarly, a long vowel can be the result of a morpheme-final /ə/ assimilating to the following vowel, and this combination then being realized as a long vowel, e.g., [keeŋaɽ] 'he will chase' (from /kə=iŋaɽ/ '3SG.M.S.NPST=chase.NCONT') or [kuurut] 'he will hold it' (from /kə=urut/ '3SG.M.S.NPST=grab/hold.NCONT'). There is no information on the behavior of morpheme-initial /ə/, as there are hardly any morphemes starting with this vowel.

In addition, there is a small number of monomorphemic roots that contain long vowels. Table 19 summarizes the attested patterns and gives an indication of their frequencies in the data set. The realizations [ii] and [əə] are not attested.

As indicated in Table 19, some long vowel realizations are assumed to result from underlying diphthongs. There is considerable evidence for the monophthongization of diphthongs in Qaqet, including evidence from productive morphological processes (such as the one illustrated in Table 18) that lead to the realization of /ai/ and /au/ as [ee] and [oo] across morpheme boundaries. Further evidence comes from the integration of loanwords containing the diphthong /ai/, which is invariably realized as [ee] in Qaqet (e.g., [leen] 'rope/line', from Tok Pisin /lain/). But note that the corresponding diphthong /au/ tends to retain its diphthong realization (e.g., [pauski] 'purse', from Tok Pisin /paus/) – a realization that is only found in loanwords. Additional evidence comes from synchronic variation in that some speakers produce long vowels, while others produce diphthongs (e.g., [teeŋ] ~ [taiŋ] 'sing.CONT'). And finally, there are indications for diachronic changes in that older sources often transcribe long vowels as diphthongs. For example, Parker and Parker (1974: 21–22) write [keenaʝi] as *kainaki* 'water'. Similarly, the orthography of place names is often suggestive of an original diphthong: *Lamarain*, *Lualait* and *Malasait* are usually pronounced [lamareen], [lualeet] and [malaseet] today. Or *Raunsepna* (pronounced [ɽaunsepna], with a diphthong) contains the word /ɽaun/ (pronounced [ɽoon], with a long vowel) 'netbags'.

Tab. 19: Long vowels within morphemes

Realization	Analysis	Frequency	Example of long vowel	Gloss
[ee]	/ii/	7 roots	[seet] /siit/	story
[ee]	/ai/	7 roots	[keena] /kaina/	water
[uu]	/uu/	2 roots	[ɣuukuk] /ɣuukuk/	sweet.potato
[oo]	/au/	4 roots	[ɽoon] /ɽaun/	netbag
[aa]	/aa/	7 roots	[laan] /laan/	bamboo.type

The diphthong /ai/ is realized [ee] in most environments, except when preceding /ɲ/ or /k/. In this environment, only [ai] is attested. In the case of /ɲ/, it is possible to argue that its palatal place of articulation has prevented the monophthongization of /ai/. In the case of /k/, a similar argument can be made. Section 2.1.1 has shown that /k/ is the only consonant that palatalizes in the environment of /i/: [ʲk] or [kʲ] when following or preceding /i/, and [ʝ] when preceding /i/ intervocalically. That is, it can be argued that this palatalization favors the realization [ai]. Note also that /ai/ and /a/ contrast with each other, i.e., there is no evidence that the realization [ai] before /ɲ/ or /k/ is an allophone of /a/. Compare e.g. /ɣuaiɲguaiɲ/ 'butterfly' with /ɣuaɲ/ 'yam', or /ⁿduɽaik/ 'chicken' with /ɽak/ 'cane leaf'. In the case of /au/, no comparable complementary distribution is found: the vast majority of cases are realized as [oo]; and the realization [au] seems to be restricted to names and loanwords.

Given the above evidence, I assume that the diphthongs /ai/ and /au/ are the main sources for [ee] and [oo]. By contrast, long vowels that do not originate in diphthongs are few: /ii/ (realized [ee]), /uu/ and /aa/. Even though it only concerns few cases, long vowels nevertheless contrast with short vowels in the same environment (illustrated in Table 20). All (near-) minimal pairs involve lexical items, with two exceptions: a contrast between /araa/ '3PL.POSS' and /ara/ '3SG.F.POSS', and between /aa/ '3SG.M.POSS' and /a/ 'NM'.

Tab. 20: (Near) minimal pairs: Long vowels vs. short vowels

Long vowel	Example (long vowel)		Example (short vowel)	
/ii/ [ee]	*siit*	stories	*sisit*	ridge
/uu/	*ɣuukuk*	sweet.potatoes	*ɣukun*	few
/aa/	*laan*	bamboo.type	*lan*	bones
	araa	3PL.POSS	*ara*	3SG.F.POSS
	aa	3SG.M.POSS	*a*	NM

It is not always straightforward to establish the phonemic structure of a given word, because both the diphthong /ai/ and the long vowel /ii/ are realized [ee]. But there are a number of reasons for positing an underlying /ii/ in some cases. First, there are reasons of symmetry: /u(u)/ and /a(a)/ are attested as both short and long vowels, while /i/ is only attested as a short vowel and /ee/ only as a long vowel. It is thus not unreasonable to assume that [ee] is the realization of /ii/.[6] Second, short vowels are predictably realized long in some environments (see section 2.3.1), and in the case of /i/, both [ii] and [ee] realizations are attested. Note especially that even the [ee] realization triggers the palatalization of a preceding /k/ (as illustrated in example 10). I take this to be evidence for [ee] being a realization of /i(i)/, as neither underlying /ai/ nor underlying /ə/ would have triggered the palatalization of a preceding /k/. Third, there are occasional variant pronunciations of [ee] as [ii], e.g., [mee] ~ [mii] 'most'. Finally, older sources sometimes write synchronic [ee] as *ii*, e.g., Parker and Parker (1974: 11) write [seetka] 'story' as *siitka*.

(10) *meekʲee*
miiki
instead
'instead' (ABL-03/09/2014)

The long vowels /uu/ and /aa/ are realized as [ʊʊ] and [aa] ~ [ɐɐ] (like their short counterparts). There is no indication that the realization [oo] could be an alternate realization of /uu/ (unlike [ee] being a realization of /ii/).

6 The short vowel /ə/ has no corresponding long vowel either. As shown in this section, /ə/ behaves differently from the other short vowels (see also section 2.3.1), and it is thus not clear if the long vowel ever existed. If it existed, its realization would have merged with that of other long vowels. On the basis of my current knowledge, it is impossible to establish evidence either for or against the existence of /əə/.

(iii) Vowel sequences

Short vowels can combine to form diphthongs both within morphemes and at morpheme boundaries. Table 21 gives an overview of the attested diphthongs. The logically possible combinations with /ə/ do not occur, and it is likely that they have merged with one of the long vowels. As discussed in (ii) above, there is evidence for such a merger involving diphthongs whose second vowel is /ə/ (but there is no information on those whose first vowel is /ə/).

Within monomorphemic words, diphthongs are not uncommon. Table 22 summarizes the patterns, indicates their frequency in the lexicon and gives some (near-) minimal pairs with words containing simple vowels. Note that Table 22 does not include those words that underlyingly contain the diphthongs /ai/ and /au/, but that are realized as the long vowels [ee] and [oo] (see Table 19 for such cases).

Tab. 21: Diphthongs

	i	**ə**	**a**	**u**
i		*iə	ia	iu
ə	*əi [ee]		*əa [aa]	*əu [uu]
a	ai ~ [ee]	*aə		au ~ [oo]
u	ui	*uə	ua	

Tab. 22: Diphthongs in monomorphemic words

Diphthong	**Frequency**	**Example**		**Near-minimal pairs**	
/ia/	18 roots	*ɟiaɽ*	scrape/paddle.NCONT	*ɟiɽ*	push
				ɣaɽu	shout.NCONT
/iu/	2 roots	*miu*	cat	*milat*	coconut.shell
				mu	put.NCONT.PST
/ai/	12 roots	*ⁿduɽaik*	chicken	*ɽak*	cane.leaf
				ⁿdaɽik	outside
/au/	1 root	*malaus*	canoe	*las*	branch
				lus	bark
/ui/	18 roots	*kui*	quoting	*kuɽi*	leave
				ki	3SG.F
/ua/	28 roots	*kua*	where	*kuɽi*	leave
				ka	3SG.M

In careful speech, diphthongs are realized as two vowels within a single syllable, but there are two kinds of exceptions (see point (ii) above). First, the diphthongs /ai/ and /au/ are usually realized as long vowels: /ai/ is realized [ee] except when preceding /ɲ/ or /k/; and /au/ is realized [oo] except in loanwords and in the word /malaus/ 'canoe' (which is not a known loanword). And second, vowel sequences at morpheme boundaries involving /ə/ are presumably all realized as long vowels. The length of a diphthong corresponds to that of a long vowel (about twice the length of a short vowel). When compared to their short vowel counterparts, we observe some assimilation between the two vowels of the diphthong: /ai/ tends to be realized as [æe], /ia/ as [eæ], /au/ as [ɑɔ] ~ [ɑo], /ua/ as [ɔɑ] ~ [oɑ], /ui/ as [ʊe], and /iu/ as [eʊ]. In normal and fast speech, diphthongs are frequently realized as short vowels plus labialization or palatalization of the preceding consonant: labialization if the first vowel of the diphthong is [u] (i.e., /Cui/ and /Cua/ are realized as [C^{w}i] and [C^{w}a]), and palatalization if it is [i] (i.e., /Cia/ and /Ciu/ are realized as [C^{j}a] and [C^{j}u]). Similarly, if the diphthong is word-initial, an initial /u/ ~ /i/ tends to be realized as [w] ~ [j], e.g., [win] '2DU' (from /uin/) or [jam] '3DU.M' (from /iam/).

Despite their frequent realization as labial or palatal glides, there are reasons to analyze them as sequences of two vowels. Recall that /k/ has an allophone [j̥] that only occurs intervocalically when preceding /i/ (see section 2.1.1). The same palatalization is observed when /i/ occurs as the first vowel in a diphthong (i.e., /ia/ and /iu/), as in [aməɽij̥iam] 'two betelnuts' (from /a=məɽik-iam/ 'NM=betelnut-DU.M'). Furthermore, section 2.1.1 has shown that /i/ triggers palatalization in a preceding or a following /k/. When /i/ occurs in this environment within a diphthong, it is lost as a segment, but still surfaces as a palatalization of /k/, e.g., [^{n}duɽa^{j}k] 'chicken' (from /^{n}duɽaik/). This phenomenon is only attested in the environment of /k/, i.e., it occurs in the same environment, regardless of whether /i/ appears as a single vowel or within a diphthong.

Sequences of two vowels are almost always realized within a single syllable, i.e., as diphthongs or long vowels. At morpheme boundaries, however, some speakers were observed to alternatively realize such sequences as two syllables separated by an epenthetic glide. For example, /kaina-im/ 'water-DU.F' is attested both as the two-syllable realization [kee.neem] and as the three-syllable realization [kee.na.jim] (with an epenthetic [j]). This phenomenon is very rare, and the conditioning factors are unknown.

Sequences of more than two vowels are attested, too. They usually occur at morpheme boundaries, but also in four monomorphemic words: /iaiβət/ [jeeβət] 'roll', /iaus/ [joos] 'spirits', /skuaik/ [sk^{w}a^{j}k] 'remove' and /ɣaiap/ /ɣajap/ (with a variant /ɣiap/) 'chickens'. Table 23 summarizes the attested patterns. In the vast majority of cases, /i/ ~ /u/ occurs in between other vowels and are realized as glides [j] ~ [w] (as in 23a). If they are preceded or followed by an identical vowel, speakers alternatively shorten this vowel and utter a diphthong (as in 23b). In some rare cases, we find assimilations in vowel quality to /i/ ~ /u/ (as in 23c). The realization as a glide is also attested if the sequence holds more than three vowels (illustrated for /i/ in 23d, and for /u/ in 23e). If the first vowel in a sequence is /i/ ~ /u/, this vowel is usually realized as a palatalization or labialization of the preceding consonant (as in 23f). Alternatively, in a few cases, an epenthetic glide is inserted following this initial /i/ ~ /u/ (as in 23g). Finally, if /ə/ occurs as the first vowel in such a sequence, it is invariably lost (as in 23h). Note that there are no examples of an underlying /ə/ in any other position.

Tab. 23: Sequences of more than two vowels

	Form	Gloss	Realization	Alternatives
23a	/a=ial/	NM=mango	[ajal]	
	/nauiɽ/	first	[nawiɽ]	
23b	/kuɽi-iam/	leave-3DU.M	[kuɽijam]	~ [kuɽiam]
	/ka=lu-uin/	3SG.M.SBJ=see-2DU	[kaluwin]	~ [kaluin]
23c	/kuɽi-uin/	leave-2DU	[kuɽiwin]	~ [kuɽuwin] ~ [kuɽuin]
23d	/ka=iaiβət/	3SG.M.SBJ=roll	[kajeeβət]	
	/ŋua=iaɽi/	1SG.SBJ=swing	[ŋuajaɽi]	~ [ŋʷajaɽi]
	/ŋua=iaiβət/	1SG.SBJ=roll	[ŋuajeeβət]	~ [ŋʷajeeβət]
23e	/ka=uaik/	3SG.M.SBJ=run	[kawaʲk]	
	/ŋua=uiɽ/	1SG.SBJ=be.first	[ŋuawiɽ]	~ [ŋʷawiɽ]
	/ŋua=uaik/	1SG.SBJ=run	[ŋuawaʲk]	~ [ŋʷawaʲk]
23f	/kia=at/	3SG.F.SBJ=fall	[kʲaat]	
	/skuaik/	remove	[skʷaʲk]	
23g	/ɽua-im/	friend-DU.F	[ɽuweem]	
23h	/kə=uamət/	3SG.M.SBJ.NPST=beat	[kuamət]	

2.2 Syllable structures

This section introduces the Qaqet syllable structure. Table 24 summarizes the attested types and gives an example of each.

The syllable structure template can thus be summarized as (C)(C)V(V)(C).

The nucleus is either a short vowel, a long vowel or a diphthong. If it is a diphthong whose first member is /i/ or /u/, this sequence can either be realized as a diphthong or as palatalization or labialization of the preceding consonant plus a simple vowel. For example, /kua/ 'where' is realized either as [kua] or as [kʷa] (see section 2.1.2).

The syllable can end in a coda consonant, but this consonant cannot be a voiced plosive, a fricative (except /s/) or /r/. This leaves the following possibilities: voiceless plosives (/p/, /t/, /k/), fricative /s/, nasals (/m/, /n/, /ɲ/, /ŋ/) and liquids (/ɽ/, /l/).

Tab. 24: Syllable structures

Type	Realization		Underlying form	
V	***a***.*mam*	fathers	*a=mam*	NM=father
VC	***ut***.*mit*	we went	*ut=mit*	1PL.SBJ=go.NCONT.PST
VV	***aa***.*lin*	sugarcanes	*a=alin*	NM=sugarcane
VVC	***ees***.*ka*	path	*a=is-ka*	NM=path-SG.M
CV	*a.**ɽa**.ɣa.ɟi*	cane leaf	*a=ɽaɣa-ki*	NM=cane.leaf-SG.F
CVC	*a.**ɽim***	buttocks	*a=ɽim*	NM=buttock
CVV	*a.**ɽia***	monitor lizards	*a=ɽia*	NM=monitor.lizard
CVVC	*a.**ɽuis***	children	*a=ɽuis*	NM=child
CCV	*da.βa **sɽu**.ra*	but grannies	*dap=a sɽu-ta*	but=NM old-PL.H
CCVC	*da.βa **sləŋ***	but gardens	*dap=a sləŋ*	but=NM garden
CCVV	*da.βa **sɽee***	but dances	*dap=a sɽai*	but=NM dance
CCVVC	***sɽiam***	name of spirit	*sɽu-iam*	old-DU.M

The syllable can have a consonant onset. In case of a simple onset, all consonants are attested. In case of a complex onset, it usually consists of an obstruent followed by a sonorant, but there are also clusters of a nasal followed by a liquid (e.g., /**mr**a.ɽik/ 'cross').[7] All complex onsets are prone to resyllabification. If the preceding syllable within the word ends in a vowel or diphthong, the first consonant of the cluster will become the coda consonant of the preceding syllable. Compare, e.g., [a**s.ɽ**u.ra] 'grannies' (from /a=sɽu-ta/ 'NM=old-PL.H') to [da.βa **sɽ**u.ra] 'but grannies (in Table 24). As discussed in section 2.1.2, it is likely that consonant clusters originated diachronically through the loss of a phonemic vowel /ə/. In some cases, this vowel no longer surfaces, and a complex onset has to be posited. In other cases, an underlying /ə/ is present in some environments, but tends to be reduced to [ᵊ] or lost altogether in fast speech. That is, consonant clusters very frequently surface on a phonetic level, e.g., [**mr**a.ma=NOUN] 'in the NOUN' (from /mət=ama=NOUN/ 'in=ART=NOUN'). A similar process is observed in coda position, where consonant clusters can surface, e.g., [ka**ts**] 'he is eating' from /ka=təs/ '3SG.M.SBJ=eat.CONT'. This phenomenon is restricted to fast speech, and the syllable template therefore does not contain complex codas.

Across clitic boundaries in fast speech, consonants tend to assimilate in their place of articulation to the following consonant. A common pattern is for the conjunc-

7 There are roots with initial consonant clusters that contradict this pattern, e.g., /**sⁿd**əm/ 'ears'. Such clusters are always resyllabified, e.g., [a**s.ⁿd**əm] 'ears' (from /a=sⁿdəm/ 'NM=ear'), and never occur in initial position.

tion /ip/ to cliticize to the following word and then to be realized as [it] (when preceding an alveolar consonant) or [ik] (when preceding a velar consonant). Otherwise, there is very little assimilation of adjacent consonants, e.g., recall that nasal + plosive clusters are not necessarily homorganic (see section 2.1.1).

Qaqet words are only rarely monosyllabic. Most roots are polysyllabic, and further syllables are added through affixation (especially noun class, gender and number suffixes, object suffixes) and cliticization (especially articles and possessors, conjunctions, prepositions, subject indexes, directionals). The patterns of word formation and their morphophonological processes are described in more detail in the following chapters.

2.3 Prosody

There is no evidence for the existence of metrically strong syllables as anchor points for post-lexical pitch accents (following Hayes 1995: 5–23 definition of lexical stress), and it is thus questionable whether Qaqet has lexical stress. There are, however, phenomena that occur at the boundaries of prosodic units: lengthening of final syllables (section 2.3.1) and pitch movements (section 2.3.2). All attested phenomena can be described with reference to such boundaries, i.e., there is currently no reason to invoke stress.

There is little information on the prosodic systems of related or neighboring languages, excepting a detailed study of Kuot (Lindström and Remijsen 2005), an East Papuan language spoken on the neighboring island of New Ireland. Kuot is said to have lexical stress, and there are minimal pairs distinguished by stress placement (Lindström and Remijsen 2005: 856–861). For Qaqet, no such minimal pairs are attested. Otherwise, however, there are remarkable similarities in the overall pitch movements (similarities and differences are highlighted throughout section 2.3.2). It is thus likely that the prosodic system of Qaqet is not unusual from an areal perspective.

2.3.1 Final lengthening

Final syllables that occur at the end of intonation units are consistently lengthened. This also includes the final syllables of words uttered in isolation or within lists, as illustrated in Figures 5 and 6 with the help of the words [akaina:] 'NM:water' and [akainaji:] 'NM:water:SG.F' (both uttered by the same speaker as non-final members of a list). In each case, the duration of the final vowel is considerably longer (250ms in both cases) than of all preceding vowels (70ms and 90ms respectively) and diphthongs (160ms and 140ms respectively). Note that this lengthening is irrespective of whether the last vowel is part of the root (as in Figure 5) or an affix (as in Figure 6).

Conversely, a final root vowel such as /a/ in /kaina/ 'water' is only realized long if it occurs in final position (as in Figure 5), but not if it occurs in non-final position preceding a suffix (as in Figure 6). In all final syllables, it is usually the vowel that is lengthened (but see below for other possibilities). Furthermore, if the syllable ends in a vowel, it is not uncommon for this vowel to occur with final aspiration, especially if it occurs before a long pause (as [akainaɟiːʰ] 'NM:water:SG.F' in Figure 7).

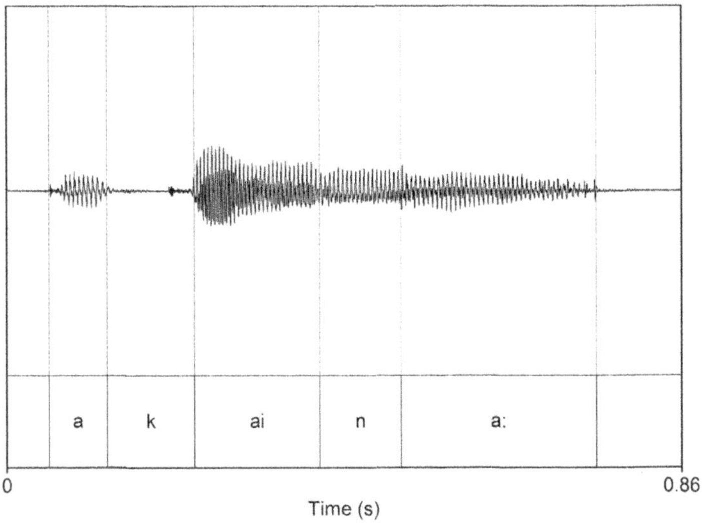

Fig. 5: Final lengthening: [akainaː] 'NM:water' (female speaker: BME)

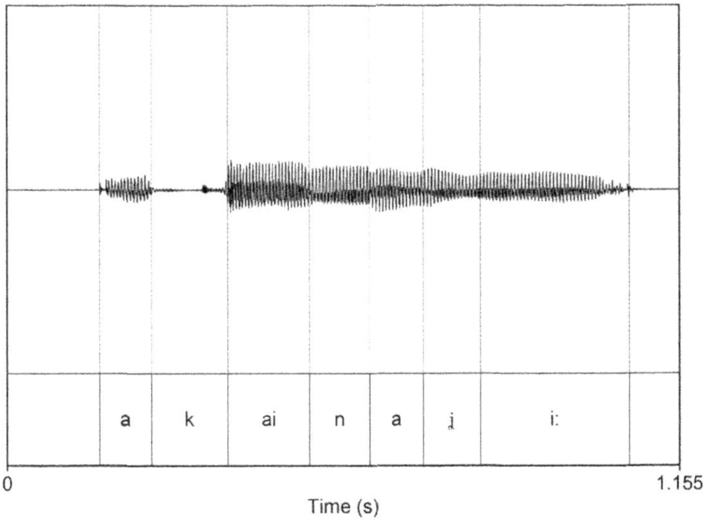

Fig. 6: Final lengthening: [akainaɟiː] 'NM:water:SG.F' (female speaker: BME)

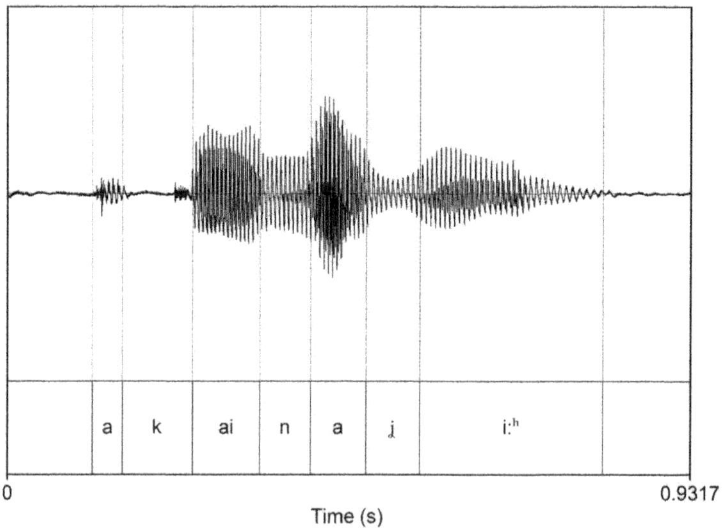

Fig. 7: Final lengthening: [akainaji:ʰ] 'NM:water:SG.F' (N11AAGSIRINIROPE-0003; male speaker: AAG)

The main exception to the lengthening of vowels are final syllables containing /ə/. Recall that this vowel is realized exceptionally short (see section 2.1.2). If it occurs in a final syllable preceding or following a sonorant or fricative, it is the consonant that is lengthened – not the vowel (see Figure 4 above for a contrastive example). If it occurs between two plosives, the vowel is realized longer than normal (albeit still shorter than other vowels in this position), and the final plosive tends to be aspirated.

This final lengthening is not analyzed as lexical stress because it disappears whenever a word is followed by other elements. This is illustrated again by means of the word [kainaji] 'water:SG.F'. Its final syllable is realized long if it precedes an intonational boundary, including words in isolation, words within lists (as in Figure 6 above), and words at the end of intonation units (as in Figure 7 above). In all other environments, its final syllable is not realized long. This is the case, e.g., when it precedes modifiers within a noun phrase (as in Figure 8 and the corresponding example 11a). And it is also frequently the case at the end of non-final prosodic units, provided that they are not separated by a pause from the next unit (as in Figure 9 and the corresponding example 11b; see section 2.3.2 for the pitch movements of non-final units). In both examples below, the final /i/ of [kainaji] is realized very short (30ms and 40ms respectively).

Given this distribution, final lengthening is analyzed here as a boundary phenomenon, not as lexical stress.

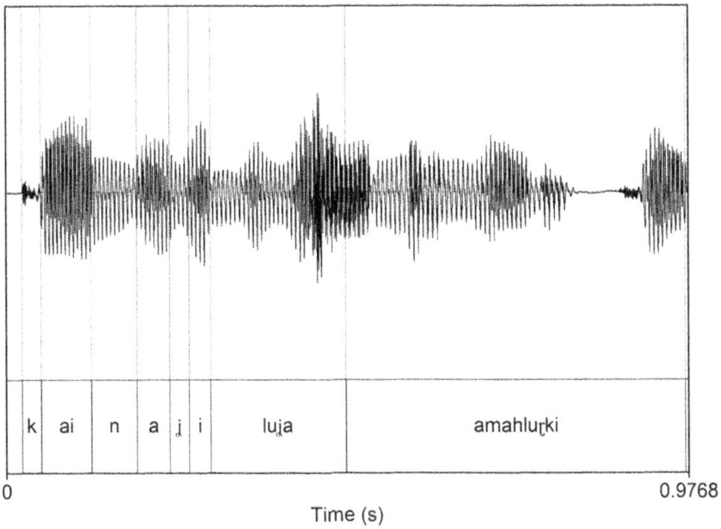

Fig. 8: Non-final syllable: [kainaʝi] 'water:SG.F' (within noun phrase) (male speaker: AAG)

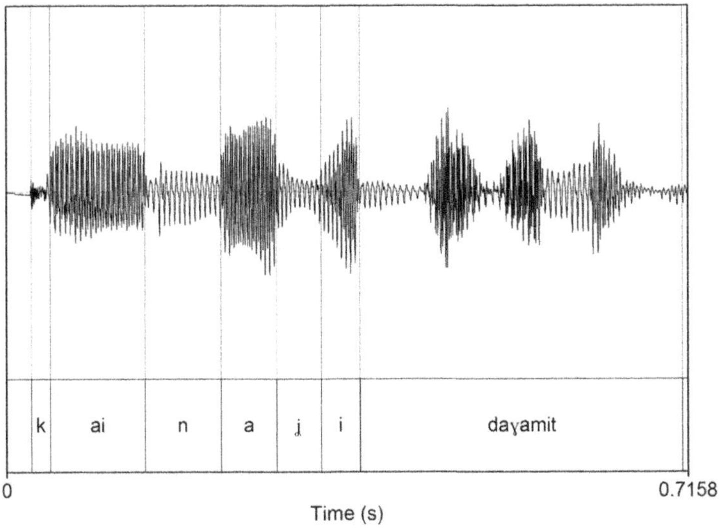

Fig. 9: Non-final syllable: [kainaʝi] 'water:SG.F' (at boundary of non-final unit) (male speaker: AAG)

(11) a. *(ama)kainaʝi luʝa amahluɽki, (...)*
(ama=)kaina-ki lu-ki-a ama=sluɽ-ki, (...)
(ART=)water-SG.F DEM-SG.F-DIST ART=big-SG.F
'(then on to) that big water (about which they say that they cannot cross it)' (N11AAGSIRINIROPE-0094)

b. *(...) kainaji, ⁿdaɣamit, (...)*
(...) kaina-ki, ⁿdə=ka=mit, (...)
water-SG.F CONJ=3SG.M.SBJ=go.NCONT.PST
'(on to) the water, and he went (and he quickly loosened the end of the rope)' (N11AAGSIRINIROPE-0080F)

2.3.2 Pitch movements

Table 25 is a summary of the attested intonation contours in Qaqet. This section presents the results of a qualitative analysis of various text types from a number of different speakers (see chapter 1.2 for details of the corpus). No quantitative analysis has been attempted. It is likely that only the most salient pitch movements were captured and that a more detailed study will unearth further prosodic types and variations within types.

Tab. 25: Intonation contours

Label	Prosody	Function
Final	final fall	declarative utterance; final member of a list
Non-final	final rise-fall	non-final unit of a declarative utterance (e.g., non-final clause, left-dislocated constituent, interjection *kuasik* 'no' & vocative); possibly also some phrasal units
Continuation	final level + glottalization	self-interruption; introducing reported speech & non-verbal demonstrations
List	final rise	non-final member of a list
Content question	fall	interrogative (content question)
Quoted content question	initial rise + final fall	reported interrogative (content question)
Polar question	final rise-fall	interrogative (polar question)
Imperative	(initial rise) + final rise	imperative

Qaqet distinguishes between final and non-final units. Final units are characterized by a falling pitch contour on the last word of the unit, while non-final units are demarcated by a rise-fall contour on their last word. These prosodic units frequently (but not necessarily) correspond to syntactic units. A final unit tends to occur at the right edge of declarative sentences, but it can also demarcate a coordinate clause within a sentence. Such clauses are alternatively realized as non-final units – and it is likely that this difference in marking is triggered by whether or not a speaker intends to portray this clause as being part of a larger unit. Other common non-final units are left-dislocated constituents, interjections such as *kuasik* 'no' and vocatives, and – less frequently – phrasal units within a clause.

Figure 10 illustrates the pitch contour of example (12): a sequence of two non-final units (12-1, 12-2) and one final unit (12-3). The two non-final units are demarcated by a very pronounced rise-fall contour (with F0 rising from around 170Hz to 250Hz and falling back to 170Hz), and the final unit ends in a slight fall (from 140Hz to 115Hz). These pitch movements are independent of pauses. It is true that final units tend to be followed by pauses, but non-final units are just as commonly found before pauses (as between the second and third unit, where there is a pause of 160ms) as without pauses (as between the first and second unit). The pitch contours leading up to such boundaries tend to be fairly flat.[8] Notably, there is no evidence for downdrift within each unit. Across the units, however, downdrift can be observed in that a final unit is usually realized at a lower frequency (in example 12, an F0 starting at 150Hz, compared to 170–180Hz in both non-final units).

(12) 1. *ɲiuas iβit nani? ŋuaβəɽsəs saɣa saməsəŋ*
ɲi=uas *i-pit* *nani=ip* *ŋua=βəɽsəs*
2SG.SBJ.NPST=watch away-up can=PURP 1SG.SBJ=loosen.NCONT
sə-ka *sə=məsəŋ*
to/with-3SG.M to/with=at.base
'watch until I can throw him down (from the tree)'

2. *^{n}dekaman pramaɣip*
^{n}də=ip=ka=man *pət=ama=ɣip*
CONJ=PURP=3SG.M.SBJ=go.inside.NCONT.PST on/under=ART=spear
'and (until) he will have speared (himself) on the spears'

3. *^{n}dəɲuaməs ^{n}dəmga*
^{n}də=ɲi=uaməs *^{n}də-ka*
CONJ=2SG.SBJ.NPST=beat:?? LOC.PART-3SG.M
'then you beat him (on the head)' (N11AAGSIRINIROPE-0061FF)

8 Some Figures in this chapter exhibit pitch movements that do not occur at audible boundaries. These are mostly triggered by segments (voiceless plosives and fricatives) and do not seem to influence the perception of pitch. I do not want to rule out the possibility that at least some of them are indicative of intermediate phrases, but the acoustic correlates of such intermediate phrases and their (possible) relationship to syntactic units have not been investigated.

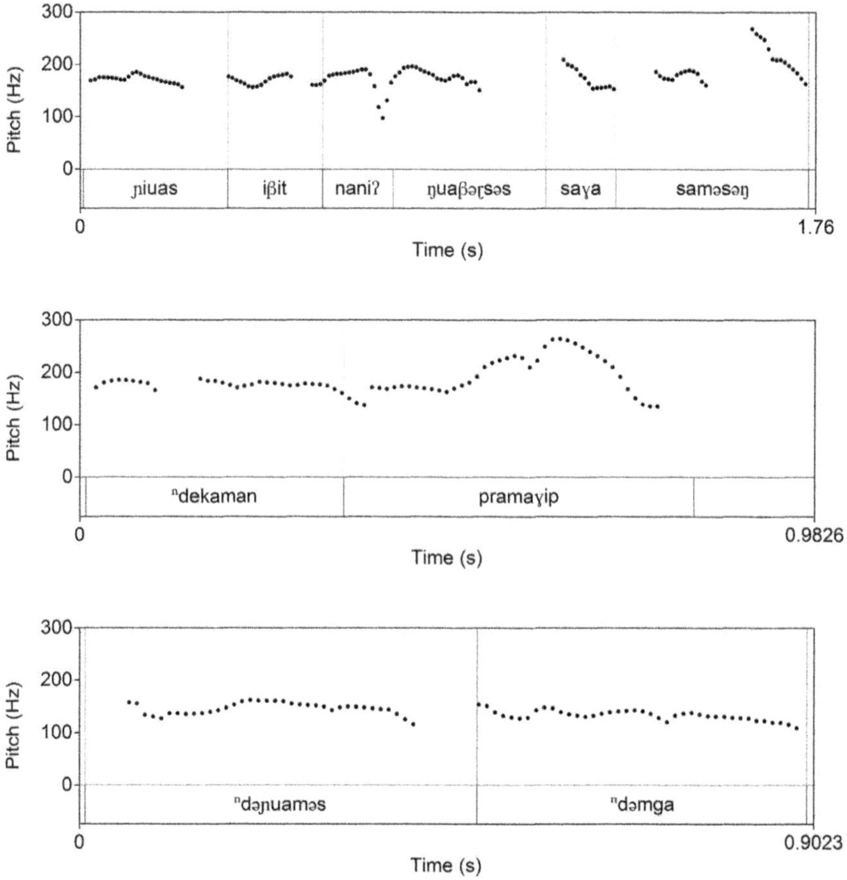

Fig. 10: Non-final and final units 1 (male speaker: AAG)

A non-final unit can also consist of a left-dislocated constituent, such as *amakainaja* 'that water' in Figure 11 and example (13).

(13) 1. *amakainaja*
ama=kaina-ki=a
ART=water-SG.F=DIST
'(at) that water'

2. *^{n}de ŋatranaim maɣamək*
^{n}də ŋa=trana=nə-im maqa-mək
CONJ 3N.SBJ=meet.CONT:RECP=from/with-3DU.F HERE-down
'they (the two branches of the water) meet each other down below here' (N11AAGBROTHERS-0037FF)

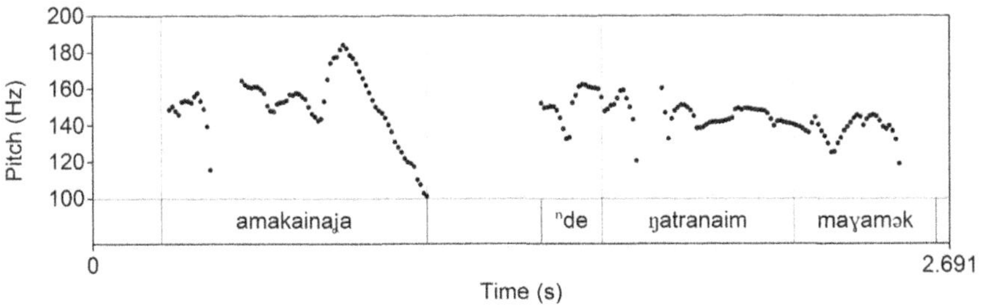

Fig. 11: Non-final unit: Left-dislocated constituent (male speaker: AAG)

The pitch movements of Qaqet final and non-final units are almost identical to those attested in Kuot. The main difference is that Kuot final units show a steep fall. Such a steep fall is sometimes also attested in Qaqet, but it is more common to have a slight fall (as in Figure 10) or even a fairly level pitch (as in 11). It is not clear at present if these different realizations correspond to different functions.

In the examples above, non-final units exhibit extreme rise-fall movements. In fast speech, however, such pitch movements are less salient, as illustrated in Figure 12 and example (14). This example contains three non-final units and one final unit. Although the non-final boundaries are audible, their acoustic cues are less pronounced. The units are not separated by pauses, and the characteristic rise-fall contour is reduced (in that the pitch movements do not exceed 130–150Hz). The contour is fairly flat, without any marked downdrift (around 140Hz from beginning to end). And the final unit is then demarcated by a clear fall on the final syllable (from 145Hz to 110Hz).

(14) 1. *^{n}desaika βəɽspəɽs naim maɣaβuk*
^{n}də=saɟi-ka βəɽspəɽs nə-im maɣa-βuk
CONJ=again-3SG.M part:REDUP from/with-3DU.F HERE-up
'and they (two rivers) part again from each other up here'

2. *^{n}dei ^{n}dep ma ^{n}gət ŋatranaim*
^{n}də=i ^{n}də=ip ma ^{n}gət ŋa=trana=nə-im
CONJ=IPFV=PURP then 3N.SBJ=meet.CONT:RECP=from/with-3DU.F
'and then they (two rivers) meet each other'

3. *^{n}deip ma ^{n}dləɣiak*
^{n}də=ip ma ^{n}gət ^{n}də=lək=ia-ka
CONJ=PURP then CONJ=take.off=other-SG.M
'and then one (of the friends) takes off'

4. *^{n}dayatit tuaɽ*
^{n}də=ka=tit *tuaɽ*
CONJ=3SG.M.SBJ=go.CONT other.side
'and he moves along one branch (of the river)' (N11AAGBROTHERS-0039)

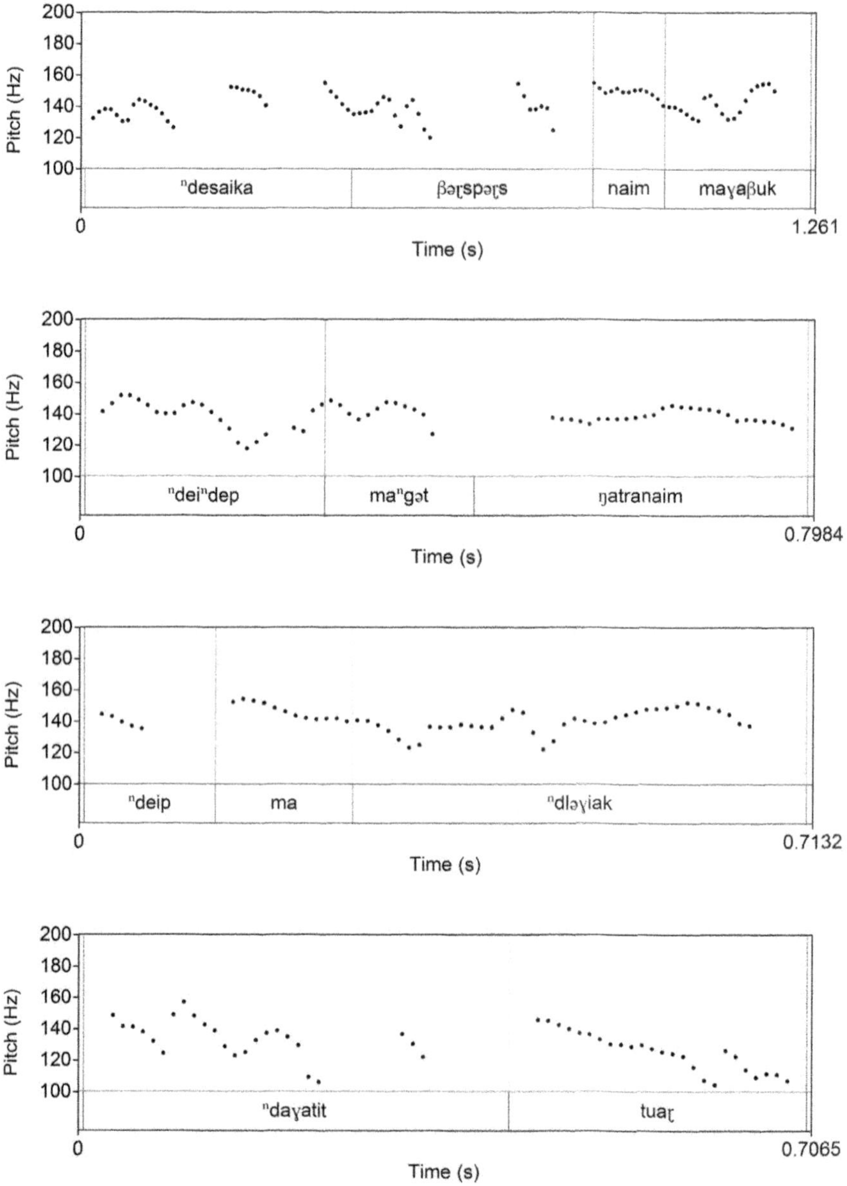

Fig. 12: Non-final and final units 2 (male speaker: AAG)

Speakers interrupt utterances when searching for words or continuations. In such cases, the pitch level is held and the last word is uttered with final glottalization. Figure 13 and example (15) illustrate this by means of word searches within a final declarative unit (with its characteristic fall at the end). The speaker interrupts this unit twice (following *lomamaʔ* and *amaləŋaʔ*), both times maintaining the pitch and adding final glottalization.

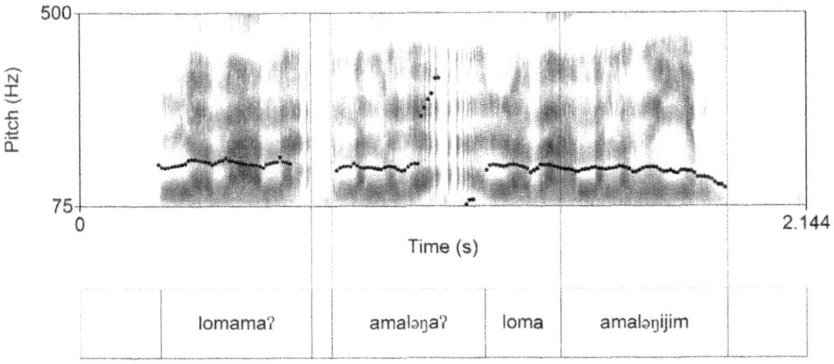

Fig. 13: Self-interruption (male speaker: AJN)

(15) *lomamaʔ.. amaləŋaʔ.. loma amaləŋijim*
lu-em-a=ama.. *ama=ləŋ(i)..* *lu-em-a* *ama=ləŋi-em*
DEM-SG.RCD-DIST=ART ART=word DEM-SG.RCD-DIST ART=word-SG.RCD
'that short.. word.. that short word' (N11AJNGENAINGMETSIQI-0029)

Interestingly, there is one word, *ma* 'thus', where the above prosodic pattern is, arguably, on its way to becoming lexicalized. This word can refer anaphorically back to an utterance or a demonstration and is then realized as [ma] (as in 16a). It can also – and more frequently – introduce reported speech or non-verbal demonstrations. In such contexts, it is invariably realized as [maʔ] (as in 16b), thus indicating that there is a verbal or non-verbal continuation following. Utterances with [maʔ] are never marked as non-final declarative units (i.e., they do not exhibit a rise-fall contour), but always occur with level pitch. Furthermore, this prosodic pattern is only attested with *ma* 'thus' – not with the word *taɣuɽa* ~ *taquɽani* 'thus', which is semantically similar and occurs in comparable contexts (as also illustrated in 16a and 16b).

(16) a. *arijip ⁿbeni ŋataɣən ma, taɣuɽa*
arik=ip *ⁿbə=ini* *ŋa=taɣən* *ma,* *taɣuaɽ=a*
supposing=PURP CONJ=SG.DIM 3N.SBJ=say.CONT thus thus=DIST
'supposing the little one says it like this [i.e., incorrectly], like this' (I12AANACLADNSOCIO2-109)

b. *ɲilu ɲiɽiŋmət maʔ* [demonstration], *tayuɽani* [demonstration]
ɲi=lu *ɲi=ɽiŋmət* *ma,* *tayuaɽ=ani*
2SG.SBJ.NPST=see.NCONT 2SG.SBJ.NPST=split:IN thus thus=DIST
'look, you have to split it like this [demonstration], like this [demonstration]' (P12ADNROPE1-045FF)

Lists have their own characteristic prosody, where each non-final member is marked by a rise (and the final member then occurs with a falling pitch, like other final units). Figure 14 and example (17) illustrate this pattern by means of an elicited example (in the context of eliciting different paradigmatic forms of a word). And example (18) (and Figure 15) is a comparable example from natural discourse between a mother and her three-year old son. The mother lists different animals and the child repeats them – both showing the rising pattern. Note that this rising pitch movement is attested only in lists, i.e., it does not seem to be a general continuation marker, and it is also absent from either NP or clausal coordination.

(17) *alaŋ, aləŋaya, aləŋiam*
a=ləŋa, *a=ləŋa-ka,* *a=ləŋa-iam*
NM=heel NM=heel-SG.M NM=heel-DU.M
'heels, one heel, two heels' (ATA-25/07/2012)

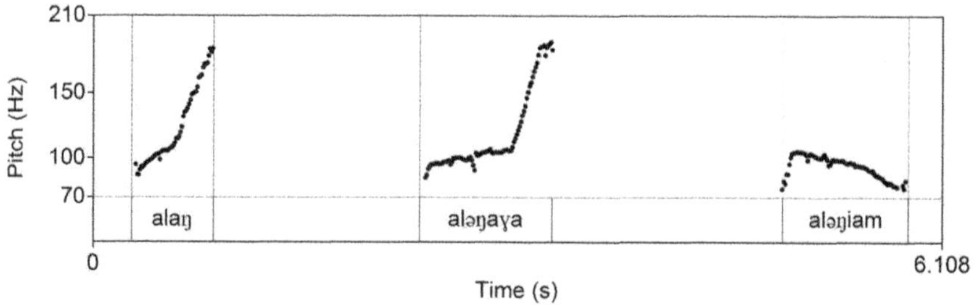

Fig. 14: Listing 1 (male speaker: ATA)

(18) 1. *ŋənama ⁿdaŋ*
ŋərə-nə=ama= ⁿdaŋ
3N.ASSOC-from/with=ART=dog
AMT: 'together with the dogs'

2. *a ⁿdaŋ*
a= ⁿdaŋ
NM=dog
YRA: 'dogs'

3. *ŋənamaanəs*
   ŋərə-nə=ama=anəs
   3N.ASSOC-from/with=ART=parrot
   AMT: 'together with the parrots'
4. *əna hanəs*
   ŋərə-nə=a *anəs*
   3N.ASSOC-from/with=NM parrot
   YRA: 'together with parrots'
5. *ŋənamaʔ.. a ^{n}brasu*
   ŋərə-nə=ama *a=^{n}brasu*
   3N.ASSOC-from/with=ART NM=eagle
   AMT: 'together with the.. eagles'
6. *^{n}brasu*
   ^{n}brasu
   eagle
   YRA: 'eagles' (LONGYDS20150516_1-942FF)

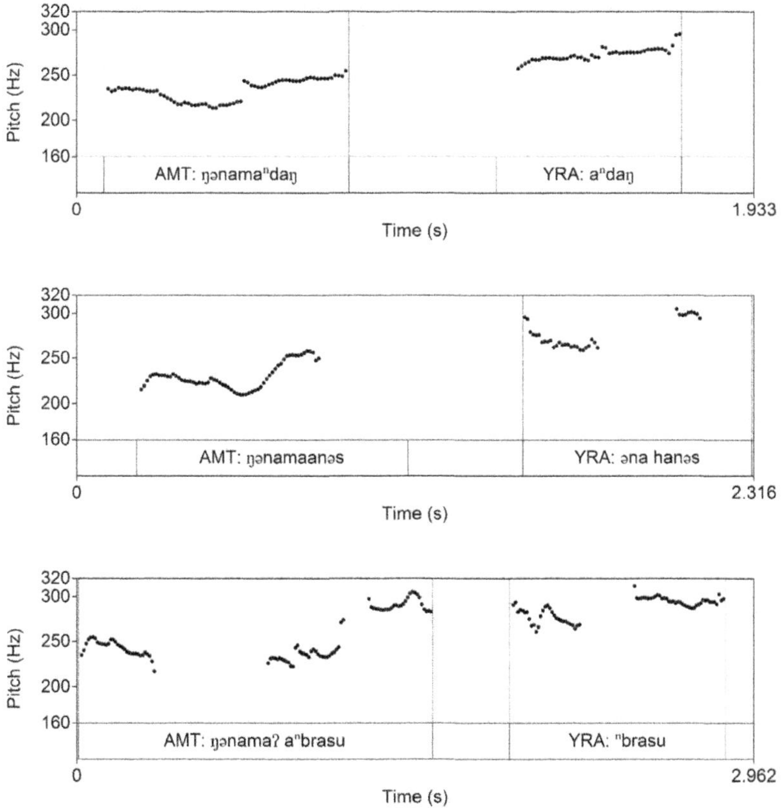

Fig. 15: Listing 2 (female speaker: AMT; child: YRA)

It is not clear if interrogatives have a unique prosody. Content questions resemble final units in that they are also characterized by a falling contour. The main difference seems to be that declarative final units tend to maintain a level pitch until the final fall, whereas interrogatives show evidence for a more general downdrift pattern. Since the attested interrogatives in the corpus consist of fairly short utterances, this suspected difference cannot be investigated further at the moment. Figure 16 and example (19) illustrate two interrogatives with the question words occurring in different positions (at the end in the first case, at the beginning in the second). In both cases, the falling contour is maintained.

(19) *ŋut kua? nəma ŋaləŋəh naŋət?*

ŋət	*kua?*	*nəma*	*ŋa=ləŋəs*	*nə-ŋət?*
3N	where	who	3N.SBJ=destroy	from/with-3N

'where is it? who damaged it?' (LONGYDS20150516_1-096FF)

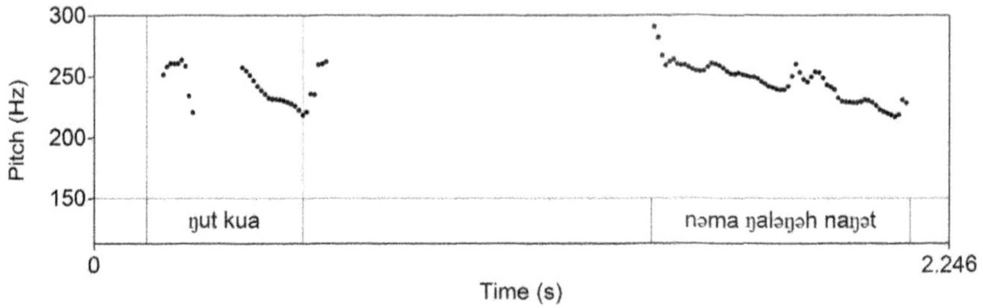

Fig. 16: Content question (female speaker: AMT)

In Kuot, by contrast, content questions exhibit an initial rise, a final fall and a maintaining of the level in between (Lindström and Remijsen 2005: 854–856). Such interrogatives are also attested in the Qaqet corpus (as illustrated in Figure 17 and example 20), but only in quoted interrogatives from narratives, i.e., Qaqet seems to distinguish prosodically between content questions and quoted content questions. Since the Kuot data also comes from narratives, it is possible that Kuot exhibits a similar distinction.

(20) *ⁿbəluŋəra nayua ama ⁿguləŋ?*

ⁿbə=lu-ŋət-a	*nə=kua*	*ama=ⁿguləŋ?*
CONJ=DEM-N-DIST	from/with=where	ART=malay.apple

'and those malay apples are from where?' (N11AAGSIRINILOBSTER2-0007)

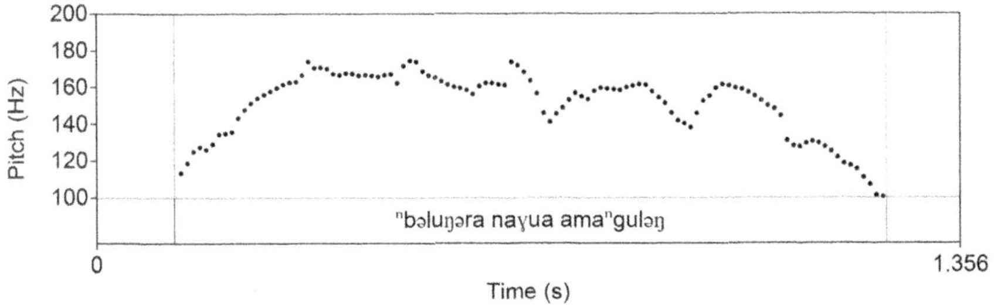

Fig. 17: Quoted content question (male speaker: AAG)

The prosody of polar questions is reminiscent of that of non-final units, and it is not clear if there is any prosodic difference between the two. Both show a rise-fall pattern on the last word. Example (21) (and Figure 18) is a short question/answer sequence; and example (22) (and Figure 19) illustrates the restriction of the rise-fall pattern to the last word of the utterance. The same pattern is attested in Kuot, too.

(21) *kua ɲinaɽi?* *mh*
kua *ɲi=naɽi?* *mh*
INTRG 2SG.SBJ.NPST=hear yes
AMT: 'do you hear?' YRA: 'yes' (LONGYDS20150516_1-858FF)

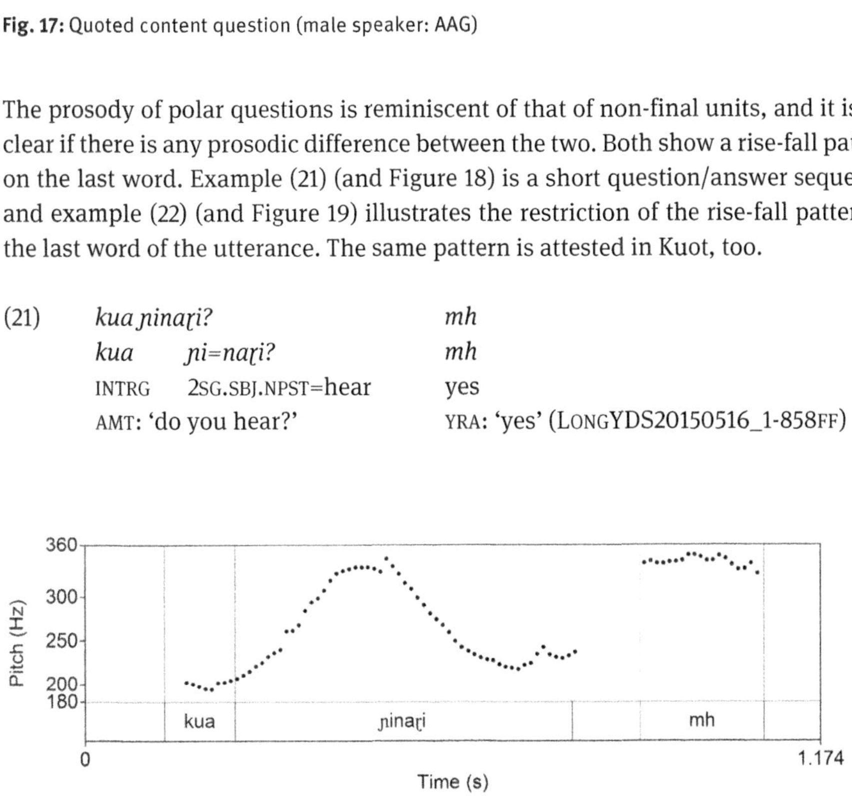

Fig. 18: Polar question 1 (female speaker: AMT; child: YRA)

(22) *kua ɲitlamaiβip? amaiβiβim?*
kua *ɲi=tlu=ama=iβip?* *ama=iβip-im?*
INTRG 2SG.SBJ.NPST=see.CONT=ART=snake ART=snake-DU.F
'do you see the snakes? the two snakes?' (LONGYDS20150516_2-011FF)

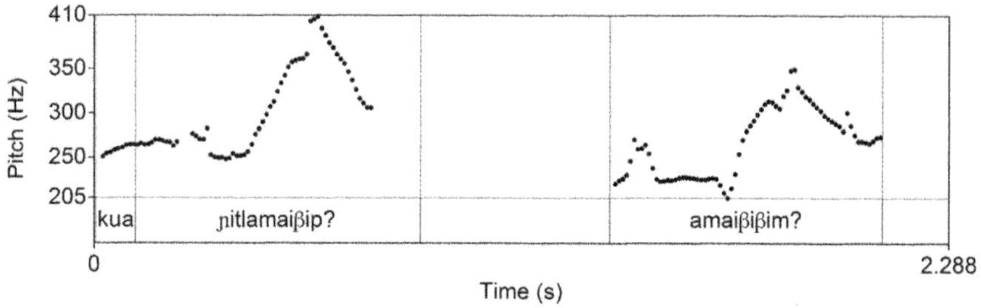

Fig. 19: Polar question 2 (female speaker: AMT)

Imperatives are characterized through a final rise. Short imperatives exhibit a continuous rise (as in example 23 and Figure 20), and longer imperatives show a downdrift pattern plus a rise on the final word (as in example 24 and Figure 21). Imperatives can also be more complex, consisting of several prosodic units (as in example 25 and Figure 22): all non-final units have a non-final prosody (i.e., a final rise-fall), and only the last unit has the imperative contour of downdrift plus final rise. Furthermore, imperatives seem to have an initial rise on their first word, but this needs further investigation. It is present in Figure 21. And it also occurs in the complex imperative in Figure 22, marking the first word of the non-final unit. Non-imperative non-final units do not exhibit such an initial rise.

(23) *ɲan*
ɲa=an
2SG.SBJ=come.NCONT.FUT
'come' (LONGYDS20150506_2-179)

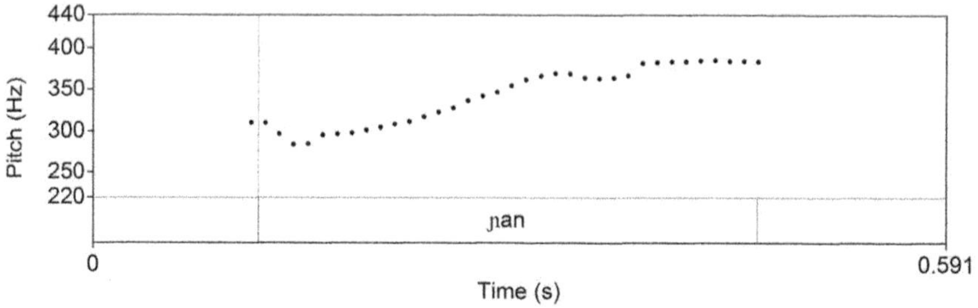

Fig. 20: Imperative 1 (female speaker: AMT)

(24) *so, ɲiruɣun ^{m}siŋan ikiranəŋ mara*

sa, *ɲi=ruɣun* *ma=siŋan*

already 2SG.SBJ.NPST=say.NCONT ART.ID=NAME

ip=ki=ranəŋ *mara*

PURP=3SG.F.SBJ.NPST=hold.NCONT here

'now, tell Singan to hold it here' (LONGYDS20150516_1-434)

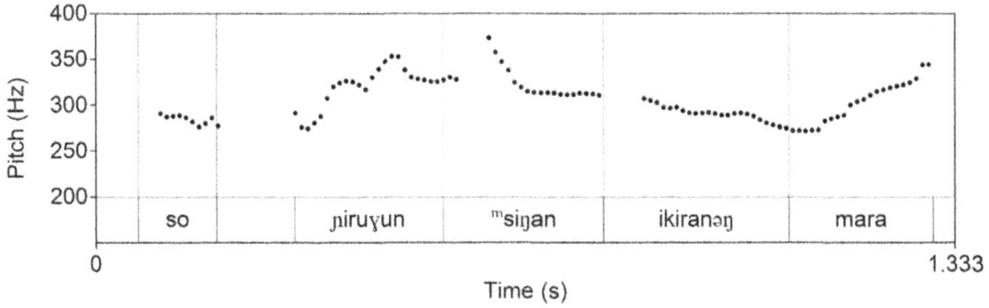

Fig. 21: Imperative 2 (female speaker: AMT)

(25) *ɲaruɣun ^{n}dəɣəɽ naniɲinəska, mrama a ^{n}biki*

ɲa=ruɣun *^{n}də=kəɽ* *nani=ɲi=nəs-ka,*

2SG.SBJ=sit.NCONT.FUT CONJ=DEONT can=2SG.SBJ.NPST=put.in.NCONT-3SG.M

mət=ama *a=^{n}bik-ki*

in=ART NM=bag-SG.F

'sit down and put it inside, into the bag' (LONGYDS20150516_1-364FF)

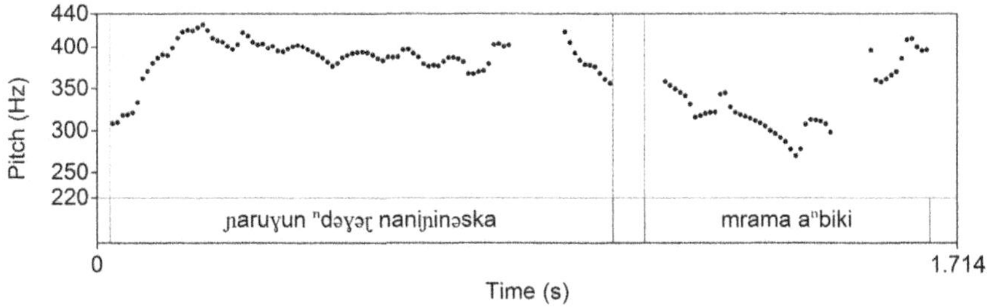

Fig. 22: Complex imperative (female speaker: AMT)

It is unknown how Kuot marks imperatives. But the Qaqet imperative pattern is very similar to the negation pattern of Kuot. In Kuot, negation is marked by a 'dip rise' pattern, with the pitch dropping to the onset of the final syllable and then rising again on its rhyme (Lindström and Remijsen 2005: 852–854). So far, no distinctive negative patterns have been observed for Qaqet.

2.4 Summary

This chapter presented Qaqet phonology. Section 2.1 discussed the phonemes, showing that Qaqet has a smallish phoneme inventory (16 consonant and 4 vowel phonemes) that includes a phonemic contrast between voiceless and voiced plosives, a phonemic contrast between /r/ and /l/, intervocalic lenition of voiceless plosives and the recent development of fricative phonemes from this process of lenition. The first two properties are usually considered characteristic of Oceanic languages, not of East Papuan languages (Dunn et al. 2008: 743). All four properties are shared by the Baining languages and Kuot, but apparently not by the other East Papuan languages of the Bismarck Archipelago (Stebbins 2009a).

Section 2.2 then summarized the syllable structures, showing that Qaqet has complex syllable structures, allowing for consonant cluster onsets and word-final consonants. The first is probably a new development, resulting from the reduction and eventual loss of /ə/ in certain environments. Both properties are attested in many East Papuan languages, but are not widespread in Oceanic languages (Lindström et al. 2007: 126).

Finally, section 2.3 described aspects of Qaqet prosody, including the lengthening of final syllables as well as an inventory of pitch movements marking (mostly) the right edge of intonation units. The prosodic structures of East Papuan languages are not well-understood, but there exists an excellent description of Kuot prosody (Lindström and Remijsen 2005). Qaqet differs from Kuot in that it does not have lexical stress, but it is otherwise remarkably similar to Kuot: the two languages seem to share the salient characteristics of final and non-final units, quoted content questions, and polar questions; and they only seem to differ in the case of negation. The remaining Qaqet units have not been described for Kuot (continuation, list, non-quoted content question, imperative) and it is thus unknown whether or not they are shared.

3 Nouns and the noun phrase

This chapter is organized around the structure of the noun phrase. Section 3.1 gives a general introduction to word classes and phrasehood in Qaqet, focusing on the word class of nouns (compared to that of adjectives) and on the noun phrase. Section 3.2 introduces heads of noun phrases: nouns, numerals and quantifiers, independent pronouns and interrogative pronouns. Sections 3.3 and 3.4 discuss, respectively, (pre-head) determiners and (post-head) modifiers. Determination is achieved through demonstrative and indefinite pronouns (which function both as heads of noun phrases and as adnominal determiners) and articles (which only function as adnominal determiners). And modification is achieved through adjectives occurring in the modifier construction, nouns occurring in the nominal modifier construction, and prepositional phrases and directionals. Section 3.5 then describes pronominal and nominal possession, and section 3.6, noun phrase coordination. Finally, section 3.7 summarizes the main points discussed in this chapter.

Qaqet has an elaborate system of noun classification: noun classes are overtly marked on nouns and pronouns, on agreeing elements within the noun phrase and on a number of argument indexes. This chapter frequently makes reference to this noun class system, but a more detailed discussion of its forms, meanings and distributions is postponed until chapter 4. Note that this grammar distinguishes terminologically between "noun class" (used in reference to the full system of classification) and "gender" (used in reference to a reduced form of the system) (see chapter 4 for details).

3.1 Introductory remarks on word classes and phrases

This section introduces the word class of nouns (section 3.1.1) and the structure of the noun phrase (section 3.1.2). Both sections also include a more general discussion on the issue of word classes and phrasehood in Qaqet. Overall, there is considerable morphosyntactic evidence for the existence of word classes and phrase structure, but there are two qualifications to be added. First, many Qaqet roots occur underived in different morphosyntactic environments. As discussed below, I do not consider such roots to be acategorial, but analyze them as cases of conversion. Second, although the constituent order within phrases tends to be rigid and contiguous, there are examples whose constituents appear in different orders, including some non-contiguous orders. It is likely that information structural considerations and/or subtle functional differences will eventually be able to account for the attested variation. For now, the number of counter-examples is too small to allow for any generalizations. Mali Baining shares the phenomenon of conversion (Stebbins 2011: 58–59, 95–97), but there is no information available on variable orders within phrases.

3.1.1 Word classes: Nouns and adjectives

Table 26 summarizes the morphosyntactic properties of nouns, comparing them to those of adjectives. This comparison is motivated by the observation that the two word classes share formal properties. Furthermore, adjectives freely convert into nouns. There are nevertheless differences, which are outlined in this section (and discussed in more detail throughout the relevant sections in chapters 3 and 4).

Tab. 26: Nouns and adjectives compared

	Noun	**Adjective**
occurs as head of NP	yes	no
- has inherent noun class	yes (most)	no
occurs as modifier within NP	yes	yes
- in modifier construction	no	yes
- in nominal modifier construction	yes	no
occurs as non-verbal predicate	yes	yes
- as non-verbal equative predicate	yes	no
- as non-verbal attributive predicate	no	yes
- non-verbal predicate takes an article (NM, ART, ART.ID)	yes	yes

The main difference between the two word classes is that only nouns can occur as heads of noun phrases. As such, only nouns can co-occur with various determiners and modifiers, as well as in all syntactic slots available to noun phrases. For example, the head noun *siit-ka* 'story-SG.M' in (1a) is preceded by a demonstrative and an article, and the noun phrase appears in direct object function. Furthermore, almost all nouns have an inherent noun class (in this case, masculine), and noun phrase elements such as demonstratives obligatorily agree in noun class with the head noun. An adjective, by contrast, can only occur in modifier position within a noun phrase. For example, the head noun in (1b) is *kaasik-ka* 'vine-SG.M', which is followed by the adjectival modifier *slurl-ka* 'big-SG.M'. The adjective does not have an inherent noun class, but agrees with that of the head noun (i.e., masculine singular in 1b).

The distribution of nouns (as heads of noun phrases) and adjectives (as modifiers within noun phrases) is fairly straightforward. They share morphological similarities in that both nouns and adjectives are marked for noun class and are preceded by articles. And they differ in that only nouns can have an inherent noun class, while adjectives always agree with the class of their head noun; there are also slight differences in the noun class paradigms of nouns and adjectives. And although the article *ama*, which introduces modifiers, is segmentally identical (and presumably diachronically related) to one of the articles introducing head nouns, it synchronically belongs to a different paradigm.

(1) a. *bradrlem luqa amasiitka*
be=ta=drlem *[lu-ka-a* *ama=siit-ka]*NP
CONJ=3PL.SBJ=know DEM-SG.M-DIST ART=story-SG.M
'and so they know [that story]NP' (I12AANACLADNSocio3-339)

b. *deqalama.. akaasika amahlurlka*
de=ka=lu=[ama.. *a=kaasik-ka* *ama=slurl-ka]*NP
CONJ=3SG.M.SBJ=see.NCONT=ART NM=vine-SG.M ART=big-SG.M
'and he sees [a.. a big vine]NP' (N11AAGSiriniRope-0013)

This seemingly clear picture is complicated by two observations. First, adjectives freely convert to nouns, in which case they occur as heads of noun phrases. For example, the head noun in (2a) is *gil-ki* 'small-SG.F' (converted from the adjective *gil* 'small'), co-occurring with a pre-head demonstrative. Such converted nouns do not have an inherent noun class, but reflect the class of their referent (i.e., a girl in (2a), thus triggering the use of the feminine noun class). Second, modification within the noun phrase is not restricted to adjectives. For example, the noun *gam-ki* 'seed-SG.F' occurs in the modifier slot in (2b), restricting the reference of *iling* 'pumpkin' (which denotes various edible parts of the pumpkin, e.g., pumpkin leaves, but also pumpkin fruits). There are subtle formal differences between adjectival and nominal modifiers (see section 3.4.2), but both can be used to modify a head noun.

(2) a. *dap, lek luqia ama.. agilki*
dap, *lek* *[lu-ki-a* *ama..* *a=gil-ki]*NP
but take.off DEM-SG.F-DIST ART NM=small-SG.F
'and [that.. little one]NP took off' (N11AAGSiriniRope-0080d)

b. *ailinggi amagamgi*
[a=iling-ki *ama=gam-ki]*NP
NM=pumpkin-SG.F ART=seed-SG.F
'[a pumpkin fruit]NP' (AJS-05/05/15)

Finally, both nouns and adjectives occur as non-verbal predicates: nouns as equative predicates (as in 3a), and adjectives, as attributive predicates (as in 3b). The two constructions share formal similarities: both have the same constituent order, and both mark their predicate by an article (which, in the case of nominal predicates, can be replaced by another pre-head determiner). But, again, there are morphosyntactic differences (e.g., the subject is introduced by a preposition in the equative construction, but not in the attributive construction), which show that these are two separate constructions (discussed in chapter 8.2 in more detail).

(3) a. *amalavu naut*
[ama=lavu]$_{\text{PRED}}$ *[ne-ut]*$_{\text{SBJ}}$
ART=adult from/with-1PL
'we are the parents' (I12AANACLADNSocio3-187)

b. *ut de amagilut*
ut *de* *[ama=gil]*$_{\text{PRED}}$*[-ut]*$_{\text{SBJ}}$
1PL CONJ ART=small-1PL
'as for us, we are small' (ATA&AEM&ACS-22/06/2011)

The brief summary above has highlighted both similarities and differences between nouns and adjectives. It is true that the Qaqet adjectives are nominal in character, sharing formal similarities with nouns. Nevertheless, there are morphosyntactic differences that warrant positing two distinct classes. Similarly, the other major word classes also have distinct morphosyntactic properties, including verbs (see chapter 5) and adverbs (see chapter 6).

While classes can thus be distinguished on formal grounds, it is necessary to add a qualification: many roots occur underived in different functions, taking on the appropriate morphology of the respective word classes. For example, the root *gep* is attested both as a noun 'pulp' (occurring in 4a as the head of a noun phrase) and as a verb 'give someone pulp' (occurring in 4b as a transitive verb). Or example (4c) features the root *siit* 'story' both as a verb ('tell a story') and as a noun ('story').

(4) a. *nyit nyiquarl tama agepka barek giahrluqa*
nyi=it *nyi=quarl*
2SG.SBJ.NPST=go.NCONT.FUT 2SG.SBJ.NPST=present.NCONT
te=ama *a=**gep**-ka* *barek* *gia=srlu-ka*
PURP=ART NM=pulp-SG.M BEN 2SG.POSS=old-SG.M
'go and give pulp (= chewed betelnut) to your grandfather' (ALR-03/06/2015)

b. *angerlnanngi kigep ama.. arluimga*
a=ngerlnan-ki *ki=**gep*** *ama..* *a=rluim-ka*
NM=woman-SG.F 3SG.F.SBJ.NPST=pulp ART NM=child-SG.M
'the mother feeds the.. the child chewed food' (ALR-03/06/2015)

c. *de nani ngusiit nurasiitka*
de *nani* *ngu=**siit*** *ne=ura=**siit**-ka*
CONJ can 1SG.SBJ.NPST=story from/with=1PL.POSS=story-SG.M
'I can tell our story' (I12AANACLADNSocio3-466)

This phenomenon is attested with a large number of roots. One possible analysis would be to argue that Qaqet roots are acategorial and that the word class distinction does not hold for the level of the root. I do not adopt this analysis, and instead assume that these are cases of conversion. The reasons for this decision are outlined below (see also Stebbins 2011: 95–97 for a similar analysis in Mali).

First, a large number of roots are attested in one word class only. Although it is likely that there are gaps in the database and that targeted elicitation will reveal more roots occurring in different classes, it nevertheless points to a pattern: roots frequently occur in one class, even if they could potentially occur in other classes, too. Furthermore, there are unidirectional conversions that point to underlying patterns: all roots that occur as adjectives also occur as nouns (conversely, there are many roots that only occur as nouns, never as adjectives). In some cases, converted forms even retain some of their original morphology: this concerns especially verbs that have different aspectual stems, which are retained when converting to other classes (see section 3.2.1 for a discussion).

And second, there are differences in meaning. Some of these differences are systematic and affect entire (sub-) classes. For example, all roots that occur as adjectives also occur as nouns. The adjective always denotes a property (as the adjectival modifier in 5a), while the corresponding noun denotes a referent characterized by that property (as in 5b). In addition, there are unpredictable meaning associations, e.g., some roots admit an abstract reading when occurring as nouns (such as *dlek* 'strong' with a reading of 'strength, confidence' in 5c), while others do not: i.e., although a semantic relationship between a property and its abstract concept is not unexpected, not all adjectives allow for this pattern. In addition, there are many meaning changes that can only be considered idiosyncratic. For example, *barl* 'big' also occurs as a verb meaning 'to be proud of something' (illustrated in 5d).

(5) a. *dinyinan damameng amabarlnget*
de=nyi=nan *de=[ama=meng*
CONJ=2SG.SBJ.NPST=put.up.CONT LOC.PART=ART=wood
*ama=**barl**-nget]*NP
ART=big-N
'then you put together the big branches' (P12ADNFIRE-026)

b. *amabarlka, deqaruqun namagilka ma*
*[ama=**barl**-ka]*NP, *de=ka=ruqun*
ART=big-SG.M CONJ=3SG.M.SBJ=say.NCONT
ne=ama=gil-ka *ma*
from/with=ART=small-SG.M thus
'then the big one, he said to the small one like this' (N11AJNGENAINGMETBROTHERS-0048)

c. *de.. dadip ngusu madlek naini*
de.. *dap=dip* *ngu=su* *[ma=***dlek**
CONJ but=FUT 1SG.SBJ.NPST=teach ART.ID=strength
*ne-ini]*NP
from/with-SG.DIM
'and.. and I will teach confidence to the little one (lit. the little one's confidence)' (I12AANACLADNSocio3-029)

d. *inani urebarl nas, navruralengiqa*
i=nani *ure=***barl** *nas,*
SIM=can 1PL.SBJ.NPST=big self
ne=pet=ura=lengi-ka
from/with=on/under=1PL.POSS=word-SG.M
'so we can be proud of our language (lit. we big/pride ourselves with our language)' (I12AANACLADNSocio2-088)

I consider the points above (i.e., the occurrence of many roots in a single word class only, the existence of patterns of conversion as well as predictable and non-predictable meaning changes) indications that the roots are not acategorial. Instead, I assume that the change in word class involves the formation of new lexemes with their own, distinct, meaning ranges. These new lexemes usually share the same morphosyntactic properties as the other members of that word class. In fact, conversion is the most common way of creating new lexemes in Qaqet. The possibilities for morphological derivation, by contrast, are very restricted.

3.1.2 Phrases: Noun phrase

Table 27 summarizes the structure of the simple noun phrase. The head of the noun phrase is either a noun or a pronoun (including independent, interrogative, demonstrative and indefinite pronouns). Nouns can take the full range of determiners and modifiers; while pronouns exhibit a number of restrictions. The head is preceded by elements with a determiner function (possessor indexes, articles, indefinite pronouns and demonstratives), which can partly co-occur. And it is followed by elements with a modifying function (adjectives, but also nouns, prepositional phrases and directionals). Again, there are co-occurrence possibilities among the modifiers. Some elements have a variable position (i.e., the demonstratives and modifiers). In both cases, the less common pattern is placed in brackets in Table 27, and the implications are discussed later in this section.

Within the noun phrase, there is agreement between the head and some of its dependents. The head is marked for noun class and number: it usually has an inherent noun class, but its class may also reflect properties of the real world referent(s).

In either case, indefinite pronouns occurring as adnominal determiners, demonstratives, and adjectives agree with the head in noun class and number. Other dependents do not agree and have an invariable form instead. Example (6a) illustrates agreement: the head noun is *qaqera* 'person', which is marked for masculine singular (reflecting the properties of its real-world male referent *Sirini*) – and both the preceding indefinite determiner *ia* 'other' and the following adjective *tlu* 'good' agree with it. In almost all cases, the noun class suffix on the noun is identical in form to the suffix on the agreeing elements, e.g., the suffix *-ka* 'SG.M' occurs both with the head noun and the agreeing elements in (6a). The only difference is found in plural nouns of the masculine and feminine classes: these nouns are unmarked (e.g., *avet* 'house' in 6b has plural reference), but the agreeing elements take an overt suffix, e.g., the neuter suffix *-nget* 'N' on the adjective *tlu* 'good' in (6b) (see chapter 4 for details).

Tab. 27: Structure of the noun phrase

1. determiners, including:	possessor index	section 3.5.1
	article	section 3.3.4
	indefinite pronoun	section 3.3.3
	demonstrative pronoun	section 3.3.2
2. (modifiers)		
3. head		section 3.2
4. (demonstrative)		
5. modifiers, including:	adjective	section 3.4.1
	noun (e.g., numeral or quantifier)	section 3.4.2
	prepositional phrase, directional	section 3.4.3

(6) a. *masirini, de iaqamaqaqeraqa amatluqa*
ma=sirini, *de* [*ia-**ka**=ama=qaqera-**ka***
ART.ID=NAME CONJ other-SG.M=ART=person-SG.M
*ama=tlu-**ka***]NP
ART=good-SG.M
'Sirini, he is [a good person]NP' (D12ADKSPIRITS-011)

b. *duqurluun bemaavramatlunget*
de=kurli-un *pe=*[*ma=avet=ama=tlu-**nget***]NP
CONJ=leave-1DU PLACE=ART.ID=house=ART=good-N
'we stay in the good houses' (N12BAMCAT-032)

The Qaqet noun phrase is thus characterized both through agreement and a fairly rigid structure: a fixed order of constituents, and a division between pre-head determination and post-head modification (including quantification). This characterization holds for the majority of cases, as most attested noun phrases exhibit this structure. There is, however, some variation.

The largest variation is found with demonstratives: they most commonly occur in pre-head position, but there is a good number of examples of demonstratives immediately following their heads. Less frequent, but also attested, is the variable position of modifiers: they mostly occur post-head, but they are also attested in pre-head position. This kind of variation is discussed further in sections 3.3.2 (for demonstratives) and 3.4 (for modifiers).

In addition, there are cases that possibly show discontinuous noun phrases. For example, an interrogative adverbial occurs between the demonstrative and the noun in (7a), or a prepositional phrase occurs between the noun and the adjective in (7b). The agreement patterns are as expected from contiguous noun phrases: the demonstrative in (7a) is marked with the suffix *-nget* 'N' (agreeing with the plural head noun); and the adjective in (7b) is marked with the suffix *-ki* 'SG.F' (agreeing with the singular feminine head noun). Syntactically, it would be possible to analyze all attested cases as two noun phrases in apposition. Under this analysis, *lungera* 'those (ones)' in (7a) would function as a demonstrative pronoun (thus being head of a separate noun phrase), and *amaguleng* 'the malay apples' would have been added as an afterthought, resulting in a structure such as 'and those ones are from where, the malay apples?' Similarly, *amaiameski* in (7b) would then function not as an adnominal modifier ('new') but as a head noun ('the new ones'). However, there are no prosodic indications that would lend support to such an analysis: such examples are uttered under a single intonation contour. By contrast, there are many clear examples of afterthoughts, which are placed in their own prosodic unit and which exhibit one of the intonation contours identified for Qaqet (see chapter 2.3).

(7) a. *belungera naqua amaguleng?*
be=lu-nget-a *ne=kua* *ama=guleng?*
CONJ=DEM-N-DIST from/with=where ART=malay.apple
'and those malay apples are from where?' (N11AAGSIRINILOBSTER2-0007)

b. *nguavan pramaluanngi navramamaket amaiameski*
ngua=van *pet=ama=luan-ki*
1SG.SBJ=buy.NCONT on/under=ART=cloth-SG.F
ne=pet=ama=maket *ama=iames-ki*
from/with=on/under=ART=market ART=new-SG.F
'I bought a new piece of cloth at the market' (ARB&BCK-11/05/15)

Since the majority of examples follows the structure outlined in Table 27 above, I see no reason to question the existence of a noun phrase in Qaqet. Nevertheless, there are enough attested counter-examples to suggest that these instantiate robust patterns that occur under specific conditions. Given the small overall number of cases, it was not possible to detect any conditioning factors. Cross-linguistically, research into discontinuous noun phrases suggests that such discontinuities often find their explanation in discourse and information structure (McGregor 1997; Schultze-Berndt and Simard 2012; see Verstraete and Louagie 2016 for an overview). And research into the variable positions of determining elements such as demonstratives suggests that this variation is linked to different interpretations: as either determining the head noun or as modifying the head noun (see Louagie 2017 for an overview). It is possible that more detailed research will reveal similar motivations for the attested patterns in Qaqet.

3.2 Heads of noun phrases

This section introduces those elements that function as heads of noun phrases: nouns (section 3.2.1), numerals and quantifiers (section 3.2.2), independent pronouns (section 3.2.3) and interrogative pronouns (section 3.2.4). In addition, demonstrative (see section 3.3.2) and indefinite pronouns (see section 3.3.3) can head noun phrases. Qaqet also has relational nouns, which diachronically developed from common nouns. Synchronically, these relational nouns cannot head noun phrases, and they are discussed in chapter 6.1.

3.2.1 Nouns

Based on their morphosyntactic properties, nouns are subdivided into three subclasses: (i) common nouns, (ii) uncountable nouns and (iii) proper nouns.

Tab. 28: Subclasses of nouns

	Common nouns	**Uncountable nouns**	**Proper nouns**
Marking of noun class & number	full possibilities	invariant form (which may or may not include noun class & number)	
Basis for selecting pronoun, person index, agreement	grammatical	grammatical	semantic
Occurs with noun marker *a* and article *ama*	yes	yes	no
Occurs with all NP determiners & modifiers	yes	yes (if semantically possible)	restricted

The meaning ranges and formal properties of these subclasses are similar to those posited for Mali Baining (Stebbins 2011: 61–62, 163–165). Their characteristic properties are summarized in Table 28 and discussed under points (i) to (iii) below. Numerals and quantifiers behave like uncountable nouns, but are discussed separately in section 3.2.2. New nouns are mostly created through conversion, but there is also overt nominalization – both possibilities are discussed under point (iv).

(i) Common nouns

All common nouns are marked for noun class and number (see chapter 4 for details of this system), Mostly, these categories take the form of overt suffixes on the noun. The only exception are plural nouns of the masculine and feminine classes, which are usually unmarked.

Most nouns are conventionally assigned to a single noun class only (although speakers can shift to other classes in order to highlight specific properties of a referent). The main exception are nouns with human reference, which do not belong to a conventionalized class, but are assigned to a class depending on the sex of their real-world referent. For example, the noun *qaqera* 'person' appears with feminine singular marking in (8a), but masculine singular marking in (8b), referring to a woman and a man respectively. It would even be possible to shift to other classes to highlight non-sex-based properties of a human referent, e.g., to the diminutive class in example (9) below.

(8) a. *dap.. amaqaqraqi amavuqi, deratiski masinap*
*dap.. [ama=qaqera-**ki** ama=vu-**ki**]NP,*
but ART=person-SG.F ART=bad-SG.F
*de=ta=tis-**ki*** *ma=sinap*
CONJ=3PL.SBJ=call.CONT-3SG.F ART.ID=NAME
'and.. there is a bad person, they call her Sinap' (D12ADKSPIRITS-031FF)

b. *de saqika iaqamqaqraqa*
*de saqi-ka [ia-**ka**=ama=qaqera-**ka**]NP*
CONJ again-3SG.M other-SG.M=ART=person-SG.M
'and he is also a (kind of) person' (D12ADKSPIRITS-053)

In all cases, the class of the noun determines the form of the pronominal reference, the person indexes and the agreement. For example, the adjective *vu* 'bad' in (8a) and the indefinite determiner *ia* 'other' in (8b) agree with their head; and the object pronoun in (8a) is co-referential with the feminine singular noun. In (8a) and (8b), the noun class and the sex of the referent happen to coincide. But in (9) below, they happen to differ: a diminutive noun class, with presumably a male or female real-world referent – and it is the diminutive class that triggers the use of the neuter subject index; the masculine or feminine indexes could not be used. This is only possible in some restricted environments, where the sex of a real-world referent can override the grammatical class: this phenomenon is observed for some possessor indexes (see chapter 4.3) and for some nominal modifiers originating in the non-verbal equative construction (see chapter 8.2.3).

(9) *kerlip ngui.. nguimini ngamraqen.. nana?*
kerl=ip *gu..* *gu-uim-**ini*** ***nga**=mraqen..* *nana?*
DEONT=PURP 1SG.POSS 1SG.POSS-child-SG.DIM 3N.SBJ=C.say what
'my.. my child must have said.. what?' (I12AANACLADNSocio2-096ff)

Common nouns are obligatorily preceded by the noun marker *a* 'NM', unless this marker is replaced by another determining element. Generally, there are no restrictions on the co-occurrence of common nouns with any of the determiners and modifiers discussed in this chapter.

Furthermore, all common nouns are countable. Often, this also includes masses and collectives, which Qaqet tends to construe as countable. For example, *kaina-ki* 'water-SG.F' belongs to the feminine class and can be marked for all number categories (e.g., it is used in its dual form to refer to two branches of a river in 10a). And uncountable nouns (see point ii below) are shifted into the noun class system to become countable (e.g., the uncountable *meng* '(fire)wood' is shifted into the diminutive class in 10b), thereby becoming countable.

(10) a. *perlsperls namakainaim*
perlsperls *ne=ama=kaina-**im***
part.CONT:REDUP from/with=ART=water-DU.F
'the two waters got parted' (N11AAGBrothers-0050)
b. *dinyatat giamengirang sagelna*
de=nya=tat *gia=meng-**irang*** *se=gelna*
CONJ=2SG.SBJ=take.CONT 2SG.POSS=wood-PL.DIM to/with=nearby
'and you move your little sticks of firewood closer' (P12ADNFire-017)

Qaqet common nouns can potentially be further subdivided into a small class of inalienably possessed nouns and a large class of alienably possessed nouns. The interpretation is not entirely straightforward, though, and a discussion is postponed until section 3.5.

(ii) Uncountable nouns

In addition to common nouns, Qaqet has a small number of nouns that have an invariant form. Semantically, this class includes nouns that refer to masses (e.g., *guvang* 'dirt'), collectives (e.g., *meng* '(fire)wood'), places (e.g., *qerleng* 'fallow garden') and abstract concepts (e.g., *gamansena* 'custom'); as well as numerals and quantifiers (see section 3.2.2) and adjectives that are converted into abstract nouns (e.g., *srlu* 'old (adj.), old age (n.)') (see section 3.4.1).

Such nouns are usually unmarked. That is, their form is identical to the plural forms of masculine and feminine nouns, and there are indications that they are conceptualized as plural (e.g., they can co-occur with the plural quantifier *burlem* 'many') (see chapter 4.2.2 for details). They differ from common nouns in the plural, however, in that they cannot be counted (i.e., they cannot co-occur with numerals), and that they do not have singular and dual forms. In addition, this subclass also contains some uncountable nouns that are overtly marked as (masculine or feminine) singular, but again, they do not have number reference. Examples are *merlen-ka* 'heaviness-SG.M' or *get-ki* 'hunger-SG.F'. There are even a few nouns like the quantifier noun *burlem* 'many' or the abstract noun *ulirl* 'heat', where unmarked and marked forms co-exist. For example, *burlem* 'many' occurs in identical environments as an unmarked noun (as in 11a) and as a feminine singular noun (as in 11b).

(11) a. *de amaburlem nangen*
de [*ama=burlem*]NP *ne-ngen*
CONJ ART=many from/with-2PL
'you are many' (P12ARSBILUM1-028)
b. *amaburlemgi naap, beap ngatit*
[*ama=burlem-ki*]NP *ne-ap,* *be=ap* *nga=tit*
ART=many-SG.F from/with-PL.RCD CONJ=PL.RCD 3N.SBJ=go.CONT
'they are many, and they are moving around' (R12ATAFROG-137)

It is very likely that the singular suffix in the above cases is lexicalized. Evidence comes from examples where such nouns function as nominal modifiers. As illustrated in (12), such nouns receive a second suffix: the abstract nouns *tres-ka* 'deliciousness-SG.M' and *vus-ka* 'tastelessness-SG.M' function as modifiers and are additionally marked for neuter and feminine singular (reflecting the class of their head noun).

(12) *amaalin amatreskanget, dav amaalinggi amavuskagi*
ama=alin *ama=tres-**ka-nget**,*
ART=sugarcane ART=tastiness-SG.M-N
dap ama=alin-ki *ama=vus-**ka-ki***
but ART=sugarcane-SG.F ART=tastelessness-SG.M-SG.F
'there are delicious sugarcanes, and there is a tasteless piece of sugarcane' (ATA&AEM&ACS-22/06/2011)

Double noun class marking is otherwise not attested in the language. Diachronically, it probably derives from prepositional structures. Compare the alternation in the non-verbal clauses in (13a) and (13b). In (13a), the abstract noun *get-ki* 'hunger-SG.F' is followed by a prepositional phrase and a pronominal object *ka* '3SG.M'. In (13b), the same noun is followed first by an unidentified consonant *m* and then by a morpheme *ka* (which can either be interpreted as the pronoun *-ka* '3SG.M' or the noun class suffix -*ka* 'SG.M'). Given this alternation, it is likely that *m* is a remnant of a preposition, possibly of *ne* 'from/with' (see also chapter 5.2.1). In some nouns, such alternations continue to co-exist (as in *get-ki(m)* 'hunger-SG.F', but also in *merlen-ka(m)* 'heaviness-SG.M'). In other nouns, *m* has become a non-analyzable part of the noun. For example, *guskim* 'breathlessness' is likely to derive from *gus-ki-m* 'breathlessness-SG.F-??', but the alternating prepositional structure is no longer attested. Furthermore, there are cases, where an underlying nasal has to be posited: notice the realization of /vus-ka-**ki**/ as [vuska**gi**] in (12) above – /ki/ would normally only be realized [gi] after a nasal, not after a vowel. Finally, there are cases like *tres-ka* 'tastiness-SG.M' (in 12 above), where no remnants of a preposition or a consonant *m* can be found – except that such nouns now seem to allow for double suffixes.

(13) a. *imiika amgetki naqa slep*

i=miika	*ama=get-ki*	***ne-ka***	*slep*
SIM=more	ART=hunger-SG.F	from/with-3SG.M	intensely

'he continues to be very hungry (lit. hunger is with him)' (N12BAMCAT-199)

b. *kames amaqalunem iqurini amagetkimga*

ka=mes	*ama=qalun-em*
3SG.M.SBJ=eat.NCONT.PST	ART=singapore-SG.RCD
i=kut-ini	*ama=get-ki-**m-ka***
SIM=inferring-SG.DIM	ART=hunger-SG.F-??-(3)SG.M

'he ate a singapore taro because he was hungry (lit. hunger is with him ~ he is a hungry one)' (AJL-04/05/2012)

I thus consider it likely that the singular suffixes of uncountable nouns are lexicalized: despite their diachronic origins as noun class suffixes, they have lost (or are in the process of losing) this functionality, and were (or are in the process of being) reinterpreted as lexicalized parts of the root. I therefore assume that such nouns occur synchronically in an invariant form.

(iii) Proper nouns

Finally, Qaqet has proper nouns. Proper nouns are usually meaningful, i.e., they are formed from existing words and expressions. Table 29 exemplifies some common patterns in personal names. As can be seen, their morphological makeup is usually transparent, although phonological changes do occur. Some changes are attested elsewhere in the language (e.g., the lenition of intervocalic plosives or the assimilation of schwa to preceding vowels, thus accounting, e.g., for the form *Murum* from underlying *mu=tem*), while others are restricted to individual names (e.g., the change from *gua* to *ga* in *Gavaik*). In some cases, a name is no longer fully transparent (e.g., in the case of *Iareksaqi*).

Tab. 29: Personal names I: Morphological structure

Name	Source	Gloss
Simple word:		
Alin	*alin*	sugarcane (noun)
Sangarl	*sangarl*	catch fish (verb)
Sunun	*sunun*	evening (adverb)
Complex word:		
Gavaik	*gua=va-ki*	1SG.POSS=thingy-SG.F ('my thingy' (noun))
Murum	*mu=te(m)*	put.NCONT.PST=PURP ('take care of' (verb))
Sagelna	*se=gelna*	to/with=nearby ('moving near' (adverb))
Complex expression, proposition:		
Sangunan	*sa=ngu-nan*	already=1SG.POSS-mother ('already my mother')
Batnaqa	*bat=ne-ka*	appear=from/with-3SG.M ('he appeared')
Iareksaqi	*ia=ngerek=se-ki*	??=alone=to/with-3SG.F ('she alone')

Regardless of their internal morphological structure, proper nouns behave alike in that they have an invariant form, i.e., they usually do not change their noun class or number to reflect properties of the referent. This is also true in the case of names formed from simple nouns. For example, the simple noun *alin* 'sugarcane' is formally a plural form (forming a paradigm with *alinngi* 'sugarcane:SG.F' and *alinim* 'sugarcane:DU.F'). As a name, however, *Alin* has a singular male referent, and there are no conventionalized overtly marked singular or dual forms of this name. While some names such as *Alin* are formally plural, other names contain an overt noun class suffix. As illustrated in Table 30, such suffixes are attested from all classes, including both sex-based and shape-based classes, and including not only singular numbers.

Noun class marking comes in two patterns. In the first pattern, the suffix gives information about the referent of the name (i.e., its sex or shape). This is the only case where a name is not invariant, but changes to another class depending on the referent. Compared to common nouns, these possibilities are restricted, though, usually involving an alternation between masculine and feminine singular. For example, *Nguinnga* 'red:SG.M' and *Nguinngi* 'red:SG.F' are used with male and female referents respectively. Alternatively, the female name *Kusaiki* 'ginger.type:SG.F' has an unmarked male counterpart *Kusak* 'ginger.type'. A similar pattern is found with names originating in verbs and complex expressions, e.g., the male name *Batnaqa* 'appear:from/with:3SG.M' (in Table 29 above) has the female counterpart *Batnaqi* 'appear:from/with:3SG.F'.[9] Or the unmarked male name *Murum* 'put.NCONT.PST:PURP' (in Table 29 above) has an overtly marked female counterpart *Murumgi* 'put.NCONT.PST:PURP:3SG.F'. Similarly, shape-based noun classes can also be used to describe a referent, e.g. *Pilangem* 'tail:SG.RCD' is not in its conventional class (which would be masculine *pilangga* 'tail:SG.M'), but rather reflects shape-based properties of the name's referent.

Tab. 30: Personal names II: Noun class marking

Name	Source	Gloss	Sex of referent	Related name
Kusaiki	*kusak-ki*	ginger.type-SG.F	female	*Kusak* 'male name'
Lemigel	*lem-igel*	mushroom-SG.EXC	male	
Luanngi	*luan-ki*	cloth-SG.F	male	
Nguinnga	*nguin-ka*	red-SG.M	male	
Nguinngi	*nguin-ki*	red-SG.F	female	
Pilangem	*pilang-em*	tail-SG.RCD	male	
Sinirang	*sin-irang*	bird.type-PL.DIM	female	

In the second pattern, the suffix is that of the conventional class of the noun, which may or may not conform to properties of the owner of the name. For example, the name *Luanngi* 'cloth:SG.F' is overtly marked for feminine (i.e., the conventional class for a piece of cloth), but has a male referent. Or *Sinirang* 'bird.type:PL.DIM' reflects properties of the birds (which are small and tend to appear in groups), not the properties of the name's referent (which is neither diminutive nor plural). Similarly, *Lemigel* 'mushroom:SG.EXC' is in the default class for mushrooms, and does not give information on the shape of the name's owner.

The morphological patterns described above are not restricted to personal names, but are attested for all proper nouns: personal names of humans, cultural heroes and spirits, place names and names of ethnic groups and languages. For example, the name of the (male) cultural hero *Genainymet* derives from *genainy=met* 'mucus=in', and the name is attested in various forms, including in its bare form

9 If a name originated in a verb or complex expression that contained a personal pronoun, it is impossible to unambiguously analyze the last morpheme. For example, the last morpheme in *Batnaqa* is *ka*, which could either be analyzed as a pronoun ('3SG.M', i.e., reflecting the diachronic origin) or a noun class suffix ('SG.M', i.e., synchronically marking the name as masculine, reflecting the sex of the male referent). Similarly, the last morpheme of *Murumgi* is *ki*, which can be analyzed either as a pronoun ('3SG.F') or as a noun class suffix ('SG.F'). For purposes of glossing, I adopt the arbitrary convention of presenting them as pronouns.

(*Genainymet*), with feminine noun class marking (*Genainymetki*), with diminutive marking (*Genainymerini*) and with both feminine and diminutive marking (*Genainymetkini*). Similarly, many other proper nouns have a transparent origin, e.g., the place name *Alaqesem* (from *alaqes-em* 'cucumber-SG.RCD') or the language name *Qavelaqa* 'Tok Pisin' (from *qavel(a)-ka* 'bush-SG.M'). Again, as with human personal names, noun class marking either gives information about the name's referent (e.g., the male spirit name *Vlengnaska* has a female counterpart *Vlengnaski*) or about the noun's conventional class (e.g., the spirit name *Vilanngi* is marked with *ki* 'SG.F', but refers to a plurality of spirits).

Although names are usually meaningful, they do not necessarily reflect properties of the current owner of the name. The common practice is to name someone after relatives and friends (who in turn were named after other relatives and friends). And while the name may have reflected characteristic properties of its original referent, this is not necessarily the case for the present referent. Given this naming practice, it is not surprising that many names are closely tied to a specific family and location, and completely absent in other Qaqet-speaking areas. It is also not uncommon to encounter non-Qaqet names that were bestowed through an association with non-Qaqet friends. This naming practice is also reflected in the culturally important concept of *nem* 'namesake, likeness': sharing a name with someone else is never co-incidental, and a special relationship between the two people ensues.

Nowadays, most people have both a Christian (usually English) baptism and/or confirmation name and a Qaqet name. The Qaqet name continues to be more common and important, and even close relatives do not necessarily know or remember the Christian name of a person. The Christian name tends to be used in official contexts only, especially when interacting with non-Qaqet officials (e.g., in school, hospital or church contexts). There is also a new practice to interpret the Christian name as the first name and the Qaqet name as the surname. This development can especially be observed on official documents. For example, in school contexts, children are enrolled with their own Christian name plus their father's Qaqet name, i.e., the father's Qaqet name is starting to become a (sur)name for all his children.

Irrespective of their origin and internal morphological complexity, proper nouns share formal properties. In all cases, the choice of pronouns, person indexes and agreement markers has a semantic basis (not a grammatical basis, as in the case of common nouns). This pattern can be most clearly shown with personal names: a female name triggers feminine forms (e.g., the subject index *kia* '3SG.F.SBJ' in 14a), while a male name triggers masculine forms (e.g., the subject index *ke* '3SG.M.SBJ.NPST' in 14b). This is also true in the case of names that include a noun class suffix. Regardless of the grammatical class, the relevant forms reflect the sex of the referent. For example, the male name *Genainymetkini* in (14b) includes the diminutive suffix *-ini* 'SG.DIM' (and probably the feminine suffix *-ki* 'SG.F'), but controls a masculine person index.

(14) a. *uantuqun masingan ikiaruqun*
uan=tuqun *ma=singan* *ip=**kia**=ruqun*
2DU.SBJ=say.CONT ART.ID=NAME PURP=3SG.F.SBJ=sit.NCONT.FUT
'you tell Singan to sit down' (LONGYDS20150517_1-457)

b. *magenainymetkini qerarles iqeksik, namalevungga*
*ma=genainymet**kini*** ***ke**=rarles*
ART.ID=NAME:SG.F:SG.DIM 3SG.M.SBJ.NPST=start.NCONT
*i=**ke**=ksik,* *ne=ama=levung-ka*
SIM=3SG.M.SBJ.NPST=climb.CONT from/with=ART=tree.type-SG.M
'Genainymetkini started to climb, into the *levung* tree' (N11AJNGENA-INGMETBROTHERS-0055)

Place names belong to the same class as their superordinate category, irrespective of their overt marking. For example, rivers are feminine and thus trigger feminine forms. In (15a), the river *Ngerlnanngi* is marked as feminine (from *ngerlnan-ki* 'woman-SG.F'), occurring as a non-verbal predicate in the equative construction whose subject is *ki* '3SG.F'. In (15b), the river name *Toriu* is not marked as feminine, but the indefinite pronoun *iaik* 'other:SG.F' nevertheless appears in its feminine form (and not in its neuter form, which would otherwise be obligatory for unmarked nouns).

(15) a. *dap kuasiqi mangerlnanngi naqia*
dap *kuasik=i* *ma=ngerlnanngi* *ne-**ki**=a*
but NEG=SIM ART.ID=NAME:SG.F from/with-3SG.F=DIST
'but it is not the case that it is the *Ngerlnanngi* river'
(LONGYJL20150805_2-597)

b. *akias nyitlu.. denyitlu giaqiama.. matoriu*
ka=kias *nyi=tlu..*
3SG.M.SBJ=actually 2SG.SBJ.NPST=see.CONT
de=nyi=tlu *gi-ia-**ki**=ama..* *ma=toriu*
CONJ=2SG.SBJ.NPST=see.CONT 2SG.POSS-other-SG.F=ART ART.ID=NAME
'actually you see.. you see one of yours.. the *Toriu* river'
(LONGYJL20150805_2-659FF)

Furthermore, there are restrictions on the co-occurrence of proper nouns with noun phrase determiners and modifiers. Most importantly, they cannot co-occur with the noun marker *a* 'NM' or the article *ama*. This noun marker is obligatorily present with all other nouns (including in their citation form), and is only absent when replaced by another determining element (see section 3.3.4). Proper nouns, by contrast, never occur with it. In vocative contexts, they occur without any article (as in 16a) or with the article *ma* 'ART.ID' (as in 16b). And in descriptive contexts, they occur with the article *ma* 'ART.ID' (as in 16c).

(16) a. *talai, dap nyi*
talai, *dap* *nyi*
NAME but 2SG
'Talai, now you' (C12VARPLAY-111)

b. *de matalai, nyi nauirl*
de ***ma**=talai,* *nyi* *nauirl*
CONJ ART.ID=NAME 2SG first
'Talai, you first' (C12VARPLAY-501)

c. *m.. m.. matalai aiaiama*
m.. *m..* ***ma**=talai* *a-ia-iam=a*
?? ?? ART.ID=NAME 3SG.M.POSS-other-DU.M=DIST
'there's two others of.. of.. Talai' (C12VARPLAY-135)

Otherwise, determination and modification are only possible when the name is taken to represent a larger category. For example, *Sirini* is the name of a cultural hero: he is usually represented as a specific individual in stories, but he is thought of as a whole category of brothers, all named *Sirini*. As such, *Sirini* can be counted (as in 17a), or be marked for indefiniteness (as in 17b). Similarly, some names can have both female and male reference, and it is thus possible to modify this name (as in 17c). Note that such contexts still trigger the use of the article *ma* 'ART.ID' that marks a referent as inherently identifiable, i.e., the referent is still conceptualized as a proper noun.

(17) a. *murl kurli masirinana malpenara*
murl *kurli* [*ma=sirini=ama* *malep-ka=ne-ta*]NP
distantly leave ART.ID=NAME=ART ten-SG.M=from/with-3PL.H
'in the past, there were ten Sirini' (N12AMVGENAINGMETBROTHERS-011)

b. *iak masirini*
[*ia-ka* *ma=sirini*]NP
other-SG.M ART.ID=NAME
'there was a Sirini' (N11AAGSIRINILOBSTER1-0001)

c. *saqika masevaqesep, de ma.. sevaqesev amaquatka, demasevaqesev amananngi*
saqi-ka *ma=sevaqesep,* *de* [*ma..* *sevaqesep*
again-3SG.M ART.ID=NAME CONJ ART.ID NAME
ama=quat-ka]NP, *de=*[*ma=sevaqesep* *ama=nan-ki*]NP
ART=man-SG.M CONJ=ART.ID=NAME ART=woman-SG.F
'and also the Sevaqesep (spirit), there is the.. male Sevaqesep, and there is the female Sevaqesep' (D12ADKSPIRITS-097FF)

Like common nouns, proper nouns are subject to regular phonological changes. As such, intervocalic plosives are lenited, e.g., the name *Katnas* is realized as *Qatnas* in

(18a). Recall, however, that there are exceptions to this rule (see chapter 2.1.1): in particular, initial plosives in loanwords are not subject to lenition. In a similar way, the foreign name *Talai* is not lenited to **Ralai* in (16b) and (16c) above. Non-initial plosives, by contrast, are always lenited, even in foreign names (as in 18b).

(18) a. *ma**q**atnas kamrenas sameseng*
*ma=**k**atnas ka=mrenas se=meseng*
ART.ID=NAME 3SG.M.SBJ=jump.NCONT.PST:SELF to/with=at.base
'Katnas jumped down' (AJS-11/06/2015)
b. *mabridge**r**a, da?*
*ma=bridge**t**=a, da?*
ART.ID=NAME=DIST right
'there's Bridget there, right?' (C12VARPLAY-278)

The above description holds for almost all proper nouns, excepting some spirit names whose morphosyntactic properties are similar to those of common nouns. Like proper nouns, spirit names usually have a transparent origin. For example, the speaker in (19a) explains the origins of the name *Nesprugumga*. But like common nouns, this spirit name obligatorily takes a determiner, e.g., the noun marker *a* (as in 19a). Another example is the spirit name *Vilanngi*, which also needs to be preceded by an article, e.g., by *ama* (as in 19c). This name is overtly marked as singular feminine (by means of *ki* 'SG.F'), but refers to a plurality of spirits. In (19b), it behaves like a common noun in that its grammatical class (singular feminine) controls agreement in the demonstrative *luqia* 'DEM:SG.F:DIST' – not its semantic class (plural). Alternatively, speakers can select the form based on the semantics: e.g., the speaker in (19c) chooses the unmarked noun *sivit* 'angry (one)' (having plural reference) – not the singular feminine form *siviraqi* 'angry:SG.F'. Speakers thus have some freedom to construe a particular expression not as a name, but as a common noun.

(19) a. ***a**nesprugumga, iqasnes praugumgi ma*
***a**=nesprugumga,*
NM=NAME:SG.M(shout.NCONT:on/under:3SG.M.POSS:fist:SG.M)
i=ka=snes pet=aa=ugum-ki ma
SIM=3SG.M.SBJ=shout.CONT on/under=3SG.M.POSS=fist-SG.F thus
'the *Nesprugumga* spirit, who shouts through his fist like this' (D12ADKSPIRITS-048FF)
b. *luqia amavilanngi de..*
*lu-**ki**-a ama=vilanngi de..*
DEM-SG.F-DIST ART=NAME:SG.F CONJ
'that *Vilan..*' (D12ADKSPIRITS-103)

c. *amavilanngi, de ama.. amasivit*
ama=vilanngi, de ama.. ama=sivit
ART=NAME:SG.F CONJ ART ART=anger
'the *Vilan*, the.. the angry ones' (I12AANACLADNSocio3-480)

(iv) Conversion and nominalization

New nouns are mostly created through conversion from adjectives and verbs, but they can also be overtly derived from verbs. Conversion or derivation from other word classes is not attested.

As discussed in section 3.1.1, conversion is a widespread phenomenon in Qaqet. In particular, all adjectives denoting a property can be converted into nouns denoting a referent of that property. These converted nouns do not belong to a conventionalized noun class (different from common nouns), and shift to different classes depending on their referent. For example, the adjective *gil* 'small' in (20a) is converted into a singular masculine noun (referring to a small boy), while the adjective *ilas* 'raw' in (20b) is converted into a neuter noun (referring to uncooked taros). This last example illustrates a further characteristic property of conversion: nouns converted from other word classes retain morphological properties from their original classes. For example, basic nouns of the masculine and feminine classes have unmarked plurals. Adjectives agreeing with such nouns, by contrast, are overtly marked by a suffix, e.g., by the neuter suffix *-nget* 'N' (see chapter 4). When adjectives are converted to nouns, they continue to exhibit these suffixes. This retention of morphology is a further indication that these nouns are not basic, but converted from another class.

(20) a. *amagilka mara, ip taqurlanyi*
*ama=**gil**-ka mara, ip taquarl=nyi*
ART=small-SG.M here PURP thus=2SG
'there is a little one here, just like you' (R12ATAFrog-010)

b. *dqatekmet nlungera, deqatsama.. amailasanget*
de=ka=tekmet ne=lu-nget-a,
CONJ=3SG.M.SBJ=do.CONT:IN from/with=DEM-N-DIST
*de=ka=tes=ama.. ama=**ilasa**-nget*
CONJ=3SG.M.SBJ=eat.CONT=ART ART=raw-N
'and he continues to work on those ones (i.e., taros), he continues to eat the.. the raw ones' (N12BAMCat-210ff)

All adjectives convert into nouns to denote a referent of that property. In addition, many (but not all) adjectives can form abstract nouns, e.g., the adjective *vu* 'bad' converts into the abstract noun 'badness' (as in 21a). Like other abstract nouns, such converted nouns are uncountable and have an invariant form. Individual adjectives also allow for conversion to nouns with unpredictable meanings, e.g., the adjective *slurl* 'big' forms the basis for the noun *slurlka* 'God' (in 21b).

(21) a. *de tika idraavu sagel raaqalatka, magenainymetkini*
de *tika* *ide=araa=***vu** *se=gel*
CONJ EMPH IPFV=3PL.POSS=bad to/with=near
araa=qalat-ka, *ma=genainymetkini*
3PL.POSS=younger.sibling-SG.M ART.ID=NAME:SG.F:SG.DIM
'and there used to be their badness towards their younger brother, Genainymetkini (i.e., they behaved badly towards him)'
(N12AMVGENAINGMETBROTHERS-015)

b. *uriaq amalanginyga iqetuqun iama.. ama.. aslurlkaalengi*
ure-ia-ka *ama=langiny-ka* *i=ke=tuqun*
1PL.POSS-other-SG.M ART=book-SG.M SIM=3SG.M.SBJ.NPST=say.CONT
i=ama.. *ama..* *a=***slurl***-ka=aa=lengi*
SIM=ART ART NM=big-SG.M=3SG.M.POSS=word
'there is one book of ours that talks about the.. the.. the word of God'
(I12AANACLADNSOCIO3-229FF)

As for verbs, no systematic conversion patterns were found, but there are many individual examples. Such nouns can be formed on the basis of simple verbs (e.g., from the transitive verb *tal* 'carry.CONT' in 22a) and complex verbs (as in 22b to 22d). For example, the noun in (22b) is formed from the intransitive verb *mestemna* (which consists of the morphemes *mes=te-na* 'eat.NCONT.PST=PURP-RECP'); and the noun in (22c) and (22d) is formed on the basis of the transitive verb *tekmet* 'do/act.CONT' (which diachronically derives from *tek=met* 'put.CONT=in'). The semantic relationships between verb and noun can be of different kinds: an instrument (as the 'handle' in 22a) or another participant involved in the event (as the 'greens' in 22b); very commonly, the noun refers to a product of the event (as the 'objects, pictures' in 22c) or the event itself (as the 'activities' in 22d). The only non-attested semantic relationship is that of actor. Otherwise, given the many possibilities, the relationship between verb meaning and noun meaning is not predictable, and some nouns allow for more than one reading (e.g., *tekmerirang* in 22c and 22d).

Verbs converting into nouns retain some of their verbal morphology – morphology that is otherwise not attested in nouns. First, verbs often have a complex structure (see chapter 5.1), including especially prepositions such as *met* 'in' (in *tekmet* 'do' in 22c and 22d) and *te* (in *mestemna* 'eat' in 22b), but also other material such as the reciprocal pronoun *-na* 'each.other' (in *mestemna* 'eat'). This complexity is retained in the converted nouns.

(22) a. *iva, dinyatu amatalkiara, luqiara*

ip=a, *de=nya=tu* *ama=**tal**-ki=iara,*
PURP=DIST CONJ=2SG.SBJ=put.CONT ART=carry.CONT-SG.F=PROX
lu-ki-iara
DEM-SG.F-PROX
'then you put the handle here, this one' (P12ARSBILUM3L-094)

b. *nyisikmet namamestemna*

nyi=sikmet *ne=ama=**mestemna***
2SG.SBJ.NPST=cut:IN from/with=ART=greens(eat.NCONT.PST:PURP:RECP)
'cut the greens' (AAS-20/06/2015)

c. *kuarl amatekmerirang, taquarl ama.. ama.. amadanggi, dakuarl amaqemgi, dakuarl ama.. amaqailka*

kua *ama=**tekmet**-irang,* *taquarl* *ama..* *ama..* *ama=dang-ki,*
INTRG ART=do.CONT:IN-PL.DIM thus ART ART ART=dog-SG.F
dap=kua *ama=qem-ki,* *dap=kua* *ama..* *ama=qail-ka*
but=INTRG ART=snake-SG.F but=INTRG ART ART=wallaby-SG.M
'maybe objects (pictures), like it's a.. a.. a dog, or maybe it's a snake, or maybe it's a.. a wallaby' (I12AANACLADNSOCIO3-246FF)

d. *ivit matekmerirang, duquas ngentuqun nengen dengen siirang*

i-pit *ma=**tekmet**-irang,* *de=kuasik* *ngen=tuqun*
AWAY-up ART.ID=do.CONT:IN-PL.DIM CONJ=NEG 2PL.SBJ=say.CONT
ne-ngen *de-ngen* *se-irang*
from/with-2PL LOC.PART-2PL to/with-PL.DIM
'when there are these activities, don't you say that you yourselves are the ones (who can do) them' (N11AJNGENAINGMETBROTHERS-0157FF)

And second, many verbs have alternating aspectual stems (see chapter 5.4.2), and nouns are always formed from one of these stems only. In all cases, it is the stem that also occurs in the multi-verb construction *raqa* 'do.properly.NCONT' ~ *taqa* 'do.properly.CONT' (see chapter 5.5). There are three possible patterns. If the verb has a special form that is only attested in this multi-verb construction, this is also the form used in all nominalizations. Examples (23a) and (23b) illustrate this pattern with the form *smis* 'C.call', occurring in both contexts. In all other contexts, one of the aspectual stems has to be used (*mis* 'call.NCONT.PST', *ris* 'call.NCONT.FUT', *tis* 'call.CONT'). Given this distribution, it could be argued that forms like *smis* 'C.call' are not converted, but overtly nominalized (by means of an initial consonant). However, most verbs do not have a special form in the multi-verb construction, and instead form their nouns from aspectual stems that are otherwise only attested in clearly verbal contexts. If the verb has a two-way stem alternation, the noun is formed from the continuous stem (as *talki* and *tekmerirang* in 22a, 22c and 22d above). If it has a three-way alternation, it is formed from the non-continuous past stem (as *mestemna* in 22b above). Verbs without stem alternation use their invariant form in nominal contexts, too (as *lil* 'write' in 23b below).

(23) a. *kuasiqini ngaraqasmisini*
kuasik=ini *nga=raqa=**smis**-ini*
NEG=SG.DIM 3N.SBJ=properly.NCONT=C.call-SG.DIM
'when he doesn't say it properly' (I12AANACLADNSocio2-037)

b. *saqi liiniip kadrlem sa.. sasmis, dap.. salil nalengiqa*
saqi *lu-ini-a=ip* *ka=drlem* *se..*
again DEM-SG.DIM-DIST=PURP 3SG.M.SBJ=know to/with
*se=a=**smis*** *dap..* *se=a=**lil***
to/with=NM=C.call but to/with=NM=write.CONT
ne=a=lengi-ka
from/with=NM=word-SG.M
'and as for that little (thought), so that he knows to.. to talk and.. to write in the language' (I12ABLAJLATASocio4-093FF)

The motivations for these patterns are unclear. In the case of nouns that are formed on the basis of their continuous stem, it could be argued that this stem conveys the more time-stable meaning of continuity and duration, and that it is this time-stability that motivates its use as a noun. However, this argument does not hold for the second group of verbs – even though they all have a continuous stem, too (e.g., *testemna* 'eat.CONT:PURP:RECP' is the continuous form of *mestemna*, but it cannot occur as a noun). There are also no differences in the relationship between verb meaning and noun meaning: all possible patterns are attested in all groups.

The morphology discussed above is clearly verbal in origin: these categories are only marked on verbs, not on basic nouns. The retention of verbal morphology is thus a further indication that Qaqet distinguishes between the word classes, and that forms are not acategorial.

In addition to conversion, Qaqet overtly derives nouns from verbs by means of the prefix *ra-* 'NMLZ'.[10] Again, the same verbal morphology that is found with converted nouns is retained with overtly derived nouns: the verb can be simple (as *mnyim* 'look.CONT' in 24a) or complex (as *snanbet* 'ask', from *snan-pet* 'ask-on/under' in 24b), and the nominal form is created on the basis of the same aspectual stems (e.g., on the basis of the continuous stem in 24a).

10 This prefix is possibly underlying *ta-*, but it invariably occurs in an intervocalic environment and therefore always surfaces as *ra-*. Its origins are unknown. Some speakers link it to the possessor indexes *ara* '3SG.F.POSS' and *araa* '3PL.POSS', but synchronically possessor index and nominalizer can co-occur (e.g., in example 24a in the text).

(24) a. *ngua deivet, guaramnyim*
*ngua de=a=ivet, gua=**ra**-mnyim*
1SG CONJ=NM=ground 1SG.POSS=NMLZ-look.CONT
'as for me, it is my view' (I12AANACLADNSocio3-409)

b. *kiaska liiranga amarasnanberirang*
*kias-ka lu-irang-a ama=**ra**-snanbet-irang*
actually-3SG.M DEM-PL.DIM-DIST ART=NMLZ-ask:ON/UNDER-PL.DIM
'there are those questions actually' (I12ABLAJLATASocio4-144)

Different from conversion, the semantic relationship between the verb and the derived noun is more restricted. If no further material is added, the nominalization is always an action nominalization. If a preposition is added, the nominalizer creates location or instrument nouns. Example (25) illustrates such a noun: *ramugunmetki* 'chair'. It is formed from the intransitive verb *mugun* 'sit', which needs a preposition to introduce a location. This kind of verbal use is illustrated in the same example with the help of the (non-related) verb *tuqun* 'sit.CONT' followed by the preposition *met* 'in'. It is this preposition that is then integrated into the nominalized form. In all cases, the preposition used in the nominalized form is the same as the one used with the verb. For example, *srlup* 'drink.CONT' introduces containers by means of *met* 'in', and the nominalized form *rasrlupmetka* 'cup' also contains this preposition (from *ra-srlup-met-ka* 'NMLZ-drink.CONT-in-SG.M'). Or *taneng* 'hold.CONT' occurs with the preposition *ne* 'from/with' to introduce an instrument, and the nominalized form *rataneng naum* 'peg' also contains this preposition (from *ra-taneng ne-em* 'NMLZ-hold.CONT from/with-SG.RCD').

(25) *nguatuqun merama ramugunmetki*
*ngua=tuqun met=ama **ra**-mugun-**met**-ki*
1SG.SBJ=sit.CONT in=ART NMLZ-sit-in-SG.F
'I'm sitting in a chair' (AJS-11/06/2015)

3.2.2 Numerals and quantifiers

The numerals three and above (but not one and two; see below) as well as the quantifiers (*burlem* 'many', *denes* 'few' and *qukun* 'few') constitute a subclass of nouns: they can head noun phrases (as in 26a), they can occur as nominal modifiers in the nominal modifier construction (as in 26b) (see section 3.4.2) and they can occur as nominal predicates in the non-verbal equative construction (as in 26c) (see chapter 8.2.3).

(26) a. *saqatira mrama.. ama.. aburlem nara*
sa=ka=tit=a *met=[ama..* *ama..*
already=3SG.M.SBJ=go.CONT=DIST in=ART ART
*a=**burlem*** *ne-ta]*NP
NM=many from/with-3PL.H
'it spreads to [the.. the.. many people]NP (lit. the manyness of them)'
(I12AANACLADNSOCIO3-338)

b. *kua amama.. angariqiving amadepguas naiving, dakua iamaqunasivim*
kua *[ama=ma..* *a=ngarik-iving* *ama=**depguas***
INTRG ART=?? NM=hand-PL.FLAT ART=three
*ne-iving]*NP, *dap=kua* *i=[ama=qunas-ivim]*NP
from/with-PL.FLAT but=INTRG SIM=ART=one-DU.FLAT
'maybe there's.. [three leaves]NP, or maybe there's [two]NP' (D12AB-DACPGARDEN-024)

c. *das nani uraburlem nairang*
de=as *nani* *[ura=**burlem**]*PRED *[ne-irang]*SBJ
CONJ=still can 1PL.POSS=many from/with-PL.DIM
'[the little ones (i.e., questions)]SBJ [are still many for us]PRED'
(I12AANACLADNSOCIO3-219)

Their morphosyntactic properties are those of uncountable nouns (see section 3.2.1): all have an invariant form, whereby most are unmarked for noun class (as *burlem* 'many' and *depguas* 'three' in the examples above), while some have an inherent noun class. For example, *burlem* 'many' has an alternative feminine singular form *burlem-ki* 'many-SG.F', and *malep-ka* 'ten-SG.M' belongs to the masculine singular noun class. As nouns, they obligatorily occur with an article (as in 26a above) or another pre-head element (e.g., a possessor index in 26c above).

Most numerals and quantifiers are nouns, but some belong to other parts of speech. First, the numeral *qunas* 'one' shares the morphosyntactic properties of adjectives (see section 3.4.1), but – like other adjectives – it can convert into a noun (as in 26b above). Second, the quantifier *mii* ~ *miis* 'most' shares the morphosyntactic properties of adverbs (see chapter 6.2), and mostly occurs outside the noun phrase (as in 27a). There are, however, occasional examples, where *mii* ~ *miis* 'most' is marked with an article (as in 27b), suggesting either a nominal origin of this quantifier or a subsequent morphosyntactic integration of the original adverb as a nominal modifier into the noun phrase. Note that *mii* ~ *miis* 'most' usually receives an interpretation of 'all, whole' or 'both' (in the case of dual referents, as in 27b), but examples such as (27c) show that it can also occur in non-exhaustive contexts. Third, the quantifier *qukun* 'few' has developed into the particle *qukun* 'a bit later' (see chapter 7.5). And fourth, Qaqet has indefinite pronouns and articles that can receive quantifying interpretations (see sections 3.3.3 and 3.3.4).

(27) a. *de ngatit, praum mii*
de *nga=tit,* *pet-em* ***mii***
CONJ 3N.SBJ=go.CONT on/under-SG.RCD most
'it continues, onto all of it (garden)' (D12ADNGARDEN-019FF)

b. *deqerl dip ngenerarraneng amalengiam amamii, atikaip..*
de=kerl *dip* *ngere-ne-ta=te=raneng*
CONJ=DEONT FUT 3N.ASSOC-from/with-3PL.H=3PL.SBJ.NPST=hold.NCONT
[ama=lengi-iam *ama=**mii**]NP,* *ka=tika=ip..*
ART=word-DU.M ART=most 3SG.M.SBJ=EMPH=PURP
'they, too, will hold on to [both languages]NP, and..' (I12AANACLAD-NSOCIO3-121)

c. *nyines amamuli mii, dap dangamadenes*
nyi=nes *ama=muli* ***mii,***
2SG.SBJ.NPST=put.in.NCONT ART=orange most
dap *de=a=ngama=denes*
but CONJ=NM=some.NSPEC=few
'put most of the oranges inside, except some few' (AJL&ADN-28/04/2015)

Tables 31 and 32 give an overview of all attested numerals and quantifiers. Table 31 includes the adjective *qunas* 'one'. And Table 32 includes all lexemes that can receive a quantifier interpretation, regardless of their part of speech. In Mali Baining, numerals are also either nouns or adjectives, but quantifiers are either adverbs or marginal members of the adjective class (but not nouns) (Stebbins 2011: 65–66, 156–160, 176–179).

Tab. 31: Numerals

	Form	**Structure**
1	*qunaska*	1 (*qunas-ka* 'one-SG.M')
2	*qunasiam*	2 (*qunas-iam* 'one-DU.M')
3	*depguas*	3
4	*rlatpes*	4
5	*ngariqit*	5 (*ngarik-it* 'hand-SG.LONG')
6	*ngariqit ngenaqa*	5 + SG.M (*ngariqit ngene*[1]*-ka*)
7	*ngariqit ngenaiam*	5 + DU.M (*ngariqit ngene*[1]*-iam*)
8	*ngariqit ngenadepguas*	5 + 3 (*ngariqit ngene*[1]*=adepguas*)
9	*ngariqit ngenarlatpes*	5 + 4 (*ngariqit ngene*[1]*=arlatpes*)
10	*malepka*	10 (*malep-ka* 'ten-SG.M')
11	*malepka ngenaqa*	10 + SG.M

	Form	Structure
12	*malepka ngenaiam*	10 + DU.M
13	*malepka ngenadepguas*	10 + 3
14	*malepka ngenarlatpes*	10 + 4
15	*malepka ngenangariqit*	10 + 5
16	*malepka ngenangariqit ngenaqa*	10 + 5 + SG.M
17	*malepka ngenangariqit ngenaiam*	10 + 5 + DU.M
18	*malepka ngenangariqit ngenadepguas*	10 + 5 + 3
19	*malepka ngenangariqit ngenarlatpes*	10 + 5 + 4
20	*maleviam*	20 (*malep-iam* 'ten-DU.M')
21	*maleviam ngenaqa*	20 + SG.M
22	...	...
30	*malev amadepguas* ~ *depguas namamalep*	10 x 3 (10 *ama*[2]=3) ~ 3 x 10 (3 *nama*[3]=10)
31	*malev amadepguas ngenaqa* ~ *depguas namamalep ngenaqa*	10 x 3 + SG.M ~ 3 x 10 + SG.M
32	...	...
40	*malev amarlatpes* ~ *rlatpes namamalep*	10 x 4 ~ 4 x 10
50	*malev amangariqit* ~ *ngariqit namamalep*	10 x 5 ~ 5 x 10
60	*malev amangariqit ngenaqa* ~ *ngariqit ngenaqa namamalep*	10 x [5 + SG.M] ~ [5 + SG.M] x 10
70	*malev amangariqit ngenaiam* ~ *ngariqit ngenaiam namamalep*	10 x [5 + DU.M] ~ [5 + DU.M] x 10
80	*malev amangariqit ngenadepguas* ~ *ngariqit ngenadepguas namamalep*	10 x [5 + 3] ~ [5 + 3] x 10
90	*malev amangariqit ngenarlatpes* ~ *ngariqit ngenarlatpes namamalep*	10 x [5 + 4] ~ [5 + 4] x 10
100	*malepka namamalep* ~ *ganemgi*	10 x 10 ~ 100 (*ganem-ki* 'parcel-SG.F')
101	*ganemgi ngenaqa*	100 + SG.M
102	...	...
110	*ganemgi ngenamalepka*	100 + 10
111	...	...
1000	*ngerlnanngi*	1000 (*ngerlnan-ki* 'woman-SG.F')

[1]*ngene* 'plus, together with', from *ngere-ne* '3N.ASSOC-from/with'
[2]*ama* 'ART'
[3]*nama* 'from', from *ne=ama* 'from/with=ART'

Tab. 32: Quantifiers

Form	Gloss	Part of speech
burlem	many	quantifier
denes	few	quantifier
qukun	few	quantifier (→ particle)
mii ~ miis	most (~ all, whole, both)	adverb (→ quantifier)
ia	other	indefinite pronoun
qa	some	indefinite pronoun
ngama	some.NSPEC	indefinite article
qama	some	indefinite article

When used in counting, the numerals are obligatorily preceded by the noun marker *a* 'NM' (as in 28a). In all other contexts, other types of articles or pre-head determiners can replace the noun marker (as in 28b). The form of the numeral *qunas* 'one' changes to reflect the noun class of the referent: the masculine class is the default class (used, e.g., in counting), but it changes to another class where appropriate (e.g., to feminine dual in the feminine dual context of 28c). Note that this change only affects the numeral *qunas* 'one' – all other numerals remain invariant, even if their morphological makeup contains a noun class suffix.

(28) a. *aqunaska, aqunasiam, adepguas (...)*
__a__=qunas-ka *__a__=qunas-iam* *__a__=depguas*
NM=one-SG.M NM=one-DU.M NM=three
'one, two, three (...)' (AAS-08/08/2015)

b. *tika butdrlem amaqunasiam, dakua amaqunaska*
tika be=ut=drlem __ama__=qunas-iam,
EMPH CONJ=1PL.SBJ=know ART=one-DU.M
dap=kua __ama__=qunas-ka
but=INTRG ART=one-SG.M
'we know two (patterns), or maybe one (pattern)' (P12ARSBILUM2-009)

c. *liimiara amaqunasim*
lu-__im__-iara ama=qunas-__im__
DEM-DU.F-PROX ART=one-DU.F
'these two (females)' (R12ATAFROG-261)

The following generalizations emerge from Table 31:

First, there are the following base forms – some of which have a transparent nominal origin: *qunas* 'one', *depguas* 'three', *rlatpes* 'four', *ngariqit* 'five' (from *ngarik-it* 'hand-SG.LONG'), *malepka* 'ten' (from *malep-ka* 'ten-SG.M'), *ganemgi* 'hundred' (from *ganem-ki* 'parcel-SG.F'), and *ngerlnanngi* 'thousand' (from *ngerlnan-ki* 'woman-SG.F'). *Ngariqit* 'five' forms the basis for 6-9, *malepka* 'ten' for the tens, *ganemgi* 'hundred' for the hundreds, and *ngerlnanngi* for the thousands.

Second, Qaqet exploits the resources of its noun class system to form all numerals containing '1' and '2': it suffixes the noun class morphemes *-ka* 'SG.M' and *-iam* 'DU.M' to the bases *qunas* 'one' (to form the numerals '1' and '2') and *malep* 'ten' (to form the numerals '10' and '20');[11] and it uses the associative structure *ngere-ne* '3N.ASSOC-from/with' with the pronouns *ka* '3SG.M' and *iam* '3DU.M' to add the digits '1' and '2'.

Third, addition is always done by means of the associative construction (see section 3.6).

Fourth, the multiples of ten (from 30 upwards) are formed in one of two ways. Either with the structure *malep ama*=NUM 'ten ART=NUM' (e.g., *malev amadepguas* '30'), or with the structure 'NUM *ne=ama=malep*' 'NUM from/with=ART=ten' (e.g., *depguas namamalep* '30'). In elicitation contexts, speakers spontaneously suggested the first possibility. In the resulting discussion, we discovered that this structure results in ambiguities for numerals above 50. For example, *amalev amangeriqit ngenaqa* in (29) could be parsed either as '10 x 5 + SG.M' (i.e., 51) or as '10 x [5 + SG.M]' (i.e., 60). When discussing this potential confusion, speakers suggested the second structure as an alternative. In natural discourse, speakers always shift away from Qaqet to Tok Pisin for higher numerals. It is thus not clear whether either of the two possibilities reflects natural language use, or whether they are *ad hoc* responses to fill perceived lexical gaps in the language.

(29) *amalev amangariqit ngenaqa*

a=malep	*ama=ngariqit*	*ngere-ne-ka*
NM=ten	ART=five	3N.ASSOC-from/with-3SG.M

'51 ~ 60' (AJL-30/04/2012)

The Qaqet numerals are not shared with Mali (Stebbins 2011: 65–66, 156–160). In terms of forms, only *depguas* 'three' and *ngariqit* 'five' are possibly cognate across the two languages. It is likely that one or both of the languages have independently innovated their numerals, especially given that some of the base numerals in both languages transparently derive from common nouns. In terms of structure, Mali combines a base-five system (forming numerals between 5 and 19) with a base-twenty system (forming numerals of 20 and above). Similarities are found in the distribution of numerals across word classes, though: numerals in both languages constitute a

11 I gloss *malep* as 'ten' (and not as 'ten/twenty'), because this form occurs in higher numerals where it can only receive the interpretation of 'ten'. By contrast, *qunas* 'one' never appears in other contexts, and it could thus equally well be analyzed as 'one/two'. I gloss it as 'one', following the pattern of *malep* 'ten'.

subclass of nouns, except for the lower numerals, which are adjectives. In Qaqet, 'one' and 'two' are adjectives; Mali also includes 'three' among its adjectives (while cognate 'three' in Qaqet is a noun).

Speakers (both adults and children) generally use Qaqet numerals below 10 – except in the context of counting. For example, in (30) below, a six-year old girl explains the rules of a game to her mother, all in Qaqet. But she shifts to Tok Pisin numerals when she starts to explain that the players need to count their stones to determine the winner.

(30) 1. *utaarl nanget pit*
ut=taarl *ne-nget* *pit*
1PL.SBJ=stand.CONT from/with-3N up
'we stand them up' (C12YMMZJIPLAY1-337)

2. *deqerl uanetlak*
de=kerl *uane=talak*
CONJ=DEONT 2DU.SBJ.NPST=play.CONT
'and you play' (C12YMMZJIPLAY1-338)

3. *dakerl uandis*
dap=kerl *uan=tis*
but=DEONT 2DU.SBJ=call.CONT
'and you call out (the numbers)' (C12YMMZJIPLAY1-339)

4. *ikua amapaip, ikua amatu, ikua amatri, ikua ama.. poa*
ip=kua *ama=**paip**,* *ip=kua* *ama=**tu**,*
PURP=INTRG ART=five PURP=INTRG ART=two
ip=kua *ama=**tri**,* *ip=kua* *ama..* ***poa***
PURP=INTRG ART=three PURP=INTRG ART four
'whether (you have) five, or two, or three or.. four' (C12YMMZJIPLAY1-340)

Ordinal numbers are formed on the basis of cardinal numbers (for 'third' and above, as in 31a) or pronouns (for 'first' and 'second', as in 31b). In both cases, the ordinal number constitutes a clause, which contains the conjunction *ip* (see chapter 8.3.4), the article *ma* 'ART.ID' and the numeral or pronoun.

(31) a. *iaqamaqaqraqaip madepguas, de ma..*
*ia-ka=ama=qaqera-ka=**ip*** ***ma=depguas**,* *de* *ma..*
other-SG.M=ART=person-SG.M=PURP ART.ID=three CONJ ART.ID
'a third person is..' (D12ADKSPIRITS-026)

b. *tesnes ip miiram*
te=snes ***ip*** ***ma=iram***
3PL.SBJ.NPST=shout.CONT PURP ART.ID=DU.DIM
'they shout a second time' (N11AAGSIRINILOBSTER1-0055)

Finally, there exist the adverbial forms *maus* ~ *miis* 'once' (illustrated in 32) and *miim* 'twice'.

(32) *nyiral metka maus*
nyi=ral *met-ka* ***maus***
2SG.SBJ.NPST-carry.NCONT in-3SG.M once
'you carry (something) in it (only) once' (P12ARSBILUM1-036)

The adverbial forms look as if they could have been formed from *ma* 'ART.ID' plus the pronouns *es* 'SG.FLAT' (resulting in *maus* ~ *miis*) and *im* 'DU.F' (resulting in *miim*), but they seem to be monomorphemic in present-day Qaqet. Adverbials of three and above have the form 'NM=NUM' (e.g., *adepguas* 'thrice').

3.2.3 Independent pronouns

A noun phrase can consist of a single independent or free pronoun, excluding any further determiners or modifiers. Table 33 summarizes the pronoun categories and forms, including for expository purposes not only the free pronouns, but most of the attested pronominal forms. The Table shows a basic two-way distinction between a noun class system (expressed in free pronouns and pronominal arguments) and a reduced gender system (expressed in possessor and subject indexes; as well as in associative pronouns not included in this Table). It also shows the mapping between the two systems. In both systems, Qaqet pronouns distinguish between singular, dual and plural number. They also distinguish between masculine and feminine in the 3SG and 3DU categories (although this distinction is collapsed in the 3DU gender), and between human and non-human (or neuter) in the 3PL category. In addition, the noun class system distinguishes a further six shape-based classes (again in singular, dual and plural number), which all trigger the neuter form in the gender system. Finally, the Table shows that the forms are largely similar across the noun class and gender systems, with the exception of some of the possessor indexes.

This section describes the distribution of free pronouns and pronominal arguments only. The possessor indexes are discussed in section 3.5.1, and the subject indexes, in chapter 5.4.1. The non-past subject index gave rise to the associative pronouns, which are illustrated in section 3.6. For details on the forms and semantics of the noun class and gender systems, see chapter 4.

The free pronouns appear in the following contexts.

They are the forms that are used in isolation, e.g., when addressing someone (as in 33a) or as one-word utterances in question/answer sequences (as in 33b).

Most commonly, the free pronouns occur in non-argument positions, usually in left-dislocated position, preceding a conjunction (as in 34a and 34b), and sometimes together with one of the particles (e.g., with *miika* 'more' in 34c) (see chapter 8.3.1 for details on these structures). If there are any preceding conjunctions or particles, free pronouns often form clitic groups with them (as in 34b and 34c). Note that this kind of environment is not restricted to pronouns: noun phrases with common nouns as heads are also frequently found in this context (as illustrated by the first unit in 34c).

(33) a. *sandra, nyi*
sandra, ***nyi***
NAME 2SG
'Sandra, you' (C12VARPLAY-076)

b. YRA: *nema?*
nema
who
AHL: *nyi!*
nyi
2SG
YRA: *ngua?*
ngua
1SG
YRA: 'who?' AHL: 'you!' YRA: 'I?' (LONGYDS20150902_2-529FF)

(34) a. *ngua de sakmetngua navraqa*
ngua *de sakmet-ngua ne=pet-ka*
1SG CONJ surprise:IN-1SG from/with=on/under-3SG.M
'as for me, I was surprised at him' (I12AANACLADNSOCIO3-430)

b. *daka, deqamira, besamuk*
*dap=**ka**, de=ka=mit=a,*
but=3SG.M CONJ=3SG.M.SBJ=go.NCONT.PST=DIST
be=se=a-muk
CONJ=to/with=DIR-across
'but as for him, he went across' (N11AAGSIRINIROPE-0087)

c. *diaramaquata, de miikra brasem amarlaunnga*
*de=ia-ta=ama=quat-ta, de miika=**ta***
CONJ=other-PL.H=ART=man-PL.H CONJ more=3PL.H
be=ta=sem ama=rlaun-ka
CONJ=3PL.SBJ=weave.NCONT ART=netbag-SG.M
'as for other men, as for them, too, they (can) weave netbags' (P12ARS-BILUM2-045)

Tab. 33: Pronouns

	Free pronoun	Pronominal argument	Possessor index	Subject index	
				Neutral	Non-past
1SG	*ngua*	*-ngua*	*gua*	*ngua*	*ngu*
2SG	*nyi*	*-nyi*	*gia*	*nya*	*nyi*
3SG.M	*ka*	*-ka*	*aa*	*ka*	*ke*
3SG.F	*ki*	*-ki*	*ara*	*kia*	*ki*
1DU	*un*	*-un*	*una*	*un*	*une*
2DU	*uin*	*-uin*	*uana*	*uan*	*uane*
3DU.M	*iam*	*-iam*	*iana*	*ian*	*iane*
3DU.F	*im*	*-im*			
1PL	*ut*	*-ut*	*ura*	*ut*	*ure*
2PL	*ngen*	*-ngen*	*ngena*	*ngen*	*ngene*
3PL.H	*ta*	*-ta*	*araa*	*ta*	*te*
3N	*nget*	*-nget*	*ngera*	*nga*	*ngere ~ nger*
SG.DIM	*ini*	*-ini*			
DU.DIM	*iram*	*-iram*			
PL.DIM	*irang*	*-irang*			
SG.RCD	*em*	*-em*			
DU.RCD	*am*	*-am*			
PL.RCD	*ap*	*-ap*			
SG.FLAT	*es*	*-es*			
DU.FLAT	*ivim*	*-ivim*			
PL.FLAT	*iving*	*-iving*			
SG.LONG	*it*	*-it*			
DU.LONG	*isim*	*-isim*			
PL.LONG	*ising*	*-ising*			
SG.EXT	*it*	*-it*			
DU.EXT	*itnem*	*-itnem*			
PL.EXT	*itnek*	*-itnek*			
SG.EXC	*igel*	*-igel*			
DU.EXC	*igrlim*	*-igrlim*			
PL.EXC	*igrling*	*-igrling*			

In non-verbal clauses (see chapter 8.2), free pronouns can occur as subjects (as in 35a). In verbal clauses, the free pronoun can co-occur with the obligatory subject index on the verb. There are two patterns. First, the free pronoun occurs in the same prosodic unit as the verb and its subject index. In such cases, the pronouns behave like noun phrases headed by nouns, and they can be analyzed as the subject of the clause. This pattern is only attested with pronouns from one of the shape-based classes (as in 35b). Second, the pronoun is set apart prosodically and syntactically in its own unit. In such cases, the pronoun arguably does not function as the subject. This pattern is possible for all pronouns, and it is the only attested pattern for pronouns that do not belong to any of the shape-based classes (as in 35c). Presumably, the difference in distribution follows from the fact that the pronouns from shape-based classes – just like common nouns – convey additional semantic information about the referent. The other pronouns, by contrast, do not add information that is not already coded in the subject index. As a result, speakers tend to use them for information structural reasons, and hence mark them in special ways. It is possible that the 3DU.M and 3DU.F pronouns distribute like the shape-based pronouns (as they add information on the sex of the referent), but there are no relevant examples in the corpus.

(35) a. *kanavet ma.. ramgi*
__ka__=ne=pet *ma..* *ramgi*
3SG.M=from/with=on/under ART.ID NAME
'he came across.. Ramgi' (N11AAGSiriniLobster2-0044)

b. *arluimirang, deirang ngerebrlany*
a=rluim-irang, *de=__irang__* *ngere=brlany*
NM=child-PL.DIM CONJ=PL.DIM 3N.SBJ.NPST=sleep
'the children, they sleep' (I12AANACLADNSocio3-326)

c. *atika ut, de utli uralengiqa imurl nevuralavurlvis*
ka=tika ***ut**,* *de* *ut=tlu=i*
3SG.M.SBJ=EMPH 1PL CONJ 1PL.SBJ=see.CONT=SIM
ura=lengi-ka *i=murl*
1PL.POSS=word-SG.M SIM=distantly
ne=pe=ura=lavu=ngere-uvis
from/with=PLACE=1PL.POSS=adult=3N.POSS-top
'as for us, we see that it is our language that came down in the past from our parents' (I12AANACLADNSocio3-156)

The free pronouns presumably gave rise to the pronominal arguments: they share the same forms and categories, and they only differ in their wordhood. The free pronouns are independent words (that may or may not cliticize to surrounding elements), while the pronominal arguments are suffixes. They are analyzed as suffixes (and not as enclitics) for two reasons. First, they invariably form a phonological word with the preceding preposition or verb. Qaqet clitics, by contrast, are more variable: the same form can usually be realized as either a proclitic or an enclitic, depending on the environment. And second, the pronominal arguments trigger phonological changes in preceding elements that are otherwise only attested in suffixes, not in enclitics. Two typical changes are illustrated in the examples below. In (36a), the basic preposition is *men* 'at', but it appears in the form *mena* when followed by a pronominal object. Similarly in (36b), the basic verb is *raneng* 'hold.NCONT', but it appears as *ranenga* when followed by a pronominal object. I assume that the suffixed forms preserve the original roots, in particular, I assume that they preserve final segments (very frequently, a final vowel *a*, as in both examples below) that were lost in the non-suffixed forms. The clearest evidence for such a diachronic scenario comes from nouns, and this development is discussed in detail in chapter 4.1.1.

(36) a. *bqurut **mena**qa*
be=ke=urut ***men**-ka*
CONJ=3SG.M.SBJ.NPST=grab.NCONT at-3SG.M
'and he grabbed at him' (N11AAGBROTHERS-0056)

b. *padip, ki**ranenga**qa*
padip, *ki=**raneng**-ka*
hopefully.FUT 3SG.F.SBJ.NPST=hold.NCONT-3SG.M
'she wants to hold him' (N11AAGSIRINIROPE-0066)

The pronominal arguments occur in three morphosyntactic contexts: as object arguments of prepositions (as in 36a above and 37a below) (see chapter 5.3.1), as object arguments of transitive verbs (as in 36b above and 37b below) (see chapter 5.2.1), and as the single argument in the agentless construction (as in 37c below) (see chapter 5.2.2).

(37) a. *bruamet naqa*
be=te=uamet *ne-**ka***
CONJ=3PL.SBJ.NPST=beat:IN from/with-3SG.M
'and they beat him (lit. beat with)' (N11AAGSIRINILOBSTER2-0078)

b. *atrik, bravlengga*
a=trik, *be=ta=vleng-**ka***
NM=trick CONJ=3PL.SBJ=kill.NCONT-3SG.M
'(it was) a trick, and they killed him' (N11AAGSIRINILOBSTER1-0081)

c. *ide qurliqa meseng*
ide *kurli-**ka*** *meseng*
IPFV leave-3SG.M at.base
'he usually stays at the bottom (of the tree)' (D12ADKSPIRITS-072)

The pronouns and pronominal arguments code information about noun class and number, and they are thus powerful tracking devices, which are commonly used to refer back to already established entities in discourse. For example, the pronoun *irang* 'PL.DIM' in (38a) occurs in subject function and refers back to the earlier introduced noun *uim-irang* 'child-PL.DIM'. Similarly in (38b), where the pronominal argument *ini* 'SG.DIM' functions as the argument of an agentless construction, referring back to *rlaun-ini* 'netbag-SG.DIM'.

(38) a. *usu uruimirang ivirang ngadrlem*
ut=su *ure-uim-**irang*** *ip=**irang*** *nga=drlem*
1PL.SBJ=teach 1PL.POSS-child-PL.DIM PURP=PL.DIM 3N.SBJ=know
'we teach our little children so that the little ones know'
(I12AANACLADNSocio3-159)

b. *kesnesnget mraarlaunini beip.. buvini*
ke=snes-nget *met=aa=rlaun-**ini***
3SG.M.SBJ.NPST=put.in.CONT-3N in=3SG.M.POSS=netbag-SG.DIM
be=ip.. *bup-**ini***
CONJ=PURP fill-SG.DIM
'he put them into his little netbag until.. the little one got filled'
(N11AAGSiriniLobster2-0020)

In fact, it is not uncommon for long stretches of discourse to rely on pronouns only for referent identification (as in (39), where the pronoun *ap* 'PL.RCD' tracks the referent *hlangap* 'bee:PL.RCD').

(39) *amah.. amahlangap nadaarlan, de nyitlaviara, amaburlemgi naap, beap ngatit*
ama.. *ama=slanga-**ap*** *ne=de=aa=rlan,*
ART ART=bee-PL.RCD from/with=LOC.PART=3SG.M.POSS=inside
de *nyi=tlu-**ap**=iara,* *ama=burlem-ki*
CONJ 2SG.SBJ.NPST=see.CONT-PL.RCD=PROX ART=many-SG.F
*ne-**ap**,* *be=**ap*** *nga=tit*
from/with-PL.RCD CONJ=PL.RCD 3N.SBJ=go.CONT
'the.. the bees(PL.RCD) from its inside, you see them(PL.RCD) here, they(PL.RCD) are many, and they(PL.RCD) are moving around' (R12ATAFrog-136ff)

3.2.4 Interrogative pronouns

Qaqet has two interrogative pronouns that function as heads of noun phrases: *nem(a)* 'who' (as in 40a) and *gi* 'what' (as in 40b). Both are overtly marked for noun class, but speakers can also resort to an unmarked form if they do not intend to presuppose anything about the identity (and hence the noun class) of the referent (as in 40c). In addition, there is a third interrogative pronoun, *kesna* 'how much, how many' that occurs in restricted nominal contexts only (see chapter 8.1.2).

(40) a. *ariaik nemgi?*
are-ia-ki ***nema**-ki?*
3SG.F.POSS-other-SG.F who-SG.F
'who is her friend?' (C12VARPLAY-270)

b. *deqatu aaqavevi.. angamagiqia?*
de=ka=tu *aa=qavep=i..*
CONJ=3SG.M.SBJ=put.CONT 3SG.M.POSS=heart=SIM
*a=ngama=**gi**-ki=a?*
NM=some.NSPEC=what-SG.F=DIST
'and he is thinking.. it's what?' (R12ATAFROG-186)

c. *nema?*
***nema**?*
who
'who?' (C12YMMZJIPlay1-110)

The morphological properties of both pronouns suggest that they have originated in nouns: both inflect for noun class, and *gi* 'what' is obligatorily marked by an article. The pronoun *nem(a)* 'who' is presumably further grammaticalized than *gi* 'what', as it cannot occur with an article (while its cognate form in Mali does occur with articles; see Stebbins 2011: 71). There are also first signs of phonetic erosion: the non-inflected form is *nema* 'who', but the base form occurring with the noun class suffixes is *nem* 'who'. Different from nouns, interrogative pronouns as heads of noun phrases do not allow for any other noun phrase elements to occur. The only exceptions are articles (in the case of *gi* 'what') and prepositional phrases (in the case of *nem(a)* 'who', see (44a) below for an example).

Both pronouns usually occur in non-verbal expressions (as in 40a and 40b above) or one-word questions (as in 40c above), but they can also occur in the other syntactic functions available to nouns, e.g., as subjects (in 41a below), objects (in 41b) or prepositional objects (as in 41c).

(41) a. *nema ngalengeh nanget?*
nema *nga=lenges* *ne-nget?*
who 3N.SBJ=destroy from/with-3N
'who damaged it?' (LONGYDS20150516_1-098)

b. *amaqasup.. aqasupka qats amagi?*
ama=qasup.. *a=qasup-ka* *ka=tes* *ama=**gi**?*
ART=rat NM=rat-SG.M 3SG.M.SBJ=eat.CONT ART=what
'the rat.. the rat is eating what?' (N12BAMCAT-218)

c. *askerl nyisnanbet te**nem**gi?*
as=kerl *nyi=snanbet* *te=**nema**-ki?*
still=DEONT 2SG.SBJ.NPST=ask:ON/UNDER PURP=who-SG.F
'you're asking about who?' (C12YMMZJIPLAY1-150)

They can furthermore function as possessors in possessive noun phrases. For example, the interrogative *nem(a)* 'who' in (42a) functions as the possessor to the indefinite pronoun *ia-ki* 'other-SG.F'. Similarly, the interrogative *gi* 'what' in (42b) functions as the possessor to the noun *nem* 'likeness'. Alternatively, speakers can express possession by means of an interrogative pronoun in a prepositional phrase (as in 42c).

(42) a. *nema ngera.. ngeriaqiara?*
nema *ngera..* *ngere-ia-ki=iara?*
who 3N.POSS 3N.POSS-other-SG.F=PROX
'whose.. thingy is this here?' (LONGYJL20150805_1-249)

b. *amapiksa, iamagiqiara.. ara.. ara.. aranem?*
ama=piksa, *i=ama=**gi**-ki=ara..*
ART=picture SIM=ART=what-SG.F=3SG.F.POSS
ara.. *ara..* *ara=nem*
3SG.F.POSS 3SG.F.POSS 3SG.F.POSS=likeness
'pictures, it's pictures of.. of.. of.. of what?' (I12AANACLADNSOCIO3-245)

c. *ailak nagel nema?*
a=ilaqa *ne=gel* ***nema?***
NM=branch from/with=near who
'whose sticks?' (C12VARPLAY-538)

The pronoun *nem(a)* 'who' asks about people (including names of people), while the pronoun *gi* 'what' asks about animals and things (as in 43a). If a speaker overtly mentions the entity in question, however, the distinction between human and non-human referents is sometimes neutralized: speakers usually use *nem(a)* 'who' – even if the referent is non-human (as the sweet potato in 43b). The use of *gi* 'what' in this context is possible (as in 43c), but infrequent.

(43) a. *dap maginget mara?*
dap *ma=**gi**-nget* *mara?*
but ART.ID=what-N here
'and what are these (things) here?' (LONGYDS20150506_1-326)

b. *maquukuqa nemnget?*
ma=quukuk=a ***nema**-nget?*
ART.ID=sweet.potato=DIST who-N
'the sweet potatoes there are what (i.e., of what kind)?'
(LONGYDS20150516_1-112)

c. *nyisnanbet naqi ip mamestemna ma**gi**nget?*
nyi=snanbet *ne-ki* *ip*
2SG.SBJ.NPST=ask:ON/UNDER from/with-3SG.F PURP
ma=mestemna *ma=**gi**-nget?*
ART.ID=greens ART.ID=what-N
'ask her about: the vegetables are what (i.e., of what kind)?'
(LONGYDS20150506_1-375)

The pronouns cannot function as interrogative determiners to a head noun. To ask about an entity, speakers either resort to a non-verbal clause (as in 43b and 43c above), or they add this entity in a prepositional phrase (as in 44a below), or they resort to a possessive construction with the interrogative as the possessed entity (as in 44b below). Again, the pronoun *nem(a)* 'who' can also be used with non-human referents in these contexts.

(44) a. *ip nemga na.. nameniam, adlek?*
ip *[nema-ka* *[ne..* *ne=men-iam]*PP*]*NP*,* *a=dlek?*
PURP who-SG.M from/with from/with=at-3DU.M NM=strength
'[who [of.. of the two]PP]NP is strong?' (L12ACMNORTHWIND-002)

b. *amalengiini ngeranemini?*
ama=lengi-ini *ngera=**nema**-ini?*
ART=word-SG.DIM 3N.POSS=who-SG.DIM
'what kind of word is this?' (LONGYDS20150506_1-728)

Interestingly, there may be indications that *nem(a)* 'who' (but not *gi* 'what') is currently being integrated as a determiner into the noun phrase. In a number of examples (like the one in (45a)), the syntactic structure is unclear: *nem(a)* 'who' semantically relates to the noun *gamansena* 'custom' and it could conceivably be interpreted syntactically as part of the noun phrase, because it agrees in noun class with the presumed head noun and because it is contiguous with it. Such examples are similar to the ones in (45b) and (45c) which differ only in that *nem(a)* 'who' can less easily be interpreted as part of the noun phrase. In (45b), the directional *ivuk* 'up' delimits the right edge of the noun phrase, suggesting a non-verbal predicate structure along the lines of 'one of our enemies up there is who' (but see section 3.1.2 on non-contiguous noun phrases). And in (45c), there is a clear prosodic break between the noun phrase and the interrogative, suggesting that the interrogative functions as an afterthought along the lines of 'talk to each other in languages, whichever ones'. I therefore tentatively assume that *nem(a)* 'who' in (45a) to (45c) does not (yet) function as a determiner.

(45) a. *daqatiqui ini ngeretekmet namagamansena nemnget?*
de=ka=tika=kui *ini*
CONJ=3SG.M.SBJ=EMPH=quoting SG.DIM
ngere=tekmet *ne=ama=gamansena* ***nema**-nget?*
3N.SBJ.NPST=do.CONT:IN from/with=ART=custom who-N
'it is said they would be following which kind of tradition?' (I12AANACLADNSocio2-142)

b. *nyaang nyiliv unangamahirlikaivuk nemga?*
nya=ang *nyi=lu=ip*
2SG.SBJ=walk.NCONT 2SG.SBJ.NPST=see.NCONT=PURP
una=ngama=sirlik-ka=i-vuk ***nema**-ka?*
1DU.POSS=some.NSPEC=meat-SG.M=AWAY-up who-SG.M
'go and see whichever enemy of ours is up there?' (N11AAGSiriniRope-0120)

c. *denyatu giaqavev idite.. tesil bana namalengi, nemnget*
de=nya=tu *gia=qavep* *i=dip=te..*
CONJ=2SG.SBJ=put.CONT 2SG.POSS=heart SIM=FUT=3PL.SBJ.NPST
te=sil *barek-na* *ne=[ama=lengi]*NP*,* ***nema**-nget*
3PL.SBJ.NPST=say.NCONT BEN-RECP from/with=ART=word who-N
'so you think that they will.. they talk to each other in which languages?' (I12AANACLADNSocio3-119)

It is likely that *gi* 'what' originated in the indefinite noun 'thingy' or 'what-cha-ma-call-it'. The present-day language regularly uses *ma* 'thingy' to replace common nouns in contexts where speakers cannot, or do not intend to, provide the specific name of an entity (as in 46a). Similarly, there is a small number of comparable examples with *gi* 'what' (as in 46b): the absence of a question intonation (see chapter 2.3.2) suggests an indefinite interpretation ('the thingies are crying') rather than an interrogative interpretation ('what is crying?'). The pronoun *nem(a)* 'who' is not attested in such contexts. Its origin is unclear, although it may be related to the common noun *nem* 'likeness', which refers to namesakes (e.g., *guanemgi* 'my female namesake, likeness' from *gua=nem-ki* '1SG.POSS=likeness-SG.F') as well as pictures and images (see 42b above for an example).

(46) a. *amaqi qirles luqa*
*a=**ma**-ki* *ki=rles* *lu-ka-a*
NM=thingy-SG.F 3SG.F.SBJ.NPST=throw DEM-SG.M-DIST
'the thingy throws down that one' (R12ADNFrog-256)

b. *ama.. amgi ngereknak, de amahlang*
ama.. *ama=**gi*** *ngere=knak,* *de* *ama=slanga*
ART ART=what 3N.SBJ.NPST=cry.CONT CONJ ART=bee
'the.. the thingies are crying, the bees' (R12BCSFROG-048)

3.3 Determination

This section discusses determination within the noun phrase. It first presents an overview of the topic (in section 3.3.1), and then introduces those elements that can occur both as pronominal heads and as adnominal determiners: demonstratives (section 3.3.2) and indefinite pronouns (section 3.3.3). The last section describes those elements that only occur as adnominal determiners (section 3.3.4).

Possessor indexes also serve a determining function and replace articles in some contexts. Their relationship to articles is discussed in the present section, but the topic of possession itself is discussed in more detail in section 3.5.

3.3.1 Overview

Qaqet noun phrases in all syntactic functions obligatorily contain a determining element in pre-head position. Even in their citation form, nouns have to be preceded by a determiner, usually by the noun marker *a* 'NM'. The only exception are proper names (of people and places) in their citation form or in vocative contexts (as in 47a).[12] In other contexts, even proper names are obligatorily preceded by the article *ma* 'ART.ID' (as in 47b).

(47) a. *sa, murumgi nyimnyim*
sa, *murumgi* *nyi=mnyim*
already NAME 2SG.SBJ.NPST=look.CONT
'now, Murumgi, look' (C12YMMZJIPLAY1-437FF)

b. *dap mamurumgi?*
dap ***ma****=murumgi?*
but ART.ID=NAME
'and what about Murumgi?' (C12YMMZJIPLAY1-536)

The Qaqet determiners are summarized in Table 34, together with comparative information on Mali. To facilitate comparison, all forms are given in IPA. It can be seen

12 In child language and child-directed speech, it is not uncommon for articles to be omitted from common nouns (see also chapter 2.1.1).

that forms are often similar (and presumably cognate) across the two languages – but their distribution and semantics do not always match. That is, the forms presumably have the same origins, but then took different language-internal developments. In the case of the demonstratives, it can be shown that they contain cognate morphology (noun class affixes and deictic roots), but that they grammaticalized from different sources; the Qaqet demonstrative base *lu* is not attested in Mali (see chapter 4.1.2). The Table also contains an interrogative pronoun, since its cognate form functions as an adnominal determiner in Mali (but not in Qaqet).

Tab. 34: Determination in Qaqet and Mali

Qaqet		**Mali**		
Form	**Gloss**	**Form**	**Gloss**	**Stebbins 2011**
Demonstratives (section 3.3.2)				
lu	DEM	–	–	p. 77–87, 175
Indefinite pronouns (section 3.3.3)				
ia	other	*iaik*	grandfather (noun)	p. 189
ɣa	some	*ɣa* ~ *ɣə*	contrastive DEM	pp. 82–84
–	–	*gua*	indefinite DEM ('some')	pp. 84–85
Articles (section 3.3.4)				
a	NM	*a*	specific	pp. 171–174
ama	ART	*?kama*	identifiable	p. 168
ma	ART.ID	*ma*	inherently identifiable	pp. 168–169
–	–	*kə*	identifiable through discourse	pp. 169–170
ɣama	some	*?kama*	identifiable	p. 168
ŋama	some.NSPEC	*aŋa, aŋama*	non-specific	pp. 170–171
Interrogative pronouns (section 3.2.4)				
gi	what	*gi*	indefinite ('which, some')	pp. 71–72, 171, 239–240

From an areal perspective, the presence of articles is especially noteworthy. They are considered a characteristic feature of Oceanic languages, not of Papuan languages (Dunn, Reesink, and Terrill 2002: 34–36; Dunn et al. 2008: 743) – but they are attested in a number of East Papuan languages (Stebbins 2009a), where they are generally considered to be Oceanic borrowings.

All determiners, including possessor indexes (see section 3.5.1), precede the head noun. The only partial exception are demonstratives, which can optionally follow the head noun. There are five possible types of combinations among the determiners, summarized in Table 35; optional morphemes are placed in brackets and morphemes in paradigmatic relationships are placed in the same column and are preceded by '~'.

Tab. 35: Distribution of determiners within the noun phrase

Pre-head			Head	Post-head
POSS ~ *a* 'NM'	*qama* 'some' ~ *ngama* 'some.NSPEC'	–	N	–
POSS ~ *a* 'NM'	*qa*-NC 'some-NC'	*ama* 'ART' (~ *ma* 'ART.ID')	N	–
(POSS)	*ia*-NC 'other-NC'	*ama* 'ART' (~ *ma* 'ART.ID')	N	–
–	DEM	*ama* 'ART' (~ *ma* 'ART.ID')	N	–
POSS ~ *a* 'NM' ~ *ama* 'ART' ~ *ma* 'ART.ID'		–	N	(DEM)

The patterns above apply to all noun phrases that have a noun as their head, but not necessarily to those that have a pronoun as their head. For pronouns, the following patterns hold (for details, see the respective sections of this grammar): Independent pronouns (section 3.2.3) and demonstrative pronouns (section 3.3.2) cannot co-occur with any of the determiners. And the co-occurrence possibilities for indefinite (section 3.3.3) and interrogative pronouns (section 3.2.4) are restricted: *ia* 'other' and *nem(a)* 'who' are optionally preceded by a possessor index; *qa* 'some' is obligatorily preceded by either a possessor index or the noun marker; and *gi* 'what' is obligatorily preceded by either *a* 'NM', *ama* 'ART' or *ma* 'ART.ID'. It is likely that these patterns reflect their different diachronic origins. Furthermore, *a* 'N', *ama* 'ART' and *ma* 'ART.ID' are also attested with predicative adjectives (see chapter 8.2.4).

Essentially, the synchronic determiners are mutually exclusive, but it is necessary to add three qualifications.

First, the article *ama* occurs in two different contexts: as determiner (in initial position of the noun phrase) and as connector (immediately preceding the head noun). As determiner, it is in complementary distribution to all other pre-head determiners: the noun marker *a*, the article *ma* 'ART.ID', the possessor indexes, the demonstratives (in pre-head position), and the complex structures incorporating indefinite articles and pronouns. As connector, it connects a pre-head indefinite pronoun (*qa* 'some', *ia* 'other') or demonstrative to the head noun; and it is presumably a diachronic part of the synchronically monomorphemic indefinite articles *qama* 'some' and *ngama* 'some.NSPEC' (from **qa-ama* 'some-ART' and **nga-ama* 'some.NSPEC-ART'). It also connects adjectival and nominal modifiers to the head noun (see section 3.4). As connector, it is not in complementary distribution to the other determiners (excepting the article *ma* 'ART.ID' in some restricted contexts). Diachronically, it is likely that the adnominal demonstratives and indefinites originated in modifier structures. As discussed in the relevant sections, demonstratives and indefinites originated as pronouns and functioned only later as adnominal determiners; in some cases, these pronouns can even be related back to common nouns. Given their nominal origins, they would have occurred in the nominal modifier construction (see section 3.4.2), thus accounting for the presence of the article *ama* as connector in both modifying and determining contexts.

Second, the indefinite articles *qama* 'some' and *ngama* 'some.NSPEC', as well as the indefinite pronoun *qa* 'some', are obligatorily preceded by either the noun marker *a* 'NM' or by a possessor index. The other indefinite pronoun, *ia* 'other', can be preceded by a possessor index (but not by the noun marker). It is likely that these co-occurrence possibilities reflect the nominal origins of these forms, with *ia* 'other' being grammaticalized further.

And third, it is likely that the noun marker *a* 'NM' is a diachronic part of the full form of the possessor indexes (e.g. *gua* from **gu-a* '1SG.POSS-NM'), and possibly also of the article *ama* (from **a-ma* 'NM-ART.ID'). Synchronically, however, there are reasons to treat them as monomorphemic.

Phonologically, the pre-head elements usually form clitic groups with the head noun. This even includes complex multimorphemic structures such as the one exemplified in (48a). It also includes demonstratives (as in 48b), although the demonstratives are the only determiners that are just as likely to occur outside such a clitic group (as in 48c).

(48) a. *nani nguarenas samet giaqammerlka*
nani *ngua=renas* *se=met*
can 1SG.SBJ=jump.NCONT.FUT:SELF to/with=in
gia=qama=*merlik-ka*
2SG.POSS=some=betelnut-SG.M
'I can jump into one of your betelnut trees' (N11AESSIRINI-0029)

b. *de.. liamamalengiami.. de magrip ngusuini remiam*
de.. ***lu-iam-a***=*ama=lengi-iam=i..*
CONJ DEM-DU.M-DIST=ART=word-DU.M=SIM
de *maget=ip* *ngu=su-ini* *te-iam*
CONJ then=PURP 1SG.SBJ.NPST=teach-SG.DIM PURP-3DU.M
'and.. those two languages that.. I then teach the little one both' (I12AANACLADNSOCIO3-053)

c. *tika savet liama amalengiam*
tika *se=pet* ***lu-iam-a*** *ama=lengi-iam*
EMPH to/with=on/under DEM-DU.M-DIST ART=word-DU.M
'it was about those two questions' (I12AANACLADNSOCIO3-093)

The determiners are considered clitics, not affixes, because they can occur as free morphemes. With the exception of the demonstratives (as in 48c above), this is rare, but possible (e.g., in 49a below). In careful speech, it is also not uncommon for a determiner to form a clitic group with a preceding preposition, and not with a following noun (as in 49b). Although, again, it is more common for the preposition to form a clitic group together with the entire noun phrase (see also chapter 5.3.1).

(49) a. *pet luqiarama.. ama ageski*
pet *lu-ki-iara=ama..* ***ama*** *ages-ki*
on/under DEM-SG.F-PROX=ART ART year-SG.F
'during this.. this year' (D12ABDACPGARDEN-070)

b. *miika bup guasakngaiam nama guvang*
miika *bup* *gua=saqang-iam* *ne=**ama*** *guvang*
more fill 1SG.POSS=eye-DU.M with/from=ART dirt
'my eyes got filled with dirt' (BMS-01/06/2015)

3.3.2 Demonstratives

The Qaqet demonstratives are morphologically complex, consisting of a demonstrative base *lu*, a noun class suffix, and a deictic root. The deictic roots are *-iara* 'PROX', *-a* 'DIST', and *mara* 'here' (usually realized as an enclitic). Chapter 4.1.2 discusses the resulting forms in more detail, including the evidence for the status of the deictic roots as suffixes or clitics. The present chapter, by contrast, focuses on the distribution of (i) the demonstrative words (occurring pronominally and adnominally), (ii) the deictic roots (occurring adverbially), and (iii) the demonstrative base *lu* (occurring adverbially).

(i) Demonstrative word

The demonstrative word occurs both pronominally and adnominally. As a pronoun, it occurs in almost all syntactic functions available to common nouns, e.g., as left-dislocated constituent (in 50a), subject (in 50b), direct object (in 50c) or prepositional object (in 50d). It can also function as the possessor within a possessive noun phrase, but not as the possessed entity (see section 3.5.2). Furthermore, the demonstrative pronoun cannot co-occur with other noun phrase elements.

(50) a. *dluqa, de naqaki qamit*
*de=**lu-ka-a**,* *de* *naka=kaki* *ka=mit*
CONJ=DEM-SG.M-DIST CONJ bit=instead 3SG.M.SBJ=go.NCONT.PST
'and as for that one, he alone went instead (of the other)'
(N11AAGSIRINILOBSTER1-0083)

b. *luqia qiatrenas*
lu-ki-a *kia=trenas*
DEM-SG.F-DIST 3SG.F.SBJ=jump.CONT:SELF
'that one jumps' (R12ADNFROG-030)

c. *tral luqa sevaaluqup dap..*
te=ral ***lu-ka-a***
3PL.SBJ.NPST=carry.NCONT DEM-SG.M-DIST
se=pe=aa=luqup *dap..*
to/with=PLACE=3SG.M.POSS=place but
'they are carrying that one to his place and..' (N11AAGSIRINILOBSTER1-0084)

d. *kurluun pet luqiaavit*
kurli-un *pet* ***lu-ki-a****=a-pit*
leave-1DU on/under DEM-SG.F-DIST=DIR-up
'we wait for that one on top' (D12ABDACPGARDEN-046)

As an adnominal demonstrative, it agrees in noun class and number with its head noun. Its position relative to the head noun is not fixed, as shown by the two contrastive examples below: it most frequently occurs at the left edge of the noun phrase (as in 51a), but there are a good number of examples where it immediately follows its head (as in 51b). In possessive structures, it obligatorily occurs in post-head position. But other than that, the factors that determine its position are not clear: the two examples below are parallel, they occur in comparable contexts, and they were uttered by the same speaker – and yet they differ in the position of the demonstrative.

(51) a. *dap luqia amakainaqi, dequas magrip nyitarlik, taqurlani nyingiarluis*
dap [***lu-ki-a*** *ama=kaina-ki*]NP, *de=kuasik*
but DEM-SG.F-DIST ART=water-SG.F CONJ=NEG
maget=ip *nyi=tarlik,* *taquarl=ani*
then=PURP 2SG.SBJ.NPST=cross.CONT thus=DIST
nyi-ne=gia=rluis
2SG.ASSOC-from/with=2SG.POSS=child
'but [that water]NP, you cannot cross it, like this, you and your children' (N11AAGSIRINIROPE-0008FF)

b. *dap makainaqi luqia, de idequas tamrarlik*
dap [*ma=kaina-ki* ***lu-ki-a***]NP, *de* *ide=kuasik*
but ART.ID=water-SG.F DEM-SG.F-DIST CONJ IPFV=NEG
ta=mrarlik
3PL.SBJ=cross.NCONT.PST
'but [that water]NP, they cannot cross it' (N11AAGSIRINIROPE-0004)

Regardless of the position of the demonstrative, the head noun is always marked by either the article *ama* or the article *ma*. Examples (52a) below and (51a) above illustrate this kind of marking for pre-head demonstratives, and (52b) below and (51b) above, for post-head demonstratives.

(52) a. *dap luqia masinepki de..*
dap [***lu-ki-a ma***=*sinepki*]NP *de..*
but DEM-SG.F-DIST ART.ID=NAME:SG.F CONJ
'but [that Sinepki]NP ..' (N12ABKSIRINI-066)

b. *keks amakainaqi luqia, deama.. ahlurlki*
ka=kias [***ama***=*kaina-ki* ***lu-ki-a***]NP,
3SG.M.SBJ=actually ART=water-SG.F DEM-SG.F-DIST
de=ama.. *a=slurl-ki*
CONJ=ART NM=big-SG.F
'[that water]NP actually, it is.. a big one' (N11AAGSIRINIROPE-0005)

Adnominal demonstratives cannot co-occur with adnominal indefinites, but they can co-occur with adjective and nominal modifiers (including quantifiers) to form complex noun phrases. The modifiers usually occur post-head, and the most common order in such complex noun phrases is thus a pre-head demonstrative and a post-head modifier (as in 53a). If the demonstrative occurs post-head, it always follows immediately after the head noun and precedes the modifier (as in 53b). Although such complex phrases are possible, it is nevertheless very rare to encounter them in natural texts. Instead, it is more common for one of the elements to function as the head of a separate noun phrase. The most typical strategy is illustrated in (53c): the noun phrase consists of a demonstrative and a head noun; and it is followed not by an adjective, but by a noun (converted from an adjective), which functions as the head of its own noun phrase, and which is separated prosodically and syntactically (by means of the conjunction *de*).

(53) a. *mani ngutlu luqa amarluimga amatluqa*
mani *ngu=tlu* [***lu-ka-a***
recently 1SG.SBJ.NPST=see.CONT DEM-SG.M-DIST
ama=rluim-ka *ama=tlu-ka]NP*
ART=child-SG.M ART=good-SG.M
'yesterday I saw [that nice boy]NP' (ARB&BCK-11/05/15)

b. *beip sagel amakainaqi luqia amahlurlki, idrelsil savraqi iquas maget trarlik*
be=ip *se=gel* [*ama=kaina-ki* ***lu-ki-a***
CONJ=PURP to/with=near ART=water-SG.F DEM-SG.F-DIST
ama=slurl-ki]NP, *ide=te=lsil*
ART=big-SG.F IPFV=3PL.SBJ.NPST=say.CONT
se=pet-ki *i=kuasik* *maget* *ta=rarlik*
to/with=on/under-3SG.F SIM=NEG then 3PL.SBJ=cross.NCONT.FUT
'then on to [that big water]NP about which they say that they cannot cross it' (N11AAGSIRINIROPE-0094)

c. *deqiavin menlauma amarlekenem, de ama.. agilem*
de=kia=vin *men=[**lu-em-a***
CONJ=3SG.F.SBJ=step.NCONT at=DEM-SG.RCD-DIST
*ama=rleken-em]*NP, *de* *[ama..* *a=gil-em]*NP
ART=branch-SG.RCD CONJ ART NM=small-SG.RCD
'she steps onto [that branch]NP, it is [a.. a small one]NP' (N11AAGSIRINI-ROPE-0070)

The above characterization holds for demonstratives containing the deictic roots *-iara* 'PROX' and *-a* 'DIST'. Demonstratives with the deictic root *mara* 'here', by contrast, only occur pronominally. As pronouns, they are attested in the same syntactic functions as the other demonstratives, e.g., in subject function (as in 54a). In addition, the corpus contains a number of examples where they are in apposition to another noun phrase (as in 54b). Such examples look similar to those of adnominal demonstratives. However, the prosodic characteristics (indicated by means of commas) identify them as occurring in their own intonation unit, usually in a non-final unit marked by a rising-falling pitch contour (see chapter 2.3.2 for prosodic units). Different from the other demonstratives, the forms containing *mara* thus seem unable to co-occur with a common noun within the same prosodic unit. I take this as evidence for them not being able to occur adnominally.

(54) a. *liamara iandit, de.. ianemalia*
lu-iam=mara *ian=tit,* *de..* *iane=mali=a*
DEM-DU.M=here 3DU.SBJ=go.CONT CONJ 3DU.SBJ.NPST=search=DIST
'these two here go, and.. they are searching now' (R12ATAFROG-095)

b. *de luqemara, amagilka, daqenamadanggi, de ianebrlany mbes*
de *[**lu-ka=mara**]*NP, *[ama=gil-ka]*NP,
CONJ DEM-SG.M=here ART=small-SG.M
de=ke-ne=ama=dang-ki,
CONJ=3SG.M.ASSOC-from/with=ART=dog-SG.F
de *iane=brlany* *mbes*
CONJ 3DU.SBJ.NPST=sleep together
'and this one here, the little one, together with his dog, the two sleep together' (R12ATAFROG-036)

It is not uncommon for the demonstrative pronouns to be further modified by directionals (see also section 3.4.3). The demonstrative is always followed directly by the directional, and the two frequently form a single phonological word (as in 55a). In addition, there are a handful of examples whose syntactic structure is unclear (as in 55b): they look like adnominal demonstratives-plus-directionals modifying a head noun, and there are no prosodic indications that the demonstrative-plus-directional does not form a single unit with the following noun. However, it is only found with a handful of examples, and only with proper nouns I therefore tentatively analyze structures as in (55b) as two noun phrases in apposition.

(55) a. *saqika luqiaavit, de dip taquarl*
saqi-ka [***lu-ki-a=a-pit***]NP, *de* *dip* *taquarl*
again-3SG.M DEM-SG.F-DIST=DIR-up CONJ FUT thus
'again [that one on top]NP, it will be the same (with it)' (D12AB-DACPGARDEN-054)
b. *dluqaavuk masirini, de ngrek saqans*
de=[***lu-ka-a=a-vuk***]NP [*ma=sirini*]NP,
CONJ=DEM-SG.M-DIST=DIR-up ART.ID=NAME
de *ngerek* *se-ka=ka=nes*
CONJ alone to/with-3SG.M=3SG.M.SBJ=shout.NCONT
'and [that one on top]NP, [Sirini]NP, he alone shouts' (N11AAGSIRINILOB-STER1-0052)

The demonstratives occur with spatial reference (as in 56a), temporal reference (as in 56b) and anaphoric reference (as in 56c). The demonstrative with the root *mara* 'here' is only attested in spatial contexts.

(56) a. YRA: *ulunget kua?*
ulu=nget *kua?*
look=3N where
AMT: *lungera*
lu-nget-a
DEM-N-DIST
YRA: 'where are they?' AMT: 'those ones' (LONGYDS20150601_1-298FF)
b. *div uneperlset pet luqiara amaageski, selauma vaapit*
dip *une=perlset* *pet* ***lu-ki-iara***
FUT 1DU.SBJ.NPST=finish.CONT on/under DEM-SG.F-PROX
ama=ages-ki *se=lu-em-a* *pe=pit*
ART=year-SG.F to/with=DEM-SG.RCD-DIST on/under=up
'we will finish it this year, that one on top' (D12ABDACPGARDEN-070)

c. *kerlka amasiitka qatit, saqatira mrama.. ama.. aburlem nara, bradrlem luqa amasiitka*
kerl-ka *ama=siit-ka* *ka=tit,*
DEONT-3SG.M ART=story-SG.M 3SG.M.SBJ=go.CONT
sa=ka=tit=a *met=ama..* *ama..* *a=burlem*
already=3SG.M.SBJ=go.CONT=DIST in=ART ART NM=many
ne-ta, *be=ta=drlem* ***lu-ka-a*** *ama=siit-ka*
from/with-3PL.H CONJ=3PL.SBJ=know DEM-SG.M-DIST ART=story-SG.M
'and the story spreads, it spreads to the.. the.. many people, and so they know that story' (I12AANACLADNSocio3-337FF)

In anaphoric contexts, the factors determining the choice of demonstrative are unclear. In spatial and temporal contexts, the contrast is between a proximal space or time (expressed in the deictic root *-iara* 'PROX') and a distal space or time (expressed in the deictic root *-a* 'DIST'), although the exact semantics of each region require further investigation. The third demonstrative containing the deictic root *mara* 'here' occurs in spatial contexts only, overlapping with the distribution of the proximal demonstrative. Given its phonological status (as a clitic, not as a suffix), its morphosyntactic distribution (as a pronoun, not as an adnominal demonstrative) and its semantics (as a spatial demonstrative only), it is likely that this demonstrative is a recent innovation, intruding into the proximal space.

(ii) Deictic roots

All three deictic roots are attested independently as adverbs. The two proximal forms have spatio-temporal meanings: *mara* 'here' occurs with a spatial meaning only (as in 57a), and *iara* 'PROX' with both spatial (as in 57b) and temporal meanings (as in 57c).

(57) a. *amadangga mara, daamam mara*
ama=dang-ka ***mara,*** *de=a-mam* ***mara***
ART=dog-SG.M here CONJ=3SG.M.POSS-father here
'the dog here, and its master here' (R12ADNFROG-276FF)

b. *tik nguameniara saruarl, de tika..*
tika *ngua=men=**iara*** *se=tuarl,*
EMPH 1SG.SBJ=come.NCONT.PST=PROX to/with=other.side
de *tika..*
CONJ EMPH
'I came here to the other side, and..' (N12BAMCAT-326)

c. *tesiit banaira, tesiit bigia*
te=siit *barek-na=**iara**,* *te=siit* *bigia*
3PL.SBJ.NPST=story BEN-RECP=PROX 3PL.SBJ.NPST=story tomorrow
'they tell stories to each other now, they tell stories tomorrow'
(I12AANACLADNSocio3-361)

The present-day distal adverb *iasi* 'DIST', by contrast, is unlikely to be related to the distal deictic root *-a* 'DIST'. This adverb is used with both spatial (in 58a) and temporal (58b) meanings.

(58) a. *kurli nyang iasiivuk*
kurli *nya=ang* ***iasi**=a-vuk*
leave 2SG.SBJ=walk.NCONT DIST=DIR-up
'leave it and go up there' (LongYDS20150601_1-274)

b. *beiviasi, beip ngilngil*
*be=ip=**iasi**,* *be=ip* *ngilngil*
CONJ=PURP=DIST CONJ=PURP morning
'until then, until morning' (N11AAGBrothers-0062)

There is, however, also an adverb *a* 'DIST', which serves text deictic functions, locating events relative to each other. It frequently marks the background event to a main event (as in 59a). As such, it commonly occurs in tail-head linkages, portraying a preceding event as completed and as background to the next event (as in 59b).

(59) a. *amaarenngia, dianebrlany*
*ama=aren-ki=**a**,* *de=iane=brlany*
ART=night-SG.F=DIST CONJ=3DU.SBJ.NPST=sleep
'it being night, they are sleeping' (N12BAMCat-085ff)

b. *deip ma, daqamrirl, kamrirla, deiva daqatit*
de=ip *maget,* *de=ka=mrirl,*
CONJ=PURP then CONJ=3SG.M.SBJ=go.down
*ka=mrirl=**a**,* *de=ip=**a*** *de=ka=tit*
3SG.M.SBJ=go.down=DIST CONJ=PURP=DIST CONJ=3SG.M.SBJ=go.CONT
'then he climbed down, having climbed down, having done this, he went' (N11AAGSiriniRope-0026ff)

This adverb also cliticizes to summarizing statements, thus framing the preceding event as completed, without necessarily introducing a new event (as in 60a). As such, it frequently cliticizes to the manner demonstrative *taquarl* 'thus', resulting in the forms *taqurla* (as in 60b) and *taqurlani* (as in 60c). The form *ani* is only attested in this context, and the exact meaning differences between *taqurla* and *taqurlani* are unknown.

(60) a. *deqerl saqava*
de=kerl *saqap=**a***
CONJ=DEONT enough=DIST
'it's enough now' (P12ADNROPE1-031)
b. *taqurla, de urlenges*
*taquarl=**a**, de ure=lenges*
thus=DIST CONJ 1PL.SBJ.NPST=destroy
'just like this, we spoil things' (I12AANACLADNSOCIO2-149)
c. *denani ngusiquat, inguraqen, itaqurlani nyitaqen*
de=nani ngu=siquat, i=ngu=raqen,
CONJ=can 1SG.SBJ.NPST=try SIM=1SG.SBJ.NPST=say.NCONT
*ip=taquarl=**ani*** *nyi=taqen*
PURP=thus=DIST(?) 2SG.SBJ.NPST=say.CONT
'I can try and say it just like you were saying it' (N11AJNGENA-INGMETSIQI-0084FF)

(iii) Demonstrative base *lu*

Finally, the demonstrative base *lu* 'DEM' functions as an adverb that occurs in spatial and temporal contexts, conveying a sense of immediacy. It usually co-occurs with the adverbs *a* 'DIST' (as in 61a), *iara* 'PROX' or *mara* 'here' (as in 61b), but it can also occur on its own or with a directional (as in 61c).

(61) a. *tikaip ngennarli brlit, datika ngenuaming lua*
*tika=ip ngen=narli brlit, dap=tika ngen=uaming **lu**=a*
EMPH=PURP 2PL.SBJ=hear IDEOPH but=EMPH 2PL.SBJ=beat:?? DEM=DIST
'when you hear (the sound) *brlit*, you strike right there and then' (N12AMVGENAINGMETBROTHERS-065)
b. *lumara, beip bigia derataarlvit, nepbang*
***lu**=mara, be=ip bigia de=ta=taarlvit,*
DEM=here CONJ=PURP tomorrow CONJ=3PL.SBJ=stand.CONT:UP
nepbang
morning
'right here and now (pointing at picture), the next day they stand up, in the morning' (R12ATAFROG-043FF)
c. *de saqika lu maamuk*
*de saqi-ka **lu** maqa-muk*
CONJ again-3SG.M DEM HERE-across
'and again right across (pointing)' (I12ABLAJLATASOCIO3-217)

It is likely that the demonstrative base originated in the verb *lu* 'see.NCONT', which gave rise to both the adverbial *lu* and the demonstrative words.

Example (62a) illustrates the presumed origin for the adverbial *lu*: a second person subject index, the verb *lu* and a spatial adverb. Such structures are commonly used as attention-directing devices in descriptions and instructions. Formally, they are imperatives, and they exhibit the typical rising pitch contour of imperatives (see chapter 2.3.2), but they also show evidence of phonetic erosion in that *nyi=lu* '2SG.SBJ.NPST=see.NCONT' tends to be realized as [ɲəlʊ] ~ [ɲʊlʊ]. Further erosion presumably gave rise to the directive particle *ulu* 'look' (illustrated in 62b). This particle was then further eroded to the adverb *lu* (as in 61a to 61c above), but still preserving its attention-getting function.

(62) a. *damamarl namadangga navraamam, benyilua*
de=ama=marl *ne=ama=dang-ka*
CONJ=ART=happiness from/with=ART=dog-SG.M
ne=pet=aa=mam,
from/with=on/under=3SG.M.POSS=father
*be=nyi=**lu**=a*
CONJ=2SG.SBJ.NPST=see.NCONT=DIST
'the dog is happy in his master's (arms), see there' (R12ADNFROG-091)

b. *ulu, nguraqasnes*
***ulu**,* *ngu=raqa=snes*
look 1SG.SBJ.NPST=properly.NCONT=put.in.CONT
'look, I'll put it properly inside' (LONGYDS20150516_1-061)

The form *ulu* 'look' presumably also gave rise to the demonstrative base *lu*. In the demonstrative word, the base *lu* is followed by a noun class suffix (originating in a third person pronoun) and a deictic root (originating in the spatial adverbs *iara* 'PROX' and *a* 'DIST'), i.e., the demonstratives originated in the structure 'see it here/there'. Their reanalysis would have taken place in contexts such as (63): *ulu* followed by a pronoun and a spatial adverb. The surface form of 'see it here/there' is nearly identical to that of 'this/that one' (e.g., *lungera*, i.e., *lu-nget-a* 'DEM-N-DIST'). Semantically, too, it is conceivable that a directive as in (63) was re-interpreted as a demonstrative.

(63) *ulungera*
ulu=nget=a
look=3N=DIST
'see it there' (LONGYJL20150805_1-011)

A further indication of the diachronic relationship between *ulu* 'look' (and hence its source verb *lu* 'see.NCONT') and the demonstrative base *lu* 'DEM' comes from examples such as (64). Example (64) is structurally ambiguous: either a verb, followed by an object suffix, followed by an adverbial enclitic (analysis 64a), or a verb followed by a demonstrative pronoun (analysis 64b). This ambiguity arises because Qaqet allows for the deletion of identical syllables across morpheme boundaries – provided that there is a semantic and diachronic relationship between the two syllables (see chapter 5.2.1). Example (64b) features two adjacent syllables *lu* (with the underlying syllable structure *nyi.lu.lu.qai.ra*), and since deletion of *lu* is allowed, we can assume a diachronic relationship between the two syllables *lu*.

(64) *nyiluqaira*

a. *nyi=lu-ka=iara*
2SG.SBJ.NPST=see.NCONT-3SG.M=PROX
'see him here' (C12ARBZJIFROG-215)

b. *nyi=lu=lu-ka-iara*
2SG.SBJ.NPST=see.NCONT=DEM-SG.M-PROX
'see this one' (C12ARBZJIFROG-215)

3.3.3 Indefinite pronouns

Qaqet has two indefinite pronouns, *ia* 'other' and *qa* 'some', which obligatorily inflect for noun class. The resulting forms are discussed in chapter 4.1.2, while this section outlines (i) their syntactic distribution and (ii) their meaning.

(i) Syntactic distribution

The two forms function both as pronouns and as determiners to a head noun. As pronouns, they occur in all syntactic functions available to nouns, e.g. as subject (in 65a), as direct object (as the first *iani* in 65b) or as prepositional object (as the second *iani* in 65b).

(65) a. *dakui iak kasil ma*

dap=kui	***ia-ka***	*ka=sil*	*ma*
but=quoting	other-SG.M	3SG.M.SBJ=say.NCONT	thus

'but (another) one would say like this' (I12AANACLADNSOCIO3-418)

b. *ngataqen deini ngamisiani, inakaini ngaman siani*

nga=taqen	*de=ini*	*nga=mis=**ia-ini**,*
3N.SBJ=say.CONT	CONJ=SG.DIM	3N.SBJ=call.NCONT.PST=other-SG.DIM
i=naka=ini	*nga=man*	*se=**ia-ini***
SIM=bit=SG.DIM	3N.SBJ=go.inside.NCONT.PST	to/with=other-SG.DIM

'he talks, and the little one says something else (= something wrong), and the little one goes a bit into another (= wrong) direction' (I12AANACLADNSOCIO2-034FF)

Both pronouns are also attested in possessive noun phrases, both as possessor and as possessed (see section 3.5). As possessed nouns, they are preceded by the possessor index (as in 66a and 66b). In the case of *qa* 'some', a pre-head element is obligatory: either the possessor index or the noun marker *a* (as in 66c). By contrast, *ia* 'other' can only be preceded by the possessor index, but not by any other element. Otherwise, no other noun phrase elements can co-occur with either of the two pronouns.

(66) a. *tika uina, davip giak karekmet na, beqarekmet nanyi raqurla*
tika *uin=a,* *dap=ip* ***gi-ia-ka***
EMPH 2DU=DIST but=PURP 2SG.POSS-other-SG.M
ka=rekmet *nana,* *be=ka=rekmet*
3SG.M.SBJ=do.NCONT:IN what CONJ=3SG.M.SBJ=do.NCONT:IN
ne-nyi *taquarl=a*
from/with-2SG thus=DIST
'it's you two now, but why your other (friend) did it, (why) he did it to you like this (we don't know why)' (N11AAGBROTHERS-0076)

b. *nyat giaqek*
*nya=tu**gia=qa-ka***
2SG.SBJ=put.CONT 2SG.POSS=some-SG.M
'put down one of yours' (C12VARPLAY-090)

c. *kua quas nyitlaqanii.. imiiki?*
kua *kuasik* *nyi=tlu=**a=qa-ini**=i..*
INTRG NEG 2SG.SBJ.NPST=see.CONT=NM=some-SG.DIM=SIM
i=miiki?
SIM=instead
'don't you remember a little something from.. from before?' (N11AAGBROTHERS-0100)

Both indefinite forms also occur as determiners to a head noun, agreeing in noun class and number with it. In such cases, the head noun is obligatorily marked by the article *ama* (as in the examples below). Furthermore, identical to their pronominal distribution, *qa* 'some' is obligatorily preceded by either the noun marker (as in 67a) or a possessor index; and *ia* 'other' either occurs initially (as in 67b) or is preceded by a possessor index (as in 67c). Such noun phrases can contain additional modifiers, e.g., adjectives (as in 67d), but they cannot contain any demonstratives or indefinite articles.

(67) a. *denyiqurlaqi raqeq ambatariqa*
de=nyi=quarl-ki *te=[a=**qa-ka***
CONJ=2SG.SBJ.NPST=present.NCONT-3SG.F PURP=NM=some-SG.M
ama=batari-ka]NP
ART=battery-SG.M
'give it [a battery]NP' (LONGYDS20150516_1-717)

b. *dav iviaqiamaltanygi iquasik magrip.. ip kiarang*
dap *ip=[**ia-ki**=ama=ltany-ki*]NP *i=kuasik*
but PURP=other-SG.F=ART=embers-SG.F SIM=NEG
maget=ip.. *ip* *kia=rang*
then=PURP PURP 3SG.F.SBJ=burn.NCONT.FUT
'but if another part of the embers won't.. burn' (P12ADNFIRE-045FF)

c. *uriaq amalanginyga iqetuqun iama..*
[*ure-**ia-ka*** *ama=langiny-ka*]NP
1PL.POSS-other-SG.M ART=paper-SG.M
i=ke=tuqun *i=ama..*
SIM=3SG.M.SBJ.NPST=say.CONT SIM=ART
'there is [one book of ours]NP that talks about the..' (I12AANACLAD-NSOCIO3-229)

d. *masirini, de iaqamaqaqeraqa amatluqa*
ma=sirini, *de* [***ia-ka**=ama=qaqera-ka* *ama=tlu-ka*]NP
ART.ID=NAME CONJ other-SG.M=ART=person-SG.M ART=good-SG.M
'Sirini, he is [a good person]NP' (D12ADKSPIRITS-011)

Both forms are likely to have a nominal origin, since their inflectional and distributional properties are similar to those of nouns (and different from those of articles). Like nouns, they are marked for noun class and they can function as heads of noun phrases. They can even function as possessed entities within the possessive construction – this context is otherwise restricted to nouns; and other pronouns (i.e., independent and demonstrative pronouns) cannot occur here. Furthermore, *qa* 'some' cannot occur without either the noun marker or a possessor index (again, similar to nouns).

The diachronic source for *qa* 'some' is unknown, but *ia* 'other' probably originated in a noun with human or kin reference. The possessed pronominal form of *ia* 'other' is frequently used in reference to friends (as in 68). Semantically, the link to 'other' is conceivably that 'friends' are conceptualized relationally as 'friends of someone', i.e., of an established referent (see point ii below). Note also that *ia* 'other' triggers the base form of the possessor index, which is otherwise only found with a handful of kin relations (see section 3.5.1). It is even possible that *ia* 'other' is cognate to Mali's kinship noun *iaik* 'grandfather' (Stebbins 2011: 189). Assuming such an origin, the pronominal use must have preceded the modifying use. The modifying use then probably originated in the apposition of two noun phrases with identical reference, similar to the structure in (68).

(68) *ip taqurlira guiaik malangmetki qiasil*
ip *taquarl=lira* [***gu-ia-ki***]$_{NP}$ [*ma=langmetki*]$_{NP}$
PURP thus=now 1SG.POSS-other-SG.F ART.ID=NAME
kia=sil
3SG.F.SBJ=say.NCONT
'like [my friend]$_{NP}$ [Langmetki]$_{NP}$ just said' (I12AANACLADNSocio3-003)

The indefinite pronoun *qa* 'some' has given rise to the complex article *aqama* 'some' (see section 3.3.4).

(ii) Semantics
Indefinite *ia* 'other' serves a determiner function in that it introduces a new referent through its relationship to another referent. For example, the speaker in (69) below talks about mythical figures and spirits, using *ia* 'other' to introduce each new referent.

Note that this form is used to refer to each member of a set, including the first one. Example (70) illustrates this use: the two protagonists are introduced by means of the dual form of *ia* 'other' in the first utterance of the narrative, and the speaker then continues to use *ia* 'other' throughout the story to compare the two protagonists (as, e.g., in the second line of 70).

(69) 1. *de.. iak, dema.. anamqa (...)*
de.. ***ia-ka,*** *de=ma..* *a=nameqa (...)*
CONJ other-SG.M CONJ=ART.ID NM=NAME
'and.. another one is.. the *Nameqa* (...)' (D12ADKSpirits-056ff)
2. *iak, deetuqun ima.. avanem (...)*
ia-ka, *de=te=tuqun* *i=ma..* *a=vanem*
other-SG.M CONJ=3PL.SBJ.NPST=say.CONT SIM=ART.ID NM=NAME
'another one, they say is.. the *Vanem* (...)' (D12ADKSpirits-061)
3. *iak, dema.. sevaqesep*
ia-ka, *de=ma..* *sevaqesep*
other-SG.M CONJ=ART.ID NAME
'another one is.. *Sevaqesep*' (D12ADKSpirits-066)

(70) 1. *iaiam, ama.. abrata vriam (...)*
ia-iam, *ama..* *a=brata* *pet-iam*
other-DU.M ART NM=brother on/under-3DU.M
'there were two ones, two.. brothers (...)' (N11AAGBrothers-0001ff)

2. *tika iviak kanak priak tirang*
tika *ip=**ia-ka*** *ka=nak*
EMPH PURP=other-SG.M 3SG.M.SBJ=cry.NCONT
*pet=**ia-ka*** *te=ia-irang*
on/under=other-SG.M PURP=other-PL.DIM
'when one cried to the other for something' (N11AAGBROTHERS-0012)

It is not uncommon for *ia* 'other' to convey a distributive reading of 'each (on their own)'. I assume that this distributive reading is a contextual reading, arising in contexts where speakers talk about a group of referents doing similar things. Example (71) illustrates how easily such a distributive reading can arise.

(71) *iaik kiaruqun siaqamarlaunnga, de iaik, de iaik*
ia-ki *kia=ruqun* *se=**ia-ka**=ama=rlaun-ka,*
other-SG.F 3SG.F.SBJ=sit.NCONT.FUT to/with=other-SG.M=ART=netbag-SG.M
de ***ia-ki,*** *de* ***ia-ki***
CONJ other-SG.F CONJ other-SG.F
'one (woman) will sit with one netbag, another (woman), another (woman) (i.e., each woman works on her own netbag)' (P12ARSBILUM2-011)

This form is furthermore used to talk about a member of a set, as illustrated in (72).

(72) *de saqika **iaq**amqaqraqa*
de *saqi-ka* ***ia-ka**=ama=qaqera-ka*
CONJ again-3SG.M other-SG.M=ART=person-SG.M
'and he is also a (kind of) person' (D12ADKSPIRITS-053)

Finally, there is the conventionalized structure *iara biari* 'all others'. It consists of the reduplicated plural form *iari* 'others' (from *ia-ta*), separated by the conjunction *be* (illustrated in 73).

(73) *dap saqika ivriari biari te.. tetaqen praqi nluqaamalengiqa ama.. ama-tokpisin*
dap *saqi-ka* *ip=are-**ia-ta*** ***be=ia-ta***
but again-3SG.M PURP=3SG.F.POSS-other-PL.H CONJ=other-PL.H
te.. *te=taqen* *pet-ki*
3PL.SBJ.NPST 3PL.SBJ.NPST=say.CONT on/under-3SG.F
ne=lu-ka-a=ama=lengi-ka *ama..* *ama=tokpisin*
from/with=DEM-SG.M-DIST=ART=word-SG.M ART ART=NAME
'and also when all her others are.. are talking to her in that language of.. of Tok Pisin' (I12AANACLADNSOCIO2-192FF)

Generally, *ia* 'other' serves a determiner function only. It does not have any reciprocal uses (as, e.g., 'each other' in English). And although there are examples where it seems to function as a modifier with the meaning of 'different' (as in 74a), speakers invariably correct such utterances in the transcription process and replace them with *ma=uqas* 'ART.ID=difference'. For example, *iaqamalengiqa* in (74a) was corrected to *amalengiqa mauqas* 'a different language'. Example (74b) illustrates the use of *mauqas* 'different'.

(74) a. *kerl iak, iaqamalengiqa*
kerl ***ia-ka,*** ***ia-ka**=ama=lengi-ka*
DEONT other-SG.M other-SG.M=ART=word-SG.M
'there would be a different one, a different language'
(I12ABLAJLATASOCIO3-102)

b. *ikua idre taqeni aqamalengiqa mauqas?*
ip=kua *ide=te* *taqen=i*
PURP=INTRG IPFV=3PL.SBJ.NPST say.CONT=SIM
a=qama=lengi-ka ***ma=uqas***
NM=some=word-SG.M ART.ID=difference
'are they saying that it is a different language?' (I12ABLAJLATASOCIO2-023)

The other indefinite pronoun, *qa* 'some', singles out a subset of an already established referent (as in 75a). It also very frequently occurs in negative contexts (as in 75b).

(75) a. *nyitaqakut, denyilaqaik*
nyi=taqa=kut,
2SG.SBJ.NPST=properly.CONT=break.ground.CONT
*de=nyi=lu=a=**qa-ki***
CONJ=2SG.SBJ.NPST=see.NCONT=NM=some-SG.F
'dig properly, and you will see some (spiders)' (LONGYDS20150601_1-357)

b. *kuasik nguats aqarang*
kuasik *ngua=tes* *a=**qa-irang***
NEG 1SG.SBJ=eat.CONT NM=some-DIM.PL
'I'm not eating anything' (N12BAMCAT-225)

The form can also acquire a contextual reading of 'something other' or 'something different', thereby overlapping with the distribution of *ia* 'other', as illustrated in the two examples below. In (76a), both indefinite pronouns occur following each other, thus strengthening the interpretation of *qa* 'some' as 'something other'. In (76b), the speakers talk about children inventing a language that is 'other than' or 'different from' the correct language.

(76) a. *kurliaik, desaqi uanukut tuanaqeng*
*kurli=**ia-ki**,* *de=saqi* *uane=kut*
leave=other-SG.F CONJ=again 2DU.SBJ.NPST=break.ground.CONT
*te=uana=**qa-nget***
PURP=2DU.POSS=some-N
'leave the other, and dig for something (other, different) of yours' (LONGYDS20150531_1-130)

b. *ah, kipurl aqeqa amalengiqa*
ah, *ki=purl* *a=**qa-ka***
INTJ 3SG.F.SBJ.NPST=invent NM=some-SG.M
ama=lengi-ka
ART=word-SG.M
'ah, she is inventing some (other, different) language' (I12AANACLAD-NSOCIO2-112)

3.3.4 Articles

This section discusses (i) the noun marker *a* 'NM', (ii) the articles *ama* 'ART' and *ma* 'ART.ID', and (iii) the indefinite articles *qama* 'some' and *ngama* 'some.NSPEC'.

(i) Noun marker

The noun marker *a* 'NM' is presumably cognate to the specific article *a* in Mali (Stebbins 2011: 171–174), but its distribution and semantics differ. In Qaqet, it can be characterized as a Stage III article (as introduced by Greenberg 1978): such an article arises when an erstwhile definite, and later specific, article occurs in more and more environments, losing its "synchronic connection with definiteness or specificity" and resulting in a form that is "a mere sign of nominality on the large majority of common nouns" (Greenberg 1978: 259). There are only very few Qaqet nouns that cannot occur with the noun marker: most proper nouns as well as all nouns that are used in vocative contexts. Otherwise, the noun marker occurs with all nouns, and also adjectives (see section 3.4.1), unless it is replaced by other determiners.

As summarized in Table 35 above, the noun marker *a* 'NM' obligatorily occurs in some contexts (preceding *qama* 'some', *ngama* 'some.NSPEC' and *qa* 'some'; unless replaced by a possessor index) and is ruled out in others (preceding *ia* 'other' and the demonstratives; and preceding nouns co-occurring with other pre-head determiners). In all other contexts (i.e., in noun phrases without other pre-head elements), it is in complementary distribution to the articles *ama* and *ma*. Its general function is to indicate nominality, and it would thus be semantically appropriate in a large number of contexts. However, since it is in opposition to the articles *ama* and *ma*, which have more specific meanings (see point ii), its distribution is governed by pragmatic principles. Speakers use the two articles if they intend to convey the more specific meanings associated with them, and only resort to the noun marker when the other meanings are not intended.

The most frequent context for the occurrence of *a* 'NM' is the citation form of all common nouns and adjectives, as illustrated by the elicited paradigm in (77a). The only exception are proper nouns, which mostly occur without the noun marker, even if they are derived from common nouns (as illustrated by means of the citation form of the place name in (77b)). There are only very few proper nouns that can occur with the noun marker (see section 3.2.1).

(77) a. *aqumga, aqumiam, aqum*
__a__=kum-ka, *__a__=kum-iam,* *__a__=kum*
NM=tree.type-SG.M NM=tree.type-DU.M NM=tree.type
'(one) *kum* tree, (two) *kum* trees, (more than two) *kum* trees' (ADN-02/09/2014)

b. *kumgi*
kumgi
NAME
'Komgi (place name, from *kum-ki* 'tree.type-SG.F')' (ADN-02/09/2014)

In connected texts, by contrast, the occurrence of the noun marker is largely restricted to non-referential contexts. For example, it frequently occurs on nouns or adjectives that are used predicatively (as in 78a). But there is always the alternative possibility to create a referential expression through the use of another article (as in 78b) (see chapter 8.2 on non-verbal clauses).

(78) a. *agetki vamaqasupka*
__a__=get-ki *pe=ama=qasup-ka*
NM=hunger-SG.F PLACE=ART=rat-SG.M
'the rat was hungy (lit. hunger is on the rat)' (N12BAMCAT-170)

b. *ik ngua, de miikamagetki nangua slep*
ip *ngua,* *de* *miika=__ama__=get-ki* *ne-ngua* *slep*
PURP 1SG CONJ more=ART=hunger-SG.F from/with-1SG intensely
'as for me, I continue to be very hungry (lit. the hunger is with me)' (N12BAMCAT-290)

The noun marker *a* also occurs in contexts where a speaker focuses on the event, not on the referent. This use is illustrated with the examples in (79) and (80). Example

(79) is an extract from a procedural text where a speaker demonstrates and explains the manufacture of ropes from vines. The referents are physically present, and she first introduces them by means of the article *ama* plus a spatial adverb (in 79-1). Following that, she keeps talking about the vines in front of her, referring to them by means of either the article *ama* or a demonstrative (as in 79-2). Following this utterance, she goes on to demonstrate how to split vines. She now focuses on the action of splitting, no longer on the referent (in 79-3 to 79-6). When she incidentally mentions the referent in this context, she marks it with the noun marker *a* (in 79-5).

(79) 1. *amamelangiara (...)*
__ama__=melang=iara
ART=vine=PROX
'the vines here (...)' (P12ADNROPE1-003)

2. *lungetmara, dinyirlingmet*
lu-nget=mara, *de=nyi=rlingmet*
DEM-N=here CONJ=2SG.SBJ.NPST=split:IN
'the ones here, you split (them)' (P12ADNROPE1-038)

3. *nyirlingmet ma*
nyi=rlingmet *ma*
2SG.SBJ.NPST=split:IN thus
'you split like this' (P12ADNROPE1-039)

4. *taqurlani ma*
taquarl=ani *ma*
thus=DIST thus
'like this' (P12ADNROPE1-040)

5. *nyirlingmet namelang*
nyi=rlingmet *ne=__a__=melang*
2SG.SBJ.NPST=split:IN from/with=NM=vine
'you split vines' (P12ADNROPE1-041)

6. *nyirlingmet taqurlani*
nyi=rlingmet *taquarl=ani*
2SG.SBJ.NPST=split:IN thus=DIST
'you split like this' (P12ADNROPE1-042)

A similar situation is illustrated in the extract below. The speaker introduces *uaik* 'birds' in (80-1) by means of an article. He then expands on these birds, referring to them with a demonstrative pronoun (in 80-2): these birds are known to detect snakes and to give away the snakes' location through singing. Following this description, the story shifts back to the protagonist, narrating how he turns himself into a snake and hides in a tree (not included in the extract). The speaker now turns to the central event in (80-3) where the birds give away the location of the protagonist. In this context, the speaker focus on the event, not on the reference of the birds – and thus marks the birds with the noun marker *a*.

(80) 1. *beip ma damuaik ngatden*

be=ip	*maget*	*de=**ama**=uaik*	*nga=tden*
CONJ=PURP	then	CONJ=ART=bird	3N.SBJ=come.CONT

'then later the birds are coming' (N12AMVGENAINGMETBROTHERS-029)

2. *lungera idengatat, pramaising (...)*

lu-nget-a	*ide=nga=tat*	pet=ama=isinga
DEM-N-DIST	IPFV=3N.SBJ=sing.CONT	on/under=ART=python

'those ones always sing about snakes (...)' (N12AMVGENAINGMETBROTHERS-030)

3. *auaik ngatden bengatat praqa.. miika*

***a**=uaik*	*nga=tden*	*be=nga=tat*
NM=bird	3N.SBJ=come.CONT	CONJ=3N.SBJ=sing.CONT
pet-ka..	*miika*	
on/under-3SG.M	more	

'birds are coming and singing about him.. on and on' (N12AMVGENAINGMETBROTHERS-033)

Similarly, it is not uncommon for the noun marker to occur with referents (especially locations) which are an integral part of the event (and thus accessible through common knowledge). For example, (81a) comes from a text about gardening. It features the first and only mention of *qerlap* 'water, bush', which is marked with the noun marker: this referent plays no further role in the narrative, but it is general knowledge that the first step in gardening is to burn and cut the bush, and all events (such as cutting the trees) take place against this background. Alternatively, such referents can be marked by an article (as in 81b), conveying a subtle semantic difference. Again, this example contains the first and only mention of *qerlap* 'water, bush', serving as the location for the canoe to travel on. But here, the speaker portrays *qerlap* 'water, bush' as a referential location (albeit one whose identity is not relevant to the story). The speaker in (81a), by contrast, focuses on the event of 'clearing the bush', portraying *qerlap* 'water, bush' as non-referential.

(81) a. *urmam katden, bqararles iaqerlap, daqatapmet pemameng*

ure-mam	*ka=tden,*	*be=ka=rarles*
1PL.POSS-father	3SG.M.SBJ=come.CONT	CONJ=3SG.M.SBJ=start.NCONT
*i=**a**=qerlap,*	*de=ka=tapmet*	*pe=ma=meng*
SIM=NM=water	CONJ=3SG.M.SBJ=cut.CONT:IN	PLACE=ART.ID=wood

'our father was coming, and he started on the bush, and he cut the trees (to make a garden)' (D12ABDACPGARDEN-007FF)

b. *ianiurlet nianamalauski sep maqerlap*
ian=iurlet *ne=iana=malaus-ki*
3DU.SBJ=pull.NCONT from/with=3DU.POSS=canoe-SG.F
se=pe ***ma****=qerlap*
to/with=PLACE ART.ID=water
'they pulled their canoe into water (to travel across the sea)' (N12BAM-CAT-131)

On the basis of the above distribution, the noun marker could be characterized as a non-referential article. But its distribution is broader: it co-occurs with indefinite specific pronouns and articles (see point iii), and it occurs with specific reference in contexts of word searches and hesitation (see below). I take this as evidence that the meaning of the noun marker *a* does not entail non-referentiality: it marks nominality, and this meaning is compatible with both referential and non-referential contexts – but since most Qaqet articles entail referentiality, the noun marker is often the only option in non-referential contexts, and thus predominantly occurs in such contexts.

The noun marker is mutually exclusive with the articles *ama* and *ma*. This differs from Mali, where the two can co-occur in some contexts (Stebbins 2011: 171–174). In Qaqet, too, there are contexts where the two (seemingly) co-occur, but the overall evidence points to them being mutually exclusive. One such context is writing, where speakers sometimes (but by no means always or mostly) write both an article and the noun marker. Example (82a) is the written original, and example (82b) is the corresponding spoken utterance, which was read from the written text and which does not contain any audible noun marker. There are only a handful of examples where both the article and the noun marker are audible in the spoken version, too (as in 82c). This example is unusual in the sense that the speaker adopts an especially careful pronunciation: there are clear pauses between the words, and he even produces the underlying plosive *t* in *qaqet* 'person' (which would normally be realized as *qaqer* preceding a vowel, even across word boundaries).

(82) a. *Siqi: ama aqaqeraqi ama atlu qi.*
Siqi: ***ama*** ***a****=qaqera-ki* ***ama*** ***a****=tlu* *ki.*
NAME ART NM=person-SG.F ART NM=good SG.F
'Siqi: a good woman.' (ADK-02/08/2012)

b. *masiqi, de amaqaqraqi amatluqi*
ma=siqi *de* ***ama****=qaqera-ki* ***ama****=tlu-ki*
ART.ID=NAME CONJ ART=person-SG.F ART=good-SG.F
'Siqi, she is a good woman' (D12ADKSPIRITS-023)

c. *savrama aqaqet araaiaus*
*se=pet=****ama*** ***a****=qaqera* *araa=iaus*
to/from=on/under=ART NM=person 3PL.POSS=spirit
'about the people's spirits' (D12ADKSPIRITS-005)

Based on the above evidence from writing, it could be argued that the noun marker is present, but tends to be elided in spoken language when preceded by an identical vowel. That is, the clitic groups *ama=a* 'ART=NM' and *ma=a* 'ART.ID=NM' would be realized as [ama] and [ma] respectively. Such an analysis is adopted by Stebbins (2011: 33; 168) for Mali. For Qaqet, I do not adopt this analysis for the following reasons.

First, the elision of identical vowels is not a regular phenomenon in the language. This can be shown with the help of vowel-initial roots such as *alin* 'sugarcane'. When the noun marker cliticizes to such a root, the result is a long vowel (as illustrated in 83a): the initial long vowel *aa* has the same length as the final vowel *i* (which is subject to final lengthening, see chapter 2.3.1), and twice as long as the medial short vowel *i*. Similarly, if an article precedes such a vowel-initial root, the result is a long vowel (as in 83b). That is, the identical vowels are both preserved. The only vowel elided regularly within vowel sequences is the vowel *e* [ə]. This can be shown with the help of the clitic group *ne=ama* 'from/with=ART' in the same example (83b), which is realized [nama]. The underlying schwa is only preserved when preceding a consonant-initial morpheme, e.g., in the clitic group *ne=ma* 'from/with=ART.ID' (in 83c).

(83) a. *aalinngi*
a=alin-ki
NM=sugarcane-SG.F
'sugarcane' (ATA-25/07/2012)
b. *ngenamaalin*
ngere-ne=ama=alin
3N.ASSOC-from/with=ART=sugarcane
'together with sugarcane' (D12ADNGARDEN-041)
c. *ngunemabridget*
ngu-ne=ma=bridget
1SG.ASSOC-from/with=ART.ID=NAME
'I together with Bridget' (C12VARPLAY-400)

Phonologically, there is thus no reason to assume that [ama] and [ma] go back to /ama=a/ and /ma=a/. Given that any root-initial lexical vowel *a* is audible when following an article, it is difficult to argue for an automatic rule of vowel elision: the fact that the noun marker *a* is not audible would rather suggest that it is not there. Furthermore, even if we posit an elision rule, we would want to analyze [ama] and [ma] in identical ways (as either both containing the noun marker or as both not containing it). But [ma] mostly (albeit not always) occurs preceding proper nouns, and they do not allow for a noun marker in their citation form. That is, one would have to argue that [ma] sometimes goes back to /ma=a/ and sometimes to /ma/.

A second piece of evidence comes from word searches: in the spoken language, this is the only context where articles and noun markers are observed to co-occur. It is not uncommon for the speaker to first utter an article *ama* or *ma*, realized with level pitch and a final glottal stop as [amaʔ] or [maʔ], signaling hesitation and the continuation of the utterance (see chapter 2.3.2). This article is then usually (but not always) followed by a pause, and then the speaker utters the noun marker and the noun. A typical example is given in (84a). Alternatively, the speaker repeats the article together with the noun (as in 84b). In the case of the article *ama*, there are no examples where the speaker does not either use the noun marker or repeat the article. In the case of the article *ma* preceding a proper noun, there is variation. If the proper noun does not admit the noun marker in its citation form, it also does not occur after a hesitation (as in 84c). If it takes the noun marker in its citation form, this marker also occurs after a hesitation (as in 84d).

(84) a. *nyaruvem namamudemgi, dakuarl ama.. alanginyis, dakuarl amagumiis*
nya=ruvem *ne=ama=mudem-ki,*
2SG.SBJ=get.ready.NCONT.FUT:PLACE from/with=ART=resin-SG.F
dap=kua ***ama..*** ***a****=langiny-es,* *dap=kua* *ama=gumi-es*
but=INTRG ART NM=paper-SG.FLAT but=INTRG ART=plastic-SG.FLAT
'you prepare the resin, or maybe the.. the paper, or maybe the plastic' (P12ADNFIRE-005FF)

b. *dinyatu ama.. amarlesirlirang ivuk*
de=nya=tu ***ama..*** ***ama****=rlesirl-irang* *i-vuk*
CONJ=2SG.SBJ=put.CONT ART ART=dry.wood-PL.DIM AWAY-up
'and you put the.. the dry sticks on top' (P12ADNFIRE-020)

c. *kanavet ma.. ramgi*
ka=ne=pet ***ma..*** *ramgi*
3SG.M=from/with=on/under ART.ID NAME
'he came across.. Ramgi' (N11AAGSIRINILOBSTER2-0044)

d. *iak, deetuqun ima.. avlengnaska*
ia-ka, *de=te=tuqun* *i=****ma..*** ***a****=vlengnaska*
other-SG.M CONJ=3PL.SBJ.NPST=say.CONT SIM=ART.ID NM=NAME:SG.M
'another one, they say is.. the *Vlengnas*' (D12ADKSPIRITS-086FF)

The above distribution suggests that speakers treat nouns following a hesitation just like nouns in isolation, and produce their citation form. This then would account for the apparent co-occurrence of articles plus noun markers. I assume that a similar explanation holds for the written language (as illustrated in examples 82a to 82c above): the written medium makes it possible for speakers to treat words as if they occur in isolation, and thus allowing for the presence of the noun marker.

(ii) Articles

Qaqet has two articles whose diachronic origins are no longer transparent: *ama* and *ma*. It is possible that the noun marker *a* is diachronically part of *ama* 'ART' (from **a-*

ma 'NM-ART.ID'), but synchronically there is no reason to analyze this article as multimorphemic. The two articles are related to the Mali articles *kama* and *ma* (Stebbins 2011: 166–171). In the case of *ma*, both form and distribution match closely. In the case of Qaqet *ama* and Mali *kama*, a re-organization of the determiner system must have taken place in one or both of the languages. In terms of forms, Mali *kama* is more likely to be cognate to Qaqet *qama* 'some' (see point iii below), but in terms of distribution, there is more overlap between Mali *kama* and Qaqet *ama* (while Qaqet *qama* 'some' is clearly restricted to indefinite contexts).

The articles occur in three contexts within the noun phrase: they mark a noun for referentiality, they connect a pre-head determiner to a noun, and they connect a post-head adjectival modifier, nominal modifier or quantifier to a noun. The articles are in complementary distribution in the first two contexts, while the last context is restricted to *ama* 'ART'. All contexts are illustrated in this section.

First, both articles function as determiners, being in complementary distribution with all other adnominal determiners and possessor indexes (see the discussion of Table 35 above). The most general (and hence frequent) article is *ama* 'ART': it occurs in all referential contexts, unless a determiner with a more specific meaning is available. The extract in (85) gives a good idea of its ubiquitousness. The speaker uses the fixed expression in (85-1) to start his story, and then uses the article *ama* in an indefinite-specific context: at the first mention of the protagonists 'cat' and 'rat' (in 85-2). He then uses *ama* in (85-3) to situate the story at a specific time (the time of the ancestors). Following that, he uses *ama* in a definite context: anaphorically tracking the previously introduced protagonists (in 85-4). From then on, he continues to use *ama* in all subsequent reference to these protagonists.

(85) 1. *asiit kararles*
a=siit *ka=rarles*
NM=story 3SG.M.SBJ=start.NCONT
'the story starts' (N12BAMCAT-007)

2. *asiitka savramamiuqi, ngenama.. aqasupka*
a=siit-ka *se=pet=**ama**=miu-ki,*
NM=story-SG.M to/with=on/under=ART=cat-SG.F
*ngere-ne=**ama**..* *a=qasup-ka*
3N.ASSOC-from/with=ART NM=rat-SG.M
'the story goes to the cat and the.. the rat' (N12BAMCAT-008)

3. *murl glamhrlura*
murl *gel=**ama**=srlu-ta*
distantly near=ART=old-PL.H
'at the time of the ancestors' (N12BAMCAT-009)

4. *de amamiuqi, ngenamaqasupka, deidianatliini*
de ***ama**=miu-ki,* *ngere-ne=**ama**=qasup-ka,*
CONJ ART=cat-SG.F 3N.ASSOC-from/with=ART=rat-SG.M
de=ide=iana=tlu-ini
CONJ=IPFV=3DU.POSS=good-SG.DIM
'the cat and the rat used to have their little friendship' (N12BAMCAT-010FF)

The article *ma* 'ART.ID' occurs in much the same contexts, except that it marks referents as inherently identifiable, i.e., it occurs especially with proper nouns. Like *ama*, it occurs at the first mention of a referent (e.g., the speaker uses it in 86-1 and 86-2 to introduce the two protagonists of her story) as well as at all subsequent mentions (e.g., in 86-4).

(86) 1. *murl masirini qatit*
murl ***ma**=sirini* *ka=tit*
distantly ART.ID=NAME 3SG.M.SBJ=go.CONT
'in the past, Sirini was going' (N11AESSIRINI-0001)

2. *bqasik nemasinavragulengga*
be=ka=sik
CONJ=3SG.M.SBJ=climb.NCONT
*ne=**ma**=sinap=ara=guleng-ka*
from/with=ART.ID=NAME=3SG.F.POSS=malay.apple-SG.M
'and he climbed into Sinap's malay apple tree' (N11AESSIRINI-0002)

3. *beqats.. amaguleng*
be=ka=tes.. *ama=guleng*
CONJ=3SG.M.SBJ=eat.CONT ART=malay.apple
'and he ate.. malay apples' (N11AESSIRINI-0003)

4. *de ma: amagamga qaat, menemasinavraarlembem*
de *ma:* *ama=gam-ka* *ka=at,*
CONJ thus ART=seed-SG.M 3SG.M.SBJ=fall.NCONT
*men=**ma**=sinap=ara=arlem-em*
at=ART.ID=NAME=3SG.F.POSS=thigh-SG.RCD
'and it happened like this: a seed fell, onto Sinap's thigh' (N11AESSIRINI-0004FF)

Speakers also choose the article *ma* 'ART.ID' when they present a common noun as a personal name. For example, *ma* in (87) indicates that *quldit* 'frog' functions as a personal name. Speakers have some freedom, though, and they can choose to not conceptualize them as personal names. This was, for example, the case in (85) above: the use of the article *ama* 'ART' indicates that *miu-ki* 'cat-SG.F' and *qasup-ka* 'rat-SG.M' are used as descriptive nouns, not as proper nouns.

(87) *ianmerianiaik maquldit*
ian=mat=iane-ia-ki ***ma**=quldit*
3DU.SBJ=take.NCONT.PST=3DU.POSS-other-SG.F ART.ID=frog
'they picked up their friend Frog' (R12ABDFROG-008)

A similar distribution is observed with locations. The article *ma* 'ART.ID' obligatorily occurs with place names (as in 88a), but speakers can also choose to mark unnamed locations with this article, thereby presenting them as inherently identifiable (as in 88b).

(88) a. *kurluriara vet marlaunsepna*
kurli-ut=iara *pet* ***ma**=rlaunsepna*
leave-1PL=PROX on/under ART.ID=NAME
'we stay here in Raunsepna' (AMB-29/06/2015)

b. *ip nyinarlip samarlaunnga, deqerl nyatit sep maqavel*
ip *nyi=narlip* *se=ama=rlaun-ka,*
PURP 2SG.SBJ.NPST=like:PURP to/with=ART=netbag-SG.M
de=kerl *nya=tit* *se=pe* ***ma**=qavel*
CONJ=DEONT 2SG.SBJ=go.CONT to/with=PLACE ART.ID=bush
'if you want (to start weaving) a netbag, you should go to the bush' (P12ARSBILUM1-008FF)

Again, as with common nouns used as proper names, speakers can alternatively choose to mark such locations with the general article *ama*. For example, the speaker in (89) below first introduces the location by means of *ama* (in 89-1), then uses *ma* (in 89-2), and then shifts back to *ama* (89-3).

(89) 1. *katra bqatit bqatit bqatit bqatit bqatit besagelama.. akainaqi*
ka=tit=a *be=ka=tit*
3SG.M.SBJ=go.CONT=DIST CONJ=3SG.M.SBJ=go.CONT
be=ka=tit *be=ka=tit*
CONJ=3SG.M.SBJ=go.CONT CONJ=3SG.M.SBJ=go.CONT
be=ka=tit *be=ka=tit*
CONJ=3SG.M.SBJ=go.CONT CONJ=3SG.M.SBJ=go.CONT
*be=se=gel=***ama..** *a=kaina-ki*
CONJ=to/with=near=ART NM=water-SG.F
'he went and went and went and went and went and went until the.. the water' (N11AAGSIRINIROPE-0002FF)

2. *dap makainaqi luqia, de idequas tamrarlik*
dap ***ma***=*kaina-ki* *lu-ki-a,* *de* *ide=kuasik*
but ART.ID=water-SG.F DEM-SG.F-DIST CONJ IPFV=NEG
ta=mrarlik
3PL.SBJ=cross.NCONT.PST
'but that water, they cannot cross it' (N11AAGSIRINIROPE-0004)
3. *keks amakainaqi luqia, deama.. ahlurlki*
ka=kias ***ama***=*kaina-ki* *lu-ki-a,*
3SG.M.SBJ=actually ART=water-SG.F DEM-SG.F-DIST
de=ama.. *a=slurl-ki*
CONJ=ART NM=big-SG.F
'that water actually, it is.. a big one' (N11AAGSIRINIROPE-0005)

Similarly, the article *ma* 'ART.ID' occurs in naming contexts, e.g., with the interrogative pronoun *gi* 'what' (see section 3.2.4): in such contexts, the speaker has identified an object and now asks for its name (as in 90a). But again, the speaker can alternatively choose to use the general article *ama* 'ART' instead (as in 90b).

(90) a. *dap maginget mara?*
dap ***ma***=*gi-nget* *mara?*
but ART.ID=what-N here
'and what are these (things) here?' (LONGYDS20150506_1-326)
b. *singan, amagiqiara?*
singan, ***ama***=*gi-ki=iara?*
NAME ART=what-SG.F=PROX
'Singan, what is this here?' (LONGYDS20150506_1-278)

The articles are only absent if determiners with more specific meanings are available. In particular, given that both articles, *ama* 'ART' and *ma* 'ART.ID', also occur in specific-indefinite contexts (e.g., at first mention), there is overlap with the indefinite pronouns and articles. They differ, however, in that their meanings are more restricted: *qa* 'some' and *qama* 'some' single out a subset from a set of identifiable referents; *ia* 'other' marks a referent as similar to another referent; and *ngama* 'some.NSPEC' occurs with non-specific referents. Speakers can thus select from a large number of determiners to frame referents in subtly different ways. This possibility is illustrated by means of the contrastive examples below. They come from the same story, and they both represent direct speech from two different protagonists (the rat in 91a, and the cat in 91b), talking about the same event. But the narrator chooses different articles, thereby framing the referent as specific-indefinite in (91a) (through the use of *ama* 'ART') but as non-specific in (91b) (through the use of *ngama* 'some.NSPEC').

(91) a. *de div uneberltiq amadaqa*
de *dip* *une=berltik* ***ama**=da-ka*
CONJ FUT 1DU.SBJ.NPST=loosen:SIDE ART=taro-SG.M
'and we will pick a taro' (N12BAMCAT-072)

b. *ip.. div undrangamadaqa*
ip.. *dip* *un=tat=a=**ngama**=da-ka*
PURP FUT 1DU.SBJ=take.CONT=NM=some.NSPEC=taro-SG.M
'and.. we will pick a taro' (N12BAMCAT-082)

In their second use, both articles connect a pre-head demonstrative or indefinite pronoun to the noun. The choice between *ama* 'ART' and *ma* 'ART.ID' follows the same principles as in their first use. For example, *ama* 'ART' precedes a common noun in (92a), while *ma* 'ART.ID' precedes a proper noun in (92b). Note, however, that *ma* 'ART.ID' is very rare in this function, as proper nouns usually do not occur with a demonstrative or indefinite pronoun.

(92) a. *de saqika iaqamqaqraqa*
de *saqi-ka* *ia-ka=**ama**=qaqera-ka*
CONJ again-3SG.M other-SG.M=ART=person-SG.M
'and he is also a (kind of) person' (D12ADKSPIRITS-053)

b. *iak masirini*
ia-ka ***ma**=sirini*
other-SG.M ART.ID=NAME
'there was a Sirini' (N11AAGSIRINILOBSTER1-0001)

Finally, there is a third context in which the article *ama* 'ART' marks post-head modifiers that have a qualifying or quantifying function. This includes adjectives (in 93a), nouns (in 93b) and numerals (in 93c) (see section 3.4).

(93) a. *div undit savramaqerleng amabarlnget*
dip *un=tit* *se=pet=ama=qerleng*
FUT 1DU.SBJ=go.CONT to/with=on/under=ART=fallow.garden
***ama**=barl-nget*
ART=big-N
'let us go to the big place' (N12BAMCAT-030)

b. *damarlaun, de tika idremsem nama.. amakaasiq amalangik*
de=ama=rlaun, *de* *tika* *ide=te=msem*
CONJ=ART=netbag CONJ EMPH IPFV=3PL.SBJ.NPST=weave.CONT
ne=ama.. *ama=kaasik* ***ama**=langik*
from/with=ART ART=vine ART=vine
'and netbags, they usually weave them from the.. the *langik* vines' (P12ARSBILUM2-016)

c. *kuasiqi amaqaqeraqa amaqunaska*
kuasik=i ama=qaqera-ka ***ama**=qunas-ka*
NEG=SIM ART=person-SG.M ART=one-SG.M
'she is not just one person' (I12AANACLADNSocio3-489)

This third use is restricted to the article *ama* 'ART'. This article is even found in contexts where the head noun is marked by another determiner, e.g., by the article *ma* 'ART.ID' (as in 94).

(94) *saqika masevaqesep, de ma.. sevaqesev amaquatka, demasevaqesev amananngi*
saqi-ka ma=sevaqesep, de ***ma**.. sevaqesep*
again-3SG.M ART.ID=NAME CONJ ART.ID NAME
***ama**=quat-ka, de=**ma**=sevaqesep* ***ama**=nan-ki*
ART=man-SG.M CONJ=ART.ID=NAME ART=woman-SG.F
'and also the Sevaqesep (spirit), there is the.. male Sevaqesep, and there is the female Sevaqesep' (D12ADKSpirits-097ff)

There are a handful of examples of *ma* 'ART.ID' occurring in this position, but they most likely constitute fixed expressions. For example, *tik mamerl* 'right' (from *tik ma=merl* 'side ART.ID=right') contains the article *ma* 'ART.ID'. But note that when it functions as a post-head modifier, the expression as a whole is marked by *ama* 'ART' (as in 95a). Another example is the modifier *mauqas* 'different', which is very likely formed from *ma=uqas* 'ART.ID=difference' (as in 95b) (see section 3.4.2 for details on this modifier).

(95) a. *dap.. giangariqis amrik mamerles*
dap.. gia=ngarik-es ***ama**=rik* ***ma**=merl-es*
but 2SG.POSS=hand-SG.FLAT ART=side ART.ID=right-SG.FLAT
'but.. your right branch' (N11AJNGenaingmetBrothers-0037)
b. *ngenenamaqaqet mauqas*
ngene-ne=ama=qaqera ***ma**=uqas*
2PL.ASSOC-from/with=ART=person ART.ID=difference
'you are together with different people' (I12AANACLADNSocio3-065)

In addition, there are cases where a noun is followed by a name marked with the article *ma* 'ART.ID'. I tentatively analyze such cases not as modification, but as two noun phrases in apposition. This analysis is supported by a number of examples where there is a prosodic break between the two nouns (as in 96a). Nevertheless, there are also cases without conclusive prosodic evidence (as in 96b).

It is possible that idiomatic expressions (such as the ones illustrated in 95 above) reflect an older stage of the language where *ama* 'ART' and *ma* 'ART.ID' were both able to introduce post-head modifiers. Supporting evidence for this possibility comes from Mali, where the cognate forms can both mark post-head modifiers (Stebbins 2011: 263–271).

(96) a. *de tika idraavu sagel raaqalatka, magenainymetkini*
de *tika* *ide=araa=vu* *se=gel*
CONJ EMPH IPFV=3PL.POSS=bad to/with=near
araa=qalat-ka, ***ma***=*genainymetkini*
3PL.POSS=younger.sibling-SG.M ART.ID=NAME:SG.F:SG.DIM
'and there used to be their badness towards their younger brother, Genainymetkini (i.e., they behaved badly towards him)' (N12AMVGENAINGMETBROTHERS-015)

b. *amaningamga magenainymetkini*
ama=ningam-ka ***ma***=*genainymetkini*
ART=younger.sibling-SG.M ART.ID=NAME:SG.F:SG.DIM
'the younger brother Genainymetkini' (N11AJNGENAINGMETBROTHERS-0068)

(iii) Indefinite articles

Qaqet has two indefinite articles: *qama* 'some' and *ngama* 'some.NSPEC'. Different from the indefinite pronouns (discussed in section 3.3.3), the indefinite articles cannot occur pronominally and they do not agree in noun class with the head noun. But indefinite articles and pronouns also share similarities: both occur as adnominal determiners (obligatorily in the case of the articles, and optionally in the case of the pronouns), they share an indefinite meaning and the two parts of speech thus cannot co-occur, and the article *qama* 'some' very likely developed diachronically from the pronoun *qa* 'some'.

Both articles are invariably preceded by either the noun marker *a* or a possessor index (see the examples below). As discussed in section 3.3.3, this distribution is suggestive of a nominal origin. The articles themselves are likely to be morphologically complex, consisting of a root (*qa* 'some' and *nga* 'some.NSPEC') plus the article *ama*. The root *qa* 'some' is also attested as the root of an indefinite pronoun, while *nga* 'some.NSPEC' is not attested elsewhere in Qaqet. But both *ngama* and *nga* are found as indefinite articles in Mali (Stebbins 2011: 170–171), thus supporting the idea that Qaqet *ngama* is morphologically complex, too.

The article *qama* 'some' has the same meaning as the indefinite pronoun *qa* 'some': it singles out subsets of an established referent, and it is attested in both affirmative (in 97a) and negative (in 97b) contexts. It is at present not clear which factors determine the distribution of *qama* 'some' as compared to that of *qa* 'some'. In terms of frequency, *qa* 'some' almost always occurs as a pronoun, but when it occurs as an adnominal determiner, it seems to occur in exactly the same contexts as *qama* 'some'.

(97) a. *ip kuarik, kelaqamanirlaqiivuq imamudemgi, de quasik*
ip *kua=arik,* *ke=lu=*
PURP INTRG=supposing 3SG.M.SBJ.NPST=see.NCONT=
*=a=**qama**=nirla-ki=i-vuk* *i=ma=mudem-ki,*
=NM=some=sun-SG.F=AWAY-up SIM=ART.ID=resin-SG.F
de *kuasik*
CONJ NEG
'supposing he can see some light up there, from the bush lamp, but no' (N11AAGBROTHERS-0053)

b. *de quas untal unaqamesmes*
de *kuasik* *un=tal* *una=**qama**=smes*
CONJ NEG 1DU.SBJ=carry.CONT 1DU.POSS=some=food
'we didn't carry any of our food' (N12BAMCAT-175)

The second indefinite article *ngama* 'some.NSPEC' is used with non-specific referents, e.g., the speaker in (98) has no specific language in mind. Given this meaning, the article very frequently (but not exclusively; see example 91b above) co-occurs with question words. It cannot occur in negative contexts.

(98) *ngulu nyitaqen angamalengiqa nana?*
ngu=lu *nyi=taqen* *a=**ngama**=lengi-ka*
1SG.SBJ.NPST=see.NCONT 2SG.SBJ.NPST=say.CONT NM=some.NSPEC=word-SG.M
nana?
what
'I see you speak whatever language?' (I12ABLAJLATASOCIO3-164)

The two indefinite articles are similar in meaning, differing only in specificity. The article *ngama* 'some.NSPEC' codes non-specificity as part of its meaning, while *qama* 'some' and the pronoun *qa* 'some' are probably neutral with respect to specificity: they almost always occur with specific readings, but seem to be compatible with non-specific readings, too – especially in negative contexts (as in example 75b above).

3.4 Modification

There are three possible structures for introducing modifiers to the noun phrase (summarized in Table 36, and illustrated with contrastive examples in 103a to 103c below): (i) the modifier construction (section 3.4.1), (ii) the nominal modifier construction (section 3.4.2) and (iii) prepositional phrases and directionals (section 3.4.3). In the modifier construction, the modifier is usually (but not always) an adjective root, which occurs post-head and agrees in noun class and number with the head. Noun roots are also attested in the modifier construction, but they most commonly occur in the nominal modifier construction. These two constructions are similar in form, and there are individual lexemes that cannot unambiguously be assigned to one or the other (discussed in section 3.4.2). Mali Baining has similar structures (Stebbins 2011: 264–280), but their distribution differs considerably: in Mali, they are used to form relative clauses and they have additional functions outside of the noun phrase.

In addition to the two modifier constructions, Qaqet also allows for prepositional phrases and directionals to modify nouns. Given their modifying function, they are discussed in this section, but their form differs considerably from that of the other two constructions.

Tab. 36: Modifiers within the noun phrase

	Structure	**Modifier**	**Agreement**
i	head + *ama* 'ART' + modifier	adjective (verb?, noun?)	yes
ii	head + *ama* 'ART' + modifier + preposition + pronoun	noun	no
iii	head + modifier	prepositional phrase, directional	no

Modifiers can co-occur, but they only rarely do so. In natural discourse, speakers clearly disprefer complex noun phrases, and they tend to prosodically and syntactically separate phrases containing more than one modifying or determining element (see section 3.3.2 for a discussion). There are thus hardly any natural examples of noun phrases with more than one modifier, and eliciting them also proved to be difficult. Among the small number of attested examples, all possible constituent orders are found. For example, prepositional phrases and directionals seem to preferably occur at the end, e.g., following the quantifying adjective *qunaski* 'one' in (99a) or the quantifying noun *depguas nara* 'three (of them)' in (99b). But there are also examples like (99c), where the pronominal head *lura* 'those ones' is followed first by a prepositional phrase and then by a quantifying noun.

(99) a. *amangerlnanda retaing amatainggi amaqunaski nama.. amiin*
ama=ngerlnan-ta te=taing [ama=taing-ki
ART=woman-PL.H 3PL.SBJ.NPST=sing.CONT ART=song-SG.F
*ama=qunas-ki ne=ama.. a=miin]*NP
ART=one-SG.F from/with=ART NM=dance
'the women are singing [one.. church song (lit. one song of dance)]NP'
(ARN-04/05/2015)

b. *adrlem ngamit samarluis amadepguas nara nep magreid eit bramit savrama sekonderi skul*
a=drlem *nga=mit* *se=[ama=rluis* *ama=depguas*
NM=know 3N.SBJ=go.NCONT.PST to/with=ART=child ART=three
ne-ta *ne=pe* *ma=greid* *eit]*NP,
from/with-3PL.H from/with=PLACE ART.ID=grade eight
be=ta=mit *se=pet=ama*
CONJ=3PL.SBJ=go.NCONT.PST to/with=on/under=ART
sekonderi *skul*
secondary school
'knowledge came to [three students from grade 8]NP and they went to secondary school' (ASS-01/06/2015)

c. *deip madsagel.. lura naimanev amadepguah nara*
de=ip *maget=de=se=gel..* *[lu-ta-a*
CONJ=PURP then=CONJ=to/with=near DEM-PL.H-DIST
ne=i-manep *ama=depguas* *ne-ta]*NP
from/with=AWAY-down ART=three from/with-3PL.H
'and then on to.. [those three (brothers) below (lit. of going down)]NP' (N11AJNGENAINGMETBROTHERS-0152)

All three types of modifiers almost always occur post-head, but there are a few examples of pre-head modifiers: (100a) illustrates a pre-head quantifying adjective, and (100b), a pre-head quantifying noun.

(100) a. *nyines amaqunaska amamuliqa merama kapka*
nyi=nes ***[ama=qunas-ka*** *ama=muli-ka]*NP
2SG.SBJ.NPST=put.in.CONT ART=one-SG.M ART=orange-SG.M
met=ama *kap-ka*
in=ART cup-SG.M
'put [one orange]NP into the cup' (AJL&ADN-28/04/15)

b. *mani ngualu aburlem nara amaqaqet iamaqurlek prara*
mani *ngua=lu* ***[a=burlem*** ***ne-ta***
recently 1SG.SBJ=see.NCONT NM=many from/with-3PL.H
*ama=qaqera]*NP *i=ama=qurlek* *pet-ta*
ART=person SIM=ART=anger on/under-3PL.H
'yesterday I saw [many people]NP, and they were angry (lit. anger was on them)' (ABL&AAN-11/05/15)

Similarly, both sentences below were offered as good descriptions of the same scenario, one containing a post-head adjective (101a), and the other, a pre-head adjective (101b).

(101) a. *mani ngupaikmet de ngualu iaqiamaavetki amaslurlki*
mani *ngu=paikmet* *de* *ngua=lu*
recently 1SG.SBJ.NPST=walk.CONT CONJ 1SG.SBJ=see.NCONT
[*ia-ki=ama=avet-ki* ***ama=slurl-ki***]NP
other-SG.F=ART=house-SG.F ART=big-SG.F
'I was walking around and saw [a big house]NP' (AJL-09/05/2012)

b. *mani ngupaikmet de ngualu iaqiamaslurlki amaavetki*
mani *ngu=paikmet* *de* *ngua=lu*
recently 1SG.SBJ.NPST=walk.CONT CONJ 1SG.SBJ=see.NCONT
[*ia-ki=**ama=slurl-ki*** *ama=avet-ki*]NP
other-SG.F=ART=big-SG.F ART=house-SG.F
'I was walking around and saw [a big house]NP' (AJL-09/05/2012)

In metalinguistic discussions, speakers suggested that post-head modifiers have a relative clause structure (i.e., 'the house that is big' in 101a above), while pre-head modifiers have an adjectival structure (i.e., 'the big house' in 101b). Such an interpretation could potentially be supported by comparative evidence: the corresponding structures in Mali admit not only individual lexemes, but also verbal and non-verbal clauses, and Stebbins (2011: 263–270) analyzes them as relative clauses. For Qaqet, however, the situation is different. Neither of the two modifier constructions admits clauses. And even though verb roots can occur as modifiers, they cannot co-occur with any of their arguments or clausal particles.

The only partial exception is the nominal modifier construction whose structure is similar to that of the non-verbal equative construction. The parallel examples below illustrate this similarity. Example (102a) features an equative clause, where the nominal predicate *depguas* 'three' is followed by the subject, which is marked by the preposition *ne* 'from/with'. And example (102b) features the nominal modifier construction, where the head noun *qaqera* 'person' is followed by the article *ama*, the noun *depguas* 'three', the preposition *ne* 'from/with', and a pronoun that is co-referential with the head noun. Given this similarity, it is possible that the equative clause constituted the source for the nominal modifier construction. The two differ, however, in that the equative clause (like all clauses) can be marked with particles (such as *saqi* 'again/also' in 102a), but the nominal modifier cannot.

(102) a. *bsaqi amademguas nara*
be=saqi [*ama=depguas*]PRED [*ne-ta*]SBJ
CONJ=again ART=three from/with-3PL.H
'and they are three again' (R12ABDFROG-134)

b. *amasiitkaira, de savrama.. aqaqeramadepguas nara*
ama=siit-ka=iara, *de* *se=pet=[ama..*
ART=story-SG.M=PROX CONJ to/with=on/under=ART
a=qaqera=ama=depguas *ne-ta*]NP
NM=person=ART=three from/with-3PL.H
'there is a story here, it goes to [th.. three people]NP' (R12ABDFROG-001FF)

Different from Mali, the Qaqet modifiers thus cannot be analyzed as clauses. And I suspect that the metalinguistic comments above reflect the word order of English rather than the underlying Qaqet structure. The comments were made by speakers who are fluent in English, and it cannot be ruled out that they equated the Qaqet post-head and pre-head adjectives with, respectively, the English post-head relative clause and pre-head adjective translation.

It is possible that the different orders allow speakers to adopt different perspectives on a situation. This point is illustrated below with the help of property concepts. Qaqet lexicalizes such concepts in both adjectives and nouns (see also section 3.4.1): different properties allow for one or the other or both. In (103a) and (103b), the properties are expressed in the post-head adjective *sesek* 'light' (in the modifier construction) and in the post-head noun *qesep-ka* 'heaviness-SG.M' (in the nominal modifier construction). In (103c), by contrast, the property is expressed in the abstract head noun *merlen-ka* 'heaviness-SG.M', which precedes a prepositional phrase (expressing the location of this concept). Discussions with speakers suggest that example (103c) focuses on the property, i.e., on the heaviness. In the other two examples, by contrast, the focus is on the referent (with the property characterizing this referent). It is possible that pre-head modifiers (as in the examples above) allow for a similar shift in perspective, i.e., an emphasis on the property, not on the referent. But this hypothesis would need further investigation.

(103) a. *tatal amaquvang amaseseknget*
ta=tal *[ama=quvang* *ama=**sesek**-nget*]NP
3PL.SBJ=carry.CONT ART=cargo ART=light-N
'they were carrying [a light cargo]NP' (ABL&AAN-11/05/2015)

b. *tatal amamengga amaqesepka vemga*
ta=tal *[ama=meng-ka* *ama=**qesep**-ka*
3PL.SBJ=carry.CONT ART=wood-SG.M ART=heaviness-SG.M
pe-ka]NP
PLACE-3SG.M
'they were carrying [a heavy tree]NP' (ABL&AAN-11/05/2015)

c. tatal amamerlennga vamaquvang
ta=tal *[ama=**merlen**-ka* *pe=ama=quvang]*NP
3PL.SBJ=carry.CONT ART=heaviness-SG.M PLACE=ART=cargo
'they were carrying [a heavy cargo]NP (lit. the heaviness in the cargo)' (ABL&AAN-11/05/2015)

3.4.1 Adjectives and the modifier construction

Adjectives constitute a distinct word class in Qaqet: although they share morphosyntactic similarities with nouns and they can freely convert to nouns, there are formal differences that justify setting up a distinct class (see section 3.1.1 for a discussion of similarities and differences).

The characteristic functions of adjectives are their occurrence as modifiers in the modifier construction and as non-verbal predicates in the attributive construction. For example, *barl* 'big' functions as a modifier in (104a): it follows the head noun, it is preceded by the article *ama*, and it is overtly marked for neuter noun class (agreeing with the unmarked plural noun *ltany* 'embers'). In (104b), the same adjective functions as a non-verbal predicate. As a predicate, it has an invariant form, e.g., it does not take neuter noun class in (104b), despite the subject being *galip* 'peanut' (i.e., an unmarked plural noun) (see chapter 8.2.4 for details of the attributive construction).

(104) a. *ditika giamengga, de nani amaltany amabarlnget, ngatdang*
de=tika *gia=meng-ka,* *de* *nani*
CONJ=EMPH 2SG.POSS=wood-SG.M CONJ can
[ama=ltany *ama=**barl**-nget]*NP, *nga=tdang*
ART=embers ART=big-N 3N.SBJ=burn.CONT
'there's your tree, and there can be a big fire, it burns' (P12ADNFIRE-037)

b. *medama.. ambarla.. ambarl.. ambarl amagaliva*
medu=ama.. *ama=barl=ama..* *ama=barl..*
past=ART ART=big=ART ART=big
*[ama=**barl**]*PRED *[ama=galip]*SBJ=a
ART=big ART=peanut=DIST
'the peanuts were b.. b.. b.. big' (D12ABDACPGARDEN-042)

In the modifier construction, the modifier obligatorily agrees in noun class and number with the head noun. In the case of unmarked plural head nouns, it takes either overt neuter agreement (in the case of non-human nouns) (as in 104a above) or plural human agreement (in the case of human nouns) (see chapter 4.2). In all other cases, the agreement suffix is identical to that of the noun class suffix on the noun. For example, *gil* 'small' takes the suffix *-irang* 'PL.DIM' in (105a) (agreeing with the diminutive plural head noun *quldit-irang* 'frog-PL.DIM'), and the suffix *-ini* 'SG.DIM' in (105b) (agreeing with the diminutive singular head noun *rleken-ini* 'branch-SG.DIM').

(105) a. *de iantaqamnyim savrama.. amaquldirirang amagilirang*

de *ian=taqa=mnyim*

CONJ 3DU.SBJ=properly.CONT=look.CONT

se=pet=[ama.. *ama=**quldit-irang*** *ama=**gil-irang**]*NP

to/with=on/under=ART ART=frog-PL.DIM ART=small-PL.DIM

'and they looked properly to [the.. the little frogs]NP' (R12ACMFROG-111FF)

b. *de saqika qiraqanbin menianamarlekenini ama.. agilini, dequas kiraqanbin senas*

de *saqi-ka* *ki=raqa=nbin*

CONJ again-3SG.M 3SG.F.SBJ.NPST=properly.NCONT=C.step

*men=[ia-ini=ama=**rleken-ini*** *ama..* *a=**gil-ini**]*NP,

at=other-SG.DIM=ART=branch-SG.DIM ART NM=small-SG.DIM

de=kuasik *ki=raqa=nbin* *se-nas*

CONJ=NEG 3SG.F.SBJ.NPST=properly.NCONT=C.step to/with-self

'again she tried to step properly on [another little.. branch]NP, but she does not step properly' (N11AAGSIRINIROPE-0135)

The modifier in this construction is almost always an adjective root (as in 104a, 105a and 105b above), but there are also examples of verb and noun roots. Such cases are infrequent, though, and it was not always possible to discern general semantic patterns. In the case of verb roots, there are a number of modifiers formed from state-change verbs (such as *nyip* 'die.NCONT'), which can easily be construed as conveying properties of referents (such as *NOUN amanyip* 'a dead NOUN'). But there are also unexpected examples, e.g., a modifier formed from the verb *qelak* '(carry.on.)shoulder.NCONT' in (106a), describing the location of the head noun's referent. If the verb has different aspectual stems, the modifier is always formed from the non-continuous stem. In the case of noun roots, a few salient semantic patterns emerge: nouns expressing gender, some abstract concepts (as in 106b), and (possibly) part/whole and type/token relationships. Synchronically, I tentatively analyze such cases as conversions of verbs or nouns to adjectives (see section 3.4.2 for a discussion and examples).

(106) a. *amangerlnanngi kital amaqalunnga amaqelaka*
ama=ngerlnan-ki ki=tal
ART=woman-SG.F 3SG.F.SBJ.NPST=carry.CONT
[*ama=qalun-ka ama=**qelak**-ka*]NP
ART=singapore-SG.M ART=shoulder.NCONT-SG.M
'the woman carries [the singapore taro on the shoulders]NP' (AMI-15/06/2015)

b. *tika masinepki amarevanngi*
tika [*ma=sinepki ama=**revan**-ki*]NP
EMPH ART.ID=NAME:SG.F ART=truth-SG.F
'he's now [a true Sinepki]NP' (N12ABKSIRINI-078)

Qaqet adjectives are thus defined by their distribution in the modifier and attributive constructions. Other morphosyntactic properties that are cross-linguistically commonly associated with adjectives are not relevant in Qaqet. In particular, Qaqet adjectives do not have comparative or superlative forms, and there is no dedicated comparative construction. Instead, comparative or superlative interpretations are left to inference. For example, the noun *dlek* 'strength' occurs as the subject of the non-verbal locative construction in (107a). It receives a superlative interpretation through the context (a competition between the wind and the sun, which is won by the sun) and through narrowing down the field to two participants (through the prepositional phrase *nameniam* 'among the two'). But nothing in the noun or in the construction entails a comparative or superlative interpretation. For example, the same noun occurs in the locative construction in (107b): this time, there is no comparative context, and therefore no comparative interpretation arises. Although, given the right context (e.g., a comparison of stories of the past with stories of the present, with the past stories being portrayed as 'stronger'), a comparative interpretation would become possible.

(107) a. *amanirlaqa, iqa de amadlek, praqa, nameniam*
ama=nirla-ka, i=ka de [*ama=**dlek***]SBJ,
ART=sun-SG.M SIM=3SG.M CONJ ART=strength
[*pet-ka*]PRED, *ne=men-iam*
on/under-3SG.M from/with=at-3DU.M
'the sun, it is it (the sun) which is the strongest of the two (lit. strength is on it among the two)' (L12ATANORTHWIND-020)

b. *de murl amadlek pamasiit*
de murl [*ama=**dlek***]SBJ [*pe=ama=siit*]PRED
CONJ distantly ART=strength PLACE=ART=story
'and the stories were strong (lit. strength was on the stories)' (I12AANACLADNSOCIO3-356)

Furthermore, there is no dedicated form or construction for conveying gradability in adjectives. Instead, speakers use particles (see chapter 7). For example, the speaker in (108) uses the particle *naka* 'bit' twice, first with a verbal clause, and then with a noun converted from an adjective. Different from Mali (Stebbins 2011: 61–66), Qaqet also does not reduplicate adjectives to express intensification.

(108) *ikatika nakairang ngererl saqamarimirang inaka amagilirang*
ip=ka=tika ***naka**=irang* *ngere=rerl*
PURP=3SG.M.SBJ=EMPH bit=PL.DIM 3N.SBJ.NPST=straighten.NCONT
se=a=qama=rim-irang *i=**naka*** *ama=gil-irang*
to/with=NM=some=taro-PL.DIM SIM=bit ART=small-PL.DIM
'and they (peanuts) grow a bit big among the taros, which are (still) a bit small' (D12ABDACPGARDEN-031)

Like Mali (Stebbins 2011: 63–66), Qaqet has a large adjective class: there are around 50 attested adjectives, mostly from the semantic types of dimension (e.g., *barl* 'big'), physical property (e.g., *ilas* 'raw'), color (e.g., *nguin* 'red'), age (e.g., *srlu* 'old') and value (e.g., *tlu* 'good'). Note that the converse does not hold true: the same semantic types are also lexicalized in abstract nouns. In some cases, an adjective converts to an abstract noun, e.g., *lkuil* 'heavy (adj.), heaviness (n.)'. In other cases, only a noun is available, e.g., the concept of 'hot' can only be expressed by a noun (*uilas* 'hotness') – while its antonym 'cold' can either be expressed by an adjective (*uis* 'cold') or a (related) noun (*uises* 'coldness').

Semantic types other than the five above are only rarely lexicalized in adjectives. There are some human propensity adjectives (e.g., *rlem* 'sad'), but this type is mostly lexicalized in abstract nouns. Furthermore, the numeral *qunas* 'one/two' is an adjective, while the higher numerals and quantifiers are nouns (see section 3.2.2). There are also some nouns that are in the process of converting into adjectives: nouns denoting gender (e.g., *quat* 'man, male') and different kinds of abstract concepts (e.g., *revan* 'truth, true') (see section 3.4.2). Furthermore, there is one complex adjective: *rik mamerl* 'right', which probably originated in a nominal expression (*tik ma=merl* 'side ART.ID=right'). Its opposite *ruarl* 'left' is a straightforward adjective.

The adjective class is an open class that admits new members. In particular, there are many color adjectives that are very likely recruited from nouns with concrete reference, e.g., *anes* 'green (adj.), parrot (n.)', *qalun* 'black (adj.), singapore taro (n.)', *qerlkerlek* 'red (adj.), blood (n.)' or *quirim* 'brown (adj.), type of taro (n.)'.[13] Other adjectives have entered the language through borrowing, e.g., some speakers use the adjective *maria* 'red' in reference to the skin color of white people – which originated

13 Although Qaqet has a large number of color adjectives, only *lauil* 'white', *nguin* 'red' and *su* 'black' have no known nominal origin.

in the name *Maria* (from the Virgin Mary). Nominal origins are also likely for adjectives from other semantic types, e.g., the adjective *rlan* 'satisfied' probably originated in the relational noun *rlan* 'inside'. Regardless of their origins, all present-day adjectives share the above morphosyntactic properties that set them apart from nouns.

It is currently possible to observe the development of a new adjective *belhat* 'huge', a borrowing from Tok Pisin (originally from *bel hat* 'hot belly', with the meaning of 'angry, impatient', but now used in local Tok Pisin with the meaning of 'huge'). In Qaqet, it frequently occurs in its own intonation unit, without adjectival or nominal morphology (as in 109a). That is, its distribution resembles that of interjections – except that it is also not uncommon for it to be marked for some nominal categories (e.g., for associative plural in 109b). In addition, there are a good number of examples where it occurs in apposition to a head noun (as in 109c): it always takes the expected article *ama* – yet there tends to be a prosodic break between the two constituents, and it does not agree with the common noun (e.g., we would expect the form *belhat-ka* 'huge-SG.M' in (109c), agreeing with the masculine singular head noun). First signs of a noun phrase structure and incipient agreement appear in contexts of the associative plural: this plural is always marked on the adjective, while the noun appears in its unmarked form (see chapter 4.2.3). For example, the associative plural appears on *belhat* in (109d), thus suggesting that it forms a syntactic unit with the preceding noun. Finally, there are a handful of examples where *belhat* is attested with full morphology, e.g., the form in (109e) is indistinguishable from that of a Qaqet adjective converted into a referential noun. It is likely that this synchronic variation points to an ongoing process whereby a non-inflecting borrowed word is gradually being integrated into the class of adjectives.

(109) a. *belhat*
belhat
huge
'huge' (LONGYDS20150516_1-158)

b. *lungetmara, belhatkena*
lu-nget=mara, ***belhat****-kena*
DEM-N=here huge-ASSOC.M
'these ones here, huge ones' (LONGYDS20150516_1-081)

c. *ani, giavaqa ambatariqa, ambelhat, nagelngua*
ani, gia=va-ka=a ama=batari-ka,
here 2SG.POSS=thingy-SG.M=DIST ART=battery-SG.M
*ama=****belhat****, ne=gel-ngua*
ART=huge from/with=near-1SG
'here, (take) your battery, the huge one, from me'
(LONGYDS20150516_2-082)

d. *aquukuq amabelhatkena*
a=quukuk *ama=**belhat**-kena*
NM=sweet.potato ART=huge-ASSOC.M
'huge sweet potatoes' (LONGYDS20150516_1-228)

e. *arsangaiama, taquarl giaiam amasakngaiam, abelhatkiam*
ara=saqang-iam=a, *taquarl* *gi-ia-iam*
3SG.F.POSS=eye-DU.M=DIST thus 2SG.POSS-other-DU.M
ama=saqang-iam, *a=**belhat**-k*[14]*-iam*
ART=eye-DU.M NM=huge-??-DU.M
'its two eyes there, just like your two eyes, huge ones' (LONGYDS20150516_1-584)

3.4.2 Nominal modifier construction

The nominal modifier construction allows nouns to occur as modifiers. Like all modifiers, nominal modifiers usually occur post-head and are preceded by the article *ama*. Additionally, they are followed by a prepositional phrase consisting of a preposition and a pronoun that is co-referential with the head noun. For example, the noun *dlek* 'strength' in (110a) modifies the head noun *meng-ka* 'wood-SG.M', preceded by the article *ama* and followed by the preposition *pe* 'on/under' and the pronoun *ka* '3SG.M' (co-referential with the masculine singular head noun). The structure exemplified in (110a) mirrors that of the locative construction, illustrated in (110b): here, the noun *dlek* 'strength' occurs in subject function, and is followed by a prepositional phrase expressing the location. Different prepositions are attested, depending on the kind of locative relationship (see chapter 8.2.2 for the locative construction, and chapter 5.3, for prepositions).

(110) a. *nguarap pamamengga amadlek pemga*
ngua=rap *pe=[ama=meng-ka*
1SG.SBJ=cut.NCONT PLACE=ART=wood-SG.M
ama=dlek *pe-ka]*NP
ART=strength PLACE-3SG.M
'I cut [a strong tree]NP (lit. a tree of strength on it)' (ABL&AAN-09/05/2015)

14 The expected form would be *belhariam* (from *belhat-iam*): the origins of *k* are unknown; but this consonant is also found in some other lexemes, e.g., in the name *Genainymet**k**ini* (the expected form is *Genainymerini*, which does exist as an alternative form). It is possible that it goes back to the noun class suffix *-ki* 'SG.F'.

b. *luqa amaqaqraqa, damadlek praqa*
lu-ka-a *ama=qaqera-ka,* *de=[ama=dlek]*SBJ
DEM-SG.M-DIST ART=person-SG.M CONJ=ART=strength
*[pet-ka]*PRED
on/under-3SG.M
'(as for) that man, he is strong (lit. strength is on him)' (ATA&AEM&ACS-22/06/2011)

Given the formal and semantic similarities, it is likely that the nominal modifier construction originated in a (relativized) non-verbal clause: a (relativized) locative clause (exemplified in the contrastive examples 110a and 110b) or a (relativized) equative clause (exemplified in 102a and 102b above). But as discussed in the introduction to this section, the modifiers cannot be analyzed synchronically as (relativized) clauses.

The nominal modifier construction differs from the modifier construction not only in its internal structure, but also in its agreement properties. There are two potential sites for agreement: the prepositional object and the modifying noun.

First, the prepositional object is a pronoun that is co-referential with the head noun. It thus invariably belongs to the same noun class as the head noun (e.g., masculine singular in 110a and 110b above). Arguably, this pattern can be synchronically analyzed as a case of agreement. That is, we would have to assume a development from a co-referential independent pronoun (functioning as a prepositional object) into an agreement morpheme (overtly marking agreement with the head noun). I cannot currently see a way of verifying or falsifying this analysis, and I therefore tentatively adopt an analysis in terms of co-reference (thus reflecting the diachronic origin).

Second, the modifying noun clearly does not agree with the head noun. It is usually an abstract noun (such as *dlek* 'strength' in the examples above), and hence not marked for noun class (see section 3.2.1 on abstract nouns). When functioning as a modifier, it never agrees with the head noun (e.g., it is not marked for masculine singular in the examples above). Furthermore, there are cases of mismatches between the noun class of the modifying noun and that of the head. This includes a number of abstract nouns that have an inherent noun class. For example, *urlin-ka* 'slipperiness-SG.M' retains its inherent masculine noun class in modifier function: in (111a), it is not marked for neuter noun class to agree with the non-human plural head noun *dul* 'stone' (different from the co-referential pronoun). Similarly, non-abstract nouns in modifier function exhibit overt noun class marking that may differ from that of the head. For example, the kinship noun *rarlim* 'firstborn' is marked for diminutive singular in (111b), even though it functions as a modifier to the masculine singular demonstrative pronoun *luqa* 'DEM:SG.M:DIST'. This demonstrative pronoun is the head of the noun phrase: it controls the masculine singular subject index on the verb, and it triggers the use of the co-referential masculine singular pronoun in the prepositional phrase.

(111) a. *mani nguat pramadul amaurlinnga vranget*
mani *ngua=at* *pet=[ama=dul*
recently 1SG.SBJ=fall.NCONT on/under=ART=stone
*ama=urlin-**ka*** *pet-**nget**]*NP
ART=slipperiness-SG.M on/under-3N
'yesterday I fell down on [the slippery stones]NP' (ABL&AAN-11/05/2015)

b. *ip ma, dluqa amararlimini naqa qeuirl*
ip *maget,* *de=[lu-**ka**-a* *ama=rarlim-**ini***
PURP then CONJ=DEM-SG.M-DIST ART=firstborn-SG.DIM
*ne-**ka**]*NP ***ke**=uirl*
from/with-3SG.M 3SG.M.SBJ.NPST=be.first.NCONT
'then [that firstborn brother]NP goes first' (N11AJNGENAINGMETBROTHERS-0100)

In a few cases, a nominal modifier structure became lexicalized as a complex noun. Sometimes, there is variation: e.g., the expression *rarlim-ini ne-ka* 'firstborn-SG.DIM from/with-3SG.M' is attested both as a nominal modifier (in 111b above) and as a head (in 112a below). And sometimes, only the complex noun is attested: e.g., the expression *lotu pe-ki* 'prayer on/under-3SG.F' (in 112b and 112c) is the conventional way to refer to a church. In the case of all complex nouns, the synchronic status of the diachronic pronouns becomes again an issue: they are the only overt indication of the class of the complex noun (e.g., feminine singular in 112c). By contrast, the class of the noun itself is irrelevant, as it does not control agreement or person indexes: e.g., the complex noun in 112c is feminine singular, and thus triggers the feminine singular possessor index *ara* '3SG.F.POSS' – the noun *lotu* 'prayer' by itself would have triggered the neuter possessor index *ngera* '3N.POSS'. That is, the original pronouns have arguably lost their pronominal status in such lexicalized expressions and developed into noun class suffixes.

(112) a. *sagel amararlimini naqa*
se=gel *ama=**rarlim-ini*** ***ne-ka***
to/with=near ART=firstborn-SG.DIM from/with-3SG.M~SG.M
'on to the firstborn brother' (N11AJNGENAINGMETBROTHERS-0152)

b. *de saqui ide ngutlu iratisavet nama.. amahlurlka aalengiqa vema.. amalotu vemgi*
de sa=kui ide ngu=tlu
CONJ already=quoting IPFV 1SG.SBJ.NPST=see.CONT
i=ta=tisavet ne=ama..
SIM=3PL.SBJ=read.CONT:TO/WITH:ON/UNDER from/with=ART
ama=slurl-ka aa=lengi-ka pe=ma..
ART=big-SG.M 3SG.M.POSS=word-SG.M PLACE=ART.ID
*ama=**lotu** **pe-ki***
ART=prayer PLACE-3SG.F~SG.F
'I say that I already see them reading the.. the word of God in the.. the church' (I12AANACLADNSocio3-239)

c. *utit ursuqup damalotu vemgi ararlan*
*ut=tit ure=suqup de=ama=**lotu***
1PL.SBJ=go.CONT 1PL.SBJ.NPST=sweep LOC.PART=ART=prayer
pe-ki ***ara**=rlan*
PLACE-3SG.F~SG.F 3SG.F.POSS=inside
'we go and sweep inside the church' (ARB-23/06/2015)

Another development leads from nouns in the nominal modifier construction to adjectives in the modifier construction. There are indications that the differences between the two constructions are not as clear-cut as described above, and that individual lexical items can cross over. The first step in such a development is illustrated in the examples below: nominal modifiers such as *burlem* 'many' normally occur with a prepositional phrase (as in 113a), but there are occasional examples without such a phrase (as in 113b).

(113) a. *de amaqaqera amaburlem nara*
*de ama=qaqera ama=**burlem** **ne-ta***
CONJ ART=person ART=many from/with-3PL.H
'(the *Vilan* spirit) is many people' (I12AANACLADNSocio3-490)

b. *bianarluis amaburlem*
*be=iana=rluis ama=**burlem***
CONJ=3DU.POSS=child ART=many
'there are their many children' (R12ADNFrog-337)

As a second step, this variation disappears and the nominal modifier always occurs without a prepositional phrase. This pattern is illustrated with *langik* 'vine' (in 114a and 114b below): this noun belongs to a larger group of nouns that never occur with a prepositional phrase when modifying another noun. Semantically, such nouns often restrict the reference of the head noun to a subset (e.g., *langik* as a subset of vines in 114a and 114b) or a part (e.g., the fruit of a pumpkin, as in 2b in section 3.1.1 above) – but not necessarily so (see the remaining examples below).

(114) a. *de amakaasika amalangika*
de *[ama=kaasik-ka* *ama=**langik**-ka]*NP
CONJ ART=vine-SG.M ART=vine-SG.M
'there's [the *langik* vine]NP' (P12ARSBILUM2-018)

b. *damarlaun, de tika idremsem nama.. amakaasiq amalangik*
de=ama=rlaun, *de* *tika*
CONJ=ART=netbag CONJ EMPH
ide=te=msem *ne=[ama..*
IPFV=3PL.SBJ.NPST=weave.CONT from/with=ART
ama=kaasik *ama=**langik**]*NP
ART=vine ART=vine
'and netbags, they usually weave them from [the.. the *langik* vines]NP' (P12ARSBILUM2-016)

Examples such as the ones above look very similar to the modifier construction, but there is still one crucial difference. In the modifier construction, the modifier agrees in noun class and number with its head. This also seems to be the case in (114a) and (114b) above: the nominal modifier is marked for SG.M in (114a) (like the singular masculine head noun), and remains unmarked in (114b) (like the unmarked plural head noun). However, both nouns happen to be inherently masculine, i.e., the above examples are not necessarily cases of agreement. The natural corpus does not contain examples where the two nouns belong to different classes, but there are some elicited examples showing a mismatch in class (as in 115a below).[15] Furthermore, both nouns in (114b) above appear in their (inherent) unmarked plural forms. In the modifier construction, by contrast, an unmarked non-human head noun always triggers overt neuter agreement in the modifier (as in 115b below).

(115) a. *akaasika amailinggi*
*[a=kaasik-**ka*** *ama=iling-**ki**]*NP
NM=vine-SG.M ART=pumpkin-SG.F
'[a pumpkin vine]NP' (CCM&AAI-31/08/15)

15 There are only very few such examples, and I cannot confidently rule out misunderstandings and/or transcription errors. For the moment, I therefore do not place too much faith in such examples, and only take them as providing additional support to the other evidence discussed in the text.

b. *damaavramatlunget*
*de=[ama=avet=ama=tlu-**nget**]*NP
CONJ=ART=house=ART=good-N
'and there are [good houses]NP' (N12BAMCAT-046)

The two nouns thus do not necessarily match in noun class, but they normally match in number, as they have the same real world referent. In the case of abstract nouns such as *revan* 'truth', there can also be variation in number. It is not uncommon for the abstract nominal modifier to remain in its invariant (i.e., formally plural) form – even if the head noun is marked for singular or dual (as in 116a). Conversely, there are examples where such a nominal modifier is marked for the same noun class and number as the head noun (as in 116b). The non-agreeing pattern in (116a) is what we would expect from the nominal modifier construction, whereas the pattern in (116b) is what we would expect from the modifier construction. That is, this variation points to a third step in the postulated development: the development of agreement in nominal modifiers.

(116) a. *dakuasiqi amaquiriam marvan*
*dap=kuasik=i [ama=quit-**iam** ama=revan]*NP
but=NEG=SIM ART=twin-DU.M ART=truth
'but they aren't [true twins]NP' (N11AAGBROTHERS-0010)
b. *de quasiqi aqamalengiini amarevanini*
*de kuasik=i [a=qama=lengi-**ini***
CONJ NEG=CONJ NM=some=word-SG.DIM
*ama=revan-**ini**]*NP
ART=truth-SG.DIM
'it's not [a true word]NP' (I12AANACLADNSOCIO2-066)

Furthermore, there are a handful of nouns like *quat* 'man ~ male' and *nan* 'woman ~ female' that always agree with their head noun (as in 117). Synchronically, such cases are probably best analyzed as cases of conversion: nouns that convert into adjectives, and that thus freely occur in the modifier construction (like all other adjectives). Diachronically, however, it seems likely that they started out as nominal modifiers, gradually shifting into the modifier construction.[16] They differ from the examples above in that they do not show any signs of variation: they never occur with a prepositional phrase, and they always agree with the head noun.

16 Presumably, a similar development also accounts for the distribution of abstract nouns that allow for double suffixation when occurring as modifiers: their inherent noun class suffix (which became lexicalized) plus an agreement suffix (see section 3.2.1).

(117) *avlengnaska amaquatka, mh, dama.. avlengnaski amananngi*
*a=vlengnas-**ka*** *ama=quat-**ka**,* *mh,* *de=ama..*
NM=NAME-SG.M ART=man/male-SG.M yes CONJ=ART
*a=vlengnas-**ki*** *ama=nan-**ki***
NM=NAME-SG.F ART=woman/female-SG.F
'the male *Vlengnas*, yes, and the.. the female *Vlengnas*' (D12ADKSPIRITS-092FF)

Finally, it is likely that the modifier *mauqas* 'different' originated in the nominal modifier construction. As modifier, it always occurs in invariant form, i.e., it is never preceded by the article *ama* or followed by a prepositional phrase (as in 118a). Nevertheless, it is likely that this modifier is multimorphemic, originating in *(a)ma=uqas* 'ART(.ID)=difference'. Compare the adverbial form *pauqas* 'differently' (as in 118b), which only retains the presumed root *uqas*, and which probably originated as a prepositional phrase (i.e., *pe=a=uqas* 'PLACE=NM=difference').

(118) a. *ngenenamaqaqet mauqas*
ngene-ne=ama=qaqera ***ma=uqas***
2PL.ASSOC-from/with=ART=person ART.ID=difference
'you are together with different people' (I12AANACLADNSOCIO3-065)

b. *ide quasiqaqek ka.. kaang pauqas, dakua..*
ide *kuasik=a=qa-ka* *ka..* *ka=ang*
IPFV NEG=NM=some-SG.M 3SG.M.SBJ 3SG.M.SBJ=walk.NCONT
pe=a=uqas, *dap=kua..*
PLACE=NM=difference but=INTRG
'normally no-one.. walks differently (i.e., wrongly), but maybe..' (I12ABLAJLATASOCIO3-040)

3.4.3 Prepositional phrases and directionals

Prepositional phrases (as in 119a) and directionals (as in 119b) can function as modifiers to a head noun. Like the other modifiers, they almost always occur post-head. Different from the others, they are not introduced by the article *ama*; and different from the modifier construction, there is no agreement. Instead, they retain the internal structure of prepositional phrases or directionals (see chapter 5.3 on prepositional phrases and chapter 6.3 on directionals), often resulting in syntactically ambiguous structures. In (119a), the context suggests that the prepositional phrase forms part of the noun phrase. Out of context, however, this example could alternatively instantiate either the locative construction (with the interpretation of 'canoes are (made) from taro') or the equative construction (with the interpretation of 'the taro is a canoe'). In (119b), the morphosyntax only allows for the noun phrase interpretation – otherwise there would have to be an overt conjunction *i* (for the interpretation of 'the child comes back from down there and says').

(119) a. *ianiurlet nianamalauski sep maqerlap, amalauski namadaqa*
ian=iurlet *ne=iana=malaus-ki* *se=pe*
3DU.SBJ=pull.NCONT from/with=3DU.POSS=canoe-SG.F to/with=PLACE
ma=qerlap, [*a=malaus-ki* ***ne=ama=da-ka***]NP
ART.ID=water NM=canoe-SG.F from/with=ART=taro-SG.M
'they pulled their canoe into water (to travel across the sea), [the canoe (made) from taro]NP' (N12BAMCAT-131FF)

b. *taquarliva, dinyinarli amarluimga naimek kasil..*
taquarl=ip=a, *de=nyi=narli* [*ama=rluim-ka*
thus=PURP=DIST CONJ=2SG.SBJ.NPST=hear ART=child-SG.M
ne=i-mek]NP *ka=sil..*
from/with=AWAY-down 3SG.M.SBJ=say.NCONT
'it's like this now, and you hear that [a child coming back from down there]NP says..' (I12ABLAJLATASOCIO3-062)

Despite their formal differences to other types of modifiers, there is overlap with the nominal modifier construction. This overlap is restricted to abstract nouns that can function both as head nouns and as nominal modifiers. Example (120a) illustrates a noun phrase containing a prepositional phrase: the head noun is *nauisaqa* 'blueness:SG.M', and the prepositional phrase specifies the location of this color. And example (120b) illustrates the nominal modifier construction: here, the head noun is *daqa* 'taro:SG.M', and the modifier consists of the noun *grlan* 'yellowness' and a prepositional phrase (with the pronominal prepositional object being co-referential to the head noun *daqa* 'taro:SG.M'). The two structures are similar in that both contain a nominal property concept and a prepositional phrase (specifying the location of the property), but they differ in the syntactic status of the property noun (as head noun in 120a and as modifier in 120b).

(120) a. *ngumnyim sagel amanauisaqa pramadam*
ngu=mnyim *se=gel* [*ama=nauisa-ka*
1SG.SBJ.NPST=look.CONT to/with=near ART=blueness-SG.M
[*pet=ama=dam*]PP]NP
on/under=ART=stone
'I am looking at [the blue mountains]NP (lit. the blueness on the mountains)' (ABL&AAN-09/05/2015)

b. *mani nguain amadaqa amagrlan pemga*
mani *ngua=in* [*ama=da-ka* [*ama=grlan*
recently 1SG.SBJ=cook.NCONT ART=taro-SG.M ART=yellowness
[*pe-ka*]PP]MODIFIER]NP
PLACE-SG.M
'yesterday I cooked [the yellow taro]NP (lit. taro of yellowness on it)'
(ABL&AAN-11/05/2015)

3.5 Possession

In possessive noun phrases, the possessor noun precedes the possessed noun, and the possessor is indexed in the form of a clitic on the possessed noun. Qaqet thus shares the typical word order of East Papuan languages – despite not sharing the concomitant verb-final constituent order and postpositions. Conversely, Qaqet does not display any of the typical Oceanic features: there are no possessive classifiers and no suffix-marked possessives, and a distinction between alienable and inalienable possession is marginal (see the discussion on possession in Dunn, Reesink, and Terrill (2002: 33–34), and the summarizing tables in Dunn et al. (2008: 743)).

This section describes first the form of the possessor indexes and their distribution (section 3.5.1) and then discusses the structure of the possessive noun phrase (section 3.5.2).

3.5.1 Possessor index

In all possessive noun phrases, both pronominal and nominal, the possessor is obligatorily indexed, usually as a proclitic on the possessed noun. Table 37 summarizes the available forms (see Table 33 above for the relationship of the indexes to the noun classes). The indexes are formed from a base plus a final vowel *a*. If the base ends in *e*, this vowel is replaced by *a*; and if it ends in any other vowel, both vowels are retained in the form of either a long vowel or a diphthong. With some exceptions (discussed below), the base forms never occur on their own.

The full form almost always cliticizes to a preceding or following element. In these contexts, it is very common for one or more of the following assimilatory processes to take place, especially in fast speech: a vowel preceding *r* tends to be lost (e.g. *ara* '3SG.F.POSS' and *araa* '3PL.POSS' are realized as *ra* and *raa* in 121c and 121e below), and final vowels are sometimes lost (e.g., *iana* '3DU.POSS' is realized as *ian* in 121a below); the long vowels in *aa* '3SG.M.POSS' and *araa* '3PL.POSS' are not always maintained;[17] and diphthongs tend to be simplified (e.g., *iana* '3DU.POSS' is frequently realized *eena* or *ina*).

Tab. 37: Possessor indexes

	SG		DU		PL	
	Base form	**Full form**	**Base form**	**Full form**	**Base form**	**Full form**
1	*gu (~ ngu)*	*gua (~ ngua)*	*une*	*una*	*ure*	*ura*
2	*gi (~ nyi)*	*gia (~ nya)*	*uane*	*uana*	*ngene*	*ngena*
3M	*a*	*aa*	*iane*	*iana*	*ara*	*araa*
3F	*are*	*ara*				
3N	*ngere*	*ngera*	=	=	=	=

The full form usually appears as a proclitic on the possessed noun (as in 121a). All preceding conjunctions or prepositions tend to also be part of the phonological word (as in 121b), and it is not even uncommon for a preceding verb or nominal possessor to be included within this clitic group (as in 121c). Alternatively, it is also possible for the possessor to form a clitic group with the preceding element(s) (especially conjunctions and prepositions), and not with the following possessed noun (as in 121d). Note also that it is common for the possessor index and the possessed noun to be separated by a hesitation pause (as in 121e), or for the possessor index to be repeated again after such a pause as a proclitic to the possessed nouns (as in 121f).

(121) a. *deiva, daqatigis ianlams*
de=ip=a, *de=ka=tigis* ***iana****=lamesa*
CONJ=PURP=DIST CONJ=3SG.M.SBJ=pluck 3DU.POSS=coconut
'later, he harvested their coconuts' (N11AJNGENAINGMETSIQI-0062)

b. *beip perlset namraarlaunini*
be=ip *perlset* *ne=met=****aa****=rlaun-ini*
CONJ=PURP finish.CONT from/with=in=3SG.M.POSS=netbag-SG.DIM
'and his little netbag got finished' (N11AAGSIRINILOBSTER1-0018)

17 This means that the contrasts between *araa* '3PL.POSS' and *ara* '3SG.F.POSS', and between *aa* '3SG.M.POSS' and *a* 'NM', are not always maintained, especially not in fast speech. Whenever the noun phrase contains a nominal possessor, the interpretation is unambiguous: the noun class of the nominal possessor determines the form of the possessor index; and the noun marker reading is ruled out. However, if there is no nominal possessor, only the discourse context can distinguish between the possible readings.

c. *besamt masinav**ra**gulengga*
*be=se=met ma=sinap=**ara**=guleng-ka*
CONJ=to/with=in ART.ID=NAME=3SG.F.POSS=malay.apple-SG.M
'and up into Sinap's malay apple tree' (N11AAGSIRINIROPE-0032)

d. *iandit savriana hlenga*
*ian=tit se=pet=**iana** sleng=a*
3DU.SBJ=go.CONT to/with=on/under=3DU.POSS garden=DIST
'they go to their garden' (N12BAMCAT-017)

e. *tenraa.. araa qalatka, bemmalk sameta*
*te-ne=**araa**.. **araa** qalat-ka,*
3PL.ASSOC-from/with=3PL.POSS 3PL.POSS younger.sibling-SG.M
be=ma=malep-ka se=met-ta
CONJ=ART.ID=ten-SG.M to/with=in-3PL.H
'they together with their.. their younger brother, and (together with him) they are ten' (N12AMVGENAINGMETBROTHERS-012)

f. *iqesnis meniana.. ianamalauski*
*i=ke=snis men=**iana**.. **iana**=malaus-ki*
SIM=3SG.M.SBJ.NPST=bite.CONT at=3DU.POSS 3DU.POSS=canoe-SG.F
'he is eating from their.. their canoe' (N12BAMCAT-202)

In most contexts, the possessor indexes appear in their full form, i.e., with a final *a*. There are only three contexts where the base forms occur (summarized in Table 38). Different from the full forms, the base forms are prefixes and always attach to the following possessed noun.

First, the base form appears with three kinship nouns that obligatorily occur in possessed form: *mam* 'man (father)' and *nan* 'woman (mother)' (as in 122a), and *uim* 'child' (as in 122b). In the case of 'child', the 1SG and 2SG forms are unexpectedly realized *ngu* [ŋu] (not *gu* [ⁿgu]) and *nyi* [ɲi] (not *gi* [ⁿgi]). The Tok Pisin loans *papa* 'father' and *mama* 'mother' also appear with the base form; the loan *pikinini* 'child' is not attested in possessed form.

(122) a. *gimam kua? ginan kua?*
***gi**-mam kua? **gi**-nan kua?*
2SG.POSS-father where 2SG.POSS-mother where
'where is your father? where is your mother?' (I12AANACLADNSOCIO3-024FF)

b. *ip nguseserl vet **ngu**imga*
*ip ngu=seserl pet **gu**-uim-ka*
PURP 1SG.SBJ.NPST=straighten:REDUP on/under 1SG.POSS-child-SG.M
'I will correct my child' (I12AANACLADNSOCIO2-165)

Tab. 38: Distribution of base form

Noun	**Gloss**	**Example (illustrated with 1SG.POSS)**		
1. Kinship nouns				
mam	father	*gumam*	*gu-mam*	1SG.POSS-man
nan	mother	*gunan*	*gu-nan*	1SG.POSS-woman
lavu (-NC)	adult/parent (-NC)	*gulavu* ~ *gualavu*	*gu-lavu* ~ *gua-lavu*	1SG.POSS-adult/parent
uim-NC	child-NC	*nguimga*	*ngu-uim-ka*	1SG.POSS-child-SG.M
uis	child	*nguis* ~ *nguauis*	*ngu-uis* ~ *ngua-uis*	1SG.POSS-child
papa	father	*gupapa*	*gu-papa*	1SG.POSS-father
mama	mother	*gumama*	*gu-mama*	1SG.POSS-mother
2. Relational nouns (see chapter 6.1)				
3. Proforms				
ia-NC	other-NC	*guiak*	*gu-ia-ka*	1SG.POSS-other-SG.M
(?) *ma*-NC	thingy-NC	*gumaqa*	*gu-ma-ka*	1SG.POSS-thingy-SG.M

All three kinship nouns have (partially) suppletive forms in some of the number categories: *lavu* 'adult/parent' (in dual and plural contexts) and *uis* 'child' (in plural contexts). These suppletive forms show variation: they usually take the full possessor index (as illustrated in 123a), and the base form is explicitly rejected in elicitation sessions. But the corpus also contains examples of these nouns with base forms (as in 123b). The 1SG and 2SG forms of *uis* 'child' again show the unexpected initial nasal consonant.

(123) a. *nevuralavurlvis*
*ne=pe=**ura**=lavu=ngere-uvis*
from/with=PLACE=1PL.POSS=adult=3N.POSS-top
'(our language that came down in the past) from our parents' (I12AANACLADNSOCIO3-156)

b. *gulaviam, uantaqen prana slep*
***gu**-lavu-iam, uan=taqen pet-na slep*
1SG.POSS-adult-DU.M 2DU.SBJ=say.CONT on/under-RECP intensely
'my parents, you talk loudly to each other' (LONGYDS20150517_1-348)

The suppletive forms are also attested in non-possessive contexts (as in 124a). In the case of the singular nouns, by contrast, speakers have to switch to distinct (albeit) related word forms in non-possessive contexts: *ngerlmamga* ~ *mamga* 'man (father)' (incorporating the noun class suffix *-ka* 'SG.M'), *ngerlnanngi* ~ *nanngi* 'woman (mother)' (incorporating the noun class suffix *-ki* 'SG.F'), and *rluim* 'child' (as in 124b).

(124) a. *nep malavu arlvis*
ne=pe *ma=**lavu*** *ngere-uvis*
from/with=PLACE ART.ID=adult 3N.POSS-top
'(the language) comes from the parents' (I12AANACLADNSocio2-087)

b. *inani nyitlamarluimirang*
i=nani *nyi=tlu=ama=**rluim**-irang*
SIM=can 2SG.SBJ.NPST=see.CONT=ART=child-PL.DIM
'you can see the little children' (I12AANACLADNSocio3-341)

Second, the base forms are found with some relational nouns, e.g., *uvis* 'top' in (123a) and (124a) above takes the base form *ngere* '3N.POSS' (not the full form *ngera*). Synchronically, relational nouns differ from possessed nouns in that they do not control agreement, person indexes or cross-referencing, i.e., they do not function as heads of possessive noun phrases. Diachronically, it is likely that they originated as possessed nouns. Their old origin is presumably reflected in the use of the base possessor index as well as in sometimes considerable fusion of possessor and relational noun, with additional loss of segments. Chapter 6.1 discusses the relational nouns in more detail.

Finally, the base forms are used with the proform *ia* 'other', as in (125a) (see section 3.3.3). All other proforms, by contrast, co-occur with the full form, e.g. *qa* 'some' (in 125b). It is possible that *ma* 'thingy' also co-occurs with the base form, but the only attested examples are in child language and child-directed speech (as in (125c) by a mother to her child, aged 2;10). Note also that Qaqet has various other nouns with related meanings, e.g., *va* 'thingy', which always occur with the full form.

(125) a. *guiang amir amahleng*
***gu**-ia-nget* *a-mit* *ama=sleng*
1SG.POSS-other-N DIR-across ART=garden
'my other gardens over there' (D12ADNGarden-069)

b. *nyitatpet giaqagel*
nyi=tatpet ***gia**=qa-igel*
2SG.SBJ.NPST=remove.skin.CONT:ON/UNDER 2SG.POSS=some-SG.EXC
'you take off some of yours' (P12ARSBilum1-024)

c. *ma bridget aremaqia*
ma *bridget* ***are**-ma-ki=a*
ART.ID NAME 3SG.F.POSS-thingy-SG.F=DIST
'it's Bridget's thingy' (C12VARPlay-032)

In the adult language, the base forms only ever occur in the contexts above. In child language and child-directed speech, however, they are attested in a wider range of contexts. Even there, it is still more common to encounter the full form – but the base forms are found, too. For example, (126a) was uttered by a child (aged 3;3); and (126b) was directed by a mother to her child (aged 3;2). In language directed to adults, these nouns would always trigger the use of the full possessor indexes. And in elicitation contexts, speakers would explicitly reject the base forms as wrong. It is at present not clear how to interpret this wider distribution in the interaction with children. Minimally, it shows that adults recognize the base forms as separable morphemes that can productively attach to nouns that would normally not take them.

(126) a. *gubias*
__gu__-bias
1SG.POSS-sore
'my sore' (LONGYDS20150601_1-352)
b. *sagel gibatri*
se=gel *__gi__=batari*
to/with=near 2SG.POSS-battery
'near your batteries' (LONGYDS20150516_1-960)

Synchronically, it can be argued that the base form occurs with inalienably possessed nouns, albeit with a very small group of nouns only. It mainly covers the core kinship terms *mam* 'man (father)', *nan* 'woman (mother)' and *uim* 'child' (with variation in their suppletive dual and plural forms) – and all three obligatorily occur in possessed form. The Tok Pisin equivalents *papa* 'father' and *mama* 'mother' also appear with the base form, but different from their Qaqet counterparts, they can occur in non-possessed form, too. A similar analysis can account for the relational nouns: they denote a search region projected from a location, and thus always occur in possessed form. In their case, we often observe fusion between the possessor and the noun, pointing to some degree of lexicalization and their older age. This is probably also true for the proform *ia* 'other', which shows a number of formal idiosyncrasies (see chapter 4.1.2 for a discussion of the paradigm).

Given their restricted distribution and fusional tendencies, I consider the base forms the original forms of the possessor indexes, which were retained in those nouns that obligatorily or frequently occurred in their possessed form. It is likely that the full forms were formed from the base forms plus the noun marker *a*. This assumption is supported by comparative data from Mali (Stebbins 2011: 181–191). The Mali possessor indexes are cognate to the Qaqet base forms, but they are augmented with the specific article *a* (cognate to the noun marker *a* in Qaqet) in those contexts that trigger the use of the specific article. That is, the base forms have a wider distribution in Mali. In Qaqet, by contrast, the distribution of the base forms is restricted, and it cannot be proven (or disproven) that the final *a* is synchronically the noun marker. For this reason, I represent the full forms in this grammar as monomorphemic, unanalyzable forms.

Mali has a larger group of inalienably possessed nouns, containing a good number of kinship nouns, bodypart nouns and relational nouns. Their morphosyntactic expression is complex: some forms of the paradigm include the specific article, some do not, and some make use of completely different forms. Stebbins (2011: 190) suggests that this variation points to an on-going change in the possessive system. Such a change is also evident when comparing cognate forms across the two languages.[18] At least some of the cognate forms in Qaqet incorporate a synchronically unanalyzable possessor index, e.g., Qaqet *ngarik* /ŋarik/ 'hand'. The cognate Mali form is *tik* 'hand', which is inherently possessed and whose citation form includes the neuter possessor index *aŋə* ~ *aŋət*, thus yielding the citation form *aŋəɹik* 'its hand'. Synchronically, the Qaqet form cannot be analyzed further: as shown in example (127), the Qaqet noun can co-occur with any possessor index in the present-day language.

(127) *lek praangarik*
lek *pet=**aa**=ngarik*
take.off on/under=3SG.M.POSS=hand
'he took off his hands' (N11AAGSIRINIROPE-0074)

Similarly, Qaqet *ngerlmam* 'man (father)' and *ngerlnan* 'woman (mother)' probably incorporate the same unanalyzable neuter possessor index. The forms *mam* 'man (father)' and *nan* 'woman (mother)' still exist in present-day Qaqet. The phonological changes in the first syllable from Qaqet *ngera* /ŋəra/ '3N.POSS' to *ngerl* /ŋəɽ/ can be explained through the reduction (and eventual loss) of the final vowel (i.e. /ŋəra/ being realized as [ŋərə] ~ [ŋərᵊ]), in combination with phonotactics, as /r/ cannot occur in syllable-final position (i.e., resulting in [ŋəɽ]). The first kind of process is attested otherwise in Qaqet, the second is not. Such a development would nevertheless explain the unusual behavior of /ɽ/: it is the only consonant that sometimes triggers lenition in following plosives, i.e., it behaves similar to vowels (see chapter 2.1.1). Furthermore, cognate Qaqet forms frequently contain an unexpected *rl* /ɽ/ that could conceivably be the last remnant of the former possessor index: *rlking* /ɽkiŋ/ 'tooth' (compare Mali *keŋ* 'tooth')), also *rluim* /ɽuim/ 'child' (compare its inalienable counterpart *uim* /uim/ 'child', as well as Mali *oem* 'child').

In addition, some Qaqet relational nouns seem to incorporate a possessor index, e.g., the relational noun *uvis* /uβis/ 'top', which is likely to be cognate to Mali *uβus* 'his head'. Like other relational nouns, it always occurs in possessed form (as in example 123a and 124a above).

The possessor index *gua* '1SG.POSS' has given rise to a noun that was formed from this index plus a noun class suffix, i.e., without any nominal base. The resulting

18 All Mali examples in this and the following paragraphs are inalienably possessed nouns, taken from Stebbins (2011: 189–191).

meaning is that of 'my friend(s)' (as in 128a). The plural form is also used as an interjection to convey empathy (as in 128b). It is not possible to replace *gua* '1SG.POSS' with any of the other possessor indexes to convey a different possessive relation (e.g., one could not use *gia* '2SG.POSS' in order to convey the meaning of 'your friend(s)').

(128) a. *guaka, dap nyisana?*
gua-ka, *dap* *nyi=sana?*
1SG.POSS-SG.M but 2SG.SBJ.NPST-do.what
'my friend, what are you doing?' (N12BAMCAT-245)

b. *lu guaqas, guari*
lu *gua=qa-es,* ***gua-ta***
DEM 1SG.POSS=some-SG.FLAT 1SG.POSS-PL.H
'mine there, sorry' (LONGYJL20150805_2-210)

All attested forms are summarized in Table 39. They show the same kind of idiosyncrasies and fusions as found with the indefinite pronouns *ia* 'other' and *qa* 'some' (see chapter 4.1.2 for details). Given their human reference, there are no forms in the neuter and shape-based noun classes.

Tab. 39: Paradigm for *gua*-NC 'my friend(s)'

	Form	Morphemes	Gloss	
SG.M	*guak* ~ *guaka*	*gua-ka*	1SG.POSS-SG.M	my male friend
SG.F	*guaik* ~ *guaiki*	*gua-ki*	1SG.POSS-SG.F	my female friend
DU.M	*guaiam*	*gua-iam*	1SG.POSS-DU.M	my two male/mixed friends
DU.F	*guavim*	*gua-im*	1SG.POSS-DU.F	my two female friends
PL.H	*guari*	*gua-ta*	1SG.POSS-PL.H	my friends; sorry

3.5.2 Possessive noun phrase

A possessive noun phrase consists obligatorily of a possessor index plus a possessed noun (as in 129a). In addition, a nominal possessor can optionally precede the possessor index and the possessed noun. The nominal possessor can be expressed by any kind of nominal or pronominal form, e.g., a common noun (as in 129b), a proper noun (as in 129c), a demonstrative (as in 129d), an interrogative pronoun (as in 129e) or an independent pronoun (as in 129f). In all cases, the noun class and number of the nominal possessor is indexed on the possessed noun.

The possessed entity is either a noun (as in 129a to 129f) or an indefinite pronoun (as in 130). Other types of pronouns cannot occur as possessed entities.

(129) a. *i buv raarlaunirang*
i *bup* [***araa***=*rlaun-irang*]
SIM fill 3PL.POSS=netbag-PL.DIM
'so that their netbags got filled' (N11AJNGenaingmetBrothers-0116)

b. *amabariqi ruimbap, de laaviara*
[*ama=bari-ki* ***are***-*uim-ap*], *de* *lu-ap-iara*
ART=bee-SG.F 3SG.F.POSS-child-PL.RCD CONJ DEM-PL.RCD-PROX
'the bee hive's children, those ones' (R12ADNFrog-177)

c. *masirini aalainnga*
[*ma=sirini* ***aa***=*lain-ka*]
ART.ID=NAME 3SG.M.POSS=line-SG.M
'Sirini's family' (N11AAGSiriniLobster2-0004)

d. *deraquarl luqiara aravang maqasing*
de=taquarl [*lu-ki-iara* ***ara***=*va-nget* *ma=qasing*]
CONJ=thus DEM-SG.F-PROX 3SG.F.POSS=thingy-N ART.ID=hair
'it's like this one's hair' (LongYDS20150601_1-424)

e. *nemga aaviskaa?*
[*nema-ka* ***aa***=*avis-ki*]=*a*
who-SG.M 3SG.M.POSS=knife-SG.F=DIST
'whose knife there?' (ATA&AEM-21/06/2011)

f. *um ngeraningaqi, de medu quasiqi qui unquhrl aqrang praqi*
[*em* ***ngera***=*ninga-ki*], *de* *medu* *kuasik=i* *kui*
SG.RCD 3N.POSS=head-SG.F CONJ past NEG=SIM quoting
une=qutserl *a=qa-irang* *pet-ki*
1DU.SBJ.NPST=plant.NCONT:?? NM=some-PL.DIM on/under-3SG.F
'the short one's (= garden) top part, we say that we haven't planted anything on it' (D12ABDACPGarden-032)

(130) *barequriaik*
*barek=ure-**ia-ki***
BEN=1PL.POSS-other-SG.F
'for our other (friend)' (P12ADNRope1-106)

Possessive noun phrases can recur. This possibility is attested in Mali (Stebbins 2011: 182), and Qaqet, too, has a fair number of such examples. However, all natural examples involve relational nouns (as *rleng* 'back' in (131a), which is possessed by *vlemga* 'pig', which in turn is possessed by *gia* '2SG.POSS'). Given that relational nouns developed from possessed nouns, I assume that such an embedding is in principle possible. But the only attested examples come from elicitation, e.g., (131b), where *lengiqa* 'language' is possessed by *lavu* 'adults/parents', which is possessed by *ura* '1PL.POSS'.

(131) a. *nani nguarenas savet giavlemgaarleng*
nani *ngua=renas* *se=pet*
can 1SG.SBJ=jump.NCONT.FUT:SELF to/with=on/under
***gia**=vlam-ka=**aa**=rleng*
2SG.POSS=pig-SG.M=3SG.M.POSS=back
'I can jump onto the back of your pig' (N11AESSIRINI-0020)

b. *uralavu araalengiqa*
***ura**=lavu* ***araa**=lengi-ka*
1PL.POSS=adult 3PL.POSS=word-SG.M
'our parents' language' (AJL-11/08/2012)

The possessed noun is the head of the possessive noun phrase. As such, it controls agreement within the noun phrase, person indexing and anaphoric tracking in subsequent clauses. For example, the head of the noun phrase in (132a) is the possessed noun *ngariqis* 'branch', which belongs to the SG.FLAT noun class: this noun class is also marked on the complex adjective *rik mamerl* 'right (side)', and it is taken up as the pronominal argument of the verb *rerl* 'straighten' in the agentless construction. Similarly, in (132b) the possessed noun is *qalembem* 'stick', which belongs to the SG.RCD noun class: again, the demonstrative *lauma* 'that one' agrees with the head noun, and the pronominal object of *ne* 'from/with' refers back to this noun. Example (132c) illustrates that the possessed noun *kaasik* 'rope/vine' triggers neuter person indexing in the associative construction – in line with its non-human plural reference. Finally, example (132d) shows that the possessed noun controls subject indexing on the verb.

(132) a. *dap.. giangariqis amrik mamerles, dinani rerl vraus vra.. savramagalipka.. aalang*
dap.. *gia=ngarik-**es*** *ama=rik* *ma=merl-**es**,*
but 2SG.POSS=hand-SG.FLAT ART=side ART.ID=right-SG.FLAT
de=nani *rerl* *pet-**es*** *pet=a..*
CONJ=can straighten.CONT on/under-SG.FLAT on/under=NM
se=pet=ama=galip-ka.. *aa=lang*
to/with=on/under=ART=galip-SG.M 3SG.M.POSS=top
'but.. your right branch, it can get stretched out on.. onto the galipnut tree's.. top' (N11AJNGENAINGMETBROTHERS-0037FF)

b. *dera.. araqalembem laumai.. ide qiats naum*
de=ara.. *ara=qalem-**em*** *lu-**em**-a=i..*
CONJ=3SG.F.POSS 3SG.F.POSS=wood-SG.RCD DEM-SG.RCD-DIST=SIM
ide *kia=tes* *ne-**em***
IPFV 3SG.F.SBJ=eat.CONT from/with-SG.RCD
'and her.. that her little stick.. with which she usually fights'
(N11AAGSIRINIROPE-0050FF)

c. *ahrlik, namramaqaqerraakaasik ngenraamengap*
a=sirlik, ne=met=ama=qaqera=araa=kaasik
NM=meat from/with=in=ART=person=3PL.POSS=vine
***ngere**-ne=araa=meng-ap*
3N.ASSOC-from/with=3PL.POSS-wood-PL.RCD
'meat, from the people's rope and wood traps' (D12ADKSPIRITS-064)

d. *araabarlka qeqsik*
*araa=barl-**ka** **ke**=ksik*
3PL.POSS=big-SG.M 3SG.M.SBJ.NPST=climb.CONT
'their eldest brother is climbing' (N12AMVGENAINGMETBROTHERS-057)

Possessive noun phrases can be complex, containing, e.g., adjectives (as in 132a above) and demonstratives (as in 132b above). Adjectives (and also other modifiers) and demonstratives follow the possessed noun and agree with it. Recall that the position of demonstratives is not fixed: they can appear pre- or post-head (see section 3.3.2). In possessive noun phrases, however, they can only ever occur following their head – it is not possible for them to precede the possessed noun or to even occur before the nominal possessor. The language thus relies both on agreement and on linear ordering to indicate a relationship between the possessed noun and its dependent elements.

The possessed noun cannot occur with a noun marker or a simple article, but it can occur with indefinite articles such as *qama* 'some' (in 133a) and with indefinite pronouns such as *ia* 'other' (in 133b). In all cases, the article has scope over the possessed noun only.

(133) a. *ati nyiguirltik guaqamasiirem*
*kaki nyi=guirltik gua=**qama**=siit-em*
instead 2SG.SBJ.NPST=turn:SIDE 1SG.POSS=some=story-SG.RCD
'it's you instead who replies to a short story of mine' (I12AANACLADNSOCIO3-348)

b. *uriaq amalanginyga iqetuqun iama..*
*ure-**ia-ka** ama=langiny-ka i=ke=tuqun*
1PL.POSS-other-SG.M ART=paper-SG.M SIM=3SG.M.SBJ.NPST=say.CONT
i=ama..
SIM=ART
'there is one book of ours that talks about the..' (I12AANACLADNSOCIO3-229)

Conversely, the possessor noun always co-occurs with an article. The form of the article is dependent on the possessor noun, not on the possessed noun. For example, a proper noun as a possessor triggers the use of the article *ma* (in 134a), while a common noun triggers the use of the article *ama* (as in 134b). Possessor nouns cannot independently be marked by demonstratives or by indefinite articles This is only possible if the possessed noun is a relational noun (see chapter 6.1).

(134) a. *maiesus aavetki*
__ma__=iesus *aa=avet-ki*
ART.ID=NAME 3SG.M.POSS=house-SG.F
'the house of Jesus' (LONGYDS20150516_1-574)

b. *kamen, bqabarl amasisterkina raavetki*
ka=men, *be=ka=barl*
3SG.M.SBJ=come.NCONT.PST CONJ=3SG.M.SBJ=break
__ama__=sister-kina *araa=avet-ki*
ART=sister-ASSOC.F 3PL.POSS=house-SG.F
'he came and broke into the house of the sisters' (AAS-01/06/2015)

3.6 Conjoined noun phrases: Associative construction

Qaqet coordinates noun phrases by means of the associative construction. This construction makes use of associative pronouns (summarized in Table 40), which usually occur as proclitics to the following noun phrase. The forms and their syntactic behavior are similar to those found in Mali (Stebbins 2011: 73–74, 179–180).

The associative pronouns are formed from a person index plus the preposition *ne* 'from/with'. The person indexes are identical to the non-past subject indexes (added for comparative purposes to Table 40; see also Table 33 in section 3.2.3 above), but we observe a loss of phonetic material in the trisyllabic forms: the full form is still attested in some cases, but not in others (marked with an asterisk in Table 40). In all cases, it is common for speakers to omit the second syllable. This second syllable consists of a sonorant (/n/ or /r/) and the vowel /ə/, followed by a syllable with an initial sonorant (/n/). In this environment, it is very common for /ə/ to be reduced or omitted altogether, resulting in a consonant cluster ([nn] or [rn]) plus subsequent simplification (to [n]) (see chapter 2.2). In the case of 1PL, this phonetic loss reveals the underlying consonant: the underlying consonant /t/ lenited to [r] in the full form *urene* (because it occurred in an intervocalic environment), but not in the reduced form *utne* (as /t/ no longer occurred intervocalically).

Tab. 40: Associative pronouns

	Associative pronouns	Subject index (NPST)
1SG	*ngune*	*ngu*
2SG	*nyine*	*nyi*
3SG.M	*kene*	*ke*
3SG.F	*kine*	*ki*
1DU	*une* (from **unene*)	*une*
2DU	*uane* (from **uanene*)	*uane*
3DU	*iane* (from **ianene*)	*iane*
1PL	*utne* ~ *urne* (from *urene*)	*ure*
2PL	*ngene* (from *ngenene*)	*ngene*
3PL.H	*tene*	*te*
3N	*ngene* (from *ngerene*)	*ngere* ~ *nger*

The associative construction is used to coordinate two noun phrases (as the first two phrases in 135a). The person index is obligatory, and its category is determined by the first conjunct (e.g., *ke* '3SG.M.ASSOC' indexes the male singular name *Sirini*). The construction cannot coordinate more than two noun phrases. Any additional noun phrase has to be added on a clausal level, e.g., through using a clausal conjunction such as *de* (as in the case of the third and fourth phrase in 135a). The head of the first noun phrase is usually a noun, but not obligatorily so. It can also be a pronoun – e.g. an independent pronoun (as in 135b).

(135) a. *savet masirini, kenemasiqi, demasinap, demaqunemgium*
se=pet *ma=***sirini***,* ***ke-ne****=ma=siqi,*
to/with=on/under ART.ID=NAME 3SG.M.ASSOC-from/with=ART.ID=NAME
de=ma=sinap, *de=ma=qunemgium*
CONJ=ART.ID=NAME CONJ=ART.ID=NAME
'about Sirini, together with Siqi, and Sinap, and Qunemgium'
(I12AANACLADNSocio3-287FF)

b. *dap parlen merain ngenangera.. angeriari*
dap *parlen* *met-***ini** ***ngere-ne****=ngera..*
but middle in-SG.DIM 3N.ASSOC-from/with=3N.POSS
ngere-ia-ta
3N.POSS-other-PL.H
'in the middle of the little one together with his.. his friends'
(I12AANACLADNSocio3-009)

The head of the second noun phrase is, again, usually a noun (as in 135a above), but it can also be a pronoun, e.g., an indefinite pronoun (as *iari* 'other:PL.H' in 135b above), a demonstrative pronoun (as in 136a below), or an independent pronoun (as in 136b below). Note that the first conjunct does not need an overt noun phrase: its identity can be indicated by the person index alone (as in both examples below).

(136) a. *de ramii ranes, iqenluraamuk*
de *ta=mii* *ta=nes,*
CONJ 3PL.H=most 3PL.SBJ=shout.NCONT
*i=**ke-ne=lu-ta-a**=a-muk*
SIM=3SG.M.ASSOC-from/with=DEM-PL.H-DIST=DIR-across
'they all shout, he together with those ones across' (N11AAGSIRINILOBSTER1-0060)

b. *dap kuasik ngenangen*
dap *kuasik* ***ngere-ne-ngen***
but NEG 3N.ASSOC-from/with-2PL
'it is not together with you' (N11AAGSIRINILOBSTER2-0038)

There is considerable independence between the two coordinated noun phrases. Both of them can occur with the full range of nominal determiners and modifiers, e.g., the second noun phrase in (137) contains a possessor index and a numeral modifier. Prosodically, there is often (but not necessarily) an intonation break between the conjuncts: a non-final pitch contour with a sharp rise-fall on the first conjunct (see chapter 2.3.2) plus a pause (as in 135a above).

(137) *kingingarl samangerlnan kinaruis amarlatpes nara*
ki=ngingarl *se=ama=ngerlnan*
3SG.F.SBJ.NPST=chase.CONT:?? to/with=ART=woman
*ki-ne=[**are**-uis* ***ama=rlatpes*** *ne-ta]*
3SG.F.ASSOC-from/with=3SG.F.POSS-child ART=four from/with-3PL.H
'she chases after the mother together with [her four children]' (N12ABKSIRINI-115)

Syntactically, the associative construction frequently occurs as an afterthought (as in 138a and 138b), providing further information on a referent. Such afterthoughts do not occur in argument function, e.g., they do not occur in subject function in the examples below. As such, they do not occur in the corresponding syntactic position (e.g., subjects would have to precede the verb) and they do not control person indexing on the verb. In (138a), the reference of the associative construction is dual masculine, which happens to be identical to that of the subject noun phrase *liama* 'DEM:DU.M:DIST' (which in turn controls the subject index *ian* '3DU.SBJ'). But in (138b), class and number of the subject index *ka* '3SG.M.SBJ' do not match that of the associative construction (whose reference is human plural).

(138) a. *de liama ianrat, kenaadanggi, be ianrat de..*
de *lu-iam-a* *ian=rat,*
CONJ DEM-DU.M-DIST 3DU.SBJ=fall.CONT
ke-ne=aa=dang-ki,
3SG.M.ASSOC-from/with=3SG.M.POSS=dog-SG.F
be *ian=rat* *de..*
CONJ 3DU.SBJ=fall.CONT CONJ
'those two were falling, he and his dog, they were falling and..' (R12ATAFROG-228FF)

b. *iknes kenaalainnga*
ip=ke=nes
PURP=3SG.M.SBJ.NPST=shout.NCONT
ke-ne=aa=lain-ka
3SG.M.ASSOC-from/with=3SG.M.POSS=line-SG.M
'and he wants to shout, he and his troops' (N11AAGSIRINILOBSTER2-0067)

By contrast, whenever the associative construction occurs in argument function, it obligatorily occurs in the corresponding syntactic slot, e.g., the subject precedes the verb (as in 139a), or the possessor precedes the possessed (as in 139b). Furthermore, any associative construction in subject or possessor function controls the person index. The coordinated phrases in (139a) are plural human, and hence trigger the subject index *ta* '3PL.SBJ' (compare the parallel example in 138b above, where the associative construction occurs as an afterthought and is thus not reflected in the subject index *ke* '3SG.M.SBJ.NPST'). And the coordinated phrases in (139b) are dual human, and hence trigger the possessor index *iana* '3DU.POSS'.

(139) a. *de qenaalainnga rans, imaurlen*
de ***ke-ne=aa=lain-ka***
CONJ 3SG.M.ASSOC-from/with=3SG.M.POSS=line-SG.M
ta=nes, *i=ma=urlen*
3PL.SBJ=shout.NCONT SIM=ART.ID=prawn
'and he and his troops shouted, the prawns' (N11AAGSIRINILOBSTER1-0062)

b. *iqerl ma.. arum, kenemasingan ianataipkia*
i=kerl ***ma..*** ***arum,*** ***ke-ne=ma=singan***
SIM=DEONT ART.ID NAME 3SG.M.ASSOC-from/with=ART.ID=NAME
iana=taip-ki=a
3DU.POSS=tape-SG.F=DIST
'it's Arum's and Singan's tape there' (LONGYDS20150516_1-594)

Semantically, the referents of both conjuncts are frequently humans (or personified humans) of equal status, thus triggering an interpretation of togetherness or joint involvement in an event. But the referents can be of any kind, including inanimate referents (as the rope and wood traps in example 140). They also do not need to be of equal status (as the human referent and his axe in example 141a below), triggering a more general accompaniment reading.

(140) *ahrlik, namramaqaqerraakaasik ngenraamengap*
a=sirlik, *ne=met=ama=qaqera=araa=kaasik*
NM=meat from/with=in=ART=person=3PL.POSS=vine
ngere-ne=araa=meng-ap
3N.ASSOC-from/with=3PL.POSS-wood-PL.RCD
'meat, from the people's rope and wood traps' (D12ADKSPIRITS-064)

The associative pronoun with the neuter person index has a wider distribution than the others. It is regularly used to add a third participant to an event. For example, there are three participants in (141a): a human referent and an axe (coordinated by means of the associative construction); following that, the speaker adds a third participant (knives) in a second clause through the use of the associative pronoun *ngene* '3N.ASSOC:from/with'. This neuter pronoun is neither co-referential with the referent of the first noun phrase (which is singular masculine) nor with the referent of the second phrase (which is singular feminine). Instead, it is an addition to the entire event, which is conceptualized as a neuter referent. This kind of context has given rise to an additive interpretation of 'too, also'. This interpretation is illustrated in (141b): the associative construction *ngenaqi* literally translates as 'it (happened) together with it (dog)', and conveys that the dog did the same thing as the deer in the preceding clause (with a more idiomatic translation of 'the dog, too'). This form is furthermore used for the higher numerals (see section 3.2.2). Note that it is not possible to use any other form in these contexts: the neuter form is obligatory even if the head is marked for a different noun class and number (e.g., for singular masculine in 141c).

(141) a. *ikiarl kenamaarepki daalang, dengenaavis*
ip=ke=qiarl
PURP=3SG.M.SBJ.NPST=paddle.NCONT
ke-ne=ama=arap-ki *de=aa=lang,*
3SG.M.ASSOC-from/with=ART=axe-SG.F CONJ=3SG.M.POSS=top
de=ngere-ne=aa=avis
CONJ=3N.ASSOC-from/with=3SG.M.POSS=knife
'he moves with an axe over his shoulders, and with his knives (lit. and it is with knives)' (N12ABKSIRINI-121FF)

b. *kiuaik segumam, dap ngenaqi qiamrenas, biqiqiuaik*
ki=uaik *se=gu-mam,* *dap*
3SG.F.SBJ.NPST=run.NCONT to/with=1SG.POSS-father but
ngere-ne-ki *kia=mrenas,*
3N.ASSOC-from/with-3SG.F 3SG.F.SBJ=jump.NCONT.PST:SELF
be=ki=qiuaik
CONJ=3SG.F.SBJ.NPST=run.CONT
'it (deer) ran with my master, and it (dog), too, jumped and is running now' (R12ABDFROG-093FF)

c. *amalepka ngenangariqit ngenaqa*
a=malep-ka ***ngere-ne=ngariqit*** ***ngere-ne-ka***
NM=ten-SG.M 3N.ASSOC-from/with=five 3N.ASSOC-from/with-SG.M
'(it's question number) sixteen (lit. ten and five and one)' (I12ABLAJLATASOCIO3-115)

The associative construction is the only means of coordinating noun phrases. Alternatively, speakers would have to resort to clausal coordination in such contexts (see chapter 8.3) (as in 142a). For all other semantic types, clausal coordinators are the only available option, e.g., to express disjunction (as in 142b).

(142) a. *saqika amabrutka, de amabrutka, damabrutki*
saqi-ka *ama=brut-ka,* ***de*** *ama=brut-ka,*
again-3SG.M ART=NAME-SG.M CONJ ART=NAME-SG.M
de*=ama=brut-ki*
CONJ=ART=NAME-SG.F
'the same with the Brutka spirit, there is the (male) Brutka, and there is the (female) Brutki' (D12ADKSPIRITS-094)

b. *taquarl ama.. ama.. amadanggi, dakuarl amaqemgi, dakuarl ama.. amaqailka*

taquarl	*ama..*	*ama..*	*ama=dang-ki,*	***dap=kua***	*ama=qem-ki,*
thus	ART	ART	ART=dog-SG.F	but=INTRG	ART=snake-SG.F
dap=kua	*ama..*	*ama=qail-ka*			
but=INTRG	ART	ART=wallaby-SG.M			

'like whether it's a.. a.. a dog, or it's a snake, or it's a.. a wallaby'
(I12AANACLADNSoci03-247)

3.7 Summary

This chapter was organized around the noun phrase in Qaqet. Section 3.1 gave a general introduction to the issues of word class (section 3.1.1) and phrasehood (3.1.2). It was shown there that Qaqet has a distinct word class of nouns, which is defined through a cluster of morphosyntactic properties: nouns occur as heads of noun phrases, (mostly) have an inherent noun class, occur as modifiers in the nominal modifier construction and as non-verbal predicates in the equative construction, and obligatorily co-occur with articles or other pre-head determiners. This cluster of properties differentiates the word class of nouns from that of adjectives, which shares some nominal characteristics. The section then continued to discuss the structure of the noun phrase, showing the typical pattern of pre-head determiners, heads and post-head modifiers. Overall, there is thus considerable evidence for the existence of both a word class of nouns and of a noun phrase. However, this section also discussed two kinds of qualifications. First, many Qaqet roots occur underived in different morphosyntactic contexts, including adjective roots that occur as nouns. It was argued that this phenomenon is a case of conversion (and not of acategoriality). Second, there is a small number of examples that deviate from the typical noun phrase structure, including examples that show a discontinuous structure. It is possible that information structural considerations play a role in the different orders, but it was not possible to offer further generalizations.

Sections 3.2 to 3.4 covered the various elements of the simple noun phrase, starting with those elements that function as heads of noun phrases: common nouns, uncountable nouns, proper nouns and derived nouns (section 3.2.1), numerals and quantifiers (section 3.2.2), independent pronouns (section 3.2.3) and interrogative pronouns (section 3.2.4). Note that most numerals and quantifiers constitute a subclass of nouns – with the main exception of the numerals 'one' and 'two', which are adjectives. In most cases, the head is obligatorily preceded by a determiner: demonstrative pronouns (section 3.3.2), indefinites pronouns (section 3.3.3) or definite and indefinite articles (section 3.3.4). The demonstratives and the indefinites function both as pronouns and as adnominal determiners; the articles only as adnominal determiners. In addition, the noun phrase can optionally contain modifiers: adjectives in the modifier construction (section 3.4.1), nouns, numerals and quantifiers in the nominal modifier construction (section 3.4.2) or prepositional phrases and directionals (section 3.4.3).

Section 3.5 discussed possession. Possessive noun phrases are formed by a possessor index that obligatorily cliticizes to the possessed noun; if a nominal possessor is present, it precedes the index and the possessed noun. This section also discussed variation in the form of the possessor index: some nouns (in particular, a handful of kinship nouns, relational nouns and proforms) have retained an older form of the possessor index. Arguably, this variation reflects a distinction between alienable and inalienable possession – although the class of inalienably possessed nouns is exceedingly small. Finally, section 3.6 showed the possibilities for conjoining noun phrases by means of the associative construction.

The forms and patterns discussed in this chapter are very similar to those of Mali Baining (as described in Stebbins 2011). But despite an overall similarity, there are considerable differences in detail, with evidence pointing both to innovations and to the re-organization of shared forms and inherited structures. Similarities and differences were noted throughout this chapter. From an East Papuan perspective, the structure of possession is of main interest: Qaqet shares the typical Papuan word order of the possessor noun preceding the possessed noun (without having retained a verb-final constituent order or postpositions), and does not exhibit any typical Oceanic features (i.e., it has no possessive classifiers, no suffix-marked possessives, and the distinction between alienable and inalienable possession is at best marginal) (Dunn, Reesink, and Terrill 2002: 33–34; Dunn et al. 2008: 743). Finally, from an areal perspective, the existence of articles is noteworthy, as they are most likely borrowings from Oceanic (Stebbins 2009a; see also Dunn, Reesink, and Terrill 2002: 34–36; Dunn et al. 2008: 743).

The next chapter continues the discussion of nouns and the noun phrase by focusing on the Qaqet noun class system: their forms and their meanings.

4 Nominal classification

Qaqet has an elaborate system of nominal classification that surfaces on nouns and pronouns, in agreement morphology and as argument indexes. The classes are thus identified through their agreement patterns, i.e., they constitute a gender system (following Corbett 1991). Qaqet has two distinct (albeit related) gender systems, and this grammar adopts the terminological distinction established by Stebbins (2011) for the Baining languages: it uses "noun class" in reference to the full system (which surfaces on nouns and independent pronouns, as object suffixes on verbs and prepositions, and on elements within the noun phrase) and "gender" in reference to a reduced system (which surfaces in the form of possessor indexes on possessed nouns, of subject indexes on verbs, and as associative pronouns).

This chapter presents the characteristics of both systems. Section 4.1 describes the noun class morphology, and section 4.2 discusses the semantics; section 4.3 illustrates the mapping of the noun classes onto the gender system; and section 4.4 gives a summary. Note that this chapter does not repeat information given in other chapters on the word classes, their membership and their distribution: nouns (chapter 3.2.1), numerals (chapter 3.2.2), independent pronouns (chapter 3.2.3), interrogative pronouns (chapter 3.2.4), demonstratives (chapter 3.3.2), indefinite pronouns (chapter 3.3.3), and adjectives (chapter 3.4.1). Other chapters also discuss agreement within the noun phrase in more detail (chapter 3.1.2), as well as the argument indexes occurring in possessive structures (chapter 3.5.1), associative structures (chapter 3.6), and verbal structures (chapter 5.2.1).

Nominal classification is characteristic of many East Papuan languages today, but the forms and semantics are very different, and cannot be reconstructed back to a common ancestor language (Dunn et al. 2008: 743; Terrill 2002). The Qaqet system described in this chapter is similar to the one found in closely related Mali and presumably in other Baining languages, and some aspects of it are possibly shared with Taulil and Butam (Stebbins 2009a). To facilitate comparison, this grammar uses as much as possible the labels employed by Stebbins (2005, 2011: 136–155) in her description of Mali.

The salient properties of Qaqet nominal classification are summarized in Table 41 and discussed in detail throughout this chapter. Qaqet has two sex-based classes (labeled masculine and feminine) and six shape-based classes (labeled diminutive, reduced, flat, long, extended and excised). Classes generally have distinct singular, dual and plural forms, but there are some syncretisms and neutralizations. The two sex-based classes are distinguished in the singular and dual, but collapsed in the plural. At the same time, the plural introduces a new distinction between human (labeled plural or plural human) and non-human (labeled neuter) referents.

Tab. 41: Nominal classification

Class	Free pronoun	Suffix on noun	Suffix elsewhere	Possessor index	Subject index	
					Neutral	Non-past
SG.M	*ka*	*-ka*		*aa*	*ka*	*ke*
SG.F	*ki*	*-ki*		*ara*	*kia*	*ki*
DU.M	*iam*	*-iam*		*iana*	*ian*	*iane*
DU.F	*im*	*-im*				
PL.H	*ta*	*Ø ~ -ta*	*-ta*	*araa*	*ta*	*te*
N	*nget*	*Ø ~ -nget*	*-nget*	*ngera*	*nga*	*ngere ~ nger*
SG.DIM	*ini*	*-ini*				
DU.DIM	*iram*	*-iram*				
PL.DIM	*irang*	*-irang*				
SG.RCD	*em*	*-em*				
DU.RCD	*am*	*-am*				
PL.RCD	*ap*	*-ap*				
SG.FLAT	*es*	*-es*				
DU.FLAT	*ivim*	*-ivim*				
PL.FLAT	*iving*	*-iving*				
SG.LONG	*it*	*-it*				
DU.LONG	*isim*	*-isim*				
PL.LONG	*ising*	*-ising*				
SG.EXT	*it*	*-it*				
DU.EXT	*itnem*	*-itnem*				
PL.EXT	*itnek*	*-itnek*				
SG.EXC	*igel*	*-igel*				
DU.EXC	*igrlim*	*-igrlim*				
PL.EXC	*igrling*	*-igrling*				

Each class has a distinct pronominal form; and each class is overtly marked by suffixes on the noun, on noun phrase elements agreeing with the noun (including adjectives, the numerals 'one' and 'two', demonstratives, indefinite pronouns, and some interrogative pronouns), and as object suffixes on verbs and prepositions. The underlying morphemes are mostly identical across all contexts, with the exception of the plural human and neuter classes: they are usually not overtly marked on the noun, but they are revealed in their pronominal forms and in their distinct agreement patterns. The LONG and EXT classes share the same singular form *it*, but the two classes have a different allomorphy (and different dual and plural forms, too).

Noun classes are furthermore mapped onto a gender system that surfaces as possessor indexes, subject indexes on the verb and (not shown in this Table) associative pronouns. In the gender system, the distinction between the masculine and feminine classes is neutralized in the dual, and the neuter class not only covers non-human plurals, but also all shape-based classes (independent of their singular, dual or plural reference).

4.1 Noun class morphology

This section describes the noun class morphology. These morphemes are suffixed to nouns and other parts of speech, and they are transparently related to the forms of the independent pronouns (summarized in Table 41 above), but they are subject to assimilatory processes when appearing as suffixes. Section 4.1.1 discusses the morphemes and their allomorphs in detail, and section 4.1.2 presents a number of proforms that contain the same underlying morphemes, but that exhibit some degree of fusion (i.e., demonstratives and indefinite pronouns).

4.1.1 Noun class suffixes

Table 42 summarizes all regular allomorphs of the noun class suffixes; the independent pronouns are subject to the same allomorphy whenever they appear as enclitics in the relevant phonological environment. Note that the plural column of the masculine and feminine classes includes a number of associative and collective plurals, which do not belong to the noun class system proper (see section 4.2.3). They are included in this section because they can replace noun class suffixes under certain conditions and because they exhibit the same kind of allomorphy.

Aside from some non-predictable forms (discussed later in this section), most of the allomorphy follows the general phonological rules of the language (see chapter 2.1.1): morpheme-initial voiceless plosives (/p/, /t/, /k/) are lenited (to [β], [r], [ɣ] ~ [ʝ]) intervocalically, and they are voiced when following a nasal. Table 43 summarizes the attested patterns. Similarly, all morpheme-final voiceless plosives are lenited when preceding a vowel-initial morpheme. Both phenomena are exemplified by means of *-pik* 'COLL.H', which is realized as *vik* [βik] in (1a) (following a vowel-final root), and as *piq* [piɣ] in (1b) (preceding a vowel-initial morpheme).

Tab. 42: Noun class suffixes and their allomorphy

	SG	DU	PL ~ N
M	*-ka* ~ *-ga* ~ *-qa*	*-iam*	Ø
F	*-ki* ~ *-gi* ~ *-qi*	*-im* ~ *-bim*	*-ta* ~ *-da* ~ *-ra* (PL.H) *-nget* (N) *-kena* ~ *-gena* ~ *-qena* (ASSOC.M) *-kina* ~ *-gina* ~ *-qina* (ASSOC.F) *-pik* ~ *-bik* ~ *-vik* (COLL.H) *-dem* (COLL.N)
DIM	*-ini*	*-iram*	*-irang*
RCD	*-em* ~ *-bem*	*-am* ~ *-bam*	*-ap* ~ *-bap*
FLAT	*-es* ~ *-bes*	*-ivim*	*-iving*
LONG	*-it* ~ *-bit*	*-isim*	*-ising*
EXT	*-it*	*-itnem*	*-itnek*
EXC	*-igel*	*-igrlim*	*-igrling*

Tab. 43: Allomorphs of noun class suffixes I: Lenition and voicing

Gloss	Allomorph after vowels	after nasals	elsewhere
SG.M	*-qa* [ɣa]	*-ga*	*-ka*
SG.F	*-qi* [ʝi]	*-gi*	*-ki*
PL.H	*-ra* [ra]	*-da*	*-ta*
COLL.H	*-vik* [βik]	*-bik*	*-pik*
ASSOC.M	*-qena* [ɣəna]	*-gena*	*-kena*
ASSOC.F	*-qina* [ʝina]	*-gina*	*-kina*

(1) a. *daqasnanbet, naarlua**vik** ma*
de=ka=snanbet, *ne=aa=rlua-**pik***
CONJ=3SG.M.SBJ=ask:ON/UNDER from/with=3SG.M.POSS=friend-COLL.H
ma
thus
'he asked his people like this' (N12ABKSIRINI-042)

b. *ketaqen sagel aaqalat**piq**a*
ke=taqen *se=gel*
3SG.M.SBJ.NPST=say.CONT to/with=near
*aa=qalat-**pik**=a*
3SG.M.POSS=younger.sibling-COLL.H=DIST
'he talks to/with his younger brothers now' (N12AMVGENAINGMET-BROTHERS-039)

In addition, a number of allomorphs exhibit an unexpected initial consonant *b* occurring after a root-final nasal *m* (but not after any other nasal) (summarized in Table 44). The distribution of this phenomenon is not predictable synchronically: it is only attested with some suffixes, and it is not a general phonological rule of the language. Interestingly, all (and only) the corresponding cognate forms in Mali have an initial *ß* (highlighted in grey in Table 45). This suggests that the initial *b* in Qaqet is a remnant of a lost consonant, which was only retained following *m* (see also the discussion of Table 57 in section 4.1.2). Note also that the singular forms of the LONG and EXT classes are identical in present-day Qaqet, but their allomorphy differs: *-it* ~ *-bit* 'SG.LONG' vs. *-it* 'SG.EXT'. This difference corresponds to a difference in Mali: only the cognate form of Qaqet *-it* 'SG.LONG' has an initial *ß* in Mali.

Table 46 illustrates the allomorphy in the environment of nasals with the help of roots that end in a nasal consonant. The suffixes chosen to illustrate this allomorphy are *-ka* 'SG.M' and *-ki* 'SG.F' (realized as voiced *-ga* 'SG.M' and *-gi* 'SG.F' when following a nasal), as well as *-iam* 'DU.M' and *-im* 'DU.F' (where only the latter has an allomorph *-bim* 'DU.F', which occurs following *m*). All noun class suffixes are highlighted in boldface. In all cases, the root-final nasals do not assimilate in place of articulation to the following velar consonants of suffixes.

Tab. 44: Allomorphs of noun class suffixes II: Insertion of *b*

Gloss	After *m*	Elsewhere
DU.F	*-bim*	*-im*
SG.RCD	*-bem*	*-em*
DU.RCD	*-bam*	*-am*
PL.RCD	*-bap*	*-ap*
SG.FLAT	*-bes*	*-es*
SG.LONG	*-bit*	*-it*

Tab. 45: Noun classes: Comparing the Qaqet and Mali forms

	Qaqet			**Mali (Stebbins 2011: 137)**[19]		
	SG	DU	PL	SG	DU	PL
M	*-ka*	*-iam*	*Ø ~ -ta*	*-ka*	*-iɔm*	*Ø ~ -ta*
F	*-ki*	*-im*	*Ø ~ -ta*	*-ki*	*-βəm*	*Ø*
DIM	*-ini*	*-iram*	*-iraŋ*	*-ini*	*-iɹɔm*	*-iɹɔŋ*
RCD	*-əm*	*-am*	*-ap*	*-βəm*	*-βam*	*-βap*
FLAT	*-əs*	*-iβim*	*-iβiŋ*	*-βəs*	*-imɛlɛm*	*-imɛlək*
LONG	*-it*	*-isim*	*-isiŋ*	*-βɛt*	*-isɛm*	*-isɛŋ*
EXT	*-it*	*-itnəm*	*-itnək*	*-ia*	*-inəm*	*-inək*
EXC	*-igəl*	*-igɽim*	*-igɽiŋ*	*-igl*	*-iglɛm*	*-iglɛŋ*

Tab. 46: Distribution of allomorphs I: Following root-final nasals

After	**Gloss**	PL	DU	SG
m	earth oven	*burlem* [ⁿbuɽəm]	*burlem**iam*** [ⁿbuɽəmiam]	*burlem**ga*** [ⁿbuɽəmga]
	cassowary	*unsim* [unsim]	*unsim**bim*** [unsimbim]	*unsim**gi*** [unsimgi]
n	singapore taro	*qalun* [ɣalun]	*qalun**iam*** [ɣaluniam]	*qalunn**ga*** [ɣalunga]
	sugarcane	*alin* [alin]	*alin**im*** [alinim]	*alinn**gi*** [alingi]
ny [ɲ]	shell/money	*qelany* [ɣəlaɲ]	*qelany**iam*** [ɣəlaɲiam]	*qelany**ga*** [ɣəlaɲga]
	step/ladder	*ilany* [ilaɲ]	*ilany**im*** [ilaɲim]	*ilany**gi*** [ilaɲgi]
ng [ŋ]	tree type	*levung* [ləβuŋ]	*levung**iam*** [ləβuŋiam]	*levung**ga*** [ləβuŋga]
	tooth	*rlking* [ɽkiŋ]	*rlking**im*** [ɽkiŋim]	*rlking**gi*** [ɽkiŋgi]

There is some variation, though, in that individual speakers sometimes do not realize a nasal as a coda consonant, but as a prenasalization of a following plosive. For example, the dual form of *mudem* 'resin' is ***mudembim*** [muⁿdəmbim], but individual speakers alternatively pronounce it as [muⁿdəⁿbim]. On morphological grounds, an

19 To facilitate comparison, both the Qaqet and Mali forms are represented here in IPA.

underlying consonant phoneme *m* has to be posited: the base form *mudem* ends in *m*, and the allomorph *-bim* 'DU.F' is only ever attested after roots ending in *m*. Phonetically, however, this nasal is sometimes only retained in the form of prenasalization (see chapter 2.1.1 for a discussion of this phenomenon).

Table 47 illustrates the patterns attested in the case of root-final non-nasal consonants, i.e., plosives, fricatives and liquids (but see chapter 2.1.1 for a discussion of the variable behavior of *rl* /ɽ/). In this context, the underlying form of the suffix *-ka* 'SG.M' surfaces with its initial voiceless plosive. If the two consonants are not identical, both consonants are preserved. If they are identical, they result in a geminate consonant that tends to be realized longer than a simple consonant in careful and normal speech, but not in fast speech (see chapter 2.1.1 for a discussion of consonant length). Different from simple plosives, such geminate plosives are not lenited intervocalically. Table 47 also shows the behavior of root-final consonants when preceding a vowel-initial suffix such as *-iam* 'DU.M': if the root ends in a voiceless plosive (but not if it ends in any other consonant), these plosives are lenited.

Tab. 47: Distribution of allomorphs II: Following root-final non-nasal consonants

After	Gloss	PL	DU	SG
p	rat	*gurup* [ⁿgurup]	*guru**viam*** [ⁿguruβiam]	*gurup**ka*** [ⁿgurupka]
t	sling	*ilat* [ilat]	*ila**riam*** [ilariam]	*ilat**ka*** [ilatka]
k	wild betelnut	*maikmaik* [maikmaik]	*maikmai**qiam*** [maikmaiɰ̥iam]	*maikmai**ka*** [maikmaikka]
s	path	*is* [is]	***isiam*** [isiam]	*is**ka*** [iska]
l	stone	*dul* [ⁿdul]	*dul**iam*** [ⁿduliam]	*dul**ka*** [ⁿdulka]

Finally, vowel-final roots trigger allomorphs with initial lenited plosives, as exemplified in Table 48 by means of the suffix *-ka* (realized as lenited *-qa* 'SG.M'). If the vowel-final root is followed by a vowel-initial suffix such as *-iam* 'DU.M', both vowels tend to be preserved. This is almost always the case when the root-final and suffix-initial vowels are non-identical (as in the first two examples of Table 48). There are occasional counter-examples, though, e.g., *brasu-iam* 'eagle-DU.M' is attested both as [ⁿbra.su.jam] and [ⁿbra.siam]. If the root-final and suffix-initial vowels are identical (as in the last example of Table 48), it is more common for the vowel to be shortened, e.g., forms like *malasi-iam* 'tree.type-DU.M' tend to be pronounced [ma.la.siam].

Again, there are variant pronunciations attested, usually from older speakers, preserving both vowels, i.e., [ma.la.si.jam] (see chapter 2.1.2 on the syllabification of vowel sequences).

Tab. 48: Distribution of allomorphs III: Following root-final vowels

Gloss	PL	DU	SG
avocado	*baata* [^{n}baata]	*baata**iam*** [^{n}baatajam]	*baata**qa*** [^{n}baataɣa]
tree type	*qablu* [ɣa^{n}blu]	*qablu**iam*** [ɣa^{n}blujam]	*qablu**qa*** [ɣa^{n}bluɣa]
tree type	*malasi* [malasi]	*malas**iam*** [malasiam ~ malasijam]	*malasi**qa*** [malasiɣa]

The allomorphy discussed so far is regular and predictable. In addition, there is allomorphy that is not entirely predictable: (i) the presence of an unexpected vowel *a* between the root and some suffixes; (ii) the presence of an unexpected vowel *a* within roots; and (iii) some irregular phonological changes and suppletion. Comparable allomorphy seems to be present in Mali, too, but their extent is unknown (mentioned briefly in Stebbins 2011: 62).

(i) Vowel *a* + suffix

Qaqet has a fairly large number of masculine and feminine nouns[20] that add an unexpected vowel *a* between the root and the singular and dual suffixes, thus resulting in the following sequences: ROOT-*a-qa* 'SG.M', ROOT-*a-qi* 'SG.F', ROOT-*a-iam* 'DU.M' and ROOT-*a-im* 'DU.F'. The vowel sequences in the dual forms are subject to regular phonological processes (see chapter 2.1.2): *aiam* 'DU.M' is realized [ajam], and *aim* 'DU.F' is realized [eem] (with a less frequent variant [ajim]). But the distribution of this vowel *a* is not predictable: all syllable structures are attested, roots can end in any vowel or consonant, and there are phonologically similar words that take the expected allomorphs. This phenomenon is exemplified in Table 49 with roots ending in a vowel, a nasal, a fricative, a liquid and a plosive. The left column displays roots with the unexpected allomorphs, and the right column displays phonologically similar roots with the expected allomorphs.

20 Comparable phenomena are also attested with some adjectives (see chapter 3.4.1), verbs (see chapter 5.2.1) and prepositions (see chapter 5.3.1).

Tab. 49: Vowel *a* + suffix I

	'egg'		'tree type'	
PL	*lu*	[lu]	*qablu*	[ɣa^{n}blu]
DU	*lu**aiam***	[luajam]	*qablu**iam***	[ɣa^{n}blujam]
SG	*lu**aqa***	[luaɣa]	*qablu**qa***	[ɣa^{n}bluɣa]
	'bamboo type'		'rope/vine'	
PL	*rlang*	[ɽaŋ]	*melang*	[məlaŋ]
DU	*rlang**aiam***	[ɽaŋajam]	*melang**iam***	[məlaŋiam]
SG	*rlang**aqa***	[ɽaŋaɣa]	*melang**ga***	[məlaŋga]
	'coconut'		'parrot'	
PL	*lames*	[laməs]	*anes*	[anəs]
DU	*lames**aiam***	[laməsajam]	*anes**iam***	[anəsiam]
SG	*lames**aqa***	[laməsaɣa]	*anes**ka***	[anəska]
	'banana flower'		'mask'	
PL	*qrarl*	[ɣraɽ]	*rmarl*	[rmaɽ]
DU	*qrarl**aim***	[ɣraɽeem]	*rmarl**im***	[rmaɽim]
SG	*qrarl**aqi***	[ɣraɽaʝi]	*rmarl**ki***	[rmaɽki]
	'year'		'banana'	
PL	*tavet*	[taβət]	*qavet*	[ɣaβət]
DU	*taver**aim***	[taβəreem]	*qaver**im***	[ɣaβərim]
SG	*taver**aqi***	[taβəraʝi]	*qavet**ki***	[ɣaβətki]

In most cases, both the singular and dual forms have the additional vowel *a*. There are, however, also cases where the vowel is present only in the singular or only in the dual form. And there are other cases where variant pronunciations are attested. Table 50 exemplifies some such nouns, highlighting in boldface those forms that exhibit the vowel *a*.

A further type of variation is found with roots ending in *k*. Some of them have an additional vowel *a* in both their singular and dual forms (as 'ginger' and 'cane leaf' in Table 51) or in one of their forms (as 'rope/vine' and 'brave person' in Table 50). At least one root ('caterpillar') shows variant realizations with and without this vowel in both singular and dual forms; and a further five roots have a vowel *a* in their dual forms, but not in their singular forms (all given in Table 51 below). In the last six cases, the absence of the vowel *a* in the singular interestingly does not cause the underlying root-final consonant *k* to surface. On the basis of the root, we would expect singular forms such as **qurlika* (from *qurlik-ka* 'caterpillar-SG.M') (just like in the case of 'rope/vine' and 'brave person' in Table 50). Instead, the geminate plosive *kk* seems to lenite to *q*. Recall that elsewhere in the language, gemination always blocks lenition. I therefore consider it more likely that forms such as *qurliqa* were not formed on the basis of the root plus the suffix plus subsequent lenition (e.g., from **qurlik-ka* => **qurlika* => *qurliqa* in this example), but rather result from the loss of the vowel *a* and the subsequent simplification of the identical consonants (e.g., *qurliqaqa* => **qurliqqa* => *qurliqa*).

Tab. 50: Vowel *a* + suffix II: Variation

Gloss	PL	DU	SG
grasshopper	*samil* [samil]	*samiliam* [samiliam]	*samil**aqa*** [samilaɣa]
rope/vine	*kaasik* [kaasik]	*kaasiq**aiam*** [kaasiɣajam]	*kaasika* [kaasikka]
rope/vine	*laanip* [laanip]	*laanivim* [laaniβim]	*laaniv**aqi*** [laaniβaʝi]
brave person	*qansak* [ɣansak]	*qansaq**aim*** [ɣansaɣeem]	*qansaki* [ɣansakki]
heel	*leng* [ləŋ]	*leng**aiam*** [ləŋajam] ~ *lengiam* [ləŋiam]	*leng**aqa*** [ləŋaɣa]

Tab. 51: Vowel *a* + suffix III: Loss of *a*

Gloss	PL	DU	SG
ginger	*qusak* [ɣusak]	*qusaq**aim*** [ɣusaɣeem]	*qusaq**aqi*** [ɣusaɣaʝi]
cane leaf	*rlak* [ɽak]	*rlaq**aim*** [ɽaɣeem]	*rlaq**aqi*** [ɽaɣaʝi]
caterpillar	*qurlik* [ɣuɽik]	*qurliq**aiam*** [ɣuɽiɣajam] ~ *qurliqiam* [ɣuɽiʝiam]	*qurliq**aqa*** [ɣuɽiɣaɣa] ~ *qurliqa* [ɣuɽiɣa]
clay	*qulek* [ɣulək]	*quleq**aiam*** [ɣuləɣajam]	*quleqa* [ɣuləɣa]
crocodile	*quvuk* [ɣuβuk]	*quvuq**aiam*** [ɣuβuɣajam]	*quvuqa* [ɣuβuɣa]
wild cocoa	*remek* [rəmək]	*remeq**aiam*** [rəməɣajam]	*remeqa* [rəməɣa]
midriff	*qalek* [ɣalək]	*qaleq**aim*** [ɣaləɣeem]	*qaleqi* [ɣaləʝi]
breast	*qumek* [ɣumək]	*qumeq**aim*** [ɣuməɣeem]	*qumeqi* [ɣuməʝi]

The corpus contains about 40 nouns that exhibit such an additional vowel *a* in at least one of their forms. Its presence or absence is conventionalized and cannot be predicted on the basis of phonological shape, syllable structure or semantics. I therefore consider it likely that *a* is part of the original root. Synchronically, Qaqet has only a handful of nouns whose roots end in *a*, and these are either known loanwords (e.g. *baata* 'avocado', from Tok Pisin *bata*) or exhibit other kinds of morphological or phonological idiosyncrasies (e.g., *daqa* 'taro' is presumably morphologically **da-ka* 'taro-SG.M', but there is no synchronic root **da* attested anywhere in the language; or *kaina* 'water' has an initial plosive *k* that does not lenite intervocalically – a phenomenon that is commonly found with loanwords, but not with native words). Conversely, there are many roots ending in other vowels. The conspicuous absence of root-final vowels *a* in the present-day language lends support to the hypothesis that this vowel was originally part of the root, but is now only retained in non-final position, e.g., preceding singular or dual suffixes.

All clear examples come from the masculine and feminine classes. This follows from the fact that the simple noun root (without any suffixes) surfaces in plural contexts – which is exactly the environment where a root-final *a* was presumably lost. By contrast, roots from other classes never occur without suffixes. Nevertheless, there are examples from other classes that are likely to have arisen in a similar way. The evidence usually comes from nouns that have related forms in the masculine and feminine classes. For example, the feminine noun *ilaqi* [ilaɟi] 'branch' does not have an unmarked plural form, but it does look as if it must have been formed from **ila-ki* 'branch-SG.F'. However, speakers explicitly relate this noun to a noun from the LONG class, *ilaqait* [ilaɣait] 'long branch', which cannot have been formed from **ila-it* 'branch-SG.LONG' (but must have been formed from *ilaqa-it* 'branch-SG.LONG'). Given the relationship between the two nouns, it is likely that *ilaqi* is a contraction of **ilaqaqi* (following the same diachronic path as the nouns discussed in Table 51 above: **ilaqaqi* => **ilaqqi* => *ilaqi*). That is, the original root (including the root-final vowel *a*) was only preserved in the suffixed forms of the LONG noun class, but not in the feminine noun.

Furthermore, *-em* 'SG.RCD' and *-es* 'SG.FLAT' are variably realized as [əm] ~ [um] and [əs] ~ [us] respectively. The distribution of [u] is partly predictable on the basis of the phonological environment (see point iii below), but there are a handful of cases where the presence of [u] cannot be explained easily. For example, *git-es* 'banana.leaf-SG.FLAT' is invariably and unexpectedly realized [^{n}girus]. It is possible that the unexpected [um] and [us] realizations are indicative of root-final vowels that were lost. This hypothesis is supported by the form *arlangus* [aɽaŋus] 'leaf of *aibika* greens', which must have been formed from **arlang**a**-es* 'aibika.greens-SG.FLAT' – the vowel-final root still surfaces in its feminine counterpart *arlang**a**qi* [aɽaŋ**a**ɟi] '*aibika* greens' (from **arlang**a**-ki* 'aibika.greens-SG.F').

(ii) Internal vowel *a*

Qaqet has a another group of about 20 nouns that also have different suffixed (singular and dual) and non-suffixed (plural) forms. In their case, the change is internal to the root: the non-suffixed form contains an internal vowel *a* in the last syllable of the root, either in place of another vowel or in addition to this vowel (forming a diphthong). The left column of Table 52 illustrates all attested patterns. In the first three patterns, the vowel *a* alternates with another vowel whose quality is predictable: *i* if followed by a palatal consonant, *u* if preceded by a velar consonant, and *e* elsewhere. It is thus likely that the basic alternation is between *a* and *e* (i.e., /ə/ in IPA); recall also that *e* is particularly susceptible to assimilation (see chapter 2.1.2). In addition, an *ai* ~ *i* alternation is attested in one root, and an *ua* ~ *u* alternation is attested in five roots.

Table 52 also demonstrates that the occurrence of the internal vowel *a* is not predictable. There are often phonologically similar nouns that do not show this alternation: the middle and right columns illustrate comparable roots without the internal vowel.

Tab. 52: Internal vowel *a*

a, e	'scraper, shell'	'door'	'spouse'
PL	*nal* [nal]	*tarl* [taɽ]	*ngerl* [ŋəɽ]
DU	*nelim* [nəlim]	*tarliam* [taɽiam]	*ngerliam* [ŋəɽiam]
SG	*nelki* [nəlki]	*tarlka* [taɽka]	*ngerlka* [ŋəɽka]
a, i	'breadfruit'	'mud'	'knife'
PL	*isany* [isaɲ]	*qurlisany* [ɣuɽisaɲ]	*sin* [sin]
DU	*isinyiam* [isiɲiam]	*qurlisanyim* [ɣuɽisaɲim]	*sinim* [sinim]
SG	*isinygi* [isiɲgi]	*qurlisanygi* [ɣuɽisaɲgi]	*sinngi* [singi]
a, u	'wild sugarcane'	'water'	'rat'
PL	*ruqap* [ruɣap]	*qerlap* [ɣəɽap]	*gurup* [^{n}gurup]
DU	*ruquviam* [ruɣuβiam]	*qerlaviam* [ɣəɽaβiam]	*guruviam* [^{n}guruβiam]
SG	*ruqupka* [ruɣupka]	*qerlapka* [ɣəɽapka]	*gurupka* [^{n}gurupka]
ai, i	'planting stick'	'wild sugarcane'	'sword grass'
PL	*qamsaik* [ɣamsaik]	*qaik* [ɣaik]	*qavik* [ɣaβik]
DU	*qamsiqiam* [ɣamsiʝiam]	*qaiqiam* [ɣaiʝiam]	*qaviqiam* [ɣaβiʝiam]
SG	*qamsika* [ɣamsikka]	*qaika* [ɣaikka]	*qavika* [ɣaβikka]
ua, u	'crab'	'tree type'	'victory leaf'
PL	*iguany* [i^{n}guaɲ]	*qirlkuany* [ʝiɽkuaɲ]	*lagun* [la^{n}gun]
DU	*igunyim* [i^{n}guɲim]	*qirlkuanyiam* [ʝiɽkuaɲiam]	*laguniam* [la^{n}guniam]
SG	*igunygi* [i^{n}guɲgi]	*qirlkuanyga* [ʝiɽkuaɲga]	*lagunnga* [la^{n}gunga]

It is unlikely that *a* is a plural infix: Qaqet does not have infixes elsewhere, most nouns do not have an overtly marked plural, and the distribution of *a* is not predictable. It is also unlikely that the singular and dual suffix vowels triggered changes in the root vowel. For example, one could argue that a suffix vowel *i* triggered the fronting of a root vowel. However, such an analysis cannot explain all attested vowel changes, nor can it explain why only a minority of nouns is affected. The alternative is thus to assume that the vowel *a* was originally part of the root, but was only retained in the non-suffixed forms. I consider this alternative to be the more likely explanation, presumably facilitated by the prosodic characteristics of Qaqet: final syllables tend to be lengthened (see chapter 2.3.1), i.e., vowels in final syllables (such as in non-suffixed forms) tend to be longer and, as a result, more target-like and less susceptible to influences from surrounding segments. Conversely, non-final syllables (such as in suffixed forms) tend to be realized considerably shorter, and vowels commonly assimilate in quality to their environment.

Such a scenario would assume the weakening of an original vowel *a* to *e* in non-final syllables (plus subsequent assimilations to palatal and velar consonants). This allophonic variation was eventually phonemicized, resulting in present-day root-internal changes. A similar development would have to be posited for the monophthongization of diphthongs. In the case of the *ai* ~ *i* alternation, the only attested example is *qamsaik* 'planting stick'. Here, the diphthong *ai* would have caused a palatalization of the following *k* [ʲk] (see chapter 2.1.2), and it is likely that this palatalized consonant in turn facilitated the retention of *i* (instead of *a*) in the suffixed forms. In the case of the *ua* ~ *u* alternation, three of the five attested examples occur after a velar consonant (such as *iguany* 'crab'), i.e., it is possible that this velar consonant facilitated the retention of *u*. In forms without velar consonants, the *u* is not stable and tends to assimilate to palatal consonants. Compare *ruany* 'knife' with its singular realizations [ruɲga] ~ [riɲga] (from *ruany-ka* 'knife-SG.M').

(iii) Irregular phonological changes and suppletion

Finally, some forms exhibit additional phonological changes.

The largest group comprises roots that end in a voiceless plosive *t*, which lenites to *r* when preceding a vowel-initial suffix. There are also comparable examples with root-final *p* (leniting to *v*) or root-final nasals. In this environment, a preceding vowel *e* is often reduced to [ᵊ], and sometimes lost altogether. This phenomenon is illustrated in Table 53 by means of the root *avet* 'house'. The reduction or loss of *e* in the environment of liquids (and sonorants in general) is very frequent (see also the discussion in chapter 2.1.2), but not inevitable; there are counter-examples such as [ɣipməriam] (from *qipmet-iam* 'trap-DU.M') or [rəknaŋəriam] (from *reknanget-iam* 'tree.type-DU.M'). In a few cases, this reduction or loss also affects the vowel *a*, as illustrated by *arap* 'axe' in Table 53. Furthermore, if the vowel is reduced or lost and if both the onset and coda consonants are liquids, then the onset consonant assimilates completely to the coda consonant. This phenomenon is illustrated with the help of *lat* 'work' whose diminutive form is *rrini* (from *lat-ini* 'work-SG.DIM').

Note that lenition has to precede vowel reduction and loss: if it were the other way, the plosive would no longer occur in an intervocalic environment, and hence would not lenite. There is only one example where the suffixed forms retain an underlying plosive: *saqang* 'eye/face'. The underlying root is presumably **sakanga* (/sakaŋa/), but the plosive *k* (/k/) surfaces as *q* ([ɣ]) intervocalically. Interestingly, the suffixed forms are realized with the underlying plosive again: **sakanga-ka* 'eye/face-SG.M' is realized as *sakngaqa* [sakŋaɣa] – presumably from *[saɣaŋaɣa] (with intervocalic lenition of /k/) via *[saɣəŋaɣa] ~ *[saɣ^{ə}ŋaɣa] ~ *[saɣŋaɣa] (with vowel reduction and loss) to [sakŋaɣa] (with the plosive surfacing again, as it no longer appears intervocalically).

Tab. 53: Lenition and vowel loss

Gloss	PL	DU	SG
house	*avet* [aβət]	*aver**im*** → *avr**im*** [aβ^{ə}rim] → [aβrim]	*avet**ki*** [aβətki]
axe	*arap* [arap]	**arav**im*** → *arev**im*** ~ *arv**im*** *[araβim] → [ar^{ə}βim] ~ [arβim]	*arep**ki*** [arəpki]
work	*lat* [lat]	**lar**iram*** → *rer**iram*** ~ *rr**iram*** *[lariram] → [r^{ə}riram] ~ [rriram]	**lar**ini*** → *rer**ini*** ~ *rr**ini*** *[larini] → [r^{ə}rini] ~ [rrini]

Some of the noun class suffixes have further variant realizations. This concerns especially the two suffixes starting with an initial vowel *e* /ə/ (*-em* 'SG.RCD' and *-es* 'SG.FLAT'), which frequently assimilates to the preceding environment. As discussed in chapter 2.1.2, [u] is a possible free variant of /ə/. Accordingly, the two suffixes tend to be realized as [um] and [us] in the environment of velar consonants and/or a preceding /u/. Usually, both realizations are attested, e.g., both [luŋəm] and [luŋum] are possible realizations of *lung-em* 'garden-SG.RCD'. Furthermore, both suffixes are realized as [im] and [is] when following either the vowel /i/ or a palatal consonant, e.g., *gumi-es* 'plastic-SG.FLAT' is realized [^{n}gumiis] and *langiny-es* 'paper-SG.FLAT' is realized [laŋiɲis]. Finally, in fast speech, the vowel *e* is sometimes deleted altogether, e.g. *sil-es* 'fern-SG.FLAT' is often realized [sils].

In the case of the suffixes *-ivim* 'DU.FLAT' and *-iving* 'PL.FLAT', the initial vowel *i* is frequently deleted, e.g., *qurlirleng-ivim* 'wild.sugarcane.leaf-DU.FLAT' tends to be realized *qurlirlengvim* [ɣuɽiɽəŋβim].

In addition, there is a small number of suppletive forms – all known forms are shown in Table 54. This includes different roots for 'adult/parent': *lavu* (used in plural and dual contexts), and *mam* 'father' and *nan* 'mother' (used in singular contexts). There are also two roots for 'taro', *nat* (as the non-suffixed form), and **da*, which forms the base for the suffixed dual and singular forms, as well as for all other noun classes (e.g., for the RCD class). Finally, the two roots for 'child' are not entirely suppletive, but they exhibit an unexplained *s* ~ *m* alternation: *rluis* (non-suffixed form) and *rluim* (all suffixed forms).

Tab. 54: Suppletive forms

PL	DU	SG
lavu 'adult'	*laviam* 'adult:DU.M'	*mam* 'father' *nan* 'mother'
nat 'taro' *dap* 'taro:PL.RCD'	*deiam* 'taro:DU.M' *dam* 'taro:DU.RCD'	*daqa* 'taro:SG.M' *dem* 'taro:SG.RCD'
rluis 'child' *rluimbap* 'child:PL.RCD'	*rluimiam* 'child:DU.M' *rluimbim* 'child:DU.F' *rluimbam* 'child:DU.RCD'	*rluimga* 'child:SG.M' *rluimgi* 'child:SG.F' *rluimbem* 'child:SG.RCD'

4.1.2 Demonstrative and indefinite pronouns

The (i) demonstrative and (ii) indefinite pronouns are overtly marked for noun class. They use the suffixes summarized in Table 41 above, but there is some fusion and erosion of segments. For this reason, the paradigms are given separately in this section. Note that this section only illustrates the morphology (see chapters 3.3.2 and 3.3.3 for a discussion of their semantics and distribution).

(i) Demonstratives

Qaqet demonstratives consist of three morphemes: a demonstrative base *lu*, a noun class suffix, and a deictic root. The deictic roots are *-iara* 'PROX' (realized as [iara] ~ [eera] ~ [ira] in free variation) and *-a* 'DIST'. In addition, the adverb *mara* 'here' is currently being integrated into the demonstrative paradigm. The resulting forms are summarized in Table 55. Note that there also exists a form without any noun class suffixes. This form is not used with nominal reference, but occurs in adverbial contexts (see chapter 3.3.2).

The deictic roots are probably cognate to those of Mali Baining, compare Qaqet *-iara* 'PROX' and *-a* 'DIST' with Mali *ụV* 'PROX' and *aβV* 'DIST'. However, the structures are different. The Qaqet demonstrative is formed by means of the demonstrative base *lu*, which is followed by the noun class suffix, which in turn is followed by the deictic root. The Mali demonstrative, by contrast, is formed from the deictic root, followed by the noun class suffix. That is, the order of deictic root and noun class suffix is reversed, and there is no separate demonstrative base *lu*. Given these differences, it is likely that they were grammaticalized independently from the same lexical items, presumably from locative adverbs. Qaqet has a proximal adverb *iara* (but the corresponding distal adverb is not **a*), and Mali has the corresponding adverbs *ụə* 'PROX' and *aβi* 'DIST' (Stebbins 2011: 77–87, 175).

Tab. 55: Demonstrative forms

	Underlying form	***-iara* 'PROX'**	***-a* 'DIST'**	***=mara* 'here'**
Ø	*lu* + deictic	*luiara*	*lua*	*lumara*
SG.M	*lu-ka* + deictic	*luqaira* [luɣeera]	*luqa*	*luqumara*
SG.F	*lu-ki* + deictic	*luqiara* [luɟeera]	*luqia*	*luqimara*
DU.M	*lu-iam* + deictic	*liamiara*	*liama*	*liamara*
DU.F	*lu-im* + deictic	*liimiara*	*liima*	*liimara*
PL.H	*lu-ta* + deictic	*luriara*	*lura*	*luramara*
N	*lu-nget* + deictic	*lungeriara*	*lungera*	*lungetmara*
SG.DIM	*lu-ini* + deictic	*liiniara*	*liina*	*liinimara*
DU.DIM	*lu-iram* + deictic	*liiramiara*	*liirama*	*liiramara*
PL.DIM	*lu-irang* + deictic	*liirangiara*	*liiranga*	*liirangmara*
SG.RCD	*lu-em* + deictic	*laumiara*	*lauma*	*laumara*
DU.RCD	*lu-am* + deictic	*laamiara*	*laama*	*laamara*
PL.RCD	*lu-ap* + deictic	*laaviara*	*laava*	*laapmara*
SG.FLAT	*lu-es* + deictic	*lausiara*	*lausa*	*lausmara*
DU.FLAT	*lu-ivim* + deictic	*liivimiara*	*liivima*	*liivimara*
PL.FLAT	*lu-iving* + deictic	*liivingiara*	*liivinga*	*liivingmara*
SG.LONG	*lu-it* + deictic	*liiriara*	*liira*	*liitmara*
DU.LONG	*lu-isim* + deictic	*liisimiara*	*liisima*	*liisimara*
PL.LONG	*lu-ising* + deictic	*liisingiara*	*liisinga*	*liisingmara*
SG.EXT	*lu-it* + deictic	*liiriara*	*liira*	*liitmara*
DU.EXT	*lu-itnem* + deictic	*liitnemiara*	*liitnema*	*liitnemara*
PL.EXT	*lu-itnek* + deictic	*liitneqiara*	*liitneqa*	*liitnekmara*
SG.EXC	*lu-igel* + deictic	*liigeliara*	*liigela*	*liigelmara*
DU.EXC	*lu-igrlim* + deictic	*liigrlimiara*	*liigrlia*	*liigrlimara*
PL.EXC	*lu-igrling* + deictic	*liigrlingiara*	*liigrlinga*	*liigrlingmara*

The source for the demonstrative base *lu* in Qaqet is very likely the verb *lu* 'see.NCONT' ~ *tlu* 'see.CONT', i.e., the demonstratives probably originated in the structure 'see it here/there' (as illustrated in 2a) (see chapter 3.3.2 for details of the diachronic scenario). In the present-day language, sequences of the verb *lu* ~ *tlu* plus a demonstrative are only sometimes realized as separate words (as in 2b). More frequently, they are fused, resulting in the loss of a syllable *lu* (as in 3c).

(2) a. *nyi sanyiluqa maraavuk*

nyi	*sa=nyi=lu-ka*	*mara=a-vuk*
2SG.SBJ.NPST	already=2SG.SBJ.NPST=see.NCONT-3SG.M	here=DIR-up

'you, you look at him up here' (C12ARBZJIFROG-137)

b. *nyitlu laumara*

nyi=tlu	*lu-em=mara*
2SG.SBJ.NPST=see.CONT	DEM-SG.RCD=here

'see this one here' (R12ATAFROG-279)

c. *saqi nyitliamara*

saqi	*nyi=tlu=lu-iam=mara*
again	2SG.SBJ.NPST=see.CONT=DEM-DU.M=here

'see these ones here again' (R12ATAFROG-272)

In terms of their regular morphophonology, the noun class suffixes in demonstratives exhibit the expected lenition of their final voiceless plosives when preceding the vowel-initial deictic roots *-iara* 'PROX' and *-a* 'DIST'. The voiceless plosives surface again in the case of *=mara* 'here', as they no longer occur intervocalically in this environment.

In addition, adjacent vowels are subject to further changes. This concerns especially the base *lu* 'DEM', which is frequently followed by a vowel-initial noun class suffix. If the initial vowel of the suffix is *a*, the result is a long vowel *aa*, e.g., *lu-am-a* 'DEM-DU.RCD-DIST' is realized as *laama* [laama]. In the case of *i*, the result is a long vowel [ee], which is represented as *ii* in the orthography (see chapter 2.1.2), e.g., *lu-im-a* 'DEM-DU.F-DIST' is realized as *liima* [leema]. Similarly, in the case of *e* /ə/, the result is a long vowel [oo], which is represented as *au* in the orthography, e.g., *lu-em-a* 'DEM-SG.RCD-DIST' is realized as *lauma* [looma]. Finally, in the case of the diphthong-initial suffix *-iam* 'DU.M', the vowel *u* is lost altogether, e.g., *lu-iam-a* 'DEM-DU.M-DIST' is realized as *liama* [liama]. Similarly, the final vowel of all vowel-final noun class suffixes is lost when preceding *-iara* 'PROX' and *-a* 'DIST', e.g., *lu-ini-a* 'DEM-SG.DIM-DIST' is realized as *liina* [leena].

In some demonstratives, lenition and vowel loss co-occur. As illustrated in Table 56, lenition must have preceded vowel loss in such cases. For example, the demonstratives *lu-ka-iara* 'DEM-SG.M-PROX' and *lu-ki-iara* 'DEM-SG.F-PROX' are realized *luqaira* [luɣeera] and *luqiara* [luʝeera] respectively. This realization is only possible if we assume that the intervocalic plosive /k/ lenited first to [ɣ] (preceding a vowel /a/) and to [ʝ] (preceding a vowel /i/). And only afterwards, the underlying vowels /a/ and /i/ were lost. If the rules were ordered differently, we would expect both proximal forms to be realized as [luʝeera] (not just the feminine form). Conversely, for the distal forms, we would expect both forms to be realized as [luɣa] (not just the masculine form).

Tab. 56: Demonstratives: Lenition and vowel loss

Underlying form	Gloss	+ Lenition	+ Vowel loss
lu-ka-iara	DEM-SG.M-PROX	*luɣaiara*	*luɣiara ~ luɣeera*
lu-ki-iara	DEM-SG.F-PROX	*lu̯jiiara*	*lu̯jiara ~ lu̯jeera*
lu-ka-a	DEM-SG.M-DIST	*luɣaa*	*luɣa*
lu-ki-a	DEM-SG.F-DIST	*lu̯jia*	*lu̯ja*

The deictics *-iara* 'PROX' and *-a* 'DIST' are considered suffixes, while *mara* 'here' is considered an enclitic. The reason for this difference in analysis is the variant realizations of *mara* (see chapter 3.3.2 for additional distributional differences). Speakers sometimes utter *mara* as a separate word, with a preceding pause and lengthening of the final syllable of the preceding word – both are indications of a word boundary (see chapter 2.3.1). Such a pronunciation is illustrated in (3a). Conversely, there are realizations where *mara* is uttered without pauses or lengthening of preceding syllables (as in 3b), and sometimes even with erosion of preceding phonetic material (as in 3c).

(3) a. *dap kurli lungut mara*
dap kurli lu-nget mara
but leave DEM-N here
'but these ones here stay' (R12ADNFROG-369)

b. *lungetmara, denyirlingmet*
lu-nget=mara, de=nyi=rlingmet
DEM-N=here CONJ=2SG.SBJ.NPST=split:IN
'these ones here, you split (them)' (P12ADNROPE1-038)

c. *lungmara*
lu-nget=mara
DEM-N=here
'this one here' (N12BAMCAT-316)

It is likely that the variant realizations are the result of diachronic developments. There are reasons to assume that all three deictics originated in adverbs, which initially continued to function as spatial adverbs (such as *mara* 'here' in 3a above). In normal speech, spatial adverbs tend to cliticize to surrounding material, i.e., they are not infrequently realized as enclitics (as in 3b). Finally, a tighter integration then triggered erosion of phonetic material (as in 3c) as well as adjustments in syllable structures. Most of the attested variation concerns consonant clusters (i.e., where *mara* cliticizes to a consonant-final suffix). Although intervocalic consonant clusters are permitted, they tend to be simplified (see chapter 2.1.1 for a discussion). Some of the clusters are simplified by losing one of the segments. This is usually the case with the cluster *mm*, e.g., *lu-em=mara* 'DEM-SG.RCD=here' is most commonly realized as [loomara] (although [loommara] is also attested). And other clusters are simplified by inserting an epenthetic [ə], e.g., both [loosmara] and [loosəmara] are equally frequent realizations of *lu-es=mara* 'DEM-SG.FLAT=here'.

A second type of variation concerns vowel quality: *lu-ka=mara* 'DEM-SG.M=here' is unexpectedly realized [luɣumara] ~ [luɣəmara]. It is likely that these realizations are triggered by the altered phonotactics. Through the cliticization of *mara*, the vowel [a] no longer occurs within the final syllable. Non-final syllables, however, are realized shorter and this presumably triggered the centralization of [a] to [ə]. And a vowel [ə] in turn frequently assimilates in quality to a preceding [u]. Similarly, *lu-ini=mara* 'DEM-SG.DIM=here' has the two realizations [leenimara] and [leenəmara], with a corresponding centralization of [i] to [ə].

I consider such variation evidence for an on-going grammaticalization process, and thus represent *mara* consistently as a clitic in this grammar (not as a suffix). By contrast, *-iara* 'PROX' and *-a* 'DIST' do not show any comparable variation, and I thus analyze them synchronically as suffixes within the demonstrative word.

(ii) Indefinite pronouns

Qaqet has two indefinite pronouns that presumably originated in nouns: they inflect for noun class; they occur also as pronouns (not only as modifiers to nouns); and *qa* 'some' cannot occur without an article (or alternatively a possessor index). That is, their inflectional and distributional properties are similar to those of nouns, and different from those of other indefinite forms (see chapter 3.3.3). The indefinite pronouns are formed from the bases *ia* 'other' and *qa* 'some', plus a noun class suffix. As the resulting forms are not entirely predictable, they are summarized in Table 57. The forms marked with a question mark are not attested in the corpus and were constructed on the basis of the available information and checked with a speaker.

The noun class suffix is always recognizable, but there are unexpected changes. The same changes are usually present in both indefinite pronouns.

In all cases, the initial /i/ of vowel-initial suffixes is lost without a trace whenever this morpheme is suffixed to the vowel-final root. This behavior is different from that observed in nouns, where long vowels at morpheme boundaries are preserved (see section 4.1.1). In the case of the indefinite pronouns, only suffix-initial diphthongs are preserved (as in *iaiam* and *qaiam*, from *ia-iam* 'other-DU.M' and *qa-iam* 'some-DU.M').

A number of forms exhibit an additional medial consonant *v* or *q*. This includes all noun classes that also have the *b*-initial allomorph (see Table 44 above), i.e., all suffixes whose cognate forms in Mali have an initial *v* (/β/). It is thus likely that the pronouns have retained an inherited consonant that was lost in other environments. Most suffixes take the expected *v* (*-im* 'DU.F', *-am* 'DU.RCD', *-ap* 'PL.RCD' and *-it* 'SG.LONG'), while two suffixes take an unexpected *q* (*-em* 'SG.RCD' and *-es* 'SG.FLAT'). It is not clear how to explain a change from *v* to *q*, and there are no comparable changes attested elsewhere in the language. It can only be observed that it concerns the only two suffixes that start with the vowel *e* – a vowel that behaves somewhat differently from other vowels in the language (see chapter 2.1.2). And in both cases, the underlying suffix vowel *e* is realized as *a* in the pronominal forms, e.g., *ia-em* 'other-SG.RCD' is realized *iaqam* (not **iaqem* or **iavem*).

Tab. 57: Indefinite pronouns

	Underlying form	***ia* 'other'**	***qa* 'some'**
SG.M	pronoun + *-ka*	*iak*	*qek*
SG.F	pronoun + *-ki*	*iaik*	*qaik*
DU.M	pronoun + *-iam*	*iaiam*	*qaiam*
DU.F	pronoun + *-im*	*iavim*	*qavim*
PL.H	pronoun + *-ta*	*iari*	*qari*
N	pronoun + *-nget*	*iang*	*qeng*
SG.DIM	pronoun + *-ini*	*iani*	*qani*
DU.DIM	pronoun + *-iram*	*iaram*	*qaram*
PL.DIM	pronoun + *-irang*	*iarang*	*qarang*
SG.RCD	pronoun + *-em*	*iaqam*	*qaqam*
DU.RCD	pronoun + *-am*	*iavam*	*qavam*
PL.RCD	pronoun + *-ap*	*iavap*	*qavap*
SG.FLAT	pronoun + *-es*	*iaqas*	*qaqas* ~ *qas*
DU.FLAT	pronoun + *-ivim*	*iavim*	*qavim*
PL.FLAT	pronoun + *-iving*	*iaving*	*qaving*
SG.LONG	pronoun + *-it*	*iavit*	*qavit*
DU.LONG	pronoun + *-isim*	*iasim* (?)	*qasim* (?)
PL.LONG	pronoun + *-ising*	*iasing* (?)	*qasing* (?)
SG.EXT	pronoun + *-it*	*iat*	*qat* (?)
DU.EXT	pronoun + *-itnem*	*iatnem* (?)	*qatnem* (?)
PL.EXT	pronoun + *-itnek*	*iatnek* (?)	*qatnek* (?)
SG.EXC	pronoun + *-igel*	*iagel*	*qagel*
DU.EXC	pronoun + *-igrlim*	*iagrlim*	*qagrlim*
PL.EXC	pronoun + *-igrling*	*iagrling*	*qagrling*

In two cases, final segments are lost: in the neuter forms *iang* and *qeng* (from *ia-nget* 'other-N' and *qa-nget* 'some-N'), and in the masculine singular forms *iak* and *qek* (from *ia-ka* 'other-SG.M' and *qa-ka* 'some-SG.M'). In slow speech, the lost segments are sometimes retained, but only rarely so. Furthermore, there is a vowel change from *a* to *e* in *qek* and *qeng*. The expected forms **qak* and **qang* are not attested.

In the case of *iari* and *qari* (from *ia-ta* 'other-PL.H' and *qa-ta* 'some-PL.H'), there is an unexpected final vowel (while the intervocalic lenition from /t/ to [r] is expected).

Finally, the feminine singular forms *iaik* [jaʲk] and *qaik* [ɣaʲk] (from *ia-ki* 'other-SG.F' and *qa-ki* 'some-SG.F') exhibit metathesis. The expected forms would be **iaqi* and **qaqi*, but these forms are not attested in isolation. However, they still surface whenever cliticization processes cause present-day *iaik* or *qaik* to be followed by a vowel within a single phonological word. For example, in (4) below, *iaik* is a proclitic to the article *ama* (plus the head noun), resulting in the pronunciation *iaqiama* [jaʝiama] (and not, as expected on the basis of the present-day form in isolation, **iaiqama* [jaiɣama]).

(4) *tika **iaqi**amavlemgi*
tika ***ia-ki**=ama=vlam-ki*
EMPH other-SG.F=ART=pig-SG.F
'it's a kind of pig' (R12ATAFROG-198)

In isolation, the expected form **iaqi* must have lost its final vowel, just like its masculine counterpart *iak* (via **iaqa* from *ia-ka* 'other-SG.M'). In both cases, the underlying plosive *k* surfaced again, as it no longer occurred in an intervocalic environment. In addition, the loss of the final vowel was not complete: in the feminine form, it left its trace in the palatalization of the plosive *k*. As discussed in chapter 2.1.1, *k* is inevitably palatalized in the environment of *i*. The same development must have taken place in the case of **qaqi*.

4.2 Noun classes: Categories

The majority of Qaqet nouns belongs to one of the two sex-based classes (masculine and feminine). Each of the two classes contains about 40% of the attested nouns, while the remaining 20% are distributed across the six shape-based classes. For each class, it is possible to establish basic semantic organizing principles: human referents in the masculine and feminine classes are assigned on the basis of being male and female respectively, while shape and size determine membership in one of the shape-based classes. However, there are large groups of nouns whose assignment is not (or no longer) semantically transparent. This is especially the case for animals, plants and inanimate referents in the masculine and feminine classes. Although there are tendencies, there are just as many counter-examples and non-transparent assignments. To a lesser extent, this observation also holds for the shape-based classes.

It is possible for a single noun root to occur in more than one class (as illustrated with some examples in Table 58). In some cases, there is a predictable change in meaning (especially if a shape-based class is involved), while in other cases, the change in meaning is not transparent. In all cases, a re-assignment to another class creates a new conventionalized lexeme, with a new, not always predictable, meaning. As such, the classes resolve patterns of polysemy. For example, the noun root *qunam* is polysemous between 'flower' and 'flour' (possibly a calque on Tok Pisin *plaua* 'flower, flour') – but *qunem-ka* 'flower-SG.M' in the masculine class refers to a 'flower', while *qunem-ki* 'flour-SG.F' in the feminine class refers to 'flour'.

This section introduces the noun class categories, their semantics and typical referents. It first discusses the two sex-based classes (section 4.2.1), as well as the distribution of the unmarked forms (section 4.2.2) and of the overtly marked plural forms (section 4.2.3). This is followed by a description of the six shape-based classes (section 4.2.4).

Tab. 58: Noun roots in different noun classes

	meng	***ilany***	***lengi***	***langiny***
M	*meng-ka* 'tree'	*ilany-ka* 'toe'	*lengi-ka* 'language'	*langiny-ka* 'book'
F		*ilany-ki* 'step, ladder'		
DIM	*meng-ini* 'stick'		*lengi-ini* 'word'	
RCD	*meng-em* 'wood trap'		*lengi-em* 'story, incantation'	
FLAT				*langiny-es* 'paper'
LONG		*ilany-it* 'leg'		
EXT				
EXC	*meng-igel* 'split tree, plank'	*ilany-igel* 'foot'		

4.2.1 Masculine and feminine classes

Qaqet has two sex-based classes, masculine and feminine, each comprising about 40% of the noun lexicon. The two classes are distinguished in the singular and dual, but their distinction is neutralized in the plural.

Most straightforwardly, the two classes are used with male and female referents respectively, including male and female humans and spirits, as well as animals whose sex is easily distinguished (e.g., hens and roosters). In such cases, the same root occurs in both classes, e.g., the noun class distinguishes between the 'girl' in (5a) and the 'boy' in (5b) – both formed from the root *rluim* 'child'. The same principle underlies the assignment of nouns that are converted from another word class and that characterize a human propensity or activity. For example, the predicate *vurek* 'tired' gave rise to the nouns *vurek-ka* 'tired man' (lit. 'tired-SG.M') and *vurek-ki* 'tired woman' (lit. 'tired-SG.F').

(5) a. *arluimgi qiatden bsagelka*
*a=rluim-**ki*** *kia=tden* *be=se=gel-ka*
NM=child-SG.F 3SG.F.SBJ=come.CONT CONJ=to/with=near-3SG.M
'the girl is coming close to him' (N11AAGSIRINIROPE-0148)
b. *dap luqa amarluimga, deqraqatekmet*
dap *lu-ka-a* *ama=rluim-**ka**,*
but DEM-SG.M-DIST ART=child-SG.M
de=ka=raqa=tekmet
CONJ=3SG.M.SBJ=properly.NCONT=do.CONT:IN
'but that boy did (tell) it in the proper way' (I12AANACLADNSOCIO3-439)

The masculine class can be considered the unmarked class, as it is used in contexts where the sex of a referent is irrelevant or unknown. For example, the masculine singular form is used in (6a) on the noun *qaqera* 'person', to refute a common misconception that a particular spirit is just a single spirit. This example is especially interesting because the spirit in question formally belongs to the feminine class: it is overtly marked for feminine, and it triggers feminine argument indexes on the verb (as in 6b). In example (6a), however, the masculine form is used in a context where the sex is not relevant.

(6) a. *kuasiqi amaqaqeraqa amaqunaska, kias amavilanngi de amaqaqera amaburlem nara*
kuasik=i *ama=qaqera-**ka*** *ama=qunas-**ka**,* *kias*
NEG=SIM ART=person-SG.M ART=one-SG.M actually
ama=vilanngi *de* *ama=qaqera* *ama=burlem* *ne-ta*
ART=NAME:SG.F CONJ ART=person ART=many from/with-3PL.H
'(the VilanFEMININE spirit) is not just one personMASCULINE, the VilanFEMININE (spirit) is actually many people' (I12AANACLADNSOCIO3-489FF)

b. *deiva, damavilanngi qiatdena*
de=ip=a *de=ama=vilann**gi*** ***kia**=tden=a*
CONJ=PURP=DIST CONJ=ART=NAME:SG.F 3SG.F.SBJ=come.CONT=DIST
'and now, the Vilan (spirit) is coming' (I12AANACLADNSocio3-527)

The masculine class is furthermore used in reference to mixed groups. This is shown with the dual masculine form *lavu-iam* 'adult-DU.M' in (7), referring to a husband and his wife.

(7) *dema genainymerini, de aalaviam masirini, qenaangerlki masiqi*
de=ma *genainymerini,* *de* *aa=lavu-**iam*** *ma=sirini,*
CONJ=ART.ID NAME:SG.DIM CONJ 3SG.M.POSS=adult-DU.M ART.ID=NAME
ke-ne=aa=ngerl-ki *ma=siqi*
3SG.M.ASSOC-from/with=3SG.M.POSS=spouse-SG.F ART.ID=NAME
'Genainymerini and his two parents, Sirini together with his wife Siqi' (D12ADKSpirits-029)

In the case of unknown referents, speakers preferably use the neuter class. Example (8) illustrates the use of the unmarked interrogative *nema* 'who' together with neuter argument indexing on the verb. Alternatively, speakers can resort to the masculine interrogative *nemga* 'who:SG.M' in contexts where the sex of the referent is unknown.

(8) *nyinarliip.. ip nema ngeretaqen*
nyi=narli=ip.. *ip* ***nema*** ***ngere**=taqen*
2SG.SBJ.NPST=hear= PURP PURP who 3N.SBJ.NPST=say.CONT
'hear.. who's talking' (ARS-12/06/2015)

While the assignment of human referents to either the masculine or the feminine class is straightforward, it is difficult to establish a clear semantic basis for the assignment of most animals, plants and inanimates.

In the case of animals, an assignment on the basis of the referent's sex is possible, but uncommon. Most animals are assigned to one class by default (see also below), and speakers use this class in all contexts where they do not explicitly focus on the sex of the referent. They can, however, shift to the other class to refer to a referent of the opposite sex. For example, *quldit-ki* 'frog-SG.F' is feminine by default, but the speaker in (9) intends to distinguish between a father and a mother frog. He therefore uses the corresponding noun class suffixes, in combination with the modifiers 'man' and 'woman'.

(9) *aqulditka amangerlmamga, kenamaqulditki amangerlnanngi*
*a=quldit-**ka*** *ama=ngerlmam-ka,*
NM=frog-SG.M ART=man-SG.M
*ke-ne=ama=quldit-**ki*** *ama=ngerlnan-ki*
3SG.M.ASSOC-from/with=ART=frog-SG.F ART=woman-SG.F
'a male frog, together with a female frog' (R12ACMFROG-107FF)

In some semantic domains, there are clear tendencies for the assignment of nouns. For example, trees, bamboos, vines, garden produce and seeds tend to be masculine, while fruits and leafy edible greens tend to be feminine. As such, masculine *vas-ka* 'breadfruit-SG.M' refers to the cultivated breadfruit tree, while feminine *vas-ki* 'breadfruit-SG.F' refers to its fruit. Or masculine *gam-ka* 'seed/fruit-SG.M' refers to seeds, while feminine *gam-ki* 'seed/fruit-SG.F' refers to fruits. Nevertheless, there are counter-examples to all tendencies. For example, *iala-ka* 'mango-SG.M' refers both to the tree and the fruit. Or both (expected) feminine *iling-ki* 'pumpkin-SG.F' and (unexpected) masculine *ngelang-ka* 'pumpkin-SG.M' refer to a similar type of edible greens (i.e., the leaves of the pumpkin fruit). Or while most cultivated root crops like *da-ka* 'taro-SG.M' or *qalun-ka* 'singapore.taro-SG.M' are masculine, *quany-ki* 'yam-SG.F' is feminine.

In the domain of artefacts and tools, we can also observe tendencies: containers, clothing, woven materials and scrapers tend to be feminine, and spears, traps and sticks tend to be masculine. For example, although bamboo plants are masculine (e.g., *kaut-ka* 'bamboo-SG.M'), sections of bamboo used as water containers and drinking vessels (e.g., *lum-ki* 'bamboo-SG.F') or as food containers (e.g., *rliin-ki* 'bamboo-SG.F') are feminine. The motivation for the attested assignments is unclear, but it is unlikely that they reflect a division in the manufacture or use of the artefacts. For example, feminine scrapers (e.g., *quarkuarik-ki* 'scraper-SG.F') are also manufactured and used by men, and masculine planting sticks (e.g., *qamsik-ka* 'planting.stick-SG.M') or drumming sticks (e.g., *qanirl-ka* 'drumming.stick-SG.M'), by women. Similarly, feminine *tek-ki* 'bark.cloth-SG.F' and *trausis-ki* 'trousers-SG.F' are both worn by men (and the first is also manufactured by men). Again, there are exceptions to the generalizations. For example, netbags woven from industrial string are feminine as expected (*ubin-ki* 'netbag-SG.F'), but netbags woven from vines are masculine (*rlaun-ka* 'netbag-SG.M'); and the masculine class also includes some containers: *botol-ka* 'bottle-SG.M' or *milat-ka* 'coconut.shell-SG.M'. Conversely, there is the feminine fighting stick *galep-ki* 'handle/club-SG.F'.

Finally, in all other domains (e.g., animals, bodyparts, geographical locations, abstract concepts), no obvious patterns emerge. In the case of animals, it is not even the case that terms for individual species belong to the same class as the generic term. For example, the generic term *uaik-ki* 'bird-SG.F' is feminine, yet bird species can be either masculine (e.g., *anes-ka* 'parrot-SG.M', *nguat-ka* 'crow-SG.M', *qeseqesek-ka* 'dove.type-SG.M') or feminine (e.g., *itup-ki* 'dove.type-SG.F', *laap-ki* 'cockatoo-SG.F', *rengirl-ki* 'parrot.type-SG.F').

Speakers can choose to assign a noun to the opposite class, in which case they highlight an unusual or untypical referent. For example, *surl-ka* 'fence-SG.M' can appear as feminine *surl-ki* 'fence-SG.F' in order to highlight an incomplete fence that has just been started around a new garden. Or *dul-ka* 'stone-SG.M' can appear as feminine *dul-ki* 'stone-SG.F' to express frustration with a particular stone. In everyday speech, such shifts are not very common, and they do not straightforwardly shed light on the semantic organization of the system. Instead, what seems to be of pragmatic importance is the fact of the shift itself. Interestingly, Dickhardt (2009: 156) observes that such shifts are a characteristic property of verbal exchanges that take place during public meetings aimed at conflict resolution. Unfortunately, our corpus does not contain recordings of such events, and it is thus not possible to investigate the patterns of shift further.

It is possible that an in-depth study will discover subtle organizational patterns, as shown by Stebbins (2005) for Mali. While there are similarities in some assignments across the two languages (e.g., the patterns reported above for Qaqet are also attested in Mali), other assignments are different. In particular, Mali has an association between the feminine class and large size, and between the masculine class and component parts of a whole. These associations do not seem to hold for Qaqet. Furthermore, even cognate lexical items do not necessarily belong to the same class, e.g., Qaqet *quainyguainy-ka* 'butterfly-SG.M' is masculine, while cognate Mali *achinggoing-ki* 'butterfly-SG.F' is feminine (Stebbins 2005: 94), or Qaqet *lamesa-ka* 'coconut-SG.M' is masculine, while cognate Mali *lamēsa-ki* 'coconut-SG.F' is feminine (Stebbins 2005: 98) (in both languages with reference to the coconut palm tree).

4.2.2 Unmarked noun

In addition to overtly marked singular and dual masculine and feminine nouns, Qaqet has unmarked nouns. These unmarked nouns can be divided into three different groups depending on their agreement and argument indexing patterns: (i) plural referents of the masculine and feminine classes (taking either plural human or neuter agreement), (ii) address terms (taking either masculine or feminine agreement), and (iii) relational nouns (not controlling any agreement).

The majority of nouns occurring in contexts (i), (ii) and (iii) are formally unmarked: they do not take any noun class suffixes, and their form is identical to that of the roots used with overt singular and dual suffixes in the masculine and feminine classes. In addition, I also include those nouns whose non-suffixed forms differ in some non-predictable ways, usually by the unexpected presence or absence of a vowel *a* (see section 4.1.1 for details). These forms distribute exactly like unmarked nouns, and I thus analyze them together. Strictly speaking, 'unmarked noun' should thus read 'noun not marked by noun class suffixes'.

(i) Plural

The contrast between the masculine and feminine classes is neutralized in plural contexts. In such contexts, nouns of both classes most commonly occur in their unmarked form, including nouns with human reference (as in 10a) as well as with non-human reference (as in 10b).

(10) a. *aqaqeramadepguas nara*
*a=**qaqera**=ama=depguas ne-ta*
NM=person=ART=three from/with-3PL.H
'three people' (R12ABDFROG-002)

b. *aavet amadepguas amaslurlnget*
*a=**avet** ama=depguas ama=slurl-nget*
NM=house ART=three ART=big-N
'three big houses' (AEM-31/05/2011)

Although both human and non-human nouns are unmarked, they show different agreement and argument indexing patterns. Nouns with human referents trigger the use of plural human forms (e.g., of the pronoun *ta* '3PL.H' in 10a above). Nouns with non-human referents (including animals), by contrast, control neuter agreement – which is not only attested with unmarked plural nouns (e.g., *nget* 'N' in 10b above) but also with singular, dual and plural nouns from shape-based classes in some contexts (see section 4.3). That is, neuter agreement neutralizes all number distinctions. However, both human and non-human unmarked nouns can be counted, and can only co-occur with numerals above two (as in both examples above). They are not attested with the numerals 'one' and 'two' (which occur with singular- and dual-marked nouns only), and all attempts at eliciting unmarked nouns with the numerals 'one' and 'two' have failed.[21]

---

21 It is not entirely clear whether plurality is semantically entailed or pragmatically inferred. Given some of the non-plural uses of unmarked nouns as well as the neuter agreement pattern, it is conceivable that their plural interpretation follows from pragmatic principles: a speaker will use dedicated singular or dual forms whenever singular or dual reference is intended – and the fact that a speaker did not use one of these forms then implicates that they are not applicable, and hence that plural reference is intended (see Levinson 2000 for a framework). There are a handful of examples that could conceivably be interpreted in this way: for example, the speaker in (i) below uses the unmarked (plural) form *ngarik* 'hand' in a dual context (and not the expected form *ngarik-isim* 'hand-DU.LONG'). A more detailed semantic and pragmatic investigation is necessary to further pursue this question.

In the case of spirits, speakers can construe them either as human (as in 11a) or as non-human (as in 11b). Both examples come from the same story from the same speaker, referring to the same event (that repeats itself in the course of the story). In the first case, the speaker portrays the spirits as human and in the second case, as non-human. As shown in the continuation of (11b), he uses *uis* 'child' to refer to the spirits – this noun would normally trigger plural human agreement.

(11) a. *dera mii rans*
*de=**ta*** *mii* ***ta**=nes*
CONJ=3PL.H most 3PL.SBJ=shout.NCONT
'and they all shout' (N11AAGSIRINILOBSTER1-0056)

b. *de nget mii ngans, kenaauis*
de ***nget*** *mii* ***nga**=nes,*
CONJ 3N most 3N.SBJ=shout.NCONT
ke-ne=aa=uis
3SG.M.ASSOC-from/with=3SG.M.POSS=child
'and they all shout, he together with his children' (N11AAGSIRINILOBSTER1-0051)

The unmarked nouns are furthermore used to form generic statements. For example, (12a) below is a generic statement about netbags. This example was immediately followed in discourse by (12b) where the speaker used singular marking in reference to the specific netbag that she and her friend were weaving at the time. I analyze such forms as generic plurals, as they allow for co-occurrence with *burlem* 'many' (as in 12c). In unambiguous contexts, this quantifier only ever occurs with plural reference (as in 12d).

(12) a. *damarlaun, de tika idremsem nama.. amakaasiq amalangik*
*de=ama=**rlaun**,* *de* *tika* *ide=te=msem*
CONJ=ART=netbag CONJ EMPH IPFV=3PL.SBJ.NPST=weave.CONT
ne=ama.. *ama=**kaasik*** *ama=**langik***
from/with=ART ART=vine ART=vine
'and netbags, they usually weave them from the.. the *langik* vines' (P12ARSBILUM2-016)

(i) *de.. lek praangarik*
de.. *lek* *pet=aa=ngarik*
CONJ take.off on/under=3SG.M.POSS=hand
'and.. he took off his hands' (N11AAGSIRINIROPE-0074)

b. *katika, tika lungerai unetmatna vramarlaunnga, de amakaasika amalangika*
ka=tika, *tika* *lu-nget-a=i* *une=tmatna*
3SG.M.SBJ=EMPH EMPH DEM-N-DIST=SIM 1DU.SBJ.NPST=work.CONT:RECP
*pet=ama=**rlaun-ka**,* *de* *ama=**kaasik-ka*** *ama=**langik-ka***
on/under=ART=netbag-SG.M CONJ ART=vine-SG.M ART=vine-SG.M
'that's it, it's (like) that, when we are working on the netbag, there's the *langik* vine' (P12ARSBILUM2-017FF)

c. *deqakias, amaburlem nama.. ama**rlaun***
de=ka=kias, *ama=burlem* *ne=ama..* *ama=**rlaun***
CONJ=3SG.M.SBJ=actually ART=many from/with=ART ART=netbag
'there are actually many kinds of.. netbags' (P12ARSBILUM2-005)

d. *de amaburlem nangen*
de *ama=burlem ne-ngen*
CONJ ART=many from/with-2PL
'you are many' (P12ARSBILUM1-028)

Finally, there is a small number of uncountable nouns that only (or preferably) occur in their unmarked form (see chapter 3.2.1 for details of this subclass of nouns). In a few cases, no other form is attested. For example, *sleng* 'garden' cannot appear with any overt noun class marking, and speakers have to resort to a distinct lexeme such as *lung-em* 'garden-SG.RCD' in order to refer to a specific garden plot. In other cases, speakers resort to one of the shape-based classes in such contexts, usually the diminutive class or the reduced class. For example, *liltem* 'domestic plant or animal' is shifted to the diminutive class (*liltem-ini* 'domestic-SG.DIM'). And in yet other cases, both unmarked and marked forms co-exist (e.g., *qerlap* 'water' ~ *qerlap-ka* 'water-SG.M').

Nouns that only or preferably occur in their unmarked form tend to refer to places (e.g., *luqup* 'place'), collectives and masses (e.g., *guvang* 'dirt') and abstract concepts and activities (e.g., *gamansena* 'custom, tradition'). Given this kind of reference, it can be assumed that unmarked nouns denote uncountable referents. This is true in the sense that they (unlike the plural nouns above) cannot co-occur with numerals. However, like other unmarked nouns, they can co-occur with the plural quantifier *burlem* 'many' (as in 13a). Qaqet only has a very small number of nouns that cannot occur with singular or dual marking; and this group is considerably smaller than in Mali, where around 300 such nouns are attested (Stebbins 2011: 139). Mostly, Qaqet has overtly marked nouns referring to places (e.g., *qavel-ka* 'bush-SG.M'), collectives and masses (e.g., *kaina-ki* 'water-SG.F'), and abstract concepts and activities (e.g., *lengi-ka* 'word-SG.M') – and all these nouns can be counted (as in 13b). Since it is lexically determined whether or not overt noun class marking is available, speakers can use both marked and unmarked nouns in reference to the same entity, e.g., the speaker in (13c) chooses both the marked noun *qavel-ka* 'bush-SG.M' and the unmarked noun *luqup* 'place' in reference to the same place.

(13) a. *sakmetngua navramasleng amaburlem*
sakmet-ngua *ne=pet=ama=**sleng*** *ama=burlem*
surprise:IN-1SG from/with=on/under=ART=garden ART=many
'I got surprised at the many gardens' (ASS-19/06/2015)
b. *perlsperls namakainaim*
perlsperls *ne=ama=**kaina-im***
part.CONT:REDUP from/with=ART=water-DU.F
'the two waters got parted' (N11AAGBROTHERS-0050)
c. *dav un ndamaqavelkaarlan, atika un denaluquviara*
dap *un* *ne=de=ama=**qavel-ka**=aa=rlan,*
but 1DU from/with=LOC.PART=ART=bush-SG.M=3SG.M.POSS=inside
ka=tika *un* *de=una=**luqup**=iara*
3SG.M.SBJ=EMPH 1DU CONJ=1DU.POSS=place=PROX
'but we are from the middle of the bush, as for us, it is our place here' (N12BAMCAT-037FF)

In the case of nouns that have both unmarked and marked forms, there seems to be a relationship between speakers choosing the unmarked (i.e., uncountable) variant and generic reference. For example, the unmarked noun *qerlap* 'water' in (14a) does not refer to any specific water, and only serves as a background for launching the canoe. Conversely, the marked noun *qerlap-ka* 'water-SG.M' in (14b) refers to the specific location of a water spirit.

(14) a. *ianiurlet naianamalauski sep maqerlap*
ian=iurlet *ne=iana=malaus-ki*
3DU.SBJ=pull.NCONT from/with=3DU.POSS=canoe-SG.F
se=pe *ma=**qerlap***
to/with=PLACE ART.ID=water
'they pulled their canoe into water' (N12BAMCAT-131)
b. *de masinepkia, de ma.. aqerlapka, de ma.. ahlurlka, de tika masinepki, de qurliqia*
de *ma=sinepki=a,* *de* *ma..* *a=**qerlap-ka**,*
CONJ ART.ID=NAME:SG.F=DIST CONJ ART.ID NM=water-SG.M
de *ma..* *a=slurl-ka,* *de* *tika* *ma=sinepki,*
CONJ ART.ID NM=big-SG.M CONJ EMPH ART.ID=NAME:SG.F
de *kurli-ki=a*
CONJ leave-3SG.F=DIST
'and Sinepki now, it is.. a water, it is.. a big (water), and Sinepki, she lives there' (N12ABKSIRINI-063FF)

All unmarked nouns discussed in this subsection are treated formally alike (in that they control human plural or non-human neuter agreement and argument indexing). Semantically, it is possible to argue that they all conceptualize their referents as plural: reference to countable plural individuals, to generic plurals, and to uncountable referents.

(ii) Address terms

Unmarked nouns are furthermore used as address terms with singular reference. For example, the speaker in (15a) uses the unmarked noun *kelmin* 'frog' (instead of the descriptive term *qalmin-ki* 'frog-SG.F') in order to address a character in a picture book. This unmarked noun has singular reference, as illustrated by the use of the second person singular pronoun *nyi* '2SG'. Of special interest here is that a handful of unmarked address terms also trigger masculine or feminine third person agreement and argument indexing (depending on the sex of the referent). This phenomenon is especially found in vocative contexts in child-directed speech, where adults sometimes address their children as *gumam* 'my father' (1SG.POSS:male) or *gunan* 'my mother' (1SG.POSS:female), followed by an instruction to the child couched in the third person (as in 15b). It is likely that this context then allowed the unmarked kinship nouns *mam ~ ngerlmam* 'father' and *nan ~ ngerlnan* 'mother' to occur in non-vocative contexts, and this pattern eventually spread to other address terms, too. As illustrated by the argument indexing on the verb in (15c), these unmarked nouns are invariably used with singular reference. To overtly mark these nouns for noun class would trigger a semantic shift to 'man' (*mam-ka* 'father-SG.M') and 'woman' (*nan-ki* 'mother-SG.F') respectively.

(15) a. *kelmin, nyiquaridi?*
__kelmin__, nyi=kuaridi?
frog 2SG=where
'frog, where are you?' (R12ADNFROG-007FF)

b. *gumam, kaang inavuk masari*
gu-__mam__, ka=ang i-na-vuk masari
1SG.POSS=father 3SG.M.SBJ=walk.NCONT AWAY-BACK-up from.there
'my father, come back down from there (lit. my father, he comes back down from there)' (LONGYDS20150601_2 079)

c. *urmam katden*
ure-__mam__ ka=tden
1PL.POSS-father 3SG.M.SBJ=come.CONT
'our father was coming' (D12ABDACPGARDEN-007)

(iii) Relational nouns

Finally, an unmarked noun is also used in the case of relational nouns (see chapter 6.1). Relational nouns are formed from full nouns, often bodypart nouns (such as *rlim-it* 'bottom/buttock-SG.LONG' in 16a), but they always occur in unmarked form in their relational use (as *rlim* 'bottom' in 16b). The examples below were chosen to illustrate the contrast between the two uses: (16a) uses the singular-marked noun to refer to the bottom part of the tree (i.e., its root or base), while (16b) uses the unmarked noun to refer to a search region relative to the tree. It would not be possible to use the singular-marked form in the second case.

(16) a. *bedemek, gelaarlimbit*
be=deng=a-mek, *gel=aa=**rlim-it***
CONJ=stop=DIR-down near=3SG.M.POSS=bottom-SG.LONG
'it stops down there near its bottom (i.e., the tree root or base)' (N11AJNGENAINGMETSIQI-0057)

b. *besavramalevunggaarlim*
*be=se=pet=ama=levung-ka=aa=**rlim***
CONJ=to/with=on/under=ART=tree.type-SG.M=3SG.M.POSS=bottom
'towards under the *levung* palm' (N11AJNGENAINGMETBROTHERS-0046)

These relational nouns do not control agreement, i.e., they cannot synchronically be considered the head of a possessive phrase. For example, in (17) below, the demonstrative agrees with the feminine noun *luqup-ki* 'place-SG.F', not with the unmarked relational noun *rlan* 'inside'. If agreement were with the unmarked noun, we would have expected the demonstrative to be *lu-nget-a* 'DEM-N-DIST'.

(17) *dluqia amaluqupkirarlan*
*de=lu-**ki**-a* *ama=luqup-**ki**=ara=**rlan***
LOC.PART=DEM-SG.F-DIST ART=place-SG.F=3SG.F.POSS=inside
'it's inside that place (not: *that inner part of the place)' (I12ABLAJLATASOCIO3-071)

4.2.3 Overt plurals

In addition to unmarked plurals, Qaqet has a number of plural morphemes that are suffixed to nouns. Again, the distinction between the masculine and feminine classes is mostly neutralized (except in the associative plural), and the relevant distinction is instead between human and non-human referents: they show distinct agreement and argument indexing patterns, and they take distinct overt plural suffixes. The following suffixes are attested and discussed in this section: (i) *-ta* 'PL.H' (human referents), (ii) *-nget* 'N' (non-human referents), and (iii) associative and collective suffixes.

(i) Human referents: *-ta* 'PL.H'

As shown in Table 41, Qaqet has an independent pronoun *ta* '3PL.H' that presumably gave rise to the plural agreement and argument indexing forms. For example, the unmarked human noun *qaqera* 'person' in (18a) triggers plural argument indexing on the verbs. In addition, some human nouns are overtly marked for plural by a suffix *-ta* 'PL.H' (as *quat-ta* 'man-PL.H' in 18b).

(18) a. *aqaqet tetliirang de ratisirang.. iurarluis*
a=qaqera ***te****=tlu-irang*
NM=person 3PL.SBJ.NPST=see.CONT-PL.DIM
de ***ta****=tis-irang.. i=ura=rluis*
CONJ 3PL.SBJ-call.CONT-PL.DIM SIM=1PL.POSS=child
'the people look at the little things, and they read the little things, (the people) who are our children' (I12AANACLADNSocio3-253)

b. *iaramaquata, de remiikradrlem samsem*
*ia-****ta****=ama=quat-****ta****,* *de* ***te****=miika =****ta****=drlem*
other-PL.H=ART=man-PL.H CONJ 3PL.SBJ.NPST=more=3PL.SBJ=know
se=a=msem
to/with=NM=weave.CONT
'some men, they also know about weaving' (P12ARSBILUM2-041)

Overt plural marking on nouns is only found with a subset of human nouns, including the salient categories of *ngerlmamda* 'men' (*ngerlmam-ta* 'man-PL.H'), *ngerlnanda* 'women' (*ngerlnan-ta* 'woman-PL.H') and *quata* 'men' (*quat-ta* 'man-PL.H'). It also includes human nouns converted from adjectives such as *barlta* 'older peers' (*barl-ta* 'big-PL.H') or *srlura* 'elders' (*srlu-ta* 'old-PL.H'). And it includes some kinship terms that are no longer widely known or used: *leselara* 'children' (*lesela-ta* 'child-PL.H'), *revista* 'in-laws' (*revis-ta* 'in.law-PL.H') and *vrlira* 'cousins' (*vrli-ta* 'cousin-PL.H'). While these nouns usually take the suffix *-ta* 'PL.H', there are also alternatives available. For example, the same speaker uses *barl-ta* 'big-PL.H' (in 19a) and *barl-pik* 'big-COLL.H' (in 19b) in reference to the same set of 'older brothers'.

(19) a. *deip ma, duqutuqun nambarlta ma*
de=ip *maget,* *de=ka=tuqun*
CONJ=PURP then CONJ=3SG.M.SBJ=say.CONT
*ne=ama=****barl-ta*** *ma*
from/with=ART=big-PL.H thus
'and then he says to the elder brothers like this' (N11AJNGENAINGMET-BROTHERS-0097)

b. *karuqun naabarlvik ma*
ka=ruqun *ne=aa=**barl-pik*** *ma*
3SG.M.SBJ=say.NCONT from/with=3SG.M.POSS=big-COLL.H thus
'he said to his elder brothers like this' (N11AJNGENAINGMETBROTHERS-0043)

The morpheme *-ta* 'PL.H' is also suffixed to human nouns that are derived from verbs. For example, it occurs on the noun *suvemda* 'teachers' in (20a), which is derived from the verb *su* 'teach'. And in (20b), it occurs on the noun *qarluqameta* 'shouters' derived from the verb *karlu* 'shout.CONT'.

(20) a. *araarisu.. suvemdaip.. tesurare.. tliiranga*
araa=ra-su.. *su=pe-**ta**=ip..*
3PL.POSS=NMLZ=teach teach=PLACE-PL.H=PURP
te=su-ta=te.. *te=lu-irang-a*
3PL.SBJ.NPST=teach-3PL.H=PURP PURP=DEM-PL.DIM-DIST
'their teach.. teachers, who.. teach them about.. about those things' (I12AANACLADNSOCIO3-250)

b. *aqarluqameta iresnes nep maiska*
*a=karlu-ka=met-**ta*** *i=te=snes*
NM=shout.CONT-3SG.M=in-PL.H SIM=3PL.SBJ.NPST=shout.CONT
ne=pe *ma=is-ka*
from/with=PLACE ART.ID=path-SG.M
'the shouters (lit. the ones shouting inside/about it) are calling out from the path' (CCM-13/06/2015)

(ii) Non-human referents: *-nget* 'N'

Non-human plural referents trigger neuter agreement and argument indexing, using forms that presumably originated in the pronoun *nget* '3N'. This is illustrated for the unmarked non-human noun *avet* 'house' in (21a) (where the adjective *tlu* 'good' is overtly marked for neuter agreement). In addition, a small number of non-human nouns are overtly marked for plural by a suffix *-nget* 'N' (as *gi-nget* 'what-N' in 21b).

(21) a. *duqurluun bemaavramatlunget*
de=kurli-un *pe=ma=avet=ama=tlu-**nget***
CONJ=leave-1DU PLACE=ART.ID=house=ART=good-N
'we stay in the good houses' (N12BAMCAT-032)

b. *aginget nget ma, tr-tr*
*a=gi-**nget*** ***nget*** *ma,* *tr-tr*
NM=what-N 3N thus SOUND
'the thingies go like this: *tr-tr*' (R12ADNFROG-290)

The overt marking of neuter nouns is largely restricted to complex nouns that were derived from predicates or prepositions plus pronouns (e.g., *nyipnget* 'spear traps', from *nyip-nget* 'die.NCONT-3N'; or *qipmetnget* 'spear traps' from *qip-met-nget* 'spear-in-3N'). In such contexts, the occurrence of neuter pronouns is expected (see chapter 3.2.3). It is thus likely that the suffixation of *-nget* 'N' to underived nouns is a new phenomenon that originated in such contexts. Further support for a more recent development comes from cases where *-nget* is suffixed to another noun class suffix (as *ngil-it-nget* 'time/space-SG.LONG-N' in 22): double noun class marking is otherwise not possible. There are also cases of disagreement among speakers. For example, *quat-nget* 'man-N' (i.e., women who have not yet given birth) was offered by some speakers as the plural form of *quat-ki* 'man-SG.F', but rejected by others. By now, the language contains a number of nouns whose origin is no longer transparent and that take the suffix *-nget* 'N' in their plural form, e.g., *rlanganget* 'bamboos', or *ginget* ~ *manget* 'what' (in 21b above).

(22) *kuanguat dengumali ramangilitnget samagaliv, ip ngu..*

kua=ngua=tit	*de=ngu=mali*		
INTRG=1SG.SBJ=go.CONT	CONJ=1SG.SBJ.NPST=search		
*te=ama=ngil-**it-nget***	*se=ama=galip,*	*ip*	*ngu..*
PURP=ART=time/space-SG.LONG-N	to/with=ART=peanut	PURP	1SG.SBJ.NPST

'maybe I will go and look for spaces among the peanuts, so that I.. (can plant some taro among the peanuts)' (D12ABDACPGARDEN-036)

(iii) Associative and collective plurals

Finally, masculine and feminine nouns can occur with associative and collective suffixes, replacing the expected plural forms (i.e., the unmarked nouns, or the nouns marked with the suffixes *-ta* 'PL.H' or *-nget* 'N'). They exhibit some peculiarities, and I do not consider them part of the noun class system proper. They do not have separate agreement and argument indexing forms, but trigger the use of either plural human or neuter forms. Furthermore, if a noun phrase consists of a noun followed by an adjective, associative and collective suffixes attach to the adjective, while the noun occurs in its expected plural form. The following forms are attested: *-kena* 'ASSOC.M', *-kina* 'ASSOC.F', *-pik* 'COLL.H' and *-dem* 'COLL.N'. Only the associative plurals are productive.

The associative plural forms *-kena* 'ASSOC.M' and *-kina* 'ASSOC.F' indicate a referent and its associates. They can be added to any proper noun to refer to a group of people associated with that person (as in 23a) or to the inhabitants of a place (e.g., *kedel-kena* 'the people of Kedel'). The label 'associative' reflects these prototypical uses as well as its presumed diachronic origins (see below). Its synchronic distribution also includes collective contexts. As such, it commonly occurs with human referents that occur in groups (as in 23b), but it can also be extended to animals (e.g., *qalmin-kina* 'a group of frogs'), artefacts (e.g., *supin-kina* 'a group of saucepans') or harvested crops (e.g., *quukuk-kena* 'a group of sweet potatoes'). This suffix is fairly frequent, and it is even attested with loanwords (e.g., *plit-kina* 'a group of plates' in 24b below, from Tok Pisin *plet* 'plate'). All such plurals are formed from masculine and feminine nouns, i.e., associative plurals cannot be formed from nouns in any of the shape-based classes. The choice of the masculine or feminine form depends on the noun class of the referent: e.g., frogs are feminine, thus triggering the feminine form *-kina* 'ASSOC.F', while sweet potatoes are masculine, thus triggering the masculine form -*kena* 'ASSOC.M'. As in other cases (see section 4.2.1), the masculine form can be considered unmarked, as it is also used in the case of mixed groups (e.g., *kedelkena* 'the people of Kedel' takes the masculine suffix *-kena* 'ASSOC.M', but includes women).

(23) a. *nyit sagel maarumgena*
nyi=it *se=gel* *ma=arum-**kena***
2SG.SBJ.NPST=go.NCONT.FUT to/with=near ART.ID=NAME-ASSOC.M
'go to Arum and his friends' (LONGYDS20150517_1 489)

b. *taquarl amananngina, iradrlem samsem amarlaun*
taquarl *ama=nan-**kina**,* *i=ta=drlem*
thus ART=woman-ASSOC.F SIM=3PL.SBJ=know
se=a=msem *ama=rlaun*
to/with=NM=weave.CONT ART=netbag
'like the women who know about weaving netbags' (P12ARSBILUM2-044)

In some cases, the associative plural is the only plural form available. For example, *nanngi* 'woman' (*nan-ki* 'woman-SG.F') only ever takes the plural form *nanngina* 'women' (*nan-kina* 'woman-ASSOC.F'). It cannot occur with the expected human plural form *-ta* (**nanda*); and the unmarked form *nan* only occurs with the different (singular) reference of 'mother'. In most cases, however, the associative plural and the expected plural co-exist, e.g., *vrli-kena* 'cousin-ASSOC.M' ~ *vrli-ta* 'cousin-PL.H', or *avis-kina* 'knife-ASSOC.F' ~ *avis* 'knife'.

In the case of human referents, the associative plural invariably triggers plural human agreement and argument indexing. For example, the noun *nanngina* 'women' in (23b) above triggers human plural subject indexing on the verb (*ta* '3PL.SBJ'). The same noun also triggers the use of the human plural possessor index *araa* '3PL.POSS' in (24a) below. In the case of non-human referents, neuter forms have to be used in these contexts, e.g., *-nget* '3N' on the predicate in (24b) or *-nget* 'N' in the demonstrative in (24c).

(24) a. *amananngina araanis amalanginy*
*ama=nan-**kina*** ***araa**=nis ama=langiny*
ART=woman-ASSOC.F 3PL.POSS=grass.skirt ART=tree.type
'the women's grass skirts are (made) of *langiny*' (AAN-08/09/2015)

b. *nyaru ama aplitkina vevanu pamalaiqi isa dengdemngera*
nya=ru *ama* *a=plit-**kina*** *pe=panu*
2SG.SBJ=put.NCONT.FUT ART NM=plate-ASSOC.F PLACE=up
pe=ama=lai-ki *i=sa* *dengdem-**nget**=a*
PLACE=ART=platform-SG.F SIM=already dry-3N=DIST
'put the plates that are already dry up on top of the board there' (BMS-14/05/1015)

c. *lungera remani abelhatkena*
*lu-**nget**-a* *temani* *a=belhat-**kena***
DEM-N-DIST underneath NM=huge-ASSOC.M
'those big ones underneath' (LONGYDS20150516_1 042)

In the case of noun phrases containing a noun followed by an adjective, the associative plural attaches to the adjective only. The preceding noun then appears in its unmarked form (as illustrated in 25a and 25b).

(25) a. *aquukuq amabelhatkena*
[*a=quukuk* *ama=belhat-**kena***]NP
NM=sweet.potato ART=huge-ASSOC.M
'huge sweet potatoes' (LONGYDS20150516_1 228)

b. *ut nama arlui.. arluis amananngina*
ut *ne=[ama* *a=rlui..* *a=rluis* *ama=nan-**kina***]NP
1PL from/with=ART NM=child NM=child ART=woman-ASSOC.F
'we together with the chil.. the female children' (AMS-22/08/2015)

The phonological status of the associative plural is not entirely clear. On the one hand, examples (25a) and (25b) above suggest that it is a clitic that attaches to the end of phrases. On the other hand, it replaces the noun class suffixes, and – in some cases – even constitutes the only available plural form. I.e., it arguably occurs in a paradigmatic relationship with the noun classes, which are suffixes. I therefore tentatively treat it as a suffix in this grammar. It is likely that the unclear phonological status reflects its diachronic origin in a free word. I assume that the associative plural grammaticalized from the associative pronouns *kena* (*ke-ne* '3SG.M.ASSOC-from/with') and *kina* (*ki-ne* '3SG.F.ASSOC-from/with') (see chapter 3.6 for details on these pronouns): the pronouns are identical in shape to the associative plural, they distinguish masculine and feminine, and they convey the meaning of 'together'. They differ, however, in their syntactic position, as they precede the associate noun phrase (as in 26) (while the associative plural follows).

(26) *iknes kenaalainnga*
ip=ke=nes
PURP=3SG.M.SBJ.NPST=shout.NCONT
ke-ne=*aa=lain-ka*
3SG.M.ASSOC-from/with=3SG.M.POSS=line-SG.M
'and he wants to shout, he and his troops' (N11AAGSIRINILOBSTER2-0067)

In addition to the associative plural, Qaqet has two collective plurals, one for human referents (*-pik* 'COLL.H') and one for non-human referents (*-dem* 'COLL.N'). Both are not productive. The first form is exclusively attested with a handful of lexemes referring to groups of humans, usually relatives: *qalat-pik* 'younger.sibling-COLL.H', *ningam-pik* 'younger.sibling-COLL.H', *rarlim-pik* 'firstborn-COLL.H', *barl-pik* 'big-COLL.H' (in reference to older siblings and cousins only), *rlua-pik* 'friend-COLL.H' and *ngerl-pik* 'spouse-COLL.H'. And the second form is only found with two lexemes: *ngarik-dem* 'arm/hand-COLL.N' (in reference to 'fingers') and *ilany-dem* 'leg/foot-COLL.N' (in reference to 'toes'). It may also be a diachronic part of some synchronically unanalyzable nouns like ***kuidem*** 'incantations'. Morphosyntactically, they behave like the associative plural, e.g., they trigger plural forms in the case of human referents (as in 27), and neuter forms, in the case of non-human referents.

(27) *nani aarluavik tenyan temga maamanu*

nani	*aa=rlua-**pik***	***te***=*nyan*
can	3SG.M.POSS=friend-COLL.H	3PL.SBJ.NPST=laugh.NCONT
te-ka	*maqa-manu*	
PURP-3SG.M	HERE-across	

'his friends can laugh at him everywhere' (I12ABLAJLATASOCIO3-164)

4.2.4 Shape-based classes

Qaqet has six shape-based classes, DIM (diminutive), RCD (reduced), FLAT (flat), LONG (long), EXT (extended) and EXC (excised), and the semantic principles for assignment to these classes are fairly transparent. There are only few nouns that exclusively belong to a shape-based class, but noun roots can easily be shifted into them to highlight a particular property of the referent. This section sketches the distribution of each of the six classes in turn.

The DIMINUTIVE class is used with small referents, and speakers regularly shift to this class to emphasize the small size of something or someone, as in (28a). Using the diminutive in this way has the additional effect of toning down the importance of the referent (as in 28b). Furthermore, this class can be used when the referent – and hence its noun class – is unknown, e.g., in (28c) where the gender of the recipient is unknown.

(28) a. *liina ima.. peinarlvisiara*
*lu-**ini**-a* *i=ma..* *pe-**ini**=ngere-uvis=iara*
DEM-SG.DIM-DIST SIM=thus PLACE-SG.DIM=3N.POSS-top=PROX
'that little one who is like this.. the little one's height is (only) to here [demonstrating height]' (N12ABKSIRINI-109FF)

b. *perlsera, quas magrip kesinnaa terlsin liina*
perlset=a, *kuasik* *maget=ip*
finish=DIST NEG then=PURP
ke=sil=ne=aa
3SG.M.SBJ.NPST=say.NCONT=from/with=3SG.M.POSS
*terles-**ini*** *lu-**ini**-a*
hide.CONT-SG.DIM DEM-SG.DIM-DIST
'it is done, he is not to talk about that little secret of his' (N12AMVGENAINGMETBROTHERS-074)

c. *nyiquarl tamasmes bareq iani*
nyi=quarl *te=ama=smes* *barek* *ia-**ini***
2SG.SBJ.NPST=present.NCONT PURP=ART=food BEN other-SG.DIM
'give the food to another one' (ALT-15/06/2015)

The REDUCED class covers referents that are short, stumpy or compact, e.g. a piece of cooked taro (as in 29a), compact bodyparts (e.g., *arlem-em* 'thigh-SG.RCD'), tightly arranged vines (as in 29b) or short stories, songs and incantations (e.g., *siit-em* 'story-SG.RCD'). Speakers regularly shift to this class if they want to highlight the compact nature of a referent, e.g., *qurel-em* 'bottle-SG.RCD' (instead of the expected *qurel-ka* 'bottle-SG.M') is used in reference to a bottle or vase of a fairly square shape. With human referents, such a shift triggers negative connotations, e.g., *gil-em* 'small-SG.RCD' in reference to a small child conveys disapproval of the child's size, contrasting with the more neutral *gil-ki* 'small-SG.F' or *gil-ini* 'small-SG.DIM'. The singular suffix is also found in names, especially in the names of ancestors and spirits that evoke disapproval. For example, it is found in the name of the cultural anti-hero known variably as *kavar-em*, *kungun-em ~ kungunemgi-em* and *ramgi ~ ramgi-em*.

(29) a. *amaqalunem bangua*
*ama=qalun-**em*** *barek-ngua*
ART=singapore-SG.RCD BEN-1SG
'a singapore piece for me' (C12VARPLAY-457)

b. *beqamit sep makaasiqem*
be=ka=mit *se=pe* *ma=kaasik-**em***
CONJ=3SG.M.SBJ=go.NCONT.PST to/with=PLACE ART.ID=vine-SG.RCD
'and he went into the vines (hiding himself)' (N12AMVGENAINGMETBROTHERS-025)

Referents in the FLAT noun class are extended in two dimensions. For example, the root *qasing* 'hair/feather' appears in the FLAT class with reference to a feather (*qasing-es*), but in the LONG class with reference to a single hair (*qasing-it*). Typical referents are all kinds of leaves and palm fronds (as in 30a), but also paper, sheets of plastic or plastic bags (as in 30b). The singular is furthermore used in reference to collectives conceptualized as spread out or aggregated over larger areas, e.g., rubbish spread on the ground, plants distributed in a garden (as in 30c) or the people of a place.

(30) a. *kua amama.. angariqiving amadepguas naiving, dakua iamaqunasivim*
kua *ama=ma..* *a=ngarik-**iving*** *ama=depguas*
INTRG ART=?? NM=hand-PL.FLAT ART=three
*ne-**iving**,* *dap=kua* *i=ama=qunas-**ivim***
from/with-PL.FLAT but=INTRG SIM=ART=one-DU.FLAT
'maybe there's.. three leaves, or maybe there's two' (D12ABDACPGARDEN-024)

b. *dakuarl ama.. alanginyis, dakuarl amagumiis*
dap=kua *ama..* *a=langiny-**es**,* *dap=kua* *ama=gumi-**es***
but=INTRG ART NM=paper-SG.FLAT but=INTRG ART=plastic-SG.FLAT
'or maybe the.. the paper, or maybe the plastic' (P12ADNFIRE-006FF)

c. *be nyitliara, iamaiameses*
be *nyi=tlu=iara,* *i=ama=iames-**es***
CONJ 2SG.SBJ.NPST=see.CONT=PROX SIM=ART=new-SG.FLAT
'and you see now that it is a new (flat) one (garden)' (D12ADNGARDEN-024FF)

The LONG class covers referents that are extended in one dimension, e.g., branches and poles, cassava or sweet potato cuttings to be planted in the garden (as in 31a), or bodyparts such as arms and legs. Note that it also includes long flexible referents (e.g., hairs), extended landscape features (e.g., ridges and cliffs, tall mountains) (as in 31b) and time (e.g. *ngil-it* 'time/space-SG.LONG') – all of which occur in the EXTENDED class in Mali. In Qaqet, the LONG and the EXTENDED classes share their singular forms (albeit with a different allomorphy, and different dual and plural forms). It is possible that this collapse in form has triggered a re-assignment of referents and a concomitant semantic re-interpretation of the classes.

More generally, the EXTENDED class is losing ground in Qaqet. It can still be identified on the basis of its paradigmatic forms and through a comparison with Mali. However, it only contains very few referents, and almost all of them are also attested in another class. In such cases, both noun classes are either used interchangeably, or a paradigmatic elicitation yields dual and plural forms in the EXTENDED class, but singular forms in another class. If referents can be conceptualized as being extended in one dimension, they also appear in the LONG class (such as *rleng-it* 'back-SG.LONG' ~ 'back-SG.EXT'), and if they can be conceptualized as being part of a whole, they also appear in the EXCISED class (especially bodyparts such as *menep-it* '??-SG.EXT' ~ *menep-igel* '??-SG.EXC' for 'eyelid', but also patches of ground).

(31) a. *denguaru amapiuqisinga, ngenama.. aquukuqising, amaslevising*
de=ngua=ru *ama=piuk-**ising**=a,*
CONJ=1SG.SBJ=put.NCONT.FUT ART=cassava-PL.LONG=DIST
ngere-ne=ama.. *a=quukuk-**ising**,*
3N.ASSOC-from/with=ART NM=sweet.potato-PL.LONG
*ama=slep-**ising***
ART= sweet.potato.plant-PL.LONG
'I plant cassava cuttings, together with.. sweet potato cuttings, sweet potato cuttings' (D12ADNGARDEN-054FF)

b. *saqika dama asisit*
saqi-ka *de=ama* *a=sis-**it***
again-3SG.M LOC.PART=ART NM=ridge-SG.LONG
'again on the mountain ridge' (N11AAGSIRINIROPE-0107)

Given this variation, it is likely that a semantic reorganization is currently taking place: the EXTENDED class is being lost, the LONG class is taking over all referents that are extended in one dimension, and the EXCISED class is covering all referents that are parts of a whole. Referents that are attested exclusively in the EXCISED class tend to be pieces that are cut or split off from a whole (e.g., planks, vines, pieces of food or garden produce) (as in 32). This class also includes feet and shoes, and some abstract concepts (such as *arin-igrling* 'noise-PL.EXC').

(32) *ingunging amamelangigrling*
i=ngu=nging *ama=melang-**igrling***
SIM=1SG.SBJ.NPST=circle.CONT ART=vine-PL.EXC
'I am weaving the split vines' (P12ADNROPE2-014)

4.3 Gender system

The noun classes discussed above surface in a number of distinct morphosyntactic environments. In addition, there are some contexts, where the noun classes are mapped onto a different system: when occurring as subject, possessor and associative indexes. I adopt Stebbins' (2011) terminology and refer to this system as a gender system, in order to distinguish it from the noun class system.

Table 59 below repeats the relevant information from Table 41 above, summarizing the forms and mappings. Mostly, the noun class and gender morphemes are similar in form, and only the origins of some possessor indexes remain unclear: *araa* '3PL.POSS' can be related to *ta* 'PL.H' (with *t* leniting to *r* intervocalically), but both the initial vowel and the long final vowel are unexpected; similarly, *a* '3SG.M.POSS' and *ara* '3SG.F.POSS' cannot be related to the corresponding noun class morphemes. Furthermore, the following categories are different across the two systems: there is a single dual gender corresponding to both the DU.M and DU.F noun classes; and the neuter gender covers the neuter noun class as well as all shape-based classes (regardless of their number).

Tab. 59: Nominal classification: Mapping noun classes onto gender

Class	Free pronoun	Suffix on noun	Suffix elsewhere	Possessor index	Subject index	
					Neutral	Non-past
SG.M	*ka*	*-ka*		*a*	*ka*	*ke*
SG.F	*ki*	*-ki*		*ara*	*kia*	*ki*
DU.M	*iam*	*-iam*		*iana*	*ian*	*iane*
DU.F	*im*	*-im*				
PL.H	*ta*	*Ø ~ -ta*	*-ta*	*araa*	*ta*	*te*
N	*nget*	*Ø ~ -nget*	*-nget*	*ngera*	*nga*	*ngere ~ nger*
Shape-based classes						

The examples below illustrate some of the mappings between noun class and gender. In (33a), both the noun and the independent pronoun are marked for the shape-based noun class PL.DIM, while the subject index appears in the neuter gender. Example (33b) shows that the neuter noun class (marked overtly on the demonstrative), just like the shape-based classes, triggers the neuter gender (on the subject index). Finally, (33c) illustrates the different forms of the SG.F noun class (*ki*) and possessor index (*ara*).

(33) a. *arluimirang, deirang ngerebrlany*
*a=rluim-**irang**,* *de=**irang*** ***ngere**=brlany*
NM=child-PL.DIM CONJ=PL.DIM 3N.SBJ.NPST=sleep
'the children, they sleep' (I12AANACLADNSOCIO3-326)

b. *i lungera ngatranyi*
i *lu-**nget**-a* ***nga**=tat-nyi*
SIM DEM-N-DIST 3N.SBJ=take.CONT-2SG
'and those (recorders) record you' (C12YMMZJIPLAY1-041)

c. *bqasnis, damalauski rarlan*
be=ka=snis, *de=a=malaus-**ki*** ***ara**=rlan*
CONJ=3SG.M.SBJ=bite.CONT LOC.PART=NM=canoe-SG.F 3SG.F.POSS=inside
'and he was eating, from inside the canoe' (N12BAMCAT-206)

As discussed in sections 4.2.2 and 4.2.3, the distinction between masculine and feminine nouns is neutralized in the plural, and instead the plural introduces a new distinction between human and non-human referents. This distinction does not extend to the mapping of the shape-based classes onto the gender system: the referents in (33a) above are plural and human, yet they control neuter gender in the subject – not plural human gender (but see the discussion below).

The majority of examples follow the mappings summarized in Table 59. The only attested mismatches involve cases where human referents in shape-based noun classes trigger masculine, feminine or plural human gender in the possessor index (but never in the subject index). Example (34a) illustrates such a mismatch: the subject noun phrase is PL.DIM, and it controls the neuter gender of the subject index, but the plural human gender of the possessor index (see also 28a above for a comparable example). This kind of mismatch is fairly frequent in the corpus, but it is not inevitable: there are also many cases where the possessor, too, appears in the neuter gender (as in 34b).

(34) a. *irang ngatirang araahdem*
irang ***nga****=tu-irang* ***araa****=sdem*
PL.DIM 3N.SBJ=put.CONT-PL.DIM 3PL.POSS=ear
'the little ones are putting their ears (to listen closely)' (I12AANACLADNSOCIO3-323)

b. *tika ama.. arluimirang angeralengiqa*
*tika ama.. a=rluim-****irang*** ***ngera****=lengi-ka*
EMPH ART NM=child-PL.DIM 3N.POSS=word-SG.M
'it is the.. the little children's language' (I12ABLAJLATASOCIO2-036)

A different kind of mismatch was already introduced in section 4.2.2: the case of address terms that are unmarked for noun class, but do not take the expected plural noun class or gender. Instead, depending on their natural sex, they trigger masculine or feminine markings. This phenomenon is illustrated in (35) by means of the two unmarked address terms *ngerlmam* 'man/father' and *ngerlnan* 'woman/mother' that trigger the dual masculine noun class (in the demonstrative) and the dual gender (in the subject and possessor indexes).

(35) *iamangerlmam, damangerlnan, de liama de.. de ianesu iana.. ianuimini*
*i=ama=ngerlmam, de=ama=ngerlnan, de lu-****iam****-a*
SIM=ART=man CONJ=ART=woman CONJ DEM-DU.M-DIST
de.. de ***iane****=su* ***iana****..* ***iane****-uim-ini*
CONJ CONJ 3DU.SBJ.NPST=teach 3DU.POSS 3DU.POSS-child-SG.DIM
'the father and the mother, those two.. they teach their.. their child' (I12AANACLADNSOCIO3-170FF)

4.4 Summary

This chapter has focused on nominal classification: section 4.1 has described the noun class morphology, section 4.2, the categories, and section 4.3, the mapping of the noun class system onto the gender system. Qaqet has two sex-based noun classes (masculine and feminine) and six shape-based noun classes (diminutive, reduced, flat, long, extended and excised), which usually have distinct singular, dual and plural forms. Only the plural of the two sex-based classes shows semantic and formal peculiarities. Semantically, it neutralizes the distinction between masculine and feminine, and instead introduces a new distinction between human and non-human referents. Formally, it is usually unmarked – but it can be marked by one of a number of distinct formatives (distinguishing between human and non-human referents, and between plurality, associative plurality and collective plurality). The noun classes are mapped onto a gender system that neutralizes some of the noun class distinctions: the dual gender does not distinguish between masculine and feminine; and the neuter gender includes non-human plurals as well as all shape-based noun classes (independent of their singular, dual or plural reference).

The noun classes surface in a large number of grammatical environments. The free pronouns distinguish noun class, and they gave rise to object suffixes on verbs and prepositions. The classes are also overtly marked by suffixes on the noun (excepting the special case of masculine and feminine plurals) and on noun phrase elements agreeing with the noun: adjectives, the numerals 'one' and 'two', demonstratives, indefinite pronouns, and some interrogative pronouns. The genders surface in the form of possessor indexes on possessed nouns, of subject indexes on verbs, and as associative pronouns. Chapters 3 and 5 give more information on these word classes and their characteristic membership and properties.

As highlighted throughout this chapter, the noun class and gender systems of Qaqet are very similar to the ones described for Mali. But while the forms are clearly cognate, there are differences in their semantic organization that warrant future comparative research: even cognate nouns do not necessarily belong to the same classes across the two languages. In addition, there are formal differences that point to different grammaticalization paths, especially in the case of the demonstrative pronouns. It remains to be seen whether and to what extent the Qaqet and Mali systems are shared with the other Baining languages, and with Taulil and Butam. In any case, the formal and semantic properties of the Qaqet and Mali systems are very different from other systems of nominal classification found in other East Papuan languages.

5 Verbs and the structure of the predicate

This chapter is organized around the word class of verbs. Verbs are clearly distinguishable from nouns and adjectives: they do not take any of the nominal morphology such as articles or noun class marking, and they cannot be heads of noun phrases or modifiers within noun phrases (but see chapter 3.1.1 on the topic of word classes and conversion in Qaqet). They are the only word class that can head intransitive and transitive predicates.

The structure of the predicate is summarized in Table 60. The subject argument is obligatorily indexed, with the index expressing information on person and tense. The index is optionally followed by the modifier *raqa* ~ *taqa* 'properly', but is more commonly followed directly by the verb stem. Qaqet verbs have up to three different aspectual stems that express information about tense/aspect. The verb stem is then optionally followed by two types of elements: verb particles and object pronouns. The term 'verb particle' is used as a cover term for a large number of (diachronic) prepositions, relational nouns, adverbs and directionals, which became incorporated into the verb, first as particles and later as suffixes. They originally served to introduce arguments in different semantic roles, or to specify the direction or manner of a verb action. Synchronically, they are often no longer fully analyzable and they constitute integral parts of complex verbs with conventionalized meanings. The final slot is filled by a suffixed pronominal form: a direct object, a reflexive or a reciprocal. This suffix is optional: it is absent with monovalent verbs, and it is mutually exclusive with an object noun phrase.

Tab. 60: Structure of the predicate

subject index	***raqa* ~ *taqa* 'properly'**	**verb stem**	**verb particle**	**object pronoun**
proclitic=	(proclitic=)	stem	(particle ~ -suffix)	(-suffix)
categories coded:				
person	manner	tense/aspect	semantic role	person
tense			direction	reflexive
			manner	reciprocal

Examples (1a) to (1c) illustrate some of the slots of the predicate: the simplest form of the predicate consisting of a subject index and a verb stem (in 1a), and more complex structures including in both examples a subject index, the modifier *taqa* 'properly' and a verb stem, plus the object pronoun *nget* '3N' in (1b) and the verb particle *met* 'in' in (1c).

(1) a. *kanes*
ka=nes
3SG.M.SBJ=shout.NCONT
'he shouted' (N11AAGSIRINILOBSTER1-0050)

b. *demiika qataqamunget*
de=miika *ka=taqa=mu-nget*
CONJ=more 3SG.M.SBJ=properly.CONT=put.NCONT.PST-3N
'and he continues to put them properly' (N11AAGSIRINILOBSTER2-0030)

c. *kataqatekmet nanget*
ka=taqa=tekmet *ne-nget*
3SG.M.SBJ=properly.CONT=do.CONT:IN from/with-3N
'he puts them properly' (N11AAGSIRINILOBSTER2-0029)

Qaqet verbs are either intransitive or transitive; there are no ditransitive verbs (in the sense that no verb can occur with three unmarked arguments, see section 5.2 for a discussion). The subject argument (covering the subject of both intransitive and transitive verbs) precedes the predicate, and is obligatorily indexed. The object argument follows: if the object is pronominal, it is suffixed to the verb stem or particle; if it is nominal, it constitutes an independent word. Qaqet thus has a fixed constituent order of AVO/SV, whereby both subject and object arguments can be omitted. In addition, there is an agentless construction that suppresses the A argument altogether (including its subject index), resulting in the structure VO. The alternation between a transitive AVO and an agentless VO structure is illustrated in (2a) and (2b). This phenomenon could alternatively be analyzed as a case of split intransitivity, with some intransitive verbs exhibiting SV order and others, VS order (see section 5.2.2 for details).

(2) a. *dianeberltiq amadaqa*
*de=iane=**berltik*** *[ama=da-ka]*OBJ
CONJ=3DU.SBJ.NPST=loosen:SIDE ART=taro-SG.M
'and they pick (lit. loosen) a taro' (N12BAMCAT-090)

b. *de berltiq iagel*
de ***berltik*** *[ia-igel]*OBJ
CONJ loosen:SIDE other-SG.EXC
'and another one got loosened' (LONGYJL20150805_1-039)

While subject and object arguments are formally unmarked, Qaqet additionally makes use of prepositions to introduce participants entailed by the verb semantics. For example, the verb *quarl* ~ *kuarl* 'present someone with something' co-occurs with the preposition *te* 'PURP' to convey the meaning of 'give' (as in 3a), and with the preposition *ne* 'from/with' to convery the meaning of 'show' (as in 3b).

(3) a. *ngenequrlaqi ramanget*
ngene=quarl-ki ***te****=a=ma-nget*
2PL.SBJ.NPST=present.NCONT-3SG.F PURP=NM=thingy-N
'you give her the thingies' (C12VARPLAY-446)

b. *beip ma, diqitaqatkuarl aruimga namamengga*
be=ip maget, de=ki=taqa=tkuarl
CONJ=PURP then CONJ=3SG.F.SBJ.NPST=properly.CONT=C.present
are-uim-ka ***ne****=ama=meng-ka*
3SG.F.POSS-child-SG.M from/with=ART=wood-SG.M
'and then, she carefully shows her son a tree' (N11AJNGENAINGMETSIQI-0017)

This chapter discusses in more detail the various properties of the predicate sketched out in the preceding paragraphs. Section 5.1 summarizes the salient properties of the verb lexicon. Section 5.2 focusses on transitivity and the marking of subject and object arguments. Section 5.3 describes prepositions and prepositional phrases, discussing the use of prepositions to introduce both adjuncts and arguments, and illustrating their further integration as verb particles and suffixes into the verb. Section 5.4 covers tense/aspect marking within the predicate. Section 5.5 introduces the modifier *raqa ~ taqa* 'properly'. Finally, section 5.6 summarizes this chapter.

The structure of the verb lexicon and the predicate are very similar to that described for Mali Baining (Stebbins 2011: 14–15, 41–57, 59–61, 100–104, 105–135, 207–216). Given the overall similarity, this chapter only points out differences, keeping in mind that some of the difference may well reflect different analytical decisions rather than structural differences between the two languages.

5.1 Verb lexicon

The Qaqet verb lexicon is characterized through a high degree of compositionality. On the one hand, there are morphologically simple verbs with general meanings whose interpretation is constrained by their combination with other elements in the clause and by contextual factors. And on the other hand, there are morphologically complex verbs with very specific meanings.

Simple verbs usually have a fairly broad meaning range, which is narrowed down through other elements. The verb *rek ~ tek* 'hold/put' is a typical example. It covers all kinds of events that involve manipulating an entity with one's hands. As a transitive verb, it receives an interpretation of 'put', e.g., 'construct, put (up)' (if the direct object is a house, as in 4a) or 'put (down)' (if the direct object is, e.g., a piece of taro). In the latter case, adding a beneficiary will evoke an interpretation of 'give (i.e., put down for the benefit of someone)' (as in 4b). The verb also occurs with various prepositions, receiving interpretations of 'put up' (when combining with *ne* 'from/with', as in 4c), 'touch, hold' (when combining with *pet* 'on/under', as in 4d) or 'shake' (when combining with *men* 'at', as in 4e). Or it combines with adverbs, receiving interpretations such as 'close in' (combining with *mirlek* 'around', as in 4f) or 'smash' (combining with *brlit* 'smashing', as in 4g).

(4) a. *bigiada ngentden ip ngenetek guaavetki*
bigiada *ngen=tden* *ip*
tomorrow 2PL.SBJ=come.CONT PURP
*ngene=**tek*** *gua=avet-ki*
2PL.SBJ.NPST=hold/put.CONT 1SG.POSS=house-SG.F
'tomorrow you come and put up my house' (ALR-17/06/2015)

b. *nyirek amaqalunem barek giaqa*
*nyi=**rek*** *ama=qalun-em*
2SG.SBJ.NPST=hold/put.NCONT ART=singapore-SG.RCD
barek *gi-ia-ka=a*
BEN 2SG.POSS-other-SG.M=DIST
'give the half singapore taro to your friend now (lit. put the singapore for his benefit)' (ALR-17/06/2015)

c. *biqitek naraqip*
*be=ki=**tek*** ***ne**=ara=qip*
CONJ=3SG.F.SBJ.NPST=hold/put.CONT from/with=3SG.F.POSS=spear
'and she plants her spears' (N11AAGSIRINIROPE-0126)

d. *kuas nyitek praqi imaliki*
kuasik *nyi=**tek*** ***pet**-ki*
NEG 2SG.SBJ.NPST=hold/put.CONT on/under-3SG.F
i=ama=lik-ki
SIM=ART=crying-SG.F
'don't hold her, she will cry' (LONGYDS20150601_1-034)

e. *damaqasupka qetek menamiuqi ma*
de=ama=qasup-ka *ke=**tek*** ***men**=a=miu-ki*
CONJ=ART=rat-SG.M 3SG.M.SBJ.NPST=hold/put.CONT at=NM=cat-SG.F
ma
thus
'and the rat is shaking the cat like this' (N12BAMCAT-107)

f. *saqika dip kirek mirlek padip kiranengaqa*
saqi-ka *dip* *ki=**rek*** ***mirlek***
again-3SG.M FUT 3SG.F.SBJ.NPST=hold/put.NCONT around
padip *ki=raneng-ka*
hopefully.FUT 3SG.F.SBJ.NPST=hold.NCONT-3SG.M
'again she will close in (on him) and wants to hold him' (N11AAGSIRINIROPE-0068)

g. *daqatek brlit, pangeraning*
*de=ka=**tek*** **brlit,** *pe=ngera=ninga*
CONJ=3SG.M.SBJ=hold/put.CONT smashing PLACE=3N.POSS=head
'and he was smashing their heads' (N11AAGSIRINILOBSTER1-0088)

The available combinations and resulting meanings are conventionalized to varying degrees. They presumably all originated in the co-occurrence of a simple verb with another element (a prepositional phrase, a relational noun, an adverb or a directional) receiving a compositional meaning. Often, the original motivation for a given combination can be (more or less confidently) reconstructed – but synchronically, many of the combinations have to be considered lexicalized, affecting the meaning and argument structure of a verb in non-predictable ways. The endpoint of this lexicalization process is the phonological integration of the simple verb and its combining element(s).

For example, the simple verb *maarl* ~ *raarl* ~ *taarl* 'stand' (in 5a) forms the basis for the complex verb *maarlvit* ~ *raarlvit* ~ *taarlvit* 'stand' (incorporating the directional *pit* 'up', as in 5b). Or the simple verb *qut* ~ *kut* 'break ground' (in 6a) forms the basis for a number of complex verbs such as *qutik* ~ *kutik* 'cut off' (incorporating the relational noun *tik* 'side', as in 6b) and *qutpet* ~ *kutpet* 'sew' (incorporating the preposition *pet* 'on/under', as in 6c).

(5) a. *daqamaarl vema.. amenggaarleng*
*de=ka=**maarl*** *pe=ma..*
CONJ=3SG.M.SBJ=stand.NCONT.PST PLACE=ART.ID
a=meng-ka=aa=rleng
NM=wood-SG.M=3SG.M.POSS=back
'and he stood behind the.. the tree' (N12ABKSIRINI-079)

b. *ianmaarlvit*
*ian=**maarlvit***
3DU.SBJ=stand.NCONT.PST:UP
'they stood up' (R12ADNFROG-284)

(6) a. *nyikut*
*nyi=**kut***
2SG.SBJ.NPST=break.ground.CONT
'you dig' (LONGYDS20150531_1-123)

b. *nyi.. nyiqutik, pemamudemini*
nyi.. *nyi=**qutik**,*
2SG.SBJ.NPST 2SG.SBJ.NPST=cut.off.NCONT:SIDE
pe=ma=mudem-ini
PLACE=ART.ID=resin-SG.DIM
'you.. you cut off a little resin' (P12ADNFIRE-013)

c. *nguqutpet gualuanngi*
*ngu=**qutpet*** *gua=luan-ki*
1SG.SBJ.NPST=sew.CONT:ON/UNDER 1SG.POSS=cloth-SG.F
'I'm sewing my dress' (AMI-08/09/2015)

In the above examples, all elements of the complex verbs are attested elsewhere in the language and hence identifiable, but this is not always the case. Sometimes, the assumed root is unattested as a simple verb. For example, there are a number of verbs that seem to contain the relational noun *tik* 'side', but that do not have a corresponding simple verb, e.g. *berltik* 'loosen' (in 7a) probably contains a synchronically unattested root **berl*. Conversely, there are cases where only the root is attested. For example, *qutserl* ~ *kutserl* 'plant' (in 7b) is likely to contain the simple verb root *qut* ~ *kut* 'break ground' plus an unknown element **serl*.

(7) a. *ianeberltiq amarimga*
*iane=**berltik*** *ama=rim-ka*
3DU.SBJ.NPST=loosen:SIDE ART=taro-SG.M
'they pick a taro' (N12BAMCAT-091)

b. *dunguqutserl ngenama.. amaquukuqaavarlen*
*de=ngu=**qutserl*** *ngere-ne=ama..*
CONJ=1SG.SBJ.NPST=plant.NCONT:?? 3N.ASSOC-from/with=ART
ama=quukuk=aa=parlen
ART=sweet.potato=3SG.M.POSS=middle
'and I plant them together with the.. the sweet potatoes there in its middle' (D12ADNGARDEN-050)

The most common formatives within complex verbs are prepositions. Other formatives (especially relational nouns, adverbs and directionals) are attested, but to a much lesser extent. And, when they occur, their contribution to the overall meaning is usually fairly transparent. For example, the meaning of *maarlvit* 'stand up' (in 5b above) transparently arises from a combination of the meanings of *maarl* 'stand' and *pit* 'up'. The contribution of prepositions, by contrast, is usually less clear. For these reasons, section 5.3 focuses on prepositions and traces the diachronic development of complex prepositional verbs in more detail: a development originating in prepositional phrases functioning as adjuncts, via prepositions introducing arguments entailed by the verb semantics, to prepositions being integrated as verb particles and suffixes into the verb.

These complex lexicalization patterns are reflected in the glossing conventions adopted in this grammar as follows. Where a preposition or another element retains some phonological independence (as in example 4 above), both the verb and the other element are glossed separately, receiving glosses that reflect their basic meanings. Where a preposition or other element has been phonologically integrated into the verb (as in examples 5, 6 and 7 above), the whole complex verb receives a single gloss reflecting its conventionalized meaning, plus additional glosses in small caps for every other element present; if their meaning is unknown, '??' is added to the gloss.

The morphological complexity of a verb does not determine its transitivity and argument structure. Both types of verbs can be intransitive (as the simple verb in 8a and the complex verb in 8b); and both can be transitive (as in 9a and 9b). Both types of verbs can introduce arguments through prepositions (as in 10a and 10b). And both can occur in constructions with reduced transitivity, such as the agentless construction that presents an event as non-controlled (as in 11a and 11b). Issues of transitivity are discussed in section 5.2.

(8) a. *biqianyip*
*be=kia=**nyip***
CONJ=3SG.F.SBJ=die.NCONT
'and it died' (N11AESSIRINI-0015)

b. *biqiamuvem*
*be=kia=**muvem***
CONJ=3SG.F.SBJ=get.ready.NCONT.PST:PLACE
'she got ready' (I12AANACLADNSOCIO3-521)

(9) a. *kamraqi*
*ka=**mat**-ki*
3SG.M.SBJ=take.NCONT.PST-3SG.F
'he picked it up' (R12ACMFROG-118)

b. *de nguguirltiqina*

de	*ngu=**guirltik**-ini=a*
CONJ	1SG.SBJ.NPST=turn:SIDE-SG.DIM=DIST

'and I pay back a small one (i.e., a small insult)' (N11AAGBROTHERS-0101)

(10) a. *lua, itatu ramamengga*

lu=a,	*ip=ta=**tu***	***te**=ama=meng-ka*
DEM=DIST	PURP=3PL.SBJ=put.CONT	PURP=ART=wood-SG.M

'there, in order that they start the fire (lit. put something for the purpose of a fire)' (P12ADNFIRE-002)

b. *bune.. untekmet tunagalip, navraarlim*

be=une..	*un=**tekmet***	***te**=una=galip,*
CONJ=1DU.SBJ.NPST	1DU.SBJ=do.CONT:IN	PURP=1DU.POSS=galip

ne=pet=aa=rlim
from/with=on/under=3SG.M.POSS=bottom
'and we.. we harvested our galipnuts, from under it' (N11AJNGENAINGMETBROTHERS-0012)

(11) a. *de biny menaqi*
de ***biny*** *men-ki*
CONJ break at-3SG.F
'and it got broken' (R12BCSFROG-058)

b. *de naqaki binymet dais*
de *naka=kaki* ***binymet*** *de=a-is*
CONJ bit=instead break:IN LOC.PART=3SG.M.POSS-end
'instead its bottom will get broken apart' (P12ARSBILUM1-037)

Finally, verbs show stem alternations that convey aspectual distinctions. Most verbs distinguish a non-continuous stem (as in 12a and 12b) and a continuous stem (as in 12c), but there are also conjugation classes that have only one (unchangeable) stem or three different stems (e.g., *mes* ~ *es* ~ *tes* 'eat' in the second clause of 12a); plus possibly additional stems occurring in other contexts. These alternations, and their relationship to the tense categories coded in the subject indexes, are discussed in section 5.4.

(12) a. *nani nguvlengnyi, denguasnyi*
nani *ngu=**vleng**-nyi,* *de=ngua=es-nyi*
can 1SG.SBJ.NPST=kill.NCONT-2SG CONJ=1SG.SBJ=eat.NCONT.FUT-2SG
'I can kill you, and eat you' (N11AESSIRINI-0010)

b. *de ianeski, meramaqulka*
de *ian=**nes**-ki,* *met=ama=qul-ka*
CONJ 3DU.SBJ=put.in.NCONT-3SG.F in=ART=bottle-SG.M
'and they put it (the frog) into the bottle' (R12ABDFROG-010)

c. *deqa plengngera, daqasnesnget mraarlaunini*
de=ka ***pleng****-nget=a,* *de=ka=**snes**-nget*
CONJ=3SG.M.SBJ kill.CONT-3N=DIST CONJ=3SG.M.SBJ=put.in.CONT-3N
met=aa=rlaun-ini
in=3SG.M.POSS=netbag-SG.DIM
'and he kept killing them, and he kept putting them in his little net-bag' (N11AAGSIRINILOBSTER1-0089)

The patterns reported above for Qaqet are reminiscent of pervasive lexicalization patterns discussed in the literature on Papuan languages (as summarized, e.g., in Foley 1986: 111–166; see especially Pawley's 1993 classic article). Complex events are often broken into more fine-grained components that are then combined in complex expressions, often in the form of serial verb constructions (where a semantically general verb combines with a more specific verb), but also in the form of a semantically more general verb combining with a more specific preposition or nominal. The rules for forming complex expressions are usually analyzable and productive, but there is a considerable amount of idiomaticity involved, determining which of the possible combinations are well-formed and meaningful. Furthermore, Papuan languages often have a multiplicity of verb stems distinguishing controlled from uncontrolled events as well as continuative from completed events. There is only one Papuan pattern that is not attested in Qaqet (Dunn, Reesink, and Terrill 2002: 38–57): stem alternations depending on person and number of arguments.

Qaqet thus seems to have inherited many semantic patterns, but the formal means of expressing them differ somewhat. Qaqet mainly uses prepositions to constrain the general meaning of verbs – not serial verb constructions (but see the discussion in section 5.5). And it uses syntactic means to distinguish between controlled and non-controlled events (in particular, the agentless construction for presenting events as non-controlled) – not verb stem alternations or inflectional morphology. It does show formal similarities to other Papuan languages, in that it employs stem alternation to convey aspectual distinctions.

5.2 Transitivity

This section discusses the issue of transitivity in Qaqet. Verbs in Qaqet can be either intransitive (allowing for at most one unmarked argument, occurring in subject function) or transitive (allowing for at most two unmarked arguments, occurring in subject and object function); there are no ditransitive verbs. All arguments can be omitted if they are recoverable from the context.

The transitivity of a verb has to be distinguished from its semantic valency. Very frequently, transitivity and valency do not match, because Qaqet makes widespread use of prepositions to introduce arguments entailed by the verb semantics. There is an on-going lexicalization process whereby prepositions that originally introduced adjuncts become integrated into the verb: they start to interact with the argument structure of individual verbs, and end up as unanalyzable verb particles or suffixes. In the intermediate stages of this development, this lexicalization process has consequences for the analysis of transitivity and grammatical relations: the question arises as to whether arguments marked by prepositions should or should not be considered (direct) objects of transitive verbs. This question cannot be easily decided. To my knowledge, there are no behavioral or coding properties that would distinguish an object from an adjunct: they both appear in post-verbal position, neither one is indexed on the verb, and there are no morphosyntactic operations such as passivization or relativization that would target only the object. The only formal difference seems to be the presence or absence of a preposition. For this reason, I take this formal difference as the determining factor: object (and subject) are defined as unmarked arguments, and the transitivity of a verb is defined in terms of the number of unmarked arguments it can co-occur with. As a result of this definition, the transitivity of a verb does not necessarily correspond to its valency.

This section focuses on transitivity as defined above. It first describes the morphosyntactic properties of subject and object (section 5.2.1), then discusses the agentless construction (section 5.2.2) and the expression of reflexive and reciprocal concepts (section 5.2.3), and finally outlines the distribution of intransitive and transitive verbs in the Qaqet lexicon (section 5.2.4). Following this discussion of transitivity, the next section then focuses on prepositions and their role in introducing arguments.

5.2.1 Grammatical relations: Subject and object

Qaqet verbs allow for at most two unmarked arguments. The subject argument precedes the verb, covering both the subject of intransitive verbs (as in 13a) and the subject of transitive verbs (as in 13b); and the object argument follows it (as in 13b). There are no ditransitive verbs that occur with two unmarked object noun phrases.

(13) a. *luqa qamit*

[*lu-ka-a*]SBJ	*ka=mit*
DEM-SG.M-DIST	3SG.M.SBJ=go.NCONT.PST

'[that one]SBJ went' (N12ABKSIRINI-118)

b. *luqa qatal luqairaavuk*

[*lu-ka-a*]SBJ	*ka=tal*	[*lu-ka-iara*]OBJ=*a-vuk*
DEM-SG.M-DIST	3SG.M.SBJ=carry.CONT	DEM-SG.M-PROX=DIR-up

'[that one]SBJ was carrying [this one]OBJ up there' (C12ARBZJIFROG-431)

Both arguments are unmarked, i.e., they do not receive any case or prepositional marking (but see section 5.3 for a discussion of prepositions). They are distinguished on the basis of the fixed constituent order of AVO/SV (but see section 5.2.2 for a discussion of the agentless construction), and the subject argument is obligatorily indexed on the verb. Note that both arguments can be freely omitted if they are recoverable from context. The following paragraphs discuss (i) the subject argument and (ii) the object argument.

(i) Subject argument

The subject argument precedes the verb, and it is obligatorily indexed on it (as illustrated in 14a). The subject slot can be filled by all types of noun phrases, including noun phrases headed by free pronouns (as in 14b). This section focusses on the marking of subjects through constituent order and subject indexes. For details on the distribution of noun phrases, see chapter 3.2.3; and for the forms and categories of the subject indexes, see chapter 3.2.3 (for the person categories) and section 5.4.1 (for the tense categories).

(14) a. *amaaren ngatit savriam*
[*ama=aren*]SBJ ***nga***=*tit* *se=pet-iam*
ART=night 3N.SBJ=go.CONT to/with=on/under-3DU.M
'[night]SBJ was falling onto them' (N12BAMCAT-159)

b. *de um ngatit ma*
de [*em*]SBJ ***nga***=*tit* *ma*
CONJ SG.RCD 3N.SBJ=go.CONT thus
'and [the short one (garden)]SBJ goes on like this' (D12ADNGARDEN-009)

While the subject index is obligatory, the subject noun phrase is not. In natural texts, a good number of examples do not contain a subject noun phrase. Often, the lexical noun phrase was mentioned in a previous clause and is thus given (as in 15a). Another common pattern is to introduce the lexical noun phrase in left-dislocated position, usually marked prosodically by a non-final intonation contour (see chapter 2.3.2) and syntactically by a conjunction (see chapter 8.3.1) (as in 15b).

(15) a. *dinyinan damameng amabarlnget, de ngatdang*
de=nyi=nan *de=ama=meng*
CONJ=2SG.SBJ.NPST=put.up.CONT LOC.PART=ART=wood
ama=barl-nget, *de* ***nga***=*tdang*
ART=big-N CONJ 3N.SBJ=burn.CONT
'then you put together the big branches, and they burn' (P12ADNFIRE-026FF)

b. *dip maliltem, de ngatit*
dip *ma=liltem,* *de* ***nga***=*tit*
FUT ART.ID=domestic.plant/animal CONJ 3N.SBJ=go.CONT
'as for the domestic plants in the future, they (will) go on' (D12ADNGARDEN-076)

The subject index presumably grammaticalized from the free pronouns, neutralizing some of the semantic distinctions found in the pronouns (see chapter 3.2.3). Since the pronouns also gave rise to noun class marking on nouns and proforms, it is not unusual for two (semantically and phonologically) related forms to follow each other: one being the noun class suffix on the lexical noun, and the other the subject index on the verb. Sometimes the syllables are identical (as in 16a), and sometimes they are at least similar (as in 16b).

(16) a. *be dip malengiqa qatit*
be *dip* *ma=lengi-**ka*** ***ka***=*tit*
CONJ FUT ART.ID=word-SG.M 3SG.M.SBJ=go.CONT
'the language will go away' (I12AANACLADNSOCIO2-170)

b. *amauaiki qiaqak nama.. amagilka bqaat*

*ama=uaik-**ki***	***kia**=qak*	*ne=ama..*
ART=bird-SG.F	3SG.F.SBJ=deceive.NCONT	from/with=ART

ama=gil-ka	*be=ka=at*
ART=small-SG.M	CONJ=3SG.M.SBJ=fall.NCONT

'the bird startled the.. the little one, and he fell' (R12BCSFROG-063)

In such environments, it is not uncommon for only the subject index to be expressed in fast speech, thus resulting in a mismatch between the overt class of the subject noun phrase and its index. For example, a non-human unmarked noun such as *lengi* 'word' (in 17a), *meng* 'wood' (in 17b) or *qasup* 'rat' (in 17c) obligatorily triggers the neuter subject index *nga* '3N.SBJ'.[22] The presence of different indexes in (17a) and (17b) (singular masculine) and in (17c) (singular feminine) therefore suggests that the nouns are underlying *lengi-ka* 'word-SG.M', *meng-ka* 'wood-SG.M' and *qasup-ki* 'rat-SG.F' – with the noun class suffix being omitted. Note that all morphophonological changes operate on the basis of the actually occurring form (not on the basis of the presumed underlying form): an initial plosive of the subject index such as *k* lenites to *q* following a vowel (as in 17a), becomes a voiced *g* following a nasal (as in 17b), and remains unchanged following a plosive (as in 17c). If it operated on the basis of the underlying form (ending in the vowel-final suffixes *-ka* 'SG.M' and *-ki* 'SG.F'), we would have expected a lenition to *q* in all three examples.

(17) a. *kuasiqi uralengi qasainis, miika*

kuasik=i	*ura=lengi*	***ka**=sainis,*	*miika*
NEG=SIM	1PL.POSS=word	3SG.M.SBJ=change	more

'our language doesn't continue to change' (I12ABLAJLATASOCIO2-167)

b. *taquarl amameng garuqun pranah*

taquarl	*ama=meng*	***ka**=ruqun*	*pet-nas*
thus	ART=wood	3SG.M.SBJ=sit.NCONT.FUT	on/under-self

'like this, the tree would shorten itself' (N11AJNGENAINGMETSIQI-0026)

c. *dama.. aqasup kiaruqun ma*

de=ama..	*a=qasup*	***kia**=ruqun*	*ma*
CONJ=ART	NM=rat	3SG.F.SBJ=say.NCONT	thus

'and the.. the rat said like this' (N12BAMCAT-262)

22 In narratives, speakers can choose to personify animals such as *qasup* 'rat', i.e., it would be possible to interpret *qasup* in (17c) as the name 'Rat', which would allow for a singular feminine subject index. There are two indications that speak against this analysis, though: in all unambiguous contexts throughout the story, *qasup* 'rat' is not treated as a proper noun; furthermore, even in this example, the choice of the articles *ama* 'ART' and *a* 'NM' shows that 'rat' is treated as a common noun (see chapter 3.2.1 on common nouns and proper nouns).

Such omissions are even attested in the case of tightly integrated words such as the demonstrative pronoun in (18): its form should have been *luqia* (from *lu-ki-a* 'DEM-SG.F-DIST'). This example illustrates a further point: it is sometimes not possible to unambiguously decide which of the syllables is omitted. For example, the omitted syllable *qia* in (18) could either be the last syllable of the demonstrative ***luqia***, or the subject index appearing as the first syllable of the verb ***qia**tes*. As reflected in the glossing, I assume that it is the subject index that is present. This decision is based on evidence from unambiguous cases. Whenever there is a prosodic word boundary, it is always before the potentially ambiguous syllable (as in 17a to 17c above). Furthermore, if the forms are phonologically non-identical, it is the form of the subject index that appears. For example, in (17c) above, the noun class suffix would have been *-ki* 'SG.F' (not *kia*).

(18) *dap luqiats amagingera?*
dap *lu=**kia**=tes* *ama=gi-nget=a?*
but DEM=3SG.F.SBJ=eat.CONT ART-what-N=DIST
'and that one eats what now?' (LONGYDS20150517_1-829)

The subject index usually appears as a proclitic to the verb (as in 19a) or to the modifier *raqa* ~ *taqa* 'properly' (as in 19b). Less frequently, the subject index is followed by a word boundary (as in 19c). Since the subject index thus shows some phonological independence, it is analyzed as a clitic (not as an affix).

(19) a. *ianemnyim pit*
***iane**=mnyim* *pit*
3DU.SBJ.NPST=look.CONT up
'they look up' (R12ADNFROG-111)

b. *de miika ianetaqamnyim*
de *miika* ***iane**=taqa=mnyim*
CONJ more 3DU.SBJ.NPST=properly.CONT=look.CONT
'and they continue to look carefully' (R12ADNFROG-315)

c. *be bigia, deian taarlvit*
be *bigia,* *de=**ian*** *taarlvit*
CONJ tomorrow CONJ=3DU.SBJ stand.CONT:UP
'and tomorrow, they get up' (N12BAMCAT-087)

Most commonly, it forms a phonological word together with the following verb. This unit is frequently preceded by other proclitics, especially conjunctions and particles (as in 20a). In fast speech, we observe the sporadic regressive assimilation of vowels in this context: the vowel of the conjunction assimilates in quality to the vowel of the pronoun (as in 20b); and sometimes the vowels of both the conjunction and the pronoun assimilate to the first vowel of the verb (as in 20c). It is also not uncommon for vowels to be omitted altogether (as in 20d).

(20) a. *dianebrlany*
__de__=iane=brlany
CONJ=3DU.SBJ.NPST=sleep
'they are sleeping' (N12BAMCAT-086)

b. ***daqa**tit tuarl*
__de__=__ka__=tit *tuarl*
CONJ=3SG.M.SBJ=go.CONT other.side
'and he moves along one branch (of the river)' (N11AAGBROTHERS-0039)

c. ***duqutu**qun nambarlta ma*
__de__=__ka__=__tu__qun *ne=ama=barl-ta ma*
CONJ=3SG.M.SBJ=say.CONT from/with=ART=big-PL.H thus
'and then he says to the elder brothers like this' (N11AJNGENAINGMET-BROTHERS-0097)

d. ***bqu**rut menaqa*
__be__=__ke__=urut *men-ka*
CONJ=3SG.M.SBJ.NPST=grab.NCONT at-3SG.M
'and he grabbed at him' (N11AAGBROTHERS-0056)

In the case of dysfluencies, the phonological word consisting of subject index and verb is usually preserved, and the subject index is repeated (as in 21a). Cases like (21b) are attested, but rare.

(21) a. *ip nani ngua.. nguatit savrama.. amahlengip ngu.. ngutmatna sranas*
ip *nani* ***ngua..*** *__ngua__=tit* *se=pet=ama..*
PURP can 1SG.SBJ 1SG.SBJ=go.CONT to/with=on/under=ART
ama=sleng=ip ***ngu..*** *__ngu__=tmatna*
ART=garden=PURP 1SG.SBJ.NPST 1SG.SBJ.NPST= work.CONT:RECP
set-nas
behind-self
'so I.. I can go to the.. the garden, and I.. I do the work by myself' (N12ABKSIRINI-052)

b. *ngua.. tiak naivuk*
ngua.. *tu=ia-ka* *ne=i-vuk*
1SG.SBJ put.CONT=other-SG.M from/with=AWAY-up
'I.. put another one down' (D12ADKSPIRITS-038)

(ii) Object argument

The object argument always follows the verb, either as a noun phrase (as in 22a) or as a pronominal suffix (as in 22b). These two are mutually exclusive, i.e., different from the subject argument, the object argument does not receive a separate index. The object suffixes originated in free pronouns, and thus distinguish all noun classes. The subject indexes, by contrast, have collapsed some of the noun class distinctions (see chapter 3.2.3). This mismatch is illustrated in example (22c): it contains two referents from the same shape-based noun class (*ini* 'SG.DIM'), once as a free pronoun in subject function and once as an object suffix. The subject index, by contrast, collapses all shape-based noun classes into a single neuter gender (*nga* '3N.SBJ').

(22) a. *biqiavleng aravlemga*
be=kia=vleng [*ara=vlam-ka*]OBJ
CONJ=3SG.F.SBJ=kill.NCONT 3SG.F.POSS=pig-SG.M
'and she killed her pig' (N11AESSIRINI-0021)

b. *atrik, bravlengga*
a=trik, *be=ta=vleng-*[*ka*]OBJ
NM=trick CONJ=3PL.SBJ=kill.NCONT-3SG.M
'(it was) a trick, and they killed him' (N11AAGSIRINILOBSTER1-0081)

c. *ivini ngatisini*
ip=[*ini*]SBJ ***nga****=tis-*[*ini*]OBJ
PURP=SG.DIM 3N.SBJ=call.CONT-SG.DIM
'so that the little one (child) says the little thing (word)' (I12AANACLADNSOCIO2-039)

The object noun phrase can form a clitic group with the preceding verb. This is especially common in the case of vowel-final verbs preceding vowel-initial noun phrases. Example (23a) illustrates a typical context: the verb *lu* ~ *tlu* 'see' preceding the article *ama* 'ART'. In other environments, no such cliticization is observed. The difference between the two environments is illustrated with the two adjacent utterances in (23b): the first object noun phrase is consonant-initial and does not cliticize to *tlu* 'see', but the second is vowel-initial and does cliticize.

(23) a. *dinyitlamaruqava*
*de=nyi=**tlu**=*[*ama=ruqap*]OBJ*=a*
CONJ=2SG.SBJ.NPST=see.CONT=ART=wild.sugarcane=DIST
'and you see the wild sugarcane now' (D12ADNGARDEN-035)

b. *de nyitlu luqaira, de nyitlamaiskaira*
de *nyi=**tlu*** *[lu-ka-iara]*OBJ,
CONJ 2SG.SBJ.NPST=see.CONT DEM-SG.M-PROX
de *nyi=**tlu**=[ama=is-ka]*OBJ*=iara*
CONJ 2SG.SBJ.NPST=see.CONT=ART=path-SG.M=PROX
'you see this one, you see the path here' (C12ARBZJIFROG-268)

In the case of the verb *lu* ~ *tlu* 'see', further phonological reduction can occur if it is followed by a demonstrative (which always starts with the syllable *lu*). This demonstrative can either occur as a separate word (as in 23b above), or it can cliticize to the verb – and in this case, its initial syllable is lost (as in 24 below). A similar loss of identical syllables was observed in the case of the subject indexes (see point i above). It is not an automatic rule, though: it is optional, and it is only attested in cases where there is a diachronic relationship between the syllables (see chapter 3.3.2 for the origins of the demonstratives).

(24) *ut**lu**qaira, brahnanbetka ilira qanauirl ingulu..*
*ut=**lu**=**lu**-ka-iara,* *be=a=ra-snanbet-ka*
1PL.SBJ=see.NCONT=DEM-SG.M-PROX CONJ=NM=NMLZ-ask:ON/UNDER-SG.M
i=lira *ka=nauirl* *i=ngu=lu..*
SIM=now 3SG.M=first SIM=1SG.SBJ.NPST=see.NCONT
'we saw this one, the question that just now was first, and I think..' (I12ABLAJLATASOCIO4-061)

There are a few cases where pronominal objects constitute independent words (as in 25a), but they almost always form a phonological word with the verb (as in 25b).

(25) a. *desa medu qaat nget nauirl*
de=sa *medu* *ka=at* ***nget*** *nauirl*
CONJ=already past 3SG.M.SBJ=fall/drop.NCONT 3N first
'and he had planted them first' (D12ABDACPGARDEN-011)

b. *kesnesnget, beqesnesnget, beip..*
*ke=snes-**nget**,* *be=ke=snes-**nget**,*
3SG.M.SBJ.NPST=put.in.CONT-3N CONJ=3SG.M.SBJ.NPST=put.in.CONT-3N
be=ip..
CONJ=PURP
'he puts them and puts them and then..' (N11AAGSIRINILOBSTER1-0010)

Although examples like (25a) above are very rare, they do exist. This variation could suggest that the pronominal objects are clitics, rather than suffixes. Despite the existence of such examples, I tentatively analyze them as suffixes because they trigger a phonological change that is otherwise only attested in the case of suffixes.[23]

There is evidence that many Qaqet roots diachronically contain a final vowel *a*, which is synchronically only preserved in those environments where the root is followed by a suffix (but not by an enclitic). The clearest evidence comes from nouns and adjectives (see chapter 4.1.1), but a similar alternation between the presence and the absence of a final vowel *a* is also observed in prepositions (see section 5.3.1) and verbs. In most contexts, a verb such as *mat* ~ *rat* ~ *tat* ~ *tmat* 'take' (and its lenited form *mar* ~ *rar* ~ *tar* ~ *tmar*) would appear without a final vowel: in the final position of an intonation unit (as in 26a), when preceding another phonological word (as in 26b), or when preceding an enclitic (as in 26c). But when it precedes a pronominal object, a final vowel *a* is invariably present (as in 26d): if it were not present, we would expect the form to be **matki* (instead of the actually attested form *meraqi* ~ *mraqi*). In nouns and adjectives, this vowel is only attested in the case of suffixes, and I therefore also analyze the pronominal objects as suffixes.

(26) a. *nyitaqa**tmat***
nyi=taqa=tmat
2SG.SBJ.NPST=properly.CONT=C.take
'pick properly' (C12VARPLAY-078)

b. *dinya**tat** giamengirang sagelna*

de=nya=tat	*gia=meng-irang*	*se=gelna*
CONJ=2SG.SBJ=take.CONT	2SG.POSS=wood-PL.DIM	to/with=nearby

'and you move your little sticks of firewood closer' (P12ADNFIRE-017)

c. *nyitaqa**tmar**ip kuasik nyilangilang*

nyi=taqa=tmat=ip	*kuasik*
2SG.SBJ.NPST=properly.CONT=C.take=PURP	NEG

nyi=ilangilang
2SG.SBJ.NPST=step/shake:REDUP
'pick properly, so that you don't disturb them' (C12VARPLAY-067)

d. *ian**meraqi***
ian=mat-ki
3DU.SBJ=take.NCONT.PST-3SG.F
'they picked it up' (R12ADNFROG-377)

23 The object suffix thus shows a closer phonological integration (as an affix) than the subject index (as a clitic). Mali Baining exhibits a comparable asymmetry (although person-marking overall is phonologically more independent than in Qaqet): Mali object pronouns can be encliticized, while subject indexes are phonologically independent words (Stebbins 2011: 42–44).

There is a small group of verbs that mark nominal and pronominal objects differently. If the object is a lexical noun phrase, it remains unmarked (as in 27a). But if it is a pronoun, it is introduced by the form *ma* (as in 27b). It is not entirely clear how to analyze this form. On the one hand, its behavior is similar to that of a preposition (see section 5.3). On the other hand, Qaqet does not have a preposition *ma*. On the basis of comparative evidence, it might be possible to relate it to one of the existing prepositions, either to *met* 'in' or to *ne* 'from/with'. In Mali, the preposition *mēt* 'inside' (cognate to Qaqet *met* 'in') has an allomorph *ma* (Stebbins 2011: 125), and the preposition *na* 'from' (cognate to Qaqet *ne* 'from/with') has an allomorph *mo* preceding some of the directionals (Stebbins 2011: 196–197). That is, it is possible that *ma* in (27b) has its origin in one of these prepositions. But regardless of its origin, the synchronic alternation is between an unmarked lexical noun phrase and a marked pronoun. It is true that some prepositions have different forms when preceding a noun or a pronoun, but there are no prepositions that alternate with zero. I therefore tentatively analyze *ma* as an overt object marker: it probably developed diachronically from a preposition, but it introduces synchronically the pronominal direct object of some verbs.

(27) a. *kaning amaququanngi*
ka=ning *ama=ququan-ki*
3SG.M.SBJ=fear.NCONT ART=owl-SG.F
'he is afraid of the owl' (R12ATAFROG-148)

b. *kaning maini*
ka=ning ***ma**-ini*
3SG.M.SBJ=fear.NCONT OBJ-SG.DIM
'he is afraid of the little one' (R12ATAFROG-126)

The object argument is not necessarily overtly realized. For example, the transitive verb *tes* 'eat' appears with a direct object in (28a), but without one in (28b). The omission of a direct object is partly conditioned by discourse structure: an object can only be omitted if it is recoverable from the context, e.g., because it is mentioned previously (as the malay apples in 28b). And it is partly conditioned by animacy: a known animate participant is not omitted, but realized as a pronoun (as in 28c). These are the most common patterns emerging from the data, but it is likely that a future in-depth study will reveal further conditioning factors.

(28) a. *kats amadaqa*
*ka=**tes*** [*ama=da-ka*]OBJ
3SG.M.SBJ=eat.CONT ART=taro-SG.M
'he eats (up) the taro' (N12BAMCAT-205)

b. *katramaguleng, deqats*
ka=tat=ama=guleng, *de=ka=**tes***
3SG.M.SBJ=take.CONT=ART=malay.apple CONJ=3SG.M.SBJ=eat.CONT
'he was picking the malay apples, and was eating (them)'
(N11AAGSIRINILOBSTER1-0034)

c. *nani ratska*
nani *ta=**tes**-[ka]*OBJ
can 3PL.SBJ=eat.CONT-3SG.M
'they can be eating him' (N11AAGSIRINILOBSTER2-0082)

5.2.2 Agentless construction

It is possible to suppress the agent argument of a transitive verb (including all its exponents, i.e. both the subject noun phrase and the subject index), leaving only the patient argument. The same pattern is available for intransitive bivalent verbs (i.e., verbs that introduce their patient argument through a preposition), but not for intransitive monovalent verbs (a few exceptions are discussed below).

In all cases, the patient is marked in exactly the same way as in the corresponding agentive utterance. For example, the verb *bup* 'fill' can occur transitively, with the patient being linked to direct object function, i.e., it is unmarked and it follows the verb (as in 29a). This verb can also appear in the agentless construction. In this case, the agent is omitted, and the patient continues to be expressed in the same way as before: either as an unmarked noun phrase following the verb (as in 29b), or as a pronominal suffix (as in 29c). A corresponding pattern is observed in the case of verbs that introduce their patient arguments by means of prepositions. For example, *sirlek* 'throw' introduces its patient argument by means of the preposition *ne* 'from/with', both when an agent is present (as in 30a) and when it is absent (as in 30b).

(29) a. *nyibuv amaglaska namasuga*
*nyi=**bup*** *[ama=glas-ka]*PATIENT *ne=ama=suga*
2SG.SBJ.NPST=fill ART=glass-SG.M from/with=ART=sugar
'you fill the glass with sugar' (BMS-01/06/015)

b. *buv aarlaunini*
bup *[aa=rlaun-ini]*PATIENT
fill 3SG.M.POSS=netbag-SG.DIM
'his netbag gets filled' (N11AAGSIRINILOBSTER1-0011)

c. *kesnesnget mraarlaunini beip.. buvini*
ke=snes-nget *met=aa=rlaun-ini*
3SG.M.SBJ.NPST=put.in.CONT-3N in=3SG.M.POSS=netbag-SG.DIM
be=ip ***bup**-[ini]*PATIENT
CONJ=PURP fill-SG.DIM
'he puts them into his little netbag until.. the little one gets filled' (N11AAGSIRINILOBSTER2-0020)

(30) a. *nyisirlek namaquvangirang*
*nyi=**sirlek*** *[ne=ama=quvang-irang]*PATIENT
2SG.SBJ.NPST=throw from/with=ART=cargo-PL.DIM
'you throw away all the things' (AMI-22/05/2015)

b. *sa sirlek naqa menari navelerles nama.. a.. a.. araalemiam*
sa ***sirlek*** *[ne-ka]*PATIENT *menari*
already throw from/with-3SG.M from.there
ne=pelerles *ne=ama..* *a..* *a..*
from/with=in.between from/with=ART ?? ??
ara=alem-iam
3SG.F.POSS=horn-DU.M
'and he got thrown down from there from between the.. the.. the.. its two horns' (R12ATAFROG-222)

Qaqet verbs thus mark their only argument in two different ways. As discussed in section 5.2.1, some verbs mark it like the subject of a transitive verb (i.e., in preverbal position and with a subject index on the verb). And as discussed above, other verbs appear in the agentless construction and mark it like the object of a transitive verb or like the prepositional object of an intransitive verb (i.e., in postverbal position, and without an index on the verb). This distribution is lexically determined, and it is possible to analyze Qaqet as having a split-intransitive system that distinguishes between a class of S_A verbs (marking their argument like a subject) and a class of S_O verbs (marking it like an object or prepositional object).

An analysis in terms of split intransitivity does capture the existence of the two patterns, but it is not clear whether the two patterns really represent two classes of verbs. If so, the two classes are not equivalent in the sense that only the S_A class contains basic intransitive verbs: some of them participate in transitivity alternations, but most of them occur only in this pattern or are arguably basic in this pattern. The S_O class, by contrast, consists almost exclusively of verbs that alternatively (and even predominantly) occur with an agent argument (as illustrated in 29 and 30 above); a few exceptions are discussed below. Furthermore, the verbs in the S_O class do not mark their patients uniformly: some occur with an unmarked argument (as in 29 above), and others, with a prepositional argument (as in 30 above). The only commonality is that the patient is marked just like the patient of the corresponding bivalent alternant.

Given the above reasoning, I prefer to think of the S_O pattern not as a class of S_O verbs, but rather as a specific argument structure construction (termed agentless construction) that is available to many verbs that have a patient or theme argument. Speakers shift to this construction to present a state change or a change of location from the perspective of the patient. In (29b) and (29c) above, the speaker first reports on an agent putting things into a netbag, and then shifts to focus on the changed state of the netbag. Or in (30b) above, the event is presented from the perspective of the protagonist of the story (the boy), not from that of a peripheral character (in this case, from that of a deer who does the throwing). In all cases, an agent is involved in the event, but the speaker chooses to suppress it and to focus on the patient, who is presented as suffering or undergoing an event outside of its control, brought about by the unmentioned agent. The function of the agentless construction is thus reminiscent of that of a passive construction – except that this construction does not share the formal properties of a passive. A possible similarity is with 'transimpersonal' constructions (Malchukov 2008), i.e., seemingly patientative intransitives that nevertheless retain transitive coding properties – except that the Qaqet construction does not show any exponent of the agent argument, not even in the form of an indefinite subject.

A comparable change of meaning is not attested in verbs that alternate between transitive and intransitive S_A patterns. Qaqet has only very few such verbs, but some do exist. In their case, the agent remains in control of the event, both in the transitive pattern (as in 31a) and in the intransitive S_A pattern (as in 31b). For example, (31b) cannot be used to describe an event where the S argument does not have control, e.g., where an inanimate object gets hidden.

(31) a. *nyit nyirerles amamerlik pemaqavel*

nyi=it *nyi=**rerles***

2SG.SBJ.NPST=go.NCONT.FUT 2SG.SBJ.NPST=hide.NCONT

ama=merlik *pe=ma=qavel*

ART=betelnut PLACE=ART.ID=bush

'go and hide the betelnuts in the bush' (BJS-17/06/2015)

b. *katirip keterles*

ka=tit=ip *ke=**terles***

3SG.M.SBJ=go.CONT=PURP 3SG.M.SBJ.NPST=hide.CONT

'he goes and hides (himself)' (R12ABDFROG-063)

Subjects of basic intransitive S_A verbs are not necessarily in control of the event, e.g., the subject of *at ~ rat* 'fall' in (32a) has no control over the falling event. Such verbs usually do not have a transitive alternant either, although a few of them do. Example (32b) illustrates the transitive use of the verb *at ~ rat* 'fall'. The transitive verb is presumably lexicalized: it probably originated as the causative alternant (literally 'make fall') of the intransitive verb, which became lexicalized as 'plant' and is now being used with all kinds of plants, not just those whose seeds are dropped.

(32) a. *de liama ianrat*
de *lu-iam-a* *ian=**rat***
CONJ DEM-DU.M-DIST 3DU.SBJ=fall/drop.CONT
'those two were falling' (R12ATAFROG-228)

b. *karar amarima*
*ka=**rat*** *ama=rim=a*
3SG.M.SBJ=fall/drop.CONT ART=taro=DIST
'he planted the taro now' (D12ABDACPGARDEN-014)

While the agentless construction is very common, it is nevertheless lexically restricted. For example, speakers do not accept *rerles* ~ *terles* 'hide' in this construction, even in situations that would be compatible with its semantics (e.g., where an inanimate entity gets hidden).

Almost all verbs occurring in the agentless construction are also attested in bivalent contexts with overt agents. To my knowledge, there are only four exceptions: *sung* 'calm', *rlu* 'move', *kurli* 'leave' and *kuasik* 'NEG'. These predicates do not alternate, and their semantics differs to some extent from that of the other predicates in this construction. It is likely that they originated in the same agentless contexts, but that they have undergone semantic change.

First, *sung* 'quiet' and *rlu* 'move' almost exclusively occur in the agentless construction – usually in imperatives directed from adults to children (as in 33a and 33b). Given their semantics, they probably originated in typical agentless contexts, such as 'get (yourself) quieted or calmed down' and 'get (yourself) moved out of the way', which were presumably considered as being outside the control (or at least willingness) of the child. In the present-day language, both now tend to appear in imperative contexts with a clear expectation that the child will obey and carry out the action, i.e., the child is expected to be the agent. In the case of *sung* 'calm', the verb can alternatively occur in the S_A intransitive pattern (as in 33c), but this is very rare. It is not possible for both an agent and a patient to be expressed (e.g., an adult calming down a child). In the case of *rlu* 'move', an S_A intransitive alternant is not attested. But it is likely to be related to the bivalent verb *rlu* 'throw (i.e., make move)' (illustrated in 33d), whose semantics now diverges from that of *rlu* 'move'.

(33) a. *sung nanyi*
sung *ne-**nyi***
quiet from/with-2SG
'you calm down' (LONGYDS20150802_1-362)

b. *rlu sanyivit*
rlu *se-**nyi**=i-pit*
move to/with-2SG=AWAY-up
'you move up there' (LONGYDS20150516_1-742)

c. *nyisung*
***nyi**=sung*
2SG.SBJ.NPST=quiet
'you calm down' (LONGYDS20150531_1-200)

d. *amakauqi qiarlu namagilka*
ama=kau-ki ***kia**=rlu* *ne=ama=gil-ka*
ART=COW-SG.F 3SG.F.SBJ=throw from/with=ART=small-SG.M
'the cow threw down the boy' (R12BCSFROG-082)

Second, *kurli* 'leave' probably originally occurred with the meaning of 'get left behind' in the agentless construction. In the present-day language, this original meaning is no longer straightforwardly attested. The closest approximation is the context exemplified in (34a): as indicated by the idiomatic free translation, it conveys a notion of negative possession, with its origins presumably in metaphorical 'get left behind/out'. Similar to *sung* 'calm' and *rlu* 'move', it is also attested in imperatives (as in 34b), probably with the original non-controlled meaning of 'get left behind', but now directed at an agent. Unlike the other two verbs, its uses were extended beyond imperative contexts, and it now constitutes a neutral way of expressing static location (as in 34c) (see chapter 8.2.2 on the locative construction). A further development must have taken place in imperative contexts: the reanalysis of the pronominal suffix. Examples (34b) and (34d) illustrate this contrast. Both are imperatives, very clearly directed at a second person. But the suffix refers to the agent in (34b) (to the one who does the staying), and to the patient in (34d) (to the one that the unexpressed agent should leave alone).[24]

24 Both (34b) and (34d) could, of course, be analyzed as '2SG/3N gets left behind', with a contextual interpretation of '2SG stays' in (34b) and '3N gets left alone' in (34d). However, given the distribution of *kurli* 'leave' in the present-day language, and especially its use in imperatives directed at second persons, I doubt that this original meaning is preserved. Note also that, in our data, this verb is not attested with a pre-verbal subject index at all, but Dickhardt (2009: 271) quotes the phrase *ngu qurli parlen* 'I stand in the middle', which contains the subject index *ngu* '1SG.NPST.SBJ'. Interestingly, this phrase is restricted to an agentive context: it is used by the mediator of a conflict who actively positions himself between the conflicting parties to attempt a resolution of their conflict.

(34) a. *landi, ngutal guapiuk, dap kurlinyi*
*landi, ngu=tal gua=piuk, dap kurli-**nyi***
NAME 1SG.SBJ.NPST=carry.CONT 1SG.POSS=cassava but leave-2SG
'Landi, I carry my cassava, and you don't have any (lit. you got left behind/out)' (LONGYJL20150805_2-333)

b. *kurlinya*
*kurli-**nyi**=a*
leave-2SG=DIST
'you stay now' (LONGYDS20150531_1-507)

c. *ide qurliqa meramameng*
*ide kurli-**ka** met=ama=meng*
IPFV leave-3SG.M in=ART=wood
'he usually stays inside the trees' (D12ADKSPIRITS-067)

d. *kurlingera*
*kurli-**nget**=a*
leave-3N=DIST
'(you) leave them now' (LONGYDS20150601_1-153)

Finally, there is *kuasik* 'NEG', which belongs to the class of particles. Many of them originated in verbs, and some can still synchronically appear with person-marking (see chapter 7.1).[25] In the case of *kuasik* 'NEG', the original verb has not only given rise to a particle, but also to the negative existential predicate. This predicate invariably appears in the agentless construction (as in 35). Given its highly grammaticalized functions, it is not surprising that *kuasik* 'NEG' does not distribute like synchronic verbs.

(35) *de quasiqaqa*
de kuasik-ka
CONJ NEG-3SG.M
'but he wasn't there' (I12AANACLADNSOCIO3-539)

To my knowledge, these four predicates are the only exceptional cases. All other verbs occurring in the agentless construction also occur in its agentive counterpart. Even in the case of these four predicates, it is possible to offer plausible scenarios for their shift in meaning. The distribution of the agentless construction thus differs considerably from that of the comparable construction in Mali Baining. Mali has many more verbs that only occur in one construction or another, and the distribution in Mali can

25 Synchronically, *kurli* 'leave' is starting to develop into a negative interjection and particle, sometimes replacing *kuasik* 'NEG'. It is possible that *kuasik* 'NEG' underwent a similar development, originating in comparable verbal contexts (see chapter 7.6).

thus more easily be described in terms of two mutually exclusive classes of intransitive verbs (see Stebbins 2011: 41–42).

5.2.3 Reflexivity and reciprocity

Qaqet expresses reflexivity and reciprocity by means of *nas* 'self' and *na* 'RECP'. Both distribute like pronouns, i.e., they occur as suffixes to verbs (thus occupying the direct object slot, as in 36a) and prepositions. Depending on the verb semantics, these prepositions introduce either arguments as in (36b) or adjuncts as in (36c).

(36) a. *bianratna mrianamudembim*
*be=ian=rat-**na*** *met=iana=mudem-im*
CONJ=3DU.SBJ=fall/drop.CONT-RECP in=3DU.POSS=resin-DU.F
'they were throwing each other into their bushlamps' (N11AAGBROTHERS-0059)

b. *taquarl amalamsaqa, deqaruqun pranah*
taquarl *ama=lamesa-ka,* *de=ka=ruqun*
thus ART=coconut-SG.M CONJ=3SG.M.SBJ=sit.NCONT.FUT
*pet-**nas***
on/under-self
'just like this, as for the coconut tree, it shall shorten itself' (N11AJNGENAINGMETSIQI-0055)

c. *kanyim nasranas*
ka=nyim *ne=set-**nas***
3SG.M.SBJ=look.NCONT from/with=behind-self
'he looked behind himself' (R12ABDFROG-046)

Being suffixes, they trigger the same kind of allomorphy as pronominal objects in a preceding verb or preposition. That is, those verbs and prepositions that have different forms before pronominal suffixes (see sections 5.2.1 and 5.3.1) also take this form before the reflexive and reciprocal suffixes. For example, the verb *pileng* 'wake' occurs as *pilenga* (in 37a), or the preposition *pet* 'on/under', as *p(e)ra* (in 37b).

(37) a. *kamaarlvit ip ke**pilenga**nas*
ka=maarlvit *ip* *ke=**pileng**-nas*
3SG.M.SBJ=stand.NCONT.PST:UP PURP 3SG.M.SBJ.NPST=wake.CONT-self
'he stood up to keep himself awake' (AJL-04/05/2012)

b. *tetaqen **pra**na i..*
te=taqen ***pet**-na* *i..*
3PL.SBJ.NPST=say.CONT on/under-RECP SIM
'they are saying to each other that..' (I12AANACLADNSOCIO3-122)

The forms express co-referentiality between the referent of the subject argument and a referent occurring in a different syntactic function (as in the examples above). In addition, both forms can be used to emphasize that the referents of the subject argument have carried out an activity either by themselves (with the reflexive, as in 38a) or together (with the reciprocal, as in 38b). In this case, the forms almost always appear within prepositional phrases following the verb. In addition, there are a few occurrences, where reflexive *nas* 'self' cliticizes to the emphasis particle *tika* (as in 38c): as indicated by the literal translation, this structure conveys again an emphasis on the subject (and not a co-referentiality between subject and object).

(38) a. *tika nani qatmatnasranas*
tika *nani* *ka=tmatna=set-**nas***
EMPH can 3SG.M.SBJ=work.CONT:RECP=behind-self
'he can be doing the work all by himself' (N12ABKSIRINI-033)

b. *ianetmatna remna*
iane=tmatna *te-**na***
3DU.SBJ.NPST=work.CONT:RECP PURP-RECP
'they work together' (N12BAMCAT-019)

c. *kequap, tikanas namakaasika*
ke=quap, *tika=**nas*** *ne=ama=kaasik-ka*
3SG.M.SBJ.NPST=tie.NCONT EMPH=self from/with=ART=vine-SG.M
'he hanged himself with a *kaasik* vine (lit. he tied (the vine), and he himself did it)' (D12ADKSPIRITS-090)

Semantically, the distribution of the reciprocal is restricted to cases of strong reciprocity, i.e., when all participants interact with each other, or at least potentially interact with each other. As such, the reciprocal is used in plural contexts (as in 39a and 39b) as well as in dual contexts (as in 39c and 39d), with all participants being equally involved in the event. For example, the speaker in (39a) explains how to let a handful of little sticks fall so that they all separate as much as possible from each other; storytelling events as in (39b) are reciprocal events in Qaqet, where people alternate in telling stories and every participant is potentially allowed to tell their own story; both participants in (39c) have an equal share in the argument; and both participants in (39d) do their equal share of chasing and being chased.

(39) a. *sa, nyat giangarik navrangerip nani verlsdem nanget navrana*
sa, *nya=at* *gia=ngarik*
already 2SG.SBJ=fall/drop.NCONT 2SG.POSS=hand
ne=pet-nget=ip *nani* *verlsdem*
from/with=on/under-3N=PURP can part.NCONT:LOC.PART
ne-nget *ne=pet-**na***
from/with-3N from/with=on/under-RECP
'now, let your hand fall from them, so that they can separate from each other' (C12VARPLAY-181)

b. *tesiit banaira, tesiit bigia*
te=siit *barek-**na**=iara,* *te=siit* *bigia*
3PL.SBJ.NPST=story BEN-RECP=PROX 3PL.SBJ.NPST=story tomorrow
'they tell stories to each other now, they tell stories tomorrow' (I12AANACLADNSOCIO3-361)

c. *dequrliama, dianeprerlsena*
de=kurli-iam=a,
CONJ=leave-3DU.M=DIST
*de=iane=prerl=se-**na***
CONJ=3DU.SBJ.NPST=argue/wrestle.CONT=to/with-RECP
'the two stay now, and they argue with each other' (N12BAMCAT-042)

d. *laianengingarl sena mragulenggaalang*
la=iane=ngingarl *se-**na***
this.day=3DU.SBJ.NPST=chase.CONT:?? to/with-RECP
met=a=guleng-ka=aa=lang
in=NM=malay.apple-SG.M=3SG.M.POSS=top
'they are now chasing each other on top of the malay apple tree' (N11AAGSIRINIROPE-0134)

If the involvement is unequal, speakers do not resort to the reciprocal. For example, the fight in (40a) is attributed to one person only, and the chasing in (40b) is asymmetrical. Similarly, adjacency relations are not expressed through the reciprocal, but are implicated through, e.g., the choice of verb (as in 40c).

(40) a. *kurli nyateski*
kurli *nya=tes-ki*
leave 2SG.SUBJ=eat.CONT-3SG.F
'don't you fight her' (C12YMMZJIPLAY1-258)

b. *dap masinepki qingarl sut*
dap *ma=sinepki* *ki=ingarl* *se-ut*
but ART.ID=NAME:SG.F 3SG.F.SBJ.NPST=chase.NCONT:?? to/with-1PL
'and Sinepki chased us' (N12ABKSIRINI-127)

c. *klainanget pramarlekenirang*
ke=lain-nget *pet=ama=rleken-irang*
3SG.M.SBJ.NPST=line-3N on/under=ART=branch-PL.DIM
'he lines them up (next to each other) on the branches'
(N11AAGSIRINILOBSTER1-0017)

In addition to their productive uses, both forms are found lexicalized as parts of complex verbs (see section 5.1 on complex verbs). For example, *sunas* 'learn' (in 41a) contains the reflexive suffix *nas* 'self'. It was formed on the basis of *su* 'teach' (in 41b), with (presumably) an original meaning of 'teach self'. Other verbs that include the reflexive are, e.g., *mrenas* ~ *renas* ~ *trenas* 'jump' or *uuknas* ~ *quuknas* 'bathe, wash self'. And verbs that contain the reciprocal are, e.g., *atmetna* ~ *ratmetna* 'meet' or *matna* ~ *ratna* ~ *tatna* 'work'. In some cases, simplex counterparts are attested (as in the alternation of *sunas* 'learn' and *su* 'teach' in 41), but in other cases, only the complex form exists.

(41) a. *de tika uruimirang ngeresunas temiam*
de *tika* *ure-uim-irang* *ngere=**sunas***
CONJ EMPH 1PL.POSS-child-PL.DIM 3N.SBJ.NPST=teach:SELF
te-iam
PURP-3DU.M
'and our little children have to learn both' (I12AANACLADNSOCIO3-094)

b. *ip ngeresuut*
ip *ngere=**su**-ut*
PURP 3N.SBJ.NPST=teach-1PL
'they teach us' (I12AANACLADNSOCIO3-380)

In addition, both are attested in idiomatic expressions. The form *nas* 'self' co-occurs with *taquarl* 'thus' in a fixed expression that conveys a return to a prior state (i.e., the prior state of 'self') (as in 42a). And *na* 'RECP' is likely to be part of the present-day adverb *gelna* 'nearby' (i.e., near each other) (as in 42b), which originated in the preposition *gel* 'near' (see section 5.3.4).

(42) a. *kua magrip.. amakainaqi qiatirip taquarlnas*
kua *maget=ip..* *ama=kaina-ki* *kia=tit=ip*
INTRG then=PURP ART=water-SG.F 3SG.F.SBJ=go.CONT=PURP
taquarl=nas
thus=self
'may it be that.. the water moves like before' (N11AJNGENAINGMETSIQI-0094)

b. *saruarl iantden, gelna namaluqup, asnaka quasiqi gelna*

se=tuarl	*ian=tden,*	***gelna***
to/with=other.side	3DU.SBJ=come.CONT	nearby

ne=ama=luqup,	*as=naka*	*kuasik=i*	***gelna***
from/with=ART=place	still=bit	NEG=SIM	nearby

'to the other side they come, nearby the place, but not too close' (N12BAMCAT-162FF)

5.2.4 Transitivity classes in the lexicon

Qaqet verbs are either intransitive or transitive. There are no ditransitive verbs, and only few ambitransitive verbs. Independent of their transitivity, many verbs allow for arguments to be introduced by prepositions: either adding an argument to an intransitive or transitive verb, or replacing the unmarked direct object with a prepositional object. This section gives a brief summary of the distribution of intransitive and transitive verbs, and the following section discusses arguments marked by prepositions.

Intransitive verbs are attested both among simple verbs (as in 43a) and complex verbs (as in 43b). As for the semantic role linked to subject function, both agent (as in 43a) and patient/theme (as in 43b) are attested, independent of whether a verb is simple or complex.

(43) a. *ip nani nyiguirl*

ip	*nani*	*nyi=guirl*
PURP	can	2SG.SBJ.NPST=return

'and then you can come back' (N12BAMCAT-272)

b. *arlaunnga qarletik*

a=rlaun-ka	*ka=rletik*
NM=netbag-SG.M	3SG.M.SBJ=turn.over:SIDE

'the netbag turned over' (ATA-30/05/2012)

An unusual characteristic of the Qaqet verb lexicon is the large proportion of bivalent verbs that are formally intransitive, resorting to a preposition to introduce their second participant. This includes especially verbs with a non-patient/theme argument such as *tekmet* 'do, act on' (as in 44a), but there are also verbs with patient/theme participants such as *tatmet* 'uproot' (as in 44b).

(44) a. *karekmet pema.. aqumqaim menaqa*

ka=rekmet	***pe****=ma..*	*a=qumeqa-im*	*men-ka*
3SG.M.SBJ=do.NCONT:IN	PLACE=ART.ID	NM=breast-DU.F	at-3SG.M

'he forms.. two breasts for him' (N12ABKSIRINI-074FF)

b. *katatmet pemamenga, beip perlsera*
ka=tatmet ***pe****=ma=meng=a,*
3SG.M.SBJ=uproot.CONT:IN PLACE=ART.ID=wood=DIST
be=ip *perlset=a*
CONJ=PURP finish=DIST
'he uprooted the trees now, and was finished now' (D12ABDACPGARDEN-009)

Transitive verbs very frequently occur with a patient or theme linked to direct object function. This observation holds mainly for simple verbs (as in 45a), but there are also examples of complex verbs (as in 45b). Such patient/theme-oriented transitive verbs are the main candidates for appearing in the agentless construction (as in 45c) (see section 5.2.2).

(45) a. *nguabiny guamerlan nep maqavel*
*ngua=****biny*** [*gua=merlana*]OBJ *ne=pe* *ma=qavel*
1SG.SBJ=break 1SG.POSS=leaf from/with=PLACE ART.ID=bush
'I broke off my leaves from the bush' (AJL-30/04/2015)

b. *kaqutik amadaqa*
*ka=****qutik*** [*ama=da-ka*]OBJ
3SG.M.SBJ=cut.off:SIDE ART=taro-SG.M
'he cut off the taro' (CMS-16/06/2015)

c. *be miika ip binybiny anirl*
be *miika* *ip* ***binybiny*** [*a=nirla*]OBJ
CONJ EMPH PURP break.REDUP NM=sun
'when the sun was rising a bit more (lit. breaking)' (N11AAGBROTHERS-0097)

Conversely, complex verbs tend to express semantic roles other than patient/theme in their direct object. For example, the simple verb *rat* 'close/cover' links a theme argument to direct object function, resulting in an interpretation of 'pushing something so that it closes' (as in 46a). Alternatively, it selects the preposition *te* 'PURP' to introduce a ground argument, with an interpretation of 'covering something' (as in 46b). This preposition has now become incorporated into the verb, resulting in the complex verb *ratem* 'close/cover:PURP', which links a ground argument to direct object function (as in 46c). Since prepositions frequently serve to introduce ground arguments, it is not surprising that complex verbs incorporating such former prepositions often retain these patterns (see section 5.3.2 for details of the lexicalization process).

(46) a. *ngurat amatarlka*
*ngu=**rat*** [*ama=tarl-ka*]OBJ
1SG.SBJ.NPST=close/cover ART=door-SG.M
'I push the door close' (CCM-13/06/2015)

b. *ngurat teguasmes*
*ngu=**rat*** ***te**=gua=smes*
1SG.SBJ.NPST=close/cover PURP=1SG.POSS=food
'I cover my food (e.g., with a cloth)' (CCM-13/06/2015)

c. *nguratem amatarlka*
*ngu=**ratem*** [*ama=tarl-ka*]OBJ
1SG.SBJ.NPST=close/cover:PURP ART=door-SG.M
'I cover the door (e.g., with a cloth)' (CCM-13/06/2015)

This difference between simple and complex verbs holds true for many verbs, but it is nevertheless only a tendency. As shown above, there are complex verbs with patient/theme arguments (as in 45b above), and simple verbs also allow for a wider variety of semantic roles. The most common patterns are reported in section 5.3 (for complex verbs) and below (for simple verbs).

One group of simple verbs alternate between linking a theme (as in 47a) or a ground role (as in 47b) to direct object function; the respective other role is optionally expressed in a prepositional phrase.

(47) a. *kuuk amakainaqi*
ka=uuk [*ama=kaina-ki*]OBJ
3SG.M.SBJ=fetch/fill.NCONT ART=water-SG.F
'he fetched the water' (AEM-02/06/2011)

b. *agilki qiuuq amaglaska namakainaqi*
a=gil-ki *kia=uuk* [*ama=glas-ka*]OBJ
NM=small-SG.F 3SG.F.SBJ=fetch/fill.NCONT ART=glass-SG.M
ne=ama=kaina-ki
from/with=ART=water-SG.F
'the girl filled the glass with water' (ACM-03/08/2012)

Furthermore, many verbs of perception (as in 48a), cognition (as in 48b) and emotion (as in 48c) are transitive and link their non-agent argument to direct object function. Verbs of speaking usually select for prepositional arguments, but some are attested with direct objects, usually taking a metalinguistic noun as direct object (as in 48d), or sometimes alternatively an addressee (as in 48e).

(48) a. *ivundrun tlamakar*
ip=un=tit=un *tlu=[ama=kar]*OBJ
PURP=1DU.SBJ=go.CONT=1DU.SBJ see.CONT=ART=car
'so that we go and see the cars' (N12BAMCAT-045)

b. *irang ngadrlem amalengiqa*
irang *nga=drlem* *[ama=lengi-ka]*OBJ
PL.DIM 3N.SBJ=know ART=word-SG.M
'they know the language' (I12AANACLADNSOCIO3-160)

c. *biqianing ama asisit*
be=kia=ning *[ama* *a=sis-it]*OBJ
CONJ=3SG.F.SBJ=fear.NCONT ART NM=ridge-SG.LONG
'and it is afraid of the ridge' (R12ABDFROG-096)

d. *ip nya.. nyamraqen liina mauqas, de..*
ip *nya..* *nya=mraqen* *[lu-ini-a]*OBJ *ma=uqas,*
PURP 2SG.SBJ 2SG.SBJ=C.say DEM-SG.DIM-DIST ART.ID=difference
de..
CONJ
'if you.. you say that one (i.e., word) differently, and..' (I12AANACLAD-NSOCIO2-062)

e. *kataqen amangerlnanngia*
ka=taqen *[ama=ngerlnan-ki]*OBJ*=a*
3SG.M.SBJ=say.CONT ART=woman-SG.F=DIST
'he tells the mother now' (N11AJNGENAINGMETSIQI-0023)

In the case of trivalent verbs, at most one argument is linked to direct object function (and the other, or sometimes both, are expressed via prepositions). The relevant argument is usually the recipient (as in 49a and 49b), although a few verbs select a theme (as in 49c).

(49) a. *nyiquarl giaqalatki ramakontainaqia*
nyi=quarl *[gia=qalat-ki]*OBJ
2SG.SBJ.NPST=present.NCONT 2SG.POSS=younger.sibling-SG.F
te=ama=kontaina-ki=a
PURP=ART=container-SG.F=DIST
'give your little sister the container now' (LONGYDS20150517_1-507)

b. *de dip ngusu nguimini rama.. amaqaqeras*
de *dip* *ngu=su* *[gu-uim-ini]*OBJ
CONJ FUT 1SG.SBJ.NPST=teach 1SG.POSS-child-SG.DIM
te=ama.. *ama=qaqera-es*
PURP=ART ART=person-SG.FLAT
'and I will teach my child the.. the Qaqet language' (I12AANACLAD-NSOCIO3-045)

c. *iqimnem aruimga sep mahausik*
i=ki=mnem [*are-uim-ka*]OBJ
SIM=3SG.F.SBJ.NPST=send/sell.CONT 3SG.F.POSS-child-SG.M
se=pe *ma=hausik*
to/with=PLACE ART.ID=hospital
'and she is sending her child to the hospital' (ARS-12/06/2015)

Ambitransitive verbs are infrequent. In most cases, such verbs have distinct (albeit related) senses, and I therefore analyze them as distinct lexemes – even though their formal properties suggest that they are diachronically related. For example, *quarl ~ kuarl* has a meaning of 'present (give, show)' when occurring transitively (as in 50a), but 'shine a light (in order to catch fish)' when occurring intransitively (as in 50b).

(50) a. *dap kequarl aarluaqa remirang*
dap *ke=quarl* [*aa=rlua-ka*]OBJ
but 3SG.M.SBJ.NPST=present.NCONT 3SG.M.POSS=friend-SG.M
te-irang
PURP-PL.DIM
'he gives his friend the little things' (N11AAGBROTHERS-0015)
b. *unekuarl meramakainaqi*
une=kuarl *met=ama=kaina-ki*
1DU.SBJ.NPST=shine.CONT in=ART=water-SG.F
'we shine into the water (to catch fish)' (N11AAGBROTHERS-0019)

Transitive verbs often omit their direct object, and thus look indistinguishable from intransitive verbs. Whenever the object is recoverable from the context, I consider such verbs to be transitive (see section 5.2.1). This analysis holds for the majority of cases, but there remains a small number of unclear cases. Some emotion verbs such as *ning ~ ngning* 'fear' are possibly ambitransitive, occurring either with a stimulus object (as in 51a) or without (as in 51b). An animate object (as in 51b) would normally not be omitted, but be expressed pronominally: its absence in (51b) could point to the verb being used intransitively. In addition, there are a few verbs such as *rerles ~ terles* 'hide' that receive a reflexive interpretation when used intransitively (see example 31 above). Mostly, though, reflexivity is overtly expressed through *nas* 'self'.

(51) a. *iqaki qengning amabariqi*
i=kaki *ke=ngning* [*ama=bari-ki*]OBJ
SIM=instead 3SG.M.SBJ.NPST=fear.CONT ART=bee-SG.F
'because he is afraid of the bees' (R12ABDFROG-059)

b. *kidatdemga, dap keqiuaik, ke.. iqengning*
ki=datdem-ka, *dap* *ke=qiuaik,*
3SG.F.SBJ.NPST=follow.CONT-3SG.M but 3SG.M.SBJ.NPST=run.CONT
ke.. *i=ke=ngning*
3SG.M.SBJ.NPST SIM=3SG.M.SBJ.NPST=fear.CONT
'it (a deer) is following him, and he is running, he.. because he is afraid' (R12ATAFROG-164)

Finally, ambitransitive verbs alternating between inchoative and causative uses are almost absent. All attested cases involve lexicalizations (as in example 32 above); otherwise, speakers resort to the agentless construction (see section 5.2.2).

5.3 Prepositions: Introducing participants

Qaqet makes extensive use of prepositions to introduce participants in different semantic roles to an event (summarized in Table 61).

Tab. 61: Prepositions and verb particles

Form	Gloss	Core semantics	Other roles
ne	from/with	source, instrument	material, partitive, addressee, theme, causee
se	to/with	goal, comitative	purpose, recipient, addressee, instrument, theme, manner complement
daleng	above	locative (superposition: above)	n/a
de	LOC.PART	locative (at part of a whole)	ground, theme/patient
gel	near	locative (proximity: near)	n/a
kut	along	locative (along)	n/a
men	at	locative (coincidence: at)	ground, theme/patient
met	in	locative (containment: in)	ground, theme/patient
pe	PLACE	locative (in a unique place)	ground, theme/patient
pet	on/under	locative (superposition: on, under; in place or time)	ground, addressee, content, theme/patient
set	behind	locative (behind)	n/a
barek	BEN	beneficiary	recipient, addressee
te	PURP	purpose	ground, theme/patient

Depending on the verb semantics, the syntactic status of the participant varies: as adjunct, as argument introduced by a preposition, or as unmarked argument. This variation is the result of a lexicalization process, whereby prepositions are first recruited to introduce arguments entailed by the verb semantics and eventually become lexicalized as verb particles and suffixes.

Section 5.3.1 focuses on the structure of the prepositional phrase: this phrase constitutes the starting point for the lexicalization process, and the basic semantics of prepositions show most clearly in their distribution in this context. Section 5.3.2 outlines the entire range of distributional possibilities of the prepositions-cum-particles, discussing the evidence for the lexicalization process. Sections 5.3.3 to 5.3.5 then describe each preposition in turn, and section 5.3.6 adds a note on other formatives.

From a comparative perspective, Qaqet and Mali share many similarities: the structure of prepositional phrases, the function of prepositions to introduce arguments as well as their further lexicalization as verb particles (see Stebbins 2011: 67–68, 105–135); and also the forms of the prepositions (as summarized in Table 62).

Tab. 62: Simple prepositions: Comparing Qaqet and Mali

Preposition	**Gloss**	**Mali (Stebbins 2011: 105–117)**[26]	
nə	from/with	*na*	from; PREP
sə	to/with	*sa*	to; with
daləŋ	above	*daer*	over
də	LOC.PART	–	
gəl	near	*gəl* ~ *gələm*	with ~ near
kut	along	–	
mən	at	*məni*	on
mət	in	*mət*	within
pə	PLACE	*pəm* ~ *pa*[27]	in ~ LOC; BEN
pət	on/under	*pət*	at
sət	behind	–	
barək	BEN	*pa*[6]	LOC; BEN
tə	PURP	*təm*	THEME; GOAL; PATH
nani	can (particle)	*nani(a)*	for
məsəŋ	at base (adverb)	*səŋ*	at the bottom of

26 To facilitate comparison, the Qaqet and Mali forms are represented here in IPA.

27 It is likely that Mali *pa* is related to both Qaqet *ba* in *barek* (in its beneficiary meaning) and *pe* (in its locative meaning). The relevant Mali examples (e.g., in Stebbins 2011: 110–111) would be rendered by Qaqet *barek* and *pe* respectively.

In most cases, the two languages have prepositions that are probably cognate, and there are only few cases where cognate forms either do not exist or where they belong to a different word class in the other language. The main difference is in the area of semantics: while the semantics of some prepositions is shared across the languages, the semantics of others is different. It is possible that some differences may turn out to be differences in analysis. But other differences are likely to be genuine differences between the languages. This includes especially the different spatial relationships expressed by the cognate spatial prepositions *mən* ~ *məni*, *pə* ~ *pəm*, and *pət*.

5.3.1 Prepositional phrases

Qaqet has thirteen prepositions that head prepositional phrases. These phrases function on a clausal level, where they usually occur in the right periphery of a clause (as in 52a) (see chapter 8.1.1 on clause structure). They also function as modifiers within noun phrases (as in 52b) (see chapter 3.4.3 on noun phrase modification), and as predicates in the non-verbal locative construction (as in 52c). They are furthermore found in a number of other non-verbal constructions (see chapter 8.2 on non-verbal clauses).

(52) a. *deruaik namenini*
de=te=uaik [***ne=men**-ini*]PP
CONJ=3PL.SBJ.NPST=run.NCONT from/with=at-SG.DIM
'they run away [from the little one]PP' (N12ABKSIRINI-111)

b. *ip nemga nameniam, de amadlek.. pemga*
ip [*nema-ka* ***ne=men**-iam*]NP, *de* *ama=dlek..*
PURP who-SG.M from/with=at-3DU.M CONJ ART=strength
pe-ka
PLACE-3SG.M
'[who amongst them]NP is the one who has strength on him' (L12ADNNORTHWIND-005)

c. *tika liirama mii vramasnanbetka amaqunaska*
tika *lu-iram-a* *mii* [***pet**=ama=snanbet-ka*
EMPH DEM-DU.DIM-DIST most on/under=ART=ask:ON/UNDER-SG.M
ama=qunas-ka]NP
ART=one-SG.M
'those two both are [inside the one question]PP' (I12AANACLADNSOCIO3-091)

Prepositions cannot be left stranded: they are obligatorily followed by a noun phrase. This includes simple noun phrases headed by a noun (as in 53a) or pronoun (as in 53b), but also complex noun phrases consisting of, e.g., a possessive structure (as in

53c). Very frequently, the prepositions co-occur with relational nouns such as *rleng* 'back' in (53d), which grammaticalized from possessive structures (see chapter 6.1 for details on relational nouns).

(53) a. *ivit naniip kaman pramaqip*
i-pit *nani=ip* *ka=man*
AWAY-up can=PURP 3SG.M.SBJ=go.inside.NCONT.PST
[***pet***=*ama=qip*]$_{PP}$
on/under=ART=spear
'and so when he spears (himself) [on the spears]$_{PP}$' (N11AAGSIRINIROPE-0127)

b. *deiva, daqatit praus*
de=ip=a, *de=ka=tit* [***pet***-*es*]$_{PP}$
CONJ=PURP=DIST CONJ=3SG.M.SBJ=go.CONT on/under-SG.FLAT
'and then, he was going [onto the flat one]$_{PP}$' (N11AJNGENAINGMETBROTHERS-0094)

c. *ngen mii ngendit prama.. amalevungga aangariqis*
ngen *mii* *ngen=tit* [***pet***=*ama..* *ama=levung-ka*
2PL most 2PL.SBJ=go.CONT on/under=ART ART=tree.type-SG.M
aa=ngarik-es]$_{PP}$
3SG.M.POSS=hand-SG.FLAT
'you all, you go [on the.. the branch of the *levung* palm]$_{PP}$' (N11AJNGENAINGMETBROTHERS-0099)

d. *iqamugun, pramamengem angerarleng*
i=ka=mugun, [***pet***=*ama=meng-em* *ngera=****rleng***]$_{PP}$
SIM=3SG.M.SBJ=sit on/under=ART=wood-SG.RCD 3N.POSS=back
'he sits [on the back of a log]$_{PP}$' (R12ADNFROG-222)

The two prepositions *ne* 'from/with' and *se* 'to/with' can also introduce directionals (as in 54a) and locational adverbs (as in 54b); and *pe* 'PLACE' is attested with directionals from the 'up' paradigm (see chapter 6). The other prepositions cannot occur in these contexts.

(54) a. *kurlip naundit samuk*
kurli=ip *nani=un=tit* [***se***=*a-muk*]$_{PP}$
leave=PURP can=1DU.SBJ=go.CONT to/with=DIR-across
'wait and we can go [(to) across]$_{PP}$' (N12BAMCAT-265)

b. *dinyirarlik seruarl*
de=nyi=rarlik [***se***=*tuarl*]$_{PP}$
CONJ=2SG.SBJ.NPST=cross.NCONT.FUT to/with=other.side
'you cross [to the other side]$_{PP}$' (N11AAGSIRINIROPE-0098)

Prepositions cannot co-occur. The only exceptions are, again, the two prepositions *ne* 'from/with' and *se* 'to/with', which are frequently followed by another preposition.[28] In such cases, they invariably receive a spatial source or goal reading (as in 55a and 55b). When occurring as simple prepositions, they are also attested in spatial contexts (as in 54a and 54b above), but such occurrences are infrequent. If they occur as simple prepositions, they usually receive a non-spatial meaning (as in 55c below).

(55) a. *kiamit, namramarliinem*
kia=mit, [***ne=met****=ama=rliin-em*]PP
3SG.F.SBJ=go.NCONT.PST from/with=in=ART=bamboo-SG.RCD
'it went [from inside the bamboo]PP' (R12ADNFROG-028)

b. *nani utit semramakainaqi*
nani ut=tit [***se=met****=ama=kaina-ki*]PP
can 1PL.SBJ=go.CONT to/with=in=ART=water-SG.F
'we can go [to the river]PP' (N12ABKSIRINI-044)

c. *deqiatit samasurlka*
de=kia=tit [***se****=ama=surl-ka*]PP
CONJ=3SG.F.SBJ=go.CONT to/with=ART=fence-SG.M
'and it continued [with the fence]PP' (D12ABDACPGARDEN-016)

As summarized in Table 63, the two prepositions can be followed by most other prepositions. The main exception is *barek* 'BEN': it is likely that its (non-spatial) beneficiary meaning is incompatible with the source and goal meanings of *ne* and *se*. Similarly, combinations with *te* 'PURP' are restricted: they do occur, but all attested cases involve lexicalizations. Again, it is likely that the non-spatial purpose meaning of the basic preposition prevents a co-occurrence. In the case of *set* 'behind', there is a shift in meaning (see below), which may prevent its productive combination with *ne* and *se*. Finally, the absence of *daleng* 'above' and *kut* 'along' might simply be gaps in the database: both prepositions are attested only very infrequently.

28 In cases of lexicalization, more combinations are attested – but these forms no longer function as prepositions (see the following sections for details). In non-lexicalized prepositional phrases, by contrast, only *ne* 'from/with' and *se* 'to/with' can occur in the first position of a complex preposition. Mali Baining allows for two further prepositions in first position, albeit in limited contexts only (Stebbins 2011: 68, 117–120).

Tab. 63: Complex prepositions

Preposition	Gloss	+ *ne* 'from/with'	+ *se* 'to/with'
daleng	above	n/a	n/a
de	LOC.PART	*nade*	*sade*
gel	near	*nagel*	*sagel*
kut	along	n/a	n/a
men	at	*namen*	*samen*
met	in	*namet*	*samet*
pe	PLACE	*nep*	*sep*
pet	on/under	*navet*	*savet*
set	behind	*naset*	n/a
barek	BEN	n/a	n/a
te	PURP	*(nare)*	*(sare)*

The resulting complex prepositions are mostly fully transparent. In terms of their form, all morphemes are identifiable, and all morphophonological changes are predictable. And in terms of their semantics, we observe a combination of the source or goal semantics of the first preposition with the spatial semantics of the second preposition.

There are two partial exceptions to the above generalization. First, *nep* (from *ne=pe* 'from/with= PLACE') and *sep* (from *se=pe* 'to/with= PLACE') unexpectedly occur without a final vowel. The resulting semantics, however, is compositional. For example, the preposition *pe* 'PLACE' introduces *qavel* 'bush' as a static location in (56a). In the case of a source or goal reading, this preposition continues to be present, preceded by *ne* 'from/with' or *se* 'to/with' respectively (as in 56b).

(56) a. *lurai, tika ide qurlira vemaqavel*
lu-ta-a=i, *tika* *ide* *kurli-ta* [***pe***=*ma*=*qavel*]$_{\text{PP}}$
DEM-PL.H-DIST=SIM EMPH IPFV leave-3PL.H PLACE=ART.ID=bush
'those ones who always stay [in the bush]$_{\text{PP}}$' (D12ADKSPIRITS-006)

b. *dinyatit sep maqavel*
de=nya=tit [***se=pe*** *ma=qavel*]$_{\text{PP}}$
CONJ=2SG.SBJ=go.CONT to/with=PLACE ART.ID=bush
'you go [into the bush]$_{\text{PP}}$' (P12ARSBILUM3L-008)

And second, the preposition *set* 'behind' is only attested in combination with *ne* 'from/with'. The simple preposition has a spatial meaning, while the complex preposition has both a compositional meaning ('from behind') and a non-compositional meaning of 'following', both in spatial (as in 57a) and temporal contexts (as in 57b).

It has furthermore developed into an adverb with a temporal meaning (illustrated in 57c).

(57) a. *de saqika qeqiuaik, nasraamam*
de *saqi-ka* *ke=qiuaik,*
CONJ again-3SG.M 3SG.M.SBJ.NPST=run.CONT
[***ne=set****=aa=mam*]PP
from/with=behind=3SG.M.POSS=father
'and it (the dog) is also running, [behind its master]PP' (R12ADNFROG-239)

b. *nasramasmes, ideresiit*
[***ne=set****=ama=smes*]PP, *ide=te=siit*
from/with=behind=ART=food IPFV=3PL.SBJ.NPST=story
'[after dinner]PP, they usually tell stories' (I12AANACLADNSOCIO3-321)

c. *de mani ureperlset naina,* [*nasat*]ADV
de *mani* *ure=perlset* *ne-ini=a,*
CONJ recently 1PL.SBJ.NPST=finish.CONT from/with-SG.DIM=DIST
nasat
later
'and we have just recently finished that one, (just a bit) [later]ADV' (D12ADNGARDEN-022FF)

Phonologically, the prepositions usually cliticize to the following element, forming a single phonological word with it. As a result of this cliticization process, the prepositions frequently do not surface in their underlying form: voiceless plosives are lenited intervocalically, and a lexical vowel /e/ (i.e., /ə/) is usually lost. For example, *pet* 'on/under' is realized *vr* in (58a), *gel* 'near' is realized *gl* in (58b), and *pe* 'PLACE' is realized as *p* and *v* (in 58c). The last column of Table 64 summarizes all such realizations.

(58) a. *kurlira* ***vr****amanirlaqa*
kurli-ta ***pet****=ama=nirla-ka*
leave-3PL.H on/under=ART=sun-SG.M
'they stayed one day' (N11AJNGENAINGMETBROTHERS-0006)

b. *tikaip nani biandres,* ***gl****ianlavu*
tika=ip *nani* *be=ian=tes,* ***gel****=iane-lavu*
EMPH=PURP can CONJ=3DU.SBJ=eat.CONT near=3DU.POSS-adult
'they can eat at their parents'' (N11AAGBROTHERS-0005)

c. ***p****aavetkia,* ***v****emaqerleng*
pe*=aa=avet-ki=a,* ***pe****=ma=qerleng*
PLACE=3SG.M.POSS=house-SG.F=DIST PLACE=ART.ID=fallow.garden
'in his home there, in the old garden' (I12AANACLADNSOCIO3-525)

In addition to these predictable changes, most prepositions exhibit an unpredictable allomorphy that is conditioned by the following element. One form is used when the preposition precedes a pronominal suffix or a preposition (Context 2 in Table 64). And another form is used elsewhere (Context 1 in Table 64). The remainder of this section describes each pattern in turn.

Tab. 64: Prepositions: Allomorphy

Citation form	Gloss	Context 1 (elsewhere)	Context 2 (pronominal suffix, preposition)	Lenited forms
ne	from/with	*ne ~ n*	*na*	n/a
se	to/with	*se ~ s*	*sa*	n/a
daleng	to/with	*daleng*	*daleng (ma)*	n/a
de	LOC.PART	*de ~ d*	*dem*	n/a
gel	near	*gel ~ gl*	*gel ~ gl*	n/a
kut	along	*kut*	*kut*	*kur ~ qur*
men	at	*men*	*mena*	n/a
met	in	*met*	*met*	*mer ~ mr*
pe	PLACE	*pe ~ p*	*pem*	*v ~ ve(m)*
pet	on/under	*pet*	*pera ~ pra*	*per ~ pr ~ ver ~ vr ~ vet*
set	behind	*set*	*sera ~ sra*	*ser ~ sr*
barek	BEN	*barek*	*ba ~ bareqa*	*bareq*
te	PURP	*te ~ t*	*tem*	*r ~ re(m)*

First, in the case of *ne ~ na* 'from/with' and *se ~ sa* 'to/with', the alternation is between *e* (i.e., [ə]) and *a* ([a]). The alternant with [ə] is present in the contexts illustrated in (59a) and (59b). In (59a), it precedes the consonant-initial element of a noun phrase, and [ə] is thus clearly audible. In (59b), it precedes the vowel-initial element of a noun phrase, and [ə] is thus lost: such vowel loss is only attested in the case of the vowel schwa – not in the case of [a] (see chapter 2.1.2). By contrast, the alternant with [a] invariably precedes a suffixed pronoun (as in 59c) or another preposition (as in 59d).

(59) a. *desaqika ngrek* ***se****ma.. ramgi qans*
de=saqi-ka *ngerek* ***se****=ma..ramgi*
CONJ=again-3SG.M alone to/with=ART.ID NAME
ka=nes
3SG.M.SBJ=shout.NCONT
'it is again only.. Ramgi who shouted' (N11AAGSIRINILOBSTER2-0059)

b. *desaqika* ***sa**maliltem*
de=saqi-ka ***se**=ama=liltem*
CONJ=again-3SG.M to/with=ART=domestic.plant/animal
'(it continues) again with plants' (D12ADNGARDEN-010)

c. *iandit* ***sa**qia*
ian=tit ***se**-ki=a*
3DU.SBJ=go.CONT to/with-3SG.F=DIST
'they now go with it' (R12ABDFROG-129)

d. ***sa**mramakainaqi*
***se**=met=ama=kaina-ki*
to/with=in=ART=water-SG.F
'to the water' (N11AJNGENAINGMETSIQI-0081)

Second, in the case of *te* ~ *tem* 'PURP', *pe* ~ *pem* 'PLACE' and *de* ~ *dem* 'LOC.PART', the alternation is between the absence and the presence of a final [m]. Example (60a) illustrates the use of *pe* (preceding a possessive noun phrase), and (60b), the use of *pem* (preceding a suffixed pronoun). Pronouns that diachronically contain an initial plosive *b* retain this consonant when suffixed to any of these three prepositions (such as synchronic *em* 'SG.RCD' (**bem*) in 60c). As discussed in chapter 4.1.1, the initial plosive *b* is only maintained following the nasal *m*, e.g., following one of the three prepositions that end in *m*. In synchronic Qaqet, it is not uncommon for the final nasal of the preposition to be lost in this environment. For example, the expected pronunciation in (60c) would have been [^{n}dəmbəm], not [^{n}də^{n}bəm]; nevertheless, the presence of *b* suggests that the underlying form of the preposition is *dem*, i.e., containing the final nasal.

(60) a. *dinyisik* ***pe**giamelanga*
de=nyi=sik ***pe**=gia=melang=a*
CONJ=2SG.SBJ.NPST=cut PLACE=2SG.POSS=vine=DIST
'you cut at your vines' (P12ADNROPE1-020)

b. *bqakiqerl kiquarik* ***pem**ga*
be=ka=kiqerl *ki=quarik* ***pe**-ka*
CONJ=3SG.M.SBJ=now 3SG.F.SBJ.NPST=hang.NCONT PLACE-3SG.M
'it lifts him up' (R12ACMFROG-076)

c. *de lik de**bem***
de *lik* *de-**em***
CONJ split/hit LOC.PART-SG.RCD
'and the short one got knocked off' (R12ADNFROG-078)

Third, in the case of *men* ~ *mena* 'at', *pet* ~ *pera* 'on/under' and *set* ~ *sera* 'behind', the alternation is between a monosyllabic and a disyllabic form ending in /a/. There is a concomitant change in that a final voiceless plosive is lenited in the disyllabic form, because it now appears intervocalically. Examples (61a) and (61b) illustrate this kind of alternation.

(61) a. *diqisnes* ***pet****luqiara*
de=ki=snes ***pet****=lu-ki-iara*
CONJ=3SG.F.SBJ.NPST=shout.CONT on/under=DEM-SG.F-PROX
'and it is barking at this one' (R12ATAFROG-216)

b. *deqasnes* ***praqi***
de=ka=snes ***pet****-ki*
CONJ=3SG.M.SBJ=shout.CONT on/under-3SG.F
'and it was barking at it' (R12ABDFROG-034)

Compare the realization in the two examples above to the realization of the phonologically similar, but non-alternating, preposition *met* 'in'. Different from *pet* 'on/under', it retains this form both in the first context (as in 62a) and in the second context (as in 62b).

(62) a. *mani qurliqi mrama.. ama..* ***met****laumiara*
mani kurli-ki met=ama.. ama.. ***met****=lu-em-iara*
recently leave-3SG.F in=ART ART in=DEM-SG.RCD-PROX
'earlier it stayed inside the.. the.. inside this one (the bottle)' (R12ATAFROG-061)

b. *dinyirltik* ***met****ki*
de=nyi=rletik ***met****-ki*
CONJ=2SG.SBJ.NPST=turn.over:SIDE in-3SG.F
'you pour (water) on it' (P12ADNFIRE-047)

Finally, the preposition *barek* 'BEN' alternates between *barek* (as in 63a) and *bareqa* (as in 63b). Again, the form preceding the pronoun ends in a final vowel [a], resulting in the lenition of the preceding plosive. The cognate preposition in Mali Baining is *pa* (Stebbins 2011: 110–111), and it is thus likely that the Qaqet form *barek* ~ *bareqa* is multimorphemic, containing a synchronically unidentifiable morpheme **rek* ~ *reqa*. Qaqet still retains the original short form in some limited contexts: *ba* precedes first and second person pronouns (as in 63c), as well as reflexive and reciprocal pronouns.

(63) a. *taquarl medu nguatis amasiaqi* ***barek****.. mabrigit*
taquarl medu ngua=tis ama=sia-ki
thus past 1SG.SBJ=call.CONT ART=chair-SG.F
barek*.. ma=bridget*
BEN ART.ID=NAME
'like earlier I pronounced (the word) 'chair' for.. Birgit' (I12ABLAJLATASOCIO2-153FF)

b. *nyilsil* ***brqa****qi, deguasiirem arlisa*
nyi=lsil ***barek****-ki,* *de=gua=siit-em*
2SG.SBJ.NPST=say.CONT BEN-3SG.F LOC.PART=1SG.POSS=story-SG.RCD
ngere-is=a
3N.POSS-end=DIST
'tell her it's the end of my short story now' (N12AMVGENAINGMETBROTHERS-079)

c. *ngua.. ngua.. nguatisini* ***ba****nyi*
ngua.. *ngua..* *ngua=tis-ini* ***barek****-nyi*
1SG.SBJ 1SG.SBJ 1SG.SBJ=call.CONT-SG.DIM BEN-2SG
'I.. I.. I say it to you' (I12AANACLADNSOCIO2-071)

The alternations described above are not predictable on phonological grounds. In the case of the alternation between *e* [ə] and [a] (for *ne* 'from/with' and *se* 'to/with'), it could be possible to argue that an underlying /a/ is weakened to [ə] in fast speech. However, if this were the only reason, we would expect variation between [ə] and [a] in all contexts – but this is not the case. Furthermore, the allomorphy occurs exactly in those contexts where other prepositions exhibit an allomorphy that cannot be explained as a weakening of /a/ to [ə].

Comparative evidence suggests that the form preceding the pronominal suffixes constitutes the original form (see Table 62 above): the cognate forms in Mali Baining almost always correspond to this form (exhibiting a final vowel or a final nasal). Similar diachronic developments are attested in nouns and adjectives (see chapter 4.1.1), and in verbs (see section 5.2.1): some noun, adjective and verb roots end in a vowel that is only preserved in suffixed forms (i.e., in forms containing a noun class suffix or an object suffix), but lost in all other environments. It is likely that a similar process also accounts for the variation among the prepositions: the presence of pronominal suffixes preserved the original form, preventing its further erosion. The clitic groups consisting of two prepositions seem to have had a similar effect. Given the limited number of combinations available (see Table 63 above), it is possible that the complex prepositions are lexicalized to some extent, and thus do not undergo the same phonological changes observed elsewhere. In other contexts, most prepositions have undergone phonetic erosion: some have lost a final vowel or nasal, and others were subject to weakening of /a/ to [ə].

In some complex verbs, the original form of the preposition is preserved, as in (64a), where the lexicalized expression *tatpem* 'cut, remove' contains the original form *pem* (not the eroded form *pe*). And in other complex verbs, the eroded form is preserved, as in (64b), where the lexicalized expression *tatnavet* 'work, help' contains *pet* (not the original form *pera*). It is likely that this variation reflects the form of the preposition at the time of lexicalization.

(64) a. *nyitatpem taqurlani*
*nyi=tat**pem*** *taquarl=ani*
2SG.SBJ.NPST=cut.CONT:PLACE thus=DIST
'you cut (it) like this' (P12ADNROPE1-029)

b. *de ngatat-navet*
de *nga=tatna**vet***
CONJ 3N.SBJ=work.CONT:RECP:ON/UNDER
'they worked (for us)' (I12AANACLADNSOCIO3-302)

5.3.2 Overview: The distributional possibilities

This section discusses the distributional possibilities of prepositions and verb particles. From a synchronic perspective, we can describe their occurrence in a number of distinct morphosyntactic environments. From a diachronic perspective, it is likely that these different environments reflect an on-going lexicalization process from prepositions to verb particles and eventually verb suffixes. This on-going lexicalization process has consequences for the morphosyntactic and semantic analysis of the forms.

Morphosyntactically, prepositions and particles exhibit different formal properties. At the two endpoints of the development, the form classes can be easily distinguished. There are, however, many individual expressions whose preposition-cum-particle cannot be clearly assigned to one class or another. This grammar adopts the convention of treating all forms as prepositions, unless there is unambiguous evidence for them being particles.

Semantically, each form has a very broad meaning range. Their basic meaning is established through analyzing their distribution in prepositional phrases that function as adjuncts. In the more lexicalized expressions, there is considerable interaction between the verb semantics and the prepositional semantics, and we observe the sometimes idiosyncratic results of meaning change. That is, the meaning of the lexicalized form is never entirely compositional, and the contribution of the prepositional semantics to the overall meaning cannot always be determined. Nevertheless, basic meaning components are often still discernable, patterns emerge and plausible diachronic developments can be posited. This grammar adopts the convention of glossing the prepositions and particles with their basic meaning.

This section summarizes the distributional possibilities, focusing on the semantic and morphosyntactic developments. It takes the preposition *te* 'PURP' as an example, but a comparable case can be made for most prepositions.

In its basic use, *te* 'PURP' introduces a non-spatial goal or purpose. In (65a), it conveys the purpose of a 'going' event. And in (65b), it adds a purpose to an 'eating' event: in this example, the direct object *luqa* 'that one' of the verb *tes* 'eat' is not overtly expressed (as it is recoverable from the preceding clause), and the preposition *te* 'PURP' introduces a third participant – a complex noun phrase that specifies the intended purpose of the meal (to be eaten as leftovers). Both utterances exemplify a prepositional phrase in adjunct function: the verb retains its basic transitivity and argument structure (intransitive in 65a, transitive in 65b), and a peripheral participant is added in a specific role (e.g., a purpose role in the case of *te* 'PURP'). Semantically, this added participant is not entailed by the verb: if the prepositional phrase were not present, such a participant would not be inferable. Phonologically, the preposition invariably forms a unit with the following noun phrase; and this noun phrase has to be overtly present.

(65) a. *deraquarl ngendit tengenameng*
de=taquarl *ngen=tit* [***te***=*ngena=meng*]PP
CONJ=thus 2PL.SBJ=go.CONT PURP=2PL.POSS=wood
'just like you are going [for your firewood]PP (i.e., collecting the firewood)' (R12ATAFROG-183)

b. *dap kuasik tika luqa, saqerlundes tunaqerlqerlek pemirang ivuneverlset*
dap *kuasik* *tika* *lu-ka-a,*
but NEG EMPH DEM-SG.M-DIST
sa=kerl=un=tes [***te***=*una=qerlqerlek*
already=DEONT=1DU.SBJ=eat.CONT PURP=1DU.POSS=leftovers
pe-irang]PP *ip=une=verlset*
PLACE-PL.DIM PURP=1DU.SBJ.NPST=finish.NCONT
'but it is not that one, we will just eat (that one) [for/as our little leftovers]PP, and we will finish (him)' (N11AAGSIRINIROPE-0123)

In a second context, the prepositional phrase interacts with the argument structure of the verb. For example, the verb *lu* ~ *tlu* 'see' is transitive, occurring with a stimulus participant mapped onto direct object function (as in 66a). Alternatively, this verb can occur with a prepositional phrase introducing a purpose participant (as in 66b). Different from the prepositional phrase in (65b) above, this phrase replaces the unmarked noun phrase in direct object function, and we observe a shift in meaning: from a stimulus reading (i.e., 'see something') to a purpose reading (i.e., 'look for something') – a shift that presumably follows from the purpose semantics of the preposition *te* 'PURP'. Arguably, this prepositional phrase could still be analyzed as an adjunct. Phonologically and syntactically, there are no differences from the clear adjuncts above. And semantically, it could be argued that the purpose participant is not entailed by the verb semantics: if no second participant is overtly present, the utterance always receives the stimulus interpretation – never the purpose interpretation (as in 66c). Nevertheless, its presence alters the argument structure of the basic verb: it becomes (arguably) intransitive, and no longer allows for a stimulus participant.

(66) a. *de qialu masirini mramagulengga*

de	*kia=lu*	*[ma=sirini]*NP	*met=ama=guleng-ka*
CONJ	3SG.F.SBJ=see.NCONT	ART.ID=NAME	in=ART=malay.apple-SG.M

'and she saw Sirini in the malay apple tree' (N11AESSIRINI-0008)

b. *urir ivurlu remgi*

ure=it	*ip=ure=lu*	[***te***-*ki*]PP
1PL.SBJ.NPST=go.NCONT.FUT	PURP=1PL.SBJ.NPST=see.NCONT	PURP-3SG.F

'let's go and look for it' (N12AMVGENAINGMETBROTHERS-042)

c. as *nguataqen ide ngutlu*

as	*ngua=taqen*	*ide*	*ngu=tlu*
still	1SG.SBJ=say.CONT	IPFV	1SG.SBJ.NPST=see.CONT

'I'm saying (it) because I keep seeing (it)' (I12AANACLADNSOCIO2-141)

In addition, there are verbs that only ever allow for a participant to be expressed in a prepositional phrase. For example, the verb *mali* 'search' needs the preposition *te* 'PURP' to introduce a second participant (as in 67a). Semantically, this participant can again be analyzed as a purpose participant, i.e., similar to the expression in (66b) above. But different from the examples above, this participant seems to be entailed by the verb semantics: there is no alternation with an unmarked direct object, and the participant is inferable even if it is not overtly present (as in 67b).

(67) a. *nyimali regiakaasik*

nyi=mali	***te***=*gia=kaasik*
2SG.SBJ.NPST=search	PURP=2SG.POSS=vine

'you search for your vines' (P12ARSBILUM1-011)

b. *iandit, dianemali*

ian=tit,	*de=iane=mali*
3DU.SBJ=go.CONT	CONJ=3DU.SBJ.NPST=search

'they go and search (for the frog)' (R12ACMFROG-017)

In all examples above, the purpose semantics of *te* 'PURP' is still clearly discernable. In other cases, a purpose reading is less obvious. For example, *te* 'PURP' introduces the theme argument of many transfer verbs, e.g., of *quarl* ~ *kuarl* 'present' in (68a), yet there is no straightforward semantic relationship between purpose and theme. Note also that it is not the case that *te* 'PURP' always introduces the theme argument – other verbs use other prepositions. In the case of *te* 'PURP', its occurrence with transfer verbs could have developed out of the contexts exemplified in (68b) and (68c). The intransitive verb *qut* ~ *kut* 'break ground' can optionally occur with a purpose adjunct (as in 68b). This structure then has probably given rise to the complex expression *qut te* ~ *kut te* 'serve', where *te* 'PURP' introduces the theme argument (as in 68c). Synchronically, this expression has conventionalized with the meaning of 'serve something to someone'. But originally, a more literal translation of (68c) would have been:

'she breaks/cuts (from the ground, e.g., from the dish) with the purpose of (it becoming) food for the benefit of her guests'.

(68) a. *ip nguaqurlanyi rembem*
ip *ngua=quarl-nyi* ***te**-em*
PURP 1SG.SBJ=present.NCONT-2SG PURP-SG.RCD
'when I gave you the short one' (N11AJNGENAINGMETSIQI-0115)

b. *uanukut tuanaivip*
uane=kut ***te**=uana=ivip*
2DU.SBJ.NPST=break.ground.CONT PURP=2DU.POSS=snake
'you dig for your worms' (LONGYDS20150531_1-001)

c. *kiaqut tamasmes bareq araqaqet*
kia=qut ***te**=ama=smes* *barek*
3SG.F.SBJ=break.ground.NCONT PURP=ART=food for
ara=qaqera
3SG.F.POSS=person
'she serves food to her guests' (AJL-04/05/2012)

The above examples illustrate that prepositions undergo meaning changes in the course of the lexicalization process. At the same time, they gradually lose their prepositional status and become verb particles (and eventually verb suffixes). Phonologically, the forms become increasingly integrated with the verb, and are often realized as enclitics to the verb. And syntactically, they no longer require prepositional objects.

For example, in the expression *qut te ~ kut te* 'serve', *te* 'PURP' can either occur as a proclitic to a prepositional object (as in 68c above) or as an enclitic to the verb without introducing a prepositional object (as in 69a below). If it still had the status of a preposition, example (69a) would not be possible. Some expressions (like *qut te ~ kut te* 'serve') allow for variation, while others no longer allow for the presence of a prepositional object at all. For example, the former preposition *te* 'PURP' is now an integral part of the complex verb *ratem* 'open:PURP'. Phonologically, it is closely integrated with the verb. Even in slow speech, it invariably forms a phonological unit with it (and it could arguably be analyzed synchronically as a suffix). And syntactically, it can no longer be followed by a noun phrase. If a second participant is to be added, speakers have to resort to the preposition *met* 'in' instead. Again, if *te* 'PURP' were functioning as a preposition, example (69b) would not be possible: Qaqet does not allow for the co-occurrence of the prepositions *te* 'PURP' and *met* 'in'.

(69) a. *kiaqutem bareq araqaqet*
*kia=qut=**te*** *barek* *ara=qaqera*
3SG.F.SBJ=break.ground.NCONT=PURP BEN 3SG.F.POSS=person
'she serves to her guests' (AJL-04/05/2012)

b. *nyiratem metki*
*nyi=ra**tem*** *met-ki*
2SG.SBJ.NPST=open.NCONT:PURP in-3SG.F
'you open it' (LONGYDS20150517_1-509)

In other cases, the integration of preposition and verb has led to a change in transitivity: the former prepositional object now functions as a direct object. For example, the complex verb *mestem ~ estem ~ testem* '(eat something) mixed with' in (70) diachronically contains the preposition *te* 'PURP'. It would have originated in contexts like (65b) above, where the verb *tes* 'eat' was followed by a purpose adjunct. But synchronically, this expression has become lexicalized, and the form *te* 'PURP' no longer functions as a preposition. As a result, the second participant is now unmarked and functions as direct object.

(70) *uandestem uanaqaluniam*
*uan=tes**tem*** *uana=qalun-iam*
2DU.SBJ=mix.CONT:PURP 2DU.POSS=singapore-DU.M
'you eat them mixed with your singapore taros' (LONGYDS20150802_1-110)

The above examples were chosen to illustrate the central issues that apply to all Qaqet prepositions. First, it is always possible to discern a basic semantics, e.g., *te* 'PURP' introduces a non-spatial goal or purpose. This basic semantics is present in prepositional phrases that function as adjuncts (as in 65 above), but it is also traceable in many of the more lexicalized expressions (as in 66 and 67). Second, there are cases where this basic semantics is not (or no longer) straightforwardly present. In some cases, relevant bridging contexts exist, thus allowing us to posit plausible diachronic scenarios for the semantic changes (as in 68b and 68c). In other cases, such evidence is not (or no longer) available. Third, I assume that the extension of meaning proceeds on a verb-by-verb basis (as sketched out in 68b and 68c). An individual verb occurs with a prepositional adjunct in its basic meaning; and if they frequently co-occur in a specific context, a process of conventionalization sets in and a complex expression arises. In the initial stages, this complex form consists of the verb plus the prepositional phrase, but over time the preposition loses its prepositional status and becomes a verb particle and eventually a suffix (as in 69 and 70). In parallel to the morphosyntactic changes, this complex expression develops a conventionalized meaning.

Given that the meaning extensions proceed on a verb-by-verb basis, no overall generalizations can be made: e.g., *te* 'PURP' was extended to mark the theme arguments of some transfer verbs, because it happened to frequently occur in contexts where such a semantic change became possible – but it has not developed into a general preposition to introduce theme arguments. This strong connection between individual verbs and prepositions, and the overall lack of generalizability, speak for an analysis in terms of lexicalization – rather than in terms of derivation (e.g., where the prepositions develop into valence-changing morphology) or even inflection (e.g., where the prepositions develop into case-marking morphology).

The above scenario has analytical consequences. In the intermediate stages of the development, the morphosyntactic status and semantics of the prepositions-cum-particles are usually indeterminable. Morphosyntactically, it is unclear whether they are best analyzed as prepositions introducing adjuncts (as in the clear cases of 65), prepositions introducing arguments (arguably, from 66 onwards), or verb particles (arguably, from 69 onwards). And semantically, it is unclear whether the prepositions-cum-particles retain their core semantics (as in 65, 66 and 67) or introduce participants in other semantic roles (arguably, from 68 onwards). As discussed above, this issue cannot easily be solved: partly because the potential criteria do not line up; and partly because we would need information about the entire distributional range of a verb. To avoid the danger of making arbitrary decisions at this point, I adopt the following conventions in this grammar: the prepositions-cum-particles are always glossed with their core meanings (e.g., *te* 'PURP', even where it arguably introduces a theme argument); they are analyzed as verb particles if they always form a phonological unit with the verb or if they can potentially occur without a noun phrase (e.g., from 68c onwards); otherwise they are analyzed as prepositions. A detailed argument structure analysis would be necessary to decide for each verb whether the preposition introduces an adjunct or an argument.[29] Such a study is beyond the scope of this grammar, though. Instead, the grammar focuses on the transitivity of a verb (defined as the number of unmarked noun phrases it can occur with) – but recognizes that there is a mismatch between its transitivity and its valency (defined as the number of arguments entailed by the verb, regardless of their morphosyntactic expression) (see also section 5.2 on transitivity).

5.3.3 Prepositions *ne* 'from/with' and *se* 'to/with'

The preposition *ne* 'from/with' is closely associated with the preposition *se* 'to/with'. Formally, they are the only prepositions that can co-occur with other prepositions and that can introduce not only noun phrases, but also directionals and adverbs (see section 5.3.1). Semantically, they have complementary spatial and accompaniment

29 Stebbins (2011: 120–132) has conducted such an analysis of the Mali lexicon, showing that 50% of the verb lexicon consists of complex verbs containing one or more prepositions-cum-particles. For Qaqet, I assume the proportion to be lower. In particular, her class of stative intransitive prepositional verbs mostly does not correspond to verbs in Qaqet, but to nouns occurring with a preposition in the non-verbal locative construction (see chapter 8.2.2). But the other two classes – active intransitive prepositional verbs and transitive prepositional verbs – are also attested in Qaqet. As discussed in the text, I am more conservative in my analysis and assume a higher degree of compositionality, but there still remains a substantial number of clear complex verbs.

readings: *ne* introducing sources and instruments, and *se* introducing goals and companions. In addition, both have developed further uses, occurring with a large number of verbs and introducing a variety of semantic roles. This section discusses each preposition in turn.

(i) Preposition *ne* 'from/with'

The glossing of *ne* 'from/with' reflects its two basic uses: introducing a spatial source ('from') or an instrument ('with'). These two uses are considered basic because their distribution is the least constrained: they are very frequent and they are attested with all types of verbs.

Most commonly, this preposition introduces the spatial source of a movement (as in 71a), and, more generally, the ground from which something is taken (as in 71b) or the material from which something is formed (as in 71c). The original source semantics has furthermore given rise to a partitive reading: the preposition *ne* 'from/with' conveys this kind of reading usually (but not necessarily) in combination with the verb particle *met* 'in' (as in 71d).

(71) a. *deqerl kiamit nameniam*

de=kerl	*kia=mit*	***ne**=men-iam*
CONJ=DEONT	3SG.F.SBJ=go.NCONT.PST	from/with=at-3DU.M

'it went from them ~ it left them' (R12ADNFROG-382)

b. *lungera, kua rabiny namerini?*

lu-nget-a,	*kua*	*ta=biny*	***ne**=met-ini?*
DEM-N-DIST	INTRG	3PL.SBJ=break	from/with=in-SG.DIM

'those ones, did they break them off from inside the little one?' (LONGYJL20150805_1-728)

c. *damarlaun, de tika idremsem namalangik*

de=ama=rlaun,	*de*	*tika*	*ide=te=msem*
CONJ=ART=netbag	CONJ	EMPH	IPFV=3PL.SBJ.NPST=weave.CONT

***ne**=ama=langik*
from/with=ART=vine

'and the netbags, they weave them from the *langik* vines' (P12ARS-BILUM2-015)

d. *kadikmet namaurlen*

*ka=dik**met***	***ne**=ama=urlen*
3SG.M.SBJ=cut:IN	from/with=ART=prawn

'he cut off some of the prawns (lit. from the prawns)' (N11AAGBROTHERS-0047)

The source semantics of *ne* 'from/with' is also visible in its use of introducing modifiers in noun phrases (as in 72a) (see chapter 3.4.3) and in adverbial phrases (as in 72b) (see chapter 6.2).

(72) a. *amalauski namadaqa*
[*a=malaus-ki* ***ne***=*ama=da-ka*]NP
NM=canoe-SG.F from/with=ART=taro-SG.M
'[the canoe (made) from taro]NP' (N12BAMCAT-132)
b. *saruarl namalevungga*
se=[*tuarl* ***ne***=*ama=levung-ka*]ADV
to/with=other.side from/with=ART=tree.type-SG.M
'to [the other side of the *levung* palm]ADV' (N11AJNGENAINGMETBROTHERS-0032)

In its second basic use, this preposition introduces an instrument (as in 73a), including non-physical instruments such as, e.g., languages (as in 73b).

(73) a. *dakua radik sametka, namaavis*
dap=kua ta=dik se=met-ka, ***ne***=*ama=avis*
but=INTRG 3PL.SBJ=cut to/with=in-3SG.M from/with=ART=knife
'or maybe they cut him, with knives' (D12ADKSPIRITS-045FF)
b. *i.. iquasik ketaqen naqamalengiqa*
i.. i=kuasik ke=taqen
SIM SIM=NEG 3SG.M.SBJ.NPST=say.CONT
ne=*a=qama=lengi-ka*
from/with=NM=some=word-SG.M
'so.. so he doesn't speak in/with any language' (I12AANACLADNSOCIO3-166)

While *ne* 'from/with' has instrumental functions, it does not have any obvious comitative functions synchronically. The only potential indication of a comitative function is its occurrence with the addressee of many speech act verbs (as in 74). Furthermore, it has given rise to the associative construction, which refers to a referent and its associates. Present-day Qaqet uses both the associative construction (see chapter 3.6) and the preposition *se* 'to/with' to convey accompaniment (see point ii below).

(74) *kitaqen naqa ma*
ki=taqen ***ne***-*ka* *ma*
3SG.F.SBJ.NPST=say.CONT from/with-3SG.M thus
'she talks to/with him like this' (N11AJNGENAINGMETSIQI-0113)

The instrumental use has probably given rise to the use of *ne* 'from/with' to introduce theme arguments of many placement verbs. It is likely that this use was originally restricted to verbs that alternated between linking either the theme argument to direct object (as in 75a) or the ground. In the latter case, the theme is added through the preposition *ne* 'from/with' (as in 75b). This alternation is reminiscent of the English *spray/load* alternation (Levin 1993: 50–51), where a locative variant (e.g., *John sprayed paint on the wall*) alternates with a *with* variant (e.g., *John sprayed the wall with paint*). In Qaqet, like in English, the choice of alternant conveys a subtle semantic difference: in the second case, the entire ground is affected by the event.

(75) a. *ngusnes amaquukuk merama ratki*
ngu=snes [*ama=quukuk*]THEME
1SG.SBJ.NPST=put.in.CONT ART=sweet.potato
[*met=ama rat-ki*]GROUND
in=ART basket-SG.F
'I put sweet potatoes into the basket' (ARS-12/06/2015)

b. *ngusnes aratki namaquukuk*
ngu=snes [*a=rat-ki*]GROUND
1SG.SBJ.NPST=put.in.CONT NM=basket-SG.F
[***ne****=ama=quukuk*]THEME
from/with=ART=sweet.potato
'I fill the basket with sweet potatoes' (ARS-12/06/2015)

In present-day Qaqet, the use of *ne* 'from/with' with theme arguments is no longer restricted to alternating verbs. It is also attested with many bivalent placement verbs such as *sirlek* 'throw/drop': they do not alternate, but they nevertheless obligatorily use this preposition to introduce their theme argument (as in 76a). It is also often possible for these verbs to occur in the agentless construction (see section 5.2.2): in this case, the agent is omitted, and the theme remains in its post-verbal position – still marked by the preposition *ne* 'from/with' (as in 76b). Furthermore, some trivalent verbs such as *quarl* ~ *kuarl* 'present' use this preposition to introduce a theme (as in 76c).

(76) a. *nyisirlek namaquvangirang*
nyi=sirlek ***ne****=ama=quvang-irang*
2SG.SBJ.NPST=throw from/with=ART=cargo-PL.DIM
'throw away the things' (AMI-22/06/2015)

b. *sa sirlek naqa menari navelerles nama.. a.. a.. araalemiam*
sa *sirlek* ***ne**-ka* *menari*
already throw from/with-3SG.M from.there
ne=pelerles *ne=ama..* *a..* *a..*
from/with=in.between from/with=ART ?? ??
ara=alem-iam
3SG.F.POSS=horn-DU.M
'and he got thrown down from there from between the.. the.. the.. its two horns' (R12ATAFROG-222)

c. *beip ma, diqitaqatkuarl aruimga namamengga*
be=ip *maget,* *de=ki=taqa=tkuarl*
CONJ=PURP then CONJ=3SG.F.SBJ.NPST=properly.CONT=C.present
are-uim-ka ***ne**=ama=meng-ka*
3SG.F.POSS-child-SG.M from/with=ART=wood-SG.M
'and then, she carefully shows her son a tree (lit. presents her son with a tree)' (N11AJNGENAINGMETSIQI-0017)

Its use with theme arguments has probably allowed this preposition to play an important role in expressing causation.[30] It is used to directly add a causee role to a number of intransitive verbs such as *maarl(vit) ~ raarl(vit) ~ taarl(vit)* 'stand' (illustrated in 77a). In their causative reading, these verbs then co-occur with the preposition *ne* 'from/with' (as in 77b and 77c): an external causer is added in subject function, and the causee is expressed as the prepositional object. This structure is compatible both with a direct causation interpretation (as in 77b) and an indirect causation interpretation (as in 77c).

(77) a. *beip tataarlvit*
be=ip *ta=taarlvit*
CONJ=PURP 3PL.SBJ=stand.CONT:UP
'and then they stand up' (N12AMVGENAINGMETBROTHERS-018)

b. *dinyitaarl nanget*
de=nyi=taarl ***ne**-nget*
CONJ=2SG.SBJ.NPST=stand.CONT from/with-3N
'you stand them (stones) up' (C12YMMZJIPLAY1-272)

30 The use of *ne* 'from/with' with causee roles is more widespread in Qaqet than in Mali: there is only one attested example of the cognate Mali preposition introducing a causee role (Stebbins 2011: 103–104, 109).

c. *nyiraarlvit nangua*
nyi=raarlvit ***ne**-ngua*
2SG.SBJ.NPST=stand.NCONT.FUT:UP from/with-1SG
'you help me stand up' (LONGYJL20150805_2-818)

This preposition furthermore is part of the indirect causation construction exemplified in (78): it consists of a subject (the causer), the verb *rekmet ~ tekmet* 'do', a prepositional phrase consisting of *ne* 'from/with' plus a noun phrase (the causee), and a separate clause introduced by a conjunction (the caused event). This construction is very productive and it can create an indirect causation reading for any kind of verb.

(78) *kirekmet **ne**majohn, beqamit kaat naivuk*
ki=rekmet ***ne**=ma=john,*
3SG.F.SBJ.NPST=do.NCONT:IN from/with=ART.ID=NAME
be=ka=mit *ka=at*
CONJ=3SG.M.SBJ=go.NCONT.PST 3SG.M.SBJ=fall.NCONT
ne=i-vuk
from/with=AWAY-up
'she made John fall down (lit. she acts on John, and he falls down)' (R12ABDFROG-098)

Finally, the preposition *ne* 'from/with' marks the subject in the non-verbal equative construction (see chapter 8.2.3).

(ii) Preposition *se* 'to/with'

As in the case of *ne* 'from/with', the glossing of *se* 'to/with' reflects its two basic uses: introducing goals ('to') and comitatives ('with'). Most commonly, this preposition introduces the spatial goals of verbs of motion (as in 79a) and caused motion (as in 79b). If a verb lexicalizes a goal semantics, this preposition is not used (as in 79c). Furthermore, if the movement is towards or in the direction of a goal, speakers do not use this preposition either: the use of *se* 'to/with' entails the attainment of the goal, i.e., the participant has reached the goal or intends to reach the goal.

(79) a. *akiqerl kiaguirla, sevraraluqup*
ka=kiqerl *kia=guirl=a,*
3SG.M.SBJ=now 3SG.F.SBJ=return=DIST
***se**=pet=ara=luqup*
to/with=on/under=3SG.F.POSS=place
'her having returned now, to her place' (I12AANACLADNSOCIO3-520)

b. *ianiurlet nianamalauski sep maqerlap*
ian=iurlet *ne=iana=malaus-ki*
3DU.SBJ=pull.NCONT from/with=3DU.POSS=canoe-SG.F
se=*pe* *ma=qerlap*
to/with=PLACE ART.ID=water
'they pulled their canoe into water' (N12BAMCAT-131)

c. *daqasnesnget, mraarlaunini*
de=ka=snes-nget, ***met***=*aa=rlaun-ini*
CONJ=3SG.M.SBJ=put.in.CONT-3N in=3SG.M.POSS=netbag-SG.DIM
'and he kept putting them in his little netbag' (N11AAGSIRINILOBSTER1-0089)

This preposition also occurs with non-motion verbs, highlighting both their orientation towards a non-spatial goal or purpose and the attainment of that goal or purpose. For example, it occurs with *lu* ~ *tlu* 'see', shifting the overall meaning towards 'find' (as in 80a). There is thus overlap with the preposition *te* 'PURP': speakers can choose either one to express a purpose reading (as in 80b and 80c). But the use of *se* 'to/with' entails attainment or an expectation of attainment, while the use of *te* 'PURP' is neutral in this respect.

(80) a. *nyalu savet lungera amaguleng nana?*
nya=lu ***se***=*pet* *lu-nget-a*
2SG.SBJ=see.NCONT to/with=on/under DEM-N-DIST
ama=guleng *nana?*
ART=malay.apple what
'how did you find those malay apples?' (N11AAGSIRINIROPE-0092)

b. *denyikut savraqi*
de=nyi=kut ***se***=*pet-ki*
CONJ=2SG.SBJ.NPST=break.ground.CONT to/with=on/under-3SG.F
'you dig for it (and find it)' (LONGYDS20150601_1-009)

c. *deqerl uanukut tuanaflaua*
de=kerl *uane=kut* ***te***=*uana=flaua*
CONJ=DEONT 2DU.SBJ.NPST=break.ground.CONT PURP=2DU.POSS=flower
'you dig for your flowers' (LONGYDS20150531_1-007)

The second basic use of *se* 'to/with' is with comitative participants. In such cases, the companion is not equally involved in the event. For example, the companion in (81a) is a dead person. Or (81b) describes an event where only the subject is doing the running, while the companion is sitting on its back. This preposition cannot be used in a situation where both participants are equally involved, e.g., where both participants are equally running. In such cases, speakers would have to resort to the associative construction instead (see chapter 3.6).

(81) a. *dap lura ramit saraa.. araamam iama.. anyipka*
dap *lu-ta-a* *ta=mit* ***se**=araa..*
but DEM-PL.H-DIST 3PL.SBJ=go.NCONT.PST to/with=3PL.POSS
araa=mam *i=ama..* *a=nyip-ka*
3PL.POSS=father SIM=ART NM=die.NCONT-SG.M
'and those ones went with their.. their father who is a.. a dead one' (N11AAGSIRINILOBSTER1-0078FF)

b. *kiqiuaik saqa*
ki=qiuaik ***se**-ka*
3SG.F.SBJ.NPST=run.CONT to/with-3SG.M
'it is running with him' (R12ABDFROG-089)

The goal and comitative meanings account for the majority of examples. In addition, this preposition is sometimes used to introduce recipients (as in 82a), addressees (as in 82b) and instruments (as in 82c). Such cases are not very frequent, though, and they likely constitute extensions from the basic semantics, either from the goal semantics (possible in 82a and 82b) or the comitative semantics (possible in 82b and 82c).

(82) a. *guak keknaq inguaguirltiqini sagelka, deqeknak*
gua-ka *ke=knak* *i=ngua=guirltik-ini*
1SG.POSS-SG.M 3SG.M.SBJ.NPST=cry.CONT SIM=1SG.SBJ=turn:SIDE-SG.DIM
***se**=gel-ka,* *de=ke=knak*
to/with=near-3SG.M CONJ=3SG.M.SBJ.NPST=cry.CONT
'my friend is crying, because I paid back something small to him, and so he is crying' (N11AAGBROTHERS-0105)

b. *ketaqen sagel aaqalatpiqa*
ke=taqen ***se**=gel*
3SG.M.SBJ.NPST=say.CONT to/with=near
aa=qalat-pik=a
3SG.M.POSS=younger.sibling-COLL.H=DIST
'he talks to/with his younger brothers now' (N12AMVGENAINGMET-BROTHERS-039)

c. *ingutaqamraqen praqip nana samatokpisin?*
i=ngu=taqa=mraqen *pet-ki=ip*
SIM=1SG.SBJ.NPST=properly.CONT=C.say on/under-3SG.F=PURP
nana ***se**=ama=tokpisin?*
what to/with=ART=NAME
'why do I talk to her properly in/with Tok Pisin?' (I12AANACLADNSOCIO2-190)

This preposition is also attested with the theme arguments of some verbs. Such arguments are usually introduced by *ne* 'from/with' (as in 83a), but some verbs alternatively allow for *se* 'to/with' (as in 83b). In the case of alternating verbs, we observe subtle differences in interpretation, suggesting that the use of *se* 'to/with' originated from its comitative semantics (as indicated by the literal translation in 83b). There are also non-alternating verbs (as in 83c), where the choice of *se* 'to/with' (instead of *ne* 'from/with') seems unmotivated – at least from a synchronic perspective.

(83) a. *diqirlan nemajohn*
de=ki=rlan ***ne***=*ma=john*
CONJ=3SG.F.SBJ.NPST=throw from/with=ART.ID=NAME
'it throws down John' (R12ACMFROG-086)

b. *karlan saaningaqi samrama.. samramabaketki*
ka=rlan ***se***=*aa=ninga-ki* *se=met=ama..*
3SG.M.SBJ=throw to/with=3SG.M.POSS=head-SG.F to/with=in=ART
se=met=ama=baket-ki
to/with=in=ART=bucket-SG.F
'(who) stuck its head into the.. the bucket (lit. it threw/moved with its head)' (R12ATAFROG-084)

c. *ide qasuam sama.. ahrlik*
ide *ka=suam* ***se***=*ama..a=sirlik*
IPFV 3SG.M.SBJ=steal to/with=ART NM=meat
'he steals the.. meat' (D12ADKSPIRITS-063FF)

Finally, it is used with speech act, cognition and emotion verbs to introduce sentential complements: activity nouns converted from verbs (as in 84a), but also basic nouns (as in 84b). As indicated in the free translations, such nouns receive a manner interpretation. It is possible that this use originated in comitative uses such as the one illustrated in (84c), where *se* 'to/with' introduces a comitative adjunct, with an overall activity interpretation.

(84) a. *kuasik kadrlem sasmisavet nalengiqa*
kuasik *ka=drlem*
NEG 3SG.M.SBJ=know
se=*a=smisavet*
to/with=NM=C.read.NCONT.PST:TO/WITH:ON/UNDER
ne=a=lengi-ka
from/with=NM=word-SG.M
'he doesn't know how to read in the language' (I12AANACLADNSOCIO3-260)

b. *ilira ngulsil savramamelangga*
i=lira *ngu=lsil* ***se****=pet=ama=melang-ka*
SIM=now 1SG.SBJ.NPST=say.CONT to/with=on/under=ART=vine-SG.M
'I just now talked about (how to weave) the *melang* vine' (P12ADNROPE2-002)

c. *iaik kiaruqun* ***s****iaqamarlaunnga*
ia-ki *kia=ruqun*
other-SG.F 3SG.F.SBJ=sit.NCONT.FUT
se*=ia-ka=ama=rlaun-ka*
to/with=other-SG.M=ART=netbag-SG.M
'one (woman) will sit with one netbag (i.e., one woman will work on one netbag)' (P12ARSBILUM2-011)

5.3.4 Spatial prepositions

The nine spatial prepositions share similar distributions, and they are therefore discussed together in this section. First, the spatial semantics of each preposition in turn is outlined: (i) *daleng* 'above', (ii) *de* 'LOC.PART', (iii) *gel* 'near', (iv) *kut* 'along', (v) *men* 'at', (vi) *met* 'in', (vii) *pe* 'PLACE', (viii) *pet* 'on/under' and (ix) *set* 'behind'. Following that, their non-spatial uses are summarized under point (x).

The prepositions *pet* 'on/under' and *pe* 'PLACE' furthermore play a role in the non-verbal locative construction, where they locate abstract concepts, serving equative and attributive functions. Other spatial prepositions are attested in this context, too, but they are much less common (see chapter 8.2 for non-verbal constructions).

(i) Preposition *daleng* 'above'

The preposition *daleng* 'above' is not very common. It describes the spatial relationship of superposition without contact, where an entity is located above another entity (as in 85a and 85b). If there is contact, speakers resort to the preposition *pet* 'on/under' instead (see point viii). In most cases, this preposition distributes like the other prepositions and directly precedes the noun phrase (as in 85a). In the case of personal pronouns, however, this pronoun is overtly marked by *ma* 'OBJ' (as in 85b) – the expected form would have been **dalengga* (from *daleng-ka* 'above-3SG.M') (see section 5.2.1 for a discussion of *ma* 'OBJ').

(85) a. *amamudemgi daleng amalaiqi*
ama=mudem-ki ***daleng*** *ama=lai-ki*
ART=resin-SG.F above ART=platform-SG.F
'the light is above the table' (ATA-07/05/2012)

b. *amaququanngi, de luqiaraavuk daleng maqa*
ama=ququan-ki, de lu-ki-iara=a-vuk ***daleng*** ***ma**-ka*
ART=owl-SG.F CONJ DEM-SG.F-PROX=DIR-up above OBJ-SG.M
'the owl, this one up there above him' (R12ABDFROG-062)

(ii) Preposition *de* 'LOC.PART'

The preposition *de* 'LOC.PART' is used for locations at parts of a whole. As such, it almost always introduces a noun phrase containing a relational noun, e.g., *is* 'end' in (86a) and (86b), both with overt nominal possessors (such as *kaasika* 'vine' in 86a) and without (as in 86b) (see chapter 6.1 on relational nouns). Such a relational noun is not obligatorily present, but even in its absence, speakers still interpret the entity to be located at a part (as indicated by the free translation in 86c). Given its meaning, this preposition is very frequently used for locations at bodyparts (as in 86d).

(86) a. *daqaiarli damakaasika ais*
de=ka=iarli ***de**=ama=kaasik-ka a-is*
CONJ=3SG.M.SBJ=swing.NCONT LOC.PART=ART=vine-SG.M 3SG.M.POSS-end
'and he swung (across) on the end of the vine' (N11AAGSIRINIROPE-0018)

b. *daqadik dais*
de=ka=dik ***de**=a-is*
CONJ=3SG.M.SBJ=cut LOC.PART=3SG.M.POSS-end
'and he cut (it) off at its end' (N11AAGSIRINIROPE-0108)

c. *kaat dama asisit*
ka=at ***de**=ama a=sis-it*
3SG.M.SBJ=fall.NCONT LOC.PART=ART NM=ridge-SG.LONG
'he fell over (the edge of) the ridge' (R12ACMFROG-089)

d. *iqaberltik damaqan*
i=ka=berltik ***de**=ama=qan*
SIM=3SG.M.SBJ=loosen:SIDE LOC.PART=ART=neck
'and he loosened the neck (of the dog) (from the container)' (R12ATAFROG-092)

The preposition *de* is very likely related to the conjunction *de* (see chapter 8.3.1). In fact, there are synchronic cases where it is impossible to decide whether *de* functions as a preposition or as a conjunction. In some cases, *de* can only be interpreted as a conjunction. For example, when it introduces verbal clauses, but also non-verbal existential clauses (as in 87a) or left-dislocated noun phrases (as in 87b). In such cases, the context does not allow for a prepositional interpretation. In (87c), by contrast, the analysis is less clear. As indicated by the alternative glossing and free translation, *de* could be analyzed either as a conjunction or as a preposition (introducing an argument of the verb *nging* 'circle').

(87) a. *saqika amabrutka, de amabrutka, damabrutki*
saqi-ka *ama=brut-ka,* ***de*** *ama=brut-ka,*
again-3SG.M ART=NAME-SG.M CONJ ART=NAME-SG.M
de*=ama=brut-ki*
CONJ=ART=NAME-SG.F
'the same with the Brutka spirit, there is the (male) Brutka, and there is the (female) Brutki' (D12ADKSPIRITS-094)

b. *de luqemara, de.. kemnyim mirleqip nguluqi quaridi?*
de *lu-ka=mara,* *de..* *ke=mnyim*
CONJ DEM-SG.M=here CONJ 3SG.M.SBJ.NPST=look.CONT
mirlek=ip *ngulu=ki* *kuaridi?*
around=PURP look=3SG.F where
'as for this one here, so.. he is looking around to see where is it?' (R12ATAFROG-073FF)

c. *ngerenging, damadangga*
ngere=nging, ***de****=ama=dang-ka*
3N.SBJ.NPST=circle.CONT ??=ART=dog-SG.M
'they are encircling (something), **and** (CONJ) it is the dog ~ they are circling **around** (PREP) the dog' (R12ADNFROG-180)

It is likely that contexts such as (87c) above constituted the bridging contexts that enabled a re-analysis. But despite the existence of such structurally ambiguous cases, the formal properties of the conjunction and the preposition differ synchronically. The conjunction introduces clauses and left-dislocated constituents (that may or may not be single noun phrases), while the preposition introduces noun phrases. The conjunction has an invariant form *de*, while the preposition has an allomorph *dem* preceding pronouns (as in 88a). Furthermore, the conjunction cannot be preceded by a preposition – but the preposition can (as in 88a, 88b and 88c). The conjunction and the preposition can even co-occur (as in 88c). And finally, the conjunction is frequently (but not necessarily) preceded by a prosodic boundary, while the preposition is usually (but not necessarily) included in the same intonation unit as the previous material.

(88) a. *de tika ip saivuk sa****dem****ga*
de *tika* *ip* *se=i-vuk* *se=****de****-ka*
CONJ EMPH PURP to/with=AWAY-up to/with=LOC.PART-3SG.M
'and it (goes) up to (the top of) it' (P12ARSBILUM3L-042)

b. *bema.. amah.. amahlangap nadaarlan*
be=ma.. *ama..* *ama=slanga-ap*
CONJ=ART.ID ART ART=bee-PL.RCD
*ne=**de**=aa=rlan,*
from/with=LOC.PART=3SG.M.POSS=inside
'and the.. the.. the bees from its inside' (R12ATAFROG-136)

c. *de sadamarlut*
de *se=**de**=ama=rlut*
CONJ to/with=LOC.PART=ART=cliff
'and on to (the edge of) the cliff' (R12ADNFROG-258)

(iii) Preposition *gel* 'near'

The preposition *gel* 'near' indicates proximity to a location. It is predominantly used with humans or personified animals that are conceptualized as locations. This includes physical coincidence or proximity (as in 89a), but also metaphorical (as in 89b) and temporal locations (as in 89c). Nevertheless, it is also attested with non-human locations (as in 89d).

(89) a. *iang mara gel mapanavu*
ia-nget *mara* ***gel*** *ma=panavu*
other-N here near ART.ID=NAME
'there's another one here near Panavu' (C12VARPLAY-168)

b. *sagel matalai, nyi*
*se=**gel*** *ma=talai,* *nyi*
to/with=near ART.ID=NAME 2SG
'on to Talai (i.e., it's Talai's turn), you' (C12VARPLAY-206)

c. *murl glamhrlura*
murl ***gel**=ama=srlu-ta*
distantly near=ART=old-PL.H
'at the time of the ancestors' (N12BAMCAT-009)

b. *katra besaivuk, sagel amangariqisa, deqa..*
ka=tit=a *be=se=i-vuk,*
3SG.M.SBJ=go.CONT=DIST CONJ=to/with=AWAY-up
*se=**gel*** *ama=ngarik-es=a,* *de=ka..*
to/with=near ART=hand-SG.FLAT=DIST CONJ=3SG.M.SBJ
'he goes up there now, to near the branch, and he..' (N11AJNGENAINGMETBROTHERS-0087FF)

The preposition has a related adverb *gelna* 'nearby', which also conveys proximity to human (as in 90a) and non-human grounds (as in 90b).

(90) a. *katit, besagelna nema.. asinepki*
ka=tit, *be=se=**gelna*** *ne=ma..*
3SG.M.SBJ=go.CONT CONJ=to/with=nearby from/with=ART.ID
a=sinepki
NM=NAME:SG.F
'he goes, to nearby.. Sinepki' (N12ABKSIRINI-068FF)

b. *saruarl iantden, gelna namaluqup*
se=tuarl *ian=tden,* ***gelna***
to/with=other.side 3DU.SBJ=come.CONT nearby
ne=ama=luqup
from/with=ART=place
'to the other side they come, nearby the place' (N12BAMCAT-162)

(iv) Preposition *kut* 'along'
The preposition *kut* 'along' is not very common. As a spatial preposition, it expresses location along a ground (as in 91). This preposition has given rise to the particle *kut* 'inferring' (see chapter 7.2).

(91) *nguatit kuramaiska*
ngua=tit ***kut**=ama=is-ka*
1SG.SBJ=go.CONT along=ART=path-SG.M
'I go along the path' (CCM-16/05/2015)

(v) Preposition *men* 'at'
The preposition *men* 'at' has a general topological meaning, conveying relationships of spatial coincidence: the entity is located in contact with the ground. This often includes attachment relations (as in 92a) as well as negative spaces such as holes (as in 92b) and locations within aggregates (as in 92c).

(92) a. *dqaquap sama.. akaasika.. aaningaqi ruarl menluqa amamengga*
de=ka=quap *se=ama..* *a=kaasik-ka..*
CONJ=3SG.M.SBJ=tie.NCONT to/with=ART NM=vine-SG.M
aa=ninga-ki *tuarl* ***men**=lu-ka-a* *ama=meng-ka*
3SG.M.POSS=head-SG.F other.side at=DEM-SG.M-DIST ART=wood-SG.M
'and he tied the.. vine's.. end at the other side **at** that tree'
(N11AAGSIRINIROPE-0023FF)

b. *iama ademga menaqa*
i=ama *adem-ka* ***men**-ka*
SIM=ART hole-SG.M at-3SG.M
'and a hole is **in** it (the tree)' (R12ATAFROG-141)

c. *iantaqamnyim sagelngera, de ianlianaik menanget*
ian=taqa=mnyim *se=gel-nget=a,*
3DU.SBJ=properly.CONT=look.CONT to/with=near-3N=DIST
de *ian=lu=iane-ia-ki* ***men**-nget*
CONJ 3DU.SBJ=see.NCONT=3DU.POSS-other-SG.F at-3N
'they were looking carefully at them now, and they saw their friend **among** them' (R12ABDFROG-123)

More generally, any kind of spatial coincidence can be expressed through *men* 'at'. Given this general meaning, there is overlap with the more specific topological prepositions, especially with *pet* 'on/under' and *met* 'in'. For example, a location 'on' a branch can alternatively be construed as coincidence (as in 93a) or as superposition (as in 93b).

(93) a. *deqamrenas samenamarlekenina*
de=ka=mrenas
CONJ=3SG.M.SBJ=jump.NCONT.PST:SELF
*se=**men**=ama=rleken-ini=a*
to/with=at=ART=branch-SG.DIM=DIST
'and he jumped **on**to the branch there' (N11AAGSIRINIROPE-0136)
b. *deqamrenas savet lauma amarlekenem de..*
de=ka=mrenas *se=**pet***
CONJ=3SG.M.SBJ=jump.NCONT.PST:SELF to/with=on/under
lu-em-a *ama=rleken-em* *de..*
DEM-SG.RCD-DIST ART=branch-SG.RCD CONJ
'and he jumped **on**to that branch and..' (N11AAGSIRINIROPE-0073)

Similarly, a location in water can be conceptualized as a coincidence relation (as in 94a) or as a containment relation (as in 94b).

(94) a. *sagelama.. asinepki, menamakainaqi, iqurliqi menama.. amakainaqi*
se=gel=ama.. *a=sinepki,* ***men**=ama=kaina-ki,*
to/with=near=ART NM=NAME:SG.F at=ART=water-SG.F
i=kurli-ki ***men**=ama..* *ama=kaina-ki*
SIM=leave-3SG.F at=ART ART=water-SG.F
'on to.. Sinepki, **in** the water, where she stays **in** the.. the water' (N12ABKSIRINI-061)

b. *dunguit semramakainaqip nguuknas*
de=ngu=it *se=**met**=ama=kaina-ki=ip*
CONJ=1SG.SBJ.NPST=go.NCONT.FUT to/with=in=ART=water-SG.F=PURP
ngu=uuknas
1SG.SBJ.NPST=wash.NCONT:SELF
'I go **in** the water and wash myself' (N12BAMCAT-283)

(vi) Preposition *met* 'in'

The preposition *met* 'in' is used for all kinds of containment relations, e.g. location within a container (as in 95a) or within a tree (as in 95b).

(95) a. *ianlu iquasiqaqi mramarliinem*
ian=lu *i=kuasik-ki* ***met**=ama=rliin-em*
3DU.SBJ=see.NCONT SIM=NEG-3SG.F in=ART=bamboo-SG.RCD
'they saw that it is not **inside** the bamboo (container)' (R12ADNFROG-041)

b. *ide qurliqa meramameng*
ide *kurli-ka* ***met**=ama=meng*
IPFV leave-3SG.M in=ART=wood
'he usually stays **inside** the trees' (D12ADKSPIRITS-067)

(vii) Preposition *pe* 'PLACE'

The preposition *pe* 'PLACE' is used in reference to places, and overlaps to some extent with the distribution of *pet* 'on/under' (see viii). The difference is that *pe* 'PLACE' introduces places that are presented as uniquely identifiable, e.g., because the place is a possessed entity, as in the first occurrence of *pe* 'PLACE' in (96a). In such cases, there is always a close association between the possessor and the possessed, which allows for, e.g., the meaning shift from 'house' to 'home' in (96a). By contrast, *pet* 'on/under' does not entail any close association, even though it can also introduce possessed places (as in 96b). More commonly, *pe* 'PLACE' introduces places that are marked with the article *ma* 'ART.ID' (as in the second occurrence of *pe* 'PLACE' in 96a), i.e., with the article used for inherently identifiable entities (see chapter 3.3.4). *Pet* 'on/under', by contrast, introduces places marked by the general article *ama* 'ART' (as in 96c).

(96) a. *ip kilu remga, paavetkia, vemaqerleng*
ip *ki=lu* *te-ka,*
PURP 3SG.F.SBJ.NPST=see.NCONT PURP-3SG.M
***pe**=aa=avet-ki=a,* ***pe**=ma=qerleng*
PLACE=3SG.M.POSS=house-SG.F=DIST PLACE=ART.ID=fallow.garden
'she looked for him, in his home there, in the old garden' (I12AANACLADNSOCIO3-524FF)

b. *iamanat pet giasleng*
i=ama=nat ***pet*** *gia=sleng*
SIM=ART=taro on/under 2SG.POSS=garden
'(about) the taro in your garden' (N12BAMCAT-081)

c. *laavuk pramasleng*
lu=a-vuk ***pet****=ama=sleng*
DEM=DIR-up on/under=ART=garden
'up there in the garden' (C12VARPLAY-397)

The preposition *pe* 'PLACE' is also used to introduce the directionals *panu* 'up' (as in 97a) and *pit* 'up' (as in 97b) (see chapter 6.3 on directionals). It is possible that its restriction to the 'up' directionals suggests that *pe* 'PLACE' includes a meaning component of superposition. Another such indication could be its overlap with *pet* 'on/under': this preposition conveys topological superposition, and it has been extended to introducing places. But synchronically, *pe* 'PLACE' is not used for topological 'on/under' relations.

(97) a. *kurliqa vevanu, dqatramaguleng*
kurli-ka ***pe****=panu,* *de=ka=tat=ama=guleng*
leave-3SG.M PLACE=up CONJ=3SG.M.SBJ=take.CONT=ART=malay.apple
'he stayed **up** there, picking the malay apples' (N11AAGSIRINIROPE-0033)

b. *deip magra, desagel luqia vaapirip saqika divunekuherl una.. unagalip nauirl*
de=ip *maget=a,* *de=se=gel* *lu-ki-a*
CONJ=PURP then=DIST CONJ=to/with=near DEM-SG.F-DIST
pe*=pit=ip* *saqi-ka* *dip=une=kutserl*
PLACE=up=PURP again-3SG.M FUT=1DU.SBJ.NPST=plant.CONT:??
una.. *una=galip* *nauirl*
1DU.POSS 1DU.POSS=peanut first
'and then, on to that one **up** there, where we will again plant our.. our peanuts first' (D12ABDACPGARDEN-058)

(viii) Preposition *pet* 'on/under'

The preposition *pet* 'on/under' has a basic spatial meaning, conveying topological 'on' and 'under' relations, i.e., a superposition relation between the located entity and the location, but it remains indeterminate as to which of the two is superposed. The default interpretation is 'on' (as in 98a), which arises in the absence of any indication to the contrary. Otherwise, both 'on' and 'under' interpretations are possible. For example, the relational noun *rleng* 'back' (in 98b) is compatible with an 'on' reading, while the relational noun *ut* 'underside' (in 98c) shifts the interpretation to an 'under' reading.

(98) a. *ip nani urit.. uri.. urit pet giangariqis*
ip *nani* *ure=it..* *ure=it..*
PURP can 1PL.SBJ.NPST=go.NCONT.FUT 1PL.SBJ.NPST=go.NCONT.FUT
pet *gia=ngarik-es*
on/under 2SG.POSS=hand-SG.FLAT
'we can go.. go.. go **on** your branch' (N11AJNGENAINGMETBROTHERS-0139)

b. *iqamugun, pramamengem angerarleng*
i=ka=mugun, ***pet****=ama=meng-em* *ngera=****rleng***
SIM=3SG.M.SBJ=sit on/under=ART=wood-SG.RCD 3N.POSS=back
'and he sits **on** the back of a log' (R12ADNFROG-222)

c. *amabalka, de qurliqa pramasiaqi rut*
ama=bal-ka, *de* *kurli-ka* ***pet****=ama=sia-ki*
ART=ball-SG.M CONJ leave-3SG.M on/under=ART=chair-SG.F
*are-****ut***
3SG.F.POSS-underside
'the ball, it is **under** the chair' (ACL-27/07/2012)

In the case of 'on' relations, *pet* 'on/under' is only ever attested when there is contact. Otherwise speakers resort to the preposition *daleng* 'above' (see point i above). In the case of 'under' relations, no such restriction was observed. For example, in (98c) above, there is no contact between the ball and the chair. Alternatively, speakers can use the adverb *temani* 'underneath' in such cases (see chapter 6.2 on adverbs).

This preposition is also used to convey a location in a place, e.g., in a garden (as in 99a) or in a town (as in 99b). In such cases, *pet* 'on/under' contrasts with *pe* 'PLACE' (see point vii).

(99) a. *deip madresnes, traaqalatka vramahleng*
de=ip *maget=de=te=snes,*
CONJ=PURP then=CONJ=3PL.SBJ.NPST=shout.CONT
te=araa=qalat-ka ***pet****=ama=sleng*
PURP=3PL.POSS=younger.sibling-SG.M on/under=ART=garden
'then they call for their younger brother in the garden' (N12AMVGENAINGMETBROTHERS-070)

b. *div undit savramaqerleng amabarlnget*
dip *un=tit* *se=**pet**=ama=qerleng*
FUT 1DU.SBJ=go.CONT to/with=on/under=ART=fallow.garden
ama=barl-nget
ART=big-N
'let us go to the big place (town)' (N12BAMCAT-030)

The preposition *pet* 'on/under' is furthermore used to express locations in time (as in 100).

(100) *ivani div unekutserl unagalip, pet luqaira amalotuqa*
ip=ani *dip* *une=kutserl* *una=galip,*
PURP=maybe FUT 1DU.SBJ.NPST=plant.CONT:?? 1DU.POSS=peanut
pet *lu-ka-iara* *ama=lotu-ka*
on/under DEM-SG.M-PROX ART=pray-SG.M
'so we might plant our peanuts **during** this week' (D12ABDACPGARDEN-068)

(ix) Preposition *set* 'behind'

The preposition *set* 'behind' is not very common: it usually occurs within the complex preposition *nasat* 'following (spatially or temporally)' (see example 57 above). As a simple preposition, it has the spatial meaning of 'behind' (as in 101).

(101) *katrama.. amagalepkia, beqiatit samasurlka, seramarima*
ka=tat=ama.. *ama=galep-ki=a,*
3SG.M.SBJ=take.CONT=ART ART=work.party-SG.F=DIST
be=kia=tit *se=ama=surl-ka,* ***set**=ama=rim=a*
CONJ=3SG.F.SBJ=go.CONT to/with=ART=fence-SG.M behind=ART=taro=DIST
'he assembled the.. the work party now, and it continued with the fence, **behind** the taro (garden)' (D12ABDACPGARDEN-021)

(x) Introducing non-spatial roles

Four of the spatial prepositions (*daleng* 'above', *gel* 'near', *kut* 'along' and *set* 'behind') are only attested in spatial contexts, but the remaining five (*de* 'LOC.PART', *men* 'at', *met* 'in', *pe* 'PLACE' and *pet* 'on/over') also occur outside of spatial contexts and introduce core participants, especially ground and patient/theme participants. Whereby different verbs select for different prepositions to introduce these participants. As illustrated below, I assume that each combination of verb and preposition was, at least originally, semantically motivated – even though synchronically it is not always possible to recover the motivation for a given combination.

I assume that the lexicalization process started with the prepositions introducing ground participants, thus reflecting their origin as introducing spatial locations. Over the course of lexicalization, the ground participants became re-interpreted in different semantic roles, especially as patient or theme participants. Such a development can be illustrated by means of the verb *ves* ~ *pes* 'close/thatch'. Synchronically, its meaning is specialized: when it selects *pet* 'on/under', it is interpreted as 'thatch (a hut)' (as in 102a); and when it selects *met* 'in', it is interpreted as 'close (a door)' (as in 102b). This distribution can be explained if we assume that it originally conveyed the more general meaning of 'put cover (on something)'. Such a verb exists in present-day Qaqet: the unrelated intransitive verb *ram* 'put cover (on something)'. This verb can occur with a prepositional phrase in adjunct function, whereby the choice of preposition depends on the spatial relationship. For example, *pet* 'on/under' introduces 'on' relations, such as putting cover 'on' a head (as in 102c). And *met* 'in' introduces 'in' relations, such as putting cover 'in' a saucepan (which is conceptualized as an 'in' relation, as it covers up a hole) (as in 102d). It is likely that *ves* 'close/thatch' originally allowed for a similar distribution – with *pet* 'on/under' for 'on' relations (such as putting cover on a hut), and *met* 'in' for 'in' relations (such as putting cover into a door frame). Eventually, these combinations became lexicalized with their specialized meanings. The participant introduced by *pet* 'on/under' (in 102a) can still be characterized as a ground or location participant. The participant introduced by *met* 'in' (in 102b) is arguably a theme participant: *tarlka* 'door' does not refer to the door frame, but to the door.

(102) a. *nyit nyives pruramidrigel*
nyi=it *nyi=ves*
2SG.SBJ.NPST=go.NCONT.FUT 2SG.SBJ.NPST=close/thatch.NCONT
***pet**=ura=midet-igel*
on/under=1PL.POSS=shelter-SG.EXC
'go and thatch our garden hut' (AMB-29/06/2015)

b. *nyang nyives meramatarlka*
nya=ang *nyi=ves*
2SG.SBJ=walk.NCONT 2SG.SBJ.NPST=close/thatch.NCONT
***met**=ama=tarl-ka*
in=ART=door-SG.M
'go and close the door' (AMB-29/06/2015)

c. *ngerram prraningaqi*
ngere=ram ***pet**=ara=ninga-ki*
3N.SBJ.NPST=cover on/under=3SG.F.POSS=head-SG.F
'it put cover **on** its head' (LONGYDS20150516_1-710)

d. *nyaram meramasupin*
nya=ram ***met**=ama=supin*
2SG.SBJ=cover in=ART=saucepan
'put cover **in** the saucepan' (AMB-16/06/2015)

Given their original spatial semantics, it is not surprising that the spatial prepositions frequently introduce ground participants. These are usually physical grounds (as in 103a), but in the case of *pet* 'on/under', they can also be non-physical grounds, e.g., addressees (in 103b) or the contents of speech acts (as in 103c).

(103) a. *nyirek prama akunngi raqasing*
nyi=rek **pet**=*ama* *a=kun-ki*
2SG.SBJ.NPST=hold/put.NCONT on/under=ART NM=corn-SG.F
ara=qasing
3SG.F.POSS=hair
'touch **at** the hair of the corn' (LONGYDS20150601_1-422)

b. *tika iviak kanak priak tiarang*
tika *ip=ia-ka* *ka=nak*
EMPH PURP=other-SG.M 3SG.M.SBJ=cry.NCONT
pet=*ia-ka* *te=ia-irang*
on/under=other-SG.M PURP=other-PL.DIM
'when one cried **to** the other for something (then the other gave it)' (N11AAGBROTHERS-0012)

c. *uruis idresu vrama.. amalengiqaamit*
ure-uis *ide=te=su* **pet**=*ama..*
1PL.POSS-child IPFV=3PL.SBJ.NPST=teach on/under=ART
ama=lengi-ka=a-mit
ART=word-SG.M=DIR-across
'our children, they teach (them) **about** the language over there' (I12AANACLADNSOCIO3-234)

The prepositions are also attested with patient/theme readings. Such readings probably developed (or are in the process of developing) from the ground readings (as illustrated for *ves* 'close/thatch' in (102) above). In fact, for many verbs, it is unclear whether the prepositional object should be interpreted as a ground or as a patient/theme. The verb *qirl* 'push' is such a verb. It frequently occurs in examples such as (104a): it is possible that *pe* 'PLACE' introduces a theme here – but alternatively, it could be argued that it introduces a ground, and that the directional phrase coerces a movement reading. In the database, there are a few examples of this verb occurring without a goal or directional phrase: in such cases, a ground interpretation is equally possible (as in 104b). It is very likely that contexts such as (104a) constitute bridging contexts that enable a reanalysis of ground participants as patient/theme participants. But for many verbs (like *qirl* 'push') it remains unclear if this reanalysis is completed.

(104) a. *ngeneqirl vemamengga imanu*
ngene=qirl ***pe****=ma=meng-ka* *i-manu*
2PL.SBJ.NPST=push PLACE=ART.ID=wood-SG.M AWAY-across
'push (at) the tree (so that it goes) across' (ALT-15/06/2015)

b. *kaqirl vamaqemgi namavuqulit*
ka=qirl ***pe****=ama=qem-ki* *ne=ama=vuqul-it*
3SG.M.SBJ=push PLACE=ART=snake-SG.F from/with=ART=stick-SG.LONG
'he touches/pushes (at) the snake with a stick' (ATA-25/07/2012)

The Qaqet verb lexicon contains many verbs that allow for alternations in the morphosyntactic expression of their participants. In the case of bivalent verbs, it is not uncommon for a verb to combine with different prepositions, or for a verb to alternate between combining with an unmarked direct object and with a prepositional object. Such alternations always entail meaning differences, and the most salient patterns are reported below.

Most commonly, a prepositional object conveys a partitive and/or atelic reading. The direct object is used when the participant as a whole is affected and the event reaches its culmination, e.g., the taro in (105a) is eaten up. And the prepositional object is used when only part of the participant is affected and the event does not reach its endpoint, e.g., the malay apples in (105b) are not eaten up. This difference in reading presumably follows from the original ground semantics of the prepositions: an action directed towards a ground can often be interpreted as partitive and/or atelic.[31]

(105) a. *kats amadaqa*
ka=tes *ama=da-ka*
3SG.M.SBJ=eat.CONT ART=taro-SG.M
'he eats (up) the taro' (N12BAMCAT-205)

b. *deqats pramagulenga*
de=ka=tes ***pet****=ama=guleng=a*
CONJ=3SG.M.SBJ=eat.CONT on/under=ART=malay.apple=DIST
'he ate **of** the malay apples there' (N11AAGSIRINIROPE-0034)

But while partitive and/or atelic readings are often present (as in the example above), they are not necessarily part of the more lexicalized expressions.

31 The available data suggests that the spatial prepositions often trigger partitive and atelic readings. It remains unclear, though, which of the readings are actually entailed semantically, and which follow from pragmatic implicatures: the partitive reading and/or the atelic reading of prepositional objects, and/or the telic reading of unmarked objects? More detailed research into argument structure and lexical aspect is needed to clarify this issue.

This includes cases, where no alternations take place. For example, *van* ~ *ban* 'buy' uses *pet* 'on/under' to introduce its theme participant (as in 106a). Presumably, it originally had a partitive reading (i.e., buying from/of the available goods), linked to atelic events. But synchronically, there is no other way of expressing the theme participant, and there is no reason to assume that the expression is atelic. Similar cases can be made for the patient/theme participants of many other verbs, e.g., of *serl* 'straighten' in (106b).

(106) a. *de dip nguvan pramaavetki amaslurlki*
de *dip* *ngu=van* ***pet**=ama=avet-ki*
CONJ FUT 1SG.SBJ.NPST=buy.NCONT on/under=ART=house-SG.F
ama=slurl-ki
ART=big-SG.F
'I will buy a big house' (AJL-23/05/2012)

b. *ivureseserl vruruis*
ip=ure=seserl ***pet**=ure-uis*
PURP=1PL.SBJ.NPST=straighten:REDUP on/under=1PL.POSS-child
'and we straighten (i.e., correct) our children' (I12AANACLADNSocio2-082)

And it includes cases of alternating verbs, where the preposition has been integrated as a particle into the verb. For example, the basic transitive verb *tat* 'take, pick up' occurs with a direct object (as in 107a). This verb forms the basis for many lexicalized expressions such as *tatpet* 'remove skin or bark' (as in 107b), which incorporates *pet* 'on/under' – presumably because removing bark involves acting on a surface. Another one is *tatmet* 'uproot' (as in 107c), which incorporates *met* 'in' – presumably because uprooting involves acting on the roots inside. In both cases, the action is directed not at the participant as a whole (as in the case of 107a), but at part of it. Nevertheless, as indicated by the continuation of (107c), such expressions do not necessarily entail atelicity.

(107) a. *dakatika qatranget taquarl iama.. aqurlitnget*
dap=ka=tika *ka=**tat**-nget* *taquarl*
but=3SG.M.SBJ=EMPH 3SG.M.SBJ=take.CONT-3N thus
i=ama.. *a=qurlit-nget*
SIM=ART NM=alive-N
'and he was picking them up like this, the.. the ones who were alive' (N11AAGSiriniLobster1-0007)

b. *iaik kitatpet*
ia-ki *ki=**tatpet***
other-SG.F 3SG.F.SBJ.NPST=remove.skin.CONT:ON/UNDER
'one removes the bark from it' (P12ARSBilum1-029)

c. *katatmet pemamenga, beip perlsera*
*ka=**tatmet*** *pe=ma=meng=a,*
3SG.M.SBJ=uproot.CONT:IN PLACE=ART.ID=wood=DIST
be=ip *perlset=a*
CONJ=PURP finish=DIST
'he uprooted the trees now, and was finished now' (D12ABDACPGARDEN-009)

The above alternations have in common that there is no change in valency: the verb remains bivalent, while the morphosyntactic expression of its second participant changes: as an unmarked direct object or as a prepositional object (introduced by different spatial prepositions). In other cases, the alternation involves a change in valency: a monovalent verb becoming bivalent through the addition of a preposition (as illustrated in 108 and 109 below).

The first example involves an alternation between a basic non-causative monovalent verb (in 108a) and a causative bivalent verb (in 108b). More commonly, speakers resort to the preposition *ne* 'from/with' for the causative alternant (see section 5.3.3), but some verbs like *guirltik* 'turn/answer' select the spatial prepositions *pet* 'on/under' or *pe* 'PLACE'. Other spatial prepositions are not attested in this type of alternation.

(108) a. *kuasik ka.. kaguirltik*
kuasik *ka..* *ka=guirltik*
NEG 3SG.M.SBJ 3SG.M.SBJ=turn:SIDE
'it (the language).. it hasn't changed' (I12ABLAJLATASOCIO2-122FF)

b. *deqaguirltik penah, amaqemgi naqa*
de=ka=guirltik ***pe**-nas,* *ama=qem-ki*
CONJ=3SG.M.SBJ=turn:SIDE PLACE-self ART=snake-SG.F
ne-ka
from/with-3SG.M
'and he changed himself, he became a snake' (N12AMVGENAINGMETBROTHERS-024)

The second example does not involve a causative alternation, but rather the addition of a ground participant. Here, the basic monovalent verb *at* 'fall' (in 109a) has become lexicalized as the bivalent verb *atmet* 'meet someone', incorporating *met* 'in' (in 109b). The presumed bridging context is illustrated in (109c). This kind of alternation is more common: it often involves the preposition *met* 'in', but other spatial prepositions are attested, too.

(109) a. *amabariqi qiaat*

ama=bari-ki	*kia=at*
ART=bee-SG.F	3SG.F.SBJ=fall.NCONT

'the beehive fell' (R12ADNFROG-149)

b. *unatmetna menamaiska*

*un=at**met**-na*	*men=ama=is-ka*
1DU.SBJ=meet.NCONT:IN-each.other	at=ART=path-SG.M

'we met each other on the road' (AJL-29/04/2015)

c. *kiaat merararluaqa*

kia=at	***met**=ara=rlua-ka*
3SG.F.SBJ=fall.NCONT	in=3SG.F.POSS=friend-SG.M

'she fell/bumped into her friend' (AJL-29/04/2015)

The patterns of alternation can be fairly complex. For example, many bivalent verbs of breaking, cutting and splitting alternate between direct objects and prepositional objects. Their direct object is the entity separated from the ground (as in 110a). And their prepositional object is the ground (as in 110b). Such verbs can also occur in the agentless construction (as in 110c). In present-day Qaqet, these verbs usually select for the spatial prepositions *men* 'at' (as in 110b and 110c) or *de* 'LOC.PART'. But diachronically, *met* 'in' must have been used for this purpose: most such verbs have lexicalized counterparts incorporating *met* 'in' – and these lexicalizations then combine with other prepositions, e.g., *ne* 'from/with' (in 110d) or a spatial preposition such as *pe* 'PLACE' (as in the agentless construction of 110e). The exact semantic difference between (110d) and (110e) is not clear. Based on their typical distributions (see section 5.3.3 for *ne* 'from/with'), it is possible that *ne* 'from/with' conveys causation and hence introduces a patient/theme participant, while *pe* 'PLACE' introduces a ground participant.

(110) a. *nguabung guavuqulka nep maqavel*

ngua=bung	*[gua=vuqul-ka]*$_{\text{OBJ}}$	*ne=pe*	*ma=qavel*
1SG.SBJ=break	1SG.POSS=stick-SG.M	from/with=PLACE	ART.ID=bush

'I broke off my stick from the bush' (AJL-30/04/2015)

b. *nani nyibung menaim?*

nani	*nyi=bung*	***men**-im?*
can	2SG.SBJ.NPST=break	at-3DU.F

'can you break the two apart?' (LONGYJL20150805_2-045)

c. *bung menamengga, de virlik pemga*

bung	***men**=a=meng-ka,*	*de*	*virlik*	*pe-ka*
break	at=NM=wood-SG.M	CONJ	fire.up	PLACE-3SG.M

'the tree got broken apart, and it burst in flame' (ATT-24/06/2015)

d. *kibungmet namameng*
*ki=bung**met*** ***ne**=ama=meng*
3SG.F.SBJ.NPST=break:IN from/with=ART=wood
'she broke the wood' (AJL-30/04/2015)

e. *miika raquarlip bungbungmt paqamaqaqeraqa ailany*
*miika taquarl=ip bungbung**met*** ***pe**=a=qama=qaqera-ka*
more thus=PURP break:REDUP:IN PLACE=NM=some=person-SG.M
aa=ilany
3SG.M.POSS=foot
'and like this, someone's leg got broken open (through thorns entering into it)' (LONGYJL20150805_2-064)

5.3.5 Prepositions *barek* 'BEN' and *te* 'PURP'

Qaqet has two prepositions that do not have spatial meanings: *barek* 'BEN' and *te* 'PURP'.

The preposition *te* 'PURP' was already discussed in section 5.3.2: its basic function is to introduce a non-spatial goal or purpose, and it has been extended to introduce the theme argument of many transfer verbs.

The preposition *barek* 'BEN' (and its short form *ba* 'BEN') introduces a beneficiary to the clause (as in 111a). Depending on the verb semantics, this added participant can also be interpreted as the recipient (as in 111b). However, in all cases, the beneficiary component continues to be present. For example, *guirltik* 'turn/answer' can only co-occur with *barek* 'BEN' if the recipient is at the same time a beneficiary – as, e.g., in (111b) where the recipient benefits from the money. If the recipient does not benefit, the preposition *se* 'to/with' is used instead – as, e.g., in (111c) (repeated from 82a above) where the payback makes the recipient cry.

This beneficiary semantics has given rise to an addressee reading with some speech act verbs (as in 112a and 112b). Example (112a) illustrates a possible bridging context, which allows for both beneficiary and addressee readings. In (112b), by contrast, only the addressee reading is available.

(111) a. *nyinin banas*
nyi=nin ***barek**-nas*
2SG.SBJ.NPST=cook.CONT BEN-self
'you cook for yourself' (P12ADNFIRE-034)

b. *nyuquarlangua daqama alanginyit, ip dip nguguirltik banyi*
nyi=quarl-ngua *de=a=qama* *a=langiny-it,*
2SG.SBJ.NPST=present.NCONT-1SG CONJ=NM=some NM=paper-SG.LONG
ip *dip* *ngu=guirltik* ***barek**-nyi*
PURP FUT 1SG.SBJ.NPST=turn:SIDE BEN-2SG
'give me some ten kina, and I will pay (it) back to you' (ALS-03/06/2015)

c. *guak keknaq inguaguirltiqini sagelka, deqeknak*
gua-ka *ke=knak* *i=ngua=guirltik-ini*
1SG.POSS-SG.M 3SG.M.SBJ.NPST=cry.CONT SIM=1SG.SBJ=turn:SIDE-SG.DIM
***se**=gel-ka,* *de=ke=knak*
to/with=near-3SG.M CONJ=3SG.M.SBJ.NPST=cry.CONT
'my friend is crying, because I paid back something small to him, and so he is crying' (N11AAGBROTHERS-0105)

(112) a. *de arik magrip saqi dip maqaqet telsil bareqarauis*
de *arik* *maget=ip* *saqi* *dip* *ma=qaqera*
CONJ supposing then=PURP again FUT ART.ID=person
te=lsil ***barek**=ara-uis*
3PL.SBJ.NPST=say.CONT BEN=3PL.POSS-child
'supposing that people will again tell (stories) to their children ~ for the benefit of their children' (I12AANACLADNSOCIO3-410)

b. *iansil bana ma*
ian=sil ***barek**-na* *ma*
3DU.SBJ=say.NCONT BEN-RECP thus
'they said to each other like this' (N12BAMCAT-054)

In all cases, this preposition introduces an adjunct. There are no examples where it has developed into a verb particle.

5.3.6 Other formatives

In most cases, verb particles and suffixes can be related to present-day prepositions. In addition, there are a few minor formatives that can be related to present-day relational nouns, adverbs and directionals. Finally, there are two recurring formatives that do not have a transparent origin: *mes* and *tik*.

The formative *mes* is found in bivalent verbs such as *dengmes* 'sharpen', *rlumes* 'throw at', *uames* 'beat against' (as in 113a) or *uukmes* 'wash', whose second participant can be considered a ground participant. Sometimes, there are related forms incorporating the preposition *met* 'in' without any apparent meaning difference, e.g., *rlumet* 'throw at' or *uamet* 'beat against' (as in 113b). The formative *mes* is also attested in Mali Baining, where it serves both to reduce affectedness in bivalent verbs (presumably similar to Qaqet) as well as to intransitivize verbs (different from Qaqet) (see Stebbins 2011: 100–101).

(113) a. *de nyuames demga*
de *nyi=**uames*** *de-ka*
CONJ 2SG.SBJ.NPST=beat:?? LOC.PART-3SG.M
'then you beat him (on the head)' (N11AAGSIRINIROPE-0062)

b. *druamet nraabarlka*
*de=te=**uamet*** *ne=araa=barl-ka*
CONJ=3PL.SBJ.NPST=beat.IN from/with=3PL.POSS=big-SG.M
'and they beat their elder brother' (N12AMVGENAINGMETBROTHERS-066)

The formative *tik* is found in a number of bivalent verbs such as *berltik* 'loosen', *guirltik* 'turn/answer', *qutik* cut off' or *rletik* 'turn over'. Again, its origins are not entirely transparent. It could be derived from the relational noun *tik* 'side' (illustrated in 114a), or from *tiqi* 'side' (as 114b). Both are very rare, and *tiqi* is only attested in elicitation contexts.

(114) a. *bqamrama.. avlemga nasramenggaarik*
be=ka=mat=ama.. *a=vlam-ka*
CONJ=3SG.M.SBJ=take.NCONT.PST=ART NM=pig-SG.M
*ne=set=a=meng-ka=aa=**tik***
from/with=behind=NM=wood-SG.M=3SG.M.POSS=side
'and he picked up the.. the pig from behind the edge of the fire' (N11AAGSIRINIROPE-0080A)

b. *agilka qarerles amaquilditki riqi anan*
a=gil-ka *ka=rerles* *ama=quldit-ki*
NM=small-SG.M 3SG.M.SBJ=hide.NCONT ART=frog-SG.F
tiqi *a-nan*
SIDE 3SG.M.POSS-mother
'the boy hid the frog from his mother' (ATA-25/07/2012)

5.4 Tense and aspect

The marking of tense and aspect is distributed over different elements in the predicate and in the clause. On a clausal level, there are particles that serve a number of different functions, including temporal and aspectual functions (see chapter 7). In addition, there are three locations for marking tense and aspect within the predicate: subject indexes (see section 5.4.1), aspectual verb stems (see section 5.4.2) and reduplicated stems (see section 5.4.3). Since subject indexes are absent in the agentless construction, the tense distinction coded by them is neutralized in this context. By contrast, the distinctions coded by aspectual and reduplicated verb stems are maintained in the agentless construction, too.

The semantic characterization of the formatives benefitted from elicitation sessions conducted with the tense/aspect questionnaire from Dahl (1985: 198–206), cross-checked against their distribution in the natural text corpus.

5.4.1 Subjects indexes: Neutral vs. non-past

The subject argument is obligatorily indexed, usually as a proclitic on the verb (see section 5.2.1). Both their forms and their meanings are almost identical to those in Mali Baining (Stebbins 2011: 44–46).

As illustrated in Table 65, there are two sets of indexes: a neutral set and a non-past set. Both sets are transparently related to the free pronouns, collapsing some of the pronominal categories: the 3DU category does not distinguish between masculine and feminine; and the 3N category includes not only non-human plurals of the masculine and feminine classes, but also all shape-based classes irrespective of their number reference (see chapters 3.2.3 and 4.3 for details).

Formally, the free pronouns, neutral indexes and non-past indexes are similar, but it is not possible to clearly establish the nature of their relationship. The free pronouns are sometimes identical to the neutral indexes (1SG, 3SG.M, 1DU, 1PL, 2PL, 3PL), sometimes, to the non-past indexes (2SG, 3SG.F), and sometimes, different from both of them (2DU, 3DU, 3N). Looking at the relationship between neutral and non-past indexes, two patterns emerge. First, many neutral indexes end in a vowel *a* (1SG, 2SG, 3SG.M, 3SG.F, 3PL, 3N), which is always absent in the non-past indexes, and sometimes also in the free pronouns. Second, many non-past indexes end in a final vowel *e* (3SG.M, 1DU, 2DU, 3DU, 1PL, 2PL, 3PL, 3N), which is absent in both the neutral indexes and the free pronouns. On the basis of this distribution, it could be speculated that the neutral index was originally either identical to the free pronouns or formed on the basis of the pronoun plus a formative **a* 'neutral', and that the non-past index was formed on the basis of a formative **e* 'non-past'; and phonetic erosion then led to the loss of this vowel in some forms. Synchronically, such erosion processes can be observed in the free variation of the 1PL and 3N non-past forms: in these cases, the form ending in *e* must still be considered basic and underlyingly present, as it triggers the lenition of *t* to *r* (i.e. **ut-e* > *ure* > *ur*, **nget-e* > *ngere* > *nger*).

Both 1PL indexes have an allomorph *ur*. In the case of the neutral index *ut* '1PL.SBJ', the variant *ur* appears regularly when preceding a vowel-initial verb (as in 115a), thus following the general lenition rules of the language (see chapter 2.1.1). In the case of *ure* '1PL.SBJ.NPST', the variant *ur* is a free variant, triggered especially by the speech rate. In fast speech, it occurs when preceding a liquid consonant (as in 115b). That is, even though the variants are identical, they occur in different environments, and can thus be distinguished.

Tab. 65: Subject indexes

	Free pronoun	Index: Neutral	Index: Non-past (NPST)
1SG	*ngua*	*ngua*	*ngu*
2SG	*nyi*	*nya*	*nyi*
3SG.M	*ka*	*ka*	*ke*
3SG.F	*ki*	*kia*	*ki*
1DU	*un*	*un*	*une*
2DU	*uin*	*uan*	*uane*
3DU.M	*iam*	*ian*	*iane*
3DU.F	*im*		
1PL	*ut*	*ut ~ ur*	*ure ~ ur*
2PL	*ngen*	*ngen*	*ngene*
3PL(.H)	*ta*	*ta*	*te*
3N	*nget*	*nga*	*ngere ~ nger ~ nge*
Shape-based classes			

(115) a. ***ur**aramaqalun*
***ut**=at=ama=qalun*
1PL.SBJ=fall/drop.NCONT=ART=singapore
'we planted singapore (taro)' (D12ADNGARDEN-006)

b. *miiki **ur**rekmeramit nauirl*
miiki ***ure**-rekmet=a-mit* *nauirl*
instead 1PL.SBJ.NPST=do.NCONT:IN=DIR-across first
'instead we work (the garden) across there first' (D12ADNGARDEN-004)

The neutral set of indexes contains a number of forms that end in a nasal *n* (1DU, 2DU, 3DU, 2PL). As discussed in chapter 2.1.1, voiceless plosives are inevitably realized voiced when following a nasal. This phenomenon is also observed in this context (as in 116a). In fast speech, the final *n* may even be omitted altogether, but the voicing assimilation remains (as in 116b). Interestingly, though, voicing is not inevitable in this context (as illustrated in the example in 116c).

(116) a. *ian**dit***
*ian=**tit***
3DU.SBJ=go.CONT
'they were going' (N12BAMCAT-129)

b. *dia**dit***
*de=ian=**tit***
CONJ=3DU.SBJ=go.CONT
'they were going' (N12BAMCAT-021)

c. *ian**tal** samek*
*ian=**tal*** *se=a-mek*
3DU.SBJ=carry.CONT to/with=DIR-down
'they were carrying it down' (N12BAMCAT-116)

It is very likely that the above irregularity in voicing assimilation is linked to the phenomenon of stem alternation in verbs. Qaqet verbs often have different stems that are marked through different initial consonants (see section 5.4.2), i.e., if assimilatory processes affected these consonants, meaning distinctions would become neutralized. For example, many verbs distinguish non-continuous and continuous stems through an alternation between initial lenited and voiceless plosive consonants, e.g., *qelak* ~ *kelak* 'carry on shoulder' in (117a) and (117b). Normally, an intervocalic plosive is obligatorily lenited, i.e., *kelak* should have appeared as *qelak* in (117b). But in this context, lenition is always blocked. In the case of voicing (as in example 116 above), an assimilation would not lead to a meaning neutralization, as there are no verb stems that express aspectual differences through an alternation between voiceless and voiced plosives. It is nevertheless possible that the rule to not assimilate the initial consonants of verbs is extended to all assimilatory processes, including voicing, thus accounting for the attested irregularities.

(117) a. *ka**qelaq** aadanggi maraavuk*
*ka=**qelak*** *aa=dang-ki* *mara=a-vuk*
3SG.M.SBJ=shoulder.NCONT 3SG.M.POSS=dog-SG.F here=DIR-up
'he shouldered his dog up here' (R12ATAFROG-243)

b. *ka**kelaqa**qa*
*ka=**kelak**-ka*
3SG.M.SBJ=shoulder.CONT-3SG.M
'he was shouldering him' (C12ARBZJIFROG-434)

In the vast majority of cases, verbs do not have different stems depending on the person category of the subject. The exception are a handful of verbs that have different forms when following a subject index ending in nasal *n* (1DU, 2DU, 3DU, 2PL). This phenomenon affects some (but by no means all) verbs whose continuous stem starts in *t* (as *tes* 'eat' in 118a and 118b). When following a subject index ending in a nasal, this initial *t* is replaced by *dr* (as *dres* 'eat' in 118b). It is likely that a voicing assimilation accounts for the presence of *d*, but this assimilation cannot explain the initial consonant cluster *dr*. Furthermore, the assimilation does not take place in all verbs. For example, *tit* 'go' (in 116a above) does not follow this pattern. Or while *tuqun* (*druqun*) 'sit' follows this pattern, homophonous *tuqun* 'say' does not.

(118) a. *nani ra**ts**ka*
*nani ta=**tes**-ka*
can 3PL.SBJ=eat.CONT-3SG.M
'they can be eating him' (N11AAGSIRINILOBSTER2-0082)
b. *ian**dres**ka*
*ian=**tes**-ka*
3DU.SBJ=eat.CONT-3SG.M
'they are eating him' (N11AAGSIRINIROPE-0156)

In addition, there are verbs with deficient paradigms: such verbs never occur following a subject index ending in *n*, and instead borrow their form from a non-related, but semantically similar, verb. For example, *an* 'come' (as in 119a) borrows its form from *men ~ ren ~ tden* 'come' (as in 119b) in these contexts. Again, there is no phonological reason for this difference. For example, homophonous *an* 'plant, drop' does occur in all person categories.

(119) a. *nyan*
*nya=**an***
2SG.SBJ=come.NCONT.FUT
'come!' (N11AJNGENAINGMETSIQI-0015)
b. *ngentden*
*ngen=**tden***
2PL.SBJ=come.CONT
'come!' (N11AJNGENAINGMETBROTHERS-0044)

The two sets of subject indexes convey a tense distinction. One of the sets overtly codes a non-past category, while the other set is neutral. For many verbs, the two sets contrast, and the neutral set thus picks up a past tense interpretation. For example, the verb *siit* 'tell a story' can combine either with the non-past index (as in 120a) or the neutral index (as in 120b), conveying non-past and past interpretations respectively.

(120) a. *de nani ngusiit nurasiitka*
*de nani **ngu=siit** ne=ura=siit-ka*
CONJ can 1SG.SBJ.NPST=story from/with=1PL.POSS=story-SG.M
'I can tell our story' (I12AANACLADNSOCIO3-466)

b. *dakatika, dunguasiit naum, de tika nguabiny saum*
dap=ka=tika, *de=**ngua=siit*** *ne-em,*
but=3SG.M.SBJ=EMPH CONJ=1SG.SBJ=story from/with-SG.RCD
de *tika* *ngua=biny* *se-em*
CONJ EMPH 1SG.SBJ=break to/with-SG.RCD
'really, I told the short story, and I cut it short' (I12AANACLADNSOCIO3-433)

In addition, there are verbs that only occur with the neutral set, even in reference to non-past events: all verbs that exhibit a three-way stem alternation – possibly because these verbs have a dedicated non-continuous future stem (see section 5.4.2). Since this neutral set can thus be used in non-past contexts, it is labeled 'neutral' (and not 'past'). The difference between the two types of verbs is exemplified below. Both utterances are answers to the question 'what are you planning to do right now?', but (121a) features the verb *ming ~ ring ~ ding* (which makes a three-way aspectual distinction) and (121b), the verb *ves ~ pes* (which makes a two-way distinction). In (121a), the speaker combines the neutral subject index with the non-continuous future stem; and in (121b), he combines the non-past subject index with the simple non-continuous stem.

(121) a. *dip nguaring guangama melangga*
dip ***ngua=ring*** *gua=ngama* *melang-ka*
FUT 1SG.SBJ=weave.NCONT.FUT 1SG.POSS=some.NSPEC vine-SG.M
'I will weave a rope for myself' (AJL-10/05/2012; SCENARIO 23 FROM DAHL 1985)

b. *nani nguves prama avetki*
nani ***ngu=ves*** *pet=ama* *avet-ki*
can 1SG.SBJ.NPST=close/thatch.NCONT on/under=ART house-SG.F
'I can thatch a house' (AJL-15/05/2012; SCENARIO 23 FROM DAHL 1985)

For those verbs that occur with either index, the neutral index is confined to past situations (as in 122a). The main exception here are conditions, as they are invariably presented with the neutral index, even if they occur in the future. For example, the first clause in (122b) features two verbs marked with the neutral subject index (*narli* 'hear' and *nes* 'shout'). This clause presents the condition for events to take place in the following two clauses, which are marked with the non-past index (*nes* 'shout').

(122) a. *imani nguarltik metki*
i=mani ***ngua****=rletik* *met-ki*
SIM=recently 1SG.SBJ=turn.over:SIDE in-3SG.F
'and yesterday I poured (water) on it' (P12ADNFIRE-050)

b. *ivit naniip ngenarlaqarang ngans, duquasik ngenenes, dap nangresa nguns*
i-pit nani=ip ***ngen****=narli=a=qa-irang*
AWAY-up can=PURP 2PL.SBJ=hear=NM=some-PL.DIM
nga*=nes, de=kuasik* ***ngene****=nes,*
3N.SBJ=shout.NCONT CONJ=NEG 2PL.SBJ.NPST=shout.NCONT
dap nani=ngerek=se(-ngua) ***ngu****=nes*
but can=alone=to/with(-1SG) 1SG.SBJ.NPST=shout.NCONT
'if/when you can hear something shouting, don't you shout (back), only I can shout (back)' (N11AAGSIRINILOBSTER2-0035FF)

The non-past category is used in future contexts, including both predictions (as in 123a) and intentions (as in 123b); and it is used in imperative contexts (as in 123c).

(123) a. *dip nyinyip*
dip ***nyi****=nyip*
FUT 2SG.SBJ.NPST=die.NCONT
'(if you eat this) you will die' (AJL-28/05/2012; SCENARIO 81 FROM DAHL 1985)

b. *de naka ngutluip ngusuini ramatokpisin*
de naka ***ngu****=tlu=ip* ***ngu****=su-ini*
CONJ bit 1SG.SBJ.NPST=see.CONT=PURP 1SG.SBJ.NPST=teach-SG.DIM
te=ama=tokpisin
PURP=ART=NAME
'a bit later, I will make sure (lit. see to it) that I teach the little one Tok Pisin' (I12AANACLADNSOCIO3-077)

c. *dequas nyivleng amaurlen*
de=kuasik ***nyi****=vleng ama=urlen*
CONJ=NEG 2SG.SBJ.NPST=kill.NCONT ART=prawn
'don't you kill the prawns' (N11AAGSIRINILOBSTER2-0012)

The non-past index is furthermore used in reference to present situations (as in 124a). Note that the boundaries of the present can be extended to include situations of the recent past. As such, particles such as *lira* 'just now' and *mani* 'recently (yesterday)' can combine with the non-past index (as in 124b) (but not necessarily so, see 122a above), while *medu* 'past' cannot (as in 124c).

(124) a. *nyitlianemalia*
*nyi=tlu=****iane****=mali=a*
2SG.SBJ.NPST=see.CONT=3DU.SBJ.NPST=search=DIST
'look they are searching now' (R12ATAFROG-065)

b. *isa lira nguquarl saqa, barequriaik*

i=sa	***lira***	***ngu**=quarl*	*se-ka,*
SIM=already	now	1SG.SBJ.NPST=present.NCONT	to/with-3SG.M

barek=ure-ia-ki

BEN=1PL.POSS-other-SG.F

'just now, I had shown (how to do) it, for our other (friend)' (P12ADNROPE1-105FF)

c. *desa medu qaat nget nauirl*

de=sa	***medu***	***ka**=at*	*nget*	*nauirl*
CONJ=already	past	3SG.M.SBJ=fall/drop.NCONT	3N	first

'and (in the past) he had planted them first' (D12ABDACPGARDEN-011)

Speakers can also use the non-past index in past situations. For example, the speakers in (125) talk about the ancient practice of story-telling, describing how their ancestors used to tell stories – and they choose the neutral index in (125a), but the non-past index in (125b). Evidence from controlled elicitations suggest that the shift to a non-past index occurs when speakers present a past situation as continuous. For example, (125c) is a typical response to a past imperfective scenario: the event is situated in the past (through the use of *murl* 'distant past'), the speaker then first presents an unbounded event (using the non-past subject index plus a continuous verb stem), and then follows up with a series of bounded events that happened in the past and within the boundaries of the walk (using neutral subject indexes plus, where applicable, non-continuous verb stems). But note that speakers can alternatively choose the neutral index for past continuous events. For example, the speaker in (125d) combines the neutral subject index with a continuous verb stem for such an event.

Given the distribution of the two subject indexes, I assume that they code tense, not aspect: the non-past index occurs in present and future contexts, while the neutral index remains neutral (and is restricted to past contexts for those verbs that contrast the two indexes). Under this analysis, there are two unexpected uses. First, speakers can (but do not have to) use the non-past index to express past imperfective events (as in 125b and 125c). And second, speakers have to use the neutral index for all conditions, even if they are set in the future (as in 122b above). These uses can be explained if we assume that Qaqet allows for a shift of the deictic center, i.e., a shift to the past, thus allowing for the use of the non-past index in past imperfective contexts (as in 125b and 125c); and to the future, thus allowing for the use of the neutral index for conditions or past-in-the-future contexts (as in 122b above). There is furthermore a tendency for the non-past index to co-occur with continuous stems, and conversely, for the neutral index to co-occur with non-continuous stems. But this tendency is likely to follow from the semantic affinity between present tense and imperfectivity, and past tense and perfectivity. Both indexes can and, in fact, commonly do co-occur with the respective other stem: the neutral index with a continuous stem (as, e.g., in 125d), and the non-past index with a non-continuous stem (as, e.g., in 124b above).

(125) a. *amahrlura, de tika murl, nep malavu arlvis, de rasiit, savet masirini*
ama=srlu-ta, de tika murl, ne=pe
ART=old-PL.H CONJ EMPH distantly from/with=PLACE
ma=lavu ngere-uvis, de ***ta****=siit, se=pet*
ART.ID=adult 3N.POSS-top CONJ 3PL.SBJ=story to/with=on/under
ma=sirini
ART.ID=NAME
'the old people, in the past, descending from the ancestors, they told stories about Sirini' (I12AANACLADNSocio3-283FF)

b. *imurl amalavu, dekiqerl tesiit nelungera amasiit*
i=murl ama=lavu, de=kiqerl ***te****=siit*
SIM=distantly ART=adult CONJ=now 3PL.SBJ.NPST=story
ne=lu-nget-a ama=siit
from/with=DEM-N-DIST ART=story
'in the past, the ancestors were telling those stories' (I12AANACLADNSocio3-311)

c. *murl vriaqamanirlaqa, de iaqamaquatka qepaikmet, de qaserlmenses i qavin amaqemgi, de qianis aailany, beiva de qamramadulka, de qarluqi naqa, be qianyip*
murl pet=a=qama=nirla-ka, de
distantly on/under=NM=some=sun-SG.M CONJ
ia-ka=ama=quat-ka ***ke****=paikmet, de*
other-SG.M=ART=man-SG.M 3SG.M.SBJ.NPST=walk.CONT CONJ
ka*=serlmenses i* ***ka****=vin ama=qem-ki,*
3SG.M.SBJ=surprise:AT:?? SIM 3SG.M.SBJ=step.NCONT ART=snake-SG.F
de ***kia****=nis aa=ilany, be=ip=a de*
CONJ 3SG.F.SBJ=bite.NCONT 3SG.M.POSS=foot CONJ=PURP=DIST CONJ
ka*=mat=ama=dul-ka, de* ***ka****=rlu-ki*
3SG.M.SBJ=take.NCONT.PST=ART=stone-SG.M CONJ 3SG.M.SBJ=throw-3SG.F
ne-ka, be ***kia****=nyip*
from/with-3SG.M CONJ 3SG.F.SBJ=die.NCONT
'once upon a time in the past, a man was walking, and he was surprised because he stepped on a snake, and it bit his leg, and then he picked up a stone and threw at it (the snake) with it (the stone), and it died' (AJL-15/05/2012; SCENARIO 181–185 FROM DAHL 1985)

d. *__ian__tekmet prianaqabany lungera*
__ian__=tekmet *pet=iana=qabany* *lu-nget-a*
3DU.SBJ=do.CONT:IN on/under=3DU.POSS=foolishness DEM-N-DIST
'they were doing that foolishness of theirs' (I12AANACLADNSOCIO3-385)

Verbs that cannot occur with the non-past index use their non-continuous future stem in future and imperative contexts (as in 126a and 126b). But since this stem also conveys aspect (i.e., non-continuity), it cannot be used for continuous future events. In such cases, the continuous stem is used and the temporal frame is left to context or is indicated by other means, e.g., by the future particle *dip* in (126c). The distribution of the non-continuous future stem furthermore differs from that of the non-past index in that it cannot occur in present contexts, nor in past continuous contexts.

(126) a. *daguaka, dakui magrip nguasnyi*
dap=gua-ka, *dap=kui* *maget=ip* ***ngua**=**es**-nyi*
but=1SG.POSS-SG.M but=quoting then=PURP 1SG.SBJ=eat.NCONT.FUT-2SG
'but my friend, I say I will then eat you' (N12BAMCAT-260)

b. *nyaris ma, pupu balar*
nya**=**ris *ma:* *pupu* *balar*
2SG.SBJ=call.NCONT.FUT thus granny NAME
'say it like this, 'granddad Balar'' (C12YMMZJIPLAY1-117)

c. *ip dip nguadingga*
ip ***dip*** *ngua=**ding**-ka*
PURP FUT 1SG.SBJ=weave.CONT-3SG.M
'so I will be weaving it' (P12ADNROPE1-104)

Similarly, these verbs use their past non-continuous stems in contexts where other verbs use the neutral index: in past contexts (as in 127a) and in conditions, including future conditions (as in 127b). Again, the distribution is not entirely equivalent, as the verb stem simultaneously expresses non-continuous aspect, i.e., past continuous events will trigger the continuous verb stem (as in 127c).

(127) a. *imeda ngune.. ngune.. gunan unmit savraarlim*
i=medu=a *ngu-ne..* *ngu-ne..*
SIM=past=DIST 1SG.ASSOC-from/with 1SG.ASSOC-from/with
gu-nan *un=**mit***
1SG.POSS-mother 1DU.SBJ=go.NCONT.PST
se=pet=aa=rlim
to/with=on/under=3SG.M.POSS=bottom
'earlier now, I and.. I and.. my mother, we went to its bottom' (N11AJNGENAINGMETBROTHERS-0011)

b. *iv amagilka qamramaqelany, de dip kevan pramaluanngi*
ip *ama=gil-ka* *ka=**mat**=ama=qelany,*
PURP ART=small-SG.M 3SG.M.SBJ=take.NCONT.PST=ART=money
de *dip* *ke=van* *pet=ama=luan-ki*
CONJ FUT 3SG.M.SBJ.NPST=buy.NCONT on/under=ART=cloth-SG.F
'if the boy gets money (in the future), he will buy a piece of cloth' (AJL-17/05/2012; SCENARIO 103 FROM DAHL 1985)

c. *murl masirini qatit*
murl *ma=sirini* *ka=**tit***
distantly ART.ID=NAME 3SG.M.SBJ=go.CONT
'in the past, Sirini was going' (N11AESSIRINI-0001)

5.4.2 Aspectual verb stems

Many Qaqet verbs have several aspectual stems that are differentiated through their initial segment(s). A verb can have up to five different forms, as exemplified with the verb 'eat' in (128): *mes* in non-continuous past contexts (as in 128a), *es* in non-continuous future contexts (as in 128b), *tes* in continuous contexts (as in 128c), *dres* in continuous contexts following a subject index ending in *n* (as in 128d), and *smes* in other contexts such as in multi-verb constructions and in nominalizations (as in 128e). Mostly, however, verbs have fewer stems.

(128) a. *amaqurlik ngames dama malasiqa*
ama=qurliqa *nga=**mes*** *de=ama* *malasi-ka*
ART=caterpillar 3N=eat.NCONT.PST LOC.PART=ART tree.type-SG.M
'the caterpillar ate from the *malasi* tree' (ABL-22/092015)

b. *dunguasnyi*
*de=ngua=**es**-nyi*
CONJ=1SG.SBJ=eat.NCONT.FUT-2SG
'I will eat you' (N12BAMCAT-273)

c. *dap ngenaqa, de qats*
dap *ngere-ne-ka,* *de* *ka=**tes***
but 3N.ASSOC-from/with-3SG.M CONJ 3SG.M.SBJ=eat.CONT
'at the same time, he was eating' (N12BAMCAT-234)

d. *lungera amaqelangeriv iandres*
lu-nget-a *ama=qelak-nget=ip* *ian=**tes(dres)***
DEM-N-DIST ART=soft-N=PURP 3DU.SBJ=eat.CONT
'the soft ones that they usually eat' (N11AJNGENAINGMETSIQI-0066)

e. *iquasiq amasmes*
*i=kuasik ama=**smes***
SIM=NEG ART=food
'there isn't anything to eat' (N12BAMCAT-178)

The opposition between aspectual stems is also maintained in the agentless construction. For example, the speakers use a continuous stem in (129a), but a non-continuous stem in (129b).

(129) a. *perlset neguasiitka*
perlset *ne=gua=siit-ka*
finish.CONT from/with=1SG.POSS=story-SG.M
'my story is ending' (P12ADNFIRE-059)

b. *tika verlset na.. namasiitka*
tika ***verlset*** *ne..* *ne=ama=siit-ka*
EMPH finish.NCONT from/with from/with=ART=story-SG.M
'the.. the story has ended' (R12ACMFROG-125)

Table 66 summarizes the patterns of stem alternation, and the following paragraphs discuss them in more detail. When citing a verb in this grammar, the following conventions are adopted: out of context, the non-continuous (or non-continuous past, where applicable) stem is cited; when referring to a specific form (e.g., in an example), the exemplified stem(s) are used; and where aspectual distinctions are under discussion, all stems are given (in the order depicted in Table 66).

The main difference is between verbs with a three-way aspectual distinction (non-continuous past, non-continuous future, continuous), those with a two-way distinction (non-continuous, continuous) and those with no distinction. The other two types of stems are marginal and their distribution is unpredictable. First, some (but not all) verbs whose continuous stem starts in *t* have an allomorph starting in *dr* when following a subject index ending in *n* (see section 5.4.1 for a discussion and exemplification). Second, a small number of verbs have an additional stem that surfaces in two contexts: in conversions and overt nominalizations (see chapter 3.2.1), and in the multi-verb construction with *raqa* ~ *taqa* 'properly' (see section 5.5). This form always starts with a consonant cluster. All other verbs use their non-continuous past stem in this context (if they make a three-way aspectual distinction), their continuous stem (if they make a two-way distinction) or their invariant stem (if they do not make any distinction).

Tab. 66: Aspectual verb stems

Alternation	**Gloss**	NCONT.PST	NCONT.FUT	CONT (after *n*)	**Other**
Three-way alternation:					
m ~ r ~ t	put	*mu*	*ru*	*tu*	NCONT.PST
m ~ r ~ (t)d	burn	*mang*	*rang*	*dang ~ tdang*	NCONT.PST
m ~ Ø ~ t	eat	*mes*	*es*	*tes (dres)*	*smes*
Two-way alternation:					
v ~ p	kill	*vleng*	=	*pleng*	CONT
r ~ t	say	*raqen*	=	*taqen (draqen)*	*mraqen*
q ~ k	dig	*qut*	=	*kut*	CONT
v ~ (C)p	burn	*ves*	=	*pes ~ spes*	CONT
v ~ (C)b	buy	*van*	=	*ban*	CONT
	step	*vin*	=	*bin*	*nbin*
q ~ (C)k	shake	*quip*	=	*kuip ~ pkuip*	CONT
q ~ (C)g	cough	*qum*	=	*mgum*	CONT
+ copy	say	*sil*	=	*lsil*	CONT
of final	chew betel	*sing*	=	*ngsing*	CONT
consonant	climb	*sik*	=	*ksik*	CONT
	blow	*is*	=	*sis*	CONT
	circle	*ing*	=	*nging*	CONT
	chew	*it*	=	*rit < *tit*	CONT
	fetch/fill	*uuk*	=	*quuk < *kuuk*	CONT
	wash	*uuk-mes*	=	*quuk-mes*	CONT
	chase	*ing-arl*	=	*nging-arl*	CONT
+ plosive	hang	*iarli*	=	*kiarli*	CONT
	see	*lu*	=	*tlu*	CONT
Invariant form:					
	loosen	*berltik*	=	=	=
	teach	*su*	=	=	=
	search	*mali*	=	=	=
	throw	*rlu*	=	=	=
	beat	*uamet*	=	=	=

The distribution of the three aspectual stems is partly predictable from the phonology of the verbs, but not entirely so. The majority of verbs make a two-way distinction between non-continuous and continuous stems. These verbs are discussed first, as their analysis sheds light on the diachronic development of the stems. They fall into three subgroups.

The first subgroup shows an alternation between a lenited consonant *v*, *r* or *q* 'NCONT' and its plosive counterpart *p*, *t* or *k* 'CONT'. This distinction is meaningful, and it is retained irrespective of the phonetic environment. For example, the initial plosive *t* in *taqen* 'say.CONT' is retained in the intervocalic environment of (130). Elsewhere, this environment obligatorily leads to the lenition of the plosive (see chapter 2.1.1). That is, we would have expected a realization as *raqen* – but this realization is blocked because of the existence of the aspectual stem *raqen* 'say.NCONT'.

(130) *deqa**taqen** prini*
*de=ka=**taqen*** *pet-ini*
CONJ=3SG.M.SBJ=say.CONT on/under-SG.DIM
'and he talks to the little one' (I12AANACLADNSocio3-013)

The verbs in the second and third subgroup suggest a possible diachronic scenario for the development of the aspectual opposition between lenited and plosive consonants (and, incidentally, for the phonemicization of the lenited consonants, see chapter 2.1.1). The two subgroups differ in the nature of the initial segment of their non-continuous stem: the verbs of the second subgroup have initial lenited consonants (just like the verbs of the first subgroup), and the verbs of the third subgroup have other initial consonants or vowels. They are similar, in that they both add a consonantal prefix in their continuous form. Both subgroups have probably retained the original formation process: an unmarked non-continuous form was opposed to a prefixed continuous form. Both forms would have occurred following a subject index, i.e., their initial consonant(s) would have frequently occurred in an intervocalic environment, and if the unmarked form had an initial voiceless plosive, this plosive would have occurred lenited. In the continuous form, by contrast, lenition would have been prevented by the consonantal prefix. The relevant environments are illustrated with the help of the (present-day) alternation of *ves* 'burn.NCONT' (from **pes*) (in 131a) and *spes* 'burn.CONT' (from **s-pes*) (in 131b). Interestingly, this verb has an alternative continuous form *pes* 'burn.CONT' occurring in free variation (as in 131c). As indicated in Table 66, some other continuous verb stems also alternate between a consonant cluster onset[32] and a simple plosive onset. It is very likely that this alternation reflects a not-yet-completed diachronic development: the loss of the prefixal consonants, and hence the simplification of consonant clusters. In the first subgroup, this process is completed, and the original allophonic variation (e.g., *pes* becoming *ves* intervocalically) was reinterpreted as a phonemic contrast between lenited (non-continuous) *ves* and non-lenited (continuous) *pes*.

32 In the case of consonant cluster onsets, we usually observe resyllabification (see chapter 2.2). For example, *respes* 'they are burning' in (131b) is morphologically *te=spes* '3PL.SBJ.NPST=burn.CONT', but is normally syllabified as *res-pes* (not **re-spes*).

(131) a. *nyi**ves** daakun angeraquis*
*nyi=**ves*** *de=a=kun* *ngera=quis*
2SG.SBJ.NPST=burn.NCONT CONJ=NM=corn 3N.POSS=skin
'burn the husks of the corn' (LONGYDS20150705_1-043)

b. *ilura re**spes** amasleng*
i=lu-ta-a *te=**(s)pes*** *ama=sleng*
SIM=DEM-PL.H-DIST 3PL.SBJ.NPST=burn.CONT ART=garden
'those ones are burning the garden' (BMS-04/08/2015)

c. *deiv ure**pes**kia*
de=ip *ure=**(s)pes**-ki=a*
CONJ=PURP 1PL.SBJ.NPST=burn.CONT-3SG.F=DIST
'we are burning it now' (D12ABDACPGARDEN-065)

The rules underlying the formation of continuous stems can be most clearly seen in the third subgroup. This subgroup contains verbs whose non-continuous form starts with a vowel or with a consonant other than a voiceless plosive (*p, t, k*) or a lenited consonant (*v, r, q*). They form their continuous stem by adding an initial consonant, which is a copy of the final consonant of the root. If the verb is vowel-initial and the copied consonant is a voiceless plosive, this plosive is lenited, compare *uuk* 'fetch/fill.NCONT' and *quuk* 'fetch/fill.CONT' (from **kuuk*) in Table 66 above. Note that the copied consonant is always the final consonant of the root, not necessarily the final consonant of the verb. For example, a complex verb such as *uukmes* 'wash.NCONT' copies the consonant *k* (i.e., the final consonant of the root *uuk* 'fetch/fill.NCONT'), and the resulting form is thus *quukmes* 'wash.CONT' (not **suukmes*). The formation is very regular, and only the behavior of vowel-final roots is not entirely predictable: there are very few such verbs, and it is impossible to discern any pattern other than that they all seem to add a plosive (both *t* and *k* are attested so far).

This process of copying final consonants also helps to explain a number of irregular continuous forms among the second subgroup and among verbs with a three-way alternation. These irregular forms have an initial voiced plosive (instead of the expected voiceless plosive). All of them end in a nasal, i.e., they would originally have formed their continuous stem by means of a nasal prefix. It is very likely that this environment then triggered an assimilation in voicing, resulting in present-day forms such as *bin* 'step.CONT' (via **npin* > **nbin*). In some cases, the continuous form still contains the original prefix (e.g., *mgum* 'cough.CONT', from **mkum*), and in other cases, the prefixed form is still attested in a different context (e.g., *nbin* 'step' is found in the 'other' column). In most cases, the voiceless plosive has disappeared altogether. But there are some verbs that retain traces of the former voicelessness: their voiced plosive is frequently not realized prenasalized (which is otherwise a regular phonetic correlate of voiced plosives, see chapter 2.1.1), and sometimes a cluster of voiceless plus voiced plosive (e.g., *td*) is audible in intervocalic environments.

All the verbs discussed so far make a two-way aspectual distinction. In addition, there are verbs with a three-way alternation. These verbs behave uniformly in that their first segment(s) alternate between *m* 'NCONT.PST', *r* ~ Ø 'NCONT.FUT' and *t* ~ *td* ~ *d* 'CONT'. As such, they are similar to the first subgroup of verbs making a two-way distinction: they have a lenited initial *r* in a non-continuous form (which is unexpectedly absent in some cases), and an initial plosive *t* in the continuous form (which is voiced in some verbs that end in a nasal consonant). They only differ in that the non-continuous category is split into a future form (formally corresponding to the single non-continuous stem in other verbs) and a past form. This past form invariably replaces the initial consonant with an *m*. The source of this consonant is unknown. Based on the evidence form verbs with a two-way distinction, we can assume that the non-continuous future form was basic, and that the continuous form was formed by means of a prefix consonant. This scenario would then suggest that *m* in the non-continuous past form must have been originally a prefix, with a subsequent simplification of the initial consonant cluster **mr* to present-day *m*. A possible indication for the existence of such a prefix is the verb *raqen* ~ *taqen* 'say'. For most speakers, this verb has two aspectual stems, plus an additional stem *mraqen* occurring in the 'other' context. But some speakers use the form *mraqen* in past contexts, too.

Finally, there are verbs that do not alternate. Their phonological structure is similar to that of the third subgroup of verbs making a two-way aspectual distinction: they usually have an initial vowel or an initial consonant other than a voiceless plosive or a lenited consonant. The non-alternating verbs are likely to contain a mix of two types of verbs. On the one hand, this group includes verbs that probably originally alternated, but that have now lost their prefix consonant without any trace. The complex verb *guirltik* 'turn/answer:SIDE' is such an example: it does not alternate, even though it is formed on the basis of the alternating verb *guirl* ~ *rlguirl* 'return'. Since complex verbs almost always follow the pattern of their root, it is very likely that *guirltik* originally had a continuous alternant **rlguirltik*, too. Furthermore, the verbs that allow for reduplication in continuous contexts (see section 5.4.3) all belong to the non-alternating verbs: it is possible that reduplication is used to recreate the lost aspectual distinction.[33] Mostly, however, there are no longer any synchronic indications that these verbs originally alternated. On the other hand, this group also includes verbs that probably never alternated. These are especially loanwords of all phonological shapes, including loanwords starting with voiceless plosives. For example, *kik* 'kick' (from Tok Pisin) does not have the expected continuous form **qik*.

33 It could even be speculated that the typologically unusual formation of continuous verb stems through consonant-copying originated in full reduplications, followed by phonetic erosion. For example, reduplication of *guirl* 'return' would yield **guirlguirl* > *rlguirl*. In the non-alternating verbs, the erosion process is completed and no trace of the reduplicated syllable remains, e.g., reduplication of *guirltik* 'turn/answer:SIDE' would yield **guirlguirltik*, which then eroded to **rlguirltik* > *guirltik*.

And it includes verbs that very likely converted from other word classes, such as *sivit* 'be angry (verb), anger (noun)', or *guarlem* 'form bubbles (verb), a bubble (noun)'.

The different aspectual stems code a distinction between continuous and non-continuous meanings.

The continuous stem is used in all kinds of imperfective contexts, including continuous contexts (as in 132a), progressive contexts (as in 132b) and habitual contexts (as in 132c). Continuous contexts sometimes trigger additional repetitions (as in 132d).

(132) a. *katika ide ianemnyim*
ka=tika *ide* *iane=**mnyim***
3SG.M.SBJ=EMPH IPFV 3DU.SBJ.NPST=look.CONT
'they keep looking' (R12ADNFROG-107)

b. *saqi nyitluiara iqiqiuaik saqa*
saqi *nyi=tlu=iara* *i=ki=**qiuaik***
again 2SG.SBJ.NPST=see.CONT=PROX SIM=3SG.F.SBJ.NPST=run.CONT
se-ka
to/with-3SG.M
'and again, see here, it is running with him' (R12ATAFROG-213)

c. *atika ide, pet masmas, daraamam, deide pet.. ke.. katit savramalat*
ka=tika *ide,* *pet* *masmas,*
3SG.M.SBJ=EMPH IPFV continuously always
de=araa=mam, *de=ide* *pet..* *ke..*
CONJ=3PL.POSS=father CONJ=IPFV continuously 3SG.M.SBJ.NPST
*ka=**tit*** *se=pet=ama=lat*
3SG.M.SBJ=go.CONT to/with=on/under=ART=work
'and always, continuously always, their father, he.. he always keeps going to work' (N12ABKSIRINI-028)

d. *katit bqatit beip sagelna*
*ka=**tit*** *be=ka=**tit*** *be=ip*
3SG.M.SBJ=go.CONT CONJ=3SG.M.SBJ=go.CONT CONJ=PURP
se=gelna
to/with=nearby
'he keeps going and going until (he arrives) nearby' (N11AAGBROTHERS-0093)

Conversely, the non-continuous stem is used in all types of perfective situations, including completed events (as the first verb in 133) as well as future events conceptualized without an internal structure (as the second verb in 133).

(133) *nguavleng gu.. gua.. gualiltem mii, de nani nyarenas saqua?*
*ngua=**vleng** gu.. gua.. gua=liltem*
1SG.SBJ=kill.NCONT 1SG.POSS 1SG.POSS 1SG.POSS=domestic.plant/animal
*mii, de nani nya=**renas** se=kua?*
most CONJ can 2SG.SBJ=jump.NCONT.FUT:SELF to/with=where
'I have killed all my.. my.. my animals and plants, so where can you jump to now (i.e., what is left for you to jump on)?' (N11AESSirini-0034ff)

For the verbs with a three-way distinction, there is an additional tense differentiation in the non-continuous category between past tense and future tense (see section 5.4.2). All other stems (i.e., the continuous stems of verbs with a three-way alternation, and both stems of verbs with a two-way alternation) are independent of tense. For example, the clause in (133) above features a non-continuous stem in a future context. Or a continuous stem can occur in both past contexts (as in 134a) and future contexts (as in 134b).

(134) a. *taquarl medu nyatisini*
*taquarl medu nya=**tis**-ini*
thus past 2SG.SBJ=call.CONT-SG.DIM
'like you were saying it the last time' (I12AANACLADNSocio2-077)
b. *de dip nyatisini*
*de dip nya=**tis**-ini*
CONJ FUT 2SG.SBJ=call.CONT-SG.DIM
'and you will be saying it' (I12AANACLADNSocio3-236)

The system of aspectual stems, as described above for Qaqet, is similar, but not identical, to the one attested in Mali (Stebbins 2011: 51–57). The two languages share the different verb classes (distinguishing between verbs that have a three-way alternation, a two-way alternation and no alternation), and they share some of the formations (especially the alternation between initial voiceless plosives and lenited consonants, as well as the occurrence of an initial *m* in the past stem of three-way alternating verbs), but Mali does not show any evidence for copying the final root consonant as a prefix consonant. Instead, Mali chooses from a small set of prefix consonants and vowels. The difference can be seen most clearly in cognate forms. For example, Qaqet shows consonant copying in the continuous stems *knak* 'cry', *mnyim* 'look' or *pnyip* 'die', while the cognate Mali stems are *tnok* 'cry', *ingim* 'search' and *ingip* 'die' (Stebbins 2011: 53). And in terms of their semantics, the stems in Mali express a tense distinction (not an aspect distinction), distinguishing between past, present and future (in the three-way alternating verbs) and present and non-present (in the two-way alternating verbs).

5.4.3 Reduplication

There are a number of verbs that make use of full reduplication in continuous contexts. For example, *del* 'knock' (illustrated in 135a) is attested reduplicated in habitual and iterative contexts (e.g., in the habitual context of 135b). In addition, a handful of verbs make use of partial reduplication in these contexts, e.g., *seserl* 'straighten' in (135c) (from *serl* 'straighten'). All attested verbs are non-alternating, i.e., they do not have dedicated aspectual stems that would occur in continuous contexts (see section 5.4.2). Given this distribution, it is likely that reduplication fills a functional gap for these verbs. Arguably, reduplication is less entrenched than the aspectual stems: the formation is very transparent, and it is largely restricted to the semantic fields of breaking and hitting (with a few exceptions). Nevertheless, reduplicated stems occur in the same contexts as continuous stems, including in non-aspectual contexts (such as in nominalizations and when following the modifier *raqa ~ taqa* 'properly').

(135) a. *luqa qadel meramatarlka*

lu-ka-a	*ka=**del***	*met=ama=tarl-ka*
DEM-SG.M-DIST	3SG.M.SBJ=knock	in=ART=door-SG.M

'that one knocked (once) at the door' (ARB-02/07/2017)

b. *ide qadeldel, kuramameng*

ide	*ka=**deldel**,*	*kut=ama=meng*
IPFV	3SG.M.SBJ=knock:REDUP	along=ART=wood

'he always hits, against trees' (D12ADKSPIRITS-058)

c. *iqatika ip.. nani qiseserl vrini*

i=ka=tika	*ip..*	*nani*
SIM=3SG.M.SBJ=EMPH	PURP	can

*ki=**seserl***	*pet-ini*
3SG.F.SBJ.NPST=straighten:REDUP	on/under-SG.DIM

'it is the case that.. she can straighten (correct) the little one' (I12AANACLADNSOCIO3-005)

There are occasional examples of continuous stems being repeated. Such examples are not only very rare, but they also differ phonologically: there is a word boundary between the repeated stems, and this word boundary then usually necessitates the insertion of an epenthetic vowel to break up a consonant cluster (as in 136). Given the small number of examples and their phonological peculiarities, it is likely that they are less grammaticalized than the reduplicated stems above. I assume that they constitute ad hoc formations serving narrative purposes in that they allow for a vivid depiction of events.

(136) *tika qepkuip pukuip*
tika *ke=***pkuip** **pkuip**
EMPH 3SG.M.SBJ.NPST=shake.CONT shake.CONT
'he keeps on shaking (the tree)' (R12ADNFROG-144)

Reduplication is especially found with verbs of breaking and hitting, i.e., with verbs that regularly occur in the agentless construction. The opposition between simple (as in 137a) and reduplicated stems (as in 137b) is also maintained in this construction.

(137) a. *de biny menaqi*
de ***biny*** *men-ki*
CONJ break at-3SG.F
'and it got broken' (R12BCSFROG-058)

b. *be miika ip binybiny anirl*
be *miika* *ip* ***binybiny*** *a=nirla*
CONJ more PURP break.REDUP NM=sun
'when the sun was rising a bit more (lit. breaking)' (N11AAGBROTHERS-0097)

5.5 Modifier *raqa* ~ *taqa* 'properly'

The predicate can optionally include the modifier *raqa* ~ *taqa* 'properly' to convey that an event was done properly, well or carefully. This modifier shows an aspectual alternation between non-continuous (*raqa*) and continuous (*taqa*), preceded by a subject index (either a neutral index or a non-past index), and followed by a verb stem. Usually, all morphemes form a single phonological word. Example (138) illustrates this structure. It features two predicates that both contain this modifier: the non-continuous stem *raqa* in the first case, and the continuous stem *taqa*, in the second. The subject indexes come from the different sets: non-past in the first case, and neutral in the second. The modifier is then followed by the verb (and a direct object, if present), and all elements together form a clitic group.

(138) *nguraqaseserl vrini, ikatika ini ngataqasmis*
*ngu=***raqa***=seserl* *pet-ini,*
1SG.SBJ.NPST=properly.NCONT=straigthen:REDUP on/under-SG.DIM
ip=ka=tika *ini* *nga=***taqa***=smis*
PURP=3SG.M.SBJ=EMPH SG.DIM 3N.SBJ=properly.CONT=C.call
'I will carefully correct the little one, so that the little one will be saying it properly' (I12AANACLADNSOCIO2-099)

The modifier behaves like any verb that exhibits a two-way distinction in its aspectual stems (see section 5.4.2): it distinguishes the stems by shifting from an initial lenited consonant *r* to an initial plosive consonant *t*; and the stems have non-continuous and continuous meanings respectively. If the modifier is absent, the aspectual contrast is coded in the verb. But if it is present, this contrast is only coded in the modifier, and the lexical verb occurs in an invariant form. The form depends on the class of the verb (see Table 66 in section 5.4.2 for the patterns). Some verbs have a dedicated stem that occurs in nominalizations and when following the modifier (e.g., *smis* 'call' in 138 above). Verbs with a three-way alternation otherwise use their non-continuous past stem (as in 139a below), verbs with a two-way alternation, their continuous stem (as in 139b), and verbs without alternation, their invariant stem (as in 139c). If a verb reduplicates (see section 5.4.3), it is always the reduplicated stem that is used in this context (e.g., *seserl* 'straighten' in 138 above).

(139) a. *kataqamunget*
*ka=taqa=**mu**-nget*
3SG.M.SBJ=properly.CONT=put.NCONT.PST-3N
'he is putting them carefully' (N11AAGSiriniLobster2-0032)

b. *miika iva, de ianetaqamnyim*
*miika ip=a, de iane=taqa=**mnyim***
more PURP=DIST CONJ 3DU.SBJ.NPST=properly.CONT=look.CONT
'and then, they keep looking carefully' (R12ADNFrog-319)

c. *ingutaqasuini*
*i=ngu=taqa=**su**-ini*
SIM=1SG.SBJ.NPST=properly.CONT=teach-SG.DIM
'I teach the little one well' (I12AANACLADNSocio3-030)

The subject index appears preceding the modifier, distinguishing between neutral and non-past. Recall that the distribution of the indexes is different for different verbs: verbs with a three-way stem alternation only co-occur with the neutral set, while all others co-occur with either set (see section 5.4.1). This distribution is also retained when the modifier is present. If the verb has a three-way alternation, only the neutral index can appear before the modifier (e.g., *smis* 'call' in 138 above triggers the use of the neutral subject index, even though it is a non-past context). For all other verbs, either index is possible, depending on the temporal setting.

The formal properties suggest that the modifier *raqa* ~ *taqa* 'properly' originated in a verb. That is, the modifier structure as a whole presumably originated in a multi-verb structure that juxtaposed two inflected verbs without any overt linker or conjunction. Present-day Qaqet does not have productive multi-verb structures of this kind, but there are a number of similarities elsewhere in the language.

First, there are a handful of idiomatic collocations of two finite verbs. The most frequent case is illustrated in (140a): the collocation SBJ=*mit* SBJ=*at* 'SBJ=fell'. This collocation does admit different subject indexes (reflecting the person category of the referent), but nothing else can be changed (e.g., it is not possible to use the continuous aspectual stems of the two verbs). Second, there is the fixed expression illustrated in (140b): an interrogative structure that consists of an invariant form *ngulu* ~ *ulu* (from *ngu=lu* '1SG.SBJ.NPST= see.NCONT') plus a fully inflected predicate (see chapter 8.1.2). Third the adverb *mii* 'most' very commonly occurs in the juxtaposed structure illustrated in (140c) (see chapter 6.2): the adverb is preceded by an independent pronoun and followed by a finite verb. And finally, a number of particles have a verbal origin and can optionally be preceded by a 3SG.M subject index, resulting in structures as in (140b) (see chapter 7.1).

(140) a. *de qiamit kiaat meseng*
de ***kia=mit*** ***kia=at*** *meseng*
CONJ 3SG.F.SBJ=go.NCONT.PST 3SG.F.SBJ=fall.NCONT at.base
'and it fell down (lit. it went and it fell)' (R12ABDFROG-045)

b. *ngulu qataqen nana?*
ngu=lu ***ka=taqen*** *nana?*
1SG.SBJ.NPST=see.NCONT 3SG.M.SBJ=say.CONT what
'what can he say (lit. I see he says what)?' (I12ABLAJLATASOCIO3-163)

c. *de nani ut mii urenesa, ngunangen*
de *nani* ***ut*** ***mii*** ***ure=nes****=a,*
CONJ can 1PL most 1PL.SBJ.NPST=shout.NCONT=DIST
ngu-ne-ngen
1SG.ASSOC-from/with-2PL
'then we all can shout out (lit. we all we shout), I together with you' (N11AAGSIRINILOBSTER1-0027)

d. *katika radrlem*
ka=tika ***ta=drlem***
3SG.M.SBJ=EMPH 3PL.SBJ=know
'they really know (them) (lit. it is the case that they know)' (I12AANACLADNSOCIO3-217)

The four structures above illustrate that Qaqet allows, or at least did allow, for the juxtaposition of two predicates (either verbal or adverbial), each appearing with its own person marker (either as a subject index or as an independent pronoun), but without any conjunction. It is likely that *raqa* ~ *taqa* 'properly' had a similar origin, but has become further integrated into the predicate: synchronically, the whole structure has only one subject index, and the morphemes usually form part of a single phonological word. Similar developments are attested in Mali Baining, albeit with non-cognate forms, suggesting that these constitute recent developments in both languages (see Stebbins 2011: 209–216).

5.6 Summary

This chapter has presented the word class of verbs and the structure of the predicate. Verbs are distinguished from other word classes in that they are the only lexical items that can head intransitive and transitive predicates.

The Qaqet verb lexicon is characterized by a high degree of compositionality, where morphologically simple verbs with general meanings combine with other elements, in particular prepositions, to form complex verbs with idiomatic, non-compositional, meanings (section 5.1).

The verb lexicon contains transitive and intransitive verbs, but no ditransitive verbs and only very few ambitransitive verbs (section 5.2.4). Both subject and object noun phrases are formally unmarked, the constituent order is SV/AVO, and the subject argument is obligatorily indexed, usually as a proclitic on the verb (section 5.2.1). In addition, some types of bivalent verbs occur in the agentless construction to convey a non-controlled situation: the subject argument and its index are omitted, and the patient continues to be expressed in the same way as before. This pattern resembles a split-intransitive system (that distinguishes between two classes of intransitive verbs, S_A verbs and S_O verbs), but there are reasons to analyze this pattern not as a lexical split, but as an argument structure alternation (section 5.2.2). Qaqet furthermore has reflexive and reciprocal pronouns that take the place of direct and prepositional objects (section 5.2.3).

The transitivity of a verb has to be distinguished from its semantic valency: many bivalent and trivalent verbs are formally intransitive or transitive, and add participants in prepositional phrases. There is a diachronic development from prepositional phrases functioning as adjuncts (section 5.3.1) via prepositions introducing arguments entailed by the verb semantics to particles and suffixes that have become lexicalized as part of a complex verb (section 5.3.2). The different prepositions (and other formatives) and their contributions to argument structure were discussed in sections 5.3.3 to 5.3.6.

The predicate also includes information on tense/aspect, which is distributed over three slots. The subject indexes code information about tense (distinguishing a non-past set from a neutral set) (section 5.4.1); the verb stems express an aspectual distinction (distinguishing continuous from non-continuous aspect; and sometimes also non-continuous future from non-continuous past) (section 5.4.2); and a subset of verbs uses reduplication to indicate continuous aspect (section 5.4.3).

Finally, the predicate can include the modifier *raqa* ~ *taqa* 'properly', which originated in a multi-verb construction that juxtaposed two inflected verbs (section 5.5).

The forms and patterns discussed in this chapter are overall very similar to those reported for Mali Baining, but there are interesting differences in detail. Furthermore, Qaqet shares pervasive lexicalization patterns reported for many Papuan languages, although the formal means sometimes differ: the compositionality of the verb lexicon, the distinction between controlled and non-controlled events, and the distinction between continuative and non-continuative events.

6 Adverbials

This chapter is organized around different subgroups of adverbials: relational nouns (section 6.1), adverbs (section 6.2) and directionals (section 6.3). These constitute distinct word classes with different morphosyntactic properties and distributions, but they have in common that they function as peripheral constituents in a clause. Prepositional phrases constitute another type of adverbial constituent. Since they were already discussed in chapter 5.3, they are not taken up again in this chapter, except when reporting on interactions between prepositional phrases and other adverbials. Section 6.4 then summarizes this chapter.

6.1 Relational nouns

Qaqet has a small group of relational nouns that occur as non-obligatory elements in prepositional phrases, e.g., *is* 'end' (in 1a) or *tik* 'side' (in 1b). They are always preceded by a possessor index, and they can optionally be preceded by a noun: such a noun is present in (1a), but absent in (1b). In all cases, the preposition is obligatory. Note that the reverse is not true: prepositional phrases do not need a relational noun (see chapter 5.3.1). If present, relational nouns mostly have spatial uses, specifying a search region (as in 1b). In some cases, this includes temporal uses, i.e., specifying a location in time (as in 1a). And in the case of *garli* 'side/topic' there are both spatial ('side') and metalinguistic ('topic') uses attested (see 5b below for an example).

(1) a. *daarenngiaris*
[*de=a=aren-ki=are-**is***]PP
LOC.PART=NM=night-SG.F=3SG.F.POSS-end
'in the middle (lit. end) of the night' (R12ADNFROG-036)
b. *de qasnesnget mraa.. aarlaunini, sraarik*
de=ka=snes-nget *met=aa..*
CONJ=3SG.M.SBJ=put.in.CONT-3N in=3SG.M.POSS
aa=rlaun-ini, [*set=aa=**tik***]PP
3SG.M.POSS=netbag-SG.DIM behind=3SG.M.POSS=side
'and he was putting them in his.. his netbag, by his side'
(N11AAGSIRINILOBSTER1-0008FF)

Table 67 lists all attested relational nouns, together with information about the form of their possessor index, related Qaqet words and corresponding relational nouns in Mali. Related Qaqet word are invariably bodypart nouns. Relational nouns in Mali have comparable morphosyntactic properties (Stebbins 2011: 189, 203–204, 313–314), and some of the forms are presumably cognate (as summarized in the last column of

Table 67), albeit not always with the same meaning. Both languages also have relational nouns that are not attested in the other language. Given both the similarities and the differences, it is likely that the structure (and some individual forms) are inherited, but that further bodypart nouns have grammaticalized independently in the two languages.

Tab. 67: Relational nouns

Form	Gloss	Possessor index	Related word (Qaqet)	Relational noun (Mali)
am	mouth	full form	*amgi* 'mouth'	*am* 'front'
garli	side	full form	?	?
is	end	base form	*is* 'buttock' (in fixed expressions only)	?
lang	top	full form	*langaqi* 'shoulder'	?
qames	front	full form	?	?
rlan	inside	full form	?	?
rleng	back	full form	*rlengit* 'back'	*thēng* 'back/top'
rlim	bottom	full form	*rlimbit* 'buttock'	?
tik	side	full form	*ngarik* 'hand'; *rik* 'hand' (in fixed expressions only)	*tik* 'side'
ut	underside	base form	?	*rut* 'base'
uvis	top	base form	*pes* 'eye/face' (in fixed expressions only)	*pēs* 'head'

The relational nouns originated as possessed (bodypart) nouns within possessive noun phrases (see chapter 3.5 for details on possessive structures). Such an origin is not only suggested by their relationship to synchronic bodypart nouns, but especially by their morphosyntactic structure. Example (2) illustrates the similarity between structures featuring a possessed noun (in 2a) and those featuring a relational noun (in 2b). The possessive noun phrase in (2a) consists of the possessor noun *levungga* 'tree.type:SG.M', the possessor index *aa* '3SG.M.POSS' (indexing the singular masculine possessor noun), and the possessed noun *ngariqis* 'hand:SG.FLAT' (which is marked for its own noun class). And the noun phrase as a whole happens to function as the complement of a preposition. The structure with a relational noun in (2b) looks superficially identical: a prepositional phrase, consisting of the preposition *pe* 'PLACE', the noun *levungga* 'tree.type:SG.M', the possessor index *aa* '3SG.M.POSS' (indexing the singular masculine noun), and the relational noun *rleng* 'back' (which is unmarked for noun class).

(2) a. *beterl vrama.. alevungga aangariqis*
be=terl *[pet=[ama..* *a=levung-ka*
CONJ=straighten.CONT on/under=ART NM=tree.type-SG.M
aa=ngarik-es]NP]PP
3SG.M.POSS=hand-SG.FLAT
'and [the.. the *levung* palm's leaf]NP got stretched' (N11AJNGENAINGMET-BROTHERS-0147)

b. *katika ngentaneng taquarl vemalevunggaarleng*
ka=tika *ngen=taneng* *taquarl*
3SG.M.SBJ=EMPH 2PL.SBJ=hold.CONT thus
*[pe=ma=levung-ka=aa=**rleng**]PP*
PLACE=ART.ID=tree.type-SG.M=3SG.M.POSS=back
'hold on like this [to the *levung* palm's back]PP' (N11AJNGENAINGMET-BROTHERS-0062)

The formal similarity of the two structures suggests that the relational nouns originated as possessed nouns in the possessive construction. Synchronically, however, the formal properties of relational nouns differ in a number of respects.

A first difference is that relational nouns can only ever occur within prepositional phrases, i.e., a preposition is obligatory, even in the absence of a head noun (as in 3).

(3) *uneqiarl daarlan*
une=qiarl *[de=aa=**rlan**]PP*
1DU.SBJ.NPST=paddle.NCONT LOC.PART=3SG.M.POSS=inside
'we scoop away [at its inside]PP' (N12BAMCAT-075)

Then there are a number of differences with regard to the possessor index. Most conspicuously, we observe the phonetic erosion of this index. For example, *ara* '3SG.F.POSS' almost always appears as *ra* (as in 4a). Similarly, *aa* '3SG.M.POSS' tends to appear as *a*, *iana* '3DU.POSS' as *ian*, *araa* '3PL.POSS' as *raa*, and *(a)ngera* '3N.POSS' as *(a)ngerl* ~ *(a)nge*. It is likely that this erosion was facilitated through relational nouns preferably forming single phonological words with preceding nouns. In the case of possessed nouns, there is variation and both possibilities are reasonably frequent: the possessed noun can either occur as an independent word (as in 2a above), or it can form a phonological word with the preceding possessor noun (see chapter 3.5 for examples). In the case of relational nouns, by contrast, it is rare to encounter examples such as (4b), where the relational noun forms an independent word. And even in such cases, it is common for phonetic erosion to occur (e.g., *ara* is again realized as *ra* in 4b).

(4) a. *de qamit bqarerlesa, vemadulki**ra**rlim*
de ka=mit be=ka=rerles=a,
CONJ 3SG.M.SBJ=go.NCONT.PST CONJ=3SG.M.SBJ=hide.NCONT=DIST
*pe=ma=dul-ki=**ara**=rlim*
PLACE=ART.ID=stone-SG.F=3SG.F.POSS=bottom
'he went and hid, at the bottom of the stone' (R12ABDFROG-071)

b. *katerles pema.. amadulki **ra**rlim*
*ka=terles pe=ma.. ama=dul-ki **ara**=rlim*
3SG.M.SBJ=hide.CONT PLACE=ART.ID ART=stone-SG.F 3SG.F.POSS=bottom
'he was hiding at the.. the bottom of the stone' (R12ACMFROG-079FF)

The possessor index obligatorily indexes the noun class of the preceding noun, but there is variation in the distribution of the neuter and plural indexes. In possessive structures, the neuter index is used if the possessor noun has a non-human plural referent (i.e., it is formally unmarked) or belongs to one of the shape-based classes. With relational nouns, by contrast, we encounter speaker variation: some speakers use the neuter index (as in 5a) in this context, and others, the plural index (as in 5b). In elicitation, most speakers consider the use of the plural index in examples such as (5b) ungrammatical, and when editing transcripts of natural speech, they tend to correct such uses. Nevertheless, the corpus contains a good number of spontaneous utterances featuring the plural index. This variation is only observed with relational nouns, never with possessed nouns.

(5) a. *damaages angerarlan*
*de=ama=ages **ngera**=rlan*
LOC.PART=ART=year 3N.POSS=inside
'in the middle of the year' (N12BAMCAT-021)

b. *de vrama.. amalotu raagarli*
*de pet=ama.. ama=lotu **araa**=garli*
CONJ on/under=ART ART=pray 3PL.POSS=side
'it is about the.. the topic (lit. side) of the church service'
(I12AANACLADNSOCIO3-228)

In the case of relational nouns, there are indications that the singular masculine index *aa* is developing into a default index. This phenomenon is illustrated in (6) below by means of the extract from a story. In (6-1), the singular feminine referent *bariqi* 'beehive' is introduced. In (6-2) to (6-5), the speaker continues to refer to the beehive by means of singular feminine forms (highlighted in boldface). Finally, in (6-6), the speaker introduces a new referent, *slangap* 'bees', locating them inside the beehive by using a prepositional phrase with a singular masculine possessor index and a relational noun. We would have expected the singular feminine index in this context, since the possessor index again picks out the beehive. Such apparent default uses of the singular masculine index are not frequent, but they do occur. Note that they are only attested if the referent is not overtly mentioned (as in 6-6 below).

(6) 1. *nyilama.. amabariqi l..*
nyi=lu=ama.. *ama=bari-**ki*** *l..*
2SG.SBJ.NPST=see.NCONT=ART ART=bee-SG.F ??
'you see the.. the beehive..' (R12ATAFROG-131)

2. *lira nyitluqi mara, meramamengga*
lira *nyi=tlu-**ki*** *mara,* *met=ama=meng-ka*
now 2SG.SBJ.NPST=see.CONT-3SG.F here in=ART=wood-SG.M
'you were just seeing it here, in the tree' (R12ATAFROG-132)

3. *de luqimara iqiaat*
de *lu-**ki**=mara* *i=**kia**=at*
CONJ DEM-SG.F=here SIM=3SG.F.SBJ=fall.NCONT
'and this one here fell' (R12ATAFROG-133)

4. *kiaat nepanu*
***kia**=at* *ne=pe=panu*
3SG.F.SBJ=fall.NCONT from/with=PLACE=up
'it fell downwards (from up)' (R12ATAFROG-134)

5. *beluqiaraamek, nyiluqiaraamek*
*be=lu-**ki**-iara=a-mek,*
CONJ=DEM-SG.F-PROX=DIR-down
*nyi=lu=lu-**ki**-iara=a-mek*
2SG.SBJ.NPST=see.NCONT=DEM-SG.F-PROX=DIR-down
'this one down there, look at this one down there' (R12ATAFROG-135)

6. *bema.. amah.. amahlangap nadaarlan*
be=ma.. *ama=h..* *ama=slanga-ap*
CONJ=ART.ID ART=?? ART=bee-PL.RCD
*ne=de=**aa**=rlan*
from/with=LOC.PART=3SG.M.POSS=inside
'and the.. the.. the bees from its inside' (R12ATAFROG-136)

Most relational nouns occur with the full form of the possessor index, subject to further erosion. In addition, there are three forms that take the base form (as *uvis* 'top' in 7a). In chapter 3.5.1, it was discussed that the base form is presumably the original form of the possessor indexes, but is synchronically only attested with a handful of inalienably possessed kinship nouns, some proforms and some relational nouns. There are a number of further indications that these three relational nouns are older than the others. In all three cases, there is considerable phonetic erosion and fusion, sometimes making it difficult to recognize the indexes. Table 68 summarizes all attested forms. In particular, observe that the neuter index *ngere* has eroded to *ngarl* ~ *arl*, and that it covers both neuter and plural contexts. There are no corresponding bodypart nouns in Qaqet, but both *uvis* 'top' and *is* 'end' are attested in fixed expressions that suggest a bodypart origin. These expressions allow for a combination with first and second person possessors, and, again, the base forms are used (as in 7b). Finally, while speakers are prepared to produce the other relational nouns without a possessor index in elicitation contexts, they never produce any of these three forms without a possessor index.

(7) a. *as pum arlvis mara*
as *pe-em* ***ngere-uvis*** *mara*
still PLACE-SG.RCD 3N.POSS-top here
'up to the short one's top is still (only up to) here [demonstrates]' (N12ABKSIRINI-026)

b. *amavriski danyis*
ama=vris-ki *de=**gi-is***
ART=nakedness-SG.F LOC.PART=2SG.POSS-end
'you have a naked bottom (lit. nakedness at your end)' (C12YMMZJI-PLAY1-419)

Tab. 68: Relational nouns: Base indexes

Base index		***is* 'end'**	***ut* 'underside'**	***uvis* 'top'**
3SG.M	*a-*	*ais*	*aut*	*auvis*
3SG.F	*are-*	*aris*	*rut*	*(a)revis*
3DU	*iane-*	*iadis*	*ianut*	*ianvis*
3PL	*ara-*	*(ng)arlis*	*arlut*	*arlvis*
3N	*ngere-*			

Relational nouns differ from many other nouns (see chapter 3.2.1), including possessed nouns, in that they are unmarked for noun class. A possessed noun is marked for the noun class appropriate to the referent. For example, the possessed noun *alem* 'horn' in (8a) is marked for dual feminine. But a relational noun is invariant: it always appears in unmarked form, regardless of the referent (as *lang* 'top' in 8b).

(8) a. *dakuasik kadrlem iqeksiqa samrama.. amakauqi araalembim*
dap=kuasik *ka=drlem* *i=ke=ksik=a*
but=NEG 3SG.M.SBJ=know SIM=3SG.M.SBJ.NPST=climb.CONT=DIST
se=met=ama.. *ama=kau-ki* *ara=**alem-im***
to/with=in=ART ART=cow-SG.F 3SG.F.POSS=horn-DU.F
'but he doesn't know that he is climbing now onto the.. the two horns of a cow' (R12ABDFROG-081FF)

b. *kasiqa, sadamamenggaalang*
ka=sik=a,
3SG.M.SBJ=climb.NCONT=DIST
*se=de=ama=meng-ka=aa=**lang***
to/with=LOC.PART=ART=wood-SG.M=3SG.M.POSS=top
'he climbed now, into the top of the tree' (C12ARBZJIFROG-335)

Finally, the relational noun does not function as a head. This differs from possessive structures, where the possessed noun is the head, controlling agreement and person indexes. For example, the pronoun in the agentless construction of (9a) picks out the possessed noun *ngariqis* 'leaf' (belonging to the singular flat class) – not the possessor noun *levungga* 'type of tree' (belonging to the singular masculine class). By contrast, the adjective in (9b) agrees with the singular masculine noun *kaasika* 'vine'. If it had agreed with the unmarked relational noun *is* 'end', we would have expected the adjective to be marked by the neuter agreement suffix *-nget*. Similarly, the agreement of the demonstrative in (9c) is with the singular feminine noun *luqupki* 'place', not with the unmarked relational noun *rlan* 'inside'.

(9) a. *dap malevungga aangariqis, desa serl vraus*
dap *ma=levung-ka* *aa=ngarik-**es**,*
but ART.ID=tree.type-SG.M 3SG.M.POSS=hand-SG.FLAT
de=sa *serl* *pet-**es***
CONJ=already straighten on/under-SG.FLAT
'and the leaf of the *levung* palm got already straightened (lit. the flat one got straightened)' (N11AJNGENAINGMETBROTHERS-0110)

b. *kadik damakaasikaais amahlurlka*
ka=dik *de=ama=kaasik-**ka**=a-is* *ama=slurl-**ka***
3SG.M.SBJ=cut LOC.PART=ART=vine-SG.M=3SG.M.POSS-end ART=big-SG.M
'he cut the end of the big vine' (N11AAGSIRINIROPE-0017)

c. *dluqia amaluqupkirarlan*
*de=lu-**ki**-a* *ama=luqup-**ki**=ara=rlan*
LOC.PART=DEM-SG.F-DIST ART=place-SG.F=3SG.F.POSS=inside
'it's inside that place' (I12ABLAJLATASOCIO3-071)

This behavior suggests that the relational noun does not function as the possessed noun in a possessive noun phrase. As such, all restrictions on modifying the possessor noun do not apply either. For example, a possessor noun cannot be independently modified by an adjective or determined by a demonstrative (see chapter 3.5.2). But no such restrictions apply to nouns preceding relational nouns (as in 9b and 9c above). Their origin in possessive structures is nevertheless still transparent in the linear order of elements. In possessive structures, adjectives and demonstratives obligatorily follow the possessed noun. In the case of relational nouns, this order is not obligatory, but it is still possible (e.g., the adjective in 9b above modifies the noun *kaasika* 'vine', but follows the relational noun).

The above discussion has shown that, despite their diachronic relationship, there are considerable synchronic differences between relational nouns and possessed nouns: relational nouns have to occur within prepositional phrases, the form and distribution of their possessor indexes show differences, they cannot be marked for noun class and they do not function as heads of possessive noun phrases. Given these differences, I consider them a separate word class. There would be some justification in analyzing them synchronically as postpositions. I have nevertheless opted for an analysis in terms of relational nouns in order to emphasize their diachronic origins as possessed nouns and their continued morphosyntactic similarity to possessive structures.

6.2 Adverbs

All attested adverbs are listed in Table 69. They are defined as a word class on the basis of their syntactic behavior, although some adverbs (in particular, spatial adverbs) exhibit additional syntactic properties and are considered distinct formal subclasses. Morphologically, all adverbs are unmarked, and there is no productive means for deriving adverbs from other word classes (even though some adverbs probably have a multimorphemic origin). Semantically, most adverbs convey information on space, time, and quantity (including frequency and collectivity). Interestingly, there are hardly any manner adverbs.

Overall, the class of adverbs is small, and there is affinity to the class of particles (see chapter 7). Adverbs and particles have different – non-overlapping – syntactic distributions, and are thus considered two distinct word classes. In terms of their semantics and functions, however, there is overlap. For example, both the adverb *mas* (in 10a) and the particle *pet* (in 10b) convey durativity. Or compare the manner adverb *valuvalu* 'slowly' and the manner particle *masna* 'quickly'. Generally, adverbs tend to modify the predicate, while particles tend to modify the entire proposition, delineating, e.g., its temporal, aspectual or modal frame, or expressing the speaker's attitude towards it. But this division is not absolute, and both adverbs and particles are attested with either function, depending on their interaction with the other elements of the clause and the pragmatic context.

(10) a. *kurlingena mas*
kurli-ngen=a ***mas***
leave-2PL=DIST continuously
'keep staying' (BMS-14/05/2015)

b. *kuas pet nyiknak*
kuasik **pet** *nyi=knak*
NEG continuously 2SG.SBJ.NPST=cry.CONT
'don't go on crying' (LONGYDS20150531_1-392)

Tab. 69: Adverbs

Space:		
a	DIST	→ distal DEM
darlik	outside	n/a
gelna	nearby (space/time)	from: PREP *gel* 'near' + PRO *na* 'RECP'
iara	PROX (space/time)	→ proximal DEM
iasi	DIST (space/time)	n/a
mara	here	→ proximal DEM
meseng	at.base	from: PREP *met* 'in' + *seng* '??'; cf. Mali *sēng* 'base' (Stebbins 2011: 118)
mirlek	around	n/a
nasat	later (space/time)	from: PREP *ne* 'from/with' + *set* 'behind'
parlen	middle	→ ?relational noun (cf. example 15)
pelerles	in.between	n/a
pusup	up.above	n/a
sanyis	far	from: PREP *se* 'to/with' + *nyis* '??'; cf. Mali *ngis* 'apart' (Stebbins 2011: 208)
temani	underneath	?from: PREP *te* 'PURP' + DIR *mani* 'down'
tuarl	other.side	n/a
Time:		
bigia	tomorrow	n/a
mabigia, bigiama	day.after.tomorrow	from: *ma* '??' + ADV *bigia* 'tomorrow'
nanima	late.evening	from: PTCL *nani* 'can' + *ma* '??'
nauirl	first	from: PREP *ne* 'from/with' + *uirl* 'be.first'
nepbang	morning, sunrise	cf. Mali *mubang* 'tomorrow' and *nēp bangang* 'at night' (Stebbins 2011: 217)
ngilngil	morning, dawn	from: REDUP of *ngil* '??'
sunun	evening	n/a
Quantity (incl. frequency, collectivity):		
maden	continuously	n/a
mas	continuously	n/a
masmas	always	from: REDUP of ADV *mas* 'continously'
maus, miis	once	?from: *ma* 'ART.ID' + PRO *es* 'SG.FLAT'

(continued on next page)

(continued from previous page)		
mbes	together	?from: PRO *(b)es* 'SG.FLAT'
mii, miis	most	n/a
miim	twice	?from: *ma* 'ART.ID' + PRO *im* 'DU.F'
ngerek	alone	n/a
slep	intensely	n/a
Manner:		
taquarl, ma	thus	n/a
valuvalu	slowly	from: REDUP of V.NCONT *valu* 'be.slow'

The Qaqet word class of adverbs is defined syntactically, and it differs syntactically from that of particles. Most saliently, adverbs and particles occur in different slots in the clause. As illustrated in example (10) above, particles always occur in the left periphery, while adverbs (just like prepositional phrases) occur in the right periphery. Adverbs can only occur in the left periphery if they are formally marked, i.e. prosodically (by a non-final rise-fall contour, see chapter 2.3.2) and/or syntactically (by means of a conjunction). This difference is illustrated in (11) for the adverb *iasi* 'DIST': it appears unmarked in its typical clause-final position in (11a), but overtly marked in initial position in (11b). Particles can optionally be marked in initial position, but they do not need to be (as in 10b above).[34]

(11) a. *deip magrip, divundiriasi*
*de=ip maget=ip, dip=un=tit=**iasi***
CONJ=PURP then=PURP FUT=1DU.SBJ=go.CONT=DIST
'then let us go there' (N12BAMCAT-036)

b. *beiviasi, de masna qamit, bquuknas*
*be=ip=**iasi**, de masna ka=mit,*
CONJ= PURP=DIST CONJ quickly 3SG.M.SBJ=go.NCONT.PST
be=ka=uuknas
CONJ=3SG.M.SBJ=wash.NCONT:SELF
'and then, he went quickly and washed himself' (N12ABKSIRINI-119)

Adverbs and particles that are semantically compatible can combine, and they frequently do so. In such cases, each can appear in its unmarked slot, as in (12a) where the particle *kerl* 'DEONT' appears to the left, and the adverb *iasi* 'DIST', to the right. Alternatively, both occur overtly marked in the left periphery. In this case, the particles

34 There are gaps in the database in that some forms are only attested overtly marked in the left periphery. It is not possible to classify such forms unambiguously as either adverbs or particles, and they are tentatively classified as particles, pending further research.

always precede the adverbs, e.g., the particles *as* 'still' and *nani* 'can' precede the adverb *iasi* 'DIST' in (12b). This is also the case if they are distributed over two intonation units, e.g., in (12c), the particles *saqi* 'again' and *dip* 'FUT' form one unit, followed by another unit containing the adverb *iasi* 'DIST'.

(12) a. *luqaira, deqerl nyimnyimiasi*
*lu-ka-iara, de=**kerl** nyi=mnyim=**iasi***
DEM-SG.M-PROX CONJ=DEONT 2SG.SBJ.NPST=look.CONT=DIST
'this one, look now' (C12ARBZJIFROG-091)

b. *as nani iasi, dunguqutserl ngenama.. amaquukuqaavarlen*
***as nani iasi,** de=ngu=qutserl*
still can DIST CONJ=1SG.SBJ.NPST=plant.NCONT:??
ngere-ne=ama.. ama=quukuk=aa=parlen
3N.ASSOC-from/with=ART ART=sweet.potato=3SG.M.POSS=middle
'(it) can still (be done) some time later, and I plant them together with the.. the sweet potatoes there in its middle' (D12ADNGARDEN-049FF)

c. *de saqika dip, iasi, denguaru amapiuqisinga*
*de **saqi**-ka **dip, iasi,** de=ngua=ru*
CONJ again-3SG.M FUT DIST CONJ=1SG.SBJ=put.NCONT.FUT
ama=piuk-ising=a
ART=cassava-PL.LONG=DIST
'and again in future, then, I plant cassava cuttings' (D12ADNGARDEN-052FF)

Particles co-occur in a specific order (see chapter 7.1), while adverbs were not observed to co-occur within a single clause. If speakers use more than one adverb, they segment them into different units (see 17b below for an example). The only exception are the demonstrative adverbs *a* 'DIST', *iara* 'PROX', *iasi* 'DIST' and *mara* 'here', which can co-occur with all other adverbs, invariably following them (as in 13).

(13) *dap ngubrlany.. ngubrlany madeniara*
dap ngu=brlany.. ngu=brlany ***maden=iara***
but 1SG.SBJ.NPST=sleep 1SG.SBJ.NPST=sleep continuously=PROX
'but I sleep.. I sleep soundly here' (N12BAMCAT-226)

The subgroup of spatial adverbs has a larger distribution than the other subgroups. They also occur in the non-verbal locative clause (as in 14a) (see chapter 8.2.2) and as complements of the two prepositions *ne* 'from/with' and *se* 'to/with' (as in 14b) (see chapter 5.3.3). Furthermore, they can be modified by phrases introduced through the preposition *ne* 'from/with' (as in 14c) (see chapters 5.3.3 and 3.4.3).

(14) a. *kidarlik*
*ki=**darlik***
3SG.F=outside
'she is outside' (C12YMMZJIPLAY1-521)

b. *dianemnyim sameseng*

de=iane=mnyim	***se=meseng***
CONJ=3DU.SBJ.NPST=look.CONT	to/with=at.base

'and they are looking to the bottom' (R12ACMFROG-105)

c. *kamas, pelerles nara.. a.. ara.. ara.. ara.. araalemiam*

ka=mas,	[***pelerles***	***ne***=*ara..*
3SG.M.SBJ=lie.NCONT.PST	in.between	from/with=3SG.F.POSS

a..	*ara..*	*ara..*	*ara..*	*ara=alem-iam*]ADV
??	3SG.F.POSS	3SG.F.POSS	3SG.F.POSS	3SG.F.POSS=horn-DU.M

'he lay [in between its.. its.. its.. its.. its.. its two horns]ADV'
(R12ATAFROG-210)

Adverbs do not exhibit any particular morphological structure: they are synchronically monomorphemic, and there are no productive means to derive adverbs. The only partial exception is reduplication, as speakers regularly reduplicate adverbs to express intensification (see 16b below for an example). Note also that there are three adverbs that are only attested in reduplicated form: *masmas* 'always' (from the adverb *mas* 'continuously'), *ngilngil* 'morning' (of unknown origin) and *valuvalu* 'slowly' (from the verb *valu* 'be slow').

Diachronically, adverbs are often multimorphemic: their known or suspected origins are indicated in the last column of Table 69. Most commonly, adverbs are formed by means of a preposition plus another element (see chapter 5.3 for details on prepositions): *gelna* 'nearby' (from the preposition *gel* 'near' and the pronoun *na* 'RECP', lit. 'near each other'); *meseng* 'at base' (from the preposition *met* 'in' plus an unknown element); *nasat* (from the prepositions *ne* 'from/with' and *set* 'behind'); *sanyis* 'far' (from the preposition *se* 'to/with' plus an unknown element); *temani* 'underneath' (possibly from the preposition *te* 'PURP' plus the directional *mani* 'down'; but see section 6.3.3); and *nauirl* (from the preposition *ne* 'from/with' and the verb *uirl* 'be first').

Some adverbs presumably include pronominal forms. The adverb *gelna* 'nearby' contains the pronoun *na* 'RECP'. And the adverbs *maus* ~ *miis* 'once' and *miim* 'twice' presumably contain an article plus the pronouns *es* 'SG.FLAT' and *im* 'DU.F'; adverbials of 'thrice' and above are formed on the basis of an article plus a numeral (see chapter 3.2.2). Furthermore, *mbes* 'together' is possibly formed from the pronoun *es* 'SG.FLAT': formally, this pronoun has an allomorph *bes* (occurring after *m*); and semantically, it is used in reference to collectives (see chapter 4.2.4).

Sometimes, an unknown formative can be isolated (e.g., the adverbs ***ma**bigia* ~ *bigia**ma*** 'day after tomorrow' and *nani**ma*** 'late evening' contain an unknown element *ma*). And sometimes a cognate form in Mali is suggestive of a multimorphemic origin (compare, e.g., the adverbs *meseng* 'at base', *sanyis* 'far' and *nepbang* 'morning' in Table 69).

Conversely, some adverbs have also given rise to other forms. This includes especially the adverbs *a* 'DIST', *iara* 'PROX' and *mara* 'here', which form the basis of the distal and proximal demonstratives (see chapter 3.3.2 and 4.1.2 for their synchronic distribution and their relationship to the demonstratives). And the adverb *parlen* 'middle' seems to be developing into a relational noun (see section 6.1). It is attested in examples like (15), where it is preceded by a preposition and the possessor index *aa* '3SG.M.POSS', yielding the interpretation of 'in its middle'. Note that it does not (yet) have the full distributional possibilities of relational nouns: it cannot occur with any possessor index other than *aa* '3SG.M.POSS', and it cannot be preceded by a head noun.

(15) *dama.. aqalunirang meraavarlen*
de=ama.. *a=qalun-irang* *met=aa=**parlen***
CONJ=ART NM=singapore-PL.DIM in=3SG.M.POSS=middle
'and the.. the singapore taros in its middle' (D12ADNGARDEN-014)

Semantically, many adverbs express space, time or both. For example, the adverb *gelna* 'nearby' specifies a location in space in (16a), but a location in time in (16b).

(16) a. *sagelna namaluqup*
*se=**gelna*** *ne=ama=luqup*
to/with=nearby from/with=ART=place
'getting closer to the place' (N12BAMCAT-236)
b. *gelnagelnaiv uneperlset nuna.. unarlaunnga*
***gelna=gelna**=ip* *une=perlset* *ne=una..*
nearby=nearby=PURP 1DU.SBJ.NPST=finish.CONT from/with=1DU.POSS
una=rlaun-ka
1DU.POSS=netbag-SG.M
'nearly nearly, we're (close to) finishing our.. our netbag' (P12ARS-BILUM2-001)

Others have only spatial semantics (as *mirlek* 'around' in 17a) or only temporal semantics (as *bigia* 'tomorrow' and *ngilngil* 'morning' in 17b).

(17) a. *draing mirlek*
de=ta=ing ***mirlek***
CONJ=3PL.SBJ=circle.NCONT around
'they circle around' (N11AAGSIRINILOBSTER1-0043)

b. *bigia de vriaqamanirlaqa, ngilngil, daqasnanbet naarluavik ma*
bigia *de* *pet=ia-ka=ama=nirla-ka,* ***ngilngil,***
tomorrow CONJ on/under=other-SG.M=ART=sun-SG.M morning
de=ka=snanbet *ne=aa=rlua-pik*
CONJ=3SG.M.SBJ=ask:ON/UNDER from/with=3SG.M.POSS=friend-COLL.H
ma
thus
'tomorrow, on the next day, early in the morning, he asked his people like this' (N12ABKSIRINI-040FF)

In addition, Qaqet has adverbs that express some form of quantification over events, including aspectual notions of continuousness and habituality (as *maden* 'continuously' in 18a), frequency (as *maus* 'once' in 18b) or intensity (as *slep* 'intensely' in 18c). This also includes information on participants acting alone or as collectives (as *mbes* 'together' in 18d).

(18) a. *kiqiuaik maden*
ki=qiuaik ***maden***
3SG.F.SBJ.NPST=run.CONT continuously
'she continues to be gone' (C12ARBZJIFROG-392)

b. *nyiral metka maus*
nyi=ral *met-ka* ***maus***
2SG.SBJ.NPST=carry.NCONT in-3SG.M once
'you carry (something) in it (only) once' (P12ARSBILUM1-036)

c. *iamagetki nangua slep*
i=ama=get-ki *ne-ngua* ***slep***
SIM=ART=hunger-SG.F from/with-1SG intensely
'I'm very hungry (lit. hunger is with me intensely)' (N12BAMCAT-254)

d. *de ianebrlany mbes*
de *iane=brlany* ***mbes***
CONJ 3DU.SBJ.NPST=sleep together
'the two sleep together' (R12ATAFROG-036)

Some of these adverbs are oriented towards the participants of an event, and two of them (*mii* ~ *miis* 'most' and *ngerek* 'alone') exhibit additional properties.

The adverb *mii* ~ *miis* 'most' can modify either an event with an interpretation of 'completely' (as in 19a) or a participant to an event with an interpretation of 'most', 'all' or 'both' (as in 19b). In the latter case, it can optionally be marked by an article, thus showing evidence for its incipient integration into the noun phrase (as in 19c) (see chapter 3.2.2 for more details on this adverb).

(19) a. *miika amagepka naqa mii*
miika *ama=gep-ka* *ne-ka* ***mii***
more ART=pulp-SG.M from/with-3SG.M most
'he was completely bruised' (N12AMVGENAINGMETBROTHERS-068)

b. *de qiamrenas, biqiavleng arakaruk mii*
de *kia=mrenas,* *be=kia=vleng*
CONJ 3SG.F.SBJ=jump.NCONT.PST:SELF CONJ=3SG.F.SBJ=kill.NCONT
ara=karuk ***mii***
3SG.F.POSS=chicken most
'and she jumped up, and she killed all her chickens' (N11AESSIRINI-0018)

c. *nyisnanbet nemaarum, savramaquvangirang amii*
nyi=snanbet *ne=ma=arum,*
2SG.SBJ.NPST=ask:ON/UNDER from/with=ART.ID=NAME
se=pet=ama=quvang-irang ***a=mii***
to/with=on/under=ART=cargo-PL.DIM NM=most
'ask Arum about all the things' (LONGYDS20150506_2 052)

Furthermore, both *mii* ~ *miis* 'most' and *ngerek* 'alone' modify nouns and pronouns, which then occur in apposition to predicates. The adverb *mii* ~ *miis* 'most' occurs in the structure exemplified in (20a): a noun or an independent pronoun, followed by the adverb, followed by the predicate (see also chapter 5.5). And *ngerek* 'alone' occurs exclusively in the structure exemplified in (20b): it is modified by a prepositional phrase introduced by the preposition *se* 'to/with', and then both precede the predicate. In either case, there is usually a tight prosodic integration of noun or pronoun, adverb and predicate: there are no prosodic phenomena that are indicative of boundaries (see chapter 2.3.2), and only hesitation pauses were observed to occur (as in 20b).

(20) a. *tikaip.. iv iammii iandit*
tika=ip.. *ip* *iam=**mii*** *ian=tit*
EMPH=PURP PURP 3DU.M=most 3DU.SBJ=go.CONT
'it is the case that.. that they both go (together)' (I12AANACLADNSOCIO3-213)

b. *deip maget, de ngrek sema.. ramgi qans*
de=ip *maget,* *de* ***ngerek*** *se=ma..* *ramgi*
CONJ=PURP then CONJ alone to/with=ART.ID NAME
ka=nes
3SG.M.SBJ=shout.NCONT
'and then, Ramgi.. alone shouts' (N11AAGSIRINILOBSTER2-0052)

The semantic fields of space, time and quantity account for almost all adverbs. In addition, there is one manner adverb, *valuvalu* 'slowly' (as in 21a), as well as two manner demonstratives, *taquarl* 'thus' and *ma* 'thus'. Qaqet more commonly expresses manner in verbs (e.g., in the verb *kaverl* 'hurry' in 21b) or in prepositional phrases (e.g., *nadlek* 'with strength' in 21c). No other semantic fields are coded in adverbs.[35]

(21) a. *kuariqip.. amaqunaski, de nani valuvalu*

kua=arik=ip..	*ama=qunas-ki,*	*de*	*nani*	***valuvalu***
INTRG=supposing=PURP	ART=one-SG.F	CONJ	can	slowly

'supposing there is.. maybe one (woman), then it (the work) can (progress) slowly' (P12ARSBILUM1-061)

b. *nyikaverl satlak*

*nyi=**kaverl***	*se=a=talak*
2SG.SBJ.NPST=hurry.CONT	to/with=NM=play.CONT

'you play quickly (lit. you hurry with playing)' (C12YMMZJIPLAY1-054)

b. *iamalurlka, qaverlset nadlek, iqasis*

i=ama=lurl-ka,	*ka=verlset*	*ne=a=**dlek**,*
SIM=ART=wind-SG.M	3SG.M.SBJ=finish.NCONT	from/with=NM=strength
i=ka=sis		
SIM=3SG.M.SBJ=blow.CONT		

'and the wind, it stopped blowing strong (lit. the strength (with which) it was blowing)' (L12ATANORTHWIND-014)

6.3 Directionals

Qaqet has a set of directionals that express downward, upward and across directions in physical space, thereby reflecting the surrounding landscape (see also chapter 1.1.3): the Qaqet mostly live and tend to their subsistence gardens in mountainous territory (with numerous valleys, mountains and ridges), and often have small cash-crop plantations in the lower regions along the coast. The directionals are very prevalent in the language: they are among the most frequent words in Qaqet, and they appear very early in the vocabulary of children.

The directional system is used both in large-scale geographical space and in small-scale space. As such, speakers can choose to focus on the overall direction towards a lower, upper or equal level: the actual path may contain other segments, but speakers would still be able to use, e.g., 'down' when moving in the direction of the

35 Qaqet differs here from Mali, which has a larger number of adverbs overall, including many manner adverbs (Stebbins 2011: 66, 208–209, 217–218). Note also that there are very few cognate forms among the Qaqet and Mali adverbs.

coast, even though they might be moving uphill at the moment of speech. Alternatively, they can choose to focus on the actual downward, upward or across movement.

The directionals almost exclusively convey the directionality of physical objects in space. A minor exception is their use to express directed gaze (as in 22).

(22) *uanenyim ivit, maavit*
uane=nyim *i-**pit**,* *maqa-**pit***
2DU.SBJ.NPST=look.NCONT AWAY-up HERE-up
'look up, up' (LONGYDS20150902_2-133)

They are furthermore used to convey direction in time: reference to a previous time is based on *mek* 'down' (as in 23a), and reference to a later time is based on *pit* 'up' (as in 23b). The directional *pit* 'up' has also given rise to the complex conjunction *ivit nani ip* 'later if/when' (as in 23c) (see chapter 8.3.4).

(23) a. *luqia namek amaageski*
lu-ki-a *ne=a-**mek*** *ama=ages-ki*
DEM-SG.F-DIST from/with=DIR-down ART=year-SG.F
'the previous (lit. from down) year' (ATA&AEM-21/06/2011)
b. *ip nyatir.. ai, nyatisinavit*
ip *nya=tir..* *ai,* *nya=tis-ini=a-**pit***
PURP 2SG.SBJ=?? hey 2SG.SBJ=call.CONT-SG.DIM=DIR-up
'when you.. hey, (when) you later (lit. up) say it' (I12AANACLADNSOCIO2-073)
c. *ivit naniip nyatit*
*i-**pit*** *nani=ip* *nya=tit*
AWAY-up can=PURP 2SG.SBJ=go.CONT
'when you can go (you come to a river)' (N11AAGSIRINIROPE-0093)

In addition to their semantic coherence, the directionals share formal properties that define them as a word class. Some of these properties are shared with adverbs, but others set them apart as a separate class.

Like other adverbials, directionals usually occur in the right periphery of the clause (as in 24a) and they can co-occur with adverbials, always following them (as in 24b, where the directional is preceded by an adverb and a prepositional phrase). Like prepositional phrases, but different from other kinds of adverbials, directionals can also occur in the modifier slot of a noun phrase, including of noun phrases in subject function (as in 24c) (see chapter 3.4.3 for details). They also occur as predicates in the locative construction (as in 23d). Different from other adverbials in this construction, they seem to be developing an incipient system of subject indexing here (see chapter 8.2.2).

(24) a. *nyiuas amek*
nyi=uas *a-**mek***
2SG.SBJ.NPST=watch DIR-down
'keep a lookout down there' (N11AAGSIRINIROPE-0059)

b. *daqatika luqaira qemnyim sagelkiaraamek*
de=ka=tika *lu-ka-iara* *ke=mnyim*
CONJ=3SG.M.SBJ=EMPH DEM-SG.M-PROX 3SG.M.SBJ.NPST=look.CONT
*se=gel-ki=iara=a-**mek***
to/with=near-3SG.F=PROX=DIR-down
'and this one is looking at her down here' (C12ARBZJIFROG-023)

c. *luqiaamek kiatranyi, dakuas nyateski*
[*lu-ki-a=a-**mek***]NP *kia=tat-nyi,*
DEM-SG.F-DIST=DIR-down 3SG.F.SBJ=take.CONT-2SG
dap=kuasik *nya=tes-ki*
but=NEG 2SG.SBJ=eat.CONT-3SG.F
'[that one down there]NP is recording you, (so) don't you fight her' (C12YMMZJIPLAY1-264)

d. *amamelangga, de qaameq, ilira nguamuqa*
ama=melang-ka, *de* *ka=a-**mek**,* *i=lira*
ART=vine-SG.M CONJ 3SG.M=DIR-down SIM=now
ngua=mu-ka
1SG.SBJ=put.NCONT.PST-3SG.M
'the vine, it is down there, where I just now put it' (P12ADNROPE1-096)

Morphologically, the directionals are marked by a directional prefix (such as *a-* 'DIR' in 24 above): these prefixes only ever occur with directionals, and directionals obligatorily occur with one of the prefixes (with a few lexicalized exceptions). Finally, like spatial adverbs, the directionals can be introduced by the prepositions *ne* 'from/with' and *se* 'to/with', but not by other prepositions (again with a few exceptions).

This section first introduces the directional paradigm (section 6.3.1), then the directional prefixes (section 6.3.2), and finally the possible combinations of prepositions with directionals (section 6.3.3).

6.3.1 The directional paradigm

The forms and semantic distinctions of the present-day Qaqet directional system are summarized in Table 70 and discussed throughout this section. There are three directions (down, up and across), and three separate forms for each direction. The main difference is between forms that entail an endpoint to a direction, and those that do not. In addition, some forms are used in reference to an intrinsic part of a referent and/or to the orientation of a referent in space.

Tab. 70: The directional paradigm

	Direction	Intrinsic part; orientation
mek	down a slope/axis to an endpoint (at lower or inside level)	lower part
manep	down a slope/axis	–
mani	–	lower part; horizontal orientation
vuk[36]	up a slope/axis to an endpoint (at upper level)	upper part
pit	up a slope/axis	upper part; vertical orientation
panu	up in mid-air	–
muk	across a slope/axis to an endpoint (at same level)	side part
mit	–	side part; orientation across a gap
manu	across a slope/axis	–

The forms are segmentally similar, suggesting that they were – originally – compositional, consisting of a base form and a suffix. Synchronically, however, they have to be analyzed as monomorphemic. On the basis of the synchronic system, it is not possible to unambiguously identify the base forms, or to assign a straightforward form/meaning correspondence to (most of) the presumed suffixes. In fact, it is likely that the present-day directional system has undergone change. This possibility is suggested by a comparison with the directional system of Mali Baining (Stebbins 2011: 68–69, 192–206) (summarized in Table 71).

Tab. 71: Directionals: Comparing Qaqet and Mali

	Qaqet			**Mali (Stebbins 2011)**		
	down	**up**	**across**	**down**	**up**	**across**
axis	*mek*	*vuk*	*muk*	*mēk*	*vuk*	*muk*
landscape				*mano*	*vono*	*mono*
endpoint				*manēp*	*vuit*	*muit*
intrinsic	*mani, mek*	*pit, vuk*	*mit, muk*			
direction (axis, landscape)	*manep*	*pit, panu*	*manu*	*mani*	*vui*	*mui*

36 It is very likely that *vuk* 'up' is underlyingly **puk*, but since this form obligatorily occurs with a vowel-final prefix, it invariably surfaces as *vuk*. I therefore represent it as *vuk*.

The forms are presumably cognate, and the overall semantics of the two directional systems is similar – but their organization and the distribution of forms over semantic categories differs considerably.

Comparing the two directional systems, it can be argued that the Mali system is more systematic in the sense that there is a clear correspondence between form and meaning across the 'down', 'up' and 'across' paradigms. The base forms (presumably *ma* ~ *mē* 'down', *vu* ~ *vo* 'up' and *mu* ~ *mo* 'across') combine with the suffixes *-k* (directionality along an axis), *-no* (directionality within a landscape) and *-(n)i* (general directionality, not entailing an endpoint); in addition, the forms derived with *-(n)i* combine with a second suffix *-t* ~ *-p* (directionality, entailing an endpoint). Assuming that such a clear correspondence reflects the original compositionality of the meaning of the base form plus the meaning of the suffix, it is arguably the Qaqet system that has undergone most of the changes, not the Mali system.

Semantically, Mali distinguishes between direction along a (vertical or horizontal) axis and direction within a landscape (i.e., down, up or across a slope). In addition, it makes an orthogonal distinction between directions entailing and not entailing a terminal endpoint, whereby the latter forms are also used for reference to an intrinsic part of a whole. In Qaqet, by contrast, the organizing principle is the presence or absence of an endpoint: there are two sets of forms, and each set conflates the two concepts of directionality along an axis and within a landscape. The Qaqet forms that express a terminal endpoint are cognate to the Mali forms that express directionality along an axis. Some of the Qaqet forms that express directionality without an endpoint are, interestingly, cognate to the Mali forms that do express such an endpoint (Qaqet *manep* 'down' and *pit* 'up'); while others are cognate to the Mali forms that express direction within a landscape (Qaqet *panu* 'up' and *manu* 'across'). The first meaning shift is systematic, and it is thus not possible to decide which of the systems represents an innovation (the Mali system, the Qaqet system or both). As for the second shift, the variety of forms in the Qaqet set would suggest that Qaqet has undergone the change.

Furthermore, both languages code directionality to an intrinsic part of a referent. In Mali, this category is expressed through the forms entailing an endpoint, while Qaqet has again recruited forms from different paradigms: *mani* 'down' (cognate to Mali *mani* 'down (without endpoint)'), *pit* 'up' (cognate to Mali *vuit* 'up (with endpoint)'), and *mit* 'across' (cognate to Mali *muit* 'up (with endpoint)'); plus the set of Qaqet forms that is otherwise used for expressing directionality with an endpoint.

Qaqet *panu* 'up' (cognate to Mali *vono* 'up (landscape)') has undergone an idiosyncratic meaning shift: this form may have originally expressed directionality without an endpoint, but is now lexicalized. And finally, Qaqet has lost three of the original forms: Mali's *mano* 'down (landscape)', *vui* 'up (without endpoint)', and *mui* 'across (without endpoint)' do not have corresponding forms in Qaqet.

The remainder of this section outlines the synchronic distribution of each of the Qaqet forms: the forms of (i) the 'down' paradigm, (ii) the 'up' paradigm and (iii) the 'across' paradigm.

(i) Down: *mek*, *manep* and *mani*

The three forms of the 'down' paradigm are *mek*, *manep* and *mani*. Their semantic differences and typical interpretations are illustrated with the help of the elicited minimal pairs in (25), and discussed below.

(25) a. *nyaruqi imek*
nya=ru-ki *i-**mek***
1SG.SBJ=put.NCONT.FUT-3SG.F AWAY-down
'put it down (onto the ground)' (AJS&ATT-15/05/2015)

b. *nyaruqi imanep*
nya=ru-ki *i-**manep***
1SG.SBJ=put.NCONT.FUT-3SG.F AWAY-down
'put it down (in the direction of the slope)' (AJS&ATT-15/05/2015)

c. *nyaruqi imani*
nya=ru-ki *i-**mani***
1SG.SBJ=put.NCONT.FUT-3SG.F AWAY-down
'put it down (an upright object on its side)' (AJS&ATT-15/05/2015)

The form *mek* conveys a downward direction along a slope or a vertical axis, entailing an endpoint. The typical endpoint is the ground level (as in 25a and 26a), but *mek* has also been extended to convey directionality with respect to an inside point (as in 26b).

(26) a. *nyaruqunimek, kerl naniip.. nyilunas mramaqiamek, nyaruqun*
*nya=ruqun=i-**mek**,* *kerl* *nani=ip..*
2SG.SBJ=sit.NCONT.FUT=AWAY-down DEONT can=PURP
nyi=lu-nas *met=a=ma-ki=a-**mek**,*
2SG.SBJ.NPST=see.NCONT-self in=NM=thingy-SG.F=DIR-down
nya=ruqun
2SG.SBJ=sit.NCONT.FUT
'sit down (on the ground), you can then.. see yourself in the thingy (camera) down there (on the ground), sit' (C12VARPLAY-440)

b. *nyitat naimek, namabiki*
nyi=tat *ne=i-**mek**,*
2SG.SBJ.NPST=take.CONT from/with=AWAY-down
ne=ama=bik-ki
from/with=ART=bag-SG.F
'pick them from inside, from the bag' (LONGYDS20150516_1-132)

In this context, *mek* contrasts with *manep*, which also conveys a direction down a slope or an axis, but without entailing an endpoint. Compare (27a) and (27b). Both examples describe a falling event down a vertical axis, but they differ in that *manep* focuses on the direction: (27a) is a typical description of a picture that depicts a boy and a dog in mid-air, just having fallen off a cliff (and not yet having reached the ground). By contrast, *mek* focuses on the endpoint of the direction: (27b) describes a picture of a beehive that had just fallen from a tree and landed on the ground, where it got broken.

(27) a. *daqamit kaarimanep*
de=ka=mit *ka=at=i-**manep***
CONJ=3SG.M.SBJ=go.NCONT.PST 3SG.M.SBJ=fall.NCONT=AWAY-down
'and it falls down' (R12ADNFROG-259)
b. *amahlang araavetki, beqiaaramek, de biny menaqi*
ama=slanga *araa=avet-ki,*
ART=bee 3PL.POSS=house-SG.F
*be=kia=at=a-**mek**,* *de* *biny* *men-ki*
CONJ=3SG.F.SBJ=fall.NCONT=DIR-down CONJ break at-3SG.F
'the hive of the bees, it fell down (to the ground), and it got broken' (R12BCSFROG-058)

The same contrast is attested when expressing a direction down a slope, usually in large-scale geographical space (as in 28a and 28b). The distribution of the two forms differs in that *manep* focuses again on the directionality (as in 28a), while *mek* focuses on the endpoint of the direction (as in 28b). This difference is also illustrated in (28c) where the speaker first uses *manep* (to indicate directionality) and then *mek* (to emphasize the endpoint of the direction).

(28) a. *kua nyinyim sagel lungera imanep?*
kua *nyi=nyim* *se=gel* *lu-nget-a*
INTRG 2SG.SBJ.NPST=look.NCONT to/with=near DEM-N-DIST
*i-**manep**?*
AWAY-down
'do you see those ones on their way down (down the mountains, in the direction of the valley)?' (LONGYJL20150805_2-017)
b. *uriaqiamek pramaluqupki, dangerlking, maqamanaqam*
*ure-ia-ki=a-**mek*** *pet=ama=luqup-ki,*
1PL.POSS-other-SG.F=DIR-down on/under=ART=place-SG.F
de=a=ngerlking, *ma=qamanaqam*
CONJ=NM=coast ART.ID=NAME
'our fellow (place) down, the place (at) the coast, Kamanakam' (I12ABLAJLATASOCIO3-045)

c. *nyirimanep sasamek*
*nyi=it=i-**manep*** *sese=a-**mek***
2SG.SBJ.NPST=go.NCONT.FUT=AWAY-down to/with:REDUP=DIR-down
'you go down (the slope), to/until (you are) down (at the hut)'
(LONGYDS20150601_1-095)

The form *manep* is also used in small-scale space whenever the direction is down a slope (as in 29). In this context, *mek* would always convey direction down the vertical axis, towards the ground – not down a slope (as in 25a above).

(29) *rlu sanyiimanep, nakarl sanyiimanep*
rlu *se-nyi=i-**manep**,* *naka=rlu* *se-nyi=i-**manep***
move to/with-2SG=AWAY-down bit=move to/with-2SG=AWAY-down
'move down, move down a bit' (C12VARPLAY-579)

In addition, the form *mek*, but not *manep*, is used in directions towards an intrinsic (i.e., bottom or lower) part of a referent. This use is illustrated in (30). Presumably, the lower part of the referent is conceptualized as an endpoint.

(30) *de nyikuav amek dais, de nyikerltep*
de *nyi=kuap* *a-**mek*** *de=a-is,*
CONJ 2SG.SBJ.NPST=tie.CONT DIR-down LOC.PART-3SG.M.POSS-end
de *nyi=kerltep*
CONJ 2SG.SBJ.NPST=strengthen.CONT
'and you tie/knit it down towards its bottom [i.e., the bottom of a netbag], and you make it strong' (P12ARSBILUM3L-028)

In this last context, there is overlap with *mani*, which exclusively occurs in reference to intrinsic parts of a referent. It is either concerned with the orientation of the referent (as in 25c above, where an upright referent is put on its side), or it expresses directionality to the lower part of a referent. This form is attested in both large-scale space (e.g., with reference to the lower part of a garden in 31a) and small-scale space (e.g., with reference to the writing at the bottom part of a picture in 31b). Note that *mani* has given rise to the topological adverb *temani* 'underneath' (see section 6.2). It is likely that the semantics of *mani*, as expressing direction towards an intrinsic part of a whole, has facilitated the development of a topological semantics. In fact, it is not uncommon for the directional and the adverb to co-occur (as in 31c).

(31) a. *tika nguamama.. amarluimirang maamani*
tika *ngua=mu=ama..* *ama=rluim-irang* *maqa-**mani***
EMPH 1SG.SBJ=put.NCONT.PST=ART ART=child-PL.DIM HERE-down
'and I placed the.. the small small shoots (of taro plants) down (in the lower part of the garden)' (D12ADNGARDEN-012FF)

b. *tamungeranema, dap tail ngenama.. amalengirangamaniip nani..*
ta=mu=ngera=nem=a, *dap*
3PL.SBJ=put.NCONT.PST=3N.POSS=likeness=DIST but
ta=il *ngere-ne=ama..*
3PL.SBJ=write.NCONT 3N.ASSOC-from/with=ART
*ama=lengi-irang=a-**mani**=ip* *nani..*
ART=word-PL.DIM=DIR-down=PURP can
'they put up their pictures now, and they marked them together with.. the words down (at the pictures' bottom parts), so that..'
(I12AANACLADNSOCIO3-248)

c. *iang maamani, remani*
ia-nget *maqa-**mani**,* *temani*
other-N HERE-down underneath
'another one down here, underneath' (LONGYDS20150516_1-032)

(ii) Up: *vuk*, *pit* and *panu*

The three forms of the 'up' paradigm are *vuk*, *pit* and *panu*. The semantic distinctions in this paradigm partly (but not completely) mirror those of the 'down' paradigm. Most straightforwardly, *vuk* 'up' is the counterpart to *mek* 'down': it expresses an upward direction along a slope or vertical axis, entailing an endpoint. In this case, the typical endpoint is any kind of top level, e.g., the top of a tree (in 32a) or upriver to the source of a river (in 32b). It is also the neutral way to express directions towards houses (as in 32c). Normally, houses are built on posts, i.e., they are raised above the ground. But in present-day Qaqet, *vuk* 'up' is used in directions towards all kinds of houses, irrespective of their actual level.

(32) a. *keksik bqeksik, beip saivuk*
ke=ksik *be=ke=ksik,*
3SG.M.SBJ.NPST=climb.CONT CONJ=3SG.M.SBJ.NPST=climb.CONT
be=ip *se=i-**vuk***
CONJ=PURP to/with=AWAY-up
'he is climbing and climbing, until (he reaches) up there'
(N12AMVGENAINGMETBROTHERS-058)

b. *sagel verlsperls namakainaqi maqavuk*
se=gel *verlsperls* *ne=ama=kaina-ki*
to/with=near part.NCONT:REDUP from/with=ART=water-SG.F
*maqa-**vuk***
HERE-up
'to near (the place where) the rivers part up here' (N11AAGBROTHERS-0044)

c. *undit savuk, sep maavetki*
un=tit *se=a-**vuk**,* *se=pe* *ma=avet-ki*
1DU.SBJ=go.CONT to/with=DIR-up to/with=PLACE ART.ID=house-SG.F
'let's go up, to the house' (N11AJNGENAINGMETSIQI-0107)

The other two forms, *pit* and *panu*, do not entail an endpoint. Most commonly, speakers resort to *pit* to convey directionality without an endpoint (as in 33a and 33b).

(33) a. *dap mamenggaa, deqa.. kamit saivit*
dap *ma=meng-ka=a,* *de=ka..* *ka=mit*
but ART.ID=wood-SG.M=DIST CONJ=3SG.M.SBJ 3SG.M.SBJ=go.NCONT.PST
*se=i-**pit***
to/with=AWAY-up
'but the tree now, it.. it went up (high)' (N11AJNGENAINGMETSIQI-0014)

b. *uanang ivit, nagelki*
uan=ang *i-**pit**,* *ne=gel-ki*
2DU.SBJ=walk.NCONT AWAY-up from/with=near-3SG.F
'walk up, (walk away) from her' (LONGYDS20150516_2-042)

The form *panu* is infrequent. In present-day Qaqet, it almost exclusively occurs with referents in mid-air (as in 34a). In addition, there are occasional examples such as (34b), which was used to describe the picture of a boy in the process of climbing a stone. It is thus possible that *panu* originally expressed direction up a slope or axis without an endpoint (which may or may not have been in mid-air), but that this original semantics shifted towards directions into mid-air.

(34) a. *dav aadangga, deqatika qemnyim sagelaviap ngatit pevanu*
dap *aa=dang-ka,* *de=ka=tika*
but 3SG.M.POSS=dog-SG.M CONJ=3SG.M.SBJ=EMPH
ke=mnyim *se=gel-ap=i=ap*
3SG.M.SBJ.NPST=look.CONT to/with=near-PL.RCD=SIM=PL.RCD
nga=tit *pe=**panu***
3N.SBJ=go.CONT PLACE=up
'and his dog, he is looking at them (bees) moving up (in the air)' (R12ACMFROG-036)

b. *kataqatmiravanu, dap madul..*
*ka=taqa=tmit=a-**panu**,* *dap* *ma=dul..*
3SG.M.SBJ=properly.CONT=C.go=DIR-up but ART.ID=stone
'he is carefully moving up, and it's a stone..' (R12ADNFROG-198)

In addition, two of the forms (*vuk* and *pit*) are used for directions towards an intrinsic (i.e., top or upper) part of a referent, e.g., the top part of a netbag (in 35a) or the top part of a plant (in 35b). The examples below illustrate this use for both *vuk* (in 35a) and *pit* (in 35b).

(35) a. *dip nyimsem praqaivuk*
dip *nyi=msem* *pet-ka=i-**vuk***
FUT 2SG.SBJ.NPST=weave.CONT on/under-3SG.M=AWAY-up
'you will weave it up (to the top of the netbag)' (P12ARSBILUM3L-055)
b. *nyaramaqeravit, demaningaqa*
*nya=rat=ama=qet=a-**pit**,* *de=ma=ninga-ka*
2SG.SBJ=take.NCONT.FUT=ART=thingy=DIR-up CONJ=ART.ID=head-SG.M
'take the upper thingy, the head [i.e., the top of the greens]'
(LONGYDS20150506_1-169)

The directional *pit* is furthermore used to express the upright orientation of a referent (as in 36). In this interpretation, *pit* distributes differently from the other directionals: it cannot be marked with any of the directional prefixes (see section 6.3.2), and it is possible that the directional *pit* 'up' is developing into an adverb *pit* 'upright' in this context.

(36) *serl vraus pit*
serl *pet-es* ***pit***
straighten on/under-SG.FLAT up
'it (the branch) got straightened up(right)' (N11AJNGENAINGMETBROTHERS-0148)

(iii) Across: *muk, mit* and *manu*

The three forms of the 'across' paradigm are *muk, mit* and *manu*. The form *muk* is the counterpart to *mek* 'down' and *vuk* 'up', as it expresses a direction that entails an end-point. As is the case in the other two paradigms, this direction can be in small-scale space along a horizontal axis, e.g., across a room (in 37a) or across from one tree to another (as in 37b). Or it can be in large-scale space, e.g., across a river (as in 37c) or across a landscape (as in 37d).

(37) a. *ngenang ngentlaqamuk ngenamabiibiqi*
ngen=ang *ngen=talak=a-**muk***
2PL.SBJ=walk.NCONT 2PL.SBJ=play.CONT=DIR-across
ngene-ne=ama=biibi-ki
2PL.ASSOC-from/with=ART=baby-SG.F
'go and play across (the room) with the baby' (LONGYDS20150517_1-184)

b. *deiva, daqatit praus, besaimuk, savramagalipkaalang*
de=ip=a, *de=ka=tit* *pet-es,*
CONJ=PURP=DIST CONJ=3SG.M.SBJ=go.CONT on/under-SG.FLAT
*be=se=i-**muk**,*
CONJ=to/with=AWAY-across
se=pet=ama=galip-ka=aa=lang
to/with=on/under=ART=galipnut-SG.M=3SG.M.POSS=top
'and then, he was going onto the flat one (branch), to across, onto the branches of the galipnut tree' (N11AJNGENAINGMETBROTHERS-0094FF)

c. *dap kurliqiamuq iqingingarl*
dap *kurli-ki=a-**muk*** *i=ki=ngingarl*
but leave-3SG.F=DIR-across SIM=3SG.F.SBJ.NPST=difficult.CONT:??
'but she stays across (the river) because she finds it too difficult (to follow him)' (N11AAGSIRINIROPE-0085)

d. *sirini qatit besamuk, savramaluqup*
sirini *ka=tit* *be=se=a-**muk**,*
NAME 3SG.M.SBJ=go.CONT CONJ=to/with=DIR-across
se=pet=ama=luqup
to/with=on/under=ART=place
'Sirini went across (the valley), to the place' (N11AAGSIRINILOBSTER2-0001)

The form *manu*, is used in similar contexts, but does not entail an endpoint, as illustrated in (38a) and (38b).

(38) a. *deip ma, diandiramanu, ianekiarl*
de=ip *maget,* *de=ian=tit=a-**manu**,*
CONJ=PURP then CONJ=3DU.SBJ=go.CONT=DIR-across
iane=kiarl
3DU.SBJ.NPST=paddle.CONT
'and then, they set off across (the ocean) and they keep paddling' (N12BAMCAT-134)

b. *nyit saqi maamanu, nyit*
nyi=it *se-ki* *maqa-**manu**,*
2SG.SBJ.NPST=go.NCONT.FUT to/with-3SG.F HERE-across
nyi=it
2SG.SBJ.NPST=go.NCONT.FUT
'go across with it, go' (LONGYJL20150805_2-245)

The form *mit* is only attested very infrequently in the corpus, always referring to intrinsic parts of a whole (as in 39a). In this context, it overlaps with the use of *muk* (as in 39b).

(39) a. *deng naqiamit, prama kautkaarlim*
deng *ne-ki=a-**mit**,* *pet=ama*
stop from/with-3SG.F=DIR-across on/under=ART
kaut-ka=aa=rlim
bamboo-SG.M=3SG.M.POSS=bottom
'it stops across (at the side part), at the bottom of the bamboo' (LONGYJL20150805_2-632)

b. *nyitaneng amuk*
nyi=taneng *a-**muk***
2SG.SBJ.NPST=hold.CONT DIR-across
'hold it across (at the side part)' (LONGYDS20150517_1-557)

More generally, the 'across' paradigm has also acquired a non-directional sense of 'over here, over there'. The form *muk* is used in all cases where the actual direction is not important (as in 40a), including in non-spatial contexts (as in 40b). And the form *manu* conveys the distributed notion of 'everywhere' (as in 40c).

(40) a. *saini ngeresiit naqa maamuk*
sa=ini *ngere=siit* *ne-ka* *maqa-**muk***
already=SG.DIM 3N.SBJ.NPST=story from/with-3SG.M HERE-across
'immediately, the little one will tell it over here (lit. across)' (I12AANACLADNSOCIO3-334)

b. *de raimuk, dluqia rarlan*
de *ta=i-**muk**,* *de=lu-ki-a* *ara=rlan*
CONJ 3PL.H=AWAY-across LOC.PART=DEM-SG.F-DIST 3SG.F.POSS=inside
'and they (the names of spirits) go there (lit. across), inside that (category)' (D12ADKSPIRITS-105)

c. *nani aarluavik tenyan temga maamanu*

nani	*aa=rlua-pik*	*te=nyan*	*te-ka*
can	3SG.M.POSS=friend-COLL.H	3PL.SBJ.NPST=laugh.NCONT	PURP-3SG.M
*maqa-**manu***			
HERE-across			

'his friends can laugh at him everywhere (lit. across)'
(I12ABLAJLATASocio3-164)

6.3.2 The directional prefixes

The directionals are almost always preceded by directional prefixes. The only two exceptions are *pit* in its non-directional use of 'upright' (see section 6.3.1) and *panu* 'up' when following certain prepositions (see section 6.3.3). Otherwise, a prefix is obligatory.

The prefixes are summarized in Table 72. They can only co-occur with directionals, and they are mostly mutually exclusive. The only exception is *na-* 'BACK', which is obligatorily preceded by either *a-* 'DIR' or *i-* 'AWAY'. From a comparative perspective, there are two prefixes that are shared by Qaqet and Mali (both in form and meaning), while other prefixes are attested in one of the languages only.

This section introduces the prefixes in the following order: (i) the prefixes *a-* 'DIR' and *i-* 'AWAY', (ii) the prefix combinations with *na-* 'BACK', and (iii) the prefixes *ma(q)a-* 'HERE' and *miasi-* 'THERE'.

Tab. 72: The directional prefixes

Qaqet	Mali (Stebbins 2011: 194–197)	Gloss	Meaning
a-	–	DIR	neutral
i-	*i-*	AWAY	away from deictic center
na-	*na-*	BACK	reversal of direction on a return trajectory
–	*tə-*	–	in the general vicinity
ma(q)a-	–	HERE	proximal to deictic center
miasi	–	THERE	distal from deictic center

(i) Prefixes *a-* 'DIR' and *i-* 'AWAY'

The prefixes *a-* 'DIR' and *i-* 'AWAY' are the most common directional prefixes: they are by far the most frequent prefixes, and they can occur with any of the directionals. The prefix *a-* 'DIR' is neutral, while *i-* 'AWAY' entails a direction away from the deictic center.

Speakers commonly use the prefix *i-* 'AWAY' when the deictic center is the here and now of the speech situation (as in 41a), including the here and now of reported speech (as in 41b). But it is also possible to assign the deictic center to a third person (as in 41c).

(41) a. *nguamatnadem **i**manu*
ngua=matnadem ***i**-manu*
1SG.SBJ=work.NCONT.PST:RECP:LOC.PART AWAY-across
'I continued planting across (away from where you and I are now)' (D12ADNGARDEN-074)

b. *daqatuqun nluraamek ma, ngenahrlika**i**manep*
de=ka=tuqun *ne=lu-ta-a=a-mek*
CONJ=3SG.M.SBJ=say.CONT from/with=DEM-PL.H-DIST=DIR-down
ma, *ngena=sirlik-ka=**i**-manep*
thus 2PL.POSS=meat-SG.M=AWAY-down
'and he was saying to those ones down (at the bottom of the tree) like this, your prey is on its way down (away from me)' (N11AAGSIRINILOBSTER2-0075)

c. *iqitaqena, de quasiqi qurlama.. amaqasupki**i**muk*
i=ki=taqen=a, *de* *kuasik=i* *kurli=ama..*
SIM=3SG.F.SBJ.NPST=say.CONT=DIST CONJ NEG=SIM leave=ART
*ama=qasup-ki=**i**-muk*
ART=rat-SG.F=AWAY-across
'she was talking now, but the.. the rat wasn't staying across (away from her)' (N12BAMCAT-311FF)

In all cases, speakers have a choice as to whether or not to frame a situation deictically. For example, when giving instructions to a second person, speakers would most frequently choose a deictic perspective (as in 42a), but this is not obligatory (as in 42b). The examples were uttered in identical contexts: a mother sitting next to her child, and instructing her to put small objects down onto the ground, i.e., arguably away from the deictic center in both cases.

(42) a. *nyatunger**i**mek, dengentlak*
*nya=tu-nget=**i**-mek,* *de=ngen=talak*
2SG.SBJ=put.CONT-3N=AWAY-down CONJ=2PL.SBJ=play.CONT
'put them down (away from us), and you all play' (C12VARPLAY-007)

b. *nyatunger**a**mek*
*nya=tu-nget=**a**-mek*
2SG.SBJ=put.CONT-3N=DIR-down
'put them down' (C12YMMZJIPLAY1-410)

Conversely, speakers preferably use a non-deictic perspective in contexts where both the speaker and the addressee are moving together (as in 43a) – but again this is not obligatory (as in 43b). In both examples, the deictic center is identical (the current place of the speakers), and the movement is away to some other place. In (43a), the speaker chooses not to focus on the deictic information, and – as the continuation of the utterance indicates – focuses instead on the path downwards. In (43b), by contrast, the speaker chooses to present a deictic point of view, emphasizing that the movement is away from the current deictic center.

(43) a. *utir**a**manep, de ma*
*ut=tit=**a**-manep,* *de* *ma*
1PL.SBJ=go.CONT=DIR-down CONJ thus
'we go down, like this [indicating the path]' (LONGYDS20150802_2-055)

b. *ee, bigia de utir**i**manev, ivurlotu*
ee, *bigia* *de* *ut=tit=**i**-manep,*
yes tomorrow CONJ 1PL.SBJ=go.CONT=AWAY-down
ip=ure=lotu
PURP=1PL.SBJ.NPST=pray
'yes, tomorrow we go down, and we will pray' (LONGYDS20150516_1-571)

Similarly, if the context involves third persons, it is more common for speakers to choose the neutral perspective (as in 44a and 44b) – but, again, the deictic perspective is possible, too (as in 44c). In (44a), both protagonists go down together, i.e., there is no obvious deictic center available, although it would have been possible to designate the current location as deictic center (as was done in 43b above). In (44b) and (44c), by contrast, one of the protagonists is moving away from the other, i.e., the speakers could have easily chosen a deictic perspective: they did so in (44c), but not in (44b).

(44) a. *iandit s**a**mek*
ian=tit *se=**a**-mek*
3DU.SBJ=go.CONT to/with=DIR-down
'they are going down' (N12BAMCAT-127)

b. *katira s**a**muqi.. iqawinim nluqai.. iqavlengga*
ka=tit=a *se=**a**-muk=i..* *i=ka=winim*
3SG.M.SBJ=go.CONT=DIST to/with=DIR-across=SIM SIM=3SG.M.SBJ=win
ne=lu-ka-a=i.. *i=ka=vleng-ka*
from/with=DEM-SG.M-DIST=SIM SIM=3SG.M.SBJ=kill.NCONT-3SG.M
'he was going now across because.. because he won against that one and.. and he killed him' (N11AAGSIRINILOBSTER1-0093)

c. *deiva, damaqasupka qaman saimek*
de=ip=a, de=ama=qasup-ka ka=man
CONJ=PURP=DIST CONJ=ART=rat-SG.M 3SG.M.SBJ=go.in.NCONT.PST
*se=**i**-mek*
to/with=AWAY-down
'and then the rat is going down (away from the cat)' (N12BAMCAT-188)

Given that Qaqet has a dedicated prefix *i-* 'AWAY' for expressing direction away from the deictic center, *a-* 'DIR' is the only available choice in contexts where a direction happens to be towards the deictic center, most notably in contexts of taking and receiving (as in 45). But as shown by (42b) and (43a) above, it also occurs in contexts where the direction is not towards the deictic center, i.e., a deictic interpretation of *a-* 'DIR' is always a contextual interpretation, and is not entailed by its semantics. In fact, directions towards the deictic center are rarely expressed by means of directionals. This shows especially in the observation that there are no attested co-occurrences of directionals with the deictic verbs *an* 'come' and *men* 'come': they would be incompatible with the semantics of *i-* 'AWAY', but not with that of *a-* 'DIR'. By contrast, directionals with either prefix are frequently attested following *mit* 'go' (as in 43 and 44 above).

(45) *nyitramaplaua **a**manep*
*nyi=tat=ama=plaua **a**-manep*
2SG.SBJ.NPST=take.CONT=ART=flower DIR-down
'pick the flowers (from) down' (LONGYDS20150802_2-184)

(ii) Prefix combinations *a-na-* 'DIR-BACK' and *i-na-* 'AWAY-BACK'

Another directional prefix, *na-* 'BACK', is only attested in combination with *a-* 'DIR' (as in 46a) and *i-* 'AWAY' (as in 46b), occurring exclusively with the set of directionals that entails an endpoint (i.e., *mek* 'down', *vuk* 'up', and *muk* 'across').

(46) a. *dav aarluaqa, de anameq iqepalui qatit daqa..*
*dap aa=rlua-ka, de a-**na**-mek*
but 3SG.M.POSS=friend-SG.M CONJ DIR-BACK-down
i=ke=palu=i ka=tit de=ka..
SIM=3SG.M.SBJ.NPST=slow.CONT=SIM 3SG.M.SBJ=go.CONT CONJ=3SG.M.SBJ
'and his friend, (moving) back up (lit. back from down), he is moving slowly and he..' (N11AAGBROTHERS-0046)

b. *ngeneiarlet merama abiki inamek*
*ngene=iarlet met=ama a=bik-ki i-**na**-mek*
2PL.SBJ.NPST=pull.NCONT in=ART NM=bag-SG.F AWAY-BACK-down
'pull the bag back up (lit. back from down)' (AJS-04/06/2015)

The prefix *na-* 'BACK' reverses the direction expressed in the directional, and at the same time entails that this reverse direction is a return trajectory. The first meaning component can be clearly seen in (46a) and (46b) above: despite the use of *mek* 'down' in both examples, the direction is upwards (i.e., from downwards). It is even possible that *na-* 'BACK' is diachronically related to the preposition *ne* 'from/with', which can introduce directionals (see section 6.3.3) and which expresses a source reading. As illustrated in (47a), its use conveys that the trajectory is away from the direction expressed by the directional, i.e., its interpretation is very similar to that of the prefix *na-* 'BACK'. But while their interpretations are similar, they are not identical. Their difference shows when they co-occur with the deictic prefix *i-* 'AWAY'. In the case of the preposition *ne* 'from/with', the deictic center is the source of the trajectory – e.g., the deictic center in (47a) is the upwards place. In the case of *na-* 'BACK', by contrast, the deictic center is the goal of the trajectory. As such, this form invariably confers a deictic interpretation onto the predicate (as illustrated in 47b, where *it* 'go' receives a 'come' interpretation).

In addition to this difference in interpretation, there are formal reasons for considering *na-* 'BACK' and *ne* 'from/with' to be separate forms synchronically: they occur in different positions (only *na-* 'BACK' can follow the prefixes *a-* 'DIR' and *i-* 'AWAY'), with different directionals (the use of *na-* 'BACK' is restricted to the set of directionals that entails an endpoint), and in different paradigmatic oppositions (only *ne* 'from/with' is opposed to *se* 'to/with').

(47) a. *kirekmet nemajohn, beqamit kaat naivuk*
ki=rekmet *ne=ma=john,*
3SG.F.SBJ.NPST=do.NCONT:IN from/with=ART.ID=NAME
be=ka=mit *ka=at*
CONJ=3SG.M.SBJ=go.NCONT.PST 3SG.M.SBJ=fall.NCONT
ne=i-vuk
from/with=AWAY-up
'she made John fall down (i.e., fall from up, away from the deictic center)' (R12ABDFROG-098)

b. *nyirinavuk*
*nyi=it=**i-na-vuk***
2SG.SBJ.NPST=go.NCONT.FUT=AWAY-BACK-up
'come back down (i.e., go from up, away to the deictic center)' (LONGYDS20150531_1-292)

The second meaning component of *na-* 'BACK', return to a previous direction, is illustrated with the examples below. The first example features two sentences from a narrative where a protagonist instructs a *levung* tree to lean across to a galipnut tree (so that he can then climb across and harvest the galipnuts). In his first instruction to the tree, the speaker chooses the directional *a-manu* 'DIR-across' (in 48-1). Following this instruction, the tree leans across, the protagonist climbs across, and the tree straightens up again. When the protagonist has finished harvesting the nuts, he instructs the tree a second time – but this time, the speakers chooses to mark the directional with *na-* 'BACK' (in 48-2), indicating that the tree should retrace its previous trajectory.

(48) 1. *kua magrip, ip nyirasamanu, savramagalipkaalang? (...)*
*kua maget=ip, ip nyi=ras=**a-manu**,*
INTRG then=PURP PURP 2SG.SBJ.NPST=lie.NCONT.FUT=DIR-across
se=pet=ama=galip-ka=aa=lang?
to/with=on/under=ART=galipnut-SG.M=3SG.M.POSS=top
'now then, will you lean across, to the top of the galipnut tree? (...)' (N11AJNGENAINGMETBROTHERS-0090)

2. *kua magrip, nyirasinamuk?*
*kua maget=ip, nyi=ras=**i-na-muk**,*
INTRG then=PURP 2SG.SBJ.NPST=lie.NCONT.FUT=AWAY-BACK-across
'now then, will you lean back across (away from across, to me, where you were before)?' (N11AJNGENAINGMETBROTHERS-0137)

A similar return trajectory is conveyed by the following, elicited, example: first *i-pit* 'AWAY-up' conveys an upward direction, and then *i-na-vuk* 'AWAY-BACK-up' conveys the reverse downward direction, returning back down from up.

(49) *amarluis tatrenas ivir inavuk*
*ama=rluis ta=trenas **i-pit** **i-na-vuk***
ART=child 3PL.SBJ=jump.CONT:SELF AWAY-up AWAY-BACK-up
'the children are jumping up and down' (AJS-11/06/2015)

(iii) Prefixes *maqa-* ~ *maa-* 'HERE' and *miasi-* 'THERE'

Finally, there are two directional prefixes that specify the endpoint of the direction as being either proximal to the deictic center (*maqa* ~ *maa-* 'HERE') or distal to it (*miasi-* 'THERE').

It is possible that these two prefixes are diachronically multimorphemic, containing a prefix consonant *m-* plus another, possibly adverbial, form. Such an origin is suggested by the prefix *miasi-* 'THERE', which has an adverbial counterpart *iasi* 'DIST'. Both the directional prefix and the adverbial can precede a directional, conveying similar interpretations: *miasi-* 'THERE' is prefixed to the directional (as in 50a), and *iasi* 'DIST' is cliticized to the entire directional word, consisting of a directional prefix and a directional root (as in 50b).

(50) a. *naka nyurlu sanget miasivuq inani ngerrat mara*

naka	*nyi=rlu*	*se-nget*	***miasi**-vuk*	*i=nani*
bit	2SG.SBJ.NPST=throw	to/with-3N	THERE-up	SIM=can

ngere=rat	*mara*
3N.SBJ.NPST=fall.CONT	here

'move them (the legs) up there a bit, so they (the sticks) can be falling here' (C12VARPLAY-174)

b. *deip maget, deiviasiivuk, deqans*

de=ip	*maget,*	*de=ip=**iasi**=i-vuk,*
CONJ=PURP	then	CONJ= PURP=DIST=AWAY-up

de=ka=nes
CONJ=3SG.M.SBJ=shout.NCONT

'and then, (going) up there (into the branches), he shouted' (N11AAGSIRINILOBSTER1-0059)

In the case of *maqa- ~ maa-* 'HERE', there is no adverbial counterpart. Semantically, the closest adverb is *mara* 'here': despite some similarity in form, there are no attested cases of *q* ([ɣ]) being an allophone of *r*, and there is thus no reason to consider these two forms related. But similar to their distal counterparts, both the proximal prefix (as in 51a) and the proximal adverb (as in 51b) occur preceding directionals. There are even examples, where adverb and prefix both co-occur (as in 51c).

(51) a. *sagel verlsperls namakainaqi maqavuk*

se=gel	*verlsperls*	*ne=ama=kaina-ki*
to/with=near	part.NCONT:REDUP	from/with=ART=water-SG.F

***maqa**-vuk*
HERE-up

'to near (the place where) the rivers part up here' (N11AAGBROTHERS-0044)

b. *aremam maraavuk, kenamagilka maraavuk*

are-mam	***mara**=a-vuk,*
3SG.F.POSS-father	here=DIR-up

ke-ne=ama=gil-ka	***mara**=a-vuk*
3SG.M.ASSOC-from/with=ART=small-SG.M	here=DIR-up

'her father up here, together with the little one up here' (R12ATAFROG-219)

c. *sa quasiqaqi mara maamek*

sa	*kuasik-ki*	***mara***	***maqa**-mek*
already	NEG-3SG.F	here	HERE-down

'she isn't down here now' (R12ATAFROG-055)

I assume that *maqa-* and *maa-* 'HERE' convey equivalent, or even identical, meanings. There are a number of cases where speakers repeat an instruction to a child, first using one form, and then the other (as in 52). Such partial repetitions, so-called variation sets (a term coined by Küntay and Slobin 1996), are a common phenomenon in child-directed speech in many languages, including Qaqet. They serve a communicative function, as caregivers produce them in order to "attract and hold the child's attention until some kind of desired response is produced – either an action or a verbalization" (Küntay & Slobin 2002: 8). As such, the forms used in variation sets cannot be interpreted as self-repairs, but rather as conveying equivalent meanings.

(52)
1. *nyiraarl* ***maa****mek*
   nyi=raarl ***maqa****-mek*
   2SG.SBJ.NPST=stand.NCONT.FUT HERE-down
   'stand down here' (LONGYDS20150802_2-231)
2. *nyiraarl* ***maqa****mek*
   nyi=raarl ***maqa****-mek*
   2SG.SBJ.NPST=stand.NCONT.FUT HERE-down
   'stand down here' (LONGYDS20150802_2-234)

The factors determining the choice of *maqa-* or *maa-* 'HERE' are not entirely clear. In some contexts, no conditioning factor was found and they seem to be in free variation. This is the case whenever they precede a directional that entails an endpoint (i.e., *mek* 'down', *vuk* 'up', and *muk* 'across'), as in (52) above. With all other directionals, only *maa-* 'HERE' is attested (as in 53).[37]

(53) *saqika guiang* ***maa****mit*
saqi-ka *gu-ia-nget* ***maqa****-mit*
again-3SG.M 1SG.POSS-other-N HERE-across
'and again, my other (gardens) here across' (D12ADNGARDEN-068)

6.3.3 Prepositions introducing directionals

Directionals can occur on their own (as the second directional *vuk* 'up' in 54), or they can be introduced by a preposition (as the first directional *mek* 'down' in 54).

37 In Mali Baining, a form *mo* is an allomorph of the preposition *na* 'from' when preceding disyllabic directionals starting in *m* (Stebbins 2011: 196–197). But it is unlikely that Qaqet *maqa-* ~ *maa-* 'HERE' is related to Mali *mo* 'from': the Qaqet form does not have a source reading; and it is attested with all directionals, independent of their syllabic and segmental structure. Conversely, all directionals can be introduced by the Qaqet preposition *ne* 'from/with'.

(54) *iandit samek, biandianaquvangivuk*
ian=tit ***se=a-mek,***
3DU.SBJ=go.CONT to/with=DIR-down
*be=ian=tu=iana=quvang=**i-vuk***
CONJ=3DU.SBJ=put.CONT=3DU.POSS=cargo=AWAY-up
'they are going down (to the beach), and they are putting their cargo up (into the boat)' (N12BAMCAT-127)

The combinatorial possibilities are restricted. Only the prepositions *se* 'to/with' (as in 55a and 55b) and *ne* 'from/with' (as in 56a and 56b) can productively introduce a directional. Furthermore, they can only introduce directionals prefixed by *a-* 'DIR' (as in 55a and 56a) or *i-* 'AWAY' (as in 55b and 56b).

(55) a. *dianmit savuk*
de=ian=mit ***se=a-vuk***
CONJ=3DU.SBJ=go.NCONT.PST to/with=DIR-up
'and they went up' (N12BAMCAT-119)
b. *bqasik saivuk*
be=ka=sik ***se=i-vuk***
CONJ=3SG.M.SBJ=climb.NCONT to/with=AWAY-up
'and he climbed up' (R12ABDFROG-078)

(56) a. *kamrenas navuk*
ka=mrenas ***ne=a-vuk***
3SG.M.SBJ=jump.NCONT.PST:SELF from/with=DIR-up
'he jumped down (lit. from up)' (N11AAGSIRINIROPE-0072)
b. *ngua.. tiak naivuk*
ngua.. tu=ia-ka ***ne=i-vuk***
1SG.SBJ put.CONT=other-SG.M from/with=AWAY-up
'I.. put another one down (lit. from up)' (D12ADKSPIRITS-038)

The resulting expressions have a straightforward compositional semantics, combining the spatial goal or source semantics of the preposition (see chapter 5.3.3 for details on their semantics and distribution) with the deictic semantics of the directional prefix and the directional semantics of the directional.

Phonologically, the prepositions are tightly integrated with the directionals: they always form a single phonological word, and the vowels of the preposition and the prefix fuse and are uttered short. As discussed in chapter 5.3.1, the prepositions *se* (i.e., /sə/) 'to/with' and *ne* (i.e., /nə/) 'from/with' have the allomorphs *sa* and *na* respectively, which surface in specific contexts. It is likely that it is these allomorphs that also occur preceding the directionals. The evidence comes from contexts where the prepositions precede the prefix *i-* 'AWAY', e.g. *saivuk* 'to up' (in 55b) and *naivuk* 'from up' (in 56b). These sequences are invariably realized as [se] (i.e., [seβuk] in 55b) and [ne] (i.e., [neβuk] in 56b). As discussed in chapter 2.1.2, a mid front vowel can arise from an underlying /ai/, but not from an underlying /əi/. In the latter case, we would have instead expected the realizations [si] (i.e., [siβuk] in 55b) and [ni] (i.e., [niβuk] in 56b). Assuming that the prepositions occur as *sa* and *na* would thus explain the vowel quality. It does not, however, explain the short vowel: we would expect a long [ee] in this context (i.e., [seeβuk] in 55b, and [neeβuk] in 56b). Given their tight phonological integration, it is conceivable that vowel shortening has taken place. In the case of original **ai* sequences (as in 55b and 56b), the vowel quality is then the last trace of this original diphthong. In the case of original **aa* sequences (i.e., of *sa* or *na* preceding *a-* 'DIR', as in 55a and 56a), there is no longer any synchronic indication of this origin: the vowel is uttered as a short [a].

There is a small number of examples where the prepositions occur reduplicated when preceding a directional (as in 57). Note that this type of reduplication is not attested in non-directional prepositional phrases.

(57) *rlu sanyivit, sasavuk*
rlu *se-nyi=i-pit,* ***sese=a-vuk***
move to/with-2SG=AWAY-up to/with:REDUP=DIR-up
'move up, to up there' (LONGYDS20150516_1-742FF)

The prepositions *se* 'to/with' and *ne* 'from/with' are the only prepositions that productively introduce directionals. In addition, there are a few cases in the 'up' paradigm that allow for other prepositions.

The most salient case is the form *panu* 'up', with its lexicalized meaning of 'up in mid-air' (see section 6.3.1). It either occurs with a directional prefix (and without a preposition) (as in 48a) or with a preposition (and without a directional prefix). In the latter case, the preposition is either the simple preposition *pe* 'PLACE' (as in 58b) (see chapter 5.3.4) or the complex prepositions *sep* (from *se=pe* 'to/with=PLACE') (as in 58c) and ***nep*** (from *ne=pe* 'from/with=PLACE') (as in 58d) (see chapter 5.3.1). This pattern is restricted to *panu* – the other two forms of the 'up' paradigm, *vuk* and *pit*, are not attested in these contexts.

(58) a. *lungeraavanu*
*lu-nget-a=**a-panu***
DEM-N-DIST=DIR-up
'that one up there' (C12VARPLAY-570)

b. *kesnes pramabariqi vevanu*
ke=snes *pet=ama=bari-ki* ***pe=panu***
3SG.M.SBJ.NPST=shout.CONT on/under=ART=bee-SG.F PLACE=up
'he is shouting at the bees up there' (R12ACMFROG-045)

c. *dap.. luqimara diqimnyim sepanu samramamengga*
dap.. *lu-ki=mara* *de=ki=mnyim*
but DEM-SG.F=here CONJ=3SG.F.SBJ.NPST=look.CONT
se=pe=panu *se=met=ama=meng-ka*
to/with=PLACE=up to/with=in=ART=wood-SG.M
'but.. this one here is looking up into the tree' (R12ATAFROG-116)

d. *kiaat nepanu*
kia=at ***ne=pe=panu***
3SG.F.SBJ=fall.NCONT from/with=PLACE=up
'it fell downwards (from up)' (R12ATAFROG-134)

In addition, both *panu* 'up' and *pit* 'up' (but not *vuk* 'up') are frequently preceded by *paa* (as in 59a) or *maa* (as in 59b). These forms are presumably related to the preposition *pe* 'PLACE' and to the directional prefix *maqa-* ~ *maa-* 'HERE' respectively, but their realizations are unexpected: it is not possible to explain the long vowel in *paa*; and it is unclear why the intervocalic environment does not trigger the lenition of *p* (of *panu* and *pit*) to *v* (i.e., *vanu* and *vit*).

(59) a. *ee, saqika luqia* ***vaapir*** *amahlenggi, deip madraquarl luqiara*
ee, *saqi-ka* *lu-ki-a* ***pe=??=pit*** *ama=sleng-ki,*
yes again-SG.M DEM-SG.F-DIST PLACE=??=up ART=garden-SG.F
de=ip *maget=de=taquarl* *lu-ki-iara*
CONJ=PURP then=CONJ=thus DEM-SG.F-PROX
'yes, also that garden up there, it will be the same as this one' (D12AB-DACPGARDEN-059)

b. *nyinyim* ***maapit****, sagel amataipki*
nyi=nyim ***maqa-??-pit,*** *se=gel*
2SG.SBJ.NPST=look.NCONT HERE-??-up to/with=near
ama=taip-ki
ART=tape-SG.F
'look up here, to the tape' (LONGYDS20150506_1-723)

Finally, Qaqet has an adverb *temani* 'underneath', which may have originated in the preposition *te* 'PURP' plus the directional *mani* 'down' (see section 6.2). Alternatively, *te* could be the only remnant of the directional prefix *tə-* 'in the vicinity of', which is productive in Mali (Stebbins 2011: 195), but not attested in Qaqet.

6.4 Summary

This chapter has introduced three types of adverbials that function as peripheral constituents in a clause: relational nouns (section 6.1), adverbs (section 6.2) and directionals (section 6.3). A fourth type, prepositional phrases, was already discussed in chapter 5.3. All adverbials share the syntactic property of occurring in the right periphery of the clause (unless they are overtly marked prosodically or syntactically), but otherwise exhibit different morphosyntactic properties.

Relational nouns occur as non-obligatory elements in prepositional phrases, usually specifying a spatial search region. They originated in bodypart nouns functioning as possessed nouns in the possessive construction, and some of their morphosyntactic properties can be attributed to this origin. Synchronically, however, there are considerable morphosyntactic differences between relational nouns and possessed nouns, suggesting an on-going grammaticalization process towards a postpositional class.

Adverbs form a fairly small word class, conveying meanings of space, time and quantity. Synchronically, adverbs are monomorphemic, although many of them probably have a multimorphemic origin. They are defined as a word class entirely in syntactic terms, and as such are set apart from the class of particles (see chapter 7). Otherwise, there is considerable heterogeneity within the adverb class, as some adverbs exhibit additional morphosyntactic properties (including spatial adverbs, as well as individual adverbs modifying participants to an event).

Finally, there is a distinct class of directionals expressing the directions of 'down', 'up' and 'across'. They have a wider distribution than other adverbials, occurring not only in the right periphery of the clause, but also as modifiers to a noun and as predicates in non-verbal constructions. Morphologically, they invariably co-occur with a directional prefix, conveying deictic information.

The adverbials discussed in this chapter interact to some extent with prepositions. Relational nouns only ever occur within prepositional phrases. And spatial adverbs as well as directionals can occur as complements of the prepositions *se* 'to/with' and *ne* 'from/with', conveying goal and source readings respectively. Non-spatial adverbs cannot be introduced by these prepositions.

7 Particles

Particles play an important role in structuring Qaqet discourse, conveying modal, temporal and aspectual information, as well as information on discourse structure and speech acts. Typologically, many of these categories tend to be expressed by inflectional marking on the predicate, and all Qaqet particles can, indeed, operate over predicates. But all particles are optional and they can occur as propositions in their own right, thus differing from the inflectional categories marked on the Qaqet predicate itself (see chapter 5.4 for the inflectional categories).

The particles share formal and semantic similarities with the class of adverbs (see chapter 6.2 for a comparison). Formally, the members of both classes are synchronically non-inflecting and morphologically simple, although a diachronic origin of particles in verbs is visible in some optional and rudimentary inflectional possibilities. And semantically, both classes convey (amongst others) temporal and aspectual information. They differ in their syntactic distribution, though: adverbs occur in the right periphery of the clause, unless they are formally marked; while particles always occur in the left periphery, co-occurring in a fixed order.

Particles are an important feature of Mali Baining discourse, too (Stebbins 2011: 93–94, 218–229). The two languages express similar kinds of meanings in their particles, but they share surprisingly few forms. In some cases, a Qaqet particle is formally and semantically similar to a form of another word class in Mali: adverbs (Stebbins 2011: 66, 208–209, 217–218) and aspect and status markers (Stebbins 2011: 88–91, 209–216). Such (non-) correspondences suggest that the particles were grammaticalized from different sources – although the general category of particles is presumably inherited.

This chapter first presents an overview of the word class of particles (section 7.1), and then describes the individual particles, organized around semantic fields: modality (section 7.2), time (section 7.3), aspect (section 7.4), discourse structure (section 7.5) and speech acts (section 7.6). Section 7.7 introduces a number of other particles that cannot be subsumed under one of the other categories; and section 7.8 summarizes the discussion.

Note that the internal subdivision of particles is not straightforward. The subdivision adopted for Mali Baining (based on the form of the particles) does not apply to Qaqet. Similarly, a classification based on co-occurrence possibilities and/or positional slots cannot easily be implemented either. For their presentation in this chapter, I therefore adopt a semantic classification.

7.1 Morphosyntactic properties

All attested particles are listed in alphabetical order in Table 73, including information on their inflectional possibilities and on possibly cognate forms in Mali.

Tab. 73: Particles

Form	Gloss	Subject marking	cf. Mali forms
ani	maybe	–	–
arik	supposing	–	–
as	still	–	*as* 'still, yet'
deng	stop	–	–
dip	FUT	–	–
ide	IPFV	–	–
kaki	instead	–	–
kerl	DEONT	*kerl (=ka)*	–
kias	actually	*(ka=) kias (-ka)*	–
kiqerl	now	*(ka=) kiqerl (-ka)*	–
kua	INTRG	–	*kue* 'where'
kuasik	NEG	–	–
kui	quoting	–	–
kurli	leave	–	*kule* 'negative imperative'
kut	inferring	*kut (-ini)*	–
la	this.day	–	–
lira	(just) now	–	–
maget	then; right	–	–
mani	recently	–	*mali* 'earlier' (?)
manima	before.yesterday	–	–
masna	quickly	–	–
medu	past	–	*mēndu* 'before'
miaqas	occasionally	–	–
miika	more	–	–
miiki	instead	–	–
murl	distantly; suddenly	–	*mir* 'long ago'
naka	bit	–	–
nani	can	–	–
padi	hopefully.PST	–	*vandi* 'desiderative'
padip	hopefully.FUT	–	*vandi* 'desiderative'
perlset	finish	–	*sot* 'finish, perfective'

Form	Gloss	Subject marking	cf. Mali forms
pet	continuously	–	*pe* 'imperfective' (?)
petpet	frequently	–	–
qukun	(bit) later	–	–
sa	already	*(ka=)*[1] *sa*	*sa* 'new event frame'
saka	immediately	*(ka=)*[1] *saka*	–
saqap	enough	–	–
saqi	again	*saqi (-ka)*	*sai* 'again'
tika	emph	*(ka=) tika*	–

[1] attested, but very rare

The particles are not obligatory, e.g., even if an event is situated in the past, a speaker is not obliged to use a past tense particle.

If a speaker chooses to use a particle, this particle occurs in the left periphery of the clause, following conjunctions and preceding all other constituents. Particles are attested in verbal clauses (as the particle combination *kui* 'quoting' and *mani* 'recently' in 1a) as well as in non-verbal clauses (as the particle combination *tika* 'EMPH', *kui* 'quoting' and *murl* 'distantly' in 1b). They can alternatively occur in a left-dislocated position: in this case, they still occur in the left periphery, but are prosodically marked by a non-final pitch contour (see chapter 2.3.2) and/or syntactically by a following conjunction (see chapter 8.3.1) (as *mani* 'recently' in 1c). Furthermore, they can form their own proposition (as the particle combination *as* 'still' and *mani* 'recently' in 1d). In fact, it is not uncommon for entire utterances to consist of particles and conjunctions only.

(1) a. *guaka, dakui manundren?*

gua-ka,	*dap=**kui***	***mani**=un=tden?*
1SG.POSS-SG.M	but=quoting	recently=1DU.SBJ=come.CONT

'my friend, wouldn't you say that we came only recently?' (N12BAM-CAT-174)

b. *katika qui murl amalavu naut, de urarletkia*

*ka=**tika***	***kui***	***murl***	*ama=lavu*	*ne-ut,*
3SG.M.SBJ=EMPH	quoting	distantly	ART=adult	from/with-1PL

de	*ura=rlet-ki=a*
CONJ	1PL.POSS=duty-SG.F=DIST

'it is said that we are the parents, it is our duty (to teach the children)' (I12AANACLADNSOCIO3-193)

c. *davip de mani, deremsem nama melang ama..*
dap=ip *de* ***mani,*** *de=ure=msem*
but=PURP CONJ recently CONJ=1PL.SBJ.NPST=weave.CONT
ne=ama *melang* *ama..*
from/with=ART vine ART
'but as for recently, we were weaving with the vines of..' (P12ARS-BILUM2-020)

d. *be nyitliara, iamaiameses, ias mania*
be *nyi=tlu=iara,* *i=ama=iames-es,*
CONJ 2SG.SBJ.NPST=see.CONT=PROX SIM=ART=new-SG.FLAT
*i=**as*** ***mani**=a*
SIM=still recently=DIST
'and you see now, that it is a new flat one (garden), that it is still of recent times' (D12ADNGARDEN-024FF)

Given that particles can form a proposition, they can be questioned or negated. For example, in the elicited dialogue in (2), the particle *arik* 'supposing' is questioned by speaker B and replaced by the particle *nani* 'can', indicating his greater certainty that the event will, indeed, happen.

(2) A: *nyitlu iarik nyarang*
nyi=tlu *i=**arik*** *nya=rang*
2SG.SBJ.NPST=see.CONT SIM=supposing 1SG.SBJ=burn.NCONT.FUT
'watch out, otherwise you may get burned'

B: *kuasiqi arik, dap katika nani*
kuasiq=i ***arik,*** *dap* *ka=**tika*** ***nani***
NEG=SIM supposing but 3SG.M.SBJ=EMPH can
'not (just) may, but (it is) sure to happen' (AJL-18/08/2014)

Particles frequently combine with each other, always in a fixed order and sometimes forming formulaic sequences. Table 74 gives an overview of these orders, based on the attested co-occurrences in the corpus of natural and elicited data. Altogether 13 particle slots have to be posited. The particles within each slot do not co-occur. Note that this does not necessarily mean that these particles cannot co-occur: some combinations are likely to be impossible on semantic grounds, but other combinations could be possible and just happen to not occur in the available data. It is likely that additional data will lead to modifications of Table 74. Particles across the two groups can combine freely in the given order, unless there are semantic restrictions.

Tab. 74: Combinatorial possibilities

Slot	Form	Gloss	See section
1	*sa*	already	section 7.4
	as	still	
2	*naka*	bit	section 7.7
	saka	immediately	
3	*tika*	EMPH	section 7.7
	kaki	instead	section 7.5
	kiqerl	now	
4	*kias*	actually	section 7.2
5	*kerl*	DEONT	section 7.2
6	*kua*	INTRG	section 7.6
7	*ani*	maybe	section 7.2
	arik	supposing	
	kui	quoting	
8	*ide*	IPFV	section 7.4
9	*miiki*	instead	section 7.5
	miika	more	
	saqi	again	
10	*kurli*	leave	section 7.6
11	*nani*	can	section 7.2
	dip	FUT	section 7.3
	la	this.day	
	lira	(just) now	
	mani, manima	recently, before.yesterday	
	medu	past	
	murl	distantly; suddenly	
12	*kuasik*	NEG	section 7.6
13	*masna*	quickly	section 7.7
	miaqas	occasionally	section 7.4
	pet, petpet	continuously, frequently	
	deng	stop	section 7.5
	perlset	finish	
	saqap	enough	
	maget	then; right	
	qukun	(but) later	

Table 74 excludes the particles *kut* 'inferring', *padi* 'hopefully.PST' and *padip* 'hopefully.FUT' (see section 7.2), because they co-occur too infrequently with other particles to be able to assign them to one of the slots. Note also that the status of some forms in slot 13 is not entirely clear: *deng* 'stop', *saqap* 'enough' and *maget* 'then' are only attested in contexts where both particles and adverbs can occur. They have been tentatively classified as particles because they are not attested in typical adverb slots (i.e., in the right periphery of the clause).

Synchronically, particles are morphologically simple and non-inflecting. Diachronically, they probably originated in verbs and this verbal origin is still visible in some of their formal properties.

Most saliently, a number of particles optionally inflect for subject. A particle like *kias* 'actually' can either appear without inflection (as in 3a), or with the subject proclitic *ka* '3SG.M.SBJ' (as in 3b), or with the subject suffix *ka* '3SG.M' in the agentless construction (as in 3c), or with both (as in 3d).

(3) a. *tika kias luqa amaqaqeraqa, de adlek*
tika ***kias*** *lu-ka-a* *ama=qaqera-ka,* *de* *a=dlek*
EMPH actually DEM-SG.M-DIST ART=person-SG.M CONJ NM=strength
'and actually that man, there is strength (on him)' (I12AANACLADNSOCIO3-511FF)

b. *iqaks amalainnga nara*
*i=**ka=kias*** *ama=lain-ka* *ne-ta*
SIM=3SG.M.SBJ=actually ART=line-SG.M from/with-3PL.H
'and they are actually the troops (lit. the line-up)' (N11AAGSIRINILOBSTER2-0051)

c. *guaka, dakiaska amagetki ngua bqe..*
gua-ka, *dap=**kias-ka*** *ama=get-ki* *ngua*
1SG.POSS-SG.M but=actually-3SG.M ART=hunger-SG.F 1SG
be=ke..
CONJ=3SG.M.SBJ.NPST
'my friend, but I was actually hungry and..' (N12BAMCAT-248)

d. *dakakiaska ngenamalavu*
*dap=**ka=kias-ka*** *ngere-ne=ama=lavu*
but=3SG.M.SBJ=actually-3SG.M 3N.ASSOC-from/with=ART=adult
'but it was actually with the adults' (I12AANACLADNSOCIO3-375)

The particle *kias* 'actually' is exceptional in that it allows for all four possibilities. Other particles only allow for either a proclitic or a suffix, but not both (see Table 73 for the distribution of subject marking). The structures in (3b) and (3c) are otherwise only attested with verbs (see chapters 5.2.1 and 5.2.2), and it is likely that each particle has retained the pattern of its original verb.

The double-marking structure exemplified in (3d) above is not attested elsewhere. It probably results from the diachronic process, with *ka* '3SG.M' no longer being interpreted as subject morphemes. Such a re-interpretation is further suggested by phonetic erosion: it is not uncommon for the proclitic *ka* '3SG.M.SBJ' to be realized as *a* (as in 4a and 4b). A comparable erosion is never found in subject morphemes cliticizing to verbs.

(4) a. ***aks*** *amalamsaqa, de qamit saivit*
ka=kias *ama=lamesa-ka,* *de* *ka=mit*
3SG.M.SBJ=actually ART=coconut-SG.M CONJ 3SG.M.SBJ=go.NCONT.PST
se=i-pit
to/with=AWAY-up
'the coconut tree actually went up high' (N11AJNGENAINGMETSIQI-0046)

b. ***akiaska*** *ama.. aqaqerasa*
ka=kias-ka *ama..* *a=qaqera-es=a*
3SG.M.SBJ=actually-3SG.M ART NM=person-SG.FLAT=DIST
'it is actually the.. the Qaqet language' (I12ABLAJLATASOCIO2-033)

If a particle inflects for subject, this morpheme is always invariable. In most cases, this morpheme is *ka* '3SG.M' (as in 5a and 5b), and once, it is *ini* 'SG.DIM' (as in 5c). This morpheme is always used, even if it does not match the subject of the main verb: e.g., the subjects of the main verbs are *ure* '1PL.SBJ.NPST' and *ta* '3PL.SBJ' in the two clauses in (5a), *ki* '3SG.F.SBJ.NPST' in (5b), and *ut* '1PL.SBJ' in (5c). Recall that both the 3SG.M category and the DIM category are attested as default noun classes, i.e., they are used in cases where the class of the referent is irrelevant or unknown (see chapters 4.2.1 and 4.2.4). It is very likely that they receive a non-referential subject interpretation here, with a more literal translation of 'it is emphasized that' (in 5a), 'it is intended that' (in 5b) and 'it is assumed that' (in 5c).

(5) a. *katika uretaqen prara iuralengiqa, katika itadrlem*
ka*=tika* ***ure****=taqen* *pet-ta*
3SG.M.SBJ=EMPH 1PL.SBJ.NPST=say.CONT on/under-3PL.H
i=ura=lengi-ka, ***ka****=tika* *ip=****ta****=drlem*
SIM=1PL.POSS=word-SG.M 3SG.M.SBJ=EMPH PURP=3PL.SBJ=know
'we say to them that (this is) our language, so that they know it'
(I12AANACLADNSOCIO3-202)

b. *deqerlka ngenamadanggi, deqiqiuaik*
*de=kerl-**ka*** *ngere-ne=ama=dang-ki,*
CONJ=DEONT-3SG.M 3N.ASSOC-from/with=ART=dog-SG.F
*de=**ki**=qiuaik*
CONJ=3SG.F.SBJ.NPST=run.CONT
'and it is together with the dog that she should be running' (R12ATAFROG-215)

c. *iqurini iutnarlip tetaqadrlem uralengiqa*
*i=kut-**ini*** *i=**ut**=narlip*
SIM=inferring-SG.DIM SIM=1PL.SBJ=like:PURP
te=taqa=drlem *ura=lengi-ka*
3PL.SBJ.NPST=properly.CONT=know 1PL.POSS=word-SG.M
'(it is done) because I assume that we want them to know our language really well' (I12AANACLADNSOCIO2-084)

There is considerable variation in the expression of the subject category: some particles can occur either with or without it; those that can occur with it are all attested with both full and reduced forms (i.e., *ka* ~ *a* '3SG.M.SBJ'); and some (like *kias* 'actually' in 3b to 3d) can express the subject either as a proclitic, as a suffix or both. It was not possible to determine any difference in meaning or use, and the variants are thus tentatively considered to be in free variation. It is likely that this variation is triggered by the grammaticalization process from full verbs to invariant particles.

The co-occurrence of particles with subject morphemes is the clearest indication of their verbal origin. In addition, they exhibit a number of other properties that are at least suggestive of a verbal origin.

First, many (but not all) initial plosives of particles are stable and do not lenite in an intervocalic environment, e.g., *tika* 'EMPH' (in 5a above) or *kias* 'actually' (in 3 and 4 above). While this phenomenon is also found in other parts of speech, it is especially salient in verbs (see chapter 2.1.1).

Second, there is a specific structure that is commonly used by narrators to indicate continuation and repetition of events: a predicate and its arguments are repeated in rapid succession several times, separated by an intervening conjunction *be*. Usually, the predicate is a verb (as in 6a), but it is also common for particles to occur in this structure. This includes particles that allow for a subject proclitic (as in 6b) as well as those that allow for a suffix (as in 6c). And it includes particles that, at least synchronically, do not contain any subject morpheme, e.g., the particle *miika* 'more' in (6d) (which is synchronically monomorphemic, although it may diachronically contain the suffix *-ka* '3SG.M').

(6) a. *katit bqatit bqatit bqatit bqatit bqatit bqatit bqatit be..*
ka=tit *be=ka=tit* *be=ka=tit*
3SG.M.SBJ=go.CONT CONJ=3SG.M.SBJ=go.CONT CONJ=3SG.M.SBJ=go.CONT
be=ka=tit *be=ka=tit*
CONJ=3SG.M.SBJ=go.CONT CONJ=3SG.M.SBJ=go.CONT
be=ka=tit *be=ka=tit*
CONJ=3SG.M.SBJ=go.CONT CONJ=3SG.M.SBJ=go.CONT
be=ka=tit *be..*
CONJ=3SG.M.SBJ=go.CONT CONJ
'he went and went and went and went and went and went and went and went and..' (N12ABKSIRINI-060)

b. *tika bqatika bqatika bqatika bqatika*
tika *be=ka=tika* *be=ka=tika*
EMPH CONJ=3SG.M.SBJ=EMPH CONJ=3SG.M.SBJ=EMPH
be=ka=tika *be=ka=tika*
CONJ=3SG.M.SBJ=EMPH CONJ=3SG.M.SBJ=EMPH
'(it went) on and on and on and on and on' (N12ABKSIRINI-102)

c. *kerlka bqerlka bqerlka bqerlka, beip maget..*
kerl-ka *be=kerl-ka* *be=kerl-ka* *be=kerl-ka,*
DEONT-3SG.M CONJ=DEONT-3SG.M CONJ=DEONT-3SG.M CONJ=DEONT-3SG.M
be=ip *maget..*
CONJ=PURP then
'(it went) on and on and on and on, and then..' (N12ABKSIRINI-083)

d. *miika bmiika bmiika bmiika bmiika, bianeprerlsena*
miika *be=miika* *be=miika* *be=miika* *be=miika,*
more CONJ=more CONJ=more CONJ=more CONJ=more
be=iane=prerl=se-na
CONJ=3DU.SBJ.NPST=argue:CONT=to/with-RECP
'(it went) on and on and on and on and on, and they wrestle each other' (N11AAGBROTHERS-0061)

Finally, there is a small number of particles such as *perlset* 'finish', which were grammaticalized from verbs that are synchronically still attested (in this case, from the verb *verlset* ~ *perlset* 'finish'). Both verb and particle are illustrated in (7a). Note that the verb distinguishes a non-continuous (i.e., *verlset*) and a continuous stem (i.e., *perlset*). The particle also uses both forms, but in this case the distribution is not conditioned by aspectual semantics, but by the phonological environment: *verlset* is used intervocalically (as in 7b), and *perlset* in all other environments (as in 7a).

(7) a. *ianverlseraqi, beip* ***perlset***
*ian=****verlset****-ki,* *be=ip* ***perlset***
3DU.SBJ=finish.NCONT-3SG.F CONJ=PURP finish
'they finished it, and it is finished' (N12BAMCAT-114)

b. *nguaring aagarliqa, de* ***verlset***
ngua=ring *aa=garli-ka,* *de* ***perlset***
1SG.SBJ=weave.NCONT.FUT 3SG.M.POSS=side-SG.M CONJ finish
'I will weave its side, and it is finished' (P12ADNROPE2-010)

Given the above discussion, it is likely that the Qaqet particles – or at least a good number of them – originated in verbs. Their verbal origin is visible in their retention of some rudimentary verbal properties. The majority of synchronic particles, however, remain uninflected, and there is no evidence for (or against) a verbal origin. Synchronically, particles thus have to be considered a distinct non-inflecting word class that is syntactically defined by their fixed position in the left periphery of the clause.

7.2 Modality

Many of the particles express epistemic, evidential and deontic meanings: (i) *ani* 'maybe', (ii) *arik* 'supposing', (iii) *kias* 'actually', (iv) *kui* 'quoting', (v) *kut* 'inferring', (vi) *nani* 'can', (vii) *kerl* 'DEONT', and (viii) *padi* 'hopefully.PST' and *padip* 'hopefully.FUT'.

(i) *ani* 'maybe'

The particle *ani* 'maybe' is only infrequently attested in the corpus. It conveys a considerable degree of uncertainty about the truth of a proposition (as in 8a). It is furthermore attested in directives and hortatives, often combining with the particle *kerl* 'DEONT' in order to tone down a suggestion (as in 8b).

(8) a. *nyitlamamenggaira, de an.. ani lamaademga mara*
nyi=tlu=ama=meng-ka=iara,
2SG.SBJ.NPST=see.CONT=ART=wood-SG.M=PROX
de *an..* ***ani*** *lu=ama=adem-ka* *mara*
CONJ maybe maybe DEM=ART=hole-SG.M here
'see the tree here, may.. maybe there's a hole here (from where the sound came)' (R12ATAFROG-254)

b. *kerl ani nani deng naura, deqerl..*
kerl ***ani*** *nani deng ne-ut=a, de=kerl..*
DEONT maybe can stop from/with-1PL=DIST CONJ=DEONT
'maybe we should stop now, and..' (I12AANACLADNSocio3-447)

(ii) *arik* 'supposing'

The particle *arik* 'supposing' marks an event as hypothetical. It commonly occurs in two types of contexts. First, it presents the hypothetical (usually undesirable) consequence of an event (as in 9).

(9) *nyitliarik nyang mramaqia*
*nyi=tlu=i=**arik*** *nya=ang*
2SG.SBJ.NPST=see.CONT=SIM=supposing 2SG.SBJ=walk.NCONT
met=a=ma-ki=a
in=NM=thingy-SG.F=DIST
'watch out, otherwise you may step on the thingy there'
(LongYDS20150517_1-192)

And second, it occurs in clauses that express a dependent circumstance to a main event, usually a condition or a causal relation: e.g., the precondition for the learning to take place in (10a), or the reason for looking into the hole in (10b). The collocation of the particle *arik* with the conjunction *ip* (as in 10a) is especially common, and it is possible that this collocation is grammaticalizing into a causal conjunction. The particle nevertheless retains its hypothetical reading in such contexts, too, and its distribution thus contrasts with that of the simple conjunction *ip* (see also chapter 8.3.4).

(10) a. *dakerl ariqiv uremsem amarlaun iv uresunas*
dap=kerl ***arik****=ip* *ure=msem ama=rlaun*
but=DEONT supposing=PURP 1PL.SBJ.NPST=weave.CONT ART=netbag
ip ure=sunas
PURP 1PL.SBJ.NPST=teach:SELF
'but supposing that we (want to) weave netbags and (want to) learn (about them)' (P12ARSBilum2-033)

b. *kemnyim samramaademga, iarik bemaqalminngiimek*
ke=mnyim se=met=ama=adem-ka,
3SG.M.SBJ.NPST=look.CONT to/with=in=ART=hole-SG.M
*i=**arik*** *be=ma=qalmin-ki=i-mek*
SIM=supposing CONJ=ART.ID=frog-SG.F=AWAY-down
'he is looking into the hole, supposing that the frog has gone down there' (R12ADNFrog-126ff)

In either context, it very commonly combines with the interrogative particle *kua* to express a hypothetical alternative (as in 11a and 11b).

(11) a. *ikuarik kiaat, dakua nana?*

*ip=**kua=arik***	*kia=at,*	*dap=kua*	*nana?*
PURP=INTRG=supposing	3SG.F.SBJ=fall.NCONT	but=INTRG	what

'supposing it may fall down, or what?' (R12ADNFROG-141)

b. *deqimali metlaumiarip kuarik kiluqi, de quasik*

de=ki=mali	*met=lu-em-iara=ip*		
CONJ=3SG.F.SBJ.NPST=search	in=DEM-SG.RCD-PROX=PURP		
kua=arik	*ki=lu-ki,*	*de*	*kuasik*
INTRG=supposing	3SG.F.SBJ.NPST=see.NCONT-3SG.F	CONJ	NEG

'it was looking inside this one (bottle) supposing that it may see it, but no' (R12ATAFROG-061)

(iii) *kias* 'actually'

The particle *kias* 'actually' (also realized as *tias*) conveys both a commitment to the truth of a statement as well as an element of surprise that it should be true, contrary to expectations. In (12a), the expectation is explicitly mentioned in the first clause, and contradicted in the second clause by means of *kias* 'actually'. Mostly, however, expectations are left implicit, as in the parallel example (12b). Since the particle emphasizes the truth of a statement, it collocates regularly with the noun *revan* 'truth' (as in 12c).

(12) a. *kuasiqi amaqaqeraqa amaqunaska, kias amavilanngi de amaqaqera amaburlem nara*

kuasik=i	*ama=qaqera-ka*	*ama=qunas-ka,*	***kias***	
NEG=SIM	ART=person-SG.M	ART=one-SG.M	actually	
ama=vilanngi	*de*	*ama=qaqera*	*ama=burlem*	*ne-ta*
ART=NAME:SG.F	CONJ	ART=person	ART=many	from/with-3PL.H

'(the Vilan spirit) is not (just) one person, the Vilan (spirit) is actually many people' (I12AANACLADNSOCIO3-489FF)

b. *deqakias, amaburlem nama.. amarlaun*

*de=ka=**kias,***	*ama=burlem*	*ne=ama..*	*ama=rlaun*
CONJ=3SG.M.SBJ=actually	ART=many	from/with=ART	ART=netbag

'there are actually many kinds of.. netbags (i.e., not just one kind, as you might have thought)' (P12ARSBILUM2-005)

c. *a.. atias arevan*
ka.. *ka=**kias*** *a=revan*
3SG.M.SBJ 3SG.M.SBJ=actually NM=truth
'it's.. it's actually the truth (contrary to what you might think)'
(I12AANACLADNSocio3-388)

(iv) *kui* 'quoting'

The particle *kui* 'quoting' attributes a statement to another authority. As such, it frequently occurs in statements about general truths (as in 13a and 13b). An overt speech act verb can be present in such contexts (as in 13a), but does not need to be present (as in 13b). Again, as with all particles, *kui* 'quoting' is not obligatory, e.g., the utterance in (13c) is almost identical to the one in (13b) – but it does not contain this particle.

(13) a. *kui retuqun iura.. amalavu naut, de saqika uralat*
kui *te=tuqun* *i=ura..* *ama=lavu*
quoting 3PL.SBJ.NPST=say.CONT SIM=1PL.POSS ART=adult
ne-ut, *de* *saqi-ka* *ura=lat*
from/with-1PL CONJ again-3SG.M 1PL.POSS=work
'they (i.e., people in general) are saying that it is our.. (that) we are the parents, (that) it is again our job (to teach the children)'
(I12AANACLADNSocio2-027)

b. *katika qui murl amalavu naut, de urarletkia*
ka=tika ***kui*** *murl* *ama=lavu* *ne-ut,*
3SG.M.SBJ=EMPH quoting distantly ART=adult from/with-1PL
de *ura=rlet-ki=a*
CONJ 1PL.POSS=duty-SG.F=DIST
'it is said that we are the parents, it is our duty (to teach the children)'
(I12AANACLADNSocio3-193)

c. *amalavu naut, de tika urarletkia*
ama=lavu *ne-ut,* *de* *tika* *ura=rlet-ki=a*
ART=adult from/with-1PL CONJ EMPH 1PL.POSS=duty-SG.F=DIST
'we are the parents, it's our duty (to teach the children)'
(I12AANACLADNSocio3-187)

The particle is used in all contexts where a speaker appeals to another authority. This includes statements about well-known truths (as in 13a and 13b above), but also any other kind of statement: e.g., the speaker in (14a) explains the functioning of a camera, and uses *kui* 'quoting' to attribute the source of information to someone else. The source in (14a) is not named, but it is equally possible to name a specific source (as in 14b).

(14) a. *iqerl kui lungera ngatranyi*
i=kerl **kui** *lu-nget-a* *nga=tat-nyi*
SIM=DEONT quoting DEM-N-DIST 3N.SBJ=take.CONT-2SG
'don't (touch it), it is said that that one is recording you' (C12YMMZJI-PLAY1-039)

b. *uniaik kiataqen itika qui uralengiqa*
une-ia-ki *kia=taqen* *i=tika* **kui**
1DU.POSS-other-SG.F 3SG.F.SBJ=say.CONT SIM=EMPH quoting
ura=lengi-ka
1PL.POSS=word-SG.M
'(like) our friend has said, she said it is our language' (I12AANACLAD-NSOCIO2-120)

The source of information is usually a third person, but it can also be another person, including a first person (as in 15).

(15) *de medu quasiqi qui unquhrl aqrang praqi*
de *medu* *kuasik=i* **kui** *une=qutserl*
CONJ past NEG=SIM quoting 1DU.SBJ.NPST=plant.NCONT:??
a=qa-irang *pet-ki*
NM=some-PL.DIM on/under-3SG.F
'we say that we haven't planted anything on it' (D12ABDACPGARDEN-032)

Finally, this particle is commonly used in impatient directives or complaints, where the authority is the first person. The following exchange between two children nicely exemplifies such a context: YJL directs ZJS's attention to a bird, but ZJS cannot find it. In the last utterance, YJL then chooses to add *kui* 'quoting', thereby emphasizing that she has already told him many times where to look.

(16) 1. ZJS: *kiqua?*
ki=kua?
3SG.F=where
ZJS: 'where is it?' (LONGYJL20150805_2-733)

2. YJL: *luqia, amauaika*
lu-ki-a, *ama=uaik-ki=a*
DEM-SG.F-DIST ART=bird-SG.F=DIST
YJL: 'that one, the bird there' (LONGYJL20150805_2-734FF)

3. ZJS: *ikiqua?*
ip=ki=kua?
PURP=3SG.F=where
ZJS: 'so where is it?' (LONGYJL20150805_2-736)

4. YJL: *luqiaavuk*
lu-ki-a=a-vuk
DEM-SG.F-DIST=DIR-up
YJL: 'that one up there' (LongYJL20150805_2-737)
5. ZJS: *kua?*
kua?
where
ZJS: 'where?' (LongYJL20150805_2-738)
6. YJL: *dakui luqiaavuk*
*dap=**kui*** *lu-ki-a=a-vuk*
but=quoting DEM-SG.F-DIST=DIR-up
YJL: 'but I told you, that one up there' (LongYJL20150805_2-739)

(v) *kut* 'inferring'

The particle *kut* 'inferring' is used in contexts where speakers present their reasoning for an assertion – a reasoning that is based on inference (as in 17a and 17b). This particle is almost exclusively attested in the form of *iqurini* (/i=kut-ini/, as in 17a), and it is likely that this form is currently grammaticalizing into a causal conjunction 'because' (see chapter 8.3.3). It is not (yet) a general causal conjunction, as it only occurs in causal contexts that also include inferential reasoning (i.e., most causal contexts do not feature this particle). Formally, a first indication of its grammaticalization is its restricted distribution: particles frequently co-occur with each other, and it is noticeable that *kut* 'inferring' almost never co-occurs with any other particle: (17b) is one of only three such examples in the entire corpus. The particle itself originated in the preposition *kut* 'along' (see chapter 5.3.4): this preposition has mainly spatial uses, but it is also used to metaphorically convey the concept of 'following someone's wishes' (as in 17c). It is possible that this metaphorical use triggered the development of an inferential meaning.

(17) a. *iqurini iutnarlip tetaqadrlem uralengiqa*
*i=**kut**-ini* *i=ut=narlip*
SIM=inferring-SG.DIM SIM=1PL.SBJ=like:PURP
te=taqa=drlem *ura=lengi-ka*
3PL.SBJ.NPST=properly.CONT=know 1PL.POSS=word-SG.M
'(it is done) because I assume that we want them to know our language really well' (I12AANACLADNSocio2-084)

b. *kuasik karaqatekmet naexam, kurini ide quasik kataqasunas*
kuasik ka=raqa=tekmet ne=a=exam,
NEG 3SG.M.SBJ=properly.NCONT=do.CONT:IN from/with=NM=exam
***kut**-ini ide kuasik ka=taqa=sunas*
inferring-SG.DIM IPFV NEG 3SG.M.SBJ=properly.CONT=teach:SELF
'he didn't do well in the exams, because I think he didn't study hard' (AJL-15/08/2014)

c. *kamit kuramam*
*ka=mit **kut**=a-mam*
3SG.M.SBJ=go.NCONT.PST along=3SG.M.POSS-father
'he did it following his father's wishes, inferring his father's wishes (lit. he went alongside his father)' (AJL-15/08/2014)

(vi) *nani* 'can'

The particle *nani* 'can' conveys notions of ability and possibility. It occurs in near-future contexts where there is an external condition that enables (or hinders) a future event. It cannot be used in cases of internal ability or capability. Often, the enabling condition is explicitly stated (as in 18a), but this is not necessarily the case (as in 18b).

(18) a. *tikanyi taqasuqaip nani qukun daqataqen praarluavik maamanu*
tika=nyi taqa=su-ka=ip ***nani*** *qukun*
EMPH=2SG.SBJ.NPST properly.CONT=teach-SG.M=PURP can later
de=ka=taqen pet=aa=rlua-pik
CONJ=3SG.M.SBJ=say.CONT on/under=3SG.M.POSS=friend-COLL.H
maqa-manu
HERE-across
'you teach him well, and later he will be able to talk (in Qaqet) to his friends everywhere' (I12ABLAJLATASocio3-159)

b. *dap nani nguksik*
dap ***nani*** *ngu=ksik*
but can 1SG.SBJ.NPST=climb.CONT
'and I can climb up' (N12AMVGenaingmetBrothers-052)

When directed at a second person, it still conveys ability (as in 19a), but it acquires additional connotations of permission in this context (as in 19b).

(19) a. *de nani nyiraqasmisini narevanu*
de ***nani*** *nyi=raqa=smis-ini*
CONJ can 2SG.SBJ.NPST=properly.NCONT=C.call-SG.DIM
ne=a=revan
from/with=NM=truth
'(if you follow my advice), you will be able to say the little (word) correctly' (I12AANACLADNSOCIO2-074)

b. *avuk, avuk nauin, avuk nauirl, ip nani sageluin*
avuk, *avuk* *ne-uin,* *avuk* *nauirl,* *ip* ***nani***
wait wait from/with-2DU wait first PURP can
se=gel-uin
to/with=near-2DU
'wait, you wait, wait first, then you can (do it afterwards)' (C12VARPLAY-064)

In addition, there are contexts where the interpretation of *nani* 'can' borders more on possibility than on ability (as in 20a and 20b).

(20) a. *inani urebarl nas, navruralengiqa*
*i=**nani*** *ure=barl* *nas*
SIM=can 1PL.SBJ.NPST=big self
ne=pet=ura=lengi-ka
from/with=on/under=1PL.POSS=word-SG.M
'so we can ~ may be proud of our language' (I12AANACLADNSOCIO2-088)

b. *ai, kiatu araqavevip nanaangilit*
ai, *kia=tu* *ara=qavep=ip*
hey 3SG.F.SBJ=put.CONT 3SG.F.POSS=heart=PURP
nani*=aa=ngil-it*
can=3SG.M.POSS=space-SG.LONG
'hey, she was thinking that it can ~ may be his place (to die now)' (I12AANACLADNSOCIO3-535)

This particle very frequently occurs in combination with the conjunction *ip*: this conjunction introduces a purpose (see chapter 8.3.4), and the particle adds the semantic component of ability (as in 21a). While it is not uncommon for them to co-occur, each one retains its own semantics, and they can each occur without the other (as in 21b and 21c).

(21) a. *ip nani ratatpem taqurlani*
ip **nani** *ta=tatpem taquarl=ani*
PURP can 3PL.SBJ=cut.CONT:PLACE thus=DIST
'and so they can remove the bark like this' (P12ADNROPE1-012)

b. *nani qukun, dinyikuap pramamelangga*
nani *qukun, de=nyi=kuap pet=ama=melang-ka*
can later CONJ=2SG.SBJ.NPST=tie.CONT on/under=ART=vine-SG.M
'a bit later, you can tie the rope' (P12ADNROPE1-051)

c. *ip nyingdemna namaburlem*
ip nyi=ingdemna ne=ama=burlem
PURP 2SG.SBJ.NPST=collect.NCONT:LOC.PART:RECP from/with=ART=many
'and so you collect them into a heap' (P12ADNROPE1-083)

(vii) *kerl* 'DEONT'

The particle *kerl* 'DEONT' is a high-frequency particle that conveys a cluster of deontic notions ranging around directiveness, with concomitant connotations of permission, necessity and desirability. It frequently occurs in utterances directed at a second person, including commands (as in 22a and 22b) and questions (as in 22c). It is not obligatory in either context, e.g., the first and last clauses in (22b) feature imperatives without this particle. But if it is present, it adds a meaning component of necessity or desirability (as in 22a and 22c) or, in combination with *nani* 'can', of permission and ability (as in 22b).

(22) a. *as kerl nyiqurlaqa*
as **kerl** *nyi=quarl-ka*
still DEONT 2SG.SBJ.NPST=present.NCONT-3SG.M
'you should give it to him' (C12VARPLAY-465)

b. *nyaruqunimek, kerl naniip.. nyilunas mramaqiamek, nyaruqun*
nya=ruqun=i-mek, **kerl** *nani=ip..*
2SG.SBJ=sit.NCONT.FUT=AWAY-down DEONT can=PURP
nyi=lu-nas met=a=ma-ki=a-mek,
2SG.SBJ.NPST=see.NCONT-self in=NM=thingy-SG.F=DIR-down
nya=ruqun
2SG.SBJ=sit.NCONT.FUT
'sit down (on the ground), you can then.. see yourself in the thingy (camera) down there (on the ground), sit' (C12VARPLAY-440)

c. *ah? nyiraqen? askerl nyisnanbet tenemgi?*
ah? *nyi=raqen?* *as=**kerl*** *nyi=snanbet*
what 2SG.SBJ.NPST=say.NCONT still=DEONT 2SG.SBJ.NPST=ask:ON/UNDER
te=nema-ki?
PURP=who-SG.F
'what? you say (what)? you're asking about who (i.e., you should ask again)?' (C12YMMZJIPLAY1-150)

This particle is also common in procedural texts, as illustrated in (23): the speaker uses it in those clauses where she introduces a new step in the procedure, portraying this step as necessary or desirable (as in 23-2 and 23-3). Again, this particle is not obligatory: e.g., the speaker chooses not to use it in the new step of 'bringing back the vines' in (23-4).

(23) 1. *ip nyinarlip samarlaunnga*
ip *nyi=narlip* *se=ama=rlaun-ka*
PURP 2SG.SBJ.NPST=like:PURP to/with=ART=netbag-SG.M
'if you want (to start weaving) a netbag' (P12ARSBILUM1-008)

2. *deqerl nyatit sep maqavel*
*de=**kerl*** *nya=tit* *se=pe* *ma=qavel*
CONJ=DEONT 2SG.SBJ=go.CONT to/with=PLACE ART.ID=bush
'you should go to the bush' (P12ARSBILUM1-009)

3. *nyatit sep maqavel, ikerl nyimali regiakaasik*
nya=tit *se=pe* *ma=qavel,* *ip=**kerl***
2SG.SBJ=go.CONT to/with=PLACE ART.ID=bush PURP=DEONT
nyi=mali *te=gia=kaasik*
2SG.SBJ.NPST=search PURP=2SG.POSS=vine
'you go to the bush, and you should search for your vines' (P12ARS-BILUM1-010)

4. *nyimali regiakaasik, regia.. regiakaasik, dinyaden sanget*
nyi=mali *te=gia=kaasik,* *te=gia..*
2SG.SBJ.NPST=search PURP=2SG.POSS=vine PURP=2SG.POSS
te=gia=kaasik, *de=nya=tden* *se-nget*
PURP=2SG.POSS=vine CONJ=2SG.SBJ=come.CONT to/with-3N
'you search for your vines, for your.. for your vines, and you bring them (back)' (P12ARSBILUM1-011FF)

Interestingly, the particle is not restricted to commands and questions directed at a second person, but is also attested in statements (as in 24a to 24c). These utterances are formally declarative utterances, but the use of the particle *kerl* 'DEONT' adds a directive component, interpreted as a directive at the addressee to act (as in 24a and 24c) or not to act (as in 24b). In all cases, the exact interpretation depends on the context. In (24a), the speaker describes a picture and uses *kerl* 'DEONT' to direct the addressee's attention to a specific scene. The utterance in the next intonation unit is then overtly addressed at the interlocutor, explicitly spelling out the intention of the speaker. Example (24b) is a simple statement about the tea being hot. The use of *kerl* 'DEONT' then turns this statement into a prohibitive utterance: note that there is no negative morphology to convey the prohibitive force, and the prohibitive interpretation is entirely due to world knowledge. Conversely, the speaker in (24c) uses *kerl* 'DEONT' to, grudgingly, grant permission to the interlocutor to take the betelnuts introduced in the previous intonation unit. In a different context, the same utterance could also have been used to withhold permission.

(24) a. *dap kerl ngenianarluis, nyilua?*
dap ***kerl*** *ngere-ne=iana=rluis,*
but DEONT 3N.ASSOC-from/with=3DU.POSS=child
nyi=lu=a?
2SG.SBJ.NPST=see.NCONT=DIST
'it is together with their children (i.e., you should look at it), do you see now?' (R12ADNFROG-332FF)

b. *as kerl auilas*
as ***kerl*** *a=uilas*
still DEONT NM=hotness
'it's still hot (i.e., you should not drink it)' (C12YMMZJIPLAY1-369)

c. *damerliqiamamuk, kerlka*
de=a=merlik-iam=a-muk, ***kerl****-ka*
CONJ=NM=betelnut-DU.M=DIR-across DEONT-3SG.M
'there's two betelnuts over there, (you) can (take them, if you must)' (LONGYDS20150516_1-471)

Finally, this particle also occurs in directives aimed at a first person. This includes hortative contexts (as in 25a), but also questions (as in 25b), statements (as in 25c) and negative statements (as in 25d).

(25) a. *deqerl utaqen prana*
*de=****kerl*** *ut=taqen* *pet-na*
CONJ=DEONT 1PL.SBJ=say.CONT on/under-RECP
'we should discuss this amongst ourselves' (I12AANACLADNSOCIO2-179)

b. *kerl amaging iamaginget?*
kerl *ama=ging* *i=ama=gi-nget?*
DEONT ART=yummy.food SIM=ART=what-N
'(let me ask) what kind of thing is *ging*?' (I12ABLAJLATASOCIO2-054)

c. *iqerl dap ngutlu de amaburlem naur, amalavu naut*
*i=**kerl*** *dap* *ngu=tlu* *de* *ama=burlem*
SIM=DEONT but 1SG.SBJ.NPST=see.CONT CONJ ART=many
ne-ut, *ama=lavu* *ne-ut*
from/with-1PL ART=adult from/with-1PL
'I see it (this kind of behavior) a lot amongst us, amongst us parents (so let's stop it)' (I12AANACLADNSocio2-132)

d. *davas kerl kuasik*
dap=as ***kerl*** *kuasik*
but=still DEONT NEG
'but it is not yet the case (so I cannot work with it yet)' (P12ADNRope2-021)

(viii) *padi* 'hopefully.PST' and *padip* 'hopefully.FUT'

The particles *padip* 'hopefully.FUT' and *padi* 'hopefully.PST' are formally and semantically very similar. Both express the wish or hope that an event takes place. In the case of *padip*, this event is hoped to take place in the future (as in 26a). And in the case of *padi*, it was hoped to have taken place in the past – but it did not, i.e., the particle receives a counterfactual interpretation (as in 26b). The particles are possibly formed on the basis of the temporal particle *dip* 'FUT' (see section 7.3). Both particles are very rare in the corpus.

(26) a. *saqika dip kirek mirlek padip kiranengaqa*
saqi-ka *dip* *ki=rek* *mirlek*
again-3SG.M FUT 3SG.F.SBJ.NPST=hold/put.NCONT around
padip *ki=raneng-ka*
hopefully.FUT 3SG.F.SBJ.NPST=hold.NCONT-3SG.M
'again she will close in (on him) and wants to hold him' (N11AAGSiriniRope-0068)

b. *padi qiaat prangua*
padi *kia=at* *pet-ngua*
hopefully.PST 3SG.F.SBJ=fall.NCONT on/under-1SG
'it (the bird) wanted to swoop down on me (but it didn't)' (LongYJL20150805_2-856)

7.3 Time

Another large group of particles expresses temporal meanings, situating events (i) in the future, (ii) on the same day or (iii) in the past. Different from the inflectional categories marked on the predicate (see chapter 5.4), these particles are always optional.

(i) Future

There is one particle that is used in reference to future events: *dip* 'FUT'. This particle is used both in prediction-based futures (as in 27a) and intention-based futures (as in 27b). It is not analyzed as an irrealis particle, as it cannot occur in, e.g., past irrealis or counterfactual scenarios. But note that there is overlap with modal particles, especially with the particle *nani* 'can', which specifies an external condition that enables an event to take place, and thus often occurs in near-future contexts (see section 7.2).

(27) a. *iqerl iv utekmet, be dip malengiqa qatit*
i=kerl *ip* *ut=tekmet,* *be* ***dip*** *ma=lengi-ka*
SIM=DEONT PURP 1PL.SBJ=do.CONT:IN CONJ FUT ART.ID=word-SG.M
ka=tit
3SG.M.SBJ=go.CONT
'so if we do this, the language will go away' (I12AANACLADNSOCIO2-170)

b. *de tika div undit, dip ngudatdemnyi*
de *tika* ***dip*** *un=tit,* ***dip*** *ngu=datdem-nyi*
CONJ EMPH FUT 1DU.SBJ=go.CONT FUT 1SG.SBJ.NPST=follow.CONT-2SG
'we will go now, I will follow you' (N12BAMCAT-051FF)

Like all particles, *dip* 'FUT' is not obligatory: there are many events that are set in the future and that are not overtly marked with *dip*. Compare the following examples, all taken from the same story and all conveying similar propositions (one character telling the other that they should go). This going event is marked in three different ways: with *dip* 'FUT' in (28a) (to explicitly situate it in the future), with *nani* 'can' in (28b) (to portray it as an ability), and unmarked in (28c) (leaving its future interpretation to context).

(28) a. *diak kasil ma, div undir ivune..*
de=ia-ka *ka=sil* *ma,* ***dip*** ***un=tit***
CONJ=other-SG.M 3SG.M.SBJ=say.NCONT thus FUT 1DU.SBJ=go.CONT
ip=une..
PURP=1DU.SBJ.NPST
'and one said to the other like this, we will go and we..' (N11AAGBROTHERS-0017FF)

b. *iansil bana ma, nani undit pramakainaqi*
ian=sil *barek-na* *ma,* ***nani*** ***un=tit***
3DU.SBJ=say.NCONT BEN-RECP thus can 1DU.SBJ=go.CONT
pet=ama=kaina-ki
on/under=ART=water-SG.F
'they said to each other like this, we can go to the river' (N11AAGBROTHERS-0028FF)

c. *dap.. luqa qepileng aarluaqa daqatuqun, undit dunekuarl*
dap.. *lu-ka-a* *ke=pileng*
but DEM-SG.M-DIST 3SG.M.SBJ.NPST=wake.CONT
aa=rlua-ka *de=ka=tuqun,* ***un=tit***
3SG.M.POSS=friend-SG.M CONJ=3SG.M.SBJ=say.CONT 1DU.SBJ=go.CONT
de=une=kuarl
CONJ=1DU.SBJ.NPST=shine.CONT
'and.. that one wakes his friend and he is saying, we go and shine a light' (N11AAGBROTHERS-0087)

Given its optionality in future contexts, it is not analyzed as a grammaticalized tense. Furthermore, like other particles, it can also occur without predicates (as in 29a), or in a left-dislocated position (as in 29b).

(29) a. *amasmesirang, ip dip savramakaska*
ama=smes-irang, *ip* ***dip*** *se=pet=ama=kas-ka*
ART=food-PL.DIM PURP FUT to/with=on/under=ART=saltwater-SG.M
'the food, (it) will (be for their journey) across the ocean' (N12BAMCAT-154FF)

b. *de saqika dip, iasi, denguaru amapiuqisinga*
de *saqi-ka* ***dip,*** *iasi,* *de=ngua=ru*
CONJ again-3SG.M FUT DIST CONJ=1SG.SBJ=put.NCONT.FUT
ama=piuk-ising=a
ART=cassava-PL.LONG=DIST
'and again in future, then, I plant cassava cuttings' (D12ADNGARDEN-052FF)

(ii) Same day

There are two particles, *la* 'this day' and *lira* 'just now', which are both used for events that take place on the same day, but which have different temporal boundaries. The particle *la* 'this day' can be used for all events that take place during the same day (including the night), either in the past (as in 30a), in the present (as in 30b) or in the future (as in 30c).

(30) a. *tikaip lunsil bana, dap kuasiqundrlem savt giahleng*
tika=ip ***la****=un=sil* *barek-na,* *dap*
EMPH=PURP this.day=1DU.SBJ=say.NCONT BEN-RECP but
kuasik=un=drlem *se=pet* *gia=sleng*
NEG=1DU.SBJ=know to/with=on/under 2SG.POSS=garden
'earlier we said to each other, that we haven't forgotten about our garden' (N12BAMCAT-080)

b. *laianengingarl sena mragulenggaalang*
la=iane=ngingarl *se-na*
this.day=3DU.SBJ.NPST=chase.CONT:?? to/with-RECP
met=a=guleng-ka=aa=lang
in=NM=malay.apple-SG.M=3SG.M.POSS=top
'they are now chasing each other on top of the malay apple tree' (N11AAGSIRINIROPE-0134)

c. *laiv undit dunekuarl, daarluaqasilm, ee*
la=ip *un=tit* *de=une=kuarl,*
this.day=PURP 1DU.SBJ=go.CONT CONJ=1DU.SBJ.NPST=shine.CONT
de=aa=rlua-ka=ka=sil=ma, *ee*
CONJ=3SG.M.POSS=friend-SG.M=3SG.M.SBJ=say.NCONT=thus yes
'(he said) tonight we will go and shine a light (to catch fish), and his friend answered like this, yes' (N11AAGBROTHERS-0082)

More generally, *la* 'this day' is used in reference to the present times, irrespective of the actual temporal reference (as in 31)

(31) *uresu uruis nadeivet, dakatika laradrlem luqa ama.. amaqaqet*
ure=su *ure-uis* *ne=de=a=ivet,*
1PL.SBJ.NPST=teach 1PL.POSS-child from/with=LOC.PART=NM=ground
dap=ka=tika ***la**=ta=drlem* *lu-ka-a*
but=3SG.M.SBJ=EMPH this.day=3PL.SBJ=know DEM-SG.M-DIST
ama.. *ama=qaqera*
ART ART=NAME
'we are teaching our children from the beginning, and these days they know about that.. Qaqet (language)' (I12AANACLADNSOCIO3-197FF)

The particle *lira* 'just now' is used for events that immediately precede the reference time. The difference between the two particles is illustrated in (32). The event in the first clause had taken place earlier in the night (a frog sleeping in a bottle, waking up and leaving), and the speaker chose *la* 'this day'. The event in the second clause took place immediately before the reference time (a boy and a dog sleeping, and having just woken up to find that the frog had left), and the speaker chose *lira* 'just now'.

(32) *de luqimara, tika ilaqibrlany maqamek, de naqaki lira liamara ianebrlany*
de *lu-ki=mara,* *tika* *i=**la**=ki=brlany*
CONJ DEM-SG.F=here EMPH SIM=this.day=3SG.F.SBJ.NPST=sleep
maqa-mek, *de* *naka=kaki* ***lira*** *lu-iam=mara* *iane=brlany*
HERE-down CONJ bit=instead now DEM-DU.M=here 3DU.SBJ.NPST=slee
'and this one here, earlier it was sleeping down here, and just now, these two here were sleeping, too' (R12ATAFROG-055)

Both particles are compatible with the non-past subject indexes: if a verb allows for these indexes, speakers can choose them in order to highlight that the past event has only just happened and that it has relevance for present events. For example, both 'sleeping' events in (32) above are marked with non-past indexes, even though they both happened in the (very recent) past (see chapter 5.4.1 for details).

While the particles have different meanings, they overlap in their reference to events that have only happened recently, thereby conveying the immediacy of this event. As illustrated in (33a) and (33b), both particles are regularly used in this context.

(33) a. *oi, nyiqurlaqi raqaik, nyi delanyams, giavim*

oi,	*nyi=quarl-ki*	*te=a=qa-ki,*
hey	2SG.SBJ.NPST=present.NCONT-3SG.F	PURP=NM=some-SG.F

nyi	*de=**la**=nya=mes,*	*gia=va-im*
2SG	CONJ=this.day=2SG.SBJ=eat.NCONT.PST	2SG.POSS=thingy-DU.F

'hey, give her one, you yourself, you have just eaten, (it was) two of yours (that you have eaten)' (LONGYDS20150506_2-187)

b. *m.. maarum nanyi, delira nyames giavim*

ma..	*ma=arum*	*ne-nyi,*	*de=**lira***	*nya=mes*
ART.ID	ART.ID=NAME	from/with-2SG	CONJ=now	2SG.SBJ=eat.NCONT.PST

gia=va-im
2SG.POSS=thingy-DU.F

'A.. Arum, you yourself, you have just eaten two of yours' (LONGYDS20150506_1-446)

(iii) Past

Qaqet has several particles that are used in reference to past events: *mani* 'recently', *manima* 'before yesterday', *medu* 'past' and *murl* 'distantly'.

The particle *mani* 'recently' is used for the recent past, starting from yesterday and extending to events within the past week or so. For example, (34a) was uttered one day after the event, while (34b) was uttered six days after the event.

(34) a. *imani nguarltik metki*

*i=**mani***	*ngua=rletik*	*met-ki*
SIM=recently	1SG.SBJ=turn.over:SIDE	in-3SG.F

'and yesterday I poured (water) on it' (P12ADNFIRE-050)

b. *mani nguamrama.. amarluis, ngulu.. uresiit savrama aqalminngi*
mani *ngua=mat=ama..* *ama=rluis,*
recently 1SG.SBJ=take.NCONT.PST=ART ART=child
ngu=lu.. *ure=siit* *se=pet=ama*
1SG.SBJ.NPST=see.NCONT 1PL.SBJ.NPST=story to/with=on/under=ART
a=qalmin-ki
NM=frog-SG.F
'recently (i.e., 6 days ago) I took the.. the children, and I see.. we were telling stories about a frog' (I12AANACLADNSOCIO3-413)

There is a formally and semantically related particle, *manima* 'before yesterday', which is very rare: the example given in (35) is the only occurrence in the entire corpus. Compare also the corresponding semantic and formal difference between the adverbs *bigia* 'tomorrow' and *mabigia* ~ *bigiama* 'after tomorrow' (see chapter 6.2).

(35) *mani guarluaqa qasil imanima amauises pemaqerlap*
mani *gua=rlua-ka* *ka=sil* *i=**manima***
recently 1SG.POSS=friend-SG.M 3SG.M.SBJ=say.NCONT SIM=before.yesterday
ama=uises *pe=ma=qerlap*
ART=coldness PLACE=ART.ID=water
'my friend said yesterday that there was coldness in the water (the day) before yesterday' (AJL-09/05/2012; SCENARIO 113 FROM DAHL 1985)

The particle *mani* 'recently' contrasts with *medu* 'past', which conveys a more distant past. The contrast between the two particles is illustrated in (36a). There is nevertheless overlap in reference, as both can be used in reference to recent events. Compare (34b) above and (36b) below: both events took place within the last week, but the speaker chose *mani* 'recently' in (34b), and *medu* 'past' in (36b). In the case of more distant events, only *medu* 'past' can be used, e.g., in reference to an event that took place four months ago in (36c).

(36) a. *lunget maamani imedu, dap lungeriara, ias mania*
lu-nget *maqa-mani* *i=**medu**,* *dap* *lu-nget-iara,*
DEM-N HERE-down SIM=past but DEM-N-PROX
i=as ***mani**=a*
SIM=still recently=DIST
'those ones (plants) down there (were) from before, but these ones, (are) still of recent times' (D12ADNGARDEN-036FF)

b. *taquarl medu nguatis amasiaqi barek.. mabrigit*
taquarl ***medu*** *ngua=tis ama=sia-ki barek.. ma=birgit*
thus past 1SG.SBJ=call.CONT ART=chair-SG.F BEN ART.ID=NAME
'like earlier I pronounced (the word) *siaqi* for.. Birgit'
(I12ABLAJLATASOCIO2-153FF)

c. *de meduun kuherlngera vet ma.. aiaqunngi mamai, ingararles naqi*
de ***medu****=un kutserl-nget=a pet ma..*
CONJ past=1DU.SBJ plant.CONT:??-3N=DIST on/under ART.ID
a=iaquan-ki ma=mai, i=nga=rarles ne-ki
NM=moon-SG.F ART.ID=May SIM=3N.SBJ=start.NCONT from/with-3SG.F
'in the past, we planted them in the.. the month of May, when it started' (D12ABDACPGARDEN-038)

Finally, *murl* 'distantly' is used for events in the distant past, both within living memory (as in 37a) and in ancestral times (as in 37b).

(37) a. *araararlimga luqa imurl karles*
*araa=rarlim-ka lu-ka-a i=****murl***
3PL.POSS=firstborn-SG.M DEM-SG.M-DIST SIM=distantly
ka=rarles
3SG.M.SBJ=start.NCONT
'their firstborn (brother), the one who started (their family) in the past'
(N12AMVGENAINGMETBROTHERS-035)

b. *murl glamhrlura*
murl *gel=ama=srlu-ta*
distantly near=ART=old-PL.H
'at the time of the ancestors' (N12BAMCAT-009)

The particle *murl* has a second meaning: it occurs at animated points in a narrative to mark an event as sudden or surprising, as illustrated by the extract in (38). Note that each surprising event in turn is marked (in 38-1, 38-2, and 38-4). This distribution differs markedly from that of its past meaning: here, the particle only ever occurs once, situating an event in the distant past, while subsequent clauses are no longer overtly marked. In this second meaning, it can also mark events that did not take place in the distant past, e.g., when narrating stories from a picture book (as in 39).

(38) 1. *saka murl kaang bqa.. kavin nanasa, damakainaqirlan*
saka **murl** *ka=ang* *be=ka..*
immediately suddenly 3SG.M.SBJ=walk.NCONT CONJ=3SG.M.SBJ
ka=vin *ne-nas=a,*
3SG.M.SBJ=step.NCONT from/with-self=DIST
de=ama=kaina-ki=ara=rlan
LOC.PART=ART=water-SG.F=3SG.F.POSS=inside
'and immediately suddenly he rushes out and he.. he himself steps now into the middle of the river' (N12ABKSIRINI-087FF)

2. *dap murl amangerlnan, dqianyimma*
dap **murl** *ama=ngerlnan,* *de=kia=nyim=ma*
but suddenly ART=woman CONJ=3SG.F.SBJ=look.NCONT=thus
'and suddenly the mother, she looks up like this' (N12ABKSIRINI-089)

3. *oi, guauiska, dap masinepkia*
oi, *gua=uis-ka,* *dap* *ma=sinepki=a*
hey 1SG.POSS=child-SG.M but ART=NAME:SG.F=DIST
'hey, my child, it's (the spirit) Sinepki' (N12ABKSIRINI-090FF)

4. *tika murl tamrenas*
tika **murl** *ta=mrenas*
EMPH suddenly 3PL.SBJ=jump.NCONT.PST:SELF
'suddenly they jumped (in fear)' (N12ABKSIRINI-092)

(39) *dap murl kaningip..*
dap **murl** *ka=ning=ip..*
but suddenly 3SG.M.SBJ=fear.NCONT=PURP
'and suddenly he got afraid because..' (R12ABDFROG-086)

7.4 Aspect

Another set of particles has loosely aspectual functions: *sa* 'already', *as* 'still', *ide* 'IPFV', *pet* 'continuously', *petpet* 'frequently' and *miaqas* 'occasionally'.

The most common such particles are *sa* 'already' and *as* 'still', which are in complementary distribution in the initial particle slot. The particle *sa* 'already' marks an event as a pre-condition for another event to take place. Typically, it occurs with reference to past events, receiving a completive interpretation (as in 40a). But it is also attested in hypothetical and future contexts. As such, it commonly occurs in conditional contexts, marking a condition (as in 40b). And it is attested in past-in-the-future contexts: the particle *sa* 'already' in (40c) locates a future event as having happened prior to another future event.

(40) a. *de qiasil ma, sanguavleng guadanggi de.. dinani nyarenas saqua?*

de	*kia=sil*	*ma,*	***sa**=ngua=vleng*
CONJ	3SG.F.SBJ=say.NCONT	thus	already=1SG.SBJ=kill.NCONT

gua=dang-ki	*de..*	*de=nani*	*nya=renas*
1SG.POSS=dog-SG.F	CONJ	CONJ=can	2SG.SBJ=jump.NCONT.FUT:SELF

se=kua?
to/with=where
'and she said like this, I have (already) killed my dog (so you cannot jump to it), so.. so where can you jump to now?' (N11AESSIRINI-0016)

b. *desa quir tuqun, desa div utekmet, taqurla, de urelenges*

*de=**sa***	*kui=ta*	*tuqun,*	*de=**sa***	*dip*
CONJ=already	quoting=3PL.SBJ	say.CONT	CONJ=already	FUT

ut=tekmet,	*taquarl=a,*	*de*	*ure=lenges*
1PL.SBJ=do.CONT:IN	thus=DIST	CONJ	1PL.SBJ.NPST=destroy

'and if it is said, if we will do (this), just like this, we spoil (things)' (I12AANACLADNSOCIO2-148FF)

c. *ip nani nyaguirl, de sa dip nyilu i nguaming amamelangga*

ip	*nani*	*nya=guirl,*	*de*	***sa***	*dip*
PURP	can	2SG.SBJ=return.NCONT	CONJ	already	FUT

nyi=lu	*i*	*ngua=ming*
2SG.SBJ.NPST=see.NCONT	SIM	1SG.SBJ=weave.NCONT.PST

ama=melang-ka
ART=vine-SG.M
'when you return, you will see that I have woven the rope' (AJL-23/05/2012; SCENARIO 107 FROM DAHL 1985)

The particle can occur in both negative statements (as in 41a) and in questions (as in 41b).

(41) a. *saqa, desa quasiqiv.. iqataaqavep*

se-ka,	*de=**sa***	*kuasik=ip..*
to/with-3SG.M	CONJ=already	NEG=PURP

i=ka=tu=aa=qavep
SIM=3SG.M.SBJ=put.CONT=3SG.M.POSS=heart
'as for him, he.. he didn't yet (know what to) think' (N12ABKSIRINI-046)

b. *saqua nyirltik nanget?*

***sa**=kua*	*nyi=rletik*	*ne-nget?*
already=INTRG	2SG.SBJ.NPST=turn.over:SIDE	from/with-3N

'have you poured it out already?' (LONGYDS20150516_1-417)

Despite its common completive interpretation, *sa* 'already' is not a typical completive particle and it is compatible with imperfective interpretations. In (42), the speaker combines this particle with *ide* 'IPFV' and non-past marking on the predicate in order to convey the interpretation that the boy telling the story properly (in the first utterance) follows from the pre-condition of his parents habitually telling him stories (in the last utterance).

(42) *dap luqa amarluimga, deqraqatekmet, de liinangerlsil, i saidresiit baqa*
dap *lu-ka-a* *ama=rluim-ka,*
but DEM-SG.M-DIST ART=child-SG.M
de=ka=raqa=tekmet,
CONJ=3SG.M.SBJ=properly.NCONT=do.CONT:IN
de *lu-ini-a=ngere=lsil,*
CONJ DEM-SG.DIM-DIST=3N.SBJ.NPST=say.CONT
i ***sa**=ide=te=siit* *barek-ka*
SIM already= IPFV=3PL.SBJ.NPST=story BEN-3SG.M
'but that boy did (tell) it in the proper way, and that little (fact) is telling (us) that they are usually telling him stories' (I12AANACLADNSOCIO3-439FF)

This particle is also observed to occur in imperatives, presenting them as if they have already been carried out (as in 43a). In imperative (as in 43b) and hortative contexts (as in 43c), it is furthermore developing into an interjection. Prosodically, the interjection is set apart from the main clause. And semantically, it no longer focuses on a prior event being completed or being a pre-condition, but rather conveys the sense that the new event will take place immediately.

(43) a. *nyi sanyiluqa maraavuk*
nyi ***sa**=nyi=lu-ka* *mara=a-vuk*
2SG already=2SG.SBJ.NPST=see.NCONT-3SG.M here=DIR-up
'you, you look at him up here' (C12ARBZJIFROG-137)

b. *sa, dengentlak*
sa, *de=ngen=talak*
already CONJ=2PL.SBJ=play.CONT
'now, you play' (C12VARPLAY-441)

c. *sa, saqi ngurarles*
sa, *saqi* *ngu=rarles*
already again 1SG.SBJ.NPST=start.NCONT
'now, I start again' (C12VARPLAY-184)

Another aspectual particle is *as* 'still', which conveys the continuity of an event. In example (44a), the speaker uses it to assert that they continue to speak their language, and have not yet switched to Tok Pisin. And in (44b), the speaker uses it to describe a story character, a child who is still small and has not yet grown. This particle frequently collocates with *kerl* 'DEONT' in imperatives, forming a fixed expression that exhorts an addressee to remain patient (as in 44c).

(44) a. *de as uretaqen uralengiqa*
de ***as*** *ure=taqen* *ura=lengi-ka*
CONJ still 1PL.SBJ.NPST=say.CONT 1PL.POSS=word-SG.M
'and we still speak our language' (I12ABLAJLATASocio2-126)

b. *as amagilem*
as *ama=gil-em*
still ART=small-SG.RCD
'(she) is still a small (child)' (N12ABKSirini-027)

c. *as kerl avuk*
as *kerl* *avuk*
still DEONT wait
'wait now' (C12VARPlay-622)

In some respects, *as* 'still' can be considered a counterpart to *sa* 'already', and the two particles are indeed mutually exclusive: *as* 'still' conveys continuity (with an event continuing to hold), while *sa* 'already' conveys change (with one event being portrayed as a pre-condition for another event to take place). This correspondence is especially salient in sequences such as the one exemplified in (45): the speaker uses *sa* 'already' in the question in (45-1), but *as* 'still' in the negative answer to this question. In fact, it is very common to encounter *as* 'still' in negated clauses (as also in 46), but not obligatorily so (see 41a above for a counter-example).

(45) 1. *saqua nyaluqa?*
sa*=kua* *nya=lu-ka?*
already=INTRG 2SG.SBJ=see.NCONT-3SG.M
'have you seen him already?' (AJL-17/05/2012; scenario 149 from Dahl 1985)

2. *as kuasik ngualuqa*
as *kuasik* *ngua=lu-ka*
still NEG 2SG.SBJ=see.NCONT-3SG.M
'I still haven't seen him ~ I haven't yet seen him' (AJL-17/05/2012; scenario 151 from Dahl 1985)

(46) *as kuasiqini ngataqen*
as *kuasik=ini* *nga=taqen*
still NEG=SG.DIM 3N.SBJ=say.CONT
'the little (baby) still doesn't speak ~ doesn't speak yet' (I12AANACLADNSocio3-150)

The particle *as* 'still' is frequently observed in combination with other particles, often without any predicate being present. Example (47) is a particularly impressive example: the four intonation units consist entirely of conjunctions and particles (excepting the adverb *iasi* 'DIST'), which together situate the event in discourse – but the event itself is never mentioned, and has to be inferred from context.

(47) *de as, as kuasik, iv as nani, as nani iasi*

de	***as,***	***as***	*kuasik,*	*ip*	***as***	*nani,*	***as***	*nani*	*iasi*
CONJ	still	still	NEG	PURP	still	can	still	can	DIST

'and still, (this piece of garden near us is) still not (planted), and so (it) can still (be planted), (it) can still (be done) some time later' (D12ADNGARDEN-046FF)

In addition, Qaqet has a number of particles that convey imperfective-type concepts. The most common such particle is *ide* 'IPFV', which is most frequently used to describe habitual or characteristic behaviors (as in 48a). As such, it can co-occur with different tenses, e.g., non-past in (48a), but past in (48b). In a negative context, it often receives an interpretation of 'never' (as in 48c).

(48) a. *idre.. uretekmet taqurla, pramaluqup*

***ide**=ure..*	*ure=tekmet*	*taquarl=a,*
IPFV=1PL.SBJ.NPST	1PL.SBJ.NPST=do.CONT:IN	thus=DIST
pet=ama=luqup		
on/under=ART=place		

'usually we.. we do it like this, in (our) place' (P12ADNFIRE-055FF)

b. *dap luqia masinepki de.. ide menara.. sangarl*

dap	*lu-ki-a*	*ma=sinepki*	*de..*	***ide***	*medu=ta..*
but	DEM-SG.F-DIST	ART.ID=NAME:SG.F	CONJ	IPFV	past=3PL.SBJ
sangarl					
catch.fish:??					

'but that Sinepki.. in the past they used to.. catch (crayfish)' (N12AB-KSIRINI-066)

c. *ide.. kuide quasiqa*

ide..	*kui=**ide***	*kuasik=a*
IPFV	quoting=IPFV	NEG=DIST

'it is said that it never.. never (happens)' (I12ABLAJLATASOCIO3-029)

While it commonly occurs in habitual contexts, it is not restricted to them: there are also many examples where it conveys continuity. For example, the utterance in (49a) was used to describe the picture of a boy and a dog looking at bees. In this context, there is overlap with the particle *pet* 'continuously' (illustrated in 49b).

(49) a. *katika ide ianemnyim*
ka=tika ***ide*** *iane=mnyim*
3SG.M.SBJ=EMPH IPFV 3DU.SBJ.NPST=look.CONT
'they keep looking' (R12ADNFROG-107)

b. *kuas pet ngenetaneng pranget, dap ngenetlak*
kuasik ***pet*** *ngene=taneng* *pet-nget,*
NEG continuously 2PL.SBJ.NPST=hold.CONT on/under-3N
dap *ngene=talak*
but 2PL.SBJ.NPST=play.CONT
'don't keep holding on to them, but play (with them)' (C12VARPLAY-384)

The particle *pet* 'continuously' is much less frequent than *ide* 'IPFV'. It is restricted to contexts of continuation and long duration (as in 49b above), and it does not convey habituality. As such, the two particles can combine (as in 50a): *ide* conveying habituality, and *pet* continuity. There is also a reduplicated form, *petpet* 'frequently'. Again, it can combine with *ide* 'IPFV' (as in 50b): *ide* conveying habituality, and *petpet* iteration and frequency. The particle *petpet* 'frequently' contrasts with the particle *miaqas* 'occasionally', which can also combine with *ide* 'IPFV' (as illustrated in 50c).

(50) a. *atika ide, pet masmas, daraamam, deide pet.. ke.. katit savramalat*
ka=tika ***ide,*** ***pet*** *masmas,* *de=araa=mam,*
3SG.M.SBJ=EMPH IPFV continuously always CONJ=3PL.POSS=father
*de=**ide*** ***pet..*** *ke..* *ka=tit*
CONJ=IPFV continuously 3SG.M.SBJ.NPST 3SG.M.SBJ=go.CONT
se=pet=ama=lat
to/with=on/under=ART=work
'and always, continuously always, their father, he.. he always keeps going to work' (N12ABKSIRINI-028)

b. *ide vetpet nguatit savramasleng nepbang*
ide ***petpet*** *ngua=tit* *se=pet=ama=sleng*
IPFV frequently 1SG.SBJ=go.CONT to/with=on/under=ART=garden
nepbang
morning
'normally I go frequently to the garden in the morning' (AJL-03/09/2014)

c. *ide miaqas nguatit samramakainaqi*
ide ***miaqas*** *ngua=tit*
IPFV occasionally 1SG.SBJ=go.CONT
se=pet=ama=kaina-ki
to/with=on/under=ART=water-SG.F
'normally I go once in a while to the river' (AJL-03/09/2014)

In addition, the two adverbs *mas* 'continuously' and *masmas* 'always' cover a comparable meaning range (see chapter 6.2).

7.5 Discourse structure

A large number of particles serve to relate events and participants to each other, thereby structuring discourse. Given that they relate events, some of them develop aspectual functions or receive contextual aspectual interpretations. Their discourse-structuring functions nevertheless predominate, and they are thus discussed together in this section. This includes (i) additive and contrastive particles, (ii) particles that terminate events, (iii) particles that sequence events and (iv) particles that set the scene for events to unfold.

(i) Additive and contrastive particles

A number of particles introduce new participants or events by relating them to previous participants or events. This includes two additive particles (*saqi* 'again' and *miika* 'more') and two contrastive particles (*kaki* 'instead' and *miiki* 'instead').

The particle *saqi* 'again' (also realized *sai* ~ *siqi* ~ *sii*) expresses repetition. If the event is carried out by the same participant, it receives an interpretation of 'again' (as in 51a). If it is carried out by a different participant, it receives an interpretation of 'too, also' (as in 51b).

(51) a. *beiva, saqika qaruqun nara ma, ila raquarl kataqen*
be=ip=a, **saqi**-*ka* *ka=ruqun* *ne-ta*
CONJ=PURP=DIST again-3SG.M 3SG.M.SBJ=say.NCONT from/with-3PL.H
ma, *i=la* *taquarl* *ka=taqen*
thus SIM=this.day thus 3SG.M.SBJ=say.CONT
'and then, he says to them like this again, just like he had said earlier' (N11AJNGENAINGMETBROTHERS-0077FF)

b. *deqaki qeqiuaik saqa, ide saqika ngenamadangga, de saqika qeqiuaik, nasraamam*
de=kaki *ke=qiuaik* *se-ka,* *ide*
CONJ=instead 3SG.M.SBJ.NPST=run.CONT to/with-3SG.M IPFV
saqi-*ka* *ngere-ne=ama=dang-ka,* *de* **saqi**-*ka*
again-3SG.M 3N.ASSOC-from/with=ART=dog-SG.M CONJ again-3SG.M
ke=qiuaik, *ne=set=aa=mam*
3SG.M.SBJ.NPST=run.CONT from/with=behind=3SG.M.POSS=father
'instead (of the boy running on his own), it (the deer) is running with him, and it is also the dog, and it (the dog) is also running, behind its master' (R12ADNFROG-235FF)

This particle is compatible with stative contexts and with negative contexts – both are illustrated in (52).

(52) *de saqika iaqamqaqraqa, dap.. saqip kuasiqiamatluqa*
de ***saqi**-ka* *ia-ka=ama=qaqera-ka,* *dap..* ***saqi**=ip*
CONJ again-3SG.M other-SG.M=ART=person-SG.M but again=PURP
kuasik=i=ama=tlu-ka
NEG=SIM=ART=good-SG.M
'and he is also a (kind of) person, but.. he is also not a good person (like the other)' (D12ADKSPIRITS-053FF)

A second additive particle is *miika* 'more', which indicates that there is an additional extent or degree to the event (as in 53a), or an additional amount (as in 53b).

(53) a. *rlusnyi miasivuk, miikaivit, miikaivit, miasivuk, miika*
rlu=se-nyi *miasi-vuk,* ***miika**=i-pit,* ***miika**=i-pit,*
move=to/with-2SG THERE-up more=AWAY-up more=AWAY-up
miasi-vuk, ***miika***
THERE-up more
'move up there, a bit more up, a bit more up, up there, more' (LONGYDS20150531_1-502FF)

b. *miika ngunarlip ngusrlup*
miika *ngu=narlip* *ngu=srlup*
more 1SG.SBJ.NPST=like:PURP 1SG.SBJ.NPST=drink.CONT
'I want to drink more' (LONGYJL20150805_3-077)

The additive meaning of this particle can give rise to contextual interpretations of continuity (as in 54a). Furthermore, if it occurs in a context where there is a change in participants, it can receive an interpretation of 'also, too' (as in 54b).

(54) a. *de miika qurliama, de miika ianmugun, de ianetaqamnyim*
de ***miika*** *kurli-iam=a,* *de* ***miika*** *ian=mugun,*
CONJ more leave-3DU.M=DIST CONJ more 3DU.SBJ=sit
de *iane=taqa=mnyim*
CONJ 3DU.SBJ.NPST=properly.CONT=look.CONT
'they kept staying now, they kept sitting, and they looked carefully (lit. they stayed more, they sat more)' (R12ABDFROG-119)

b. *diaramaquata, de miikra brasem amarlaunnga*
de=ia-ta=ama=quat-ta, *de* ***miika**=ta*
CONJ=other-PL.H=ART=man-PL.H CONJ more=3PL.H
be=ta=sem *ama=rlaun-ka*
CONJ=3PL.SBJ=weave.NCONT ART=netbag-SG.M
'as for other men, as for them, too, they (can) weave netbags (not only the women)' (P12ARSBILUM2-045)

The two contrastive particles, *kaki* 'instead' (also realized *aki*) and *miiki* 'instead', both single out an intended event (as in 55a) or participant (as in 55b) from among a group of alternative events or participants, contrasting it with the possible alternatives. The alternatives can be explicitly stated in a negated clause (as in 55c), but it is much more common to leave them implicit, inferable from the context (as in 55a and 55b).

(55) a. *de ama.. aaleng nanget, iqaki lira qarek brlit pangeraning*
de *ama..* *a=aleng* *ne-nget,* *i=**kaki*** *lira*
CONJ ART NM=weakness from/with-3N SIM=instead now
ka=rek *brlit* *pe=ngera=ninga*
3SG.M.SBJ=hold/put.NCONT smashing PLACE=3N.POSS=head
'and they were.. dead, because instead (of leaving them alive), he had just now smashed their heads' (N11AAGSIRINILOBSTER2-0025FF)

b. *deqaki mapanavu, nyitlu, deqerl mpanavu qesiquat*
*de=**kaki*** *ma=panavu,* *nyi=tlu,* *de=kerl*
CONJ=instead ART.ID=NAME 2SG.SBJ.NPST=see.CONT CONJ=DEONT
ma=panavu *ke=siquat*
ART.ID=NAME 3SG.M.SBJ.NPST=try
'it's Panavu ('s turn) instead (not yours), watch out, Panavu is trying' (C12VARPLAY-466)

c. *kuasik iqiading amamelangga inaqaki qibrlany*
kuasik *i=kia=ding* *ama=melang-ka*
NEG SIM=3SG.F.SBJ=weave.CONT ART=vine-SG.M
*i=naka=**kaki*** *ki=brlany*
SIM=bit=instead 3SG.F.SBJ.NPST=sleep
'she is not weaving a rope, and instead she is sleeping a bit' (AJL-10/05/2012; SCENARIO 84 FROM DAHL 1985)

The particle *miiki* 'instead' has an almost identical distribution to that of *kaki* 'instead', except that it adds an element of emphasis or surprise. This difference is illustrated in example (56). The first clause contains *kaki* 'instead' conveying contrast, but without surprise: the event was, in fact, expected. The last clause then contains *miiki* 'instead', conveying contrast as well as surprise: the expectation did not materialize.

(56) *aki medu nguatu guaqavev idip kerekmet mavit, de miiki qeraqatekmet*
kaki *medu* *ngua=tu* *gua=qavep* *i=dip*
instead past 1SG.SBJ=put.CONT 1SG.POSS=heart SIM=FUT
ke=rekmet *mavik,* *de* ***miiki***
3SG.M.SBJ.NPST=do.NCONT:IN badly CONJ instead
ke=raqa=tekmet
3SG.M.SBJ.NPST=properly.NCONT=do.NCONT:IN
'instead (of him doing well) I expected that he will do badly, and instead (I find to my surprise that) he does well' (AJL&ADN-20/08/2014)

(ii) Terminating events

Three particles indicate that an event has ended. The most common such particle is *perlset* 'finish', which occurs at the end of a larger episode, e.g., an entire story (as in 57a), a major step in a procedural text, or an argument in a discussion. It is not used to indicate the completion of a simple event – in such cases, speakers would always resort to *sa* 'already' (see section 7.4). This particle transparently grammaticalized from the verb *verlset* ~ *perlset* 'finish', which is still synchronically attested (see section 7.1). The verb frequently occurs in the agentless construction (as in 57b), where it has a similar distribution to that of the particle: examples (57a) and (57b) were uttered in identical contexts, but they differ formally in that the verb requires an overt subject argument (*siitka* 'story'). The verb furthermore maintains a distinction between two aspectual stems (*verlset* 'finish.NCONT' ~ *perlset* 'finish.CONT'), which is lost in the particle: here, the alternation between *v* ~ *p* is conditioned entirely by the phonological environment, with *v* occurring intervocalically (as in 57a). Given their similar distribution, it is likely that the occurrence of the verb in the agentless construction (as in 57b) facilitated its grammaticalization as a particle (as in 57a).

(57) a. *katika verlsera*
ka=tika ***perlset****=a*
3SG.M.SBJ=EMPH finish=DIST
'it (the story) has really ended' (R12ADNFROG-389)
b. *tika verlset na.. namasiitka*
tika ***verlset*** *ne..* *ne=ama=siit-ka*
EMPH finish.NCONT from/with from/with=ART=story-SG.M
'the.. the story has really ended' (R12ACMFROG-125)

A second such particle is *deng* 'stop', which introduces an endpoint. It frequently marks the end of a story (as in 58a), and thus has a similar distribution to that of *perlset* 'finish'. There is a subtle meaning difference, though: *deng* 'stop' marks an event as being the last or final event, while both the particle and the verb *verlset* ~ *perlset* 'finish' mark an episode as having ended. This difference is illustrated in (58b). Given its meaning, *deng* 'stop' very frequently receives a contextual interpretation of 'until' (as in 58c). The particle can also occur reduplicated, intensifying its meaning (as in 58d).

(58) a. *tika denga*
tika ***deng**=a*
EMPH stop=DIST
'it (the story) has ended' (D12ADKSPIRITS-108)

b. *bedeng, inyaverlser inyain banas*
*be=**deng**, i=nya=verlset i=nya=in*
CONJ=stop SIM=2SG.SBJ=finish.NCONT SIM=2SG.SBJ=cook.NCONT
barek-nas
BEN-self
'and lastly, you have finished and you (can) cook for yourself' (P12ADNFIRE-040FF)

c. *atika un denaluquviara, imurl, bedeng*
ka=tika un de=una=luqup=iara, i=murl,
3SG.M.SBJ=EMPH 1DU CONJ=1DU.POSS=place=PROX SIM=distantly
*be=**deng***
CONJ=stop
'as for us, it is our place here, from the past, until now (lit. which (starts in) the past and stops)' (N12BAMCAT-038FF)

d. *bqatika vramaarenngi vramaarenngi, beip dengdeng ingilngil*
be=ka=tika pet=ama=aren-ki
CONJ=3SG.M.SBJ=EMPH on/under=ART=night-SG.F
*pet=ama=aren-ki, be=ip **dengdeng** i=ngilngil*
on/under=ART=night-SG.F CONJ=PURP stop:REDUP SIM=morning
'(it was) really (like this) during the whole whole night, until (lit. and it stops) early morning' (N11AAGBROTHERS-0096)

Like *perlset* 'finish', *deng* 'stop' has its transparent origin in a verb occurring in the agentless construction (as in 59).

(59) *de qiamen, de deng naqia*
*de kia=men, de **deng** ne-ki=a*
CONJ 3SG.F.SBJ=come.NCONT.PST CONJ stop from/with-3SG.F=DIST
'it (deer) came and it stopped now (at the edge of the cliff)' (R12ATAFROG-226)

A third particle, *saqap* 'enough', also conveys the end of an event, with the added connotation that as much as necessary was done to reach its completion (as in 60a). When it is directed at a second person, it usually has the negative connotation of 'more than enough' (as in 60b). Like *perlset* 'finish' and *deng* 'stop', this particle has its origin in a verb occurring in the agentless construction (as in 60c).

(60) a. *deqerl saqava*
de=kerl ***saqap****=a*
CONJ=DEONT enough=DIST
'it's enough now (I have done all I can)' (P12ADNROPE1-031)

b. *saqap denyit nyaruqun maamuk*
saqap *de=nyi=it* *nya=ruqun*
enough CONJ=2SG.SBJ.NPST=go.NCONT.FUT 2SG.SBJ=SIT.NCONT.FUT
maqa-muk
HERE-across
'enough now, you go and sit over here' (LONGYDS20150506_1-682)

c. *uiau, tika saqap naqia*
uiau, *tika* ***saqap*** *ne-ki=a*
INTJ EMPH enough from/with-3SG.F=DIST
'*uiau*, she's had enough now' (C12YMMZJIPLAY1-447)

(iii) Sequencing events

There are two particles that sequence events. The most common such particle is *maget* 'then' (often shortened to *mã* or *get*), which structures the story line by introducing new events. Individual speakers differ considerably in how frequently they choose to use this device, but the overall pattern is similar: it only ever marks an event that advances the story line further. For example, (61) is an extract from a narrator who very frequently uses *maget* 'then'. It introduces each new event, but it is absent whenever the narrator steps out of the story line: *maget* 'then' never appears in direct speech attributed to the story characters, nor in the elaboration of events (e.g., of the 'going' event in lines 61-4 to 61-6).

(61) 1. *kurlira vramanirlaqa*
kurli-ta *pet=ama=nirla-ka*
leave-3PL.H on/under=ART=sun-SG.M
'they stayed one day' (N11AJNGENAINGMETBROTHERS-0006)

2. *deip maget, daqaruqun ma (...)*
de=ip ***maget****,* *de=ka=ruqun* *ma (...)*
CONJ=PURP then CONJ=3SG.M.SBJ=say.NCONT thus
'and then, he said like this (...)' (N11AJNGENAINGMETBROTHERS-0007FF)

3. *beip maget, deratit*
be=ip ***maget****,* *de=ta=tit*
CONJ=PURP then CONJ=3PL.SBJ=go.CONT
'and then, they were going' (N11AJNGENAINGMETBROTHERS-0013FF)

4. *lek mara, deratit*
   lek *ma-ta,* *de=ta=tit*
   take.off OBJ-3PL.H CONJ=3PL.SBJ=go.CONT
   'they took off, and they were going' (N11AJNGENAINGMETBROTHERS-0014)
5. *tatit bratit bratit bratit bratit be..*
   ta=tit *be=ta=tit* *be=ta=tit*
   3PL.SBJ=go.CONT CONJ=3PL.SBJ=go.CONT CONJ=3PL.SBJ=go.CONT
   be=ta=tit *be=ta=tit* *be..*
   CONJ=3PL.SBJ=go.CONT CONJ=3PL.SBJ=go.CONT CONJ
   'they were going and going and going and going and going and..' (N11AJNGENAINGMETBROTHERS-0015)
6. *tamena, vramagalipkaarlim*
   ta=men=a,
   3PL.SBJ=come.NCONT.PST=DIST
   pet=ama=galip-ka=aa=rlim
   on/under=ART=galipnut-SG.M=3SG.M.POSS=bottom
   'they now came to the bottom of a galipnut tree' (N11AJNGENAINGMET-BROTHERS-0016)
7. *deip maget, daabarl taruqun ma (...)*
   de=ip ***maget****,* *de=aa=barl* *ta=ruqun* *ma (...)*
   CONJ=PURP then CONJ=3SG.M.POSS=big 3PL.SBJ=say.NCONT thus
   'and then, his older brothers said like this (...)' (N11AJNGENAINGMET-BROTHERS-00017FF)

This particle frequently occurs in its own intonation unit, preceded by the conjunctions *deip* (as in 61-2 and 61-7), *beip* (as in 61-3) or *ip* (not illustrated), and followed by the conjunctions *de* (as in 61-2, 61-3 and 61-7) or *be* (not illustrated) (see chapter 8.3 on conjunctions). It is likely that the prosodic segmentation and the conjunctions contribute to the sequential interpretation of the utterances. But there are also examples where *maget* 'then' occurs in different contexts, often combining with other particles (as in 62). That is, it is likely that the particle *maget* 'then' itself expresses a sequential meaning, too.

(62) *dap kuinquas magriv ursiqavit*
   dap *kui=nani=kuasik* ***maget****=ip* *ure=sik=a-pit*
   but quoting=can=NEG then=PURP 1PL.SBJ.NPST=climb.NCONT=DIR-up
   'but it is said that we then cannot climb up' (N11AJNGENAINGMETBROTHERS-0049)

A second, less frequent particle has a similar function: *qukun* 'later' sequences events, conveying the additional notion that the next step follows only a bit later (as in 63). It probably originated in the quantifier *qukun* 'few' (see chapter 3.2.2).

(63) *nani qukun, dinyikuap pramamelangga*
nani **qukun**, *de=nyi=kuap* *pet=ama=melang-ka*
can later CONJ=2SG.SBJ.NPST=tie.CONT on/under=ART=vine-SG.M
'a bit later, you can tie the rope' (P12ADNROPE1-051)

The particle *maget* 'then' (but not *qukun* 'later') is used in a second function: to signal agreement. For example, in the exchange between two speakers in (64), *maget* appears among many other utterances, all conveying agreement. If it is negated, it signals disagreement (as in 65b). Interestingly, the speaker in (65b) explicitly opposes *maget* 'then' (signaling agreement) to the particle *kuasik* 'NEG' (signaling disagreement), presenting them as antonyms.

(64) 1. ATA: *taqurla*
taquarl=a
thus=DIST
ATA: 'like this now' (I12ABLAJLATASOCIO2-094)

2. ABL: *mh, tika*
mh, *tika*
INTJ EMPH
ABL: 'mh, that's it' (I12ABLAJLATASOCIO2-095FF)

3. ATA: *magra*
maget*=a*
then/right=DIST
ATA: 'right' (I12ABLAJLATASOCIO2-097)

4. ABL: *tika magra*
tika ***maget****=a*
EMPH then/right=DIST
ABL: 'that's it, right' (I12ABLAJLATASOCIO2-098)

(65) a. *ah, kuasik maget*
ah, *kuasik* ***maget***
INTJ NEG then/right
'ah, that's not okay' (I12AANACLADNSOCIO3-165)

b. *ip kua magra, dap kua quasik*
ip *kua* ***maget****=a,* *dap* *kua* *kuasik*
PURP INTRG then/right=DIST but INTRG NEG
'whether it (the answer) is yes or no' (I12ABLAJLATASOCIO2-017)

(iv) Setting the scene

The particle *kiqerl* 'now' (also realized as *tiqerl*) has a scene-setting function. In narratives, it marks episodes that set the scene for later events to unfold. For example, the narrator in (66) uses this particle in the first clause to establish the setting, and then addresses his audience to ensure that they understand. Following this scene-setting episode, he then continues with the story line. This particle is not obligatory in such contexts, and its occurrence is restricted to decisive moments of a narrative, just before exciting or surprising events are about to take place – e.g., the scene in (66) is the background to a frog escaping.

(66) *atiqerla, damaarenngiaris, nyitlamaiaqunngi maraavuk?*
*ka=**kiqerl**=a,* *de=ama=aren-ki=are-is,*
3SG.M.SBJ=now=DIST LOC.PART=ART=night-SG.F=3SG.F.POSS-end
nyi=tlu=ama=iaquan-ki *mara=a-vuk?*
2SG.SBJ.NPST=see.CONT=ART=moon-SG.F here=DIR-up
'now it's in the middle of the night, do you see the moon up here?'
(R12ATAFROG-023)

Its scene-setting function overlaps to some extent with that of the distal demonstrative adverb *a* (see chapter 3.3.2). This adverb occurs frequently in tail-head linkages, where it portrays a preceding event as completed and as background to the next event. It thus very frequently co-occurs with the particle, e.g. in (66) above. Their interaction is illustrated in more detail in (67) below. Example (67-1) is a declarative utterance that reports an event on the story line (a spirit returning to her place). In (67-2) and (67-3), the narrator mentions this returning event again (once with the original verb *guirl* 'return', and once with the general motion verb *mit* 'go') and marks them with the demonstrative *a* and, in (67-2), he additionally uses the particle *kiqerl* 'now'. These two repeated clauses do not add new information, but instead serve to set the scene for the last clause in (67-3) (the spirit preparing for battle).

(67) 1. *biqiaguirl*
be=kia=guirl
CONJ=3SG.F.SBJ=return.NCONT
'she returned' (I12AANACLADNSOCIO3-519)

2. *akiqerl kiaguirla, sevraraluqup*
*ka=**kiqerl*** *kia=guirl=**a**,*
3SG.M.SBJ=now 3SG.F.SBJ=return=DIST
se=pet=ara=luqup
to/with=on/under=3SG.F.POSS=place
'her having returned now, to her place' (I12AANACLADNSOCIO3-520)

3. *dap.. iani, deqiamira, biqiamuvem*
dap.. *ia-ini,* *de=kia=mit=**a**,*
but other-SG.DIM CONJ=3SG.F.SBJ=go.NCONT.PST=DIST
be=kia=muvem
CONJ=3SG.F.SBJ=get.ready.NCONT.PST:PLACE
'and.. as for the little (man), she (spirit) having gone, she (spirit) got ready (to battle the man)' (I12AANACLADNSocio3-521)

The particle *kiqerl* 'now' is also attested outside of narrative contexts, occurring in utterances directed at second persons. In such cases, it usually adds a sense of frustration (as in 68).

(68) *melangga, akiqerl miika nyi, delra ngutaqen ip kurlinyi nyimnyim inamuk*
melangga, *ka=**kiqerl*** *miika* *nyi,* *de=lira* *ngu=taqen*
NAME 3SG.M.SBJ=now more 2SG CONJ=now 1SG.SBJ.NPST=say.CONT
ip *kurli-nyi* *nyi=mnyim* *i-na-muk*
PURP leave-2SG 2SG.SBJ.NPST=look.CONT AWAY-BACK-across
'Melangga, it's always you, I have just said that you should stop looking across' (C12VARPlay-476)

7.6 Speech acts: Negatives and interrogatives

Several particles overtly signal speech acts of negation (*kuasik* 'NEG' and *kurli* 'leave') and interrogation (*kua* 'INTRG').

The particle *kuasik* 'NEG' (often realized *kuas*) is the main means of conveying negation: it negates any type of verbal (as in 69a) or non-verbal clause (as in 69b), including declarative (as in 69a and 69b), imperative (as in 69c) and interrogative speech acts (as in 69d). It also frequently occurs in its own intonation unit, asserting the negative outcome of a preceding event (as in 69e).

(69) a. *as kuasiqini ngadrlem*
as ***kuasik**=ini* *nga=drlem*
still NEG=SG.DIM 3N.SBJ=know
'the little one still doesn't understand' (I12AANACLADNSocio3-142)

b. *iamalevungga, dequas aqamarleken praqa*
i=ama=levung-ka, *de=**kuasik*** *a=qama=rleken*
SIM=ART=tree.type-SG.M CONJ=NEG NM=some=branch
pet-ka
on/under-3SG.M
'the *levung* palm, it doesn't have any branches on it (lit. branches are not on it)' (N11AJNGenaingmetBrothers-0050)

c. *kuas nyiknaqa, qatika uina*
kuasik *nyi=knak=a,* *ka=tika* *uin=a*
NEG 2SG.SBJ.NPST=cry.CONT=DIST 3SG.M.SBJ=EMPH 2DU=DIST
'don't cry, it's (only) the two of you now' (N11AAGBROTHERS-0075)

d. *kua quas nyitlaqanii.. imiiki?*
kua **kuasik** *nyi=tlu=a=qa-ini=i..*
INTRG NEG 2SG.SBJ.NPST=see.CONT=NM=some-SG.DIM=SIM
i=miiki?
SIM=instead
'don't you remember a little something from.. from before?'
(N11AAGBROTHERS-0100)

e. *kemali mrama.. ama.. a.. ama.. pemaavetki, de quasik*
ke=mali *met=ama..* *ama..* *a..* *ama..*
3SG.M.SBJ.NPST=search in=ART ART NM ART
pe=ma=avet-ki, *de* **kuasik**
PLACE=ART.ID=house-SG.F CONJ NEG
'he is searching in the.. the.. the.. the.. in the house, but no (he didn't find it ~ it isn't there)' (R12ATAFROG-082FF)

This particle very likely originated in the negative existential predicate *kuasik*, which occurs in the agentless construction (see also chapter 5.2.2). In fact, it is not always straightforward to determine whether the form is used as a predicate or as a particle. In the case of pronominal referents, its analysis as a predicate is unambiguous: the referent is the subject of the existential clause, it can be of any noun class (e.g., masculine in 70a, but feminine in 70b), it is suffixed to the predicate, and the predicate appears in its non-final form of *kuasiqa* (see chapter 5.2.1 for the distribution of the final vowel *a*). In the case of nominal referents, by contrast, there is structural ambiguity. The noun phrase *aqamadum* 'a taro piece' in (70c) could either be interpreted as a subject noun phrase, with *kuasik* 'NEG' as the existential predicate (yielding an interpretation of 'there is no X'). Alternatively, it could be interpreted as a non-verbal equative clause, with *kuasik* 'NEG' as the particle (yielding an interpretation of 'it's not X'). Presumably this kind of context constituted the bridging context between the existential predicate use and the particle use.

(70) a. *de quasiqaqa*
de **kuasik**-*ka*
CONJ NEG-3SG.M
'but he wasn't there' (I12AANACLADNSOCIO3-539)

b. *de sa qiamira, quasiqaqi mara*
de *sa* *kia=mit=a,* **kuasik**-*ki* *mara*
CONJ already 3SG.F.SBJ=go.NCONT.PST=DIST NEG-3SG.F here
'she has already gone now, she is not here' (R12ATAFROG-053)

c. *kuasiq aqamadum, tapiuqem*
kuasik *a=qama=da-em,* *tapiuk-em*
NEG NM=some=taro-SG.RCD cassava-SG.RCD
'there isn't any piece of taro, there's a piece of cassava
~ it's not a piece of taro, it's a piece of cassava' (LONGYDS20150601_1-452)

The form *kuasik* 'NEG' is additionally used as a negative interjection, as illustrated in the exchange in (71).

(71) 1. ZSD: *ah, sangunan, nyilang*
ah, *sangunan,* *nyi=ilang*
INTJ NAME 2SG.SBJ.NPST=shake
ZSD: 'ah, Sangunan, you moved it' (C12VARPLAY-634)
2. XCS: *kuasik*
kuasik
NEG
XCS: 'no (I didn't move it)' (C12VARPLAY-635)

While the particle *kuasik* 'NEG' is the most common means of conveying negation, there are indications that a new negative particle, *kurli* 'leave', is emerging. This form occurs in similar contexts to *kuasik* 'NEG', but in different frequencies. It is most commonly used as a predicate in the agentless construction (as in 72a) (see chapter 5.2.2 for details on this predicate), and it is also frequently attested as a prohibitive interjection (as in 72b). In addition, there are a few examples where it seems to occur with a prohibitive meaning in a particle slot: compare the parallel examples in (72c) (with *kurli* 'leave') and (72d) (with *kuasik* 'NEG'). Given the small number of cases, it is likely that examples such as (72c) constitute innovations.

(72) a. *kurliqaavuk*
kurli*-ka=a-vuk*
leave-3SG.M=DIR-up
'he stays up (in the tree)' (N12AMVGENAINGMETBROTHERS-028)
b. *ai, kurli, kurli*
ai, ***kurli,*** ***kurli***
INTJ leave leave
'hey, leave it, leave it' (C12VARPLAY-243)
c. *kurli nyateski*
kurli *nya=tes=ki*
leave 2SG.SBJ=eat.CONT-3SG.F
'don't you fight her' (C12YMMZJIPLAY1-258)

d. *dakuas nyateski*
*dap=***kuasik** *nya=tes-ki*
but=NEG 2SG.SBJ=eat.CONT-3SG.F
'don't you fight her' (C12YMMZJIPLAY1-264)

Finally, Qaqet overtly marks interrogation by means of the particle *kua* 'INTRG' (also realized *kuarl*). This particle marks polar questions (as in 73a), and is mutually exclusive with question words (see chapter 8.1.2). Given the formal similarity, it is possible that *kua* 'INTRG' is related to the clause-final question word *kua* 'where' (illustrated in 73b).

(73) a. *kua nyitlu?*
kua *nyi=tlu?*
INTRG 2SG.SBJ.NPST=see.CONT
'do you see?' (R12ATAFROG-157)
b. *nani nyatit kua?*
nani nya=tit ***kua?***
can 2SG.SBJ=go.CONT where
'where can you go?' (N12ABKSIRINI-050)

This particle is also attested outside of interrogative contexts proper, marking available alternatives. This includes indirect polar questions (as in 74a), but also declarative utterances presenting alternatives. In such cases, speakers either mark each alternative with *kua* 'INTRG' (as in 74b), or all except the first (as in 74c).

(74) a. *kuas nyadrlem, ip kuaiaavetkia*
kuasik nya=drlem, ip ***kua****=i=aa=avet-ki=a*
NEG 2SG.SBJ=know PURP INTRG=SIM=3SG.M.POSS=house-SG.F=DIST
'you don't know whether (or not) it is his house now' (D12ADKSPIRITS-015FF)
b. *katik divut duremsem amarlaun, iquarl amaquatka, (...), dap kuarl amananngi*
ka=tika dip=ut de=ure=msem ama=rlaun,
3SG.M.SBJ=EMPH FUT=1PL CONJ=1PL.SBJ.NPST=weave.CONT ART=netbag
*i=***kua** *ama=quat-ka, (...) dap* **kua** *ama=nan-ki*
SIM=INTRG ART=man-SG.M but INTRG ART=woman-SG.F
'it is the case that we (all), we will weave netbags, whether it's a man, (...), or whether it's a woman' (P12ARSBILUM2-037FF)

c. *taquarl ama.. ama.. amadanggi, dakuarl amaqemgi, dakuarl ama.. amaqailka*
taquarl ama.. ama.. ama=dang-ki, ***dap=kua*** *ama=qem-ki,*
thus ART ART ART=dog-SG.F but=INTRG ART=snake-SG.F
dap=kua *ama.. ama=qail-ka*
but=INTRG ART ART=wallaby-SG.M
'like whether it's a.. a.. a dog, or it's a snake, or it's a.. a wallaby' (I12AANACLADNSocio3-247)

In addition, there is a second particle, *ulu* 'look', which is currently grammaticalizing into an interrogative particle (see chapter 8.1.2).

7.7 Other particles

This section introduces the remaining four particles that cannot easily be assigned to one of the semantic groups: (i) *tika* 'EMPH', (ii) *saka* 'immediately', (iii) *naka* 'bit' and (iv) *masna* 'quickly'.

(i) *tika* 'EMPH'

The particle *tika* 'EMPH' is a high-frequency particle, which is used to emphasize a statement or an opinion. As such it occurs in a large variety of contexts.

It commonly occurs in answers to questions, confirming that the answer is a true representation of the world. Compare the parallel examples (75a) (without the particle) and (75b) (with the particle): (75a) was uttered as part of the story-line narrating the sequence of events, while (75b) was uttered as a response to a question from the audience.

(75) a. *dianmuqi*
de=ian=mu-ki
CONJ=3DU.SBJ=put.NCONT.PST-3SG.F
'and they kept it (as a pet)' (R12ADNFrog-020)

b. *tika ianmuqia*
tika *ian=mu-ki=a*
EMPH 3DU.SBJ=put.NCONT.PST-3SG.F=DIST
'they really kept it now (as a pet)' (R12ADNFrog-050)

Despite its frequent occurrence in answers, it cannot be analyzed as a focus particle: it does not generally mark new information, it never marks contrastive information, and it is not restricted to this context. Another frequent context is its use to emphasize well-known truths, such as statements about customary activities and traditional knowledge (as in 76a). But it can be used to emphasize any kind of statement (as in 76b). And it is compatible with any kind of tense or aspect-marking on the predicate.

It also frequently occurs to mark the beginning (as in 77a) or the end (as in 77b) of a story or longer statement.

(76) a. *de qatika, idamalavu*
de *ka=**tika**,* *ide=ama=lavu*
CONJ 3SG.M.SBJ=EMPH IPFV=ART=adult
'it really is usually the parents (who teach the children)' (I12AANACLADNSOCIO3-133)

b. *de naqatika, dinya.. nyiral metka maus, de naqaki binymet dais*
de *naka=ka=**tika**,* *de=nya..* *nyi=ral*
CONJ bit=3SG.M.SBJ=EMPH CONJ=2SG.SBJ 2SG.SBJ.NPST=carry.NCONT
met-ka *maus* *de* *naka=kaki* *binymet* *de=a-is*
in-3SG.M once CONJ bit=instead break:IN LOC.PART=3SG.M.POSS-end
'then really, you.. you carry (something) in it (only) once, (because) instead its bottom will get broken apart' (P12ARSBILUM1-036FF)

(77) a. *perlsera, datika uriak*
perlset=a, *dap* ***tika*** *ure-ia-ka*
finish=DIST but EMPH 1PL.POSS-other-SG.M
'it's finished now, but there really is another (question) of ours (to answer)' (I12ABLAJLATASOCIO3-183)

b. *tika verlsera*
tika *perlset=a*
EMPH finish=DIST
'it (the story) has really ended' (N12BAMCAT-334)

This particle not only occurs in statements, but also in imperatives where it adds emphasis and force to the directive (as in 78a). And it occurs in hortatives, emphasizing and confirming the intention of the speaker to carry out the activity (as in 78b).

(78) a. *atika nyimali imanep*
*ka=**tika*** *nyi=mali* *i-manep*
3SG.M.SBJ=EMPH 2SG.SBJ.NPST=search AWAY-down
'really, search down there' (C12VARPLAY-562)

b. *atika uretaing praum*
*ka=**tika*** *ure=taing* *pet-em*
3SG.M.SBJ=EMPH 1PL.SBJ.NPST=sing.CONT on/under-SG.RCD
'really, we will sing a short (song)' (I12AANACLADNSOCIO3-455)

Speakers also use this particle to confirm or signal agreement with somebody else's statement (as in 79-4).

(79) 1. AAN: *damataqatekmet pemga*
de=ama=taqa=tekmet *pe-ka*
CONJ=ART=properly.CONT=do.CONT:IN PLACE-SG.M
AAN: '(they are) people who do things properly' (I12AANACLADNSOCIO3-401)

2. ADN: *ee*
ee
yes
AAN: 'yes' (I12AANACLADNSOCIO3-402)

3. ACL: *mh*
mh
INTJ
ACL: 'mh' (I12AANACLADNSOCIO3-403)

4. ADN: *tika*
tika
EMPH
ADN: 'really' (I12AANACLADNSOCIO3-404)

There is some overlap with the particle *kias* 'actually' (see section 7.2), as both frequently occur in statements that report on how the world is. But while *kias* conveys a speaker's commitment to the truth, *tika* serves to add emphasis to the conviction that the statement is true. As such, the two can co-occur (as in 80a). Similarly, there is overlap with *kerl* 'DEONT' (see section 7.2), as both communicate intentions of first person referents. Again, they can co-occur (as in 80b), with *kerl* portraying a statement as constituting an invitation to act (in this case, an invitation by the speaker to herself to continue weaving), whereas *tika* places emphasis on the speaker's intention to carry out the activity.

(80) a. *tika kias luqa amaqaqeraqa, de adlek*
tika ***kias*** *lu-ka-a* *ama=qaqera-ka,* *de* *a=dlek*
EMPH actually DEM-SG.M-DIST ART=person-SG.M CONJ NM=strength
'and actually that man, there is strength (on him)' (I12AANACLADNSOCIO3-511FF)

b. *de qatikaqerl nguading daisiara, tika nguading taqurlani*
de *ka=**tika**=**kerl*** *ngua=ding*
CONJ 3SG.M.SBJ=EMPH=DEONT 1SG.SBJ=weave.CONT
de=a-is=iara, *tika* *ngua=ding* *taquarl=ani*
LOC.PART=3SG.M.POSS-end=PROX EMPH 1SG.SBJ=weave.CONT thus=DIST
'I have really finished weaving this end (of the rope), and I continue weaving like this' (P12ADNROPE2-012FF)

(ii) *saka* 'immediately'

The particle *saka* 'immediately' conveys a sense of immediacy. As such, it is used in future contexts indicating that an event is about to take place (as in 81a). But is also used in past dramatic contexts, again conveying the immediacy of the situation (as in 81b).

(81) a. *ip saka nani nyiraing praum*
ip ***saka*** *nani* *nyi=raing* *pet-em*
PURP immediately can 2SG.SBJ.NPST=sing.NCONT on/under-SG.RCD
'you can immediately sing a short (song)' (I12AANACLADNSocio3-450)

b. *de qasaka qaning amaququanngi*
de *ka=**saka*** *ka=ning* *ama=ququan-ki*
CONJ 3SG.M.SBJ=immediately 3SG.M.SBJ=fear.NCONT ART=owl-SG.F
'and he immediately became scared of the owl' (R12ABDFrog-053)

(iii) *naka* 'bit'

The particle *naka* 'bit' (also realized as *na*) introduces an element of quantification to the event (as in 82a and 82b). It can also quantify over participants, singling out one of the participants (as in 82c). And it can receive a contextual temporal interpretation, indicating a time shortly before or after (as in 82d). There are a few examples where it could be interpreted as conveying attenuation, e.g., *naka* 'bit' in (82b) could arguably downplay the actual distance. But such cases are not common and they always allow for an alternative quantificational interpretation, too.

(82) a. *de naka ngatit pit*
de ***naka*** *nga=tit* *pit*
CONJ bit 3N.SBJ=go.CONT up
'it (the taro) grows a bit' (D12ABDACPGarden-023)

b. *as naka qui amaigules*
as ***naka*** *kui* *ama=igules*
still bit quoting ART=farness
'it is said that it is still a bit far away' (N12BAMCat-165)

c. *dluqa, de naqaki qamit*
de=lu-ka-a, *de* ***naka****=kaki* *ka=mit*
CONJ=DEM-SG.M-DIST CONJ bit=instead 3SG.M.SBJ=go.NCONT.PST
'and as for that one, he alone went instead (of the other)'
(N11AAGSiriniLobster1-0083)

d. *de naka ngutluip ngusuini ramatokpisin*
de **naka** *ngu=tlu=ip* *ngu=su-ini*
CONJ bit 1SG.SBJ.NPST=see.CONT=PURP 1SG.SBJ.NPST=teach-SG.DIM
te=ama=tokpisin
PURP=ART=NAME
'a bit later, I will make sure (lit. see to it) that I teach the little one Tok Pisin' (I12AANACLADNSocio3-077)

(iv) *masna* 'quickly'

Finally, the particle *masna* 'quickly' conveys a manner interpretation. It is attested both in simple (as in 83a) and reduplicated forms (as in 83b).

(83) a. *sa, de saqi masna nyitat*
sa, *de* *saqi* **masna** *nyi=tat*
already CONJ again quickly 2SG.SBJ.NPST=take.CONT
'okay, pick again quickly' (C12VARPlay-658)

b. *masmasna ngentat*
masmasna *ngen=tat*
quickly:REDUP 2PL.SBJ=take.CONT
'pick quickly' (C12VARPlay-648)

7.8 Summary

This chapter has focused on particles, which are defined syntactically as a word class: they occur in the left periphery of the clause, and they can co-occur with each other in fixed orders. They are synchronically non-inflecting and morphologically simple, but many of them probably originated diachronically in verbs. Some of them still retain verbal properties, notably restricted possibilities for subject inflection. The particles express information on modality, time, aspect, discourse structure, speech act and some other categories. As such, they frequently have scope over predicates, but they can also occur as propositions in their own right. All particles are optional, and speakers choose them to structure discourse. Qaqet shares the word class of particles and its overall discourse-structuring function with Mali Baining, but the two languages share only very few forms.

8 Clauses

This chapter introduces the different clause types: the structure of simple (verbal) clauses (section 8.1), non-verbal clauses (section 8.2) and clause linking (section 8.3). Section 8.4 then summarizes this chapter.

8.1 Simple clauses

Different aspects of the structure of simple clauses have been discussed in more detail elsewhere in this grammar, and this section serves to bring together the available information on clause structure (section 8.1.1) and speech acts (section 8.1.2). The focus of the presentation is on verbal clauses, but non-verbal clauses allow for the same peripheral constituents, and they are negated and questioned in the same way.

8.1.1 Verbal clauses

The different constituents of a verbal clause combine in the fixed order summarized in Table 75.

Tab. 75: Clause structure

1	Conjunction(s)	see section 8.3
2	Particle(s)	see chapter 7
3	Subject	see chapter 5.2.1
4	Verb	see chapter 5
5	Direct object	see chapter 5.2.1
6	Prepositional object(s) (entailed by verb semantics)	see chapter 5.3
7	Prepositional phrase(s), Relational noun(s), Adverb(s)	see chapters 5.3, 6.1, 6.2
8	Directional(s)	see chapter 6.3

In all verbal clauses, the constituent order is AVO ~ SV. This verb-medial order is a common areal pattern in New Britain and New Ireland, and Qaqet does not exhibit any evidence for a verb-final order, which is otherwise widespread among Papuan languages, including East Papuan languages (Dunn, Reesink, and Terrill 2002: 32–33, 36–37; Dunn et al. 2008: 743).

Example (1a) illustrates the intransitive SV order, while (1b) illustrates the one potential exception to this order: the agentless construction. This construction could be analyzed as exhibiting VS constituent order. However, as discussed in chapter

5.2.2, there are reasons to not adopt this analysis and to instead assume a VO constituent order. With respect to non-verbal clauses, there is more variation, including two constructions whose subject follows the predicate (e.g., the attributive construction exemplified in 1c) (see section 8.2).

(1) a. *asiitka qerarles*
a=siit-ka *ke=rarles*
NM=story-SG.M 3SG.M.SBJ.NPST=start.NCONT
'the story starts' (N11AJNGENAINGMETSIQI-0001)
b. *buv aarlaunini*
bup *aa=rlaun-ini*
fill 3SG.M.POSS=netbag-SG.DIM
'his netbag gets filled' (N11AAGSIRINILOBSTER1-0011)
c. *samabarl lungera*
sa=ama=barl *lu-nget-a*
already=ART=big DEM-N-DIST
'that one is already big' (LONGYJL20150805_1-265)

In transitive clauses, a direct object follows immediately after the verb (as in 2a). Recall that Qaqet makes widespread use of prepositions to introduce semantic arguments of a verb (see chapter 5.3): such arguments also follow the verb (as in 2b). Qaqet does not have any ditransitive verbs, but there are trivalent verbs that introduce arguments through prepositions. In such cases, the unmarked direct object precedes the prepositional phrase (as in 2c). If a prepositional phrase introduces a participant that is not entailed by the verb semantics, it follows to the right (as in 2d).

(2) a. *kua nyi.. nyadrlem amaququanngi?*
kua *nyi..* *nya=drlem* *[ama=ququan-ki]OBJ?*
INTRG 2SG 2SG.SBJ=know ART=owl-SG.F
'do you.. you know the owl?' (R12ATAFROG-149)
b. *ianmali ramaqulditki*
ian=mali *[te=ama=quldit-ki]PP*
3DU.SBJ=search PURP=ART=frog-SG.F
'they searched for the frog' (R12BCSFROG-014)
c. *dap kequarl aarluaqa remirang*
dap *ke=quarl* *[aa=rlua-ka]OBJ*
but 3SG.M.SBJ.NPST=present.NCONT 3SG.M.POSS=friend-SG.M
[te-irang]PP
PURP-PL.DIM
'he gives his friend the little things' (N11AAGBROTHERS-0015)

d. *ee, qemali raamamiara mramamengga*
ee, ke=mali *[te=aa=mam]*ARGUMENT*=iara*
yes 3SG.M.SBJ.NPST=search PURP=3SG.M.POSS=father=PROX
*[met=ama=meng-ka]*ADJUNCT
in=ART=wood-SG.M
'yes, he searches for his master here in the tree' (C12ARBZJIFROG-229)

The relative ordering of the peripheral elements of the clause has been discussed and illustrated in more detail in the preceding chapters: particles (chapter 7.1), prepositional phrases (chapter 5.3), prepositional phrases including relational nouns (chapter 6.1), adverbs (chapter 6.2) and directionals (chapter 6.3); conjunctions will be discussed in section 8.3. All peripheral elements can occur in all types of clauses, including non-verbal clauses.

Usually, only a small number of the available slots is actually filled. And it is very common for one or more element to be left-dislocated: particles (as in 3a), subjects (as in 3b), direct objects (as in 3c), prepositional phrases (as in 3d), directionals (as in 3d and 3e) or adverbs (as in 3f). The structure of left-dislocation is discussed in section 8.3.1.

(3) a. *de naqatika, dinya.. nyiral metka maus*
de ***naka=ka=tika,*** *de=nya..* *nyi=ral*
CONJ bit=3SG.M.SBJ=EMPH CONJ=2SG.SBJ 2SG.SBJ.NPST=carry.NCONT
met-ka *maus*
in-3SG.M once
'then really, you.. you carry (something) in it (only) once' (P12ARS-BILUM1-036)

b. *dap maramgi, de qamrenas*
dap ***ma=ramgi,*** *de* *ka=mrenas*
but ART.ID=NAME CONJ 3SG.M.SBJ=jump.NCONT.PST:SELF
'and Ramgi, he jumped' (N11AAGSIRINIROPE-0141)

c. *damarlaun, de tika idremsem namalangik*
*de=**ama=rlaun,*** *de* *tika* *ide=te=msem*
CONJ=ART=netbag CONJ EMPH IPFV=3PL.SBJ.NPST=weave.CONT
ne=ama=langik
from/with=ART=vine
'and the netbags, they weave them from the *langik* vines' (P12ARS-BILUM2-015)

d. *dap.. imuk pramagalipkaarlim, de qurlama.. alevungga*
dap.. ***i-muk*** ***pet=ama=galip-ka=aa=rlim,***
but AWAY-across on/under=ART=galipnut-SG.M=3SG.M.POSS=bottom
de *kurli=ama..* *a=levung-ka*
CONJ leave=ART NM=tree.type-SG.M
'and.. across at the bottom of the galipnut tree, a.. a *levung* palm is (there)' (N11AJNGENAINGMETBROTHERS-0023)

e. ***miasivuk**, de sa nguaistem naqi*
miasi-vuk, *de* *sa* *ngua=istem* *ne-ki*
THERE-up CONJ already 1SG.SBJ=blow.NCONT:PURP from/with-3SG.F
'up there, I already extinguished it (the fire)' (P12ADNFIRE-052)

f. *be bigia, deian taarlvit*
be ***bigia,*** *de=ian* *taarlvit*
CONJ tomorrow CONJ=3DU.SBJ stand.CONT:UP
'and tomorrow, they get up' (N12BAMCAT-087)

8.1.2 Speech acts

The different speech acts are marked through prosody and/or through particles and question words, but they do not differ syntactically: affirmative and negative statements, as well as questions and commands, exhibit identical syntactic structures.

The following near-minimal pairs illustrate the use of particles: an unmarked affirmative statement (in 4a), a negative statement marked by the particle *kuasik* (in 4b), and a polar question marked by the particle *kua* (in 4c).

(4) a. *de radrlem*
de *ta=drlem*
CONJ 3PL.SBJ=know
'and they know it' (I12AANACLADNSOCIO3-251)

b. *de quasik kadrlem sasmisavet nalengiqa*
de ***kuasik*** *ka=drlem* *se=a=smisavet*
CONJ NEG 3SG.M.SBJ=know to/with=NM=C.read:TO/WITH:ON/UNDER
ne=a=lengi-ka
from/with=NM=word-SG.M
'and he doesn't know how to read in the language' (I12AANACLADNSOCIO3-257)

c. *kua ngendrlem?*
kua *ngen=drlem?*
INTRG 2PL.SBJ=know
'do you know it?' (N11AJNGENAINGMETBROTHERS-0156)

There are also no differences between verbal and non-verbal clauses. For example, *kuasik* 'NEG' negates both the verbal clause in (5a) and the non-verbal clause in (5b). At the same time, a pitch contour of a final rise-fall marks both utterances as polar questions.

(5) a. *kuas nyitluini?*
kuasik *nyi=tlu-ini?*
NEG 2SG.SBJ.NPST=see.CONT-SG.DIM
'you don't see it?' (LONGYJL20150805_2-708)

b. *kuas amangerlnanngia?*
kuasik *ama=ngerlnanngi=a?*
NEG ART=NAME=DIST
'it's not Wara Pukpuk?' (LONGYJL20150805_2-621)

Negation was discussed in chapter 7.6: it is marked through the particles *kuasik* or *kurli*, and there is no characteristic negative intonation pattern (see also chapter 2.3.2 for a discussion).

Commands directed at a second person are exclusively marked prosodically through a final rise (see chapter 2.3.2), and there are no dedicated imperative particles (but see chapter 7.2 for various modal particles that can be used in commands). Commands directed at a first or third person do not differ prosodically from declarative clauses. In verbal clauses, commands are framed with the non-past subject indexes or the non-continuous future stem (depending on the type of verb), as in (6a) (see chapter 5.4.1 for their overall distribution). In the case of prohibition, speakers resort to the same negative particles as in all other cases (as in 6b). Furthermore, some verbs commonly occur in the agentless construction in imperative contexts (as in 6c) (see chapter 5.2.2).

(6) a. *nyitaqen*
nyi=taqen
2SG.SBJ.NPST=say.CONT
'talk' (C12YMMZJIPLAY1-539)

b. *kuas nyiknaqa*
kuasik nyi=knak=a
NEG 2SG.SBJ.NPST=cry.CONT=DIST
'don't cry' (N11AAGBROTHERS-0075)

c. *sung nangen*
sung ne-ngen
quiet from/with-2PL
'be quiet' (C12VARPLAY-082)

Questions are marked through a number of different question words, which are summarized in Table 76. In addition, questions are marked prosodically: the interjection through a rising pitch contour, tag and polar questions through a final rise-fall, and content questions through a falling contour (see chapter 2.3.2). In the case of polar questions, the particle is not obligatory, and the pitch contour alone can convey the question.

Tab. 76: Question words

Category	Form	Translation
interjection	*ah* [ă:]	ah, huh
tag question	*da*	right
polar question	*kua*	INTRG
content question	*nema*	who, which
	gi	what
	kesna	how much, many
	kesnanda	when
	kua	where
	nana	what, how
	ip nana	why (lit. PURP what)
interrogative verb	*sana*	do what

The interjection *ah* is used to initiate repairs, i.e., addressees use it to signal to the speaker that they should repeat their utterance (as illustrated in the exchange in 7). Segmentally, it exhibits a low-front vowel, which is cross-linguistically common for this kind of interjection. Prosodically, however, it differs from the typical pattern in that it does not exhibit the language-specific question intonation of either a polar question or a content question (see Dingemanse, Torreira, and Enfield 2013).

(7) 1. YRA: *amaiauskiara?*
ama=iaus-ki=iara?
ART=spirit-SG.F=PROX
YRA: 'is it a spirit here?' (LONGYDS20150516_1-787)
2. AMT: *ah?*
ah?
INTJ
AMT: 'huh?' (LONGYDS20150516_1-788)

3. YRA: *aiaus?*
a=iaus
NM=spirit
YRA: 'spirits' (LONGYDS20150516_1-789)
4. AMT: *aiaus?*
a=iaus?
NM=spirit
AMT: 'spirits?' (LONGYDS20150516_1-790)
5. YRA: *mh*
mh
INTJ
YRA: 'yes' (LONGYDS20150516_1-791)

Tag questions are formed by means of the clause-final question word *da* 'right', seeking confirmation (as illustrated in the exchange in 8).

(8)
1. ATA: *dap.. deqaki dsaqui uankuarl nama.. ama.. ama.. ama.. amapiksaqa, da?*
dap.. *de=kaki* *de=sa=kui* *uan=kuarl*
but CONJ=instead CONJ=already=quoting 2DU.SBJ=present.CONT
ne=ama.. *ama..* *ama..* *ama..* *ama=piksa-ka,* ***da?***
from/with=ART ART ART ART ART=picture-SG.M right
ATA: 'but.. you have already given an.. an.. an.. an.. an example, right?' (I12ABLAJLATASOCIO2-068)
2. AJL: *mh*
mh
INTJ
AJL: 'yes' (I12ABLAJLATASOCIO2-069)

Polar questions are formed with the help of the particle *kua* 'INTRG' (see chapter 7.6 for details). Alternatively, they are only indicated prosodically by means of a rise-fall on the final syllable(s) of the utterance (as in 5 and in 7-1, 7-3 and 7-4 above).

Content questions are formed through different *in situ* question words. There are two interrogative pronouns, *nema* 'who, which' and *gi* 'what', which have retained nominal morphology, occur as heads of noun phrases and stand in place of the questioned entity (see chapter 3.2.4 for details). A third interrogative pronoun is *kesna* 'how much, many', which has retained only minimal nominal properties, occurring in a subset of those contexts where numerals and quantifiers occur (see chapter 3.2.2). It obligatorily takes an article, and it occurs either as a nominal modifier to a head noun (as in 9a) (see chapter 3.4.2 on nominal modifiers), or as a nominal predicate in the equative construction (as in 9b) (see section 8.2.3).

(9) a. *nyatit segianirl amaqesna?*
nya=tit *se=[gia=[nirla]*HEAD
2SG.SBJ=go.CONT to/with=2SG.POSS=sun
*[ama=**kesna**]*NOMINAL.MODIFIER*]*NP*?*
ART=how.much/many
'you go for how many days?' (ABL&AAN-01/05/2015)
b. *aqesna namaminit?*
*[a=**kesna**]*PRED *[ne=ama=minit]*SBJ*?*
NM=how.much/many from/with=ART=minute
'how many minutes (lit. the minutes are how many)?'
(LONGYDS20150516_1-338)

In addition, there are a number of clause-final question words: *kesnanda* 'when', *kua* 'where', *nana* 'what, how' and *ip nana* 'why'. They occur unmarked in the clause-final adverbial slot (as in 10a), or alternatively in the marked left-dislocated position (as in 10b).

(10) a. *dip nyatit kesnanda?*
dip nya=tit ***kesnanda**?*
FUT 2SG.SBJ=go.CONT when
'when will you go?' (ATA&AEM-21/06/2011)
b. *dap kesnanda, deqamen?*
dap ***kesnanda**, de=ka=men?*
but when CONJ=3SG.M.SBJ=come.NCONT.PST
'but when did he come (lit. but when was it that he came)?'
(LONGYJL20150805_1-742)

The question word *kesnanda* 'when' asks about time (as in 10a and 10b above). It was presumably formed on the basis of *kesna* 'how much, many', but the origins of its second element are unknown, and its synchronic distribution differs from that of *kesna*.

The interrogative *kua* 'where' asks about a location (as in 11a). In this function, it is sometimes replaced by the longer form *kuaridi* 'where' (as in 11b), which is presumably formed on the basis of *kua* plus an unknown element. The form *kua* (but not *kuaridi*) combines with the prepositions *ne* 'from/with' and *se* 'to/with' to ask about the source and the goal respectively (as in 11c and 11d). The latter form can also be used to ask about a reason (as in 11e). The question word *kua* 'where' is presumably related to the particle *kua* 'INTRG' that forms polar questions, but the two forms have different distributions and functions synchronically (see chapter 7.6).

(11) a. *maqulditki, dequrliqi qua?*
ma=quldit-ki, *de=kurli-ki* ***kua?***
ART.ID=frog-SG.F CONJ=leave-3SG.F where
'the frog, where is it?' (R12BCSFROG-001)

b. *nyiquaridi?*
*nyi=**kuaridi?***
2SG=where
'where are you?' (R12ADNFROG-008)

c. *biak kamen naqua?*
be=ia-ka *ka=men* ***ne=kua?***
CONJ=other-SG.M 3SG.M.SBJ=come.NCONT.PST from/with=where
'another one comes from where?' (I12AANACLADNSOCIO3-125)

d. *de nani nyarenas saqua?*
de *nani* *nya=renas* ***se=kua?***
CONJ can 2SG.SBJ=jump.NCONT.FUT:SELF to/with=where
'so where can you jump to now?' (N11AESSIRINI-0035)

e. *nyi, nyitaneng praqi saqua?*
nyi, *nyi=taneng* *pet-ki* ***se=kua?***
2SG 2SG.SBJ.NPST=hold.CONT on/under-3SG.F to/with=where
'you, why are you holding it?' (C12VARPLAY-443)

The interrogative *nana* 'what, how' is used to ask about manner. It can form a question on its own (as in 12a), but it can also question a clause (as in 12b and 12c). More generally, it is used as an open question for more information (as in 12d). And it combines with the conjunction *ip* 'PURP' to ask about a reason (as in 12e).

(12) a. *damalavu rasil ma, nana?*
de=ama=lavu *ta=sil* *ma,* ***nana?***
CONJ=ART=adult 3PL.SBJ=say.NCONT thus what
'and the parents asked like this, what (happened) ~ how (did it happen)?' (N11AAGBROTHERS-0104)

b. *ulu dip ngurekmet neguauis nana?*
ulu *dip* *ngu=rekmet* *ne=gua=uis*
look FUT 1SG.SBJ.NPST=do.NCONT:IN from/with=1SG.POSS=child
nana?
what
'what ~ how will I do with my children?' (N12ABKSIRINI-032)

c. *tararlik nana?*
ta=rarlik ***nana?***
3PL.SBJ=cross.NCONT.FUT what
'how will they cross?' (N11AJNGENAINGMETBROTHERS-0120)

d. *amaplaua nana?*
ama=plaua ***nana**?*
ART=flower what
'what (do you mean), flowers?' (LONGZDL20160117_2-471)

e. *ingutaqa suqi ip nana?*
i=ngu=taqa *su-ki* ***ip*** ***nana**?*
SIM=1SG.SBJ.NPST=properly.CONT teach-3SG.F PURP what
'why (for what purpose) do I teach her properly?' (I12AANACLADNSOCIO2-189)

All content questions can optionally be marked with an initial particle *ngulu* ~ *ulu* 'look'. This particle presumably originated in the inflected verb *ngulu* 'I see', which is often used by older speakers in combination with a 'where' question (illustrated in 13a). Younger speakers almost always use the eroded form *ulu* in this context (as in 13b). It is most frequently observed in the context of 'where' questions, but there are occasional examples of its co-occurrence with all other question words, too (as in 13c; see also 12b above). Given its still restricted distribution, the analysis of *ngulu* ~ *ulu* 'look' is not straightforward: speakers recognize it as an inflected verb, but its beginning phonetic erosion and spread to a larger number of interrogative contexts suggests that it is currently grammaticalizing into an interrogative particle (see also chapter 7.6). The form *ulu* is furthermore used as a directive interjection (illustrated in 13d), and it has presumably given rise to the demonstrative base *lu* (see chapter 3.3.2 for details).

(13) a. *de ngulamadangga qua?*
de ***ngu=lu**=ama=dang-ka* ***kua**?*
CONJ 1SG.SBJ.NPST=see.NCONT=ART=dog-SG.M where
'where is the dog? (lit. I see the dog where?)' (C12ARBZJIFROG-272)

b. *uluqi qua?*
***ulu**=ki* ***kua**?*
look=3SG.F where
'where is it?' (LONGYJL20150805_1-595)

c. *ulu div undit dangamaginget?*
ulu *dip* *un=tit* *de=a=ngama=**gi**-nget?*
look FUT 1DU.SBJ=go.CONT LOC.PART=NM=some.NSPEC=what-N
'we will travel in what?' (N12BAMCAT-063)

d. *ulu uaniaqamek*
ulu *uane-ia-ka=a-mek*
look 2DU.POSS-other-SG.M=DIR-down
'look one of yours is down there' (LONGYDS20150516_1-437)

Finally, Qaqet has an interrogative verb, *sana* 'do what', which is used to ask about activities (as in 14).

(14) *dap nyisana?*
*dap nyi=**sana**?*
but 2SG.SBJ.NPST=do.what
'what are you doing?' (N12BAMCAT-222)

8.2 Non-verbal clauses

Non-verbal clauses in Qaqet are used to convey existence, location and direction, possession, equation and attribution: the existential construction (section 8.2.1), the locative construction (section 8.2.2), the equative construction (section 8.2.3), and the attributive construction (section 8.2.4) (summarized in Table 77). Note that Qaqet does not have a dedicated possessive construction, and speakers resort instead to the existential or the locative constructions to convey predicative possession. In addition, there is the so-called agentless construction, which shares similarities with some non-verbal constructions, most notably the final position of its only argument. This construction is included for comparative purposes in Table 77, but it was already discussed in chapter 5.2.2.

The general characteristic of all attested non-verbal clauses is the absence of a copula or other (defective) verbal element. Instead, Qaqet relies on syntax: the existential consists of a single noun phrase, and the other constructions juxtapose subject and predicate, whereby the order of constituents differs across the different constructions. Subjects are usually noun phrases, but the equative construction marks its subject by means of a preposition. And subjects are never cross-referenced on the predicate. The constructions furthermore differ in the types of predicates they admit. Table 77 summarizes the properties of each construction.

The related language Mali shares the general characteristics of non-verbal clauses: a juxtaposition of constituents, and a split between constructions with a post-verbal subject (conveying equation and attribution) and those with a pre-verbal subject (conveying location and possession) (Stebbins 2011: 48–51).

The non-verbal constructions do not contain any verbal elements and as such they differ from the agentless construction, which is added for comparative purposes to Table 77: it is a verbal construction, and it does not admit any nominal morphology. For example, the equative predicate (in 15a) and the attributive predicate (in 15b) both obligatorily occur with determiners such as articles. By contrast, the verb in the agentless construction cannot occur with any nominal morphology (as in 15c). Furthermore, such predicates also occur in straightforward verbal clauses (as in 15d).

Tab. 77: Non-verbal clauses

Construction	Syntax	Predicate
Existential	[subject]$_{NP}$	–
Locative	[subject]$_{NP}$ + [predicate]$_{ADV\sim PP\sim DIR}$	adverbial (including prepositional phrase, directional)
Equative	[predicate]$_{NP}$ + [subject]$_{PP*}$	NP with head noun or quantifier
Attributive	[predicate]$_{ADJ}$+ [subject]$_{NP}$	adjective
Agentless	[predicate]$_{V}$ + [object]$_{NP\sim PP}$	verb (see chapter 5.2.2)

*subject is obligatorily marked by preposition *ne* 'from/with'

(15) a. *de amaburlem nangen*
de [***ama***=*burlem*]$_{PRED}$ [*ne-ngen*]$_{SBJ}$
CONJ ART=many from/with-2PL
'you are many' (P12ARSBILUM1-028)

b. *de amavureknyi*
de [***ama***=*vurek*]$_{PRED}$-[*nyi*]$_{SBJ}$
CONJ ART=tired-2SG
'you are tired' (AJL-23/05/2012)

c. *perlset neguasiitka*
[*perlset*]$_{PRED}$ [*ne*=*gua*=*siit-ka*]$_{OBJ}$
finish.CONT from/with=1SG.POSS=story-SG.M
'my story is ending' (P12ADNFIRE-059)

d. *besak divunperlset naqaira*
be=*saka* *dip*=*un*=[*perlset*]$_{PRED}$ *ne-ka*=*iara*
CONJ=immediately FUT=1DU.SBJ=finish.CONT from/with-3SG.M=PROX
'and we will soon finish it' (P12ARSBILUM1-069)

Given their predicative nature, all non-verbal clauses can occur with all types of particles (see chapter 7). For example, the locative construction in (16a) co-occurs with the temporal particle *dip* 'FUT', and the attributive construction in (16b) with the modal particles *kias* 'actually' and *kua* 'INTRG'.

(16) a. *kasil idiv amauises pemaqerlav iara*
ka=*sil* *i*=***dip*** [*ama*=*uises*]$_{SBJ}$
3SG.M.SBJ=say.NCONT SIM=FUT ART=coldness
[*pe*=*ma*=*qerlap*]$_{PP}$ *iara*
on/under=ART.ID=bush PROX
'he said that there will be coldness in the water now' (AJL-09/05/2012)

b. *akias kua amaslurlnyi!*
*ka=**kias*** ***kua*** *[ama=slurl]*PRED-*[nyi]*SBJ*!*
3SG.M=actually INTRG ART=big-2SG
'haven't you grown!' (AJL-15/08/2014)

8.2.1 Existential construction

The existential construction consists of a single noun phrase, without any dedicated morphemes conveying existence. This noun phrase frequently co-occurs with particles (such as *nani* 'can' in 17a, or *dip* 'FUT' in 17b), but not necessarily so (as in 17c). If a referent is recoverable from context, it is omitted altogether. For example, the second clause in (17a) does not overtly express the mosquitos (which were introduced in the preceding clause) – not even by using a pronoun. The existential interpretation has to be inferred in such cases.

(17) a. *nani manirlaqa, denani quasik*
*nani [ma=nirla-ka]*NP*, de=nani kuasik*
can ART.ID=sun-SG.M CONJ=can NEG
'if there is sun, there won't be (mosquitos)' (LONGYDS20150601_1-378)

b. *bigia de quasik magriv aqani ngeruuknas idiv amaqaiki be div amauises*
bigia de kuasik maget=ip a=qa-ini
tomorrow CONJ NEG then=PURP NM=some-SG.DIM
*ngere=uuknas i=dip [ama=qaik-ki]*NP
3N.SBJ.NPST=wash.NCONT:SELF SIM=FUT ART=rain-SG.F
*be dip [ama=uises]*NP
CONJ FUT ART=coldness
'tomorrow no-one washes himself (because) there will be rain and there will be coldness' (AJL-09/05/2012)

c. *nyan, imanirlaqa*
*nya=an, i=[ma=nirla-ka]*NP
2SG.SBJ=come.NCONT.FUT SIM=ART.ID=sun-SG.M
'come, there's sun' (LONGYDS20150601_2-071)

The noun phrase can be complex, containing, e.g., possessive pronouns (as in both 18a and 18b), modifiers (as in 18a) or relational nouns (as in 18b).

(18) a. *kua uanataipki amatluqi?*
*kua [uana=taip-ki ama=tlu-ki]*NP*?*
INTRG 2DU.POSS=tape-SG.F ART=good-SG.F
'is there your good tape (i.e., do you have a good tape)?'
(LONGYDS20150516_1-552)

b. *kua de gialar angerarlan?*
kua de [gia=lat ngera=rlan]NP?
INTRG CONJ 2SG.POSS=work 3N.POSS=inside
'is there the inside of your work (i.e., do you have work ~ are you working)?' (AJL-15/05/2012)

Qaqet does not have a dedicated construction to express predicative possession. Instead, speakers either resort to the locative construction (see section 8.2.2) or to the existential construction. In the latter case, the occurrence of possessive person indexes (as in the examples above) often triggers a translation as a possessive predicate. Such an interpretation is likely to be a contextual interpretation, though, as indicated by the alternative progressive translation in (18b) above. Nevertheless, it is very common for the existential construction to receive a possessive interpretation. This is especially the case in the structure exemplified in (19a) and (19b) below: a left-dislocated noun phrase, followed by the existential construction, which in turn appears with a possessor index.

(19) a. *ngua de guarletki*
ngua de [gua=rlet-ki]NP
1SG CONJ 1SG.POSS=duty-SG.F
'as for me, there is my duty (i.e., I have a duty)' (I12AANACLADNSOCIO2-163)

b. *dap ngua de guasleng*
dap ngua de [gua=sleng]NP
but 1SG CONJ 1SG.POSS=garden
'as for me, there is my garden (i.e., I have a garden)' (N12BAMCAT-071)

Qaqet has a dedicated negative existential predicate, *kuasik* 'NEG' occurring in the agentless construction (as in 20), which gave rise to the negative particle *kuasik* (see chapters 5.2.2 and 7.6).

(20) *de quasiqaqi*
de kuasik-ki
CONJ NEG-3SG.F
'she isn't there' (R12ATAFROG-107)

8.2.2 Locative construction

The locative construction consists of a subject noun phrase preceding an adverbial. It expresses location and direction, and it is also used to convey possession, equation and attribution.

The Figure (i.e., the entity to be located) is linked to the subject noun phrase. It can be any kind of pronoun (e.g., an independent pronoun in 21a or 21c, a demonstrative pronoun in 21b) or noun; and it can also be omitted if it is given through the discourse (as in the question/answer sequence in 23 below). The adverbial, by contrast, is obligatory. It expresses the Ground (i.e., the entity with respect to which the Figure is located), which can be an adverb (as in 21a), a prepositional phrase (as in 21b), or a directional (as in 21c).

(21) a. *nget tuarl*
[*nget*]SBJ [*tuarl*]ADV
3N other.side
'they are on the other side' (D12ADNGARDEN-070)

b. *tika liirama mii vramasnanbetka amaqunaska*
tika [*lu-iram-a* *mii*]SBJ
EMPH DEM-DU.DIM-DIST most
[*pet=ama=snanbet-ka* *ama=qunas-ka*]PP
on/under=ART=ask:ON/UNDER-SG.M ART=one-SG.M
'those two (questions) both are inside the one question' (I12AANACLADNSOCIO3-091)

c. *iqerl tengning imasinepki, deqiavuk*
i=kerl *te=ngning* *i=ma=sinepki,*
SIM=DEONT 3PL.SBJ.NPST=fear.CONT SIM=ART.ID=NAME:SG.F
de=[*ki*]SBJ*=*[*a-vuk*]DIR
CONJ=3SG.F=DIR-up
'they fear Sinepki, she is up there' (N12ABKSIRINI-067)

The subject noun phrase is usually not indexed on the predicate, and the only partial exception are directional predicates. In most cases, the subject of a directional predicate is either a pronoun (as in 21c above) or a noun (as in 22a below). But there are a handful of examples that contain both a noun and a pronoun (as in 22b). It is possible that examples such as (22b) reflect a developing system of subject indexing on the directional predicate. For the moment, however, there are too few attested cases to pursue this possibility any further.

(22) a. *kaki amaqasupkaimek, bqa.. kanis daaqerlimgi*
kaki [*ama=qasup-ka*]SBJ*=*[*i-mek*]DIR, *be=ka..*
instead ART=rat-SG.M=AWAY-down CONJ=3SG.M.SBJ
ka=nis *de=aa=qerlim-ki*
3SG.M.SBJ=bite.NCONT LOC.PART=3SG.M.POSS=nose-SG.F
'instead a rat is down there, and it.. it bit on his nose' (R12ADNFROG-130)

b. *masirini qaamuk mramagulengga*
[*ma=sirini*]SBJ [***ka***]??=[*a-muk*]DIR [*met=ama=guleng-ka*]PP
ART.ID=NAME 3SG.M=DIR-across in=ART=malay.apple-SG.M
'Sirini is over there in the malay apple tree' (N11AAGSIRINILOBSTER1-0039)

The locative construction basically expresses static location. As such, it occurs both in 'where' question (as in 23-1) and in the answer to such questions (as in 23-2).

(23) 1. *uluqi qua?*
ulu=[*ki*]SBJ [*kua*]INTRG*?*
look=3SG.F where
'where is it?' (LONGYDS20150601_1-019)
2. *meramasupinngi*
[*met=ama=supin-ki*]PP
in=ART=saucepan-SG.F
'in the saucepan' (LONGYDS20150601_1-020)

All attested prepositions can occur in the locative construction, including complex prepositions that are formed through adding the prepositions *ne* 'from/with' or *se* 'to/with' to one of the spatial prepositions (see chapter 5.3). These complex prepositions invariably convey a dynamic reading. For example, (24a) illustrates motion from a location, and (24b), motion towards a location.

(24) a. *ee, tika uralengiqa.. nep malavu arlvis*
ee, *tika* [*ura=lengi-ka*]SBJ..
yes EMPH 1PL.POSS=word-SG.M
[*ne=pe* *ma=lavu* *ngere-uvis*]PP
from/with=PLACE ART.ID=adult 3N.POSS-top
'yes, our language.. comes from the parents' (I12AANACLADNSOCIO2-086FF)
b. *asiitka savramamiuqi, ngenama.. aqasupka*
[*a=siit-ka*]SBJ [*se=pet=ama=miu-ki*]PP,
NM=story-SG.M to/with=on/under=ART=cat-SG.F
ngere-ne=ama.. *a=qasup-ka*
3N.ASSOC-from/with=ART NM=rat-SG.M
'the story goes to the cat and the.. the rat' (N12BAMCAT-008)

The locative construction is also commonly used in possessive contexts. As indicated by the bracketing and free translations below, I see no reason to analyze the possessive use as a separate function of the locative construction: the formal properties are identical, and the spatial interpretation continues to be available. Instead, I consider the possessive interpretation a contextual interpretation. Example (25a) illustrates a typical context that can be interpreted as a possessive relation. And example (25b) illustrates a dynamic change of possession, conveyed through adding the preposition *ne* 'from/with': the sticks were given from Bridget, but they do no longer belong to her.

(25) a. *iamalevungga, dequas aqamarleken praqa*
i=ama=levung-ka, *de=kuasik* *[a=qama=rleken]*$_{SBJ}$
SIM=ART=tree.type-SG.M CONJ=NEG NM=some=branch
[pet-ka]$_{PP}$
on/under-3SG.M
'the *levung* palm, it doesn't have any branches on it (lit. branches are not on it)' (N11AJNGENAINGMETBROTHERS-0050)

b. *nagel nema? nagel mabridget?*
[ne=gel *nema]*$_{PP}$*?* *[ne=gel* *ma=bridget]*$_{PP}$*?*
from/with=near who from/with=near ART.ID=NAME
'(the sticks) come from who? (they) come from Bridget?' (C12VARPLAY-549FF)

The preposition *ne* 'from/with' has a second, comitative, sense. Again, this sense is present in the locative construction whenever *ne* 'from/with' occurs as the only preposition (as in 26a). It is very likely that this use has given rise to the associative construction, which conveys accompaniment (as in 26b). They not only have a similar meaning, but they also share a number of formal properties: the order of morphemes is identical; and both make use of the preposition *ne* 'from/with'. Synchronically, however, they have to be analyzed as different constructions: the associative construction coordinates noun phrases; it makes use of a set of associative person indexes that is not identical to that of the independent pronouns (albeit similar); these indexes are obligatory and they are affixes (see chapter 3.6 for details of the associative construction).

(26) a. *atikara namerrini*
ka=tika=[ta]$_{SBJ}$ *[ne=ama=lat-ini]*$_{PP}$
3SG.M.SBJ=EMPH=3PL.H from/with=ART=work-SG.DIM
'it is the case that they are with the little work (i.e., they have the little work)' (N12ABKSIRINI-082)

b. *kinamadangga*
ki-ne=ama=dang-ka
3SG.F.ASSOC-from/with=ART=dog-SG.M
'she with the dog' (I12AANACLADNSOCIO3-422)

The locative construction is furthermore intruding into the domains of equation and attribution. Qaqet has distinct non-verbal constructions for both, but speakers can alternatively shift to the locative construction to convey a dynamic reading. Example (27a) illustrates a typical context: a nominal subject (*ualsing* 'charcoal'), a preposition (*pet* 'on/under') and a pronominal location (*ki* '3SG.F'). The literal translation is thus 'charcoal is on it', but a more idiomatic translation is 'it becomes charcoal'. It is also possible for the subject to be a quantifier (as *malep* 'ten' in 27b) or a noun converted from an adjective (as *barl* 'big' in 27c) – which would normally occur in the equative and attributive constructions respectively. Again, they occur with dynamic readings in the locative construction. In (27b), the speaker uses the locative construction to highlight the dynamicity of reaching the number 'ten' (through adding another person). And in (27c), speakers prefer the translation 'fat(ness)' (instead of 'big(ness)'), arguing that this sentence conveys change – and presumably considering 'fatness' to be a changeable property (and 'bigness', a more time-stable property).

(27) a. *inyiluiaiqiam ualsing praqi*
i=nyi=lu=[ia-ki=ama *ualsing*]SBJ [*pet-ki*]PP
SIM=2SG.SBJ.NPST=see.NCONT=other-SG.F=ART charcoal on/under-3SG.F
'if you see one (log), which has become charcoal (lit. charcoal is on it)'
(P12ADNFIRE-048)

b. *tenraa.. araa qalatka, bemmalk sameta*
te-ne=araa.. *araa* *qalat-ka,*
3PL.ASSOC-from/with=3PL.POSS 3PL.POSS younger.sibling-SG.M
*be=[ma=malep-ka]*SBJ [*se=met-ta*]PP
CONJ=ART.ID=ten-SG.M to/with=in-3PL.H
'they together with their.. their younger brother, and (together with him) they are ten ~ they become ten (lit. ten are inside them)'
(N12AMVGENAINGMETBROTHERS-012)

c. *abarl praqi*
[*a=barl*]SBJ [*pet-ki*]PP
NM=big on/under-3SG.F
'she has become fat (lit. bigness is on her)' (ATA&AEM&ACS-22/06/2011)

In the case of many lexical items, speakers can choose between using the equative and attributive constructions or using the locative construction. In addition, there are lexical items, where speakers do not have such a choice: only the locative construction can be used. This includes a small number of lexicalized expressions such as *amadang praqa* 'he is a hunter (lit. dogs are on him)' in (28a), which contains the preposition *pet* 'on/under' and which is the conventionalized way of referring to a 'hunter'. And it especially includes nominal expressions that convey property concepts (as in 28b). In such cases, the dynamic reading is not necessarily present.

(28) a. *luqaira, de amadang praqa*
lu-ka-iara, *de* *[ama=dang]*SBJ *[pet-ka]*PP
DEM-SG.M-PROX CONJ ART=dog on/under-SG.M
'as for this one, he is a hunter (lit. dogs are on him)' (ACM-06/08/2012)

b. *de murl amadlek pamasiit*
de *murl* *[ama=dlek]*SBJ *[pe=ama=siit]*PP
CONJ distantly ART=strength PLACE=ART=story
'and the stories were strong (lit. strength was on the stories)' (I12AANACLADNSOCIO3-356)

I analyze all cases above as instantiations of the locative construction,[38] consisting of a nominal subject and a prepositional phrase. The subject is always a noun – either a lexical noun (as in 27a, 28a and 28b), a quantifier (as in 27b) or a noun arising through conversion from an adjective (as in 27c). Nouns, quantifiers and adjectives share a number of formal properties, and there is independent evidence that adjectives convert into nouns (see chapter 3.1.1). In most cases, the nominal and adjectival forms are identical, but there are also a handful of cases where Qaqet uses different forms. Compare, for example, the adjective *uis* 'cold' (used in the attributive construction) and the noun *uises* 'coldness' (used in the locative construction). In such cases, the locative construction always features the nominal form, never the adjectival form.

The prepositions *pet* 'on/under' and *pe* 'PLACE' are by far the most frequent prepositions occurring with equative and attributive interpretations. But other prepositions are attested, too, albeit in smaller numbers. For example, *uulirl mramamengga* 'the hotness is in the fire' (from *a=ulirl met=ama=meng-ka* 'NM=hotness in=ART=wood-SG.M') makes use of the preposition *met* 'in', conveying an inside locative relation. And expressions conveying human propensity frequently make use of the preposition *ne* 'from/with', e.g., *aneng naqa* 'laziness is with him' (from *a=neng ne-ka* 'NM=laziness from/with-3SG.M').

To summarize the discussion, the locative construction expresses a locative relationship, and it can also be used to convey possession, equation and attribution. In the case of possession, there is no dedicated possessive construction. Speakers instead resort to the locative construction, thereby conceptualizing possession as a spatial relation (when using spatial prepositions) or an accompaniment (when using the

38 The alternative possibility would be to analyze these cases as consisting of a non-verbal predicate (a noun, adjective or quantifier), and a subject that is introduced by a preposition. This is a possible analysis, too: such a constituent order is attested in both the equative and the attributive construction; and prepositions introduce subjects in the equative constructions. However, as discussed in the text, I consider the overall evidence to be in favor of the locative analysis. This decision has the additional advantage that the morphosyntax provides unambiguous criteria for identifying the constituents – whereas the alternative possibility introduces the danger of relying on subjective assessments as to whether a specific case is locative or equative/attributive in meaning.

comitative preposition); alternatively, they can use the existential construction (see section 8.2.1). In the case of equation and attribution, there are separate non-verbal constructions (see sections 8.2.3 and 8.2.4), but they are not available for all lexical items. For these items, speakers have to resort to the locative construction. For others, speakers can shift to the locative construction to highlight a dynamic reading.

In the case of location, speakers can alternatively resort to the verb *kurli* 'stay/leave' in the agentless construction (see chapter 5.2.2). This possibility is especially frequent in the case of subjects that are human or personified animals (as illustrated in 29).

(29) *saqi de qurliqi ruarl mramameng*
sa=ki *de* ***kurli**-ki* *tuarl* *met=ama=meng*
already=3SG.F CONJ leave-3SG.F other.side in=ART=wood
'as for her already, she stays on the other side in the trees' (N12BAMCAT-312)

8.2.3 Equative construction

The equative construction expresses proper inclusion, equation and quantification. As discussed in chapter 3.2.2, the morphosyntactic properties of quantifiers and numerals are (almost) identical to those of nouns, and they are thus probably best analyzed as a subclass of nouns.

In the equative construction, the predicate is either a noun (as in 30a) or a quantifier (as in 30b). In either case, the predicate obligatorily precedes the subject, and the subject is introduced by the preposition *ne* 'from/with'. This preposition is used both with pronominal subjects (as in 30a) and nominal subjects (as in 30b).

(30) a. *amalavu naut*
[*ama=lavu*]PRED [*ne-ut*]SBJ
ART=parent from/with-1PL
'we are the parents' (I12AANACLADNSOCIO3-187)

b. *deqakias, amaburlem nama.. amarlaun*
de=ka=kias, [*ama=burlem*]PRED [*ne=ama..*
CONJ=3SG.M.SBJ=actually ART=many from/with=ART
ama=rlaun]SBJ
ART=netbag
'there are actually many kinds of.. netbags' (P12ARSBILUM2-005)

The respective questions are formed in the same way, as illustrated in (31a) (for nouns) and (31b) (for quantifiers).

(31) a. *nemgi nanyi?*
nem-ki ne-nyi?
who-SG.F from/with-2SG
'who are you?' (ABL&AAN-01/05/2015)

b. *aqesna namaminit?*
a=kesna ne=ama=minit?
NM=how.much/many from/with=ART=minute
'how many minutes (lit. the minutes are how many)?'
(LONGYDS20150516_1-338)

Given their nominal character, both the predicate and the subject are marked for noun class. Since the two nouns designate different entities in the world, their noun classes do not necessarily match, and each noun retains its inherent noun class. For example, the predicate in (32a) is the feminine noun *smeski* 'food:SG.F', while the subject is a masculine pronoun (referring back to the singular masculine noun *lengiqa* 'word:SG.M'). Or the predicate in (32b) is the singular noun *lainnga* 'line:SG.M' (having a collective reference to the family line), while the subject is a plural pronoun.

(32) a. *uralengiqa iuras.. urasmeski naqa, amatok-pisin*
*ura=lengi-ka i=ura=s.. ura=smes-**ki***
1PL.POSS=word-SG.M SIM=1PL.POSS=?? 1PL.POSS=food-SG.F
*ne-**ka**, ama=tok-pisin*
from/with-3SG.M ART=NAME
'our language, (the one) which is our.. it is our food, Tok Pisin'
(I12AANACLADNSOCIO3-105)

b. *iqaks amalainnga nara*
*i=ka=kias ama=lain-**ka** ne-**ta***
SIM=3SG.M.SBJ=actually ART=line-SG.M from/with-3PL.H
'and they are actually the troops (lit. line-up)' (N11AAGSIRINILOBSTER2-0051)

Aside from coincidental matches (where the inherent noun classes of subject and predicate happen to match), matches are found only in those cases, where the predicate has no inherent noun class, but takes on the noun class of its referent. Mostly (but not exclusively, see below), these are nouns converted from adjectives. For example, the adjective *gil* 'small' converts into the noun *gil* 'small one', which can be marked for any noun class, e.g., *gilka* 'a small (singular masculine) one' or *gilki* 'a small (singular feminine) one'. When such nouns occur in the equative construction, the noun class of subject and predicate usually match (as in 33a and 33b). If the subject is a speech act participant, the predicate noun would still change depending on the noun class of the referent. For example, the pronoun *nyi* '2SG' does not distinguish gender, but this information is coded in the predicate noun (in 33c and 33d).

(33) a. *ka de amagilka naqa*

ka	*de*	*ama=gil-**ka***	*ne-**ka***
3SG.M	CONJ	ART=small-SG.M	from/with-3SG.M

'as for him, he is a small one' (ATA&AEM&ACS-22/06/2011)

b. *ki de amagilki naqi*

ki	*de*	*ama=gil-**ki***	*ne-**ki***
3SG.F	CONJ	ART=small-SG.F	from/with-3SG.F

'as for her, she is a small one' (ATA&AEM&ACS-22/06/2011)

c. *nyi de amagilka nanyi*

nyi	*de*	*ama=gil-**ka***	*ne-**nyi***
2SG	CONJ	ART=small-SG.M	from/with-2SG

'as for you, you are a small one (singular masculine)' (ATA&AEM&ACS-22/06/2011)

d. *nyi de amagilki nanyi*

nyi	*de*	*ama=gil-**ki***	*ne-**nyi***
2SG	CONJ	ART=small-SG.F	from/with-2SG

'as for you, you are a small one (singular feminine)' (ATA&AEM&ACS-22/06/2011)

Nevertheless, even though the noun classes tend to match in the above cases, mismatches are also attested: whenever one of the constituents is marked with a shape-based noun class, the other can be marked with a gender-based noun class. For example, the predicate in (34) is the kinship noun *rarlim* 'firstborn', which does not have an inherent noun class. In (34), it is marked for diminutive, while the subject is masculine. It would be possible to change either the predicate (to masculine) or the subject (to diminutive), but the speaker chose different markings, thereby highlighting different aspects of the referent: the diminutive tones down its importance, and the masculine gives information on its sex.

(34) *amararlimini naqa*

*ama=rarlim-**ini***	*ne-**ka***
ART=firstborn-SG.DIM	from/with-3SG.M

'he is the firstborn' (N11AJNGENAINGMETBROTHERS-0064)

In the case of predicate numerals and quantifiers, there is a match in number, though not necessarily in noun class. The numerals 'one' and 'two' use the base form *qunas*, marked for the appropriate noun class. In their case, the subject and numeral predicate match in number and noun class, e.g., both are dual feminine in (35a). Most numerals above 'two' as well as most quantifiers are unmarked for nouns class. If they occur as predicates, the subject noun phrase obligatorily occurs in its plural form – but there are no restrictions on its noun class, e.g., plural human (in 35b) or plural diminutive (in 35c). Finally, the numerals 'ten' and 'twenty' as well as some quantifiers have an inherent (singular or dual) noun class. In their case, the subject is plural, thus matching the number value, but not the overt noun class. For example, *burlem* 'many' can interchangeably occur unmarked as *burlem* (in 35c) or with inherent singular feminine marking as *burlemgi* (in 35d). In either case, the subject has to be plural.

(35) a. *de amaqunasim, navim*
*de ama=qunas-**im**, ne-**im***
CONJ ART=one-DU.F from/with-3DU.F
'and they (dual feminine) are two' (P12ARSBILUM3L-023)

b. *dakatika madepguas nara*
*dap=ka=tika ma=depguas ne-**ta***
but=3SG.M.SBJ=EMPH ART.ID=three from/with-3PL.H
'and they (plural human) are three now' (R12ADNFROG-366)

c. *das nani uraburlem nairang*
*de=as nani ura=burlem ne-**irang***
CONJ=still can 1PL.POSS=many from/with-PL.DIM
'the little ones (plural diminutive) are still many for us' (I12AANACLADNSOCIO3-219)

d. *amaburlemgi naap*
*ama=burlem-**ki** ne-**ap***
ART=many-SG.F from/with-PL.RCD
'they (plural reduced) are many' (R12ATAFROG-137)

8.2.4 Attributive construction

The attributive construction expresses attribution. It is similar to the equative construction in that the predicate precedes the subject. They differ, however, in that the attributive predicate is always an adjective, and in that it is followed directly by the subject (without an intervening preposition); furthermore, the two constructions have different patterns for marking noun class.

The following two examples illustrate the difference between the attributive construction (in 36a) and the equative construction (in 36b) by means of the form *barl* 'big'. In (36a), it occurs in its base form as an adjective, and it is followed directly by the subject noun phrase. In (36b), by contrast, it occurs as the converted noun *barl* 'older one' plus appropriate noun class marking (in this case, the plural human noun class). Being a nominal predicate, it obligatorily requires the subject to be introduced by a preposition.

(36) a. *sep mabarl amarluisa*
se=pe *[ma=barl]*PRED *[ama=rluis]*SBJ*=a*
to/from=PLACE ART.ID=big ART=child=DIST
'when the children are big' (I12AANACLADNSocio3-118)

b. *kuasik ngenan senas iamabarlt nangen*
kuasik *ngen=an* *se-nas* *i=[ama=barl-ta]*PRED
NEG 2PL.SBJ=put.up.NCONT to/with-self SIM=ART=big-PL.H
*[ne-ngen]*SBJ
from/with-2PL
'don't pride yourselves, just because you are the older ones'
(N11AJNGenaingmetBrothers-0159)

The corresponding question is formed by means of the question word *nema* 'who' (or *gi* 'what'), which is placed at the end of the clause (as in 37) (see chapter 3.2.4 for details on these two interrogative pronouns).

(37) *maquukuqa nemnget?*
ma=quukuk=a *nema-nget?*
ART.ID=sweet.potato=DIST who-N
'the sweet potatoes there are what (i.e., of what kind)?'
(LongYDS20150516_1-112)

The predicate adjective always has an invariant form, i.e., it is not marked for noun class and number. For example, the predicate *barl* remains invariant, even though the subject is human plural (in 36a above), masculine dual (in 38a below) or feminine singular (in 38b below).

(38) a. *amaququanngi, ama.. ama.. ama.. amabarl arasakngaiam*
ama=ququan-ki, *ama..* *ama..* *ama..* *[ama=barl]*PRED
ART=owl-SG.F ART ART ART ART=big
*[ara=saqang-iam]*SBJ
3SG.F.POSS=eye/face-DU.M
'the owl, its eyes are.. are.. are.. are big' (R12ATAFrog-150)

b. *abarl gianingaqi*
*[a=barl]*PRED *[gia=ninga-ki]*SBJ
NM=big 2SG.POSS=head-SG.F
'your head is big' (CCK&AGR-27/06/2015)

The above examples illustrate nominal subjects. Proforms such as demonstrative or indefinite pronouns behave in the same way as nouns. Personal pronouns, by contrast, are suffixed directly to the adjective (as in 39a and 39b).

(39) a. *iasamaremasngua*
i=as=[ama=remas-ngua]
SIM=still=ART=smelly-1SG
'because I'm still smelly' (N12BAMCAT-263)

b. *kurluun pramarim ip mabarlngeri..*
kurli-un pet=ama=rim ip [ma=barl-nget]=i..
leave-1DU on/under=ART=taro PURP ART.ID=big-3N=SIM
'we (won't) wait for the taros to be big..' (D12ABDACPGARDEN-029)

In the case of pronominal subjects, there is a potential ambiguity, which is exemplified in (40) below. The expression *mavureka* could either instantiate the attributive construction, parsing as *ma-vurek-ka* 'ART.ID-tired-3SG.M' (with a translation of 'it is tired'). Alternatively, it could be a referential noun occurring in left-dislocated position, parsing as *ma-vurek-ka* 'ART.ID-tired.one-SG.M' (with a translation of 'the tired one'). The context may make one or the other interpretation more likely, but there is no formal difference between the two options. This ambiguity arises because adjectives convert into nouns (e.g., *vurek* 'tired (adjective)' and 'tired one (noun)'), and because the personal pronouns and the noun class suffixes are largely identical in form (e.g., *ka* '3SG.M (personal pronoun)' and 'SG.M (noun class suffix)'). The only unambiguous cases are speech act participants (as in 39a above) and the neuter category (as in 39b above): they can only instantiate the attributive construction, because there do not exist any corresponding noun class suffixes (see chapters 3.2.3 and 4 for the different forms).[39]

(40) *dap sa aadangga, de miika mavureka, daqabrlany*
*dap sa aa=dang-ka, de miika ma=vurek-**ka**,*
but already 3SG.M.POSS=dog-SG.M CONJ more ART.ID=tired(one)-??
de=ka=brlany
CONJ=3SG.M.SBJ=sleep
'but his dog, it was really tired, and it slept
~ but his dog, as for the really tired one, it slept' (R12ADNFROG-206)

8.3 Clause linking

Semantically, Qaqet expresses different kinds of relationships between clauses through the extensive use of discourse-structuring particles (discussed in chapter 7)

39 The neuter form *nget* 'N' is also attested as a noun class suffix. That is, utterances containing a neuter form are potentially ambiguous, too. However, as discussed in chapter 4.2.3, this phenomenon is a new development: *nget* as a noun class suffix is found with very few nouns only; and most such nouns have a transparent origin in predicates.

and conjunctions (discussed in this section). Prosodically, the different kinds of relationships are signaled in identical ways (see chapter 2.3.2). Usually, all non-final clauses receive a non-final intonation contour (consisting of a final rise-fall), and the final clause, a final contour (consisting of a final fall). Alternatively, speakers can choose to mark all clauses with a final contour, i.e., they can choose to not mark their relationship prosodically. Morphosyntactically, there is no difference between non-final and final clauses, or between clauses that contain particles or conjunctions, and those that do not. In fact, there is no clear evidence for any form of subordination.

Clauses can be juxtaposed without any conjunctions, but such cases are uncommon and are usually accompanied by some other indication of their relationship. Example (41a) illustrates a typical case: the two clauses (one containing a verb of thinking, and the other, the content of the thought) are juxtaposed, and the intervening demonstrative adverb *taquarl* 'thus' signals the relationship between the two. Another demonstrative adverb, *ma* 'thus', is especially common in this context, often following verbs of speaking, perception or cognition (as in 41b). It belongs formally to the class of adverbs (see chapter 6.2), but it is arguably developing into a conjunction that introduces speech and thought. It is marked through a unique prosody: a level tone plus glottalization (see chapter 2.3.2 for details).

(41) a. *kiatraqavep, taqurlani, qiraqanbin senas*

kia=tu=ara=qavep,	*taquarl=ani,*
3SG.F.SBJ=put.CONT=3SG.F.POSS=heart	thus=DIST
ki=raqa=nbin	*se-nas*
3SG.F.SBJ.NPST=properly.NCONT=C.step.on	to/with-self

'she thought, like this, (that) she balanced herself properly'
(N11AAGSIRINIROPE-0136)

b. *luqaamuk masirini qasil ma, ngenahrlikaimanep*

lu-ka-a=a-muk	*ma=sirini*	*ka=sil*
DEM-SG.M-DIST=DIR-across	ART.ID=NAME	3SG.M.SBJ=say.NCONT

ma,	*ngena=sirlik-ka=i-manep*
thus	2PL.POSS=meat-SG.M=AWAY-down

'that Sirini over there said like this, your prey is on its way down'
(N11AAGSIRINILOBSTER1-0070)

The overall patterns of clause linking are similar to those found in Mali Baining (Stebbins 2011: 15–16, 91–93, 248–280), but they are unusual from a Papuan perspective. Many Papuan languages are known to employ multi-verb constructions, clause-chaining, switch reference, and/or subordination (Dunn, Reesink, and Terrill 2002: 36; Foley 1986: 167–205). As for (mono- or biclausal) multi-verb constructions, it is possible that Qaqet had such constructions in the past, but they have given rise to synchronic modifiers (see chapter 5.5) and particles (see chapter 7.1). And there is no evidence for the existence of either clause-chaining or switch reference. Since both are usually associated with an AOV constituent order, it is probably not surprising that they are absent in Qaqet. More surprising is the absence of any clear cases of subordination. Qaqet does have tail-head linkage, which is common in Papuan and neighboring languages (Dunn, Reesink, and Terrill 2002: 36–37), but again, tail-head linkage is achieved through the linking of two main clauses (see chapters 3.3.2 and 7.5).

Table 78 gives an overview of the Qaqet conjunctions and the presumably cognate forms in Mali.

Tab. 78: Conjunctions

Form	Function	cf. Mali
de	additive; left-dislocation	*da* 'additive'
be	additive (close relationship)	–
dap	contrastive	*dak* 'adversative'
–	–	*ura* 'disjunctive'
i	simultaneity	*i* 'reason', *ia* 'relator'
ip	purposive	*va* ~ *iva* ~ *diva* 'purposive'
–	–	*dai* 'consequence'
–	–	*asika* 'conditional'

Qaqet conjunctions are often formally and semantically similar to their Mali Baining counterparts. In some cases, one of the languages lacks a conjunction found in the other. In particular, Qaqet does not have a disjunctive conjunction. Instead, it uses the contrastive conjunction *dap* in combination with the particle *kua* 'INTRG' for this purpose. There is also no distinct conjunction for expressing consequence (which can be conveyed in Qaqet through the additive conjunctions) and condition (which can be conveyed in Qaqet through the purposive conjunction in combination with particles).

The major difference between the two languages is that Mali allows for embedded clauses. Interestingly, Mali uses three relators for this purpose (*ia*, *ma* and *ama*), which all have counterparts in Qaqet. The relators *ma* and *ama* are presumably cognate to the Qaqet articles *ma* and *ama*. In Qaqet, these articles play a role in connecting determiners and modifiers to the noun phrase – but they cannot be used to add (relative) clauses to the noun phrase (see chapter 3.3.4). And the relator *ia* is presumably cognate to the Qaqet conjunction *i* marking simultaneity – but again, different from Mali, this conjunction does not serve to embed clauses.

All conjunctions occur in clause-initial position, although they may be packaged prosodically with the preceding clause or else appear in their own intonation unit (see section 8.3.1 for a discussion and exemplification of the attested patterns). The conjunctions are mutually exclusive, with the exception of *ip* 'PURP', which can be preceded by *de*, *be* or *dap*. No other combinations are possible.

This section introduces the additive conjunctions *de* and *be* (section 8.3.1), the contrastive conjunction *dap* (section 8.3.2), the simultaneous conjunction *i* (section 8.3.3) and the purposive conjunction *ip* (section 8.3.4).

8.3.1 Addition

Qaqet employs two additive conjunctions, *de* and *be*: they have similar distributions, but *de* is more frequent and occurs in a larger number of contexts. It is discussed first, and then compared to the distribution of *be*.

The conjunction *de* sequences discourse by introducing each subsequent event. The extract in (42) is a typical example. (42-1) is the first utterance after an extended direct speech: here, the conjunction *de* forms part of the fixed expression *deip maget* 'and then', marking the beginning of a new episode (see chapter 7.5 for the distribution of the particle *maget* 'then'). The second occurrence of *de* in (42-1) is discussed below (as marking the preceding element as left-dislocated). Following that, each subsequent event is introduced by the simple conjunction *de* (in 42-2 and 42-3). Then, the first clause in (42-4) describes an event that occurs simultaneously to the one in (42-3) (the child of the *Brutka* coming across *Sirini* doing something), i.e., it does not introduce a subsequent event and the conjunction is absent. But it is again present in the second clause, which reports a subsequent event to the first clause (i.e., *Sirini* first picking the fruits, then eating them). In (42-5), the narration returns to the next event featuring the child of the *Brutka*, and again the narrator uses the conjunction *de*. The pattern illustrated by this extract is very typical of Qaqet discourse: *de* is almost always present in such contexts – unless it is replaced by another conjunction (e.g., by the conjunction *be* in the second clause of 42-5). It is very rare not to encounter any conjunction in this kind of context.

(42) 1. *deip maget, dleqama.. abrutka iaqama.. aarluimga*
de=*ip* *maget*, **de**=*lek*=*ama..* *a*=*brutka*
CONJ=PURP then CONJ=take.off=ART NM=NAME:SG.M
ia-ka=*ama..* *aa*=*rluim-ka*
other-SG.M=ART 3SG.M.POSS=child-SG.M
'and then, one.. a child of the.. the *Brutka* (spirit) took off' (N11AAGSIRINILOBSTER1-0029FF)

2. *daqapaikmet*
de=*ka*=*paikmet*
CONJ=3SG.M.SBJ=walk.around.CONT:IN
'and he wandered around' (N11AAGSIRINILOBSTER1-0031)

3. *de qanavet ma.. sirini mrama.. agulengga.. aalangiqa*
   de *ka=ne=pet* *ma..* *sirini*
   CONJ 3SG.M=from/with=on/under ART.ID NAME
   met=ama.. *a=guleng-ka..* *aa=langa-ka*
   in=ART NM=malay.apple-SG.M 3SG.M.POSS=shoulder-SG.M
   'and he came across.. Sirini in the.. the malay apple tree's.. top' (N11AAGSiriniLobster1-0032ff)
4. *katramaguleng, deqats*
   ka=tat=ama=guleng, ***de****=ka=tes*
   3SG.M.SBJ=take.CONT=ART=malay.apple CONJ=3SG.M.SBJ=eat.CONT
   'he (i.e. Sirini) was picking the malay apples, and was eating (them)' (N11AAGSiriniLobster1-0034)
5. *daqamit, bqasil, braqama.. abrutka*
   de*=ka=mit,* ***be****=ka=sil..*
   CONJ=3SG.M.SBJ=go.NCONT.PST CONJ=3SG.M.SBJ=say.NCONT
   barek=ama.. *a=brutka*
   BEN=ART NM=NAME:SG.M
   'and he (i.e. the child of the *Brutka*) went and said, to the.. the Brutka (spirit)' (N11AAGSiriniLobster1-0035ff)

The above extract also exhibits some typical prosodic characteristics. They are discussed here for the conjunction *de*, but the characteristics hold true for all Qaqet conjunctions. In many cases, the conjunction forms a prosodic unit with the clause it introduces. There is always a prosodic boundary between the two clauses, whereby the preceding clause can either be marked by a non-final prosodic contour (i.e., a final rise-fall) or a final prosodic contour (i.e., a final fall). That is, speakers can choose whether or not to portray an utterance as being part of a larger episode (see chapter 2.3.2 for details) – but this choice does not impact upon the use of the conjunction *de*, which is present in either case. Furthermore, there is usually also a clear pause preceding the conjunction.

Throughout the corpus, there are nevertheless many instances that differ from the prosodic pattern described above. These differences are mainly of two kinds. First, there is a large number of examples that exhibit only minimal cues to a prosodic boundary: i.e., the pitch movements indicating prosodic boundaries are reduced and/or there are no pauses. Example (42-4) is such a case in point: there is no pause, and the pitch movements preceding the conjunction *de* are barely perceptible. A similar case is (42-5) (this time concerning the conjunction *be*). Usually, a boundary is audible (represented by a comma in the above examples), but there remain a number of unclear cases.

And second, the conjunctions often serve as floor-holders and are followed by hesitation pauses. These pauses can be minimal (as in 43a), but they can also be very extensive (as in 43b). It is also not uncommon for dysfluencies to occur at this point, with conjunctions being repeated several times (as in 43c).

(43) a. *liamara iandit, de.. (0.07) ianemalia*
lu-iam=mara *ian=tit,* ***de..*** *iane=mali=a*
DEM-DU.M=here 3DU.SBJ=go.CONT CONJ 3DU.SBJ.NPST=search=DIST
'these two here go, and.. they are searching now' (R12ATAFROG-095)

b. *kalu savrianaqulditkia, de.. (0.8) kamraqi*
ka=lu *se=pet=iana=quldit-ki=a,*
3SG.M.SBJ=see.NCONT to/with=on/under=3DU.POSS=frog-SG.F=DIST
de.. *ka=mat-ki*
CONJ 3SG.M.SBJ=take.NCONT.PST-3SG.F
'he saw their frog, and.. he picked it up' (R12ACMFROG-117FF)

c. *nyaruqun, de.. de.. de.. de.. dama.. uh demabridget, kimnyim sagelngen*
nya=ruqun, ***de..*** ***de..*** ***de..*** ***de..*** ***de****=ama..*
2SG.SBJ=sit.NCONT.FUT CONJ CONJ CONJ CONJ CONJ=ART
uh ***de****=ma=bridget,* *ki=mnyim* *se=gel-ngen*
INTJ CONJ=ART.ID=NAME 3SG.F.SBJ.NPST=look.CONT to/with=near-2PL
'sit down, and.. and.. and.. and.. and the.. uh and Bridget, she will be looking at you' (C12VARPLAY-437)

The conjunction *de* not only introduces verbal clauses (as in the examples above), but any kind of proposition. Example (44-4) illustrates a typical case. Such examples often look superficially like noun phrase coordination (e.g., 'days and nights' in this case). However, in each case, there are indications that the linking continues to operate on a clausal level. For example, the content of the utterance in (44-4) is essentially a condensed paraphrase of the content expressed in the three preceding clauses (in 44-1, 44-2 and 44-3). Syntactically, the propositions are often marked by particles or adverbs, which do not operate on a phrasal level (e.g., the particle *tika* 'EMPH' in 44-4). And prosodically, there is a boundary between the two units. Given all indications together, utterances such as (44-4) are analyzed as a linking of two existential clauses (which are not overtly marked in Qaqet; see section 8.2.1). On a functional level, there is nevertheless some overlap with noun phrase coordination (see chapter 3.6 for details).

(44) 1. *amanirl ngatit savriam, pramakaska*
ama=nirla *nga=tit* *se=pet-iam,*
ART=sun 3N.SBJ=go.CONT to/with=on/under-3DU.M
pet=ama=kas-ka
on/under=ART=saltwater-SG.M
'the days (lit. suns) were going down on them, at sea' (N12BAMCAT-146FF)

2. *damaaren ngatit savriam, pramakaska*
de=ama=aren nga=tit se=pet-iam,
CONJ=ART=night 3N.SBJ=go.CONT to/with=on/under-3DU.M
pet=ama=kas-ka
on/under=ART=saltwater-SG.M
'and the nights were going down on them, at sea' (N12BAMCAT-148)
3. *iandit*
ian=tit
3DU.SBJ=go.CONT
'they (the cat and the rat) were going' (N12BAMCAT-149)
4. *tika amanirl, damaaren, dav iandit*
*tika ama=nirla, **de**=ama=aren, dap ian=tit*
EMPH ART=sun CONJ=ART=night but 3DU.SBJ=go.CONT
'it was really days, and it was nights, but they were (still) going' (N12BAMCAT-150)

The conjunction *de* is furthermore used in a second context: as marking the boundary between a left-dislocated element and the clause. Such left-dislocations are very frequent in Qaqet discourse. Often, the left-dislocated element is a noun phrase that is co-referential with the subject (as in 45a) or with any other argument of the verb (as the prepositional object in 45b). It is even possible for more than one participant of the event to be left-dislocated (as in 45c).

(45) a. *aqasupka, de qebrlany*
*a=qasup-ka, **de** ke=brlany*
NM=rat-SG.M CONJ 3SG.M.SBJ.NPST=sleep
'(as for) the rat, it is sleeping' (N12BAMCAT-197)
b. *amalengiqa, de as uraneng praqa*
*ama=lengi-ka, **de** as ure=raneng*
ART=word-SG.M CONJ still 1PL.SBJ.NPST=hold.NCONT
pet-ka
on/under-3SG.M
'(as for) the language, we will still hold on to it' (I12ABLAJLATASOCIO2-128)
c. *luqaira, de aaqulditki, de qatalki*
*lu-ka-iara, **de** aa=quldit-ki,*
DEM-SG.M-PROX CONJ 3SG.M.POSS=frog-SG.F
***de** ka=tal-ki*
CONJ 3SG.M.SBJ=carry.CONT-3SG.F
'(as for) this one [the boy], and (as for) his frog, he carries it' (C12AR-BZJIFROG-579)

The left-dislocated elements do not function as arguments in the clause, as evidenced by the distribution of argument indexing. In the case of direct objects, the index and the direct object noun phrase are in complementary distribution (see chapter 5.2.1). But a left-dislocated noun phrase can co-occur with an object index on the verb, e.g., the index *ki* '3SG.F' and the dislocated noun phrase pick out the same referent in (46a). In the case of subjects, the situation is slightly different, as subject noun phrases and subject indexes co-occur. However, there are restrictions on subject noun phrases consisting of independent pronouns (see chapter 3.2.2). In the case of dislocated noun phrases, by contrast, no such restrictions apply, and any independent pronoun can appear in this slot (as the pronoun *ki* '3SG.F' in 46b).

(46) a. *dav aadanggi, de nyitluqi maraamuk*
dap ***aa=dang-ki,*** *de* *nyi=tlu-**ki***
but 3SG.M.POSS=dog-SG.F CONJ 2SG.SBJ.NPST=see.CONT-3SG.F
mara=a-muk
here=DIR-across
'and (as for) his dog, you see it over there' (R12ATAFROG-190)

b. *dap ki, de qiamrenas*
dap ***ki,*** *de* ***kia**=mrenas*
but 3SG.F CONJ 3SG.F.SBJ=jump.NCONT.PST:SELF
'but (as for) her, she jumped out' (R12ATAFROG-056)

Left-dislocation is not restricted to participants in an event, but is also found for all other kinds of elements, including adverbs (as in 47a), prepositional phrases (as in 47b), and particles (as in 47c).

(47) a. *nanima sunun, diandit iv ianebrlany, biana.. ianaavetki*
nanima *sunun,* ***de**=ian=tit* *ip*
late.evening evening CONJ=3DU.SBJ=go.CONT PURP
iane=brlany, *be=iana..* *iana=avet-ki*
3DU.SBJ.NPST=sleep CONJ=3DU.POSS 3DU.POSS=house-SG.F
'late evening time, they are going to sleep, and (it is in) their.. their house' (N11AAGBROTHERS-0008)

b. *priang amanirl, duqurli amaqalmin*
pet=ia-nget *ama=nirla,* ***de**=kurli* *ama=qalmin*
on/under=other-N ART=sun CONJ=leave ART=frog
'on one day, a frog was (there)' (I12AANACLADNSOCIO3-420)

c. *ip nani qukun, de barek liina*
ip *nani* *qukun,* ***de*** *barek* *lu-ini-a*
PURP can later CONJ BEN DEM-SG.DIM-DIST
'so (it) can (be) later, (that I teach it) for that little one' (I12AANACLAD-NSOCIO3-078)

The second additive conjunction is *be*: it also serves to introduce subsequent events, but it does not mark left-dislocated elements. This pattern is illustrated in (48). The utterance in (48-2) starts a new episode, and the speaker uses *be* as part of the fixed expression *beip maget* 'and then'. The entire expression is left-dislocated, and the following clause is marked by the conjunction *de* – it is not possible for *be* to occur in this second context.

(48) 1. *kataqen amangerlnanngia*
ka=taqen *ama=ngerlnan-ki=a*
3SG.M.SBJ=say.CONT ART=woman-SG.F=DIST
'he tells the mother now' (N11AJNGENAINGMETSIQI-0023)
2. *beip maget, diqitaqen amalengiima ma*
***be**=ip* *maget,* ***de**=ki=taqen*
CONJ=PURP then CONJ=3SG.F.SBJ.NPST=say.CONT
ama=lengi-em=a *ma*
ART=word-SG.RCD=DIST thus
'and then, she says a short incantation now like this' (N11AJNGENAINGMETSIQI-0024FF)

While there is overlap between *be* and *de* in the sequencing of discourse, they have subtly different meanings: *be* entails a close conceptual relationship between the sequences, while the semantics of *de* are more general, and do not give information about the closeness of the relationship. By itself, *de* does not indicate a remote relationship – but as it pragmatically contrasts with *be*, it often receives such an interpretation.

For example, the utterance in (48-2) above is a direct consequence of the utterance in (48-1), and the narrator thus chooses to use *be*: the son has just asked the mother to speak a short incantation, and the mother follows up on this request in (48-2).

Similarly, *be* is used in (49a) to assert the close relationship between getting up to kill oneself and to then die; while the neutral conjunction *de* introduces this entire sequence of closely-related events. Example (49b) illustrates another typical context for the use of *be*: the narrator repeats a predicate and its argument in rapid succession to indicate the repetition of the event, and uses *be* to mark each repetition.

(49) a. *deip ma, diqiamrenas, biqiadik sametnas, biqianyip*
de=ip *maget,* ***de**=kia=mrenas,*
CONJ=PURP then CONJ=3SG.F.SBJ=jump.NCONT.PST:SELF
***be**=kia=dik* *se=met-nas,* ***be**=kia=nyip*
CONJ=3SG.F.SBJ=cut to/with=in-self CONJ=3SG.F.SBJ=die.NCONT
'and then, she jumped up, and she cut her (head) off, and she died' (N11AESSIRINI-0037FF)

b. *iandit biandit biandit biandit biandit, besavrama.. alamsaqa*
ian=tit ***be**=ian=tit* ***be**=ian=tit*
3DU.SBJ=go.CONT CONJ=3DU.SBJ=go.CONT CONJ=3DU.SBJ=go.CONT
***be**=ian=tit* ***be**=ian=tit,*
CONJ=3DU.SBJ=go.CONT CONJ=3DU.SBJ=go.CONT
***be**=se=pet=ama..* *a=lamesa-ka*
CONJ=to/with=on/under=ART NM=coconut-SG.M
'they were going and going and going and going and going, and (it is) to the top of the.. the coconut tree' (N11AJNGENAINGMETSIQI-0041)

8.3.2 Contrast

The conjunction *dap* is used to set up a contrast between two propositions. For example, in (50a), both the participants (cat and rat) and the events (paddling and sleeping) contrast. But it is also possible to use the conjunction to contrast participants only (as in 50b) or events only (as in 50c). Note that the contrasting proposition need not be overtly expressed and can be left implicit. For example, the speaker uses *dap* in (50d) to express a contrast to the unexpressed thought that the event took place a long time ago.

(50) a. *amiuqakiarl siam, dap ma.. aqasupka, de qebrlany*
a=miu-ka=ka=kiarl *se-iam,*
NM=cat-SG.M=3SG.M.SBJ=paddle.CONT to/with-3DU.M
dap *ma..* *a=qasup-ka,* *de* *ke=brlany*
but ART.ID NM=rat-SG.M CONJ 3SG.M.SBJ.NPST=sleep
'the cat paddles the two of them, and as for the.. as for the rat, it is sleeping' (N12BAMCAT-195FF)

b. *kuarl amaging, dap kuarl amatata*
kuarl *ama=ging,* ***dap*** *kuarl* *ama=tata*
INTRG ART=yummy.food but INTRG ART=meat
'whether it is *ging*, whether it is *tata*' (I12ABLAJLATASOCIO2-081)

c. *deqerl kui nyiraqamraqena, dap miika quasiqi nyiraqasmis amalengiini, taquarlip..*
de=kerl *kui* *nyi=raqa=mraqen=a,*
CONJ=DEONT quoting 2SG.SBJ.NPST=properly.NCONT=C.say=DIST
dap *miika* *kuasik=i* *nyi=raqa=smis*
but more NEG=SIM 2SG.SBJ.NPST=properly.NCONT=C.call
ama=lengi-ini, *taquarl=ip..*
ART=word-SG.DIM thus=PURP
'you may have (wanted) to say it properly, but you didn't quite say the little word correctly like..' (I12AANACLADNSOCIO2-057)

d. *guaka, dakui manundren?*
gua-ka, **dap**=*kui* *mani=un=tden?*
1SG.POSS-SG.M but=quoting recently=1DU.SBJ=come.CONT
'my friend, wouldn't you say that we came only recently?' (N12BAM-CAT-174)

Given its contrastive function, it can often be translated as English 'but' – but one should be careful not to equate the forms in the two languages. For example, the speaker in (51-2) uses *dap* to set up a contrast between two mythical figures, *Siqi* and *Genainymerini*. Both of them are good people, though, and a translation with English 'but' is not possible in this context.

(51) 1. *masiqi, de amaqaqraqi amatluqi*
ma=siqi *de* *ama=qaqera-ki* *ama=tlu-ki*
ART.ID=NAME CONJ ART=person-SG.F ART=good-SG.F
'Siqi, she is a good woman' (D12ADKSPIRITS-023)
2. *dap.. iaqamaqaqraqaip madepguas, de ma.. genainymerini*
dap... *ia-ka=ama=qaqera-ka=ip* *ma=depguas,*
but other-SG.M=ART=person-SG.M=PURP ART.ID=three
de *ma..* *genainymerini*
CONJ ART.ID NAME:SG.DIM
'while.. a third person is.. Genainymerini (who is also a good person)' (D12ADKSPIRITS-025FF)

8.3.3 Simultaneity

The conjunction *i* establishes a close link between two propositions that are not separated in time. As such, it occurs in two salient contexts: to link two or more events that occur simultaneously, and to give additional information on an event. Examples (52a) and (52b) illustrate the first context: two events that occur at the same time.

(52) a. *keksik, be sasari, iqetlamaademgiara*
ke=ksik, *be* *sasari,*
3SG.M.SBJ.NPST=climb.CONT CONJ to.there
i=*ke=tlu=ama=adem-ki=iara*
SIM=3SG.M.SBJ.NPST=see.CONT=ART=hole-SG.F=PROX
'he is climbing, to (up) there, and (being up there) he is looking into the hole here' (R12ADNFROG-119)

b. *nyiluqaiara, iqeksik namadanggaira*
nyi=lu-ka=iara, ***i****=ke=ksik*
2SG.SBJ.NPST=see.NCONT-3SG.M=PROX SIM=3SG.M.SBJ.NPST=climb.CONT
ne=ama=dang-ka=iara
from/with=ART=dog-SG.M=PROX
'see him here, he is climbing together with the dog here' (C12AR-BZJIFROG-215)

And examples (53) and (54) illustrate the second context: an elaboration. Example (53-1) asserts that the protagonist is stealing, and (53-2) elaborates on the act of stealing. Or in (54a), there is an elaboration on the meaning of *laviam* 'parents'. In cases where the elaboration is on a preceding noun phrase, the clauses can sometimes look like relative clauses (as in 54a or 54b). However, they are not relative clauses, and they do not form part of the noun phrase. In all cases, they invariably occur following the entire clause (e.g., following adverbs such as *taquarl* 'thus' in 54b). Furthermore, there are many cases like (53), where the elaboration is not on a noun phrase, and where an interpretation as a relative clause is not possible. Since there are no formal or functional differences between cases like (53) and cases like (54), I consider both to instantiate the same construction.

(53) 1. *deip maget daqa.. kesuam*
de=ip maget de=ka.. ke=suam
CONJ=PURP then CONJ=3SG.M.SBJ 3SG.M.SBJ.NPST=steal
'and then he.. he is stealing' (N12BAMCAT-200FF)

2. *iqesnis meniana.. ianamalauski*
i*=ke=snis men=iana.. iana=malaus-ki*
SIM=3SG.M.SBJ.NPST=bite.CONT at=3DU.POSS 3DU.POSS=canoe-SG.F
'he is eating from their.. their canoe' (N12BAMCAT-202)

(54) a. *amalaviam, iamangerlmam, damangerlnan, de liama de..*
ama=lavu-iam, ***i****=ama=ngerlmam, de=ama=ngerlnan,*
ART=adult-DU.M SIM=ART=man CONJ=ART=woman
de lu-iam-a de..
CONJ DEM-DU.M-DIST CONJ
'it is the parents, the father and the mother, those two..' (I12AANACLADNSOCIO3-169FF)

b. *dakatika qatranget taquarl iama.. aqurlitnget*
dap=ka=tika ka=tat-nget taquarl
but=3SG.M.SBJ=EMPH 3SG.M.SBJ=take.CONT-3N thus
i*=ama.. a=qurlit-nget*
SIM=ART NM=alive-N
'and he was picking them up like this, the.. the ones who were alive' (N11AAGSIRINILOBSTER1-0007)

Given the right context, such an elaboration can receive a causal interpretation (as in 55a). In fact, the conjunction *i* commonly collocates with the particle *kut* 'inferring' in causal contexts (as in 55b) (see also chapter 7.2).

(55) a. *masangunan kiawin, iqiamramadepguas*
ma=sangunan kia=win, ***i****=kia=mat=ama=depguas*
ART.ID=NAME 3SG.F.SBJ=win SIM=3SG.F.SBJ=take.NCONT.PST=ART=three
'Sangunan won, (because) she picked three' (C12VARPLAY-159)

b. *nguatu guaqavep taqurla, iqebrlany iqurini iamavureka*
ngua=tu gua=qavep taquarl=a,
1SG.SBJ=put.CONT 1SG.POSS=heart thus=DIST
i=ke=brlany ***i=kut-ini*** *i=ama=vurek-ka*
SIM=3SG.M.SBJ.NPST=sleep SIM=inferring-SG.DIM SIM=ART=tired-SG.M
'I am thinking like this now, he is sleeping, and it is because he is tired' (AJL&ADN-25/05/2012; SCENARIO 58 FROM DAHL 1985)

An elaboration can provide a large variety of circumstantial information, such as time (as in 56a) or manner (as in 56b).

(56) a. *lunget maamani imedu*
lu-nget maqa-mani ***i****=medu*
DEM-N HERE-down SIM=past
'those ones (plants) down there (were) from before' (D12ADNGARDEN-036)

b. *katden imaguskimgaira*
ka=tden ***i****=ma=guskim-ka=iara*
3SG.M.SBJ=come.CONT SIM=ART.ID=breathlessness-SG.M=PROX
'he is coming, being short of breath' (N12ABKSIRINI-121)

Furthermore, the conjunction *i* commonly marks propositions that are introduced by speech act verbs (as in 57a), verbs of perception (as in 57b), verbs of cognition (as in 57c), verbs of emotion (as in 57d) or phasal verbs (as in 57e).

(57) a. *tetuqun i amaburlemgi*
te=tuqun ***i*** *ama=burlem-ki*
3PL.SBJ.NPST=say.CONT SIM ART=many-SG.F
'they say that it is many (people)' (I12AANACLADNSOCIO3-259)

b. *de utlui miiki lungeriara raqurla*
*de ut=lu=****i*** *miiki lu-nget-iara taquarl=a*
CONJ 1PL.SBJ=see.NCONT=SIM instead DEM-N-PROX thus=DIST
'we saw that these ones were like this (like those ones)' (D12ADNGARDEN-080)

c. *be qiadrlem iammelanggaamek*
*be kia=drlem **i**=ama=melang-ka=a-mek*
CONJ 3SG.F.SBJ=know SIM=ART=vine-SG.M=DIR-down
'and she knows that the rope is down there' (P12ADNROPE1-107)

d. *iqerl tengning imasinepki, deqiavuk*
*i=kerl te=ngning **i**=ma=sinepki,*
SIM=DEONT 3PL.SBJ.NPST=fear.CONT SIM=ART.ID=NAME:SG.F
de=ki=a-vuk
CONJ=3SG.F=DIR-up
'they fear Sinepki, she is up there' (N12ABKSIRINI-067)

e. *nyirarles i nyading*
*nyi=rarles **i** nya=ding*
2SG.SBJ.NPST=start.NCONT SIM 2SG.SBJ=weave.CONT
'you start weaving' (P12ADNROPE1-092)

Given this distribution, this conjunction could arguably be analyzed as a complementizer, introducing complement clauses. Again, I do not adopt such an analysis, and instead assume that this distribution follows from its basic semantics of simultaneity. As such, *i* can be replaced by another conjunction, conveying a different interpretation. For example, the conjunction *ip* also marks propositions introduced by speech act verbs (as in 58a) and perception verbs (as in 58b). In this case, it retains its purposive reading, communicating intentions and wishes. Note also that the complex verb *narlip* 'like' (in 58c) was formed on the basis of *narli* 'hear, feel' plus the conjunction *ip*.

(58) a. *lira ngutaqen ip nyatuqun*
*lira ngu=taqen **ip** nya=tuqun*
now 1SG.SBJ.NPST=say.CONT PURP 2SG.SBJ=sit.CONT
'I'm telling you now to sit down' (C12VARPLAY-631)

b. *tika uretluip tadrlem amatok-pisin*
*tika ure=tlu=**ip** ta=drlem ama=tok-pisin*
EMPH 1PL.SBJ.NPST=see.CONT=PURP 3PL.SBJ=know ART=NAME
'we have to see to it that they know Tok Pisin' (I12AANACLADNSOCIO3-207)

c. *deip nyinarlip nyikavrla*
*de=ip nyi=narl**ip** nyi=kaverl=a*
CONJ=PURP 2SG.SBJ.NPST=like:PURP 2SG.SBJ.NPST=hurry.CONT=DIST
'if you want to be quick now' (P12ARSBILUM1-027)

In fact, a conjunction is not necessary at all in this context. It is just as common to juxtapose two clauses (as in 59a), or to indicate the relationship through a particle or an adverb (as in 59b).

(59) a. *binyilu qaat meseng*
be=nyi=lu *ka=at* *meseng*
CONJ=2SG.SBJ.NPST=see.NCONT 3SG.M.SBJ=fall.NCONT at.base
'see he fell down' (R12ATAFROG-151)

b. *de ianlu ma: angerlmamga, qena.. angerlnan*
de *ian=lu* ***ma:*** *a=ngerlmam-ka,*
CONJ 3DU.SBJ=see.NCONT thus NM=man-SG.M
ke-ne=a.. *a=ngerlnan*
3SG.M.ASSOC-from/with=NM NM=woman
'and they see this: the father, together with the.. the mother' (R12ADNFROG-303FF)

There is also no evidence that the second clause is an argument of the first. There is no structural difference depending on whether a conjunction is present (as in 57 and 58 above) or absent (as in 59 above). This includes the possibility to have an overt direct object argument, even in cases where the conjunction is present (as shown for *i* in 60a, and for *ip* in 60b).

(60) a. *nyilamadangga iqerl qatit*
nyi=lu=ama=dang-ka ***i****=kerl* *ka=tit*
2SG.SBJ.NPST=see.NCONT=ART=dog-SG.M SIM=DEONT 3SG.M.SBJ=go.CONT
'see the dog moving' (C12ARBZJIFROG-290)

b. *ai, kiatu araqavevip nanaangilit*
ai, *kia=tu* *ara=qavep=****ip***
hey 3SG.F.SBJ=put.CONT 3SG.F.POSS=heart=PURP
nani=aa=ngil-it
can=3SG.M.POSS=space-SG.LONG
'hey, she was thinking (lit. put her thought) that it may be his place (to die now)' (I12AANACLADNSOCIO3-535)

The conjunction *i* is commonly used in yet another context: following particles, especially the particle *kuasik* 'NEG' (as in 61a). Again, it is not obligatory in this context (as illustrated in 61b). And again, this use can be subsumed under its general meaning of simultaneity.

(61) a. *kuasiqi amakarkia*
*kuasik=****i*** *ama=kar-ki=a*
NEG=SIM ART=car-SG.F=DIST
'there's no car now (lit. it is not the case, there are cars)' (C12VARPLAY-305)

b. *dap kui quasiqamaquIditkia*
dap kui kuasik=ama=quldit-ki=a
but quoting NEG=ART=frog-SG.F=DIST
'but there's no frog now' (R12ABDFROG-019)

8.3.4 Purpose

The conjunction *ip* introduces a purpose clause. Depending on the context, it can receive an intentional reading (as in 62a), but not necessarily so (as in 62b)

(62) a. *saqi undirip nka unemnem uniarang nauirl*
*saqi un=tit=**ip** naka une=mnem*
again 1DU.SBJ=go.CONT=PURP bit 1DU.SBJ.NPST=sell.CONT
une-ia-irang nauirl
1DU.POSS-other-PL.DIM first
'we again go to sell a little of our small ones first' (D12ABDACPGARDEN-052)

b. *kuasiqaqamadleq ikraneng senas, amalkuil de..*
*kuasik=a=qama=dlek **ip**=ka=raneng se-nas,*
NEG=NM=some=strength PURP=3SG.M.SBJ=hold.NCONT to/with-self
ama=lkuil de..
ART=heavy CONJ
'there isn't any strength (in him) so that he (can) hold himself (on the branches), there is heaviness (in him), and..' (N11AAGSIRINILOBSTER1-0068)

The purpose clause is morphosyntactically an independent clause: it can be marked for any tense/aspect or polarity, and its subject can be co-referential with the subject of the preceding clause (as in 62a above), but does not need to be (as in 63a below). The conjunction is also used to introduce goal phrases (as in 63b). And it is used to form the 'why' question (see section 8.1.2).

(63) a. *nguraqaseserl vrini, ikatika ini ngataqasmis*
ngu=raqa=seserl pet-ini,
1SG.SBJ.NPST=properly.NCONT=straigthen:REDUP on/under-SG.DIM
***ip**=ka=tika ini nga=taqa=smis*
PURP=3SG.M.SBJ=EMPH SG.DIM 3N.SBJ=properly.CONT=C.call
'I will carefully correct the little one, so that the little one will be saying it properly' (I12AANACLADNSOCIO2-099)

b. *saiandirip saruarl*
*sa=ian=tit=**ip*** *se=tuarl*
already=3DU.SBJ=go.CONT=PURP to/with=other.side
'they go to (reach) the other side' (N12BAMCAT-143)

Given its purpose reading, it is often set in the future, co-occurring with the particles *nani* 'can' or *dip* 'FUT' (as in 64a). It furthermore often follows speech act or perception verbs (as in 64b). In such cases, it looks similar to a complementizer, but there are reasons to not analyze it as a complementizer (see the discussion in section 8.3.3 above).

(64) a. *amasmesirang, ip dip savramakaska*
ama=smes-irang, ***ip*** ***dip*** *se=pet=ama=kas-ka*
ART=food-PL.DIM PURP FUT to/with=on/under=ART=saltwater-SG.M
'the food, (it) will (be for their journey) across the ocean' (N12BAMCAT-154FF)

b. *tasil ip nyatuqun taqurlani*
ta=sil ***ip*** *nya=tuqun* *taquarl=ani*
3PL.SBJ=say.NCONT PURP 2SG.SBJ=sit.CONT thus=DIST
'they said that you (should) sit like this (i.e., properly)' (C12YMMZJI-PLAY1-291)

Another common context is the collocation of *ip* with conjunctions and/or particles that sequence events. In some cases, both the sequential meaning (of the other conjunction and/or particle) and the purpose meaning (of *ip*) are present (as in 65a). But there are also many cases where only the sequential reading is present, without any purpose reading (as in 65b and 65c). It is likely that these now constitute fixed expressions with their own non-compositional meaning.

(65) a. *bqatit bqatit, besamrama.. akainaqi, deip ma, daqasangarl*
be=ka=tit *be=ka=tit,*
CONJ=3SG.M.SBJ=go.CONT CONJ=3SG.M.SBJ=go.CONT
be=se=met=ama.. *a=kaina-ki,* ***de=ip*** ***maget,***
CONJ=to/with=in=ART NM=water-SG.F CONJ=PURP then
de=ka=sangarl
CONJ=3SG.M.SBJ=catch.fish:??
'he was going and going, to the.. river, to then catch (prawns)' (N11AAGSIRINILOBSTER1-0003FF)

b. *daqamrirl iasimek, deip maget, de qataqen prama.. alevungga*
de=ka=mrirl *iasi=i-mek,* ***de=ip***
CONJ=3SG.M.SBJ=go.down DIST=AWAY-down CONJ=PURP
maget, *de* *ka=taqen* *pet=ama..* *a=levung-ka*
then CONJ 3SG.M.SBJ=say.CONT on/under=ART NM=tree.type-SG.M
'he climbed down there, and then, he says to the.. *levung* palm'
(N11AJNGENAINGMETBROTHERS-0131FF)

c. *pemaqerleng, deiva, dama.. amavilanngi*
pe=ma=qerleng, ***de=ip=a,*** *de=ama..*
PLACE=ART.ID=fallow.garden CONJ=PURP=DIST CONJ=ART
ama=vilanngi
ART=NAME:SG.F
'in an abandoned garden, and then, there was a.. a Vilan (spirit)'
(I12AANACLADNSOCIO3-476)

The conjunction is furthermore used in a second context: to introduce conditional clauses. It is possible that this second use can be analyzed as a contextual interpretation of its basic purposive meaning. Most examples continue to allow for a purpose reading (as in 66a). Nevertheless, there are cases where a purpose reading is no longer obvious. For example, the person in (66b) does not intend to move the objects: she intends to pick up the objects carefully, and the whole purpose is to not accidentally touch and move any of the other objects. Such examples suggest that the conjunction is developing a second, conditional, sense. There are very few such cases, though, and there is always additional material that could trigger the conditional readings. In (66b), it is probably the presence of *ivit* 'upon (doing X)' in the first clause. In fact, it is very common for speakers to resort to the fixed expression *ivit nani ip* in conditional contexts, as in (66c), which has a more literal translation of 'upon spearing himself' (see chapter 6.3 for a discussion of *ivit*). Another common collocation in this context is *ariq ip*, as in (66d) (see also chapter 7.2).

(66) a. *ip.. ip nyarekmet pramarlaunnga, dinyatit sep maqavel*
ip.. ***ip*** *nya=rekmet* *pet=ama=rlaun-ka,*
PURP PURP 2SG.SBJ=do.CONT:IN on/under=ART=netbag-SG.M
de=nya=tit *se=pe* *ma=qavel*
CONJ=2SG.SBJ=go.CONT to/with=PLACE ART.ID=bush
'in order to.. to make a netbag, you go into the bush'
~ 'if.. if you (want to) make a netbag ...' (P12ARSBILUM3L-007FF)

b. *ivit kitat, beip nyilang, de ngenenes praqi*
i-pit *ki=tat,* *be=**ip*** *nyi=ilang,*
AWAY-up 3SG.F.SBJ.NPST=take.CONT CONJ=PURP 2SG.SBJ.NPST=shake
de *ngene=nes* *pet-ki*
CONJ 2PL.SBJ.NPST=shout.NCONT on/under-3SG.F
'when she picks (it) (lit. upon her picking it), and if she moves (it), then you shout at her' (C12VARPLAY-601)

c. *ivit naniip kaman pramaqip, de nyaramagalepki metka*
i-pit ***nani=ip*** *ka=man*
AWAY-up can=PURP 3SG.M.SBJ=go.inside.NCONT.PST
pet=ama=qip, *de* *nya=ru=ama=galep-ki*
on/under=ART=spear CONJ 2SG.SBJ=put.NCONT.FUT=ART=club-SG.F
met-ka
in-3SG.M
'and so when he spears (himself) on the spears, then you hit the fighting stick on him' (N11AAGSIRINIROPE-0127FF)

d. *dakatika ariqiv ur amarluis naut, de uretluiv uredlek*
dap=ka=tika ***arik=ip*** *ut* *ama=rluis* *ne-ut,*
but=3SG.M.SBJ=EMPH supposing=PURP 1PL ART=child from/with-1PL
de *ure=tlu=ip* *ure=dlek*
CONJ 1PL.SBJ.NPST=see.CONT=PURP 1PL.SBJ.NPST=strength/strong
'but supposing that (we want to consider) us young people, we must see to it that we stand up strong (and learn the different patterns)' (P12ARSBILUM2-029FF)

Finally, the conjunction *ip* is used to introduce ordinal numbers (see chapter 3.2.2).

8.4 Summary

This chapter has presented a brief introduction to Qaqet clause structure, covering both verbal and non-verbal clauses. Non-verbal clauses are used extensively to convey existence, location and direction, possession, equation and attribution. Note that Qaqet does not make use of any copula in its non-verbal constructions. Instead, it relies on syntax alone, juxtaposing the constituents.

The order of elements in a clause is fixed. Verbal clauses have a constituent order of AVO ~ SV: this order is unexpected from a Papuan perspective, but it is commonly found in Oceanic and non-Oceanic languages of New Britain and New Ireland. The non-verbal locative construction also shares the order of the subject preceding the predicate. In addition, Qaqet has two constructions that exhibit the reversed order of the predicate being followed by the subject: the non-verbal equative and attributive constructions.

Both verbal and non-verbal clauses can occur with the same peripheral elements: conjunctions and particles in the left periphery, and prepositional phrases, relational nouns, adverbs and directionals in the right periphery. Furthermore, the clause structure of affirmative statements is identical to that of negative statements, questions and commands. The different speech acts are marked through prosody and/or through particles and question words, but not through syntax.

In Qaqet discourse, it is common for one or more elements of a clause to be left-dislocated, including particles, arguments, prepositional phrases, directionals and adverbs. This left-dislocation is marked prosodically (through a final rise-fall) and segmentally (through the conjunction *de*).

Finally, this chapter has discussed the available mechanisms for clause linking. Qaqet combines main clauses with each other, making use of prosodic marking plus a variety of particles (discussed in chapter 7) and conjunctions (discussed in this chapter) to indicate different kinds of semantic relationships. There is no clear evidence of subordination, and Qaqet does not employ any of the typical Papuan constructions of serialization, clause-chaining or switch reference.

Appendix: Text collection

This appendix contains three texts of different genres, with the aim of illustrating connected Qaqet discourse: a conversation (text 1), a narrative story (text 2), and a descriptive text (text 3).

Text 1: Teaching the Qaqet language

This text is an extract from a longer conversation between three elder women, the community leaders AAN (born ca. 1943), ACL (born 1955) and ADN (born ca. 1952) discussing a number of sociolinguistic questions. In this extract, they discuss the parents' responsibility for teaching the Qaqet language to their children. The discussion was video-recorded on 17 MAY 2012, and it is archived with the Endangered Languages Archive under the identifier I12AANACLADNSocio.

(1) ADN *pet liina*
pet *lu-ini-a*
on/under DEM-SG.DIM-DIST
'about that one (question)'

(2) ADN *de qatika idamalavu*
de *ka=tika* *ide=ama=lavu*
CONJ 3SG.M.SBJ=EMPH IPFV=ART=adult
'it really is usually the parents (who teach the children)'

(3) ADN *de tika nani.. tetaqen praraa.. arauis*
de *tika* *nani..* *te=taqen* *pet=araa..*
CONJ EMPH can 3PL.SBJ.NPST=say.CONT on/under=3PL.POSS
ara-uis
3PL.POSS-child
'when.. they talk to their.. children'

(4) ADN *namalengiqa*
ne=ama=lengi-ka
from/with=ART=word-SG.M
'in the language'

(5) ACL *mh*
mh
INTJ
'mh'

(6) ADN *iqui murl tasalini*
i=kui murl ta=sal-ini
SIM=quoting distantly 3PL.SBJ=give.birth-SG.DIM
'when they give birth to the little one'

(7) ADN *derasalini, utaqen prini iquasiqini.. ngadrlem*
de=ta=sal-ini, ut=taqen pet-ini
CONJ=3PL.SBJ=give.birth-SG.DIM 1PL.SBJ=say.CONT on/under-SG.DIM
i=kuasik=ini.. nga=drlem
SIM=NEG=SG.DIM 3N.SBJ=know
'they give birth to the little one, (and) we talk to the little one who doesn't.. understand'

(8) ACL *as kuasiqini ngadrlem*
as kuasik=ini nga=drlem
still NEG=SG.DIM 3N.SBJ=know
'the little one still doesn't understand'

(9) ADN *a'ee*
a'ee
INTJ
'true'

(10) ACL *de sa rataqen prini*
de sa ta=taqen pet-ini
CONJ already 3PL.SBJ-say.CONT on/under-SG.DIM
'(but) they already talk to the little one'

(11) ADN *kuasiqini.. kuasiqini ngataqen*
kuasik=ini.. kuasik=ini nga=taqen
NEG=SG.DIM NEG=SG.DIM 3N.SBJ=say.CONT
'the little one (still) doesn't.. the little one (still) doesn't talk'

(12) ACL *mh*
mh
INTJ
'mh'

(13) ADN *naqatika qui ini..*
naka=ka=tika kui ini..
bit=3SG.M.SBJ=EMPH quoting SG.DIM
'it is said that the little one..'

(14) ACL *as kuasiqini..*
as kuasik=ini..
still NEG=SG.DIM
'the little one still doesn't..'

(15) ADN *ee*
ee
yes
'yes'

(16) ACL *as kuasiqini ngataqen*
as kuasik=ini nga=taqen
still NEG=SG.DIM 3N.SBJ=say.CONT
'the little one still doesn't speak'

(17) ADN *dakatika utaqen prinia namalengiqa*
dap=ka=tika ut=taqen pet-ini=a
but=3SG.M.SBJ=EMPH 1PL.SBJ=say.CONT on/under-SG.DIM=DIST
ne=ama=lengi-ka
from/with=ART=word-SG.M
'but we are talking to the little one now in the language'

(18) AAN *de ngenetat*
de ngene=tat
CONJ 2PL.SBJ.NPST=take.CONT
'and you will pick it up'

(19) ADN *ee*
ee
yes
'yes'

(20) ADN *de ngenetat*
de ngene=tat
CONJ 2PL.SBJ.NPST=take.CONT
'and you will pick it up'

(21) ADN *dap.. atika ut, de utli uralengiqa imurl nevuralavurlvis*
dap.. ka=tika ut, de ut=tlu=i
but 3SG.M.SBJ=EMPH 1PL CONJ 1PL.SBJ=see.CONT=SIM
ura=lengi-ka i=murl
1PL.POSS=word-SG.M SIM=distanly
ne=pe=ura=lavu=ngere-uvis
from/with=PLACE=1PL.POSS=adult=3N.POSS-top
'but.. as for us, we see that it is our language that came down in the past from our parents'

(22) ACL *mh*
mh
INTJ
'mh'

(23) ADN *de tika, div uresu ur.. usu uruimirang ivirang ngadrlem*

de	*tika,*	*dip*	*ure=su*	*ure..*	*ut=su*
CONJ	EMPH	FUT	1PL.SBJ.NPST	1PL.POSS	1PL.SBJ=teach

ure-uim-irang	*ip=irang*	*nga=drlem*
1PL.POSS-child-PL.DIM	PURP=PL.DIM	3N.SBJ=know

'we ourselves will teach our.. we teach our little children so that the little ones know'

(24) ADN *irang ngadrlem amalengiqa*

irang	*nga=drlem*	*ama=lengi-ka*
PL.DIM	3N.SBJ=know	ART=word-SG.M

'(so that) they know the language'

(25) ACL *mh*

mh

INTJ

'mh'

(26) ACL *nadeivet*

ne=de=a=ivet

from/with=LOC.PART=NM=ground

'from the beginning'

(27) ADN *nadeivet*

ne=de=a=ivet

from/with=LOC.PART=NM=ground

'from the beginning'

(28) ADN *saqi quasik magrip, kurlinger iqatika qua lek katir iamadengengga*

saqi	*kuasik*	*maget=ip,*	*kurli-nget*	*i=ka=tika*
again	NEG	then=PURP	leave-3N	SIM=3SG.M.SBJ=EMPH

kua	*lek*	*ka=tit*	*i=ama=dengeng-ka*
INTRG	take.off	3SG.M.SBJ=go.CONT	SIM=ART=dumb.person-SG.M

'and again the little one can't be left (to pick it up) alone, (otherwise) he will take off and go on (in life) becoming a dumb person'

(29) ACL *ah, kuasik maget*

ah,	*kuasik*	*maget*
INTJ	NEG	then/right

'ah, that's not okay'

(30) ADN *i.. iquasik ketaqen naqamalengiqa*

i..	*i=kuasik*	*ke=taqen*
SIM	SIM=NEG	3SG.M.SBJ.NPST=say.CONT

ne=a=qama=lengi-ka

from/with=NM=some=word-SG.M

'so.. so he doesn't speak in/with any language (of his own)'

(31) ACL *mh*
mh
INTJ
'mh'

(32) ADN *dakatika i.. amalaviam*
dap=ka=tika i.. ama=lavu-iam
but=3SG.M.SBJ=EMPH SIM ART=adult-DU.M
'but it is the case that.. it is the parents'

(33) ADN *iamangerlmam, damangerlnan*
i=ama=ngerlmam, de=ama=ngerlnan
SIM=ART=man CONJ=ART=woman
'the father and the mother'

(34) ADN *de liama de.. de ianesu iana.. ianuimini*
de lu-iam-a de.. de iane=su iana..
CONJ DEM-DU.M-DIST CONJ CONJ 3DU.SBJ.NPST=teach 3DU.POSS
iane-uim-ini
3DU.POSS-child-SG.DIM
'(it is) those two.. they teach their.. their child'

(35) ADN *tamalengiqa*
te=ama=lengi-ka
PURP=ART=word-SG.M
'in the language'

(36) AAN *mh*
mh
INTJ
'mh'

(37) ADN *ias kui murl ngenesal.. tasalini ama.. ama.. ama.. amaanguanini*
i=as kui murl ngene=sal..
SIM=still quoting distantly 2PL.SBJ.NPST=give.birth
ta=sal-ini ama.. ama.. ama.. ama=anguan-ini
3PL.SBJ=give.birth-SG.DIM ART ART ART ART=baby-SG.DIM
'and still when you give birth.. (when) they give birth to a.. a.. a.. a small baby'

(38) ADN *dakatika nani iandraqen prini namalengiqa*
dap=ka=tika nani ian=taqen pet-ini
but=3SG.M.SBJ=EMPH can 3DU.SBJ=say.CONT on/under-SG.DIM
ne=ama=lengi-ka
from/with=ART=word-SG.M
'it's the case that they (the parents) talk to the little one in the language'

(39) ACL *mh*
mh
INTJ
'mh'

(40) ADN *be nangere.. ngereknak*
be nani=ngere.. ngere=knak
CONJ can=3N.SBJ.NPST 3N.SBJ.NPST=cry.CONT
'when he.. he cries'

(41) ADN *de tika retaqen prini*
de tika te=taqen pet-ini
CONJ EMPH 3PL.SBJ.NPST=say.CONT on/under-SG.DIM
'they talk to the little one'

(42) ADN *namalengiqa*
ne=ama=lengi-ka
from/with=ART=word-SG.M
'in the language'

(43) ADN *be nangeresana*
be nani=ngere=sana
CONJ can=3N.SBJ.NPST=do.what
'whatever he does'

(44) ADN *i amaanguanini quasiqi ngeretaqen*
i ama=anguan-ini kuasik=i ngere=taqen
SIM ART=baby-SG.DIM NEG=SIM 3N.SBJ.NPST=say.CONT
'the baby, (even though) he doesn't talk (yet)'

(45) ADN *de tika retaqen prini namalengiqa*
de tika te=taqen pet-ini
CONJ EMPH 3PL.SBJ.NPST=say.CONT on/under-SG.DIM
ne=ama=lengi-ka
from/with=ART=word-SG.M
'they will talk to him in the language'

(46) ADN *de.. atika ut*
de.. ka=tika ut
CONJ 3SG.M.SBJ=EMPH 1PL
'and.. it's us'

(47) ADN *amalavu naut, de tika urarletkia*
ama=lavu ne-ut, de tika ura=rlet-ki=a
ART=adult from/with-1PL CONJ EMPH 1PL.POSS=duty-SG.F=DIST
'we are the parents, it's our duty'

(48) ADN *iv uresu uruimini*
ip ure=su ure-uim-ini
PURP 1PL.SBJ.NPST=teach 1PL.POSS-child-SG.DIM
'that we teach our child'

(49) ADN *tamalengiqa*
te=ama=lengi-ka
PURP=ART=word-SG.M
'in the language'

(...)

(50) ACL *katika qui murl amalavu naut, de urarletkia*
ka=tika kui murl ama=lavu ne-ut,
3SG.M.SBJ=EMPH quoting distantly ART=adult from/with-1PL
de ura=rlet-ki=a
CONJ 1PL.POSS=duty-SG.F=DIST
'it is said that we are the parents, it is our duty'

(51) ACL *ikatika uresu uruis, itadrlem*
ip=ka=tika ure=su ure-uis,
PURP=3SG.M.SBJ=EMPH 1PL.SBJ.NPST=teach 1PL.POSS-child
ip=ta=drlem
PURP=3PL.SBJ=know
'that we teach our children, so that they know'

(52) ACL *iqerl araa.. ah, atika amaqaqeraraa lengiqa*
i=kerl araa.. ah, ka=tika ama=qaqera=araa
SIM=DEONT 3PL.POSS INTJ 3SG.M.SBJ=EMPH ART=person=3PL.POSS
lengi-ka
word-SG.M
'because it is their.. ah, it is the language of the Qaqet'

(53) ACL *katika*
ka=tika
3SG.M.SBJ=EMPH
'that's it'

(54) ACL *uresu uruis nadeivet, dakatika laradrlem luqa ama.. amaqaqet*
ure=su ure-uis ne=de=a=ivet,
1PL.SBJ.NPST=teach 1PL.POSS-child from/with=LOC.PART=NM=ground
dap=ka=tika la=ta=drlem lu-ka-a
but=3SG.M.SBJ=EMPH this.day=3PL.SBJ=know DEM-SG.M-DIST
ama.. ama=qaqera
ART ART=person
'we are teaching our children from the beginning, and these days they know about that.. Qaqet (language)'

(55) ACL *de amalengiqa luqa*
de ama=lengi-ka lu-ka-a
CONJ ART=word-SG.M DEM-SG.M-DIST
'it's that language'

(56) ACL *kerl ariqip kuasiq ur.. u.. u.. uretaqen prara neluqa ama.. ama.. amalengiqa, de qatika qua la qurlira raqurla?*

kerl arik=ip kuasik ure.. ure..
DEONT supposing=PURP NEG 1PL.SBJ.NPST 1PL.SBJ.NPST
ure.. ure=taqen pet-ta
1PL.SBJ.NPST 1PL.SBJ.NPST=say.CONT on/under-3PL.H
ne=lu-ka-a ama.. ama.. ama=lengi-ka,
from/with=DEM-SG.M-DIST ART ART ART=word-SG.M
de ka=tika kua la kurli-ta taquarl=a?
CONJ 3SG.M.SBJ=EMPH INTRG this.day leave-3PL.H thus=DIST
'if we.. we.. we.. we don't speak to them in that.. that.. that language, will they just be left like that (to pick up the language on their own)?'

(57) ACL *la utaqen nana?*

la ut=taqen nana?
this.day 1PL.SBJ=say.CONT what
'what did we just say (earlier in the discussion)?'

(58) ACL *katika uretaqen prara iuralengiqa, katika itadrlem*

ka=tika ure=taqen pet-ta
3SG.M.SBJ=EMPH 1PL.SBJ.NPST=say.CONT on/under-3PL.H
i=ura=lengi-ka, ka=tika ip=ta=drlem
SIM=1PL.POSS=word-SG.M 3SG.M.SBJ=EMPH PURP=3PL.SBJ=know
'we say to them that (this is) our language, so that they know it'

(59) ACL *amaqaqet*

ama=qaqera
ART=person
'the Qaqet (language)'

(...)

(60) AAN *tika uretluip tadrlem amatokpisin*

tika ure=tlu=ip ta=drlem ama=tokpisin
EMPH 1PL.SBJ.NPST=see.CONT=PURP 3PL.SBJ=know ART=tok.pisin
'we (also) have to see to it that they know Tok Pisin'

(61) ACL *mh*

mh
INTJ
'mh'

(62) ADN *mh*

mh
INTJ
'mh'

(63) AAN *saqika raquarl ama.. amaqaqet*
saqi-ka taquarl ama.. ama=qaqera
again-3SG.M thus ART ART=person
'again it's just like (with).. the Qaqet (language)'

(64) ADN *amaqaqet*
ama=qaqera
ART=person
'the Qaqet (language)'

(65) AAN *tikaip.. iv iammii iandit*
tika=ip.. ip iam=mii ian=tit
EMPH=PURP PURP 3DU.M=most 3DU.SBJ=go.CONT
'it is the case that.. that they both go (together)'

(66) ACL *iammii iandit*
iam=mii ian=tit
3DU.M=most 3DU.SBJ=go.CONT
'they both go (together)'

(67) AAN *iandit parlenna*
ian=tit parlen-na
3DU.SBJ=go.CONT middle-RECP
'they go together hand in hand'

(68) ACL *mh*
mh
INTJ
'mh'

(69) AAN *katika radrlem*
ka=tika ta=drlem
3SG.M.SBJ=EMPH 3PL.SBJ=know
'they really know (them)'

Text 2: A story of Sirini and Sinap

This text illustrates a traditional Qaqet narrative. Traditional stories revolve around the cultural hero Sirini and/or members of his family (for collections of such stories, see Bley 1914; Hesse 2007: 2–63). Sirini is the embodiment of the moral values of Qaqet society (see Dickhardt 2009: 150–177; Hesse 2007: 1–2): he is a hard-working gardener who provides generously for his family and community; he takes responsibility, and he shows respect, modesty and shame; and he is a clever person who is able to fight against his evil antagonists. One of these antagonists is Sinap. AEM (born 1980) told this story of Sirini and Sinap to me, her husband ACS (born ca. 1982), her in-law ATA (born ca. 1952) and a number of children. The narrative was audio-recorded on 02 JUN 2011, and it is archived with the Endangered Languages Archive under the identifier N11AESSirini.

(1) *murl masirini qatit*
murl *ma=sirini* *ka=tit*
distantly ART.ID=NAME 3SG.M.SBJ=go.CONT
'in the past, Sirini was going'

(2) *bqasik nemasinavragulengga*
be=ka=sik
CONJ=3SG.M.SBJ=climb.NCONT
ne=ma=sinap=ara=guleng-ka
from/with=ART.ID=NAME=3SG.F.POSS=malay.apple-SG.M
'and he climbed into Sinap's malay apple tree'

(3) *beqats.. amaguleng*
be=ka=tes.. *ama=guleng*
CONJ=3SG.M.SBJ=eat.CONT ART=malay.apple
'and he ate.. malay apples'

(4) *de ma*
de *ma*
CONJ thus
'and it happened like this'

(5) *amagamga qaat, menemasinavraarlembem*
ama=gam-ka *ka=at,*
ART=seed-SG.M 3SG.M.SBJ=fall.NCONT
men=ma=sinap=ara=arlem-em
at=ART.ID=NAME=3SG.F.POSS=thigh-SG.RCD
'a seed fell, onto Sinap's thigh'

(6) *iqimsem rarlaunnga*
i=ki=msem *ara=rlaun-ka*
SIM=3SG.F.SBJ.NPST=weave.CONT 3SG.F.POSS=netbag-SG.M
'while she is weaving her netbag'

(7) *de qiaang sadarlik, be qianyim*
de *kia=ang* *se=darlik,* *be* *kia=nyim*
CONJ 3SG.F.SBJ=walk.NCONT to/with=outside CONJ 3SG.F.SBJ=look.NCONT
'and she went outside, and she looked'

(8) *de qialu masirini mramagulengga*
de *kia=lu* *ma=sirini* *met=ama=guleng-ka*
CONJ 3SG.F.SBJ=see.NCONT ART.ID=NAME in=ART=malay.apple-SG.M
'and she saw Sirini in the malay apple tree'

(9) *de qiaruqun naqa ma*
de kia=ruqun ne-ka ma
CONJ 3SG.F.SBJ=say.NCONT from/with-3SG.M thus
'and she said to him like this'

(10) *nani nguvlengnyi, denguasnyi*
nani ngu=vleng-nyi, de=ngua=es-nyi
can 1SG.SBJ.NPST=kill.NCONT-2SG CONJ=1SG.SBJ=eat.NCONT.FUT-2SG
'I can kill you, and eat you'

(11) *ingulu nani nyiqiuaik nana?*
i=ngu=lu nani nyi=qiuaik nana?
SIM=1SG.SBJ.NPST=see.NCONT can 2SG.SBJ.NPST=run.CONT what
'because how can you run away now?'

(12) *daqasil ma*
de=ka=sil ma
CONJ=3SG.M.SBJ=say.NCONT thus
'and he said like this'

(13) *nani nguarenas savet giadanggirarleng*
nani ngua=renas se=pet
can 1SG.SBJ=jump.NCONT.FUT:SELF to/with=on/under
gia=dang-ki=ara=rleng
2SG.POSS=dog-SG.F=3SG.F.POSS=back
'I can jump onto the back of your dog'

(14) *deip maget, diqiadik menaradanggi*
de=ip maget, de=kia=dik men=ara=dang-ki
CONJ=PURP then CONJ=3SG.F.SBJ=cut at=3SG.F.POSS=dog-SG.F
'and then, she cut her dog'

(15) *biqianyip*
be=kia=nyip
CONJ=3SG.F.SBJ=die.NCONT
'and it died'

(16) *de qiasil ma, sanguavleng guadanggi de.. dinani nyarenas saqua?*
de kia=sil ma, sa=ngua=vleng
CONJ 3SG.F.SBJ=say.NCONT thus already=1SG.SBJ=kill.NCONT
gua=dang-ki de.. de=nani nya=renas
1SG.POSS=dog-SG.F CONJ CONJ=can 2SG.SBJ=jump.NCONT.FUT:SELF
se=kua?
to/with=where
'and she said like this, I have killed my dog, so.. so where can you jump to now?'

(17) *nani nguarenas savet giaqamakarukirarleng*
nani ngua=renas se=pet
can 1SG.SBJ=jump.NCONT.FUT:SELF to/with=on/under
gia=qama=karuk-ki=ara=rleng
2SG.POSS=some=chicken-SG.F=3SG.F.POSS=back
'I can jump onto the back of one of your chickens'

(18) *de qiamrenas, biqiavleng arakaruk mii*
de kia=mrenas, be=kia=vleng
CONJ 3SG.F.SBJ=jump.NCONT.PST:SELF CONJ=3SG.F.SBJ=kill.NCONT
ara=karuk mii
3SG.F.POSS=chicken most
'and she jumped up, and she killed all her chickens'

(19) *deip ma, diqiasil ma, sanguavleng guakaruk, de nani nyarenas saqua?*
de=ip maget, de=kia=sil ma,
CONJ=PURP then CONJ=3SG.F.SBJ=say.NCONT thus
sa=ngua=vleng gua=karuk de nani
already=1SG.SBJ=kill.NCONT 1SG.POSS=chicken CONJ can
nya=renas se=kua?
2SG.SBJ=jump.NCONT.FUT:SELF to/with=where
'and then, she said like this, I have killed my chickens, so where can you jump to now?'

(20) *nani nguarenas savet giavlemgaarleng*
nani ngua=renas se=pet
can 1SG.SBJ=jump.NCONT.FUT:SELF to/with=on/under
gia=vlam-ka=aa=rleng
2SG.POSS=pig-SG.M=3SG.M.POSS=back
'I can jump onto the back of your pig'

(21) *diqiamrenas, biqiavleng aravlemga*
de=kia=mrenas, be=kia=vleng
CONJ=3SG.F.SBJ=jump.NCONT.PST:SELF CONJ=3SG.F.SBJ=kill.NCONT
ara=vlam-ka
3SG.F.POSS=pig-SG.M
'and she jumped up, and she killed her pig'

(22) *diqiasil ma, nguavleng gua.. guavlemga, de nani nyarenas saqua?*
de=kia=sil ma, ngua=vleng gua..
CONJ=3SG.F.SBJ=say.NCONT thus 1SG.SBJ=kill.NCONT 1SG.POSS
gua=vlam-ka, de nani nya=renas
1SG.POSS=pig-SG.M CONJ can 2SG.SBJ=jump.NCONT.FUT:SELF
se=kua?
to/with=where
'and she said like this, I have killed my.. my pig, so where can you jump to now?'

(23) *nani nguarenas savet giapusiqaarleng*
nani ngua=renas se=pet
can 1SG.SBJ=jump.NCONT.FUT:SELF to/with=on/under
gia=pusi-ka=aa=rleng
2SG.POSS=cat-SG.M=3SG.M.POSS=back
'I can jump onto the back of your cat'

(24) *diqiamrenas, biqiavleng arapusiqa*
de=kia=mrenas, be=kia=vleng
CONJ=3SG.F.SBJ=jump.NCONT.PST:SELF CONJ=3SG.F.SBJ=kill.NCONT
ara=pusi-ka
3SG.F.POSS=cat-SG.M
'and she jumped up, and she killed her cat'

(25) *daqa.. qiasil ma, nguavleng guapusiqa, de nani nyarenas saqua?*
de=ka.. kia=sil ma, ngua=vleng
CONJ=3SG.M.SBJ 3SG.F.SBJ=say.NCONT thus 1SG.SBJ=kill.NCONT
gua=pusi-ka, de nani nya=renas
1SG.POSS=cat-SG.M CONJ can 2SG.SBJ=jump.NCONT.FUT:SELF
se=kua?
to/with=where
'and he.. she said like this, I have killed my cat, so where can you jump to now?'

(26) *nani nguarenas samet gialamsaqa*
nani ngua=renas se=met gia=lamesa-ka
can 1SG.SBJ=jump.NCONT.FUT:SELF to/with=in 2SG.POSS=coconut-SG.M
'I can jump into your coconut tree'

(27) *deip de qiasil ma, nguavleng gua.. gualamsaqa*
de=ip de kia=sil ma, ngua=vleng
CONJ=PURP CONJ 3SG.F.SBJ=say.NCONT thus 1SG.SBJ=kill.NCONT
gua.. gua=lamesa-ka
1SG.POSS 1SG.POSS=coconut-SG.M
'then she said like this, I have killed my.. my coconut tree'

(28) *nguarap pegualamsaqa, de nani nyarenas saqua?*
ngua=rap pe=gua=lamesa-ka de nani
1SG.SBJ=cut.NCONT PLACE=1SG.POSS=coconut-SG.M CONJ can
nya=renas se=kua?
2SG.SBJ=jump.NCONT.FUT:SELF to/with=where
'I have chopped down my coconut tree, so where can you jump to now?'

(29) *nani nguarenas samet giaqammerlka*

nani *ngua=renas* *se=met*
can 1SG.SBJ=jump.NCONT.FUT:SELF to/with=in
gia=qama=merlik-ka
2SG.POSS=some=betelnut-SG.M
'I can jump into one of your betelnut trees'

(30) *deip diqiasil ma*

de=ip *de=kia=sil* *ma,*
CONJ=PURP CONJ=3SG.F.SBJ=say.NCONT thus
'then she said like this'

(31) *nguarap peguamerliqa, de nani nyarenas saqua?*

ngua=rap *pe=gua=merlik=a* *de* *nani*
1SG.SBJ=cut.NCONT PLACE=1SG.POSS=betelnut=DIST CONJ can
nya=renas *se=kua?*
2SG.SBJ=jump.NCONT.FUT:SELF to/with=where
'I have chopped down my betelnut trees now, so where can you jump to now?'

(32) *nani nguarenas samet giaqamamengga, samet giameng*

nani *ngua=renas* *se=met*
can 1SG.SBJ=jump.NCONT.FUT:SELF to/with=in
gia=qama=meng-ka, *se=met* *gia=meng*
2SG.POSS=some=tree-SG.M to/with=in 2SG.POSS=tree
'I can jump into any one of your trees, into your trees'

(33) *diqiamrenas biqiarap prameng mii*

de=kia=mrenas *be=kia=rap*
CONJ=3SG.F.SBJ=jump.NCONT.PST:SELF CONJ=3SG.F.SBJ=cut.NCONT
pe=ara=meng *mii*
PLACE=3SG.F.POSS=tree most
'and she jumped up and chopped down all her trees'

(34) *diqiasil ma, sanguarap, pegua.. gua.. guameng amii, dungua.. nguavleng gua.. gua.. gualiltem mii*

de=kia=sil *ma,* *sa=ngua=rap,*
CONJ=3SG.F.SBJ=say.NCONT thus already=1SG.SBJ=cut.NCONT
pe=gua.. *gua..* *gua=meng* *a=mii,* *de=ngua..*
PLACE=1SG.POSS 1SG.POSS 1SG.POSS=tree NM=most CONJ=1SG.SBJ
ngua=vleng *gua..* *gua..*
1SG.SBJ=kill.NCONT 1SG.POSS 1SG.POSS
gua=liltem *mii*
1SG.POSS=domestic.plant/animal most
'and she said like this, I have already chopped down all my.. my.. my trees, and I.. I have killed all my.. my.. my animals and plants'

(35) *de nani nyarenas saqua?*
de nani nya=renas se=kua?
CONJ can 2SG.SBJ=jump.NCONT.FUT:SELF to/with=where
'so where can you jump to now?'

(36) *daqasil ma, nani nguarenas sep nyapes*
de=ka=sil ma, nani ngua=renas
CONJ=3SG.M.SBJ=say.NCONT thus can 1SG.SBJ=jump.NCONT.FUT:SELF
se=pe gia=pes
to/with=PLACE 2SG.POSS=eye/face
'and he said like this, I can jump onto your head'

(37) *deip ma, diqiamrenas, biqiadik sametnas*
de=ip maget, de=kia=mrenas, be=kia=dik
CONJ=PURP then CONJ=3SG.F.SBJ=jump.NCONT.PST:SELF CONJ=3SG.F.SBJ=cut
se=met-nas
to/with=in-self
'and then, she jumped up, and she cut her (head) off'

(38) *biqianyip*
be=kia=nyip
CONJ=3SG.F.SBJ=die.NCONT
'and she died'

(39) *de masirini qamrirl*
de ma=sirini ka=mrirl
CONJ ART.ID=NAME 3SG.M.SBJ=go.down
'and Sirini climbed down'

(40) *bqamet masinap*
be=ka=mat ma=sinap
CONJ=3SG.M.SBJ=take.NCONT.PST ART.ID=NAME
'and he picked up Sinap'

(41) *daqamuqi vraavetki*
de=ka=mu-ki pe=ara=avet-ki
CONJ=3SG.M.SBJ=put.NCONT.PST-3SG.F PLACE=3SG.F.POSS=house-SG.F
'and he put her into her house'

(42) *daqarlusep pemaavetki saqi*
de=ka=rlusep pe=ma=avet-ki
CONJ=3SG.M.SBJ=set.light:TO/WITH:PLACE PLACE=ART.ID=house-SG.F
se-ki
to/with-SG.F
'and he burned down the house over her'

(43) *daqamit*
de=ka=mit
CONJ=3SG.M.SBJ=go.NCONT.PST
'and he went'

Text 3: Weaving netbags

This text is a descriptive text about netbags, known as *bilum* in Tok Pisin: the ubiquitous Papua New Guinean bags of all shapes and sizes and for all occasions – for carrying personal items, garden or market produce, and sometimes babies. The Qaqet version is made of dried and split creepers woven into a bowl-like shape. This extract comes from a longer recording of two women, ADN (born ca. 1952) and ARS (born 1983), engaged in weaving a netbag. After demonstrating the procedures, ARS narrated the following extract. It was video-recorded on 22 MAY 2012, and it is archived with the Endangered Languages Archive under the identifier P12ARSBilum.

(1) *uh, une.. gelnagelnaiv uneperlset nuna.. unarlaunnga, dav unarlaunnga, de ama.. abarl-daremengga*
uh, une.. gelna=gelna=ip une=perlset
INTJ 1DU.SBJ.NPST nearby=nearby=PURP 1DU.SBJ.NPST=finish.CONT
ne=una.. una=rlaun-ka,
from/with=1DU.POSS 1DU.POSS=netbag-SG.M
dap una=rlaun-ka, de ama.. a=barl-daremengga
but 1PL.POSS=netbag-SG.M CONJ ART NM=netbag.type
'uh, we.. nearly nearly, we're (close to) finishing our.. our netbag, and our netbag (type), it is (called) the.. *barl-daremengga*'

(2) *dap ma.. amarlaun*
dap ma.. ama=rlaun
but ART.ID ART=netbag
'the.. the netbags'

(3) *deqakias, amaburlem nama.. amarlaun*
de=ka=kias, ama=burlem ne=ama.. ama=rlaun
CONJ=3SG.M.SBJ=actually ART=many from/with=ART ART=netbag
'there are actually many kinds of.. netbags'

(4) *iut, biari, de utdrlem sama.. amarlaun mii*
i=ut, be=ia-ta, de ut=drlem se=ama..
SIM=1PL CONJ=other-PL.H CONJ 1PL.SBJ=know to/with=ART
ama=rlaun mii
ART=netbag most
'and we, some (of us), we know about.. all (kinds) of netbags'

(5) *naqatika ut, biari, de utdrlem ama.. tika butdrlem amaqunasiam, dakua amaqunaska*
naka=ka=tika ut, be=ia-ta, de ut=drlem ama..
bit=3SG.M.SBJ=EMPH 1PL CONJ=other-PL.H CONJ 1PL.SBJ=know ART
tika be=ut=drlem ama=qunas-iam, dap=kua ama=qunas-ka
EMPH CONJ=1PL.SBJ=know ART=one-DU.M but=INTRG ART=one-SG.M
'and we, others (of us), we only know.. we know two (patterns), or maybe one (pattern)'

(6) *iariip ma.. amaburlemgi naut, de div ure.. iaik kiaruqun siaqamarlaunnga, de iaik, de iaik*
ia-ta=ip ma.. ama=burlem-ki ne-ut, de dip
other-PL.H=PURP ART.ID ART=many-SG.F from/with-1PL CONJ FUT
ure.. ia-ki kia=ruqun
1PL.SBJ.NPST other-SG.F 3SG.F.SBJ=sit.NCONT.FUT
se=ia-ka=ama=rlaun-ka, de ia-ki, de ia-ki
to/with=other-SG.M=ART=netbag-SG.M CONJ other-SG.F CONJ other-SG.F
'some of us (come together) in.. in large numbers, and we will.. one (woman) will sit with one netbag, another (woman), another (woman) (i.e., each woman works on her own netbag)'

(7) *i amarlaun, de tika iak, de iak*
i ama=rlaun, de tika ia-ka, de ia-ka
SIM ART=netbag CONJ EMPH other-SG.M CONJ other-SG.M
'the netbags, another (netbag) another (netbag) (i.e., different kinds of netbags)'

(8) *dap ngrek sauniara, de naqatika unmerama.. abarl-daremengga*
dap ngerek se-un=iara, de naka=ka=tika
but alone to/with-1DU=PROX CONJ bit=3SG.M.SBJ=EMPH
un=mat=ama.. a=barl-daremengga
1DU.SBJ=take.NCONT.PST=ART NM=netbag.type
'but we two are alone here, and so we just took up the.. the *barl-daremengga*'

(9) *damarlaun, de tika idremsem nama.. amakaasiq amalangik*
de=ama=rlaun, de tika ide=te=msem
CONJ=ART=netbag CONJ EMPH IPFV=3PL.SBJ.NPST=weave.CONT
ne=ama.. ama=kaasik ama=langik
from/with=ART ART=vine ART=vine
'and netbags, they usually weave them from the.. the *langik* vines'

(10) *katika*
ka=tika
3SG.M.SBJ=EMPH
'that's it'

(11) *tika lungerai unetmatna vramarlaunnga, de amakaasika amalangika*
tika lu-nget-a=i une=tmatna
EMPH DEM-N-DIST=SIM 1DU.SBJ.NPST=work.CONT:RECP
pet=ama=rlaun-ka, de ama=kaasik-ka ama=langik-ka
on/under=ART=netbag-SG.M CONJ ART=vine-SG.M ART=vine-SG.M
'it's (like) that, when we are working on the netbag, there's the *langik* vine'

(12) *davip de mani, deremsem nama melang ama.. amamalasi, dap kuarl amalamii.. alamiip*
dap=ip de mani, de=ure=msem ne=ama
but=PURP CONJ recently CONJ=1PL.SBJ.NPST=weave.CONT from/with=ART
melang ama.. ama=malasi, dap kuarl ama=lamiip.. a=lamiip
vine ART ART=tree.type but INTRG ART=tree.type NM=tree.type
'but as for recently (just now), we were weaving with the vines of.. *malasi*, and maybe of.. *lamiip*'

(...)

(13) *kuariqip naanarlip de.. kuas turahlurla*
kua=arik=ip nani=un=narlip de.. kuasik
INTRG=supposing=PURP can=1DU.SBJ=like:PURP CONJ NEG
te=ura=slurl=a
PURP=1PL.POSS=big=DIST
'if we want to.. (I'm) not (talking) about our old people now'

(14) *dakatika ariqiv ur amarluis naut*
dap=ka=tika arik=ip ut ama=rluis ne-ut
but=3SG.M.SBJ=EMPH supposing=PURP 1PL ART=child from/with-1PL
'but supposing that (we want to consider) us young people'

(15) *de uretluiv uredlek*
de ure=tlu=ip ure=dlek
CONJ 1PL.SBJ.NPST=see.CONT=PURP 1PL.SBJ.NPST=strength/strong
'we must see to it that we stand up strong (and learn the different patterns)'

(16) *div uredlek samagi?*
dip ure=dlek se=ama=gi
FUT 1PL.SBJ.NPST=strength/strong to/with=ART=what
'we will stand up strong for what?'

(17) *div uredlek samarlaunnga*
dip ure=dlek se=ama=rlaun-ka
FUT 1PL.SBJ.NPST=strength/strong to/with=ART=netbag-SG.M
'we will stand up strong (and learn) about the netbag'

(18) *i urahlurla, de radrlem, dav ut, taqurlani, vet lu.. lu.. lausiara amalimbes, de quasiqutdrlem amarlaun*

i	*ura=slurl=a,*	*de*	*ta=drlem,*	*dap*	*ut,*	*taquarl=ani,*
SIM	1PL.POSS=big=DIST	CONJ	3PL.SBJ=know	but	1PL	thus=DIST

pet	*lu..*	*lu..*	*lu-es-iara*	*ama=lim-es,*
on/under	DEM	DEM	DEM-SG.FLAT-PROX	ART=young-SG.FLAT

de	*kuasik=ut=drlem*	*ama=rlaun*
CONJ	NEG=1PL.SBJ=know	ART=netbag

'because our old people, they know, but we, like these.. these.. these young people, we don't know about netbags'

(19) *dakerl ariqiv uremsem amarlaun iv uresunas*

dap=kerl	*arik=ip*	*ure=msem*	*ama=rlaun*
but=DEONT	supposing=PURP	1PL.SBJ.NPST=weave.CONT	ART=netbag

ip	*ure=sunas*
PURP	1PL.SBJ.NPST=teach:SELF

'but supposing that we (want to) weave netbags and (want to) learn (about them)'

(20) *taquarlunetmatnaira ngenama.. amahrluqi*

taquarl=une=tmatna=iara	*ngere-ne=ama..*
thus=1DU.SBJ.NPST=work.CONT:RECP=PROX	3N.ASSOC-from/with=ART

ama=srlu-ki
ART=old-SG.F

'just like we are working here together with the.. the old woman'

(21) *katik divut duremsem amarlaun, iquarl amaquatka*

ka=tika	*dip=ut*	*de=ure=msem*	*ama=rlaun,*
3SG.M.SBJ=EMPH	FUT=1PL	CONJ=1PL.SBJ.NPST=weave.CONT	ART=netbag

i=kuarl	*ama=quat-ka*
SIM=INTRG	ART=man-SG.M

'it is the case that we (all), we will weave netbags, whether it's a man'

(22) *dap ma navramarlaunnga, dap kuarl amananngi*

dap	*ma*	*ne=pet=ama=rlaun-ka*	*dap*	*kuarl*
but	thus	from/with=on/under=ART=netbag-SG.M	but	INTRG

ama=nan-ki
ART=woman-SG.F

'about a netbag like this, or whether it's a woman'

(23) *tika*

tika

EMPH

'that's it'

(24) *iaramaquata, de remiikradrlem samsem*
ia-ta=ama=quat-ta, de te=miika=ta=drlem
other-PL.H=ART=man-PL.H CONJ 3PL.SBJ.NPST=more=3PL.SBJ=know
se=a=msem
to/with=NM=weave.CONT
'some men, they also know about weaving'

(25) *ama.. amarlaun*
ama.. ama=rlaun
ART ART=netbag
'the.. the netbags'

(26) *taquarl amananngina, iradrlem samsem amarlaun*
taquarl ama=nan-kina, i=ta=drlem se=a=msem
thus ART=woman-ASSOC.F SIM=3PL.SBJ=know to/with=NM=weave.CONT
ama=rlaun
ART=netbag
'like the women who know about weaving netbags'

(27) *diaramaquata, de miikra brasem amarlaunnga*
de=ia-ta=ama=quat-ta, de miika=ta
CONJ=other-PL.H=ART=man-PL.H CONJ more=3PL.H
be=ta=sem ama=rlaun-ka
CONJ=3PL.SBJ=weave.NCONT ART=netbag-SG.M
'as for other men, as for them, too, they (can) weave netbags'

(28) *atika verlsera*
ka=tika perlset=a
3SG.M.SBJ=EMPH finish=DIST
'it's finished now'

(29) *verlset dalengi ngarlisa, savramarlaunnga*
verlset de=a=lengi ngere-is=a,
finish.NCONT LOC.PART=NM=word 3N.POSS-end=DIST
se=pet=ama=rlaun-ka
to/with=on/under=ART=netbag-SG.M
'it's the end of the story, about the netbag'

References

Anonymous. 1984. *A siit na ura lengi barak ama ruis i re sunas per ama luqup* [Our language for the children to learn]. Kokopo: Summer Institute of Linguistics.

Anonymous. 2006. *Alsil iini sever ama HIV ngen ama AIDS* [Talking about HIV and AIDS]. Kokopo: Summer Institute of Linguistics.

Bley, Bernhard. 1914. Sagen der Baininger auf Neupommern, Südsee. *Anthropos* 9. 196–220, 418–448.

Burger, Friedrich. 1913. *Die Küsten- und Bergvölker der Gazellehalbinsel. Ein Beitrag zur Völkerkunde von Neuguinea unter besonderer Hervorhebung rechtlicher und sozialer Einrichtungen* (Studien und Forschungen zur Menschen- und Völkerkunde, 12). Stuttgart: Strecker & Schröder.

Chung, Kyung-Ja & Chul-Hwa Chung. 1996. Kuot grammar essentials. In John M. Clifton (ed.), *Two non-Austronesian grammars from the Islands* (Data Papers on Papua New Guinea Languages), 1–75. Ukarumpa: Summer Institute of Linguistics.

Corbett, Greville G. 1991. *Gender* (Cambridge Textbooks in Linguistics). Cambridge: Cambridge University Press.

Dahl, Östen. 1985. *Tense and aspect systems*. Oxford: Basil Blackwell.

Dickhardt, Michael. 2008. Die Feuertänze der Baining. In Ines de Castro, Katja Lembke & Ulrich Menter (eds.), *Paradiese der Südsee. Mythos und Wirklichkeit*, 98–101. Hildesheim & Mainz: Roemer- und Pelizaeus-Museum; Philipp von Zabern.

Dickhardt, Michael. 2009. *Schau nur, und also wirst du dich wandeln! Eine Studie zur Kulturanthropologie der Moralität unter den Qaqet-Baining von Raunsepna, Neubritannien, Gazellehalbinsel, Papua-Neuguinea*. Göttingen: Georg-August-Universität Habilitationsschrift.

Dickhardt, Michael. 2012. Die mit den Geistern tanzen. Maskentänze, Identität und Moral unter den Qaqet-Baining (Gazellehalbinsel, Neubritannien, Papua-Neuguinea). *Mitteilungen der Berliner Gesellschaft für Anthropologie, Ethnologie und Urgeschichte* 33. 15–31.

Dingemanse Mark, Francisco Torreira & Nick J. Enfield. 2013. Is "huh?" a universal word? Conversational infrastructure and the convergent evolution of linguistic items. *PLoS One* 8.11: e78273. doi:10.1371/journal.pone.0078273.

Donohue, Mark & Simon Musgrave. 2007. Typology and the linguistic macrohistory of Island Melanesia. *Oceanic Linguistics* 46(2). 348–387.

Dunn, Michael, Robert A. Foley, Stephen C. Levinson, Ger Reesink & Angela Terrill. 2007. Statistical reasoning in the evaluation of typological diversity in Island Melanesia. *Oceanic Linguistics* 46(2). 388–403.

Dunn, Michael, Stephen C. Levinson, Eva Lindström, Ger Reesink & Angela Terrill. 2008. Structural phylogeny in historical linguistics: Methodological explorations applied in Island Melanesia. *Language* 84(4). 710–759.

Dunn, Michael, Ger Reesink & Angela Terrill. 2002. The East Papuan languages: A preliminary typological appraisal. *Oceanic Linguistics* 41(1). 28–62.

Dunn, Michael, Angela Terrill, Ger Reesink, Robert A. Foley & Stephen C. Levinson. 2005. Structural phylogenetics and the reconstruction of ancient language history. *Science* 309. 2072–2075.

Fajans, Jane. 1983. Shame, social action, and the person among the Baining. *Ethos* 11(3). 166–180.

Fajans, Jane. 1985. The person in social context: The social character of Baining 'psychology'. In Geoffrey M. White & John Kirkpatrick (eds.), *Person, self, and experience. Exploring Pacific ethnopsychologies*, 367–397. Berkeley: University of California Press.

Fajans, Jane. 1993. The alimentary structures of kinship: Food and exchange among the Baining of Papua New Guinea. In Jane Fajans (ed.), *Exchanging products: Producing exchange* (Oceania Monographs, 43), 59–75. Sydney: Sydney University Press.

Fajans, Jane. 1997. *They make themselves: Work and play among the Baining of Papua New Guinea*. Chicago: The University of Chicago Press.

Fajans, Jane. 1998. Transforming nature, making culture: Why the Baining are not environmentalists. *Social Analysis* 42(3). 12–27.

Foley, William A. 1986. *The Papuan languages of New Guinea* (Cambridge Language Surveys). Cambridge: Cambridge University Press.

Frye, Henrike. In prep. *Talking with children in Qaqet (a Papuan language of Papua New Guinea)*. Cologne: University of Cologne dissertation.

Futscher, Otto. 1959. *Taulil-Grammatik und naturwissenschaftliche Sammelarbeiten (Neubritannien, Südsee)* (Micro-Bibliotheca Anthropos, 30). Posieux & Freiburg: Anthropos Institut.

Greenberg, Joseph H. 1978. How does a language acquire gender markers? In Joseph H. Greenberg (ed.), *Universals of human language (Vol 3: Word structure)*, 47–82. Stanford: Stanford University Press.

Hayes, Bruce. 1995. *Metrical stress theory: Principles and case studies*. Chicago & London: University of Chicago Press.

Hellwig, Birgit. 2012-13. Qaqet corpus at the *Endangered Languages Archive*. https://elar.soas.ac.uk/Collection/MPI188145.

Hellwig, Birgit. To appear. Child language documentation: A pilot project in Papua New Guinea. *Language Documentation and Conservation*.

Hellwig, Birgit, Carmen Dawuda, Henrike Frye & Steffen Reetz. 2014-19. Qaqet corpus at the *Language Archive Cologne*. http://hdl.handle.net/11341/00-0000-0000-0000-202A-0@view.

Hesse, Karl. 2007. *A Jos! Die Welt, in der die Chachet-Baininger leben. Sagen, Glaube und Tänze von der Gazelle-Halbinsel Papua-Neuguineas* (Quellen und Forschungen zur Südsee, 2). Wiesbaden: Otto Harrassowitz Verlag.

Hesse, Karl & Theo Aerts. 1996. *Baining life and lore*. Port Moresby: University of Papua New Guinea Press.

Hiery, Hermann Joseph. 2007. Die Baininger. Einige historische Anmerkungen zur Einführung. In Karl Hesse, *A Jos! Die Welt, in der die Chachet-Baininger leben. Sagen, Glaube und Tänze von der Gazelle-Halbinsel Papua-Neuguineas* (Quellen und Forschungen zur Südsee, 2), VII-XXIX. Wiesbaden: Otto Harrassowitz Verlag.

Küntay, Aylın, and Dan I. Slobin. 1996. Listening to a Turkish mother: Some puzzles for acquisition. In Dan I. Slobin, Julie Gerhardt, Amy Kyratzis & Jiansheng Guo (eds.), *Social interaction, social context, and language: Essays in honor of Susan Ervin-Tripp*, 265–286. Mahwah, NJ: Lawrence Erlbaum Associates.

Küntay, Aylın & Dan I. Slobin. 2002. Putting interaction back into child language: Examples from Turkish. *Psychology of Language and Communication* 6(1). 5–14.

Ladefoged, Peter. 2001. *Vowels and consonants: An introduction to the sounds of languages*. Oxford: Blackwell.

Ladefoged, Peter & Ian Maddieson. 1996. *The sounds of the world's languages*. Oxford: Blackwell.

Landi, John & George Arigini. 1983a. *Kisim save long ritim Qaqet* [Learn to read Qaqet]. Kokopo: Summer Institute of Linguistics.

Landi, John & George Arigini. 1983b. *A siit na ura lengi* [Stories in our language]. Kokopo: Summer Institute of Linguistics.

Landi, John & George Arigini. 1983c. *Ure sunas 1–4* [We teach ourselves 1–4]. Kokopo: Summer Institute of Linguistics.

Landi, John & George Arigini. 1987a. *Radingki ara siit* [Radingkis stories]. Kokopo: Summer Institute of Linguistics.
Landi, John & George Arigini. 1987b. *lang ama siit* [Sample stories]. Kokopo: Summer Institute of Linguistics.
Landi, John & George Arigini. 1987c. *Uure lil taqurani na ma Qaqet ara lengi* [We write like this in Qaqet]. Kokopo: Summer Institute of Linguistics.
Laufer, Carl. 1946/49. Rigenmucha, das Höchste Wesen der Baining (Neubritannien). *Anthropos* 41/44(4/6). 497–560.
Laufer, Carl. 1950. Die Taulil und ihre Sprache auf Neubritannien. *Anthropos* 45(4/6). 627–640.
Laufer, Carl. 1959a. Jugendinitiation und Sakraltänze der Baining. *Anthropos* 54(5/6). 905–938.
Laufer, Carl. 1959b. P. Futschers Aufzeichnungen über die Butam-Sprache (Neubritannien). *Anthropos* 54(1/2). 183–212.
Laufer, Carl. 1959c. P. Otto Futscher M.S.C., Taulil-Grammatik und naturwissenschaftliche Sammelarbeiten aus Neubritannien (Südsee) (Micro-Bibliotheca Anthropos, Vol. 30.) *Anthropos* 54(1/2). 213–217.
Leipold, Andreas. 2008. *Das erste Jahr der Hamburger Südsee-Expedition in Deutsch-Neuguinea (1908–1909)*. Bremen: Europäischer Hochschulverlag.
Levin, Beth. 1993. *English verb classes and alternations: A preliminary investigation*. Chicago & London: The University of Chicago Press.
Levinson, Stephen C. 2000. *Presumptive meanings: The theory of generalized conversational implicature*. Cambridge, MA & London: MIT Press.
Lindström, Eva. 2002. *Topics in the grammar of Kuot: A non-Austronesian language of New Ireland, Papua New Guinea*. Stockholm: Stockholm University dissertation.
Lindström, Eva & Bert Remijsen. 2005. Aspects of the prosody of Kuot, a language where intonation ignores stress. *Linguistics* 43(4). 839–870.
Lindström, Eva, Angela Terrill, Ger Reesink & Michael Dunn. 2007. The languages of Island Melanesia. In Jonathan S. Friedlaender (ed.), *Genes, language, and culture history in the Southwest Pacific* (Human Evolution Series, 5), 118–140. New York: Oxford University Press.
Louagie, Dana. 2017. The status of determining elements in Australian languages. *Australian Journal of Linguistics* 37(2). 182–218.
Lynch, John, Malcolm Ross & Terry Crowley. 2002. *The Oceanic languages* (Curzon Language Family Series, 1). London: Curzon Press.
Malchukov, Andrej. 2008. Split intransitives, experiencer objects and 'transimpersonal' constructions: (Re-)establishing the connection. In Mark Donohue & Søren Wichmann (eds.), *The typology of semantic alignment*, 76–100. Oxford: Oxford University Press.
Marley, Alexandra. 2013. *Language Use amongst the Qaqet Baining: A sociolinguistic study of language choices in an ethnolinguistic minority in Papua New Guinea*. Melbourne: La Trobe University MA thesis.
McGregor, William. 1997. Functions of noun phrase discontinuity in Gooniyandi. *Functions of Language* 4(1). 83–114.
Meng, Chenxi. 2018. *A grammar of Tulil*. Melbourne: La Trobe University dissertation.
Misaqi, Gaius. 1987. *A siiriram* [Two sample stories]. Kokopo: Summer Institute of Linguistics.
Misaqi, Gaius. 1990. *Langinka 1* [(Qaqet Baining) primer 1]. Rabaul: National Department of Education (Division of Education, Department of East New Britain).
Müller, Hermann. 1915/16. Erster Versuch einer Grammatik der Sulka-Sprache, Neu-Pommern (Südsee). *Anthropos* 10/11. 75–97, 523–552.
Parker, Diana, Steve Simpson & Elyce D. Cobb. 1992. *Ure sunas. Qaqet Baining alphabet and number book*. Ukarumpa and Rabaul: Summer Institute of Linguistics and National Department of Education (Division of Education, Department of East New Britain).

Parker, James & Diana Parker. 1974. A tentative phonology of Baining (Kakat dialect). In Richard Loving (ed.), *Phonologies of four Papua New Guinea languages* (Workpapers in Papua New Guinea Languages, 4), 5–43. Ukarumpa: Summer Institute of Linguistics.

Parker, James & Diana Parker. 1977. *Baining grammar essentials*. Ukarumpa: Summer Institute of Linguistics. Unpublished manuscript.

Parkinson, Richard. 1907. *Dreißig Jahre in der Südsee: Land und Leute, Sitten und Gebräuche im Bismarckarchipel und auf den deutschen Salomoinseln*. Stuttgart: Strecker & Schröder.

Pawley, Andrew. 1993. A language which defies description by ordinary means. In William A. Foley (ed.), *The role of theory in language description* (Trends in Linguistics, Studies and Monographs, 69), 87–129. Berlin and New York: Mouton de Gruyter.

PNG Bible Translation Association. 1976. *Mak aa lengi sa pet ma Iesus Kristus* [Gospel of Mark]. Kokopo: Summer Institute of Linguistics.

PNG Bible Translation Association. 1978. *Ama Judakana ara tekmerirang* [How the Jews lived; translated from Pasin bilong ol Juda]. Kokopo: Summer Institute of Linguistics.

PNG Bible Translation Association. 1996. *A slurlka aa langinka ama iameska: A lengi ama atlunget bareq ama Qaqet* [The New Testament in the Qaqet-Baining language of Papua New Guinea]. Papua New Guinea: PNG Bible Translation Association.

PNG Bible Translation Association. 2004a. *Ma Iesus ka riktik dama laurlka* [Jesus calms the storm]. Kokopo: Summer Institute of Linguistics.

PNG Bible Translation Association. 2004b. *Ama samariaqa ama atluqa (Luk 10: 30–37)* [The Good Samaritan]. Kokopo: Summer Institute of Linguistics.

PNG Bible Translation Association. 2004c. *Ma Iesus ka ngil ver ama rleniam ian pes (Mataio 20: 29–34)* [Jesus heals two blind men]. Kokopo: Summer Institute of Linguistics.

PNG Bible Translation Association. 2005. *Ama siitka sevet ma Kristus i qa men* [A Christmas book]. Kokopo: Summer Institute of Linguistics.

PNG Bible Translation Association. 2006. *Ama langinka saver ama aiquan* [Monthly calender]. Kokopo: Summer Institute of Linguistics.

Pool, Gail. 2015. *Lost among the Baining: Adventure, marriage and other fieldwork*. Columbia: University of Missouri Press.

Pool, Jeremy. 1984. Objet insaisissable ou anthropologie sans objet? Field Research among the Northern Baining, New Britain (1969–1970). *Journal de la Société des Océanistes* 40(79). 219–233.

Qaqet Literacy Project. 2004a. *Mali re ama ailaing iising* [Looking for legs]. Kokopo: Summer Institute of Linguistics.

Qaqet Literacy Project. 2004b. *A slangaqi qi rarlma ama arlem de ama apngipki* [Flies cause sickness and death]. Kokopo: Summer Institute of Linguistics.

Qaqet Literacy Project. 2012. *A qelvaqa ama gilka* [Little caterpillar]. Kokopo: Summer Institute of Linguistics.

Qaqet Literacy Project. n.d. *Gua punini* [My turtle]. Kokopo: Summer Institute of Linguistics.

Rascher, Matthäus. 1900. *Versuch zu einer Grammatik des Bainingischen*. Unpublished manucript.

Rascher, Matthäus. 1904. Grundregeln der Bainingsprache. *Mitteilungen des Seminars für Orientalische Sprachen zu Berlin* 7(1). 31–85.

Rascher, Matthäus. 1909. *Baining (Neupommern), Land und Leute* (Aus der deutschen Südsee, 1). Münster: Verlag der Aschendorff'schen Buchhandlung.

Reesink, Ger. 2005. Sulka of East New Britain: A mixture of Oceanic and Papuan traits. *Oceanic Linguistics* 44(1). 145–193.

Reetz, Steffen. In prep. *Motivations for code-switching among Qaqet-speaking adults in Kamanakam, East New Britain Province, Papua New Guinea*. Cologne: University of Cologne dissertation.

Rohatynskyj, Marta A. 2000. The enigmatic Baining: the breaking of an ethnographer's heart. In Sjoerd R. Jaarsma & Marta A. Rohatynskyj (eds.), *Ethnographic artifacts: Challenges to a reflexive anthropology*, 174–194. Honolulu: University of Hawai'i Press.

Rohatynskyj, Marta A. 2001. On knowing the Baining and other minor ethnic groups of East New Britain. *Social Analysis* 45(2). 23–40.

Ross, Malcom. 1994. Areal phonological features in north central New Ireland. In Tom Dutton & Darrell T. Tryon (eds.), *Language contact and change in the Austronesian world* (Trends in Linguistics. Studies and Monographs, 77), 551–572. Berlin: Mouton de Gruyter.

Ross, Malcom. 1996. Contact-induced change and the comparative method: cases from Papua New Guinea. In Mark Durie & Malcolm Ross (eds.), *The comparative method reviewed: Regularity and irregularity in language change*, 180–217. New York: Oxford University Press.

Ross, Malcom. 2001. Is there an East Papuan phylum? Evidence from pronouns. In Andrew Pawley, Malcolm Ross & Darrell Tyron (eds.), *The boy from Bundaberg: Studies in Melanesian linguistics in honour of Tom Dutton* (Pacific Linguistics, 514), 301–321. Canberra: Pacific Linguistics.

Ross, Malcom. 2005. Pronouns as a preliminary diagnostic for grouping Papuan languages. In Andrew Pawley, Robert Attenborough, Jack Golson & Robin Hide (eds.), *Papuan pasts: Cultural linguistic and biological histories of Papuan-speaking peoples*, 15–65. Canberra: Pacific Linguistics.

Schmidt, Wilhelm. 1904. Eine Papuasprache auf Neupommern. *Globus* 86(5). 79–80.

Schmidt, Wilhelm. 1905. Die Bainingsprache, eine zweite Papuasprache auf Neupommern. *Globus* 87. 357–358.

Schneider, Cindy. 2011. Why field linguists should pay more attention to research in applied linguistics. *Australian Journal of Linguistics* 31(2). 187–209.

Schneider, Cindy. 2015. Micro-level planning for a Papua New Guinean elementary school classroom: "copycat" planning and language ideologies. *Current Issues in Language Planning* 16(3). 335–354.

Schneider, Joseph. 1962. *Grammatik der Sulka-Sprache (Neubritannien)* (Micro-Bibliotheca Anthropos). Posieux & Freiburg: Anthropos Institut.

Schultze-Berndt, Eva & Candide Simard. 2012. Constraints on noun phrase discontinuity in an Australian language: The role of prosody and information structure. *Linguistics* 50(5). 1015–1058.

Spriggs, Matthew. 1997. *The Island Melanesians* (The Peoples of South-East Asia and the Pacific). London: Wiley-Blackwell.

Stanton, Lee. 2007. *Topics in Ura phonology and morphophonology, with lexicographic application.* Christchurch: University of Canterbury MA thesis.

Stebbins, Tonya N. 2004. Mali Baining perspectives on language and culture stress. *International Journal of the Sociology of Language* 169. 161–175.

Stebbins, Tonya N. 2005. Nominal classification in Mali. *Anthropological Linguistics* 47(1). 77–131.

Stebbins, Tonya N. 2009a. The Papuan languages of the Eastern Bismarcks: Migration, origins and connections. In Bethwyn Evans (ed.), *Discovering history through language. Papers in honour of Malcolm Ross* (Pacific Linguistics, 605), 223–243. Canberra: Pacific Linguistics.

Stebbins, Tonya N. 2009b. Semantics of clause linking in Mali. In R. M. W. Dixon & Alexandra Y. Aikhenvald (eds.), *The semantics of clause linking: A cross-linguistic typology* (Explorations in Linguistic Typology, 5), 356–379. Oxford: Oxford University Press.

Stebbins, Tonya N. 2011. *Mali (Baining) grammar: A language of the East New Britain Province, Papua New Guinea* (Pacific Linguistics, 623). Canberra: Pacific Linguistics.

Stebbins, Tonya N. & Mark Planigale. 2010. Explaining the unknowable: accessibility of meaning and the exegesis of Mali Baining songs. *Australian Journal of Linguistics* 30(1). 141–154.

Stebbins, Tonya N. & Julius Tayul. 2009. *Mali (Baining) texts* (Pacific Linguistics, 606). Canberra: Pacific Linguistics.

Stebbins, Tonya N. & Julius Tayul. 2012. *Mali (Baining) dictionary: Mali-Baining amēthamon angētha thēvaik*. Canberra: Pacific Linguistics.

Stehlin, Johannes. 1905/06. *Wörterbuch: Baining-Deutsch*. Unpublished manuscript.

Terrill, Angela. 2002. Systems of nominal classification in East Papuan languages. *Oceanic Linguistics* 41(1). 63–88.

Tharp, Douglas. 1996. Sulka grammar essentials. In John M. Clifton (ed.), *Two non-Austronesian grammars from the Islands* (Data Papers on Papua New Guinea Languages), 77–179. Ukarumpa: Summer Institute of Linguistics.

Tiqa, Sevarin, A. Kaltaumen & Diane Parker. 1983. *Langinka 1–2* [Primer 1–2]. Kokopo: Summer Institute of Linguistics.

Tiqa, Sevarin, A. Kaltaumen & Diane Parker. 1996. *A langinka bareq ama Qaqet* [Qaqet primer]. Rabaul: National Department of Education (Division of Education, Department of East New Britain).

Verstraete, Jean-Christophe & Dana Louagie. 2016. Noun phrase constituency in Australian languages: A typological study. *Linguistic Typology* 20(1). 25–80.

Volmer, Hermann. 1926. *Wörterbuch: Baining-Deutsch*. Unpublished manuscript.

Volmer, Hermann. 1928. *Grammatik des Bainingschen*. Unpublished manuscript.

Wurm, Stephen A. 1982. *Papuan languages of Oceania* (Ars Linguistica, 7). Tübingen: Narr.

Index